Film

A Critical Introduction

Film

A Critical
Introduction

Maria Pramaggiore   Tom Wallis

PEARSON

and

Editorial Director: Jason Jordan
Series Editor: Molly Taylor
Editorial Assistant: Michael Kish
Marketing Manager: Mandee Eckersley

For related titles and support materials, visit our online catalog at www.ablongman.com.

Between the time website information is gathered and then published, it is not unusual for some sites to have closed. Also, the transcription of URLs can result in unintended typographical errors. The publisher would appreciate notification where these errors occur so that they may be corrected in subsequent editions.

Printed in China

This book was designed and produced by
Laurence King Publishing Ltd, London
www.laurenceking.co.uk

Every effort has been made to contact the copyright holders, but should there be any errors or omissions, Laurence King Publishing Ltd would be pleased to insert the appropriate acknowledgment in any subsequent printing of this publication.

Editor: Richard Mason
Picture Researcher: Tim Nicholson
Designer: Newton Harris
Typesetting: Marie Doherty

Front cover/Back cover: Kate Winslet and Jim Carrey in *Eternal Sunshine of the Spotless Mind*, 2004. Copyright Focus Features/The Kobal Collection/Davis Lee

Frontispiece: Burt Lancaster and Claudia Cardinale, *The Leopard*, 1963. Dalton Nicholson Collection. Twentieth Century Fox, 1963.

Contents

Part Two
FILM ANALYSIS *31*

Preface

Film: A Critical Introduction proposes that film is an art form and a cultural institution worthy of serious intellectual consideration. It demystifies the process of academic inquiry for students who love movies but may not possess the tools for creating interpretive arguments.

Teaching film studies is more exciting and challenging than ever. New technologies that make films—and information about films—readily available have produced a flurry of interest in the medium. Viewers can watch DVDs with special features and commentary tracks, and they can find information on the Web ranging from official studio sites to reviews by individual fans. Even casual film enthusiasts now want to learn how to describe the cinematic techniques used by their favorite directors. Not surprisingly, film studies instruction is growing at every educational level.

This textbook is designed for students who possess a broad range of information but don't have the framework for understanding cinema as an aesthetic and cultural institution. The book provides that framework by focusing on the skills of analysis and argument that are critical to an intellectual engagement with the medium. The material helps readers master film techniques and terminology. It highlights research skills and rhetorical strategies, enabling students to build comprehensive, thoughtful interpretations of films. And rather than limiting a discussion of writing to a single chapter, it encourages readers to build their interpretive skills at the same time that they enhance their knowledge of form, visual style, and sound.

● How this Textbook is Organized

This book is divided into three parts. Part One introduces readers to the importance of film analysis, offering helpful strategies for discerning the ways in which films produce meaning.

In Part Two, individual chapters examine the fundamental elements of film, including narrative form, *mise en scène*, cinematography, editing, sound, and alternatives to narrative cinema. Each chapter introduces basic terms, techniques, and concepts, then goes much further, showing readers how this information can be used to interpret films. In Chapters 3–7, *Techniques in Practice* sections model the way that specific details (for example, the choice of a lens) can be used as the basis for interpreting a scene or film. In addition, end-of-chapter film analyses address one of that chapter's larger topics in relation to a specific film, such as *The Grand Illusion*, *Devil in a Blue Dress*, *Triumph of the Will*, and *Meshes of the Afternoon*.

The book's emphasis on forming arguments culminates in Chapter 9, "Writing About Film". This chapter presents a detailed account of four different approaches to writing about film, including the research paper and the popular review.

Part Three moves beyond textual analysis to explore film as a cultural institution. This section of the book introduces readers to essential areas of film studies research: the Hollywood style, ideology, stardom, genre, *auteur* theory, and the contemporary film industry. Each chapter is organized around the explicit and implicit questions that film critics and scholars ask when they investigate cinema's role in culture. Each chapter also includes examples of popular and scholarly writing about film.

● Special Features of this Textbook

Techniques in Practice sections in Chapters 3–7 use key concepts and film techniques to analyze and interpret a scene, a film, or several films. These sections reinforce the idea that the ultimate goal of mastering definitions and concepts, and paying close attention to details, is to formulate rich interpretations.

Inset boxes in Chapters 3–7 help students understand the filmmaking process, including industry personnel and trades.

Film Analysis end-of-chapter essays in Chapters 2–8 address a broad topic area of the chapter (for example, setting) in a carefully developed analysis of one or two films. *Sidebars* draw attention to rhetorical strategies, demystifying the process by which writers move from gathering details to generating ideas and organizing an argument.

Samples of published film scholarship and criticism throughout Part Three illustrate important modes of inquiry in film studies (for example, ideological criticism) and familiarize readers with the conceptual and rhetorical diversity of writing about film.

Works Consulted lists at the ends of chapters point students to possibilities for further research.

Examples drawn from a wide variety of films engage the reader's interest without sacrificing intellectual rigor. While the book focuses on narrative filmmaking, it also offers in-depth discussions and analyses of avant-garde and documentary films, and features a number of important narrative films made outside Hollywood.

An extensive glossary succinctly defines the terms and concepts discussed in each chapter.

● Supplements

Instructor's Manual
This manual is designed to ease the time-consuming demands of instructional preparation, enhance lectures, and provide helpful suggestions to organize the course. It features chapter overviews, detailed lecture outlines, student learning objectives, lecture launchers, and sample syllabi.

Companion Web Site with Online Study Guide
This Web site features practice tests and Web resources. The Companion Website can be viewed at: www.ablongman.com/pramaggiore1e.

PowerPoint Presentation Package
This package consists of a collection of lecture outlines and graphic images keyed to every chapter in the text, and is available on the web at: http://suppscentral.ablongman.com.

Acknowledgements

Writing this book would have been impossible without the support, input, and energy of many, many other people. We thank North Carolina State University's College of Humanities and Social Sciences for release time to work on the project. We are grateful for the insights offered by film studies colleagues at North Carolina State and elsewhere, including Joe Gomez, Andrea Mensch, Devin and Marsha Orgeron, Jim Morrison, Jans Wager, and Greg Johnson.

We were lucky to work with knowledgeable and supportive editors at Laurence King and Allyn and Bacon, especially Karen Dubno, Lee Greenfield, Richard Mason, Matthew Taylor, Molly Taylor, and Michael Kish. We were amazed by Tim Nicholson's feats of image acquisition and his unflappable good humor as he managed to turn the process of obtaining picture permissions into an art form in itself. We also thank Nick Newton for transforming our prosaic text and hard-won images into an aesthetically pleasing whole.

To Todd Morgan and Todd Platt: thank you for sharing your seemingly boundless DVD library. To our adopted family—the entire cast of characters at the Player's Retreat, including Deborah Wyrick, Andrea Gomez, Leila May, Don Palmer, Robert McMillan, Steve Luyendyk, Dave Luyendyk, and Steve Edelstein—we couldn't have done it without you. We also gratefully acknowledge the unfailing support of our given families.

Finally, we thank the readers whose constructive feedback was invaluable as we revised several drafts of this book. They are: Henry B. Aldridge, Eastern Michigan University; Linda Anthon, Valencia Community College; Charles V. Eidsvik, University of Georgia; Cynthia Erb, Wayne State University; Walton Jones, University of California, San Diego; Dann L. Pierce, University of Portland; Catherine L. Preston, University of Kansas; Tarshia L. Stanley, Spelman College; and David Alan Williams, Texas Tech University.

Maria Pramaggiore
Tom Wallis

September 2004

Part One

Introduction to Film Analysis

Film is a complex art form and cultural institution whose influence spans the 20th century and transcends it. In its infancy, film depended on the technology of the industrial revolution and the business model associated with the penny arcade. In its maturity, the cinema emerged as a global entertainment industry, instigating and taking advantage of technological developments in photography, sound recording, and, eventually, electronic and digital imaging. The cinema not only contributed to a mass culture of entertainment and celebrity; it also provided a forum for education and critique through the tradition of social documentary, and served as a medium of personal expression in the form of avant-garde films and home movies.

Many film lovers value movie spectacles that transport them to a magical world of romance, drama, and adventure. Others seek out challenging films that provide a rigorous intellectual and aesthetic experience. This book contends that these two desires are not mutually exclusive: the most profound moments of immersion in cinema art also invite audiences to ponder social, aesthetic, moral, and intellectual questions.

In Part I, Chapter One provides an overview of the book's approach. Chapter Two introduces the foundation of film interpretation. It helps readers to develop strategies for critical reading and analysis so that they may better understand the way films build meaning through the systematic use of details. It also lays out the goal of film analysis: the clear and convincing description, evaluation, and interpretation of films.

Baz Luhrmann's *Moulin Rouge* with Nicole Kidman.

Chapter 1

Introduction

Last night I was in the Kingdom of Shadows.

Maxim Gorky, on attending his first film screening

Watching a movie takes most viewers out of their everyday lives and transports them to a different world, a realm that Russian writer Maxim Gorky called "the Kingdom of Shadows." When 35 mm films are projected in a movie theater, a powerful beam of light passes through translucent celluloid to produce those "shadows," the larger-than-life images on the big screen. Whether people watch a film in a movie theater or the digitized version at home on a DVD, they continue to visit Gorky's kingdom (fig. **1.1**). They immerse themselves in the lives of fictional characters, develop opinions about historical events, and become captivated by artistic combinations of color, light, and sound. Because films engage viewers on an emotional level, some people criticize the cinema as escapist entertainment. Yet others praise it as an imaginative art form that allows people to realize their dreams and fantasies. The reality is that films do both of these things, and more.

This book maintains that watching films can be both emotionally satisfying and intellectually stimulating. It offers essential tools for developing a critical approach to the film

1.1 "The Kingdom of Shadows": viewers lose themselves in a film.

medium, based on knowledge about the way films are made and the way they can be interpreted in aesthetic, technological, and cultural contexts. One premise of this book is that moviegoers who learn to analyze films and to build sound, thoughtful interpretations will enhance their experience (and enjoyment) of the cinema. This book is not intended to turn every reader into a professional critic or scholar. But it does emphasize that training in film helps viewers to understand and enjoy their experiences of film. The more viewers know about how films are made, why certain films have been celebrated and others ridiculed, and how movies contribute to culture, the better they are able to understand and interpret the films they see.

One of this book's major concerns is film analysis, and one of its main aims is to help readers identify the major elements of film art and recognize the way those elements work together to produce meaning. The book also emphasizes the value of critical reading, which means putting those analytical skills to use by examining and questioning a film's organization and visual style. A viewer who reads a film critically asks questions such as: does this film conform to the accepted conventions of a particular **genre** (such as the Western) or does it move beyond them? Does it tell a story in a conventional manner, or does it overturn expectations about structure or characters? Does the film's "look" enhance its themes, or do visual elements introduce irony or tension?

But the book also encourages students to develop the skills necessary to build sound written interpretations. The writing process helps to clarify thoughts and organize ideas. By focusing on writing skills, the book emphasizes the importance of constructing thoughtful interpretations.

How This Book Is Organized

The book's introductory section, Part I, concludes with Chapter Two, which offers some strategies for embarking on film analysis. First, it considers the kinds of expectations that viewers bring to a film and then asks whether or not the film satisfies those expectations. Second, it looks at how a film's use of details and repetition can give clues about its underlying structure and meaning. As an example of film analysis in action, Chapter Two concludes with a short essay on the meaning contained in historical references in Carl Franklin's *Devil in a Blue Dress* (1995). This is the first in a series of end-of-chapter analyses that the reader will find in Chapters Three through Eight.

Part II introduces the basic tools for performing film analysis. Chapters Three through Eight lay out the characteristics of a film's formal mode of organization, visual style, and sound. These

1.2 *Lord of the Rings* computer game, an example of "industry convergence".

chapters help readers recognize film techniques, describe these techniques using film studies terminology, and understand the part each of them plays in the film's overall organization. Each chapter ends with a "Film Analysis" essay exploring one of the chapter's topics in relation to a specific film, similar to the analysis of *Devil in a Blue Dress* at the end of Chapter Two. Sidebars that accompany each analysis identify rhetorical techniques the writer has used to organize and develop ideas and emphasize major points. Part II concludes with Chapter Nine, which focuses on writing about film. The chapter presents some ground rules for interpreting films in four contexts: the scene analysis, the film analysis paper, the research paper, and the film review. After completing Part II, readers should be able to write a textual analysis of an individual film that describes, evaluates, and interprets the text's formal mode of organization, sound, and visual style.

Part III moves from the textual analysis of individual films to examine cinema more broadly as a cultural institution, discussing in Chapters Ten through Twelve subjects such as the relationship between social context and film style, the connection between movies and ideology, and phenomena such as the **star system**. Chapters Thirteen and Fourteen then investigate the relationship between films and two other important cultural institutions: popular structures for storytelling (genres) and the social and aesthetic role of the filmmaker, or **auteur** (a director whose *oeuvre* reveals a consistent artistic vision), as artist and celebrity. Part III concludes with Chapter Fifteen, which discusses film as an industry, focusing on new technologies and industry convergence—the blending of cinema with other entertainment industries (fig. **1.2**). Over the past twenty years, these technological, economic, and social developments have exercised a tremendous influence on the way people experience the cinema as a cultural institution.

Each chapter in Part III includes excerpts from essays by film scholars and critics that serve as examples of published film writing for academic and popular audiences. By the time readers have completed this section, they will be prepared to formulate questions related to cinema as a cultural institution and to conduct independent research on film studies topics. Together, Parts II and III help readers develop the analytical, critical reading, and rhetorical skills to describe, interpret, and evaluate a film at the textual level and to engage current issues in film and media studies by moving beyond the individual text to consider film's broader cultural significance.

● Technical Tips

- Although interpreting films requires knowledge of visual principles and sound design as well as narrative form, the discipline of film studies has adopted some of the terminology of literary studies, for example, describing films as "texts" and interpretations as "readings."
- The first time a technical term is used, it appears in boldface. All boldface terms are defined in the glossary.

- At the end of every chapter, "Works Consulted" provides references to material consulted for the chapter and for the Film Analysis.
- A bulleted list under "Summary" appears at the end of Chapters Two through Eight.
- Chapters Two through Eight contain inset boxes on various topics, including the terms that describe aspects of film production and personnel.
- The first time a film is mentioned, its title is accompanied by the name of the director and the release date. Titles of most foreign-language films appear in English first, then in the original language (or as a transliteration). Subsequent references are in English only. If a film is more generally known by its original-language title, the English translation is given in parentheses the first time the film is mentioned.
- Asian names appear according to the name under which the director's work has become known: Akira Kurosawa (surname second) and Wong Kar Wai (surname first). When conducting research on film directors, readers should consider the fact that book and journal publishers, DVD manufacturers, and webmasters may use both systems.

Works Consulted

Gorky, Maxim. "The Kingdom of Shadows," in Gilbert Adair, *Movies*, pp. 10–13. London and New York: Penguin, 1999.

2

An Approach to Film Analysis

How can you still enjoy movies, I am often asked [. . .], when you spend all your time analyzing them and researching them? All I can say in response is that I enjoy movies more than ever, but admittedly, in a very different way from my very first excursions into the illuminated darkness.

Andrew Sarris

When a college student tells a friend about seeing Stanley Kubrick's *Dr. Strangelove* (1964; fig. **2.2**), a black comedy about nuclear deterrence, what information does he convey? When a film reviewer writes about that film, does she present the same ideas as the friends who informally share their opinions? And when a film scholar writes an essay about that film, would he adopt the same approach as the casual viewer or the popular critic?

It seems likely that these three viewers would discuss the same film in different ways. Is one of them "right"? Casual viewers might focus on whether they formed a personal connection to characters or enjoyed a particular performance, such as George C. Scott's comic turn. Were the special effects exciting? If so, they may decide to see more Kubrick films. By contrast, critics and scholars place their observations in a specialized framework. They use their knowledge of film to formulate interpretations about what the film means,

2.1 The black monolith from *2001: A Space Odyssey*, a motif and symbol.

on the level of the story and on broader cultural and aesthetic levels.

A film critic would evaluate the film using criteria such as story coherence, technical innovations, and notable performances, perhaps comparing this film to other work by the same **director**. (Even film critics will differ in their approaches: a film critic writing in 2006 would probably use different evaluative criteria from one writing the year the film was released, because *Dr. Strangelove* has come to be recognized as an important classic.) A film scholar might write an essay arguing that *Dr. Strangelove* represents an important moment in cinema history when independent film production blossomed as the Hollywood studio system declined.

2.2 Slim Pickens adds humor in Kubrick's black comedy *Dr. Strangelove*.

Any viewer's ability to find meaning in a film is based on knowledge, cultural experiences, preferences, formal training, and expectations. But the significance a viewer derives from a film also depends upon the choices the filmmaker has made. For example, a director may rely on **genre conventions** or she may revise them, introducing unexpected characters or situations. The more a spectator knows about the pattern, and the significance of deviating from it, the more he will understand and appreciate the film.

This chapter introduces two ideas that are essential to film analysis. The first one is that expectations influence filmmakers' choices and viewers' experiences of films. Those expectations involve many aspects of a film, including its formal mode of organization, genre, stars, and director. The second idea is that filmmakers present information, elicit emotions, and suggest ideas by orchestrating details in a systematic way. A close analysis of the way such details are used can therefore provide clues about the film's underlying structure and themes. Another way for a filmmaker to create meaning is through references to people, events, or issues outside the film itself, and this chapter also looks at ways of analyzing how these references work. The chapter ends with a look at how an understanding of a film's structure and themes can form the basis for different sorts of statements about it, and, in particular, for making interpretive claims about it. Alongside this is a discussion of how the choices a filmmaker makes—for example, the way she uses details to create meaning—all go to form her own distinctive style.

● Understanding Audience Expectations

All film viewers bring expectations to their experiences of film. Someone who goes to a Farrelly Brothers film for a laugh brings vastly different expectations than someone attending an Ingmar Bergman retrospective hoping to be challenged intellectually.

Viewers form expectations about movies by learning about and experiencing film, visual art, and culture.

Most viewers form expectations about the *kind* of film they plan to see. Will it tell a story or present an argument, or will it consist of abstract images set to a soundtrack? These expectations relate to a film's mode of organization. In narrative fiction films, viewers expect to see stories about human characters whose circumstances produce comedy or tragedy, or both. If these viewers planned to see a documentary instead, they would expect the film to present real-world events, and they might expect to be given factual information about a historical or contemporary situation. If these viewers saw an **avant-garde film**, they might not expect to see a story at all, since avant-garde film-makers see film as a visual art form rather than a storytelling medium.

If viewers expect all films to tell stories, they may be disappointed or confused by documentaries and avant-garde films. As film scholar Scott MacDonald points out, "by the time most people see their first avant-garde film, they have already seen hundreds of films in commercial theaters and on television and their sense of what a movie is has been almost indelibly imprinted in their conscious and unconscious minds" (MacDonald, p. 1). What's most important, however, is to recognize that, despite their differences, each mode of organization is amenable to analysis and interpretation using the tools provided in this book.

Expectations and Modes of Organization

Narrative fiction films are organized by the cause and effect logic of storytelling: they present characters who encounter obstacles as they attempt to achieve their goals. Viewers identify with characters and understand the choices they make, even if they themselves wouldn't make the same ones. In the Austin Powers films (Jay Roach 1997, 1999, 2002), a 1960s British spy is resurrected and must learn how to navigate the post-Cold War era while foiling the dastardly plans of his nemesis, Dr. Evil. Powers is motivated by pride in his image as a successful, swinging, James Bond type. The fact that he dresses and behaves according to the values and sartorial style of the 1960s creates obstacles for him and comic moments for the audience (see figs. 4.24, 4.25).

Most filmgoers expect to encounter characters such as Austin Powers whose motivations are clear. But filmmakers may flout the rules, and this may enhance or detract from the viewer's enjoyment. For example, a director may present a character with unclear motivations. In *Once upon a Time in the West* ("*C'era una volta il West*"; Sergio Leone 1968), audiences may be puzzled as to what motivates Harmonica (Charles Bronson) to pursue Frank (Henry Fonda) because Leone withholds crucial information until the film's conclusion.

A character with unclear motivations can be intriguing. In Michelangelo Antonioni's mystery *Blow-Up* (1966), the audience never learns why Jane (Vanessa Redgrave) was involved in a murder, or why the victim was killed. That missing information is consistent with the film's focus on a self-absorbed photographer (David Hemmings) who must learn that his camera does not help him see, understand, and control reality. Viewers who wish to be challenged appreciate the way some films provide variations on the standard pattern.

Viewers generally expect a narrative film to offer a conclusion that resolves conflicts. Some critics claim that Hollywood films end happily because profit-oriented studio executive refuse to risk alienating audiences. Yet even independent-oriented film producers Bob and Harvey Weinstein of Miramax forced filmmaker Charles Burnett to "substitute a less blunt and despairing ending after some test-marketing" of *The Glass Shield* (1995) (Rosenbaum, p. 161). Many independent directors work against the traditional happy ending. John Sayles' *Limbo* (1999) concludes without making clear whether or not a family stranded in the Alaskan wilderness will be rescued. The conclusion of Stanley Kubrick's *A Clockwork Orange* (1970) finds that the criminal protagonist Alex De Large (Malcolm McDowell) has not been rehabilitated, but instead seems to have reverted to his initial state of anti-social aggression. These open-ended conclusions or circular narratives may leave audiences with lingering questions, not **closure**.

Some documentary films tell stories, although the stories originate in real world events. These films may satisfy many of the expectations regarding characters, conflicts, and resolution that viewers bring to narrative fiction films. *Hoop Dreams* (Steve James 1994) documents the high school careers of Arthur Agee and William Gates, two young African-American men who want to become professional basketball players. As the stories unfold, the film raises questions about educational opportunity, professional sports, and race in contemporary America. *Hoop Dreams* allows these ideas to emerge from stories connected to two individuals who invite the viewer's identification just as characters in a fictional story might do.

Other documentaries present explicit or implicit statements about the real world events they depict. Viewers expect to weigh the information presented and draw conclusions, rather than simply enjoy the unfolding of a story. Some documentaries inform and persuade audiences by presenting facts and logical arguments, while others address viewers on an emotional level through interviews and re-enactments, and some do both. In *Bowling for Columbine* (2002), Michael Moore presents his perspective on gun violence in the U.S., interviews experts and average people, and presents statistics on the number of gun-related deaths and injuries in the U.S. every year. Many documentary enthusiasts look forward to the information they acquire from documentaries and marvel at the real-world people and events that sometimes rival the plots of even the most imaginative narrative fiction films.

Other documentaries explore their subject matter through a less direct approach. *Winged Migration* ("*Le Peuple migrateur*"; Jacques Cluzaud and Michel Debats 2001) observes a real-world phenomenon—the migration of birds—without appearing to persuade the audience to accept an explicit message. Even so, the film contains an implicit idea: that birds are a unique and interesting life form and may be threatened by human activities such as hunting and industrial pollution.

Avant-garde films move even farther away from the conventions of narrative film. Avant-garde filmmakers explore the aesthetic capabilities of the film medium, seeing it as similar to painting, sculpture, or dance. They rarely tell stories or present arguments and, instead, make meaning through symbols and metaphors. A viewer of avant-garde films

would expect that basic elements of the film medium, such as **composition** (the arrangement of visual elements in the frame), editing patterns, and sound, will carry great significance, while characters or events are given less importance. Film enthusiasts who are open to a non-narrative exploration of sound and vision may enjoy the experimental works of filmmakers such as Stan Brakhage, whose mesmerizing short film *Black Ice* (1993; fig. **2.3**) consists of nothing but abstract, pulsating images.

Whether a filmmaker creates a narrative, documentary, or avant-garde film, he or she is aware of audience expectations. For their part, viewers bring expectations about the type of film they are seeing and may be delighted or disturbed by a filmmaker's choices.

2.3 An abstract image from Brakhage's *Black Ice*.

Expectations about Genres, Stars, and Directors

When viewers plan to see a narrative fiction film, they probably arrive with specific expectations regarding the type of story the film will tell. Those expectations are based on their knowledge of film genres, movie stars, and directors. Filmmakers anticipate that viewers have expectations and they may or may not choose to fulfill them. Director Clint Eastwood satisfies viewers expecting to see a classical Western when, at the conclusion of *Unforgiven* (1990), he stages a dramatic, revenge-driven shootout in which the film's hero uses his skill with a gun to subdue an entire town. But directors also thwart expectations, as Robert Altman does in *McCabe and Mrs. Miller* (1971), when he suggests that large industrial corporations, not individual pioneers, controlled the Wild West. The film's setting in the muddy and snowy northwest defies the look of the traditional Western, and the shootout at the film's conclusion does not glorify the hero's gunslinging prowess.

2.4 Baz Luhrmann's *Moulin Rouge* revived the musical while challenging its conventions.

Most films satisfy some, but not all, genre expectations. Giving audiences what they expect may please them, but it also has the potential to bore them. James Bond films depend on certain familiar elements (beautiful women and megalomaniac villains) but also include innovations (exotic locales, updated weapons technologies, and changing political conflicts). Baz Luhrmann's *Moulin Rouge* (2001; fig. **2.4**) reinvigorated the musical genre by breaking rules and pairing contemporary popular music with a nineteenth-century storyline.

Another important influence on expectations is the star system, a marketing process that studios, talent agencies, and the press use to transform actors into brand name products. Viewer expectations come into play because fans enjoy seeing their favorite actors in the same kind of role again and again. Arnold Schwarzenegger rose to fame as the Terminator, not as the *Kindergarten Cop* (Ivan Reitman 1990), and Clara Bow became known as the "It Girl" because of her repeated portrayals of a spunky, sexy, working-class girl (fig. **2.5**). Actors may be associated with genres: John Wayne is linked to Westerns (fig. **2.6**), Judy Garland to musicals, and Humphrey Bogart to detective films. A movie starring Tom Cruise elicits expectations of an action-packed extravaganza, whereas viewers might expect a film featuring Denzel Washington to be a character drama involving suspense and action. A typical Julia Roberts film revolves around romance and women's empowerment, whereas a film featuring Will Smith typically involves comedy and action.

The public forms expectations about directors as well. Alfred Hitchcock is known as the master of suspense, whereas Woody Allen films are associated with New York City settings, neurotic characters, and self-deprecating jokes. The name Busby Berkeley conjures up images of elaborate musicals, and John Ford is synonymous with the Western. James Cameron, David Fincher, and John Woo are known for action-oriented films such as *The Terminator* (1984, 1991) *Se7en* (Fincher 1995) and *Face/Off* (Woo 1997). Ang Lee, a director who made several movies about family crises, including *The Wedding Banquet* ("*Hsi Yen*"; 1993), *Eat Drink Man Woman* ("*Yin shi nan nu*", 1994), and *The Ice Storm* (1997) combined his background in character-driven films with action-oriented martial arts in *Crouching Tiger, Hidden Dragon* ("*Wo Hu Zang Long*"; 2000).

In order to analyze a film, one must consider viewer expectations and take note of which expectations are met and which ones are modified or rejected. Did Clint Eastwood satisfy expectations about the Western genre in *Unforgiven*, or did he modify the standard formula? If there are modifications, what are the effects of those choices?

In order to answer questions such as these, the viewer must take note of the seemingly minor details that are critical for conveying meaning. Paying close attention to patterns of repetition is one way to identify the most crucial details, the ones that relate to a film's themes and structure. Just as classical music, a

2.5 *(above)* Clara Bow, the "It Girl".

2.6 *(below)* John Wayne in *Stagecoach*, a classic Western.

temporal art form, is organized by the repetition of musical phrases, films use visual and sound details to organize the flow of information.

● The Orchestration of Detail

Certain details seem to demand the viewer's attention. Those details may relate to a storyline or characters, or they may arise from the visual or sound aspects of the film. Usually, details claim attention because they are prominent. One way for a filmmaker to assure that audience attention will be focused on a detail is to repeat it.

Motifs

When any detail takes on significance through repetition, it is called a **motif**. Filmmakers may employ any film element to develop a motif, including (among others): lines of dialogue, gestures, costumes, locations, props, music, color, and composition.

Motifs have a variety of functions. They can provide information about characters and reinforce the significance of an idea. In *Citizen Kane* (Orson Welles 1941), the last word spoken by newspaper magnate Charles Foster Kane (Orson Welles)—"rosebud"—serves as a motif. The fact that nobody knows what Kane meant by the word motivates Mr. Thompson (William Alland) to interview Kane's friends, ex-wife, and business associates. The repetition of "rosebud" unifies stories that five different narrators tell about Kane's life. Finally, the physical object the word refers to sheds light on Kane's hidden desires (fig. **2.7**). In *American Beauty* (Sam Mendes 1999), roses function as a motif that suggests a youthful passion for beauty that middle-aged Lester Burnham (Kevin Spacey) is desperate to revive.

Motifs can also encourage spectators to compare and contrast characters, plot events, objects, or situations. When an eerie black monolith appears in a prehistoric sequence and returns in the second and fourth parts of *2001: A Space Odyssey* (Stanley Kubrick 1968; fig. **2.1**, p. 6) viewers compare those moments in space and time. The film questions whether humankind has made progress over the span of recorded time, and the recurring image of the mysterious monolith acts as a concrete object to use as a point of comparison and a potent symbol for generating interpretations.

Once established, motifs may evolve, suggesting change and development in a character or situation. In Alfred Hitchcock's

2.7 The Rosebud motif revealed in *Citizen Kane.*

Notorious (1946), Alicia Huberman (Ingrid Bergman) is introduced as a party girl. Hitchcock shows Alicia drinking to excess in an early scene at her Florida home. When she falls in love with T. R. Devlin (Cary Grant), she attempts to change her ways. Having a drink at a café with Devlin, she declines a second round. But Devlin ridicules her, doubting her ability to leave the past behind. So Alicia changes her mind and orders a double. Throughout the film, Devlin and Alicia both question whether she can change her ways. The drinking motif, which evolves over the course of the film, helps to develop this theme.

An analysis of motifs in *The Sixth Sense* (M. Night Shyamalan 1999) might begin with the recognition that the color red appears repeatedly. A viewer can isolate this visual motif by compiling a list detailing each instance of the use of that color. To uncover the meaning of that motif, he must reintegrate the visual effect with story events to arrive at the interpretation that red is used to signify the presence of death.

Repetition can also serve an important function in documentary films. Documentary filmmakers may repeat images to highlight their significance, as Albert and David Maysles do in *Gimme Shelter* (1970), a documentary about the Rolling Stones' American tour in 1969. The filmmakers repeat scenes that show a man being attacked near the stage during the Altamont concert. The first time, the viewer sees the images as part of the performance. But the images reappear in the next scene, where the filmmakers and band members watch the concert footage on an editing table. This repetition emphasizes the significance of the tragic incident and provides viewers with access to the band's reactions to the event.

Repetition can also create meaning in avant-garde films. Hollis Frampton's *Nostalgia* (1967) is based on the repetition of a simple, disjointed act: while the camera is trained on a photograph, a **voice-over** describes an image. Over time, it becomes apparent that the voice-over does not describe the image it accompanies but, rather, the next photograph in the series. At the end of each description, the photograph is burned. The burning motif signals the transition to a new combination of words and image but also comments on the ephemeral nature of photographic images and memories.

Parallels

Filmmakers sometimes use the repetition of details to create **parallels.** A parallel arises when two characters, events, or locations are compared through the use of a narrative element or visual or sound device. When this happens viewers are encouraged to consider the similarities and differences. In *Steamboat Bill, Jr.* (Charles Reisner and Buster Keaton 1928), Bill Jr. (Buster Keaton) goes to have his hair cut. At the barbershop, a friend of his from college is also having her hair styled. A profile shot of Keaton and the woman with the same haircut draws a parallel between the two characters (fig. **2.8**). The joke is meant to suggest that Bill is not manly, a fear his father harbors because Bill is a college boy. The comic parallel of the haircut seems to confirm his father's suspicion. This being a Buster Keaton comedy, Bill ultimately gets the girl, despite (or perhaps because of) their identical haircuts.

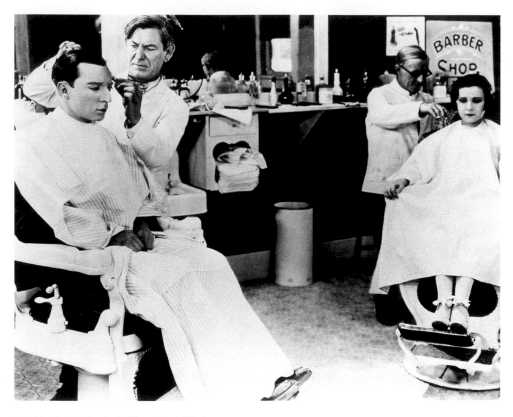

2.8 Identical haircuts in *Steamboat Bill, Jr.*

A parallel may reveal that characters who seem diametrically opposed to one another actually share some underlying characteristics. At the conclusion of *The Empire Strikes Back* (Irvin Kershner 1980), Luke Skywalker loses his hand during the light saber battle with Darth Vader. He later has it replaced with an artificial hand. The robotic limb suggests a physical commonality between the two: Luke has become more like Vader, a robotic figure who is never seen without his rigid, artificial outer covering. This parallel supports the theme that the two Jedi are similar in their mastery of the force, which one uses for good and the other for evil. It also reinforces the fact that Darth Vader is Luke's father, a fact Vader reveals during their battle.

A **shot** at the conclusion of Akira Kurosawa's *High and Low* (*"Tengoku to jigoku"*; 1962) compares two seemingly opposed characters, the wealthy businessman Mr. Gondo (Toshiro Mifune) and a kidnapper whose ransom demands have ruined Gondo financially. In the final scene, as the kidnapper screams at Gondo, it becomes clear that his motivation for the crime was that he resented and envied Gondo's wealth and position. During their interaction, the filmmaker captures the two men's faces together in a glass pane. The image suggests that the men may be more alike than it seems: they share an ability to pursue a goal ruthlessly. Gondo has exercised this ability in the business world and the kidnapper has done so as a criminal. Although the viewer's sympathies lie with Gondo, the scene adds complexity to this hard-edged businessman who has fallen from power.

Parallels can also play an important role in non-narrative films. In Walter Ruttmann's *Berlin, Symphony of a Great City* (*"Berlin, die Sinfonie der Großstadt"*; 1927), a quick **cut** between shots of police officers and dolls in a store window bobbing their heads up and down suggests their common physical posture and makes a humorous comment on the behavior of the police (figs. **2.9**, **2.10**).

In avant-garde films, parallels may work as metaphors, suggesting the common characteristics of two images. *Un Chien Andalou* (*"An Andalusian Dog"*; Luis Buñuel and Salvador Dalí 1929) compares a shot of clouds slicing across the moon with one depicting

the filmmaker Luis Buñuel slicing a human eye (figs. **2.11**, **2.12**). The image functions as a metaphor for the way the movie intends to assault its viewers, and the film certainly did shock contemporary audiences with its irrational, anti-narrative structure.

Details and repetition can form patterns that contribute to a film's meaning. In a narrative fiction film, these elements may explain a character's motivation, present themes, and contribute to the overall flow of the story. In documentaries, they may encourage viewers to make connections between ideas or to reconsider their initial thoughts about an event. In avant-garde films, repetition can organize the flow of images and sound, and may create connections between seemingly dissimilar images. As a result, paying attention to repetition, motifs, and parallels can help viewers to recognize a film's deeper structure.

2.9 *(left)* Bobbing dolls in *Berlin, Symphony of a Great City* (*"Berlin, die Sinfonie der Großstadt"*).

2.10 *(right)* Police officers in *Berlin, Symphony of a Great City.*

Details and Structure

One way to create a framework for meaning is to pay attention to the way the film begins and ends, and the way it unfolds in sections. Each section forms a part of the underlying

2.11 *(left)* Clouds slicing across the moon in *Un Chien Andalou* (*"An Andalusian Dog"*).

2.12 *(right)* An eye being sliced in *Un Chien Andalou.*

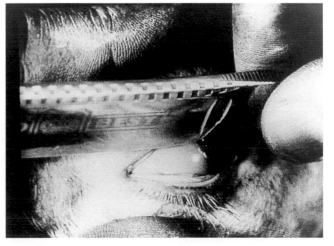

structure of a film. A full analysis of the film reunites the parts and considers the way they interact to produce meaning.

Parallels in Openings and Closings

Parallels that invite viewers to compare the beginning and end of a film provide information about its overall structure. In Jafar Panahi's *The Circle* ("*Dayereh*"; 2000), the opening and closing shots are eerily similar, suggesting that events have gone full circle. The effort that several characters have expended over the course of the film may have been in vain. In *Winged Migration*, the filmmaker begins and ends with scenes of birds in the same location, emphasizing the cyclical, endlessly repeated pattern of migration. *Rear Window* (Alfred Hitchcock 1954) begins and ends in the same location, but the differences between the two scenes convey a great deal about the changes the two main characters have undergone.

Structure and Turning Points

Just as popular songs conform to a familiar pattern—the alternation between verse and chorus—so narrative feature films tend to flow according to a standard structure. Analyzing a narrative film involves dividing the story into beginning, middle, and end and tracking important **turning points**. Even before mastering the complexities of narrative form (the subject of Chapter Three), it is possible to recognize turning points that signal the end of one section of the film and the beginning of another. In the example from *Notorious*, Alicia's decision to limit her drinking signals her desire for change, but Devlin's callous response undermines her courage and she experiences a setback.

Directors signal important moments such as these through camerawork, editing, and sound as well as through dialogue and action. The camera may linger on a shot to suggest its importance, or dramatic music may underscore a particularly significant action. Sometimes an editing transition such as a **fade-out**, where the image slowly recedes until the screen is completely black, reinforces the notion that a major shift has taken place. This is the case in *The Sixth Sense*, for example, where a fade signifies the passage of time between the night Malcolm Crowe (Bruce Willis) is shot and the day he meets Cole (Haley Joel Osment).

When Malcolm visits Cole in the hospital, he shares a secret with the boy, who until this point has resisted Malcolm's attempts to help him. But Cole reciprocates: he tells Malcolm he sees dead people. Cole expresses his trust in the psychologist, and the focus of the film shifts from Malcolm's quest to discover what is troubling the boy to figuring out what Malcolm can do to help him. The director calls attention to this moment: as Malcolm begins to open up, the camera moves slowly toward him, emphasizing Malcolm's emotions. Furthermore, Cole, who had turned his face away, turns back toward Malcolm in a **close-up**, signifying his willingness to share his secret in return. Becoming attuned to significant turning points such as this one, and to how they are created, helps viewers gain a better understanding of a film's structure.

Documentary films can be divided into parts as well. Frederick Wiseman's *Domestic Violence* (2001) opens with scenes of a man abusing his wife. A turning point occurs when the film begins to observe several women as they arrive at a domestic violence shelter and begin their recovery process. A shift—but not necessarily progress—signals the film's conclusion. Wiseman returns to yet another scene of domestic abuse: the police respond to a call where a man admits that he is likely to become physically abusive to his domestic partner but refuses to leave his home.

Repetition and Non-chronological Structure

In a documentary, a turning point may be based on a change from one topic to another. Alternatively, documentaries may be structured according to the various points of view brought to bear on an issue: the arguments for going to war could be positioned before or after the arguments for avoiding war. One of the most famous documentaries about the Holocaust, Alain Resnais's *Night and Fog* ("*Nuit et Brouillard*"; 1955) can be divided into parts according to certain visual attributes. The events occurring in Nazi Germany before and during World War II are depicted in black and white, while postwar images are filmed in color. Rather than presenting a straightforward chronology, Resnais interweaves the troubling events of the past and the apparent tranquility of the present, creating a strong visual contrast that also suggests that the past lives on.

Avant-garde films can be divided into sections as well. The turning points may be subtle, however, signaled by changes in the photographic properties of images, in the way the images and sound relate to one another, or in editing patterns that alter the film's rhythm or pace. Yoko Ono's *No. 4 (Bottoms)* (1966) is an 80-minute film entirely composed of images of rear ends walking away from the camera. At a certain point, Ono repeats some images, changing the viewer's relationship to them. Scott MacDonald argues that "once the film develops this mystery of whether a particular bottom has been seen before, the viewer's relationship with the bottoms becomes more personal: we look not to see a new bottom but to see if we 'know' a particular bottom already" (MacDonald, p. 26).

The goal of examining the relationship between details and structure is to arrive at a comprehensive analysis that takes into account the way seemingly minor elements combine to produce the overall design of a film. Viewers also must consider the details filmmakers include when they make references to people or events outside the film. Recognizing the importance of these references deepens the audience's understanding of the work.

● Creating Meaning Through the World Beyond the Film

Films can also convey meaning by making reference to people and events that exist outside the world of the film. Viewers may understand plot details, character motivation, or themes better because of references to historical events, to other films. and to works of art. In some cases, those references are crucial to the audience's full understanding of the film, but in others, references may function simply as inside jokes.

Historical Events and Cultural Attitudes

Narrative films convey fictional stories, yet they frequently make reference to actual historical events. A film set in a particular era, for example the U.S. Civil War, will more than likely include well-known events such as the burning of Atlanta (depicted in *Gone with the Wind*; Victor Fleming 1939) or the battle at Petersburg (in *Cold Mountain*; Anthony Minghella 2003). Similarly, a number of movies have been made about epic battles in World War II, the Korean War, the Vietnam War, and the Gulf War. Some films, such as *Patton* (Franklin J. Schaffner 1970) and *Born on the Fourth of July* (Oliver Stone 1989), are based on historical figures. Others, such as *The Best Years of Our Lives* (William Wyler 1946) and *Three Kings* (David O. Russell 1999), use war to explore social issues. Films such as *Hiroshima, Mon Amour* ("*Hiroshima, My Love*"; Alain Resnais 1959) and *Plenty* (Fred Schepisi 1985) depict the effects of war, but not necessarily combat, on individuals and societies.

In some cases, references to historical events may be very subtle and easy to miss, such as the newspaper headline that Jake Gittes (Jack Nicholson) reads early in Roman Polanski's *Chinatown* (1973). The film is set in 1937 in Los Angeles, and Jake's newspaper announces the recent victory of Seabiscuit, a famous underdog racehorse, at the nearby Santa Anita racetrack (fig. **2.13**).

Sometimes a director may refer to an attitude or a social context rather than an event. The title of *American Beauty* and the film's rose motif refer not only to a particular kind of rose but also to the Grateful Dead, a musical group who put out an album with the same title. The Grateful Dead's music represents a lifestyle that Lester Burnham wants to revisit: rebellion against convention during the freewheeling 1960s.

In some cases, of course, because of their familiarity with historical events, viewers may take issue with a filmmaker's dramatization of a historical episode. Some filmmakers have been accused of forwarding an interpretation of events rather than an accurate representation of facts, though it can also be argued that any set of historical "facts" is subject to interpretation. Oliver Stone, whose *JFK* (1991) depicted the 1963 assassination of President John F. Kennedy, came under attack for presenting speculative history. Film historian David Cook shows just how complex the question of accuracy is when he writes:

> [. . .] many critics accused [*JFK*] of attempting to rewrite history. But, in addition to some certifiably paranoid speculation, Stone puts more *accurate* information about the assassination and its aftermath on screen in 189 minutes than most contemporary audiences would have encountered in their lifetimes. (Cook, p. 953; emphasis in original)

2.13 Jake (Jack Nicholson) reads the newspaper in *Chinatown*.

Chapter 2: An Approach to Film Analysis

More recently, *A Beautiful Mind* (Ron Howard 2000), based on Sylvia Nasar's biography of Nobel prize-winning mathematician John Nash, provoked controversy by avoiding certain aspects of its subject's life contained in the book.

Yet it would surely be impossible for any film—especially a narrative film, seeking to tell a story—to give an exhaustive depiction of events. Certain characters, events, and issues may be modified for dramatic effect, and audiences should consider why the filmmaker makes certain choices: to create or avoid controversy, perhaps, or to improve the flow of the story?

Stars as References

Films also refer to entities outside themselves through movie stars. Chapter Twelve examines the star system, so it's sufficient for this discussion to observe that actors often repeat and reprise roles and that directors may expect audiences to make connections with those previous roles. Casting Al Pacino as Big Boy in *Dick Tracy* (Warren Beatty 1990) was doubly comical, first because of Pacino's over-the-top performance, but second, because he parodied his performances as gangsters and undercover cops in previous films, including *The Godfather* films (1972, 1974, 1990; fig. **2.14**), *Serpico* (Sidney Lumet 1973), and *Scarface* (Brian De Palma 1983). In *La Femme Nikita* (Luc Besson 1991) Jeanne Moreau plays the woman who teaches Nikita to use her feminine wiles in lethal ways, possibly reminding viewers of Moreau's early roles as a sexually adventurous and independent woman in *The Lovers* ("*Les Amants*"; Louis Malle 1959), *Jules and Jim* ("*Jules et Jim*"; François Truffaut 1962), and *The Bride Wore Black* ("*La Mariée était en noir*"; François Truffaut 1968).

2.14 Al Pacino in *The Godfather*—a more sinister role than Big Boy in *Dick Tracy*.

Public Figures and Celebrities as References

Films can also make reference to public figures. Steven Soderbergh's *Traffic* (2000) includes scenes with U.S. Senators Orrin Hatch and Don Nickles in order to add another layer of meaning to a story line concerned with the U.S. war on drugs (fig. **2.15**). Sinead O'Connor, a well-known Irish pop musician, plays the Blessed Virgin Mary in *The Butcher Boy* (Neil Jordan 1997). Director Neil Jordan's choice may remind viewers of O'Connor's public attack on the Catholic Church in a controversial 1992 television performance on "Saturday Night Live," where she ripped apart a photograph of the Pope. Casting O'Connor as a Catholic icon adds irony to the film.

Intertextual References

Films also sometimes make **intertextual references**, or references to other films or works of art. Films of the French New Wave are known for their numerous references to French

2.15 American Senators add a historical dimension to *Traffic*.

and American films. In Jean-Luc Godard's *Band of Outsiders* ("*Bande à Part*"; 1964), the filmmaker playfully references Jacques Demy's *Umbrellas of Cherbourg* ("*Les Parapluies de Cherbourg*"; 1964) and Charlie Chaplin's *The Immigrant* (1917). *Run Lola Run* (Tom Tykwer 1999) makes a pointed visual reference to Alfred Hitchcock's *Vertigo* (1958). In a scene where Lola (Franka Potente) gambles at a casino to earn the money her boyfriend needs, the camera comes to rest on a painting of a woman. The shot resembles a scene in Hitchcock's film where a blonde Madeleine Elster (Kim Novak) sits before a portrait of the raven-haired Carlotta Valdez (figs. **2.16**, **2.17**). The woman's hairstyle—a spiral French twist—is a prominent detail that may help viewers to connect the two films.

It's reasonable to ask whether this, or any, intertextual reference functions merely as a visual trick, designed to gratify viewers who recognize the portrait and distinctive hairstyle. In this case, the reference to *Vertigo* has several interpretations that make it meaningful. The hairstyle contributes to a visual motif in the film involving a spiral pattern. As she hurries down the stairs of her apartment building and through the Berlin streets, Lola's

2.16 Kim Novak and the portrait in *Vertigo*.

Chapter 2: An Approach to Film Analysis

path creates spirals. Furthermore, the film's structure resembles a spiral. Physically, Lola begins at the same point in each segment, performs the same actions, but always ends up at a different point, which suggests the idea of slightly imperfect circle, or spiral. In some versions, Lola and her boyfriend are killed, but they return to life when the story begins again. The spiral motif and bringing characters back to life link the film to *Vertigo*, which has a repetitive structure in which characters seem to die and come back to life.

2.17 The portrait in *Run Lola Run* references Hitchcock's *Vertigo*.

Avant-garde and Documentary References

Avant-garde films also make references to the world outside films and to other films. Bruce Conner's *A Movie* (1958) and Chick Strand's *Cartoon la Mousse* (1979) are **compilation films** composed entirely of scenes from other films (see figs. 8.29, 8.30). The film segments contribute meaning based on their look, their original content and context, and the way they are juxtaposed with new images.

In one sense, all documentaries make reference to the world beyond film because they are based on historical events. Michael Moore's *Roger and Me* (1989) documents the closing of a GM plant in Flint, Michigan. Errol Morris's *The Thin Blue Line* (1988) looks at a Texas murder and its aftermath. *Rock Hudson's Home Movies* (Mark Rappaport 1993) looks at cinema culture by examining Rock Hudson's Hollywood career and his gay identity. The filmmaker suggests that Hudson's success depended on the public's ignorance about his sexuality whereas gay viewers saw Hudson as a gay icon from his earliest screen roles.

Meaningful References with Objects

Films also refer to real-world objects. Characters may drive a particular kind of vehicle, wear clothing made by a specific designer, and consume popular brands of beer and soft drinks. Often these references are the result of lucrative business deals called **product placement**. Corporations agree to pay film studios a fee to feature products in a film. In Steven Spielberg's *E.T: The Extra-Terrestrial* (1980), the script called for the alien to become hooked on M&Ms. But the Mars corporation was anxious about linking its product to a repulsive alien, so the production company turned to the makers of a new product, Reese's Pieces. *E.T* caused a tremendous sensation, sending the demand for Reese's Pieces soaring and paving the way for a wave of product placement agreements (Monaco, p. 589).

The important question to ask is whether or not familiar products serve a purpose in terms of the film's meaning: do they help to form motifs, do they add significance? In *Men with Guns* (1997), a John Sayles film about peasants caught between warring guerrillas and government troops in an unnamed Central American country, ubiquitous Coke machines suggest that this large U.S. corporation has found a way to make a profit even from very poor people (fig. **2.18**). And in this region of the world the company may be the face of the U.S. The Coca-Cola company also plays a role in creating satire in Kubrick's *Dr. Strangelove*, when an army colonel refuses to steal the machine's change for another officer to make a pay telephone call to the U.S. President to avert a nuclear disaster (fig. **2.19**). He is reluctant to raid the coin box because the machine is the property of an American corporation. Such references to name-brand products should not be rejected out of hand as meaningless; they may serve a function in terms of character and story.

2.18 *(top)* Coke as social commentary in *Men with Guns.*

2.19 *(bottom)* A Coke machine as social satire in *Dr. Strangelove.*

● The Goal of Film Analysis: Articulating Meaning

The purpose of film analysis— breaking a film down into component parts to see how it is put together—is to make statements about a film's themes and meaning. Those statements take three different forms, each one related to a different level of meaning. The first type of statement is descriptive: a **descriptive claim** is a neutral account of the basic characteristics of the film. Most descriptions of narrative fiction films involve plot events. "In *The Matrix* (Wachowski Brothers 1999), Neo (Keanu Reeves) is jolted out of his everyday existence as a computer programmer and exposed to the reality that powerful computers control human existence. He learns to master physical combat to fight the computer program that keeps humans ignorant of their plight." By putting together a series of descriptive claims, this viewer has arrived at a **plot summary**, a sequential

Film Style

For film critics who distinguish content from style, style is defined as the way the content of a film is presented to the audience. A romance story can be presented as a heartbreaking, melodramatic ordeal, with scenes of crashing ocean waves set to classical music, or as a whimsical romp that involves rides on Ferris wheels and 1960s pop music. For many filmmakers and critics, however, the story is inseparable from the way it is told, and style cannot be easily disengaged from subject matter.

Film scholars have long divided narrative fiction films into three stylistic categories: **classical**, **realist**, and **formalist**. The classical style includes the type of films made under the Hollywood studio system, in which the story is paramount. The various elements of film art (including lighting, editing, and sound) do not call attention to themselves as aesthetic devices: instead, they contribute unobtrusively to the smooth flow of the story. The goal is to invite viewers to become a part of the story, not to remind them that they are watching a film. Most commercial releases adopt a classical style, seeking to entertain audiences by immersing them in a fictional world.

Realist films reject some of the rules of classical narrative in terms of characters, stories, and structure. Films made in a realist style do not privilege the story at the expense of

2.20 The realistic presentation of the battle scene at Burpelson in *Dr. Strangelove*.

details that evoke characters, places, and eras. Their stories generally involve average, everyday people. Their plots may seem to digress, as filmmakers strive for spontaneity and immediacy rather than a highly crafted structure. In Vittorio De Sica's *Umberto D* (1952), a scene much discussed by filmgoers involves a maid going through her morning routine. Her actions have no real consequences for the story; so, in a classical film that scene would be "wasted time." In this film, the scene establishes the texture of this minor character's daily life. Ironically, a realist style may be experienced as a more obtrusive style because it allows character and environment to take precedence over storytelling. Despite its name, realism is not reality. Like classicism, it is a style produced by a combination of techniques. Realist films may adopt a different approach to stories than classical films, but they do not necessarily present a "truer" vision of reality. A case in point is the Jules Dassin film *Naked City*. Hailed for its gritty realism when it was released in 1947, audiences fifty years later can't help but notice the artificiality of the talky voice-over.

Formalist films are self-consciously interventionist. They explore abstract ideas through stories and characters. As such, these films generally rely on unusual visual techniques that call attention to themselves as artistic exploration. Formalist films such as Resnais's *Last Year at Marienbad* ("*L'année dernière à Marienbad*"; 1961), Andrej Tarkovsky's *Solaris* (1968), and *American Splendor* (Shari Springer Berman and Robert Pulcini 2003) self-consciously distance viewers from characters and plot. They raise philosophical questions about the nature of identity and reality and represent the most dramatic departure from classical style.

Some films intentionally blend more than one style. A notable example is Kubrick's *Dr. Strangelove*, which juxtaposes realist immediacy in combat scenes (fig. **2.20**) with a studied formalism in scenes of General Jack D. Ripper's office, where stagey, dramatic lighting and extreme camera angles give visual form to Ripper's insanity (fig. **2.21**).

2.21 Ripper's office in *Dr. Strangelove*—a formalist approach.

Another less tangible factor that contributes to style is the **tone** of a film. Whereas mood defines a feeling, tone is the attitude behind the film. A film may be ironic, encouraging viewers to take a distanced, critical look at the characters, for example, or it may have a nostalgic tone, where the past seems superior to the present day. Tonal shifts are important as well: Roberto Benigni's *Life is Beautiful* ("*La vita è bella*"; 1998) uses cinematography to signal the tonal shift from early scenes depicting two characters falling in love (fig. **2.22**) to later scenes that show the same characters imprisoned in a Nazi concentration camp (fig. **2.23**). The pastel colors, golden light, and soft focus of the early scenes of screwball romance give way to a cold blue environment, harsh gray light, and painfully precise focus.

2.22 *(top)* Golden hues in the early scenes of *Life is Beautiful* ("*La vita è bella*").

2.23 *(bottom)* Harsh grays and blues dominate the late scenes of *Life is Beautiful*.

account of the important events in a film. Descriptive statements do not present judgments or discuss the significance of events. But descriptions may go beyond events and refer to genre: "*The Matrix* seems more like a Western than a Sci-Fi film," or "The action sequences in *The Matrix* look like those in Hong Kong action films" (fig. **2.24**).

An **evaluative claim** presents a judgment. An evaluative statement expresses the author's belief that the film is good, bad, or mediocre: he or she may give it a grade of "A," "F," or "C." The "two thumbs up" formula of Ebert and Roeper and the four- or five-star, or A, B, C, D scales used by other film critics present evaluative claims (fig. **2.25**). An example of an evaluative claim is the statement: "*The Matrix* is a great film." But this is a weak evaluative claim because the speaker has not established any criteria for the evaluation: the listener does not know why the speaker thinks *The Matrix* is great. Without that information, does the evaluation have credibility?

A stronger evaluative claim includes the reasons why the evaluation is positive or negative. "*The Matrix* is a great film because it includes exciting scenes of physical combat." This statement is more convincing than the first assertion because it provides the basis for the judgment. Evaluative claims are always based on the evaluator's criteria, even if they remain unstated. Here, the unstated but implicit criterion is that exciting action scenes make a film great. Given the tremendous diversity of viewer preferences, it's important to be clear about evaluative criteria. Transparency helps to prevent disputes arising from different beliefs and underlying assumptions.

An **interpretive claim** presents an argument about a film's meaning and significance. Interpretive claims address a film's themes and abstract ideas. They do more than simply identify a film's themes; they go further, making an argument about what the film does with those themes. For example, after careful critical analysis, a filmgoer might conclude that one theme in *The Matrix* relates to technology. An interpretive claim might suggest: "*The Matrix* questions the notion of technological progress by showing that technology actually controls people rather than the other way around."

Another theme of the same film is the importance of individuals working together to accomplish goals. Are the two themes related to one another? They may be. So a more complex interpretive claim might be: "Although an over-reliance on technology proves dangerous, the film finally assures viewers that a small group of people united by a common purpose can defeat the most powerful technological system."

This statement is by no means the only interpretive claim someone might make about *The Matrix*. There can be many descriptions and interpretations of any one film. The viewer who appreciates the film's action sequences might make this interpretive claim: "*The Matrix* uses Hong Kong cinema-style action sequences to show that ultimately, resistance to an oppressive technological system is based on physical strength." (Note the difference between

2.24 A scene from *Once upon a Time in China, Part II* (Hark Tsui 1992), a typical Hong Kong action movie.

2.25 Critics grade films in *Entertainment Weekly*.

Critical Mass

Here's how a sampling of critics from across the country grade 10 current releases.

	JAMI BERNARD N.Y. Daily News	TY BURR Boston Globe	MIKE CLARK USA Today	JOANNA CONNORS Cleveland Plain Dealer	ROGER EBERT Chicago Sun-Times	LIAM LACEY Toronto Globe and Mail	MICK LASALLE San Francisco Chronicle	TODD McCARTHY Variety	CARRIE RICKEY Philadelphia Inquirer	RENE RODRIGUEZ The Miami Herald	ENTERTAINMENT WEEKLY	EW READERS*	CRITICS' AVERAGE
BAADASSSSS!	—	A-	B	—	A-	B+	B	B-	B	—	A-	B	B+
CONTROL ROOM	—	—	—	B+	—	—	—	B-	—	—	B-	B	B
▲ DAY AFTER TOMORROW	C+	C+	C-	C+	B-	C	B	C+	C	D	C+	B	C+
HARRY POTTER...	A-	B+	B	A	A-	A-	B-	A-	B+	B+	B+	A-	B+
RAISING HELEN	C+	C-	D+	—	C	C-	C-	—	C	C	C+	B-	C
SAVED!	—	—	C+	A-	B	—	B	—	—	—	B	B+	B
SHREK 2	A-	B	B	B	B+	B	C+	B	A-	B-	A-	A-	B
SOUL PLANE	D	D	—	B-	—	—	B-	—	D+	C	C-	C-	C-
SUPER SIZE ME	B+	B+	B	—	B	B+	B+	—	A-	—	A	A-	B+
TROY	B	C	B	C-	C-	C	B	C+	B	C+	C	B+	C+

*EW READER GRADES come from the Front Row, EW's online reader panel. If you'd like to join, go to frontrowpanel.com/join.

this statement and the descriptive statement that simply compared the film to Hong Kong action films.) Another viewer might not agree that the film presents physical might as the only means of resisting dehumanization, claiming instead: "*The Matrix* suggests that the powers of the mind and body must be integrated in order for humans to overcome obstacles."

How should a third person listening to these statements determine which interpretation is correct? Although films support multiple interpretations, they do not generally support diametrically opposed claims. Some claims have greater validity than others. To be convincing, any interpretive claim must be well supported by details from the film. And constructing valid interpretive claims is not a simple matter: a serious interpretation demands a thorough consideration of all aspects of the film that support or weaken the claim.

To determine which interpretive claim about *The Matrix* is strongest (that is, which claim is best supported by the film), consider the way the film depicts the relationship between ideas and physical prowess. Is it true that Neo's physical skills (along with those of Morpheus and Trinity) are the only basis for their success? Are there scenes, moments, or lines of dialogue suggesting that action must be combined with analysis or contemplation? A film like this one may look simple, but a careful examination of details, structure, and tone may reveal implicit or hidden ideas that are not obvious at first.

● The Importance of Developing Interpretive Claims

One of the most challenging and rewarding aspects of studying film is developing interpretive claims. Whereas a brief description may be helpful when deciding whether or not to see a film, interpretive claims move the conversation to a new level. Interpretation takes into account the complexity of films, capturing the way films affect viewers long after they have left the theater or turned off their DVD player. Because interpretive claims grow out of description and analysis, they take account of the way that stories, characters, camera angles, sound effects, and other elements of film art interact to produce intense emotional and thought-provoking experiences.

Interpreting films also helps to develop logical thinking and writing skills. Making an interpretive claim about a favorite film is fun, but it also demands organization and keen insight. Finally, interpretations link films to larger issues. For example, the question implicit in the two conflicting interpretations of *The Matrix*—the film's view of the proper relation between physical action and contemplative thought—ought to generate discussion about subjects that are important to the world outside the movie theater.

Part II of this book offers the essential tools for describing and analyzing films, beginning with a discussion of narrative form, and moving through visual elements and sound. Developing the ability to recognize specific visual, sound, and storytelling techniques and their effects on viewers is critical to constructing clear and thoughtful interpretive claims. By the end of Part II, readers should be able to formulate a sound, comprehensive interpretive argument about a film, using the proper terminology to describe the film techniques covered in Chapters Three through Eight.

● Summary

- Viewer expectations about formal organization, stars, director, and genre influence their experience of films.
- Filmmakers anticipate expectations and may satisfy some expectations and offer novel approaches to others.
- Paying careful attention to repeated details helps to uncover important aspects of character, story, and structure.
- Motifs (any significant repeated element) and parallels (which ask viewers to compare and contrast two distinct characters, situations, or locations) are particularly important instances of repetition that, among other things, signal turning points and structure.
- Films produce meaning by making reference to history, to real world locations, objects, or people, to other arts forms, and to other films.
- Three types of written statements provide information about a film's meaning: descriptive, evaluative, and interpretive statements.
- Film style emerges from the interaction of a film's formal mode of organization, its subject matter, and its visual and sound elements. Three styles are differentiated according to specific traits: classical (invested in clear storytelling), realist (interested in exploring characters and capturing life), and formalist (overt intervention that calls attention to the process of representation).

Film Analysis • Reading Significant Details

To analyze a film, viewers must be active, which means paying attention to details, asking questions, and not taking anything for granted. If possible, viewers should watch a film twice before analyzing it in writing or in discussion, using the first viewing to simply watch the film and taking notes the second time through. If only one screening is possible, then viewers should take notes during the first screening and watch a scene or listen to an exchange of dialogue more than once if it seems significant. Develop a system to chart the way motifs are established and developed.

The essay below looks at the ways that Carl Franklin's *Devil in a Blue Dress* uses historical references to add significance to the story. To comprehend references fully, viewers must first take note of them and then follow up by asking questions and conducting research.

2.26 A subtle allusion to African-American cinema history in *Devil in a Blue Dress*.

Study Notes offer tips about note-taking and paying attention to details.

Historical References in *Devil in a Blue Dress*

Carl Franklin's *Devil in a Blue Dress* tells the story of Easy Rawlins (Denzel Washington), an African-American man living in Los Angeles in 1948 who has recently been laid off from his job. He agrees to do some private investigation work for a white man named Allbright (Tom Sizemore); his job is to find a woman named Daphne Monet (Jennifer Beals). Over the course of the film, the director includes several references to actual locations and historical events that help viewers to understand the racially segregated world Easy Rawlins must navigate.

The film's locations reflect historical patterns of racial separation in Los Angeles. Easy has returned from World War II and, under the auspices of the GI Bill, bought a home in Watts. Several times in the film, he goes to Central Avenue, a lively urban area with shops and nightclubs. Easy has friends in the bars on Central Avenue and fluid **tracking shots** show that he is comfortable enjoying the lively nightlife among the throngs of people.[1]

By contrast, when Easy meets Allbright at the Malibu Pier, a tracking shot depicts him with his jacket zipped up, obviously uncomfortable in a predominantly white area of town. Furthermore, a static camera and cuts emphasize the way two young white men harass and physically trap Easy because he is talking to a white woman. Later, when Easy meets Daphne Monet at the Ambassador Hotel, there is a "white only" section. The film's references to historical locations inform viewers about segregation in 1940s Los Angeles. They show that Easy lives in a divided city: he is comfortable and welcome in some areas, but not in others.[2]

The film also contains a historical reference to African-American visual culture during the 1940s. As Easy drives down the street, a theater marquee visible behind him bears the title of the film *The Betrayal*, made by the pioneering black filmmaker Oscar Micheaux in 1948 (fig. **2.26**). In creating Easy's world, director Carl Franklin makes evident the thriving culture of the predominantly African-American South Central section of L.A.[3] This movie theater is part of Easy's territory: along with his own home, this neighborhood is the area where he is most relaxed.

Devil in a Blue Dress also calls attention to another historical event of the late 1940s that relates to the theme of racial segregation. As Mark Berrettini points out in his essay on the film, Easy intentionally misstates Daphne Monet's name when he asks friends about her, calling her "Delilah" and "Dahlia" so as to appear casual about his inquiry (Berrettini, p. 76).[4] The first name is a biblical reference to a dangerous woman, which Daphne seems to be. But the second name refers to a shocking and real L.A. crime, the "Black Dahlia" murder, unsolved since 1947 (Berrettini, p. 76). The victim, Elizabeth Short, was presented as a woman of loose morals who deserved her tragic fate. Easy's misnaming attaches those same associations to Daphne Monet. And most of the characters see Daphne this way, although Easy and the audience eventually learn the she is not what she seems to be. The reason why Daphne is dangerous is not because of loose morals, but because she represents a challenge to the strict segregation of black and white people.

Devil in a Blue Dress uses references to historical events, locations, and people to add layers of meaning to the story. The references not only create a fuller picture of postwar L.A., but also help viewers to understand more fully the crucial role racial segregation plays in Easy's story.

3 Take note of historical locations or figures such as Oscar Micheaux. Conduct research to determine whether the reference is significant. On-line sources may point you to general information, whereas essays in scholarly film journals develop interpretations that bear on the film's themes.

4 The keener the attention to detail, the better the analysis. For example, the author of the journal article cited interprets a historical reference based on a character pretending to forget another character's name. Many viewers would not question the significance of the "mistake."

Works Consulted

Berrettini, Mark. "Private Knowledge, Public Space: Investigation and Navigation in *Devil in a Blue Dress*," *Cinema Journal*, 39/1 (Fall 1999), pp. 74–89.

Cook, David. *A History of Narrative Film*, 3rd edn. New York: Norton, 1996.

MacDonald, Scott. *Avant Garde Film: Motion Studies*. Cambridge: Cambridge University Press, 1993.

Monaco, James. *How to Read a Film*, 3rd edn. New York and Oxford: Oxford University Press, 2000.

Rosenbaum, Jonathan. "The World According to Harvey and Bob," in *Movies as Politics*, pp. 159–65. Berkeley and Los Angeles, CA: University of California Press, 1997.

Sarris, Andrew. *The Primal Screen*. New York: Simon and Schuster, 1973.

Film Analysis

Part II provides readers with the analytical tools needed to interpret films. These tools include identifying the elements of film art and the terminology that film scholars and filmmakers use to describe film techniques. Part II also helps readers to develop the skills necessary to write a comprehensive textual analysis.

Chapters Three through Seven offer readers a thorough understanding of five components of film: narrative form (the way the story is structured), mise en scène (or cinematic staging), cinematography, editing, and sound. These chapters explore a wide variety of films, yet they all emphasize narrative as a mode of organizing visual and sound elements. Chapter Eight focuses specific attention on documentary and avant-garde films, emphasizing the fact that these films, even if they do not tell a story, also orchestrate visual and sound details to produce meaning according to definable organizing principles.

Part II also offers several opportunities for readers to build their writing skills. Film analyses at the end of Chapters Three through Seven offer examples of film writing and provide useful tips on topics such as logic and organization and incorporating outside research. Chapter Nine focuses on using the skills and information acquired by working through Chapters Three through Eight to describe, evaluate, and interpret films. Chapter Nine emphasizes the importance of writing clearly and persuasively about movies both in an academic context and for a general audience.

Filmy image texture in the opening of *McCabe and Mrs. Miller.*

3

Narrative Form

One should not tell stories as straight-line narratives. There are so many other possibilities, and film would only enrich them.

Peter Greenaway

*T*wo recent films involve characters who discover the lives they have been living are elaborate fictions. Those discoveries take place at different points in the two films, however. In *The Matrix*, Neo learns early on that the world he inhabits is a computer program designed to keep people content so their bodies can be farmed by machines. When he learns the truth, Neo joins a group of people fighting the powerful system that maintains the world of false appearances.

In *Vanilla Sky* (Cameron Crowe 2001), David (Tom Cruise) experiences the fast-paced life of a wealthy New Yorker. He has friends and girlfriends, but suffers a disfiguring car

3.1 Nature is an obstacle to be overcome in *A Perfect Storm*.

accident, and experiences a downward emotional spiral. His attempts to maintain friendships and pursue a new relationship all seem to fail. At the film's conclusion, David learns that all of his experiences since the accident have been figments of his imagination. Shortly after the accident, his brain was cryogenically preserved and he has been suspended in a dreamy afterlife for many years. He may choose to continue in that state, or re-enter reality.

Neo's awakening occurs early in the film, while David's takes place at the end. Does this difference matter to the viewer, and should it? To answer this question, one must develop an understanding of the rules of **narrative** form.

Chapter Two argued that learning to read details is critical to film analysis, since they form the basis for a film's organization and meaning. This chapter looks at one important mode of organization: narrative form. The primary purpose of narrative form is to tell a story, the driving force behind literary genres such as novels, short stories, and stage plays. But comic strips and even some poetry and music can be organized according to the rules of narrative form. Becoming familiar with the role of narrative as a structuring device allows viewers to grasp character change and development, recognize parallels and motifs, and most importantly, to synthesize these details to build an interpretation of a film's themes.

Although most feature films are organized according to principles of narrative form, there are other types of films which are organized differently. Chapter Eight examines some alternatives to narrative fiction film. This chapter offers a definition of narrative and looks at some of the key concepts employed when analyzing narrative form. It then goes on to examine the structure that most conventional narrative films take, and at some alternatives to that structure. The chapter ends by looking at some of the perspectives from which a film can be narrated, or appear to be narrated.

Defining Narrative

A narrative is an account of a string of events occurring in space and time. Not merely a cluster of random elements, a narrative presents an ordered series of events connected by the logic of cause and effect. For example, when Neo learns that the Matrix controls human life (cause), he decides to join Morpheus and Trinity in their quest to defeat it (effect). Neo's character traits, including his values and beliefs, contribute to his decision. A different character might refuse to get involved, preferring the false sense of security the Matrix provides. Narratives piece events together in a linear fashion that clearly shows the audience the reasons for, and the consequences of, character behavior. This logic of cause and effect ties together character traits, goals, obstacles, and actions.

Narrative films generally focus on human characters and their struggles. Characters possess traits, face conflicts, perform actions, and undergo changes that enable or hinder their pursuit of a specific goal. The goal may be concrete or abstract, lofty or banal: in some cases it may be finding love; in others it may be saving humanity or arriving safely at a destination. Russian narrative theorist Tzvetlan Todorov argued that all narratives involve the disruption of a stable situation, which makes restoration of equilibrium an important

The Screenplay

The process of making a feature film begins with an original or an adapted **screenplay**, written by a screenwriter, based on fictional events or non-fiction source material. A screenplay that has not been commissioned—one that a screenwriter submits for consideration—is called a **spec script**. Screenplays usually go through a number of revisions, modified by script doctors, specialists in a particular area, such as dialogue. During **pre-production**, the director adds information (numbering scenes, determining camera placement, cuts, and sound cues) to produce the **shooting script**, which is the day-to-day guide the director and cinematographer use during production. After each day of shooting, the script supervisor maintains a detailed log of the scenes filmed that day.

goal. Even when a conclusion restores equilibrium, chances are good that characters attain stability only after undergoing important changes: for example, after reconsidering goals and the means of attaining them and facing down internal demons or external challenges.

Characters encounter obstacles to attaining goals: these obstacles arise from within, from other characters, from non-human characters (in horror and science fiction), and from forces of nature (disaster films; fig. **3.1**, *A Perfect Storm*; Wolfgang Peterson 2000). They may be concrete physical challenges (scaling a mountain), the actions and desires of others (a lover's rejection), or internal psychological or emotional issues (fear of commitment). In some cases the characters may not achieve the goal they are pursuing: events, or their own failings, may conspire against them.

Many narrative films involve characters overcoming obstacles on more than one level. The *Lord of the Rings* trilogy (Peter Jackson 2001, 2002, 2003) offers an example. The primary obstacle the Fellowship faces is the physical challenge posed by the Dark Lord Sauron and his Orcs, yet each character also faces internal challenges as the group moves toward its collective goal. Frodo, for example, must resist the lure of the ring.

Filmmakers orchestrate story details in a systematic way to produce a meaningful and enjoyable experience for the audience. They establish and explore characters and their conflicts using the panoply of cinematic techniques available, including dialogue, music, visual effects, locations, costumes, colors, and editing. This chapter focuses specifically on the narrative choices available to screenwriters and film directors and helps readers to recognize the conventions of classical narrative form as well as alternatives to those conventions. The next section discusses how filmmakers often combine elements that do not exist in the story world with their fictional narratives.

Framing the Fictional World: Diegetic and Non-Diegetic Elements

Narrative films often include elements that exist outside the fictional world of the story—such as the opening or closing credits, or background music. The implied world of the story, including settings, characters, sounds, and events, is the **diegesis**. Elements that exist outside the diegesis are called **non-diegetic** or **extradiegetic** devices. The audience is aware of these non-diegetic components of the film, but the characters, of course, are not.

Filmmakers use non-diegetic elements for several reasons: they may draw attention to aspects of the narrative from a position outside the story, they communicate with the audience directly, and they engage viewers on an emotional level.

Most narrative films tell a story by simply showing a sequence of actions, but others include a narrator, who may or may not be one of the characters in the film. A non-diegetic narrator, one who is not a character in the story, may not seem to have a vested interest in explaining events a certain way and thus may appear to be objective. Non-diegetic narrators address the audience in *Band of Outsiders* ("*Bande à part*"; Jean-Luc Godard 1964), *Babe* (Chris Noonan 1995), and *Dogville* (Lars Von Trier 2003).

A non-diegetic voice-over narrates *The Royal Tenenbaums* (Wes Anderson 2001). In the same film, a non-diegetic visual device creates an analogy between the narration and the act of reading stories aloud to children. A large printed page opens new "chapters" of the film (fig. **3.2**).

The opening of *Star Wars* (George Lucas 1977) consists of a written explanation of the history behind the film's events. Those words reeling off into space are not a part of the diegesis.

Narration by a character from the fictional world, such as Holly (Sissy Spacek) in *Badlands* (Terrence Malick 1974) or Cher (Alicia Silverstone) in *Clueless* (Amy Heckerling 1995) is a diegetic element, even if the character narrates from a point in time that is earlier or later than the events depicted. (A full treatment of this diegetic technique appears in the discussion of character subjectivity later in this chapter.)

Music may function as a diegetic or a non-diegetic element. Often filmmakers use non-diegetic music (without a source in the story world) to accompany action or romantic scenes. The music communicates directly to viewers on an emotional level, enhancing the actions depicted.

The distinction between diegetic and non-diegetic elements can be played for comedy. In *I'm Gonna Git You Sucka* (Keenen Ivory Wayans 1988), a spoof of 1970s black action films, macho hero John Spade (Bernie Casey) is accompanied by a theme song. Audiences may assume that, like Issac Hayes's wildly popular theme music for *Shaft* (Gordon Parks 1971), Spade's theme is non-diegetic. Yet in this parody, the music *is* part of the diegesis: a live band follows Spade wherever he goes and plays his song. By the end of the film, Spade's son and protégé Jack (Keenen Ivory Wayans) has hired a hip hop ensemble to produce his own live soundtrack (fig. **3.3**).

3.2 The book device in *The Royal Tenenbaums*.

3.3 Wayans's band provides humor in *I'm Gonna Git You Sucka.*

Non-diegetic narration and music accomplish several things: they frame the diegesis (providing information from a vantage point unavailable within the story world), interrupt the diegesis (distancing viewers or creating humor), and enhance the mood of the diegesis (reinforcing moments of danger or romance).

Within the Diegesis: Selecting and Organizing Events

Feature films typically have a **running time,** or **screen time** of between 90 and 180 minutes. But the stories they tell rarely take place in that amount of time. "Real time" films such as *Nick of Time* (John Badham 1995) or *Cleo from 5 to 7* (Agnès Varda 1962), in which the events take exactly as long as the film's running time to unfold, are rare exceptions to this rule.

How do filmmakers tell stories that span entire lives in this short period of time? Buck Henry, screenwriter of *The Graduate* (Mike Nichols 1967) and *To Die For* (Gus Van Sant 1995), explains: "the secret of a film script is compression" (Peacock, p. 111). That is, films do not depict every moment of their characters' lives; in fact, they omit a great deal. Days, months, or even years may pass in the blink of an eye, or during a fade-out.

Simply put, filmmakers choose to present certain events and leave others out. This seemingly obvious principle of storytelling is so important to narrative form that Russian literary theorists created two terms to describe the fact that a writer (or, in this case, a screenwriter) transforms a complete, chronological story (the ***fabula***) into an abbreviated, reorganized version of events that plays out on screen for the audience (the ***syuzhet***).

The *syuzhet* refers to the selection and ordering of the actions explicitly presented on screen. The *fabula* is the chronological narrative, in its entirety, that implicitly stands behind the events depicted. The *fabula* includes events that take place during the span of time of the *syuzhet* that are implied but not overtly represented. The *fabula* also incorporates a character's **backstory** (a character's formative experiences before the beginning of the *syuzhet*). Some film scholars prefer the terms **plot** (*syuzhet*) and **story** (*fabula*). But, because viewers typically use "plot" and "story" indiscriminately to mean "narrative," these admittedly unusual Russian terms are better suited to the precise terminology of film analysis.

In *Citizen Kane*, viewers do not see the events of Charles Foster Kane's life between about age eight and age twenty-five; the *syuzhet* omits these details. But the young man's activities during that decade are not simply left to the imagination. Mr. Bernstein, Jed Leland, and Kane himself all mention the fact that Kane was expelled from several universities. Kane's mischievous pranks and subsequent expulsions are never shown, but the viewer is aware of them. In this complex film, many *fabula* events are eliminated from the *syuzhet*. For example, a newspaper headline announces the deaths of Emily Norton Kane and Junior, but the tragic event is not dramatized.

The significance of the difference between *fabula* and *syuzhet* is not simply that events are left out. Instead, the important question is: what is the effect of these choices? Does it change a viewer's perception of a character or the flow of action that certain events are represented while others are not?

The *syuzhet* entails more than simply eliminating events from the *fabula*—it also involves re-ordering events. The *syuzhet* can begin at any point within the *fabula*, including the end. *Citizen Kane* and *Memento* (Christopher Nolan 2001) begin at the end of the *fabula* and move backward in time. Filmmakers may use **flashbacks** and **flashforwards**, scenes from the past or future that interrupt the film's present tense, to rearrange the chronology of the *fabula*. Repositioning events influences the way the audience understands them.

In *Out of the Past* (Jacques Tourneur 1947), Jeff (Robert Mitchum) tells his fiancée, Ann (Rhonda Fleming), about his former life of crime in several long flashbacks. Those flashbacks appear after the film's opening scenes have presented Jeff as an ordinary man living in a small town. By manipulating the order of events—showing his present life first and then showing his past—the *syuzhet* encourages viewers to sympathize with Jeff. They see him as an upstanding citizen before they learn he was a criminal.

The flashbacks emphasize the fact that Jeff's past intrudes into his current life. The re-emergence of his past disrupts Jeff's equilibrium, and he takes action to prevent his former associates from coming back into his life. But no matter how hard he tries, Jeff cannot escape the consequences of his past. In this example, the screenwriter reorders the *fabula* in order to control viewers' engagement with the main character. It also leads viewers to the central theme of the film, which is signified by the title and underscored by the flashback structure.

The notion that Jeff cannot escape his criminal past marks this film as a *film noir*, a French term meaning "black film." *Film noir* emerged in a cycle of American films of the 1940s and '50s that focused on social outcasts: criminals, private detectives, and losers trapped in violent circumstances. By and large, *films noirs* have a downbeat tone and pessimistic world view, matched by a bold, expressionist visual style that makes effective use of darkness and shadows.

Fabula events that are omitted from the *syuzhet* may have a strong bearing on the narrative. In Orson Welles's *Touch of Evil* (1958), a late *film noir*, a criminal suspect finally confesses to a crime. Prior to the confession, he had maintained his innocence, even though police captain Hank Quinlan (Orson Welles) had framed him for the crime. The confession is not presented in the *syuzhet* but is mentioned in an aside to Mike Vargas (Charlton Heston), another official who opposes Quinlan and his corrupt methods. Oddly enough, the confession vindicates Quinlan. True, he violates ethical principles and breaks laws by framing suspects. Yet, after the suspect confesses, Quinlan's repeated claim that he only frames the guilty rings true.

What might have been the consequences of including the confession in the *syuzhet*? Would giving that moment dramatic emphasis cause the audience to admire Quinlan's flawed approach? By leaving the confession out of the *syuzhet*, the film balances the discovery of the truth with Quinlan's violation of laws and procedures. Quinlan is not applauded for having the right instincts about the suspect. The tension between following procedures (associated with Vargas) and doing whatever is necessary to apprehend criminals (Quinlan's approach) is a central conflict in the film. The decision to leave the confession out of the *syuzhet* contributes to the ambiguous nature of the conflict.

The *syuzhet* may also manipulate the frequency of events (how many times an act occurs). A single *fabula* event may be depicted more than once, sometimes from the perspective of several characters, as with Susan Alexander's opera debut in *Citizen Kane*. The film presents the debut twice, once from Susan's perspective and once from Jed Leland's.

In Jim Jarmusch's *Mystery Train* (1989), three narratives are connected by the repetition of three sounds: a DJ's introduction to Elvis Presley's "Blue Moon," a train whistle heard as the train crosses a bridge, and a gunshot inside the Memphis hotel where the characters are staying. Each of these events occurs once in the *fabula* (where events are chronological and can only take place once) but three times in the *syuzhet*. Using a sound repetition makes this device subtle, but it still may jar viewers because it indicates that, although the viewer experiences the *syuzhet* as three separate stories unfolding sequentially, they are happening simultaneously.

The distinction between the *fabula* and *syuzhet* makes clear that each event represented in a film has been selected for dramatization and has been ordered systematically—there are no accidents. The *syuzhet* may distill, condense, and expand on *fabula* events, giving writers and directors great latitude in portraying characters and events. The *syuzhet* need not chronicle every moment in the *fabula*, and it usually emphasizes the importance of some moments relative to others. When analyzing a narrative film, take note of the *fabula* events that have been left out of the *syuzhet*, changes in chronology, and events that may occur more than once; they often reveal important aspects of structure, character, and theme.

● Narrative Structure

The standard pattern that shapes narrative films is the **three-act structure**. Act One introduces characters, goals, and conflict(s) and ends with a first turning point, which causes a shift to Act Two. A turning point, which may be signaled through dialogue, setting, or other visual or sound techniques, represents a moment when an important change has occurred that affects a character or situation. Generally, at this point the main character (the **protagonist**) modifies the methods by which she plans to attain her goals, or changes those goals altogether. In Act Two, the protagonist meets obstacles, possibly arising from the actions of another central figure who opposes her, called the **antagonist**. The conflicts increase in number and complexity, leading to a major turning point, referred to as the climax. Act Three presents the **dénouement**, a series of events that resolves the conflicts that have arisen—not always happily. When the concluding moments of the film tie up all the loose strands, leaving no unanswered questions, the film is said to provide closure.

However, film scholar Kristin Thompson has recently argued that both classical and contemporary Hollywood films actually exhibit a **four-part structure** (fig. **3.4**). The parts, which are of roughly equal length, are demarcated by turning points linked to character goals. The main difference between the three-act model and Thompson's four-part structure is that she locates a critical turning point at the midway point—the "dead center" of the film.

In the four-part structure, the introduction leads to an initial turning point, which is followed by a complicating action. This leads in turn to the central turning point at the halfway mark. After that shift, a period of development takes place; this is where the protagonist clearly struggles toward goals. That struggle leads to the climax, followed by the resolution and epilogue.

3.4 Three- and four-part narrative structures.

Three-Act Structure	Four-Part Structure (Thompson)
Act One: Exposition leads to turning point	1. Exposition leads to turning point
Act Two: Complications lead to climax	2. Complicating action leads to major turning point at halfway mark
	3. Development: struggle toward goal leads to climax
Act Three: Action leading to resolution	4. Epilogue

At the beginning of a film, audiences find themselves thrust into a fictional world of characters and actions they cannot fully understand. To help orient viewers at the opening of a film, filmmakers often impart a great deal of information in a relatively short period of screen time. The very opening of the film, dense with narrative details, is called the **exposition**. The exposition brings viewers "up to speed" on place, time, characters, and circumstances. The exposition is not synonymous with the first act, however. The first act includes the exposition but generally is longer, because it also sets up the film's primary conflict.

The exposition of *Rear Window* introduces the audience to a group of people living in the New York apartment building where protagonist L.B. Jeffries (Jimmy Stewart) lives. The cast of characters includes a dancer, a sculptor, a couple with a dog, a composer, and some sunbathers. After **panning** across the courtyard, taking note of these neighbors through Jeffries' open window, the camera cuts to a large thermometer and then tracks backward into Jeffries' apartment. The camera sweeps through the interior, as if examining its contents with curiosity. In a brief amount of screen time, Hitchcock conveys a good deal of information: Jeffries' name (written on his leg cast), his profession (adventure photographer), his physical state (explained by the photograph of the automobile accident), and his ambivalence about romance (the positive and negative photograph of a glamorous woman).

Spectators may absorb some of this information without even being aware of doing so. This dialogue-free exposition—Jeffries is asleep—lays the groundwork for all the events that occur in the film. It introduces Jeffries' physical predicament, his voyeuristic tenden-

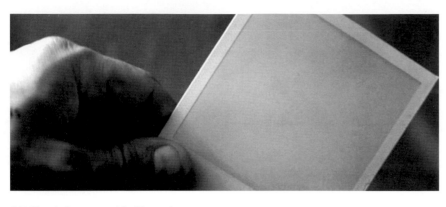

3.5 Time being reversed in *Memento*.

cies, and the stifling summer temperatures that bring people and their secrets out into the courtyard. Introducing details in the exposition and exploiting them later is an example of the conscious placement and repetition of information.

The exposition of Christopher Nolan's *Memento* (2001) orients audience members to the fictional world in a different way. The exposition does not provide information about characters or motivation, but, instead, offers a clue as to how to read this unusually structured film. The *syuzhet* reverses the chronological sequence of most of the events in the *fabula*. The *syuzhet* begins with the final *fabula* event and works backward in time (though flashbacks ensure the *syuzhet* is not simply a reversal of the chronology of the *fabula*). In the opening scene, the erasure of an image on a Polaroid photograph conveys to the audience the fact that time is moving in reverse (fig. **3.5**). This moment draws on viewers' knowledge about the way Polaroid cameras work and inventively presents the film's time frame in purely visual terms.

Narrative details are important throughout the film, not only in the exposition. Typically, critical transitions between acts are marked by lines of dialogue, changes in setting, or major events that suggest a shift in character or circumstance. In *The Wizard of Oz* (Victor Fleming 1939), Dorothy's now legendary line "We're not in Kansas anymore" draws attention to the dramatic shift in her circumstances at the end of Act One, after the cyclone has carried her to the land of Oz. In *The Fly* (David Cronenberg 1986), scientist

3.6 A sign of trouble to come in *The Fly*.

Seth Brundle (Jeff Goldblum) begins to sprout large hairs on his back after experimenting with teleportation (fig. **3.6**). Although he and his girlfriend are aware of this odd turn of events, they do not yet realize it is an early indication of his second act transition from human to Brundlefly, as he eventually calls himself.

In the screwball comedy *Bringing Up Baby* (Howard Hawks 1938), the setting demarcates a classical three-act structure. Would-be lovers Susan (Katharine Hepburn) and David (Cary Grant) meet in New York in Act One, then drive to Connecticut where, in the second act, they face a number of complications that prevent them from attaining their divergent goals. One of Susan's goals is to be with David, so she achieves a partial victory by getting him to Connecticut and keeping him there. They return to New York in the film's very brief third act for a resolution of their romance.

● ●

Techniques in Practice: Narrative Structure in *Stagecoach*

John Ford's *Stagecoach* (1939) is an example of a film with a conventional narrative structure. Based on "Stage to Lordsburg," an Ernest Haycox short story published in *Collier's* magazine in 1937, the film's three-act structure is marked by events and shifts in geographical setting. The film follows a group of people traveling by stagecoach from the town of Tonto to Lordsburg. The *syuzhet* contains several **lines of action** (or **plotlines**) that converge. Many conventional narrative films combine two narrative paths, with one involving romance and the other concerned with a professional goal, a civic duty, or the attainment of a long-held dream. Here, the two lines of action that assume prominence are the stagecoach journey and Ringo Kid's quest for revenge.

The exposition introduces eight residents of Tonto as they prepare for the journey. Director John Ford makes it clear that each one of this diverse group of stagecoach passengers has an individual motivation for the trip. Dallas (Claire Trevor) is a prostitute who has been expelled from Tonto by the self-righteous Law and Order League. The pregnant Lucy Mallory (Louise Platt) intends to join her husband, a cavalry soldier, while Gatewood (Berton Churchill), a banker, has stolen money from his bank and is using the trip to make his getaway. The gambler Hatfield (John Carradine) has a personal reason for making the trip (he recognizes Lucy Mallory). Doc Boone (Thomas Mitchell), an amiable drunkard, has been evicted by his landlady.

Although each character has a specific motivation for going, they all share the goal of reaching Lordsburg. The central conflict facing the travelers emerges when a cavalry report comes in that Geronimo has been active in the area. The threat of hostile Indians—a stereotype and staple of the classical Western—represents an external obstacle to the achievement of that goal.

The first act concludes with an important turning point. Ringo Kid flags the stagecoach down after it has left Tonto. He wants to ride to Lordsburg to find the Plummer brothers and avenge the deaths of his brother and father. Although he appears later than the other characters, Ringo's desire for revenge becomes a central line of action. (In fact, Sheriff Curly Wilcox anticipated Ringo's appearance early in the first act, when he tells coach driver Buck that, because Ringo broke out of jail and might be looking for the Plummers, the Sheriff must accompany the stage.) Curly, who sympathizes with Ringo because he knew his father, takes Ringo into "custody." Ringo's goal is clear and his obstacles are external (Sheriff Curly, the Plummer brothers, the law). Goals and conflicts are well established as the stage heads toward Dry Fork, the first stop on the journey.

The second act involves complications for both lines of action. The geographical journey west is complicated by the Indian threat and clashes among the travelers.

3.7 *(top left)* The climax of *Stagecoach*: Geronimo's attack.

3.8 *(top right)* Gatewood is arrested near the end of *Stagecoach*: justice is served.

3.9 *(bottom)* Ringo and Dallas head for the border in *Stagecoach*, providing closure.

At the first stop in Dry Fork, Lucy Mallory, Hatfield, and Gatewood make their distaste for Dallas apparent. Furthermore, the travelers are divided on whether they should forge ahead to Lordsburg, given the threat of attack. They travel to Apache Wells, where, with the help of Doc Boone and Dallas, Lucy Mallory gives birth. The baby's arrival is an added complication, but the event forces Ringo to acknowledge his feelings for Dallas. After leaving Apache Wells, the stagecoach must ford a river because Geronimo and his men have ransacked the next town, Lee's Ferry. Reminding them of their vulnerability, the event tests their physical ability and builds tension around the increased possibility of an attack.

Throughout the second act, Ringo encounters an internal obstacle because he develops romantic feelings for Dallas. Their relationship threatens to interfere with his plan for revenge and introduces suspense: can Ringo still carry out his plans, or will he run away with Dallas? If he goes after the Plummers and survives, what kind of future could Ringo and Dallas have if he is arrested?

The climax occurs when Geronimo attacks the stagecoach between Lee's Ferry and Lordsburg (fig. **3.7**). The passengers ward off the Indians just long enough for the cavalry to rescue them. This resolves the line of action associated with the stagecoach journey: the dénouement traces the arrival of the stage in Lordsburg as various characters meet their fates. Hatfield has been killed in the attack, Lucy and her baby will be reunited with her husband, and Gatewood is arrested (fig. **3.8**). But director John Ford defers the climax of the second line of action, which involves Ringo's revenge. In Lordsburg, Ringo faces down the Plummers and kills them. The conclusion offers closure on all levels: Ringo exacts his revenge, and then he and Dallas (with the help of Doc Boone and Sheriff Curly) escape to his ranch in Mexico (fig. **3.9**).

Chapter 3: Narrative Form

Stagecoach may be examined in terms of Thompson's four-part structure. The primary difference lies in the analysis of Act Two. After the exposition, the first turning point (Ringo's arrival) signals the start of the complicating action for both lines of action. What event marks the major turning point halfway through the film? What goals do the characters dedicate themselves to achieving after that turning point, in the section Thompson calls development? How are the lines of action resolved?

● ●

Alternatives to Conventional Narrative Structure

Not all narrative films conform to a three-act or four-part structure. Remaining attentive to narrative, visual, and sound details that signal turning points makes it possible to discern alternative narrative structures. In unconventional narratives, turning points signal narrative shifts, even though they do not form the basis for a three- (or four-) act structure.

In *Full Metal Jacket* (Stanley Kubrick 1987), a two-part structure is reinforced by a change in setting and a parallel. An abrupt transition from training camp to combat takes place when, after a fade, the film moves the action from Parris Island, South Carolina, to Da Nang, Vietnam. The geographical shift represents an important change in the protagonist's goal: in the first half of the film, Joker (Matthew Modine) must learn how to survive marine training camp both mentally and physically. In the second, he must learn how to survive his tour of duty in Vietnam. Several parallels signal the two-part structure: each segment begins with a popular song and ends with a protracted scene of violent death.

Another variation on structure is the use of **frame narration**. This technique, used in *The Cabinet of Dr. Caligari* ("*Das Kabinett des Dr. Caligari*"; Robert Wiene 1919), consists of a character who narrates an embedded tale to onscreen or implied listeners. This allows for the creation of two distinct dieseses, and there may be complicated interactions between the two. The narrator may or may not be a character within the embedded tale, and may or may not appraise the events with objectivity.

In *Caligari*, Francis (Friedrich Feher) tells a rapt listener the fantastic tale of the mysterious Dr. Caligari (Werner Krauss), a man who travels with a somnambulist (sleepwalker), whose mind he controls. Under Caligari's spell the sleepwalker, Cesare (Conrad Veidt), terrorizes an entire town, killing Francis's best friend and kidnapping his fiancée. As Francis narrates this bizarre story, the embedded tale unfolds in flashbacks. The film's shocking conclusion returns to the circumstances of Francis's narration and casts doubt on his reliability: he is a paranoid madman living in a mental institution. Caligari is actually the benevolent hospital director.

Citizen Kane also uses a frame narration. Thompson's search for Rosebud (which involves four different living narrators in addition to Thatcher's memoir and the opening newsreel) represents the frame. Kane's complex, multilayered life story is the embedded tale. Generally, the frame narration does not evolve into as detailed a story as the embedded tale. But Bryan Singer's *The Usual Suspects* (1995) merges two narratives that carry equal emotional weight: the frame narration's cat-and-mouse game of the interrogation of Verbal Kint (Kevin Spacey) and the embedded tale's depiction of the doomed heist.

Another important alternative is the **episodic** narrative. In episodic narratives, events are not tightly connected in a cause-and-effect sequence and characters do not focus on a single goal. Character actions may appear to be unmotivated, with hours or days unfolding in a spontaneous flow, and the movie may seem to digress. These films are sometimes referred to as "a day in the life of . . . ," which suggests the way they equalize the importance of many events, rather than singling out dramatic turning points and climaxes. An episodic structure emphasizes the repetition of everyday events rather than the dramatic accumulation of tension toward a moment of crisis. Some episodic narratives conclude without resolving the conflicts; if this is the case, the film is said to be **open-ended.**

The 400 Blows ("*Les Quatre Cents Coups*"; François Truffaut 1959) is an episodic film that revolves around the daily experiences of a young boy named Antoine Doinel (Jean-Pierre Léaud). The routine of the boy's school and home life are elaborated in scenes of school, home, and time with friends. Although a conflict exists between Antoine and his parents, Antoine's goals are unclear.

Instead of setting up the characters and conflicts, the film's exposition establishes a state of mind. It shows schoolboys passing around a provocative calendar of women, establishing Antoine's age—somewhere within the traumatic stage of life known as puberty—and his boredom and restlessness at school. The film chronicles Antoine's daily life without highlighting important events. He goes to school, he does chores at home, he runs errands, overhears a conversation about the horrors of childbirth, and gets ready for bed. The next day he does not go to school, an obvious break in his routine that acts as a turning point, although the reasons for it are obscure. Antoine wanders aimlessly with his friend René (Patrick Auffray), riding a carnival centrifuge, seeing a film, and playing pinball.

While out in the city, Antoine sees his mother kissing a stranger, a shocking moment whose significance is not immediately clear. Nothing in Antoine's life changes overtly because of this act, though a conventionally structured film might emphasize this traumatic moment as an important turning point through camera or sound techniques, which Truffaut avoids. In a conversation shortly afterward, Mme. Doinel speaks to Antoine about keeping secrets from his father, and offers him money should he do well in school. He labors over an essay but is accused of plagiarism and suspended. Antoine moves into René's apartment and the boys' high jinks ultimately land Antoine in jail.

Although cause-and-effect relations are in evidence in this sequence of events—Antoine's misbehavior has consequences—the protagonist's motivations and goals are not clear. He is inarticulate and engages in bad behavior without a specific target; when he does have a target, it seems inappropriate. For example, he steals a typewriter from his father's workplace, even though his father has played a benign and positive role in his life (fig. **3.10**).

Sent to an observation center for juvenile delinquents, Antoine opens up to the psychologist, revealing an underlying emotional conflict that explains, in retrospect, much of his anti-social behavior. His parents married because his mother was pregnant, and

Antoine learned from his grandmother that his mother wanted to have an abortion. When Antoine defies the family code of secrecy and writes a letter home that contains the truth about the kiss he witnessed, his mother visits him and informs him that he will be sent to Labor Detention (a boot camp). Antoine runs away, but officials pursue him. At the film's conclusion, Antoine finds himself at the beach, making an earlier line of dialogue significant in retrospect. Antoine had told René he would like to join the navy so he could see the ocean. Another case where dialogue is significant only in retrospect is the conversation Antoine overhears about childbirth.

3.10 Antoine steals his father's typewriter in *The 400 Blows* ("*Les Quatre Cents Coups*").

The film defies conventional narrative form in a number of ways. The film focuses on Antoine's relationships rather than his actions. For example, he and René care more about one another than do any adults in the film. Scenes do not build conflict, but defuse it. Antoine does not respond to the illicit kiss he witnesses, but avoids the matter. The escape to René's apartment serves as a digression, a way to avoid the conflict at home. But these scenes also show the boys having fun.

Antoine and René's carnival ride suggests the cyclical character of Antoine's life: little forward progress is made. When he finally does name the conflict within his family, the information only retrospectively explains the tension between Antoine and his mother. Finally, while the events of the conclusion are clear—his parents assert their authority to send him away and Antoine escapes—their significance is not. Antoine resists the imposition of parental and governmental authority and runs away. At the end of the film, his future is uncertain (see fig. 4.14).

● Variations on Narrative Conventions: Beyond Structure

The two-part, frame/embedded tale, and episodic structures of *Full Metal Jacket*, *Dr. Caligari*, and *The 400 Blows* offer alternatives to standard narrative construction. But there are a number of other ways films sometimes resist and rewrite the rules of narrative.

The principles of narrative that govern commercial feature films emerged from the practices and preferences of Hollywood filmmakers in the early part of the twentieth century. Commercial Hollywood's studios established a formula for making popular films that tell stories and refined these rules over several decades. The "rules" for classical Hollywood narrative film include:

- Clarity. Viewers should not be confused about space, time, events, or character motivations.
- Unity. Connections between cause and effect must be direct and complete.
- Characters. They should invite viewer identification, be active, and seek goals.
- Closure. Third acts and epilogues should tie up loose ends and answer all questions.
- "Unobtrusive craftsmanship" (Thompson, p. 9). Stories are told in a manner that draws viewers into the diegesis and does not call attention to the storytelling process.

A number of narrative filmmaking traditions have modified or rejected the rules of the dominant Hollywood method of storytelling. Art films, independent films, non-Western films, and unconventional Hollywood films represent alternatives to the standard form, to the delight of many and the dismay of others. The ways that they challenge convention are suggested below. Any film may exhibit one or more of these features, and may do so in a subtle or dramatic way.

- Lack of clarity. Multiple, conflicting lines of action, inconsistent characters, extreme degree of character subjectivity. Examples: *Citizen Kane*, *The Conversation* (Francis Ford Coppola 1974), *Mystery Train*, *Rashomon* (Akira Kurosawa 1950), *Run Lola Run*, *Thin Red Line* (Terence Malick 1998)
- Lack of unity. Broken chain of cause and effect. Examples: *Last Year at Marienbad* ("*L'Année dernière à Marienbad*"; Alain Resnais 1961), *Memento*, *Mulholland Drive* (David Lynch 2001), *Reservoir Dogs* (Quentin Tarantino 1992)
- Open-endedness. Questions are left unanswered or conflicts unresolved. Examples: *The 400 Blows*, *L'avventura* ("*The Adventure*"; Michelangelo Antonioni 1960), *Limbo* (John Sayles 1999), *The Italian Job* (Peter Collinson 1969), *Blow-Up*
- Unconventional characterizations.
  - Audience is distanced from characters rather than invited to identify. Examples: *Badlands* (Terence Malick 1973), *The Conversation*, *Dead Man* (Jim Jarmusch 1996); *Persona* (Ingmar Bergman 1966)
  - Characters contemplate or talk about action rather than taking action. Examples: *Cleo from 5 to 7*, *My Dinner with Andre* (Louis Malle 1981), *Slacker* (Richard Linklater 1991), *Stranger than Paradise* (Jim Jarmusch 1983), *Waking Life* (Richard Linklater 2001)
  - Character goals are unclear. Examples: *The Graduate*, *The 400 Blows*
  - Narrators may be unreliable. Examples: *Dr. Caligari*, *Rashomon*, *The Usual Suspects* (Bryan Singer 1995)
- Intrusions, direct address to the audience and other devices call attention to narrative as a process. Examples: *American Splendor*, *Just Another Girl on the IRT* (Leslie Harris 1993), *The Nasty Girl* ("*Das schreckliche Mädchen*"; Paul Verhoeven 1990), Dogville (Lars von Trier 2003), *Persona*, *The Usual Suspects*, *Natural Born Killers* (Oliver Stone 1994)

Perspective and Meaning

A narrator can play a crucial role in novels and short stories. By establishing a position or angle of vision on the story events—a perspective—the narrator determines whether the reader has access to the same information that characters possess. Stories narrated in the **first person** use the pronoun "I" and limit readers to a single character's knowledge and understanding of events. **Third-person** narration refers to a story conveyed from a position outside any single character's experiences. In literature, the use of "he" and "she" signals the narrator's third-person perspective. A third-person narration can be relatively limited—where the reader's access to information is limited to that of a few characters—or **omniscient** ("all-knowing"), where the reader has more information than any character.

Films treat narration differently. Although characters occasionally address the audience using the first person "I" in a voice-over, films rarely use a first-person narration throughout an entire film. *Lady in the Lake* (Robert Montgomery 1946), a *film noir* featuring Phillip Marlowe (played by Montgomery), adopts a first-person narration throughout (fig. **3.11**). The camera literally points at everything the protagonist sees. But the viewer's inability to see the main character inhibits identification, despite the first-person

3.11 The use of a mirror in *Lady in the Lake* fails to make the first-person narrative convincing.

voice-over. Seeing everything that Marlowe sees (including a glimpse of himself in the mirror) is not sufficient to ensure viewer engagement with the character or immersion in the unfolding story.

Most films employ a system of **restricted narration**, which conveys external events as well as the knowledge, thoughts, and feelings of one or two major characters without the intervention of an explicit narrator. The story seems to unfold rather than to be narrated to the audience. Viewers experience the story from the perspective(s) of a few major characters. They become aligned with those characters because the film imparts the information, knowledge, and experiences that those characters have.

Within an overall framework of restricted narration, directors sometimes provide viewers with information that main characters do not possess. These selective moments of omniscience—where viewers gain more knowledge than major characters—usually occur in scenes that do not include the protagonist(s). Viewers consider the story details presented in such scenes as well as the significance of the uneven distribution of information among the characters in their understanding of the narrative.

In Hitchcock's *North By Northwest* (1959), the audience grows perplexed along with advertising executive Roger Thornhill (Cary Grant) as he is plagued by an apparent case of mistaken identity. Thugs who believe he is a man named Kaplan repeatedly terrorize him. At the end of the first act, a brief scene clarifies the situation for the audience, but not for Thornhill. Kaplan is a fictional government agent, a decoy for a real spy positioned within an enemy organization and Thornhill is an innocent bystander caught up by mistake. The audience now knows more than Thornhill about the bizarre events of the past few days and may worry that he is somewhat defenseless against the trouble that

3.12 Alex and Mrs Sebastian discuss Alicia in *Notorious*.

undoubtedly awaits him. Yet viewers still do not possess complete omniscience. What is the nature of the government operation? Whom can Thornhill trust? And who is the agent on the inside?

Filmmakers play with restricted narration through these shifts in perspective for several reasons: to explain story events of which the character is unaware, to align viewers with other important characters, and to create suspense. The fact that the audience has more information than Alicia Huberman and T.R. Devlin in *Notorious* is critical to building the suspense of the film's second half. Over the course of several scenes, viewers learn that Alex Sebastian (Claude Rains) and Mrs. Sebastian (Madame Konstantin)—Alicia's husband and mother-in-law and the targets of her investigation—have discovered that Alicia is a government agent and have begun poisoning her (fig. **3.12**). Neither Alicia nor Devlin (her supervisor and love interest) suspects her cover has been blown, so they are unaware of any danger. The audience may despair of Alicia making it out alive and wonder whether Devlin will catch on in time to save her. If Hitchcock had limited the viewer to Alicia's perspective, the audience would be just as unaware of the danger as she is and the suspense would have been eliminated.

Furthermore, by providing the audience with more information than his two protagonists possess, Hitchcock ties the spy and the romance plotlines together. Viewers are likely to become frustrated when the lovers clash over Alicia's illness, which affects their relationship as well as their mission. Devlin misinterprets Alicia's sickness as a hangover, thinking she has reverted to her old drinking ways. Alicia responds rebelliously; she encourages him in his misperception, angry that he refuses to see that she has changed. Because the omniscient perspective makes the audience aware of the actual jeopardy that Alicia faces, it casts a different light on Devlin's treatment of Alicia. Not only is he petty and unfair, but his inability to control his personal feelings seems likely to cost Alicia her life. By manipulating perspective, Hitchcock lays the emotional groundwork that prepares the audience for Devlin's final confrontation with the Sebastians and his reconciliation with Alicia (fig. **3.13**).

3.13 Devlin and Alicia are reconciled in *Notorious*.

Character Subjectivity

"Point of view" is a term sometimes used in a literary context to describe the overall system of narration in a novel, poem, or short story. But in film, the term designates a very specific and limited use of camera to indicate perspective. A **point-of-view shot** occurs when the audience temporarily shares the visual perspective of a character or a group of characters. Simply put, the camera points in the direction that the character looks, simulating her field of vision.

Point-of-view shots do not necessarily result in the audience understanding or sympathizing with a character. Subjective engagement may result from a simple point-of-view shot, but usually a deeper connection is accomplished through a pattern of shots or a combination of narrative, visual, and sound elements.

A scene in which the camera adopts a character's point of view but does not offer much in the way of subjective insight comes in the final sequence of *Full Metal Jacket*. Several shots are presented from the point of view of the unseen sniper who shoots two American marines, Eight Ball (Dorian Harewood) and Doc (Jon Stafford). But the scene does not invite viewers to share the sniper's thoughts and feelings; it merely shows the audience what the sniper sees. The shot portraying the sniper's point of view is followed by extreme close-ups of the two marines the sniper has shot. The close-ups are in slow motion, exaggerating their pain, which further undermines any connection to the sniper.

Point-of-view shots can align viewers with characters (see figs. 3.17, 3.18). They help to explain the way characters experience the world, validate characters' interpretations of events, and provide information about motivation. In *Broken Blossoms* (D.W. Griffith 1919), shots from the point of view of Lucy (Lillian Gish) communicate the young girl's fear of men. The camera adopts the girl's point of view as her abusive father, Battling, approaches her. The sexual connotations of his physical abuse are made clear later, when the girl is about to be kissed by Cheng (Richard Barthelmess). Cheng loves her and has saved her life, but a shot of Cheng from Lucy's point of view shows Cheng in a similar position to her father in the earlier scene. In addition to point-of-view shots, the director uses the actors and setting to create a physical parallel between the two men (figs. **3.14**, **3.15**).

Point-of-view shots can inform audiences about characters even if they reveal a *mis*interpretation. In *Days of Heaven* (Terence Malick 1979), Bill (Richard Gere) kisses his former lover Abby (Brooke Adams) on the cheek as a gesture of farewell. The next shot reveals that Abby's husband, The Farmer (Sam Shepard), is watching. His point-of-view shot (from a great distance) emphasizes his misunderstanding: he interprets the kiss as a threat to his relationship with Abby. Here a point-of-view shot allows viewers to understand a character's thoughts but does not limit their knowledge to that character's misinterpretation.

Diegetic sound techniques such as voice-over narration or a character's direct

3.14 *(top)* Battling approaches Lucy in *Broken Blossoms.*

3.15 *(bottom)* Cheng approaching Lucy in *Broken Blossoms* visually recalls the earlier scene.

Chapter 3: Narrative Form

address to the camera can be used to place audiences more firmly within a character's subjectivity. Voice-overs, when characters step outside the flow of events to talk to themselves, to an implied listener, or to the audience, expose audiences to a character's thoughts. Voice-overs are a distinctive characteristic of *film noir*, and are featured in *The Big Sleep* (Howard Hawks 1946) and *Lady from Shanghai* (Orson Welles 1947). Voice-overs allow characters to reflect back on their lives in *Badlands* (Terence Malick 1974), *Goodfellas* (Martin Scorsese 1990), and *The Virgin Suicides* (Sofia Coppola 1999), where one narrator uses the plural "we" to convey the shared thoughts and feelings of a group of boys.

3.16 Chantel addresses the audience directly in *Just Another Girl on the IRT.*

In *Just Another Girl on the IRT*, Chantel (Ariyan Johnson 1992) tells the audience in no uncertain terms who she is and what she stands for, speaking directly to the camera as she would to one of her friends (fig. **3.16**). The direct address also serves a thematic purpose, because Chantel want to tell her story in order to counteract the culture's stereotyped images of young African-American women.

Sound may align viewers with a character at a less conscious level than point-of-view shots. In the opening shot of *The Conversation*, viewers hear odd, scrambled sounds that do not correspond to the images in front of them, which depict a crowd in San Francisco's Union Square. Several moments into the scene, it becomes clear that the sounds are distortions produced by recording equipment. They are diegetic sounds, but they are heard only by the characters taping the conversation of two characters in the square.

● ●

Techniques in Practice: Noticing Shifts in Perspective

Some films, such as Hitchcock's *Psycho* (1960), contain significant shifts in perspective. The film's early scenes focus on Marion Crane (Janet Leigh), her relationship with Sam (John Gavin), and her theft of $40,000 from her workplace. The importance of Marion's perspective is reinforced when Marion encounters a Highway Patrol officer. The scene, composed of several point-of-view shots, emphasizes the idea that the film is concerned with Marion's thoughts and actions (see figs. 6.1, 6.8).

The audience soon learns that the film will not continue to privilege Marion's perspective, however, because she is murdered. This aspect of the film shocked audiences at the time. Rare is the film in which the protagonist, the character whose perspective the audience has shared, is killed at all, much less a third of the way into the film!

3.17 *(top left)* Norman spies on Marion in *Psycho*.

3.18 *(top right)* A point-of-view shot reveals what Norman sees in *Psycho*.

3.19 *(bottom left)* Marion's car slowly sinks in *Psycho*, seen from Norman's point of view.

3.20 *(bottom right)* A close-up of Norman watching anxiously in *Psycho*.

But the transition from Marion's perspective to that of Norman Bates (Anthony Perkins) does not occur simply as a result of Marion's death. Several scenes prior to the famous shower scene where Marion dies, the camera has already begun to adopt Norman's point of view (fig. **3.17**). When Norman reads Marion's pseudonym in the hotel register, the audience shares his point of view and understands that he knows Marion has lied to him. When Norman looks through a hole in the wall to spy on Marion, the audience also shares his point of view (fig. **3.18**).

After Marion's death, when Norman hides the evidence, point-of-view shots may evoke audience sympathy for him. The scene alternates between point-of-view shots that align the audience with Norman as he watches Marion's car stubbornly refusing to sink into the pond (fig. **3.19**) and close-ups of Norman, at first worried (fig. **3.20**), and then, when the car goes under, relieved.

The remainder of the film departs from an exclusive focus on Norman, adopting his perspective as well as that of Marion's sister Lila (Vera Miles), who has come to investigate her disappearance. So, the film asks viewers to make the shift not only from Marion's perspective to Norman's but also to Lila's. Furthermore, in order to prolong suspense and close the film with a twist, Hitchcock makes masterful use of restricted narration, preventing the audience from learning one critical aspect of Norman's story—the true nature of his relationship with his mother—until the end of the film.

Figure **3.21** summarizes the elements of narrative form covered in this chapter. Like all narrative art forms, narrative films depend on characters, conflicts, and cause-and-effect logic. But, unlike stories, novels, and plays, narrative films uniquely depend on visual and sound elements to establish place and time, develop characters, suggest themes and ideas, and create mood. The next chapter examines a film's integrated program of visual design, which determines the overall "look of the film," a complex element of film art referred to as *mise en scène*.

3.21 Narrative Form.

Elements of narrative	Characters, actions, time, place, causality
Selection and ordering of narrative elements	*Syuzhet*: events selected, arranged, and presented on screen; *fabula*: all events that explicitly and implicitly underlie the *syuzhet*, in chronological order
Presentation of the fictional world	Diegetic: part of the implied story world; non-diegetic: exists outside story world
Dramatic structure	Three-act, four-part, frame/embedded, episodic
Perspective	First-person, third-person (restricted, omniscient, or a combination)

● Summary

- The diegesis consists of the world of the story. Non-diegetic elements allow the filmmaker to communicate with the audience directly, rather than through characters or other aspects of the fictional world.
- The distinction between the *syuzhet* and the *fabula* is critical for understanding the significance of the order and selection of events. The *syuzhet* contains all represented events whereas the *fabula* consists of a complete and chronological accounting of all represented and implied events.
- Many narrative films conform to a three-act or four-part structure. Alternatives to this model include two-part structures, frame/embedded tale, and episodic narratives.
- Some films adopt, and others discard, conventions of narrative form, such as unity, clarity, sympathetic, action-oriented characters, closure, and unobtrusive craftsmanship.
- Most narrative films use restricted narration, providing objective and subjective information to viewers. When viewers know more than characters about an event, that knowledge affects their response to the character and may generate suspense.
- Point-of-view shots may or may not align viewers with characters. They may encourage viewers to understand and sympathize with characters, as do character voice-overs and direct address (both diegetic elements).
- Narrative films tend to privilege the perspective of one or two main characters. As they unfold, they may shift between or among characters.

Film Analysis • Analyzing Narrative Structure

The essay below analyzes narrative form in Akira Kurosawa's *Rashomon* (1950). The author argues that the structure, characters, and conclusion of the film depart from the classical model.

Before beginning any writing assignment, it's important to make an outline. An outline is a blueprint: it should contain the main idea and indicate the structure of ideas that supports that main point. An outline of the essay below identifies the thesis statement and traces the writer's organizational logic.

Thesis: *Rashomon* offers an alternative to traditional narrative form through its structure, characters, and lack of closure.

I. Structure

A. define conventional three-act structure so reader understands basis for comparison

B. identify structural departures in *Rashomon* and explain how they differ from traditional structure

   1. *Rashomon* is composed of a frame story and an embedded story

   2. the embedded story unfolds through repetition, whereas frame story proceeds with conventional beginning, middle, and end

II. Characters

A. define the two salient features of classical model for comparison purposes: characters are action-oriented and invite identification

B. present details that show the ways characters in *Rashomon* function differently

   1. frame story emphasizes contemplation over action (it consists of telling stories to pass the time)

   2. the film offers opportunities for identification *and* distancing (the audience may not identify with the woodcutter when his point of view is challenged; characters in the embedded story are inconsistent)

III. Closure

A. conventional narratives generally answer all questions

B. here, questions are left unanswered: thwarting viewer's ability to determine "the truth"

C. the embedded story is not resolved, though the frame story achieves partial resolution

The Narrative Complexity of *Rashomon*

Based on a 1921 story by Ryunosuke Akutagawa entitled "In a Grove," Akira Kurosawa's *Rashomon* (1950) is notable for several reasons. One reason is its importance to film history. It was the first Japanese film to gain international recognition when it won the Grand Prize at the Venice Film Festival and the Academy Award for best foreign film. The second reason is the film's striking narrative organization. One critic states that the film is "as brilliant in its multifaceted plot as a cut gem" (Zunser, p. 37). *Rashomon* represents an alternative to traditional narrative form in three ways: through its structure, characters, and conclusion.

Rashomon departs from a traditional three-act structure, organized in a linear fashion with a beginning, middle, and end. Instead, Kurosawa's film has a layered structure composed of a frame narration and an embedded story. The events are set in twelfth-century Japan, at a time when, the film states, "famines and civil wars had devastated the ancient capital." The frame story focuses on three men—a woodcutter, a Buddhist priest, and a commoner—who wait out a thunderstorm, sheltered by the ruined Kyoto city gates (fig. **3.22**). The woodcutter tells the others of an incident that he has witnessed three days earlier. The other two men listen to the embedded story, which describes a violent encounter between a samurai, his wife, and a bandit.

The embedded tale unfolds in flashbacks. But the woodcutter's version of the story is not the only one depicted. A total of four flashbacks show the same events from different perspectives: that of the woodcutter, the samurai, the wife, and the bandit. (The samurai Takehiro, who has been killed, communicates his version through a medium.)

Whereas the frame story is structured by cause and effect (the men wait for the rain to let up and tell stories in the meantime), the embedded tale is structured differently. Because the same events are repeated four times, from different perspectives, the cause-and-effect logic becomes confusing. Each

3.22 The woodcutter, priest, and commoner find shelter at the city gates in *Rashomon*.

narrator tells a different story, raising the following questions: what were the motivations of the samurai, wife, and bandit (causes), and what actually happened (effects)?

The second way in which *Rashomon* offers an alternative to traditional narrative form is through its characters. In conventional Hollywood narratives, characters rarely spend time contemplating the world; they are more likely to take action. But the "actions" of the three characters in *Rashomon*'s frame story are storytelling, sharing opinions, and waiting for the rain to end. *Rashomon* highlights the importance of abstract ideas more than action. The frame story points to the ambiguous nature of reality and the human capacity for altruism. The embedded story has its share of action, including robbery, sexual assault, and sword fighting. Yet, as those actions are reported over and over again by the four narrators, they become secondary to the philosophical questions raised about the nature of reality.

Rashomon confounds the classical narrative model by making it difficult to identify with its characters. In traditional narrative films, the main character, generally a complex but likeable figure, attracts the sympathy and identification of the audience. In *Rashomon*, the woodcutter resembles a conventional protagonist in that he does state a clear motivation for his storytelling: he seeks clarity. His first line in the film is "I can't understand it," expressing his desire to make sense of the events he has witnessed (fig. **3.23**). But the commoner calls that motivation into question, and undercuts audience identification with the woodcutter when he accuses the woodcutter of lying to protect himself.

Furthermore, the characters in the embedded story are inconsistent. With each telling, their traits, goals, and motivations change, which makes it difficult for the viewer to develop a stable sense of identification with the samurai, his wife, or the bandit.

Finally, the film's conclusion offers a stunning example of open-endedness rather than the closure typical of traditional narratives. While the frame narration offers a sense of resolution (the rain subsides, the men find a baby, and the woodcutter

3.23 The woodcutter provides just one version of events in *Rashomon*.

decides to adopt the child), the clashing flashbacks provide no obvious way to ascertain the truth of the embedded story. It is difficult for the audience to determine which version (and which narrator) to believe. The truth about what actually happened in the embedded story remains in doubt and thus unresolved.

In these three aspects—narrative structure, characters, and conclusion—Kurosawa's *Rashomon* departs from classical narrative form in innovative ways. The layered narrative, unusual characterizations, and open-ended conclusion have all contributed to the film's ability to fascinate viewers for many decades, and to inspire films such as *Hero* (Zhang Yimou 2004).

Works Consulted

Barbarow, George. "*Rashomon* and the Fifth Witness," in *"Rashomon": Akira Kurosawa, Director*. New Brunswick and London: Rutgers University Press, 1987, pp. 145–8.

Buscombe, Edward. *Stagecoach*. London: British Film Institute, 1992.

Gras, Vernon and Marguerite (ed.). *Interviews: Peter Greenaway*. Jackson, MI: University of Mississippi Press, 2000.

Richie, Donald, ed. *"Rashomon": Akira Kurosawa, Director*. New Brunswick and London: Rutgers University Press, 1987.

Richie, Donald, ed. *Focus on "Rashomon"*. Englewood Cliffs: Prentice-Hall, 1972.

Thompson, Kristin. *Storytelling in the New Hollywood*. Cambridge: Harvard University Press, 1999.

Thompson, Kristin. *Storytelling in Film and Television*. Cambridge: Harvard University Press, 2003.

Zunser, Jesse. Review of *Rashomon*, in *Focus on "Rashomon."* Englewood Cliffs: Prentice-Hall, 1972, pp. 37–8.

4

Mise en Scène

What matters is the way space is cut up, the precision of what happens within the magical space of the frame, where I refuse to allow the smallest clumsiness.

Federico Fellini

Francis Ford Coppola's *The Godfather* (1972) opens with a wedding. Connie (Talia Shire), the daughter of Don Vito Corleone (Marlon Brando), marries Carlo Rizzi (Gianni Russo) at the Corleone estate outside New York City. About halfway through the film, Vito's son Michael (Al Pacino), who is hiding from enemies in Sicily, marries a young woman named Apollonia in the small town of Corleone. Although both scenes depict Corleone family weddings, they look very different. The first scene is a lavish reception held on the lawn of the imposing Corleone mansion. Connie wears an

4.1 Connie's lavish wedding in *The Godfather.*

extravagant wedding gown (fig. **4.1**) while hundreds of guests drink copiously and feast on lasagne.

By contrast, in the scene of Michael and Apollonia's wedding, the actual ceremony is shown at the small village church (fig. **4.2**). The wedding party parades through the dusty streets of the rustic countryside. The bride and groom circulate among their guests, serving them candy, before dancing together in the town square. This comparison raises a question related to the use of visual details: what significance can be derived from the fact that these two weddings look so different?

Narrative and visual elements work together to establish differences between the two Corleone weddings. Connie's

4.2 Michael's humble village wedding in *The Godfather*.

wedding emphasizes the secular (non-religious) aspects of the event. First, the scene does not depict the wedding ceremony. Also, Vito takes care of business matters during the reception, as well-wishers ask him for favors. Costumes and props—including the fancy automobiles parked nearby—tell viewers that the guests are affluent. By contrast, the scene of Michael's wedding foregrounds the marriage by showing the priest blessing the couple in the church. A small number of people attend their reception. Everyone is dressed simply, including the groom, who wears a black suit instead of a tuxedo. As they serve their guests, the wedding couple, not the ostentatious display of wealth, takes center stage. These details of setting, costume, and props imply that, in America, wealth and business take precedence over family and community. This conflict between business and family assumes great significance over the course of the *Godfather* trilogy, becoming one of its major themes.

This chapter explores the way filmmakers carefully orchestrate visual details such as these to develop characters, support themes, and create mood. The chapter focuses on the integrated design program, called *mise en scène*, by examining four major components: setting, the human figure, lighting, and composition. It then looks at two specific styles of *mise en scène*: that associated with German Expressionist cinema of the 1920s and the French style of the 1930s known as Poetic Realism. These distinctive approaches suggest different ways in which *mise en scène* creates fictional worlds that viewers find compelling.

The term *mise en scène* (pronounced "meez ahn sen") originated in the theater and literally means staging a scene through the artful arrangement of actors, scenery, lighting, and props—everything that the audience sees. In a film, the *mise en scène* is designed by a production designer, working in collaboration with the film director. In a narrative film,

Designing the Look of the Film

The *mise en scène* is determined during pre-production and production and involves the work of many people. The production designer's careful planning contributes greatly to the coherence of the *mise en scène*. The director and production designer make decisions about how the story world will look well before principal photography begins. The art director supervises the construction of scale models and computer graphics to preview possibilities. Location scouts travel to find locations. A construction coordinator directs carpenters who build sets according to the specifications in blueprints drawn up by set designers; set decorators find the appropriate materials to make the space a plausible environment and translate the production

designer's themes into visual details. Set dressers work during shooting, arranging the items on the set.

Casting directors audition actors and extras. Costume designers present sketches to the director for approval, and wardrobe supervisors acquire and manage costumes. Makeup artists and hairdressers work with actors to achieved the desired physical appearance for the characters. The property master is responsible for finding and maintaining props. The director runs rehearsals with actors before shooting begins to work on **blocking** (the plan for actors' movements), choreography (in action sequences or song and dance numbers), and the subtleties of each actor's performance.

mise en scène creates the look of the world of the story. In documentary films, directors do not usually control their environment, but they can choose which elements to focus on. Avant-garde filmmakers may dispense with a story altogether, yet they still arrange the elements in the frame according to aesthetic principles described in this chapter.

Each element of the *mise en scène*—the setting, the human figure, lighting, and composition—influences the viewer's experience of the story, characters, space, and time. Filmmakers use details in a systematic, integrated manner not only to create a world on screen, but also to indicate character development, present motifs, amplify themes, and establish mood.

● Setting

Setting refers to the places where the film's action unfolds. These places may be general or specific locations, real or imaginary places. In *Notorious*, events occur in two cities: Miami, Florida, and Rio de Janeiro, Brazil. In each city there are a number of specific locations as well: the Miami County Courthouse, Alicia Huberman's house, and, in Rio, Alicia's apartment, the race track, the government offices, and Alex Sebastian's house. The change in setting from Miami to Rio marks a turning point in the narrative when Alicia commits to changing her life by becoming a government agent.

Alicia's apartment and Alex's house are sets built on a studio soundstage (a large, warehouse-like structure that houses sets and provides optimum control over lighting and sound when filming). Constructing a set provides filmmakers with the maximum degree of control over their shooting environment. On an indoor set, directors and cinematographers do not have to contend with bad weather, noise, and unreliable lighting conditions. These are precisely the conditions that pose challenges to documentary filmmakers!

A constructed set can be built to the filmmaker's precise specifications. For Marcel Carné's *Children of Paradise* ("*Les Enfants du Paradis*"; 1945), an outdoor set was constructed on a studio back lot to simulate a nineteenth-century Paris street. In order to use the small space to convey the feel of a bustling city block, the builders constructed a line of two-story buildings that diminished in size from the foreground to the background (fig. **4.3**). To maintain proportions, Carné had small-scale carriages built and employed dwarves as extras in the distant areas of the shot. This production technique is called **forced perspective**: filmmakers construct and arrange buildings and objects on the set so that they diminish in size dramatically from foreground to background. Because the human eye uses the relative size of objects as a gauge of depth, the large disparity in size between foreground and background objects creates the illusion of greater depth.

Most commercial films contain scenes shot on location; for example, in Ridley Scott's *Blade Runner* (1982) the Bradbury building grounds the film's futuristic Los Angeles setting in a familiar, present-day structure. Locations may be easily recognizable spots, such as the Grand Canyon in *Thelma and Louise* (Ridley Scott 1991) or New York's Dakota apartment building (fig. **4.4**) in Roman Polanski's *Rosemary's Baby* (1969).

An actual geographical location may be used to represent another place altogether. Stanley Kubrick filmed *Eyes Wide Shut* (1999) in London, although the story is set in New York City. Francis Ford Coppola filmed the Vietnam War epic *Apocalypse Now* (1979) on location in the rainforests of the Philippines.

4.3 *(top)* Constructed set of a city street, from *Children of Paradise* ("*Les Enfants du Paradis*").

4.4 *(bottom)* A corridor in New York's Dakota building, from *Rosemary's Baby*.

Filmmakers also use **computer-generated imagery** (CGI) to create settings: the ocean in *Titanic* (James Cameron 1997) was generated by computers. Whether the production design involves built sets, location shooting, and/or CGI, viewers must believe in the fictional world before them. Scott Ross of Industrial Light and Magic says "the role that we need to play, and we really try hard to do so, is that we help define what the director is trying to get across on film" (Arden). Deciding whether to construct sets, to use locations, and/or to take advantage of newer computer technologies is part of the creative challenge of filmmaking. These decisions also relate to the business of filmmaking, as location shooting is often complex, time-consuming, unpredictable, and more expensive than shooting on a set.

Describing Setting: Visual and Spatial Attributes

The visual characteristics of a setting evoke responses from the audience. Do events take place inside buildings or outdoors? Are settings living spaces, work places, or public spaces? Are they spacious or cramped, sunny and bright, or dim and shadowy? Are they full of bits and pieces or empty?

At first glance, an open, bright, exterior setting might suggest limitless possibilities, as in the rock climbing scene that opens *Mission:Impossible 2* (John Woo 2000), whereas a dark, cramped interior, like that in the opening of *Memento*, may connote entrapment. But an open space can also serve as a site of horror, as it does in the rural farm setting in *Night of the Living Dead* (George A. Romero 1967; fig. **4.5**). The *contextual* use of any setting is important to interpreting *mise en scène*. The context for interpretation includes the actions taking place there as well as the way the setting relates to other settings used throughout the film.

The director or location scout chooses particular spaces for their visual and spatial attributes. Those qualities inevitably transmit cultural meanings as well as emotional implications. The stately but hollow beach house in *Interiors* (Woody Allen 1978) reflects material wealth and emotional distance. The seedily nondescript Los Angeles apartment occupied by Jerry and Lois Kaiser (Chris Penn and Jennifer Jason Leigh) in *Short Cuts* (Robert Altman 1993) indicates their lower middle-class status. Settings need not be ornately decorated or breathtakingly beautiful to offer insight into the lives of characters.

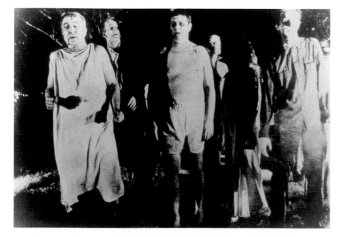

4.5 *Night of the Living Dead*: open space as the site of horror.

The Functions of Setting

The primary functions of setting are to establish time and place, to introduce ideas and themes, and to create mood. In a period film, the setting recreates a place and time; visual details are especially important when the time period is essential to the film's story and themes. Historical research contributed to the meticulous depiction of New York City in the 1870s in Martin Scorsese's *The Age of Innocence* (1993), a film about the struggle between love and obligation in high society. The settings, which speak to the ritualized behavior of this group of people, were integral to the representation of the protagonist's decision to remain with his wife and suppress his passionate love for another woman—a choice that might be difficult for contemporary audiences to understand. Director Scorsese said, "the setting's important only to show why this love is impossible" (Cocks and Scorsese, p. vii). Even the most "accurate" representations are subject to creative license. In the case of *The Age of Innocence*, the city of Troy, New York, was used as an exterior location for action set in Manhattan.

Daughters of the Dust (Julie Dash 1990), filmed on location on the Georgia and South Carolina Sea Islands, accurately depicts the places where the Gullah culture thrived. The ocean setting introduces ideas and themes: it reinforces the connection between the Peazant family and their African ancestors and their separation from the world of the mainland U.S. (see fig. 5.43).

Certain genres are linked to settings and time periods. Westerns are located in the American Southwest in the late nineteenth century, whereas gangster films typically evoke a modern, urban environment. Other genres, such as romantic comedies, are less dependent on geography or historical period.

As with any element of filmmaking, directors sometimes choose to use settings that work against expectations. Although musicals can take place anywhere, the singing and dancing that define the genre often take place in stylized, theatrical settings. But musicals such as *Dancer in the Dark* (Lars von Trier 2000) and *Billy Elliot* (Stephen Daldry 2000) contain numbers choreographed amid urban neighborhoods (fig. **4.6**), factories, and prisons. These films inventively test the genre's boundaries by emphasizing the incongruity of bleak settings as the backdrop for musical extravaganzas.

Settings need not refer to existing locations or actual historical periods: instead they may evoke a generic sense of place or stand for implicit ideas. The large, bustling, but unspecified city in F.W. Murnau's *Sunrise* (1927) is important mainly because it provides a contrast to the bucolic countryside where the main characters live. The city is never named. In this film, it is less important to know the specific location of the city than to recognize it as a source of excitement that ultimately allows a husband and wife to rediscover their love for one another.

Settings help to determine the mood of a scene or an entire film. In *Blade Runner*, scenic devices establish the degraded

4.6 Dancing in the streets in *Billy Elliot*.

4.11 *(top)* Ada expresses herself by playing the piano on the beach in *The Piano*.

4.12 *(bottom)* The brown-toned interior of Stewart's house in *The Piano*.

4.13 The beach provides a setting for a clash of generations in *Bhaji on the Beach*.

Rider (Niki Caro 2002), and *Troy* (Wolfgang Peterson 2004). The following examples illustrate the importance of context.

In *The Piano* (Jane Campion 1993) Scottish settler Stewart (Sam Neill) leaves the piano that his mail-bride Ada (Holly Hunter) has brought with her from Scotland behind on the New Zealand beach after she arrives there with her belongings. When she returns to that spot with Mr. Baines (Harvey Keitel) and her daughter Flora (Anna Pacquin), her joy at being reunited with her beloved instrument (fig. **4.11**) is enhanced by the setting. The beach's bright open space offers a visual contrast to the dense, green forest and the dim, wood-walled interiors of the settlers' homes (fig. **4.12**). Ada smiles and moves fluidly as she plays the piano and Flora dances wildly to the music. Ada and Flora's movements and smiling facial expressions underscore feelings of openness and provide insight into their emotions. In this film, the beach represents, among other things, the intense pleasure of creative self-expression.

Bhaji on the Beach (Gurinder Chadha 1994) also features a beach setting. Its inclusion in the film's title signals its central importance. The story follows a diverse group of South Asian women as they take a day trip to Bristol, England. In comparison to the cramped bus ride in the opening of the film, the beach offers freedom of movement and privacy (fig. **4.13**). These are thematically important because the mature women in the group, who adhere to Indian traditions, often disapprove of the younger women, who have grown up in Britain and have adopted Western behavior.

But the beach is not a space of vast, wild, unspoiled beauty as it is in *The Piano*; alongside expanses of sand, fast food restaurants and a strip club appear. The women exhibit various levels of comfort with the informality of the beach and its tourist attractions, highlighting the theme of the generational and cultural differences that divide the women.

The final scene of *The 400 Blows* finds the troubled young protagonist, Antoine Doinel, running from a juvenile detention center to the beach. The setting seems incongruous after the urban streets that have served as the character's usual environment. The beach does not promise the unfettered freedom conventionally associated with that setting. Instead, the

slowness of Antoine's movements and a final **freeze frame** render the scene ambiguous (fig. **4.14**). Will he escape to freedom? Does the ocean signify an opportunity for rebirth, or does it represent yet another boundary? The uncertainty of the final moment on the beach contributes to the film's non-traditional narrative structure.

In the opening scene of *Black Girl* ("*La Noire de . . .*", Ousmane Sembene 1966), a young Senegalese woman named Diouana (Mbissine Thérèse Diop) leaves Senegal, a former French colony, and travels to France by ocean liner to work for a wealthy family. Once in Nice, however, she realizes that her function there is not to care for the children, as she had been told, but to serve as maid and cook. The family neglects to pay her salary and their constant demands make her a virtual prisoner in the stifling apartment (fig. **4.15**). She has few opportunities to leave the apartment, much less explore the beach. Depressed and desperate, Diouana decides to take her life.

Under the circumstances, a beach scene depicting carefree vacationers who sun themselves and read newspapers (fig. **4.16**) must be interpreted ironically. Only the privileged are permitted to frolic on the beach; their servants remain inside. The scene of the beach highlights Diouana 's exploitation and her invisibility.

In these examples, beach settings produce meaning within a specific context. In *Black Girl*, the beach represents a dead end rather than a site of transcendence, as it seems to be for Ada in *The Piano*. In *Black Girl* and *Bhaji on the Beach*, the beach setting highlights cultural conflicts. In *The 400 Blows*, the beach setting and the freeze frame raise more questions about where Antoine is headed than they answer.

4.14 Antoine contemplates his future in *The 400 Blows* ("*Les Quatre Cents Coups*").

4.15 Diouana mopping the floor in *Black Girl* ("*La Noire de . . .*").

4.16 Carefree vacationers on the beach in *Black Girl*.

● The Human Figure

As the above examples suggest, actors' performances contribute a great deal to a film's meaning. Most narrative feature films tell stories about human beings and the conflicts they face. Casting (the selection of actors), acting style, and the placement and movement of figures influence the viewer's response to fictional characters, their strengths and weaknesses, and their hopes and fears.

Casting

Choosing actors is one of the most important decisions a director can make. Usually a casting director organizes auditions, but "A-list" actors are generally cast without the indignity of an audition. Their agents negotiate with directors and studio executives, sometimes discussing the star's wishes regarding the casting of other actors and desired changes in the script.

Well-known stars can earn more than $20 million per film, but the price may be worth it because attaching a popular celebrity to a project helps to secure financing. Some prominent actors occasionally work "for scale" (the minimum wage for professional actors) if they like a particular script or because they enjoy the experience of making low-budget films. Filmmakers may be limited in their casting choices for other reasons. Alfonso Cuarón—director of *Y Tu Mamá También* ("And Your Mother As Well" 2001)—was hired to direct the third *Harry Potter* film, *Prisoner of Azkaban* (2004), but was not permitted to hire different actors or alter the production design because that would have risked alienating the fans of the popular *Harry Potter* series.

The practice of **typecasting**—repeatedly casting an actor in the same kind of role—offers benefits to stars and studios. Stars sometimes prefer roles that will play to their strengths and reinforce their image. At the same time, because actors' fees represent a large percentage of production costs, and because audiences often go to movies to see favorite stars, studio executives prefer to minimize risk and to stick with a "sure thing" in terms of casting.

So, for example, Harrison Ford portrayed an ironic swashbuckler in both the *Star Wars* and the *Indiana Jones* series in the late 1970s and early 1980s. Hugh Grant became a star playing the upper-class, aloof, but self-deprecating romantic hero in *Four Weddings and a Funeral* (Mike Newell 1993) and *Notting Hill* (Roger Michell 1999).

Sometimes actors deliberately choose roles that work against type. This can be a risky proposition, since fans may refuse to accept this shift from their familiar frame of reference. Meg Ryan, who became a household name playing winsome romantic leads in comedies such as *When Harry Met Sally* (Rob Reiner 1989), *Sleepless in Seattle* (Nora Ephron 1993), and *You've Got Mail* (Nora Ephron 1998), found it difficult to depart from that image. Her *When a Man Loves a Woman* (Luis Mandoki 1994), where she played an alcoholic, *Addicted to Love* (Griffin Dunne 1997), a black comedy, and *Proof of Life* (Taylor

Hackford 2000), an action-adventure film, were box office failures. This is not to say that actors are incapable of moving beyond typecasting, but that commercial considerations may limit their opportunities to do so.

Acting Style

Actors bring a public image and their previous roles with them, but they also bring training in a particular acting style. In early cinema, stage acting techniques influenced film acting and a highly emotive, almost pantomime style prevailed. In silent films, facial and bodily expressions were the primary means of conveying the story. Whereas actors on the stage rely on physical presence and projection to a live audience, film actors contain their expressiveness for the camera to pick up.

The most influential school of film acting is **Method acting**, a style based on the theories of Russian theater director Constantin Stanislavski, who brought a new, psychological realism to character depiction in the early twentieth century. "The Method" was further developed by the Group Theatre of the 1930s, committed to presenting plays to promote social awareness and activism. Many Group Theatre practitioners went on to become stage and film actors and directors associated with the Actors' Studio, founded in New York in 1947 and run by Lee Strasberg since 1948. Method actors get into character, inhabiting their psychological reality. They immerse themselves in the feelings of the character and then connect those emotions to their own experiences to realize the performance. Prominent method actors include Marlon Brando, James Dean (fig. **4.17**), Julie Harris, and Robert De Niro. Method acting has become one style within a large array of training options that actors may engage with to develop their craft.

Film scholar Barry King identifies several categories of actors, based on the way their performances are perceived by audiences. Impersonation describes the work of actors who seem to disappear into their roles: actors with this ability to transform themselves include Meryl Streep, Sean Penn, and Julianne Moore. Personification refers to the work of actors who remain themselves or always play themselves and may have scripts written specifically to exploit their particular attributes. Katharine Hepburn, John Wayne, Cary Grant, and Tom Cruise belong in this category. Technical acting refers to the mastery of external details of a character such as an accent or physical trait, as evident in Peter Sellers' and Jim Carrey's work.

4.17 James Dean, a leading exponent of "The Method".

Actors' performances also depend on the narrative: protagonists are presented in lead roles; their sidekicks, friends, and other lesser personages are played out in supporting roles. **Character actors** often play the same supporting roles in many films, but they generally do not achieve the widespread recognition enjoyed by lead actors. Examples of character actors include Franklin Pangborn, Steve Buscemi, Thelma Ritter, Phillip Seymour Hoffman, and Maggie Smith. **Extras** are hired to appear anonymously, often in crowd scenes (although computer graphics allow special effects technicians to create crowd scenes in post-production). **Cameos** are brief appearances by well-known actors playing themselves. Ensemble acting is based on an equitable distribution of the work and the glory. Directors such as Robert Altman, Woody Allen, Mike Leigh, and Christopher Guest often collaborate with large ensembles.

Acting Brechtian: Distancing the Audience

An actor's skill in bring a character to life—his ability to make audience members believe in the character—is essential to involving viewers in a realist film. But some filmmakers reject the conventions of realism. Directors such as Rainer Werner Fassbinder, Jean-Luc Godard, and Alain Resnais have explored the film medium as a process of representation. Uninterested in the psychological believability of characters, they draw on German dramatist Bertolt Brecht's ideas about acting, which emphasize the artifice, not the authenticity, of performance (fig. **4.18**). Brecht's Epic Theater was an attempt to stimulate the audience's critical thought processes, not their emotions, by calling attention to the aesthetic and political frameworks that produce stories and characters. **Brechtian distanciation** refers to the destruction of the theatrical illusion for the purpose of eliciting an intellectual response in the audience.

4.18 Bertolt Brecht in the late 1940s.

An example of a Brechtian approach is David Lynch's *Mulholland Drive* (2001). The actors' performances are intentionally opaque: they do not reveal their characters' inner thoughts or emotions. Rita (Laura Harring) is a blank slate because a car accident has robbed her of her identity. Betty (Naomi Watts) assumes the role of a Nancy Drew detective to help Rita. Adam (Justin Theroux) acts the role of a film director as scripted by powerful movie moguls. Ironically, in the one scene where viewers might feel connected to Betty, she is reading for a part in a film! In the audition—a performance—Betty expresses more emotion than she does in the rest of the film. Lynch's use of anti-realist acting, combined with a fragmented narrative that originates in one character's dreams, forces viewers to pull away from the story and constantly to ask questions about the "reality" of the characters and events.

Actors' Bodies: Figure Placement

In rehearsal, directors work with the actors to block the action, establishing movements that change their physical relationships with other actors and with the camera. **Figure placement and movement**—what audiences see on screen—can produce artful compositions, provide information about characters and their relationships, develop motifs, and reinforce themes.

Directors treat actors' bodies as elements of the visual field. Figures who tower over other characters, for example, may dominate them in some other way in the film, whereas characters who meet each other on the same physical level (high/low) and plane of depth (foreground/background) may exhibit a more equitable relationship. Characters who occupy the foreground gain visual prominence through their apparent proximity to the viewer. They may assume a greater narrative importance as well. The analysis below looks at how figure placement in Orson Welles's *Citizen Kane* conveys the ongoing predicament of the film's central character.

● ●

Techniques in Practice: Figure Placement in *Citizen Kane*

A scene in *Citizen Kane* illustrates the way the careful positioning of actors produces meaning. In the Colorado boarding house scene, characters are positioned in ways that provide insight into their relationships and suggest Charles Foster Kane's motivations later in his life.

As the Kanes and Mr. Thatcher (George Coulouris) discuss Charles's future, Mary Kane (Agnes Moorehead) sits very close to the camera. The banker Thatcher is seated behind her, while her husband, Jim Kane (Harry Shannon), moves between the foreground and middle ground of the shot. Charles, who can be heard as he plays outside in the snow, is visible through the window. The prominence of Mary Kane underlines her position of authority. She makes the decision to send her son Charles away to grow up as Thatcher's ward, believing that she is acting in his best interests.

Mary and Jim Kane disagree about the decision. Their difference of opinion on this matter is signified by dialogue as well as figure placement. Moving around in the middle ground, Jim mutters his opposition to Mary's plan. After he learns that the agreement with the bank will provide him with a sum of money, however, he decisively walks away from Mary and Thatcher. He resigns himself to the decision Mary has made with the statement, "It's all for the best." His movement is closely linked to his self-serving line of dialogue. He closes the window, severing his relationship with his son. Charles can no longer be heard.

Mary immediately stands up, moves to the window, and opens it. She calls to Charles as she tells no one in particular that she has had his trunk packed for a week. Opening the window reverses the action Jim has taken, suggesting the tension between them. Mary is troubled by her decision to send the boy away, a fact that becomes evident when she re-establishes the connection to her son. Her movements and dialogue contradict her earlier stoicism, providing insight into her mixed feelings. The viewer gains access to Mary's emotions through her movement and proximity to the camera.

Similarly, Charles's movements compellingly narrate the early years of his life in visual terms. Even when Charles can be seen through the window, he is positioned between the

4.22 Joe says goodbye to his car in *Sunset Boulevard*.

4.23 Henry Fonda resembles Lincoln in *Young Mr. Lincoln*.

Thief), the bicycle is a not only a means of transportation for Antonio Ricci (Lamberto Maggiorani), but also a symbol of the desperate situation facing the people of postwar Italy. When Ricci's bicycle is stolen, he loses his job. Similarly, for Joe Gillis in *Sunset Boulevard*, the repossession of his car reinforces his dependence on Norma; when his car is towed away, he says that he feels his legs have been cut off (fig. **4.22**).

Actors' Bodies: Makeup

Makeup and hairstyles establish time period, reveal character traits, and signal changes in characters. Makeup was used in early cinema simply to make actors' faces visible. But improvements in film stock and lighting mean that makeup is now used to enhance or minimize an actor's prominent features or to simulate youth or advanced age.

Makeup can alter an actor's appearance so that he or she more closely resembles a historical figure, thus enhancing a film's claim to historical accuracy. This was the case with Henry Fonda in *Young Mr. Lincoln* (John Ford 1939; fig. **4.23**) and Ben Kingsley in *Gandhi* (Richard Attenborough 1982).

In *Monster* (2003), Patti Jenkins's drama about serial killer Aileen Wuornos, actress Charlize Theron sat for several hours of makeup application every day. Makeup artist Toni G applied liquid latex to Theron's face to create the look of sun-damaged skin. Theron recreated Wuornos emotionally and physically, and she earned an Academy Award for her performance.

Makeup and **prostheses** (three-dimensional makeup attached to faces and bodies) may produce comical or frightening effects. For his role in *Roxanne* (Fred Schepisi 1987), Steve Martin wore a huge prosthetic nose, an essential physical feature of his character, C.D. (a reference to Cyrano de Bergerac, the hero of the original play by Edmond Rostand, on which the film is based). In the *Austin Powers* films, Mike Myers plays several characters (Powers, Dr. Evil, and Fat Bastard) with the help of makeup, costumes, hairstyle, and prostheses (figs. **4.24**, **4.25**).

Horror film monsters and science fiction creatures pose great challenges for makeup artists and costume designers. To become the monster in *Frankenstein* (James

Whale 1931), Boris Karloff sat for many hours while technicians applied layers of makeup and prostheses; his bulky costume included weights in his shoes, which helped him create the monster's distinctive shuffle (fig. **4.26**). In *Van Helsing* (Stephen Sommers, 2004) Shuler Hensley wore at least fifteen facial prostheses and leg extensions that added more than eight inches to his height to re-create the terrifying image of the Frankenstein monster. In *The Grinch* (Ron Howard 2000), Jim Carrey not only donned a full-body costume that transformed him into a furry green monster, but he also wore contact lenses that dramatically changed the color of his eyes.

Digital effects that are added in post-production also modify an actor's appearance. In *The Mask* (Charles Russell 1994), **morphing** accomplishes Jim Carrey's grotesque transformation. Images of actors may be altered in a variety of ways using computer graphics programs: for example, an image can be scanned into the computer and unwanted elements digitally "painted out" of the image or the background.

An actor may undertake serious physical changes in order to play a role. Renee Zellweger gained some much-publicized weight to play the title character in two *Bridget Jones* films. Jared Leto lost weight to portray a heroin addict in *Requiem for a Dream* (Darren Aronofsky 2000), as did Adrian Brody when he played a Holocaust survivor in *The Pianist* (Roman Polanksi 2002). Silent film star Lon Chaney was known as the "man of a thousand faces": he earned that reputation because he physically transformed himself for each role.

In *The Hunchback of Notre Dame* (Wallace Worsley 1923) and *The Phantom of the Opera* (Rupert Julian 1925), he depicts outcasts with physical disabilities. As Alonzo in *The Unknown* (Tod Browning 1927), he pretends to be armless, then has both arms amputated in an unsuccessful and pitiful attempt to win the love of a fellow circus performer (fig. **4.27**).

4.27 Lon Chaney as Alonzo in *The Unknown*.

Techniques in Practice: Physicality in *Raging Bull* and *Ali*

When Robert De Niro convinced Martin Scorsese to film *Raging Bull* (1980) and to cast him as boxer Jake La Motta, the actor understood the importance of rendering the psychology and emotions of the character through his physicality. In the film, La Motta is obsessed with maintaining his body at the peak of perfection. The film's grueling fight scenes required De Niro to train, develop his stamina, and mold his physique: the actor even entered amateur boxing matches. La Motta's body obsession extends to experiments with sexual temptation. He asks his wife, Vickie (Cathy Moriarty), to seduce him, but then resists in order to prove he has control over his body.

As he ages, it becomes evident that La Motta's self-control is a form of narcissism: he uses his powerful physique to control others. He begins to use his body aggressively outside the ring. When jealousy overcomes him, he physically attacks friends, his wife, and his brother. He intentionally destroys an opponent's face because his wife admired the boxer's looks. Mary Pat Kelly writes that De Niro's La Motta is "so unconscious of his own feelings and emotions that he can speak only through violence" (Kelly, p. 121). In the later stages of his life, La Motta indulges himself by drinking, smoking, and overeating, all of which contribute to his grossly overweight body. Both his youthful physical perfection and his aging decrepitude are attributable to his complete self-absorption. De Niro's physical transformation has inspired actors ever since. Commenting on his intensive training for his role as Achilles in *Troy*, Brad Pitt remarked, "Ever since De Niro put on 60 pounds for *Raging Bull*, that set the course. He screwed us all, really" ("Brad Pitt").

A slightly different challenge faced Will Smith in taking on the role of Muhammad Ali, the former world heavyweight boxing champion (fig. **4.28**). In *Ali* (2001), director Michael Mann decided to limit the plot events to the ten years leading up to Ali's historic "Rumble in the Jungle"—the challenge match in Zaire where he recaptured his title from George Foreman. Concentrating on a shorter timespan in the boxer's life did not necessarily make Smith's job simpler, however. Like La Motta, Ali's self-expression extended beyond the physical contest inside the ring.

Like De Niro, Smith trained physically for the role, putting on 35 pounds. But just as important as rendering Ali's graceful athleticism was Smith's ability to capture Ali's distinctive manner of speaking and presenting himself in public. Famous for his social consciousness and his rhyming zingers, Ali was a public figure with an intellectual approach and a political perspective on racism and the Vietnam War. Smith paid particular attention to Ali's vocal qualities: the

4.28 Will Smith in the title role in *Ali*.

slightly raspy voice, the rhythmic manner of speaking, and the ironic tone. *New Yorker* film critic David Denby writes that Smith's performance "gets the right Kentucky music in [Ali's] voice" and captures the "slow moving meditativeness of a big bodied man" (Denby, p. 27). De Niro and Smith were successful in their depictions of boxers not only because they undertook physical training, but also because they considered the way each man used his physicality in his boxing career and in his life outside the ring.

● Lighting

Light is an essential requirement of filmmaking. Without light entering the camera lens, no image would be recorded. Lighting is an element of *mise en scène* because it illuminates the set and the actors and can be designed to create certain moods and effects. But it is also related to issues of cinematography, since the photochemical properties of film stock, the use of lenses and filters, and lab processing techniques all affect the look of a film. Lighting furthers the audience's understanding of characters, underscores particular actions, develops themes, and establishes mood.

Light exhibits three attributes: quality (hard or soft), placement (the direction from which the light strikes the subject), and contrast (high or low). **Hard light**, produced by a relatively small light source positioned close to the subject, tends to be unflattering

4.29 *(top)* Harsh lighting emphasizes the imperfections of Michael Caine's face.

4.30 *(bottom)* Soft, diffuse light minimizes details and flatters Jayne Mansfield.

because it creates deep shadows and emphasizes surface imperfections (fig. **4.29**). **Soft light**, from a larger source that is diffused (scattered) over a bigger area or reflected off a surface before it strikes the subject, minimizes facial details, including wrinkles (fig. **4.30**). Unless a character is intended to appear plain or unattractive, cinematographers use soft light so that the actors' faces appear in the most attractive way. Skilled Hollywood cinematographers produce flattering renderings of stars by taking special care with quality and the positioning of light sources.

Available light (or natural light) from the sun can be hard or soft, depending on time of day, time of year, angle of the sun, cloud cover, and geographical location. It may also vary in color. According to Sandi Sissel, Director of Photography for Mira Nair's *Salaam Bombay!* (1988), "You can take a lens with absolutely no filtration and point it, and you'll get footage back from Moscow that will be grayish blue and you will get footage back from India that will be golden" (LoBrutto, p. 175).

One reason why early U.S. filmmakers settled in southern California in the 1910s was the golden-hued quality of the light there. Cinematographers generally agree that the most beautiful light falls during what cinematographer Nestor Almendros has called the "magic hour": just before sunrise and just after sunset, when the diffusion of the sun's light produces glowing images (fig. **4.31**).

The direction of light (or positioning of lighting sources) also produces a variety of different effects. A light source directly in front of the subject (frontal lighting) creates a flat effect, washing out facial detail and creating shadows directly behind the subject (fig. **4.32**). Lighting from either side of the subject produces a sculptural effect, rendering three dimensions by making volume and texture visible (fig. **4.33**). Lighting from behind separates the subject from the background (fig. **4.34**).

Most filmmakers supplement natural lighting with artificial light for greater control over the illumination of the image. Documentary and low-budget feature films, however, often favor natural light, their choices partly dictated by consideration of

4.31 *(above)* Diffused lighting at the "magic hour" in *Days of Heaven*.

4.32 *(below)* Frontal lighting washes out facial detail from Greta Garbo in *Mata Hari* (1931).

cost and limitations of the shooting environment (particularly important for documentary filmmakers who wish to minimize the disruptiveness of their presence). Independent filmmaker Lenny Lipton pithily sums up the commercial film industry's approach to lighting. He writes, "If you are interested in lighting a bottle of cola so that it glimmers and glistens, or if your concern is to light a starlet's face so that she looks fantastically like a piece of stone, you will go to very nearly insane lengths to control the lighting" (Lipton, p. 218).

In the Hollywood studio era, a system of lighting was developed that would allow cinematographers to do just that. **Three-point lighting** has remained a standard approach to lighting. The method is designed to ensure the appropriate level of illumination and to eliminate shadows (figs. **4.35**, **4.36**). The primary source of light is the key light, the frontal lighting source aimed at the subject from a range of positions. The key light can be set up next to the camera or moved away from it on either side, approaching a 45°

4.33 *(left)* Side lighting produced a sculptural effect in this shot of Hardy Kruger.

4.34 *(right)* Back lighting makes Kruger stand out from the background.

4.35 *(left)* Joan Crawford: precise effects of three-point lighting.

4.36 *(center)* Marlene Dietrich here is artfully lit.

4.37 *(right)* Merle Oberon was known for her characteristic gleaming eyes, produced by "obie" lights.

angle on the camera–subject axis. The closer the key light gets to 45°, the more the subject will be illuminated from the side, which produces sculptural effects.

The fill light is a light (or light-reflecting surface) positioned on the opposite side of the subject from the key light. Its purpose is to eliminate the shadows cast by the key light and to regulate the degree of contrast. The back light (aimed at the subject from behind and above) visually separates subject from background. When used with minimal key or fill lighting, the backlight produces a silhouette effect.

In addition to these three sources of light, eye lights are aimed directly into the eyes of an actor to produce a gleam in the eye (fig. **4.37**). These are also called obie lights, named for Merle Oberon, the actress for whom they were developed. Side lights or kicker lights model the subject in three dimensions by illuminating it from either side.

Chapter 4: *Mise en Scène*

Image contrast—one of the most important factors in establishing mood—depends on the relative intensity of the key light to the fill light (key/fill), also known as the lighting ratio. **High-key lighting** refers to a lighting design in which the key to fill ratio is 2:1 or lower. In this configuration, the fill light is nearly as intense as the key light. Thus it eliminates virtually all of the shadows cast by the key light and provides an even illumination of the subject, with most facial details washed out (fig. **4.38**). High-key lighting tends to create a hopeful mood, appropriate for light comedies and for cheery scenes in musicals such as *The Sound of Music* (Robert Wise 1965).

4.38 High-key lighting sets the optimistic mood of *The Sound of Music*.

Natural-key lighting (or normal lighting) is produced with a ratio of key to fill light between 4:1 and 8:1. Here the key light is somewhat more intense than the fill light, so the fill is no longer able to eliminate every shadow (fig. **4.39**).

Low-key lighting is produced by increasing the intensity of the key light relative to the fill. In low-key lighting, the lighting ratio (key/fill) is between 16:1 and 32:1. The much greater intensity of the key light makes it impossible for the fill to eliminate shadows, producing an image with a number of shadows (often on characters' faces) and high contrast (many grades of lightness and darkness; fig. **4.40**).

Low-key lighting creates a somber or forbidding mood and is often used in crime dramas and *films noirs*. It is also the favored lighting style for gothic horror films because

4.39 *(left)* Shadows from *The Godfather* show the effect of natural-key lighting.

4.40 *(right)* Low-key lighting creates a shadowy interior in *The Big Sleep*.

4.41 Low-key lighting can also set the mood for horror films such as *Phantom of the Opera* (1925).

it adds a sense of gloom to any setting (fig. **4.41**). Note that several lighting styles maybe used in a single film: as the Von Trapp family escapes from the Nazis in *The Sound of Music*, low-key lighting helps shift the film's mood from the brighter scenes to signify the danger involved.

Notice that the terminology of high- and low-key lighting is counterintuitive: a higher ratio of key to fill is in fact a low-key lighting set up.

● Composition

The last aspect of *mise en scène* examined in this chapter is composition, defined as the visual arrangement of the objects, actors, and space within the frame. A filmmaker's treatment of composition may reiterate underlying themes and ideas, but may also be chosen to produce a striking visual effect.

Balance and Symmetry

The space of the frame can be thought of as a two-dimensional space, where principles of visual art can be brought to bear. One important principle is to ensure there is balance or symmetry within the frame. The frame can be partitioned horizontally, on a left–right axis, and vertically, from top to bottom. A balanced composition has an equitable distribution of bright and dark areas, striking colors, objects and/or figures. In classical Hollywood films, symmetry was often achieved by centering actors in the shot (fig. **4.42**).

In one scene in *Rebel without a Cause* (Nicholas Ray 1955), balance is achieved through figure placement. Jim (James Dean) stands on a sofa, while his parents, on either side of him, plead with him to tell them where he has been. In the closing moments of *Devil in a Blue Dress*, the tall palm trees that line Easy Rawlings' street create balance and harmony, signifying a return to order (fig. **4.43**).

By contrast, an unbalanced composition leads the viewer's eye in a particular

4.42 Katharine Hepburn in the center of the frame in *Holiday*.

direction by giving greater emphasis to a bright or dark area of the frame, to an object or actor, or to an area of color. Asymmetry may suggest a lack of equilibrium, but, as with all aspects of *mise en scène*, the composition must be interpreted in context.

The closing shot of Michelangelo Antonioni's *L'Avventura* (1960) divides the frame into two parts: on the right, a flat wall appears; on the left, a man and woman sit with their backs to the camera and stare into the distance, where a mountain appears (fig. **4.44**). This composition creates several contrasts: the wall seems to have only two dimensions, whereas the left side of the frame offers depth. The uniform texture of the wall is at odds with the way the couple's dense, dark clothing distinguishes them from the horizon. The flat surface and right angles of the wall contrast with the diagonal formed by the seated man and the standing woman. These visual tensions result in the viewer repeatedly scanning the image without his eyes coming to rest in any one place, a form of visual open-endedness.

Lines and Diagonals

Graphic elements such as lines play a role in composition. The human eye tends to respond to diagonal lines, vertical lines, and horizontal lines in decreasing degrees of emphasis. All three may be used as compositional elements, but a diagonal line carries the most visual weight.

A dramatic use of a diagonal line occurs in the opening shot of *Rebel without a Cause*, where Jim lies sprawled on a street. Director Ray was influenced by Impressionist painter Edouard Manet's *Le Torero mort* ("Dead Bullfighter," 1864) in arranging the shot (fig. **4.45**). The diagonal figure takes advantage of the width of the image but also uses the line of Dean's foreshortened body to lead the viewer's eye into the depth of the frame.

In Sergei Eisenstein's *Battleship Potemkin* ("*Broneonosets Potyomkin*"; 1925), the famous Odessa Steps sequence relies on the opposition between strong diagonal lines, associated with the sweeping advance of the Imperial troops, and the horizontal

4.43 *(top)* On the set: the tree-lined street provides symmetry in *Devil in a Blue Dress*.

4.44 *(bottom)* The closing shot of *L'Avventura*.

Composition

83

4.52 Chiaroscuro evokes drama at the tense climax of *The Third Man*.

Light and Dark

Arranging light and dark areas in the frame is an important aspect of composition and can contribute to balance. Using contrasting areas of lightness and darkness to create compositional effects is referred to as **chiaroscuro**, after a classical painting technique. In *The Third Man* (Carol Reed 1949), Harry Lime (Orson Welles) meets his fate in a beautifully lit underground tunnel (fig. **4.52**).

Color

Production designers develop a color palette, or range of colors, appropriate to the subject matter or the mood of the film. In doing so, they take into account the way audiences respond to the properties of color. When white light is refracted, it produces colors along a spectrum from red to violet, each with a different wavelength. Because viewers perceive reds, yellows, and oranges as warm (vibrant with energy), and blues and greens as cool (relaxing rather than exciting), filmmakers choose to incorporate colors into sets, costumes, and props according to the effect they are seeking to create.

Like any other visual technique, color in the *mise en scène* may function as a motif. Nicholas Ray repeatedly uses the color red to suggest the fusion of existential anguish and sexual urges of the younger generation in *Rebel without a Cause*. Red appears in Jim's jacket (fig. **4.53**), Judy's coat and lipstick, and in the simulated explosion of the galaxy at

4.53 A red jacket sets the tone in *Rebel without a Cause*.

the Observatory. In *Do the Right Thing* (Spike Lee 1989), the viewer is repeatedly reminded of the heat of the summer's day by the use of red and yellow in costumes and in the set (fig. **4.54**).

Saturation refers to the strength of a hue (red, green, blue, yellow, etc.). **Desaturated** colors are less pure; they contain more white than saturated colors and thus they look grayish, pale or washed out. In Steven Soderbergh's *The Limey* (1999), desaturated color establishes the characterless environment of Los Angeles and contributes to a downbeat mood as Wilson (Terence Stamp) searches for his daughter's killers (fig. **4.55**).

Wong Kar Wai's *In the Mood For Love* ("*Fa yeung nin wa*"; 2000) uses saturated hues to depict the sensual, colorful dresses and neon lights of Hong Kong in the 1960s (fig. **4.56**). In doing so, the film makes visual reference to American films about Asia set in that period and filmed in Technicolor, including *Love is a Many-Splendored Thing* (Henry King 1955) and *The World of Suzie Wong* (Richard Quine 1960; fig. **4.57**).

While conventional cultural associations may attach to certain colors that appear in the *mise en scène*—black for mourning, for example—it is

4.54 *(top)* Reds and yellows emphasize the summer heat in *Do the Right Thing*.

4.55 *(center)* Desaturated color creates a washed-out look in *The Limey*.

4.56 *(bottom)* Saturated color in *In the Mood for Love* ("*Fa yeung nin wa*") evokes Technicolor films about Asia from the 1960s.

important in forwarding interpretations to consider the contextual use of color in relation to cultural norms, narrative elements, and other visual techniques.

● Two Approaches to *Mise en Scène*

The Frame in Two Dimensions: *mise en scène* in German Expressionism

Several German films released in the decade immediately following World War I (1918–1928) were so visually distinctive that contemporary critics lauded their merits, making the Weimar Republic's film industry one of the first internationally recognized national cinemas. Robert Wiene's horror classic *The Cabinet of Dr. Caligari* (1919) helped make the German film industry Hollywood's most serious competitor. French critics coined the term *Caligarisme* to describe films made in this style, but most film critics and scholars use the term **German Expressionism**, named for the Expressionist movement in painting and sculpture that began in Germany before World War I. Along with *The Golem* ("*Der Golem*"; Paul Wegener 1920), *Dr. Mabuse, The Gambler* ("*Dr Mabuse, der Spieler*"; Fritz Lang 1922), *Metropolis* (Fritz Lang 1926), *Nosferatu* (F.W. Murnau 1922), *The Last Laugh* ("*Der letzte Mann*"; F.W. Murnau 1922), and *Faust* (F.W. Murnau 1926), Weine's film is recognized as one of the canonical examples of German Expressionist cinema.

Film scholars have debated whether the style was a reflection of German culture and psychology or simply a creative response to financial constraints. Lotte Eisner and Siegfried Kracauer argue that *Caligari* reflects German interests in mysticism and ominously foretells the coming of Hitler, whereas Thomas Elsaesser contends that the German film studio, Universum Film Aktiengesellschaft (UFA), was strapped for cash during production of *Caligari* and opted to build intentionally primitive sets. Some argue that the German film industry used stylized set designs and cinematography to distinguish German art films from more pedestrian Hollywood fare. What no one disputes, however, is that the dramatic use of *mise en scène* is one of the primary reasons German Expressionism was, and is, so visually distinctive and important to film history.

The film's macabre story (which involves a murderous madman and a sleepwalker), chiaroscuro lighting, diagonal lines, and bizarre, artificial sets give the film a distinctive look (fig. **4.58**). The combination of visual elements conveys a world out of balance and suggests extreme states of subjectivity—that is, states of feeling rather than being. The visual system externalizes characters' unbalanced perceptions of the world.

The sets in *Caligari* reflect contemporary experiments in the visual arts, namely the emphasis on distortion, jagged shapes, and irregu-

4.58 Edgy angles and chiaroscuro lighting heighten the tension in *The Cabinet of Dr. Caligari* ("*Das Kabinett des Dr. Caligari*").

4.59 Francis is hounded by text in *The Cabinet of Dr. Caligari*.

larity in Expressionist painting, sculpture, and theater. Artists such as Ernst Ludwig Kirchner, Max Pechstein, and Käthe Kollwitz explored the ways distorted lines and shapes convey profound emotions in figurative paintings, lithographs, prints, and woodcuts. Hermann Warm, one of the three set designers on *Caligari* (all of whom were Expressionist artists), felt that "films must be drawings brought to life" (quoted in Ellis and Wexman, p. 54). The emphasis on the frame as a two-dimensional surface appears throughout *Caligari*, in sets where shadows are actually painted on. This idea is taken to its ultimate extreme in a scene where a deranged character is hounded by text that appears all around him on screen (fig. **4.59**). The screen becomes a writing surface.

Since the 1920s, many filmmakers have used *mise en scène* to depict extreme states of subjectivity. Few films, however, reproduce the weird, two-dimensional frame of *Caligari*. A crazily snarled mess of tubes and wires in Terry Gilliam's *Brazil* (1985) reflects an entire social order gone mad. In one of the film's most memorable scenes, two men from the central office

4.60 Francis's apocalyptic dream, from *The Butcher Boy*.

pay a visit to the protagonist's apartment in order to repair his ducts. The tangle of bulging and belching tubes and pipes behind the wall is a metaphor for the chaos and disorder below the surface of this authoritarian dystopia. *The Butcher Boy* (Neil Jordan 1997) presents the disturbed inner world of Francis Brady, who grows up in a small village in post-World War II Ireland. In a dream, he witnesses the detonation of a nuclear bomb (whose mushroom cloud rises above a postcard-perfect image of rural Ireland), then roams the gray, charred landscape, encountering bizarre pig carcasses and space aliens. The *mise en scène* renders Francis's trauma with startling and surreal immediacy (fig. **4.60**).

Combining *Mise en Scène* and Camerawork: The Frame in Three Dimensions in French Poetic Realism

André Bazin, one of the co-founders of the influential French film journal *Cahiers du Cinéma* ("Cinema Notebooks"), celebrated films that made dramatic use of three-dimensional space. He described this approach as a *mise en scène* aesthetic—one that emphasized movement through choreography within the scene rather than through editing.

Although Bazin focused on the importance of *mise en scène*, he also discussed cinematography. His ideas show that elements of film are inevitably interrelated and that analysis and interpretation must take into account the fact that film techniques work together, combining to produce an overall experience for the viewer. Using Bazin's ideas to discuss the *mise en scène* aesthetic and French Poetic Realism thus serves as a conclusion to this chapter and an introduction to the next chapter on cinematography.

Bazin celebrated the films of French Poetic Realism because they emphasize the space of the story world: the setting and the arrangement of figures. The films of three of the most important directors of French cinema during the 1930s—Marcel Carné, Julien Duvivier, and Jean Renoir—emphasize the complex interplay between individuals and society. Whereas Hollywood favored stories about individuals transcending social limitations, French Poetic Realist films depicted characters whose fates are determined by their social milieu.

These filmmakers used *mise en scène* to illuminate the possibilities and limitations of characters trapped by social circumstance. In *Pépé le Moko* (Julien Duvivier 1937), the title character, a criminal, finds himself psychologically trapped in the sprawling casbah of Algiers, the very environment that affords him his freedom from the law. Pépé (Jean

Gabin) has fallen in love with a traveling socialite; he sacrifices his freedom, and ultimately his life, when he leaves the casbah in order to be with her. A common feature of Poetic Realist films was the depiction of characters such as Pépé whose desires are at odds with society.

Two visual characteristics of Poetic Realism convey this theme: careful construction of the *mise en scène* and elaborate camera movement. Because these films explore how environment shapes human behavior and destiny, set designers paid attention to minute, yet meaningful, details. Unlike German Expressionism's self-consciously artificial *mise en scène*, that of Poetic Realism depicts realistic and identifiable environments. Poetic Realism's set designs are not distorted or artificial, yet they invest the image with atmosphere. In *The Rules of the Game* ("*La Règle du jeu*"; 1939), Renoir repeatedly emphasizes the intricately adorned rooms and hallways of a lavish French château (fig. **4.61**).

Bazin analyzed *The Grand Illusion* ("*La Grande Illusion*"; Jean Renoir 1937) in terms of its detailed *mise en scène*: "[The film's] realism is not the result of simple copying from life; rather, it is the product of a careful re-creation of character through the use of detail *which is not only accurate but meaningful as well*" (Bazin, p. 63; emphasis added). Bazin's statement explains how Poetic Realism earned its name. The setting is realistic in that it reproduces the experience of the lived world, and it is poetic because the careful orchestration of visual techniques heightens the characters' psychological reality, making it tangible to viewers.

Technological factors played a role in determining the look of Poetic Realism. Given the movement's emphasis on detailed, realistic, and atmospheric settings, cinematographers were faced with the challenge of capturing the fine details of the *mise en scène* in three-dimensional space. In French films during the 1930s, camera mobility rapidly increased. In 1930, about one shot in ten involved a moving camera, whereas in 1935, one shot in three involved a moving rather than a stationary camera.

Camera movements combine with a carefully constructed set to produce emotional and intellectual depth in Jean Renoir's *The Crime of Monsieur Lange* ("*Le Crime de Monsieur Lange*"; 1935). Amédée Lange (René Lefèvre) works for a floundering publishing house, whose owner, Batala (Jules Berry), callously seduces women and swindles his workers and investors. When Batala disappears and is presumed dead, Lange transforms the publishing company into a thriving cooperative that treats its workers, investors, and readers with respect. One night, in the midst of a

4.61 A carefully orchestrated shot from Renoir's *The Rules of the Game* ("*La Règle du jeu*"), an example of Poetic Realism.

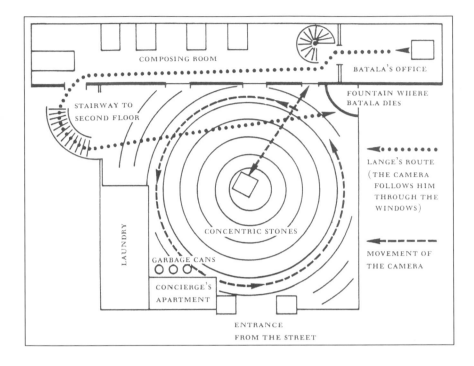

COMPOSING ROOM

BATALA'S OFFICE

FOUNTAIN WHERE
BATALA DIES

STAIRWAY TO
SECOND FLOOR

LANGE'S ROUTE
(THE CAMERA
FOLLOWS HIM
THROUGH THE
WINDOWS)

LAUNDRY

CONCENTRIC STONES

MOVEMENT OF
THE CAMERA

GARBAGE CANS

CONCIERGE'S
APARTMENT

ENTRANCE
FROM THE STREET

4.62 A sketch by André Bazin of the complex camera movement in *The Crime of Monsieur Lange* ("*Le Crime de Monsieur Lange*").

4.63 *(left)* The climax of *The Crime of Monsieur Lange*: Lange exits screen right.

4.64 *(center)* The climax of *The Crime of Monsieur Lange*: the camera pans across the courtyard.

4.65 *(right)* The climax of *The Crime of Monsieur Lange*: a three-shot of Lange, Batala, and Valentine.

celebratory staff party, Batala suddenly returns to stake his claim on the now prosperous company. Lange, unwilling to allow his former boss to ruin the cooperative spirit of the enterprise, shoots him.

What is most striking about the climactic scene is its choreography (fig. **4.62**). The episode begins with Batala trying to seduce Lange's new romantic interest, Valentine (Florelle), in a dark, cobblestoned courtyard, while the staff revelry continues unabated across the way (only Lange and Valentine are aware of Batala's presence). As Batala corners Valentine, the camera cranes up to film Lange in the company office, two flights above the courtyard. He is stunned and distraught over Batala's demands. As Lange resolutely marches out of the office, the camera tracks his movement through the building and down the stairs. When Lange reaches the courtyard, he exits the frame at screen right (fig. **4.63**), while the camera moves in the opposite direction, panning to the left. Instead of following Lange's movement, the camera pans across the courtyard (fig. **4.64**), nearly completing a circle, until it finds Lange, Batala, and Valentine (fig. **4.65**). Then Lange fires the gun.

The scene is a potent example of Poetic Realism's use of a mobile camera to explore the *mise en scène* in three dimensions and to establish emotional and psychological connections among people and events. The camera's careful attention to Lange's trek heightens the tension by postponing his inevitable confrontation with Batala. The camera's sweep of the courtyard symbolically collects the neighborhood's inhabitants, most notably the workers. This camera movement and the detailed set are crucial to the film's defense of Lange's character. He does not act out of self-interest—instead, Lange acts on behalf of all of his partners. Batala's murder becomes a communal act.

As this comparison of German Expressionism and French Poetic Realism suggests, analyzing a film's *mise en scène* can be a challenging enterprise, requiring attention to details of setting, figure placement, lighting, and composition, as elements of the overall production design. Furthermore, these examples show that visual elements work in concert to produce meaning. Rich interpretations grow out of the serious contemplation of the interaction of aesthetic elements. The next chapter considers another important visual element: cinematography.

● Summary

- *Mise en scène* (setting the scene or staging the action) is an integrated design program that establishes the "look" of a film.
- The setting refers to the location of the action, which can be filmed on location or artificially constructed on a soundstage. Sets can be digitally enhanced. The spatial attributes of settings contribute meaning, often by developing characters and their conflicts and suggesting themes.
- The human figure encompasses actors, including casting, acting style, figure placement and movement, and costumes, props, and makeup.
- Lighting can affect not only the look but also the mood of a film. Hollywood's standard three-point lighting produces bright, clear images with minimal shadows, whereas the low-key lighting characteristic of *film noir* makes use of shadows and contrast to convey intrigue and danger. The dramatic lighting schemes often used in horror films contribute to the audience's feelings of shock and unease.
- Composition is the art of using graphic elements such as balance, line, foreground and background, light and dark, and color to convey information, emotions, and meaning.
- German Expressionism and French Poetic Realism are different film styles that each depend on a distinctive *mise en scène*.

● ●

Film Analysis ● The Functions of Space

This analysis focuses on the way a single aspect of *mise en scène* (the use of spatial oppositions) performs two functions: to develop characters and reinforce themes.

Learning how to describe specific details that support interpretive claims makes papers more engaging and convincing. These detailed descriptions must be clearly and logically linked to each of the paper's major ideas. Study Notes point out the way the author uses detailed descriptive claims to support interpretive claims.

4.66 *(top)* Thelma's room is full of clutter at the beginning of *Thelma and Louise*.

4.67 *(bottom)* Louise packs neatly in *Thelma and Louise*.

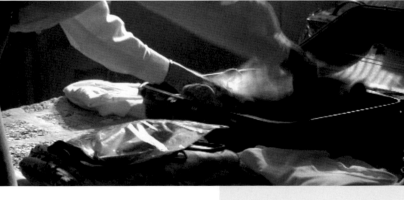

Spatial Oppositions in *Thelma and Louise*

Ridley Scott's *Thelma and Louise* employs spatial oppositions to develop characters and to further one of the film's primary themes: the women's increasing independence. Initially, an opposition between settings highlights the differences between the two main characters. Over the course of the film, however, Thelma (Geena Davis) and Louise (Susan Sarandon) begin to share the same spaces as they drive into the open landscape of the Southwest. Their growing independence from the world they have left behind is made evident through contrasts between the settings they occupy and the settings inhabited by the men who pursue them. The film culminates in the two women's decision to keep going into an unconfined space rather than be imprisoned by the world they have left behind.[1]

The film opens with a contrast between the two protagonists, helping the audience to understand their personalities. Each woman appears in a kitchen. Louise, at work as a waitress in a bright, noisy, commercial kitchen at a diner, calls her friend Thelma. As she talks to Louise on the phone, Thelma paces back and forth in her kitchen at home: a dark, confining, and messy room in the home she shares with her husband, Darryl (Christopher McDonald).[2] The fact that Louise works and Thelma stays at home is made clear in this spatial opposition and is reinforced by two other aspects of *mise en scène*: costumes and props. Thelma wears a sloppy bathrobe and eats a candy bar while Louise wears a white uniform. Louise is associated with hard work and discipline while Thelma is shown as childish and disorganized.

The scene of the two women packing reinforces the contrast between them. The camera shows Thelma and Louise in their respective domestic spaces: Thelma dashes around the bedroom of her suburban house, packing everything she owns. Louise packs neatly in an apartment filled with light and mirrors, and free of the clutter that overwhelms Thelma's bedroom (figs. **4.66**, **4.67**).

4.68 Thelma takes over at the wheel, late in *Thelma and Louise*.

When the women head out to spend the weekend at the hunting cabin of Louise's friend, the spaces they inhabit change a great deal. They stop at the Silver Bullet, a Country and Western bar. After Louise shoots and kills Harlan (Timothy Carhart), they stop at coffee shops and gas stations and stay in a series of anonymous hotel rooms. These settings are facsimiles of the domestic spaces they left behind (kitchens and bedrooms), but they are also public spaces. Importantly, Thelma and Louise share these spaces, which they did not do in the opening scenes.[3]

As the film progresses, the women spend more of their time together in the car, a space that at first differentiates the women but later unites them. In the early scenes of the film, Louise always drives, while Thelma is content to ride in the passenger seat and put her feet up on the dashboard. After the shooting, Thelma drives the car wildly until Louise asks her to pull over. Louise does not trust Thelma with her car. Gradually, however, Thelma assumes more of the driving duties, taking some control over the shared space and the direction of their journey (fig. **4.68**). The moment when Thelma begins to drive occurs just after J.D. (Brad Pitt) robs them; Thelma takes responsibility by dragging Louise into the car and driving away.[4]

Late in the film, the women drive rather than stopping in hotels. They venture into the uninhabited areas of the desert Southwest (fig. **4.69**). The open landscape replaces diners and hotel rooms. This shift becomes most apparent after they stop in the

3 Here the author draws a contrast between early and late scenes in the film, using specific visual evidence to argue that the use of space changes over time. Without describing the difference in context (for example, when the details appear in the narrative), the claim could not be supported.

4 The author cites a specific moment and visual detail to establish the turning point where the use of the space of the car changes dramatically.

4.69 Thelma and Louise are surrounded by space in the empty desert landscape in *Thelma and Louise*.

middle of the night. Louise walks away from the car to take in the panorama of the rock formations in the empty desert landscape; the loose framing shows that she is surrounded by emptiness.[5] The women spend the night on the road, having freed themselves from the confines of their homes and hotel rooms.

As the women move away from Arkansas geographically and psychologically, the men who pursue them become more confined in terms of the spaces they occupy.[6] The spatial opposition between Thelma and Louise has disappeared, and a new one takes its place: the opposition between the two women on the one hand and the Arkansas State Police/FBI and the men in their lives—Darryl and Jimmy (Michael Madsen)—on the other. The men are increasingly shown in offices and domestic spaces. Detective Hal Slocum (Harvey Keitel) first appears outside in the parking lot at the Silver Bullet. His second scene finds him at the office. Eventually, he moves into Darryl and Thelma's house, along with FBI agents who have set up shop in Darryl and Thelma's home, tapping the phone and watching videos (fig. **4.70**). Intermittent rainstorms emphasize the crowded and confining environs of the household. The increasing control and freedom the women exercise in relation to the bright, open desert landscape contrasts with the men who are tracking them—they move from police stations and offices into the tightly framed space of the Dickinson home.

The final scene uses the Grand Canyon to suggest the independence and freedom the women have attained. Rather than go to prison, or even return to the homes, apartments, workplaces, or hotel rooms they have left behind, they choose to keep driving into the open space. Whether or not viewers understand or agree with the women's decision, the logic of their flight into the canyon is unassailable, given the pattern of spatial opposition developed throughout the film.

4.70 FBI men tightly framed at Darryl's house in *Thelma and Louise*.

Works Consulted

Arden, Darlene. "The Magic of ILM." www.darlenearden.com/articleILM.htm

Bazin, André. *Jean Renoir.* New York: Simon and Schuster, 1971. Trans. 1973.

Bizony, Piers. "Shipbuilding," in *The Making of "2001: A Space Odyssey."* New York: Random House, 2000, pp. 43–54.

"Brad Pitt goes to extremes in *Troy*." Reuters. May 13, 2004. http:msnbc.msn.com/id/4953083. 6/20/2004.

Cocks, Jay, and Martin Scorsese. *"The Age of Innocence": The Shooting Script*. New York: Newmarket Press, 1995.

Denby, David. Review of *Ali*. *The New Yorker*, January 28, 2002, p. 27.

Eisner, Lotte. *The Haunted Screen*. Berkeley, CA: University of California Press, 1952. Trans. 1969.

Ellis, Jack C., and Virginia Wright Wexman. *A History of Film*, 5th edn. Boston: Allyn and Bacon, 2002.

Elsaesser, Thomas. *Weimar Cinema and After: Germany's Historical Imaginary*. New York: Routledge, 2000.

Fellini, Federico. *Fellini on Fellini*, trans. Isabel Quigley. Cambridge and New York: Da Capo Press, 1996.

Gibson, Pamela Church. "Film Costume," in *The Oxford Guide to Film Studies*, ed. John Hill and Pamela Church Gibson. Oxford and New York: Oxford University Press, 1998, pp. 36–42.

Horn, John. "Producers Pursue a *Potter* with Pizzazz." *Raleigh News and Observer*, January 25, 2004, p. 3G.

Kelly, Mary Pat. *Martin Scorsese: A Journey*. New York: Thunder's Mouth Press, 1991.

King, Barry. "Articulating Stardom," *Screen*, 26/5 (1985), pp. 27–50.

Kracauer, Siegfried. *From "Caligari" to Hitler: A Psychological History of the German Film*. Princeton, NJ: Princeton University Press, 1971.

Lipton, Lenny. *Independent Filmmaking*. New York: Simon and Schuster, 1983.

LoBrutto, Vincent. *Principal Photography: Interviews with Feature Film Cinematographers*. London and Westport, CT: Praeger, 1999.

McDonald, Paul. "Film Acting," in *The Oxford Guide to Film Studies*, ed. John Hill and Pamela Church Gibson. Oxford and New York: Oxford University Press, 1998, pp. 30–36.

Mottram, James. *The Making of "Memento."* London: Faber and Faber, 2002.

Naremore, James. *Acting in the Cinema*. Berkeley, CA: University of California Press, 1990.

Scott, Walter. "Personality Parade." *Parade Magazine*, June 13, 2004, p. 1.

Sklar, Robert. *Film: An International History of the Medium*, 2nd edn. New York: Harry N. Abrams, 2002.

5

Cinematography

The history of light is the history of life, and the human eye was the first camera.

Josef Von Sternberg

Steven Soderbergh's *Traffic* looks at the effects of illegal drug use in the United States and Mexico. One plotline revolves around Bob Wakefield (Michael Douglas), who is the head of the U.S. Drug Enforcement Agency and learns that his teenage daughter has become addicted to drugs. Another plotline traces official corruption and drug trafficking in Mexico, while a third concerns the activities of a wealthy Miami drug dealer and his wife. The multiple plotlines are connected by a common theme: the destructive impact of drugs on individuals, families, and communities. Yet each line of action has a distinct visual style. Scenes of Mexico are golden-hued with washed-out images, whereas scenes

5.1 Golden-hued scenes of Mexico, from *Traffic*.

depicting the Wakefield family in Cincinnati have a bluish-gray cast and a wide range of tones (figs. **5.1**, **5.2**).

Soderbergh, who acted as director and as director of photography (DP), deliberately produced these effects by his choice of film stock, and by manipulating the lighting, using filters, and processing the film in particular ways. These aspects of filmmaking, which involve photographic or electronic procedures for producing images, fall under the general heading of cinematography.

Most audience members would be able to follow the multiple plotlines of *Traffic* without the visual cues Soderbergh provides, so why would he go to such lengths to produce these effects? One answer is that cinematography can do more than just support the narrative; it also can contribute to the viewer's emotional response and aesthetic experience.

5.2 This Miami scene from *Traffic* uses natural light.

Cinematography techniques work with a film's mode of organization (narrative, documentary, or avant-garde), with its *mise en scène* and editing, and with its sound to produce meaning in an integrated way. The most powerful uses of cinematography do more than simply display technical expertise: they provoke emotional, intellectual, and aesthetic responses.

Cinematographers "speak" to the audience in visual terms, using images as expressively as writers use words. To grasp the full import of visual expression, viewers must move beyond selective vision, which is the tendency to notice only those things they want to see, they expect to see, and they are used to seeing. Veteran DP Edward Lachman, who worked on *The American Friend* ("*Der amerikanische Freund*"; Wim Wenders 1977), *Desperately Seeking Susan* (Susan Seidelman 1985), and *The Virgin Suicides*, observes, "We rely so heavily on the written word to translate an idea we don't trust how images can express an idea" (LoBrutto, p. 123). This statement defines the challenge and the artistry of cinematography. Well-respected cinematographers such as Gregg Toland, Garrett Brown, and Haskell Wexler have inventively experimented with the tools of cinematography. By constantly testing and improving on the art and technology of image making, cinematographers expand the aesthetic possibilities of cinema.

This chapter examines the ways filmmakers use cinematography to develop characters, tell a story, produce a distinctive look, suggest ideas, and evoke emotions. Although it addresses many technical aspects of filmmaking, the chapter is not designed to instruct would-be cinematographers in their craft. Interested readers are encouraged to consult *American Cinematographer* magazine and the *American Cinematographer's Manual* for instruction in filmmaking techniques.

In this chapter, the effects of a technique (that is, the way it works in concert with other aspects of the film) are more important than the methods used to achieve it. When building an interpretive claim about a film, the first order of business is to identify a technique using the proper terminology. Second, the viewer moves beyond description, developing ideas about the technique as it works in relation to other elements to produce meaning. Understanding how a technique emerged and developed, and how it has been used in various contexts, enhances interpretation, but is not central to it.

During the first 100 years of cinema, cinematography was synonymous with photography, a photochemical process. As electronic technologies such as **analog** and **digital video** recording have eclipsed traditional methods, cinematography has come to include many non-photographic processes such as computer-generated imagery, or CGI. Although digital technologies now augment photography-based processes and may replace them entirely, photography defined the visual language of film's first century. Therefore, this chapter examines photographic processes as well as newer digital technologies. The next section compares the technologies of film and video. The remainder of the chapter examines four elements of cinematography: **camerawork** (the operation, placement, and movement of the camera), **lenses** and **filters**, **film stock**, and **special visual effects**. Lastly, there is a look at the cinematographic effects made possible by the advent of digital film technology, and at the broader impact of that technology on film style.

● Film and Video: A Comparison

Creating film images involves photographic and chemical processes. Exposing film stock to light passing through a lens **aperture** (a circular opening that can be enlarged or constricted) causes a chemical reaction in the light-sensitive silver halide particles in the film. Developing the exposed film in a chemical bath produces a **negative**; on black-and-white film, dark colors will appear white; on color film, a color will appear as its complementary color (for example, red will appear green). The film negative is then printed to another roll of film to produce a **master positive**. Until the late 1920s, contact printing was used to make master positives: developed film was sandwiched with raw film stock and a light beam aimed through the layers. The **optical printer**, developed in the late 1920s, projects the image from the developed film onto raw film stock and, until recently, was the primary means of creating special visual effects (fig. **5.3**). Most master positives are used for special effects because of their excellent image quality. With each successive generation, there is a loss of quality. Copying a master negative onto reversal film produces a negative from which **release prints** (used in movie theaters) are struck.

In exhibition, projectors aim a beam of light through each frame of the release print as it advances. The light beam strikes a reflective screen on which viewers see the images. The film is wound around a platter, and a claw mechanism pulls each frame into place at a speed of 24 frames per second. Because projectors are equipped with a two-bladed shutter, each frame is flashed twice, and viewers watch 48 images per second (figs. **5.4**, **5.5**). The rapid succession of individual images creates the illusion of motion. The ability to perceive the sequence as continuous is believed to derive from two properties of human vision: **persistence of vision**, which argues that the brain holds an image for a few seconds after it's gone, and the **phi phenomenon** whereby the eye perceives two lights flashing on and off as one light moving. A running joke regarding visual perception appears in David Fincher's *Fight Club* (1999). Tyler Durden (Brad Pitt) works as a film projectionist and splices single frames of pornographic images into commercial films before projecting them. These shocking sights disturb audience members, but they don't know why they are upset, since the images pass by so quickly that they do not consciously register them.

For audiences, the advantages of film over video images are many. One is the high resolution, or density of the image. There are approximately 18 million **pixels** (picture elements) per frame of 35 mm film, compared to 300–400,000 in a video image. On film, a higher degree of detail will be apparent in dark and light areas relative to those of video images, owing to its wider **exposure latitude** or dynamic range (thirteen stops, compared to nine on video). Another difference involves color: colors generally appear flatter and harsher on video than on film.

The disadvantages of film are primarily borne by filmmakers and exhibitors. Using film is slow and expensive. The equipment is expensive and bulky, and storing and shipping 35

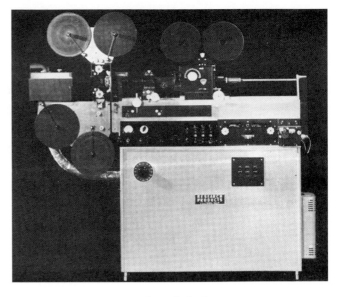

5.3 An optical printer.

5.4 *(left)* A strip of exposed film.
5.5 *(right)* 35-mm film projectors.

mm film prints are inconvenient. For non-theatrical viewing, film poses a great problem: it is difficult for individuals to purchase and maintain the equipment for film projection.

Video cameras record an electronic signal onto tape; the signal is stored either in waves (analog video) or in a binary code of ones and zeros (digital video). Video images are created by **charge coupler devices** (CCDs), silicon chips with thousands of sensors that convert light to an electronic signal. Video cameras use three CCDs—red, green, and blue— to create a full spectrum of color. Digital video can be compressed and stored on computers, where computer algorithms can encode information about an image without necessarily storing each pixel. The code can, for example, create a blue sky by describing a large number of pixels with the same color attribute across the top of a specific image.

Video monitors, including television sets, have three electron beams (one each for red, green, and blue) housed in a cathode ray tube. When a signal comes in (from an antenna, cable, satellite dish, VCR, or DVD player), each of the three beams scans the image across the screen horizontally one line at a time, illuminating light-emitting phosphors. The frequency of the scan allows the image to appear as a single, integrated frame. Until recently, video monitors used **interlaced scanning**, which meant that each frame was scanned as two fields: one consisting of all the odd-numbered lines, the other all the even lines. Newer cameras and monitors use **progressive scanning**, meaning each frame is treated as a single field.

The standard video format in the U.S., NTSC (National Television Standards Committee), produces 525 scan lines and a scanning rate of 29.97 frames per second; PAL, used in Europe and elsewhere, uses 625 scan lines at 25 frames per second. **Telecine** machines transfer film to video formats. To convert film (shot at 24 fps) to video (which is exhibited at nearly 30 fps), the film is slowed down slightly as it is run through telecine (to 23.976 fps) and an extra frame is created. This process is called a 3:2 pull-down. This is not necessary when converting film to the PAL format.

Transferring film to video also can involve image manipulation, such as **panning and scanning**, a process of re-shooting a widescreen film in order to convert it to the television **aspect ratio**, which looks more like a square than a rectangle (see fig. 5.89 for a comparison of aspect ratios). Panning and scanning selects parts of the image from the widescreen frame, and thus alters—some would say, ruins—the original composition and editing. The alternative is **letterboxing**, which preserves the original aspect ratio, but reduces the overall size of the image (figs. **5.6**, **5.7**). Letterboxing has become more common on DVDs—some offer a panned and scanned and a letterboxed version of the same film. With the advent of HDTV (high-definition television), with its aspect ratio of 1.78 to 1, widescreen films (at 1.85:1) may not suffer as greatly in the process of transfer.

For filmmakers, the traditional disadvantages of video relative to film include lower resolution and less control over **depth of field** (see fig. 5.49). But new video cameras, with variable frame rate capabilities (including 24 fps) and smaller CCDs are better able to simulate the look of film (Wheeler, p. 60). For consumers, a problem arises with video formats because analog video images degrade each time a copy is made, and videotape deteriorates rapidly. The metal oxide that is cemented to the plastic tape flakes off over time and, with it, the image.

Digital videotape is stronger and longer-lasting because its metal particles are embedded in the tape and protected with several coatings. An even longer-lasting alternative, however, is the DVD. The digital signal can be copied without loss of quality, or easily imported and exported as a file to a hard drive (through FireWire© or IEEE 1394 connections between cameras and computers). The ease of use of digital cameras, combined with the availability of relatively inexpensive editing software, has made filmmaking accessible to more people. Distribution can be as easy as uploading a file to the internet.

The future of digital image making, storage, and distribution seems assured. HDTV broadcasting began in the U.S. in 1998. International agreements signed in 1993 determined that the HDTV broadcast standard would be digital, suggesting the potential for the integration of digital technologies for film viewing, including DVD, digital cable, and satellite.

5.6 *(top)* Thelma eyes JD in *Thelma and Louise.*

5.7 *(bottom)* After panning and scanning, JD is cut out of the frame in *Thelma and Louise.*

● Camerawork: The Camera in Time and Space

Creating Meaning in Time: The Shot

Cinematography involves both the spatial characteristics of the frame and the temporal, or time-dependent, character of the film medium. Narrative fiction films tell stories, documentaries recount and observe events, avant-garde films create new combinations of image and sounds; all of these different types of film unfold in space and time before the viewer.

The shot, a single uninterrupted series of frames, is film's basic unit of expression: an image whose meaning unfolds over time. Shots vary in length, theoretically, from the briefest exposure of a single film frame to the uninterrupted exposure of a full roll of motion picture film. In Hitchcock's *Rope* (1948), the exposure of a roll of film without cuts yielded shots of about eight minutes in length. Editing several shots together produces a **scene**, which is a coherent narrative unit: one which has its own beginning, middle, and end.

5.8 A series of storyboards.

In order to use the time they have on the set efficiently, directors and cinematographers generally plan each shot ahead of time. One method for planning shots is the **storyboard**—a series of drawings that lays out the film sequentially (fig. **5.8**). Some directors, such as Brian De Palma, use photographs as storyboards. Others, such as Jim Jarmusch, reject storyboards and even shot lists, preferring to improvise ("Interview" 2004). The DP designs **set-ups**, positioning actors, the camera, and lighting arrangement for each shot.

Films are generally not shot in chronological order, and, except on very low-budget productions, every shot is filmed more than once. Each version is called a **take**. In post-production, the editor and director choose which takes will appear in the film. Those takes not included in the final print are called **out-takes**. *Me, Myself, and Irene* (Farrelly Brothers 2000) includes comic out-takes showing actors making mistakes over the final credits. *A Bug's Life* (John Lasseter and Andrew Stanton 1998) and *Chicken Run* (Peter Lord and Nick Park 2000) make this practice doubly humorous by providing out-takes of animated characters, who, by definition, do not make mistakes!

Uninterrupted shots of more than one minute are called **long takes**. Orson Welles's *Touch of Evil* is renowned for its opening shot, a long take that follows the movements of a newly married couple on foot and a car with a bomb in its trunk as they cross the Mexico–U.S. border (fig. **5.9**). The long take creates tension as two lines of action merge on narrative and visual levels. Robert Altman's *The Player* (1992) pays its respects to Welles with an inside joke: a continuous shot of eight minutes in length that opens the film and introduces the audience to action on a Hollywood studio back lot. The camera sweeps by characters, who reverently describe Welles's feat in *Touch of Evil*.

5.9 The celebrated crane shot at the beginning of *Touch of Evil*.

Long takes build dramatic tension, emphasize the continuity of time and space, and allow directors to focus on the movement of actors in the space of the *mise en scène*. A long take defines the fate of Irish immigrants in Martin Scorsese's *Gangs of New York* (2002). A camera sweeps along lines of young Irish men disembarking from the boats in New York harbor and eavesdrops on transactions taking place at tables where military recruiters offer the men their citizenship if they join the Union army. The camera reverses its motion,

Chapter 5: Cinematography

following the men as they trudge back onto ships, headed for the U.S. South. A final reversal of motion occurs as the camera follows the return of the soldiers in pine coffins, which are removed from the boat and piled upon the dock (figs. **5.10**, **5.11**).

Scorsese is known for dramatic long takes. Another depicts the courtship of a young couple in *Goodfellas*. As Henry (Ray Liotta) and Karen (Lorraine Bracco) enter the famous New York nightclub the Copacabana, the camera moves fluidly, following them into the pandemonium of the kitchen and through the labyrinthine passages of the building on their way to the packed club. The relentless continuity of the shot, which takes about three minutes, conveys Karen's confusion and exhilaration as she is unwittingly drawn into Henry's world of organized crime.

Unlike *Gangs of New York*, where the long take collapses time and space (and defines the soldiers' fate), this long take

5.10 *(top)* A crane shot from *Gangs of New York*: loading coffins.

5.11 *(bottom)* A crane shot of the dock, from *Gangs of New York*: new conscripts are on the left.

exaggerates them. The rapid-fire sequence of greetings and continuous movement into the club dramatize what would otherwise be an unremarkable experience for the characters, lengthening it and marking it as an exciting moment.

Altering Time: Slow and Fast Motion

Cinematographers manipulate the speed of filming to compress or expand time. Unless special effects are desired, the standard recording speed is 24 frames per second. By reducing or increasing the camera's recording speed, and then projecting the film at 24 frames per second, filmmakers can affect the viewer's perception of time.

To produce **slow motion**, the camera records images at a speed faster than that at which it is projected. When the film is projected at the standard rate, the action appears to be slowed down. One minute of film recorded at 36 fps has a greater number of frames than one minute of film recorded at 24 fps. When projected at 24 fps, the 36 fps footage will take longer than one minute to screen, drawing out the action. Slow motion lengthens the duration of an action and seems to break down human movement into its component parts.

This effect has been used for both comic and dramatic purposes. In *The Naked Gun* (David Zucker 1988), a parody of police action films, new lovers run along a beach. When a jogger runs in the opposite direction and rams into their joined hands, slow motion

From Stop Motion to Animation

Stop-motion photography (**pixilation**) is the technique underlying all film **animation** (fig. **5.12**). As early as 1906–7, J. Stuart Blackton used stop motion to animate objects and hand drawings in one-reel films for Vitagraph, and French filmmaker Emile Cohl combined animation and live action (Crafton, p. 71; Cook, p. 52). Animators soon developed a process using transparent overlays called **cels** (for "celluloid") to separate moving figures from static backgrounds, which avoided the problem of drawing each frame individually. Still, cel animation is a labor intensive and time-consuming process, and it remained the standard technique for animated films until the 1990s.

Animated short films were exhibited along with newsreels and fiction features, providing "humor, slapstick spectacle, animal protagonists, and fantastic events" (Crafton, p. 72). Disney Studios developed the iconic figure of Mickey Mouse during the 1920s, and Warner Brothers created Porky Pig, Elmer Fudd, Daffy Duck, and Bugs Bunny in the 1930s and 1940s. Disney Studios achieved commercial success with animated features such as *Snow White and the Seven Dwarfs* (David Hand 1937), *Pinocchio* (Ben Sharpsteen and Hamilton Luske 1940), and *Fantasia* (Ben Sharpsteen 1940; fig. **5.13**).

After a long decline, animation experienced a renaissance during the 1990s. When it was on the point of eliminating its

5.12 *(above)* Stop-motion photography animates insects in *The Cameraman's Revenge*.

5.13 Animals as characters in *Fantasia*, one of Disney's most successful animated features.

5.14 Rotoscoping and computer graphics animate live action in *Waking Life*.

animation division in the 1990s, Disney (having moved into live-action feature films) did an about-face and purchased Pixar Studios (originally the computer graphics division of LucasFilm). Pixar's success with *Toy Story* (John Lasseter 1995), the first computer-animated feature, re-energized commercial animation. Since then, several such films have earned critical acclaim, including *Princess Mononoke* ("*Mononoke Hime*"; Hayao Miyazaki 1997), *Spirited Away* ("*Sen to Chihiro no Kamikakushi*"; Hayao Miyazaki 2001), and *Toy Story 2* (John Lasseter 1999). In 2003, Pixar's animated *Finding Nemo* (Andrew Stanton and Lee Unkrich) was the highest-grossing film in the U.S., earning $340 million. The increasingly popular Japanese style of animation, called **anime**, grew out of the film and television

work of Osamu Tezuka during the 1950s and 1960s. Anime can be distinguished from most styles of animation because it is not necessarily aimed at young audiences.

As part of the revitalization of animation through computer graphics, Richard Linklater took the artistry of the **rotoscope** to a new level in *Waking Life* (2001). The rotoscope projects photographs or footage onto glass so that images can be traced by hand as templates for cartoon characters (Rickitt, p. 141). After Linklater shot and edited a live action version of *Waking Life* on digital video, a team of animators used a computer program to trace over and color the entire film on a computer monitor. Working with a variety of animators in this way meant that each of the different scenes in the film has its own visual style (fig. **5.14**).

exaggerates the physical comedy. In this case, slow motion has established and undercut the scene's traditional romantic elements. In contrast, in David Fincher's *Panic Room* (2002), Meg Altman (Jodie Foster) temporarily escapes from the fortress-like panic room where she and her daughter have been hiding from intruders. As she looks for her cell phone, slow motion lengthens the duration of Meg's desperate search and increases the scene's sense of urgency, because both Meg and her daughter are vulnerable when the panic room door is open.

To produce **fast motion**, cinematographers record images at a slower speed than the speed of projection. Before cameras were motorized, this was called **undercranking** the camera. Fewer frames are exposed in one minute when shooting at a speed of 16 fps than at a speed of 24 fps. When projected at 24 fps, that action takes less than a minute on screen and appears unnaturally rapid.

5.15 "Trick" photography: Orlock is exposed to the sun in a double exposure from *Nosferatu*.

F. W. Murnau used fast motion in *Nosferatu* (1922) to indicate the supernatural speed with which Count Orlock (Max Schreck) loads a group of coffins onto a cart as he prepares to leave his castle for England (fig. **5.15**). After Orlock climbs into one of the coffins, stop-motion photography (also called pixilation) is used to make it appear as though the coffin lid leaps to the top of the coffin. The technique involves photographing a scene one frame at a time and moving the model between each shot. The process was used to animate the beasts in *King Kong* (Merian C. Cooper and Ernest B. Schoedsack 1933) and *Mighty Joe Young* (Ray Harryhausen 1949). **Go-motion**, a technique developed by Industrial Light and Magic, builds movement into single frames. In this process, the puppet or model is motorized and moves when the camera's shutter is open, creating a sense of blur. The technique was used for the whales in *Star Trek IV: The Voyage Home* (Leonard Nimoy 1986).

Accelerating and Freezing Time: Time Lapse and Frozen Moments

Time-lapse photography is a process of recording a very small number of images over a long period of time—say, one frame per minute or per day. Time-lapse nature photography can present a flower blooming or storm clouds moving across the sky in a matter of seconds.

Contemporary filmmakers have developed sophisticated methods for manipulating time. An impressive effect developed during the 1990s is called a **frozen time moment**, or a bullet-time moment. These terms refer to a shot where a single action is viewed simultaneously from multiple vantage points around the action. The technique was first used in the martial arts scenes in *The Matrix*. To create this effect, more than 122 still cameras were arranged around the action, timed and calibrated in order to capture still images of the action at the same instant. Those still images were then used as a blueprint in digital post-production, where technicians "interpolated" additional frames. They create additional images to simulate the motion that could occur in between the actual stills. Combining the stills with the interpolated frames allowed them to extend the duration of the shot. The result is a "time-frozen subject seen from changing perspectives" (Martin, p. 70). *The Matrix* employed a crew of 40 photographers, 4–5 computer graphics designers, and 95–100 digital effects artists. Note that this stunning effect was created by combining traditional still photography with the latest digital post-production technology.

The Camera and Space: Height, Angle, and Shot Distance

Whereas the length of a take and slow and fast motion influence the viewer's sense of time, the positioning and movement of the camera affect the viewer's understanding of space. Camera placement and movement determine the way viewers perceive characters, events, and objects in the world on screen. Viewers can be forced to adopt the perspective of a single character (for example in Coppola's *The Conversation*), may be implicated in voyeurism (as in Hitchcock's *Rear Window*), and can be made to see the world through the eyes of a vicious killer (as in John Carpenter's *Halloween*, 1978).

Three important variables for any shot are camera height, angle on the action, and distance from the action. These choices convey information, form motifs, introduce ideas, and create mood. Michael Chapman, DP for *Taxi Driver* (Martin Scorsese 1976) and *Raging Bull*, feels that "camera angles tell us emotional things in ways that are mysterious" (Schaefer and Salvato, p. 124). Camera placement may evoke a wide range of emotions: the position of the camera may compel intimacy or establish a sense of distance from characters and situations.

Camera Height

The camera's height most frequently approximates an eye-level view of the action (fig. **5.16**), but **eye-level shots** are usually combined with intermittent shots from higher and lower vantage points. This height convention can assume a variety of forms. Japanese filmmaker Yasuhiro Ozu consistently places the camera at about three feet above the ground. For Western viewers, this vantage point may appear unusual, but this camera height is at the approximate eye level of the action taking place, as characters sit on the floor (fig. **5.17**). In Stanley Kubrick's *The Shining* (1980), DP Garrett Brown used a floor-level camera to follow a child, Danny Torrance (Danny Lloyd), as he rides around the interior of the sinister

5.16 *(top)* An eye-level scene from *The Philadelphia Story*.
5.17 *(bottom)* A very different eye-level scene from *Tokyo Story*.

5.18 A camera at water level gives the swimmer's viewpoint in *Jaws*.

Overlook Hotel on his Big Wheel. Brown comments on the surreal effect of this low camera placement: "The fact that we were below the kid and the vanishing point toward which we were moving was hidden behind him gave this whole sequence a fantastic quality" (LoBrutto, p. 149). Another film that makes effective use of an unconventional eye-level shot is *Jaws* (Steven Spielberg 1975), in which the camera's height approximates a swimmer's perspective, skimming the water's surface (fig. **5.18**).

Camera Angle

Another aspect of camera position is angle. In most shots, the camera is level. **High-angle shots**, where the camera is positioned above the character or action and aimed downward, tend to minimize the subject. In *Notorious*, when Alex Sebastian confides to his mother that he has married a spy, the camera adopts an extremely high angle in a close-up, emphasizing his panic, claustrophobia, and inefficacy (fig. **5.19**). High-angle shots may also be taken at a distance from the subject. Gordon Parks Jr.'s *Superfly* (1972) opens with a high-angle shot of two junkies about to ambush an unsuspecting Youngblood Priest (Ron O'Neal), introducing the dangerous urban setting of the film. The high angle and the great distance between the camera and the action (a **long shot**) combine to limit the viewer's emotional engagement with the characters. When film techniques encourage spectators to step back from the story or characters in terms of their emotional

5.19 A high-angle shot of Alex Sebastian in *Notorious*.

Chapter 5: Cinematography

engagement—as this camera positioning does—the effect is said to distance the viewer.

Low-angle shots, which position the camera below the subject, aiming upward, often exaggerate the size and volume of the subject, including the human body. If a ceiling is visible in an interior shot, as is common in the films of John Ford, the camera has probably been positioned at a slightly low angle (fig. **5.20**). In Sergio Leone's *For a Few Dollars More* ("*Per qualche dollari in più*"; 1965), a gunfight early in the film uses the contrast between level shots, low-angle shots, and high-angle shots to distinguish between bounty hunter Colonel Mortimer (Lee Van Cleef) and the man he is hunting. Low-angle shots of Mortimer imply his mastery of the situation. Even from a distance, he looms large in the frame because of the low angle. Level shots from behind Mortimer approximate his perspective, and they neither minimize nor exaggerate the wanted man. Finally, high-angle shots of the man tumbling to the ground after Mortimer shoots him emphasize his defeat (figs. **5.21**, **5.22**, **5.23**).

A **canted** or **Dutch angle** leans to one side. Generally, the subject creates a diagonal line in the frame. A canted angle often signifies a moment of imbalance or loss of control. Near the end of *Out of Sight* (Steven Soderbergh 1998), canted angles suggest an ironic reversal after Jack Foley (George Clooney) robs a former prison associate Richard Ripley (Albert Brooks) of $5 million in diamonds

5.20 *(above)* An interior shot, showing the ceiling, from *The Searchers*.

5.21 *(below)* A level shot of Mortimer in *For a Few Dollars More* ("*Per qualche dollari in più*").

5.22 *(bottom left)* A low-angle shot of Mortimer in *For a Few Dollars More*.

5.23 *(bottom right)* A high-angle shot of Mortimer's victim in *For a Few Dollars More*.

5.24 A canted angle used near the end of *Out of Sight*.

(fig. **5.24**). When Foley returns to the house to prevent other thieves from harming Ripley, one of the thieves discovers him sneaking in. A canted angle depicts the stand-off as the thug holds a gun on him from the bottom of a staircase.

An **overhead shot**, also called a bird's eye shot, gives a unique perspective on the action from above. In *Spider-Man* (Sam Raimi 2002) overhead shots depict the boundless strength and enthusiasm of Peter Parker (Tobey Maguire) as he tests his new-found spider powers by catapulting himself across New York rooftops. In *Psycho*, Hitchcock uses an overhead shot to startle viewers and maintain the secret regarding Mother's identity (see fig. 6.4).

Overhead shots are not always explained by plot events, however. A director may include these shots in order to distance the spectator from the characters or action. After the final shootout in *Taxi Driver*, when police arrive at the apartment where Iris (Jodie Foster) lives, a cut to an overhead shot depicts the police and Travis Bickle (Robert De Niro) from above. The overhead angle combines with the static *mise en scène*—even the actors are frozen—to distance viewers from the action. To realize this shot, Scorsese's crew cut a hole in the ceiling above the room where the action takes place and shot the scene through the opening.

Camera Distance

Camera distance refers to the space between the camera and its subject, which can determine how emotionally involved the audience becomes with characters. In an **extreme long shot** (XLS) the human subject is very small in relation to the surrounding environment (fig. **5.25**). In a **long shot** (LS) from Agnès Varda's *Cleo from 5 to 7* (*Cléo de 5 à 7*, 1961), the camera captures the figure of protagonist Cleo (Corinne Marchand) in its entirety. It is prominent because it occupies relatively more space in the frame, but is still entirely within the frame (fig. **5.26**). A **medium long shot** (MLS) from *Holiday* captures the human figure from the knees up (fig. **5.27**). A **medium shot** (MS) from *Capturing the Friedmans* situates the human body in the frame from the waist up (fig. **5.28**); a

5.25 An extreme long shot in the opening sequence of *Lord of the Rings: The Two Towers*.

5.26 *(top)* A long shot from *Cleo from 5 to 7.*

5.27 *(center left)* A medium long shot from *Holiday.*

5.28 *(center right)* A medium shot from *Capturing the Friedmans.*

5.29 *(bottom)* A medium close-up of Bob Dylan from *Don't Look Back.*

medium close-up (MCU) from the chest up (fig. 5.29). A close-up (CU) closes in on a section of the body, such as the face, torso, legs, or hands (fig. 5.30). An extreme close-up (XCU) will depict only a body part such as an eye, ear, or finger (see fig. 6.23).

Medium shots and close-ups tend to produce a greater sense of intimacy by allowing viewers to focus on actors' faces and character emotions, whereas long shots tend to emphasize the environment and the space that surrounds the characters. However, the effect of any shot distance must be interpreted in context. In *The Graduate*, the two main characters, Benjamin Braddock (Dustin Hoffman) and Mrs. Robinson (Anne Bancroft), frequently mask their emotions.

5.30 *(left)* A close-up of John Travolta from *Blow Out.*

5.31 *(right)* Anne Bancroft as an expressionless Mrs. Robinson in the foreground of *The Graduate.*

Immediately after a scene in which Mrs. Robinson makes a pass at Ben that he rejects, Ben and Mr. Robinson (Murray Hamilton) have a conversation about Ben's experience with women. A close-up of Mrs. Robinson's face as she listens betrays no emotion; this close-up does not provide immediate access to her feelings (fig. **5.31**). Is she sad? Angry? Bemused? Here, it is the relation between the conversation in the background and the close-up, which isolates Mrs. Robinson, that creates the emotional texture of the scene. As with most shots, narrative events, composition, other elements of *mise en scène* and camera distance contribute to the overall effect.

Most filmmakers vary shot distance, not only to serve the needs of the narrative, but also to create patterns, develop motifs, and support themes. John Cassavetes uses close-ups for spontaneity and emotional intimacy in character-driven films such as *Faces* (1968) and *A Woman under the Influence* (1974).

Filmmakers can also use shot distance to convey abstract ideas. Carl Theodor Dreyer depends almost exclusively on close-ups and medium shots of Joan of Arc and her interrogators in *The Passion of Joan of Arc* ("*La Passion de Jeanne d'Arc*"; 1928). The

5.32 *(left)* A close-up emphasizes this scene of psychological combat from *The Passion of Joan of Arc* ("*La Passion de Jeanne d'Arc*").

5.33 *(right)* A two-shot of Alma and Elisabeth in *Persona.*

Chapter 5: Cinematography

narrative focus on Joan's trial and use of close-ups emphasize Joan's spiritual power, not her military prowess. Dreyer's consistent use of close-ups heightens the psychological combat between Joan and the judges (fig. **5.32**). Dreyer championed the close-up because he believed the soul is visible in the human face.

Ingmar Bergman's *Persona* uses close-ups of two characters to suggest the intensity of their relationship. Emotionally troubled actress Elisabeth Vogler (Liv Ullman) and her nurse Alma (Bibi Andersson) seem to trade and merge their identities through several of Bergman's visual motifs. The use of tightly framed **two-shots**—in which both women's faces are visible in close-up—creates a visual metaphor for that merging (fig. **5.33**).

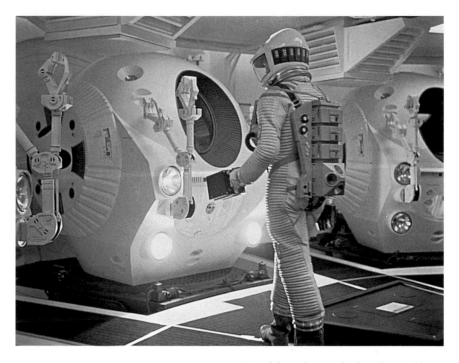

5.34 A long shot emphasizes the machine-filled universe in *2001: A Space Odyssey*.

In contrast, in *2001* Stanley Kubrick uses long shots to de-emphasize the significance of human beings and their aspirations, symbolized by machines and computers. Long shots of astronauts Dave Bowman (Keir Dullea) and Frank Poole (Gary Lockwood) show their insignificance in relation to the mechanical and computerized environment they have helped to create, especially in the context of the vast universe (fig. **5.34**). The final shots of the film, which involve extreme close-ups of a human figure, produce a startling counterpoint to Kubrick's consistent use of long shots. Close-ups of the star child suggest the human potential for rebirth.

Camera Movement: Exploring Space

In addition to height, angle, and shot distance, camera movement is another cinematographic element that can affect the meaning of shots and scenes. A camera that remains in the same position may produce a sense of stagnation, as is the case with DP Tom DeCillo's static camera in Jim Jarmusch's *Stranger than Paradise*. In contrast, a moving camera may encourage viewers to become involved in a character's physical or psychological sensations, as in Scorsese's *Raging Bull*, or may act as a counterpoint to the action. In Jean Renoir's *The Rules of the Game*, a moving camera transports the viewer through a grand French estate. The camera reveals parallels between wealthy aristocrats and their servants, moving across class boundaries that the characters themselves cannot transcend. The process of shifting the camera's height, angle, or distance to account for changes in character position is called **reframing**.

5.35 The burning house in *The Life of an American Fireman.*

Horizontal and Vertical Movement

Some camera movements are horizontal and vertical. A **pan** is the horizontal turning motion of a camera fixed to a tripod, a movement typically used to show an expanse of landscape, whether it be a vast canyon or a crowded city street. An important moment in film history occurred when Edwin Porter included a pan in *The Life of an American Fireman* (1903). Porter's camera pans to follow firefighters as they rush to a fire; the moving camera finally rests on the burning house (fig. **5.35**). This pan integrated camerawork and narrative development, as film historians Gerald Mast and Bruce Kawin explain:

> This was not a simple matter of panning to cover a wide subject, like a city skyline; what it did was discover the logic for the pan, making a camera movement part of the film's dramatic strategy—because it followed a moving object and because it kept the burning house out of the frame until the moment Porter chose to reveal it. (Mast and Kawin, p. 39)

A **swish pan** occurs when a pan is executed so quickly that it produces a blurred image, indicating rapid activity or, sometimes, the passage of time. In Spike Lee's *Do the Right Thing*, a swish pan adds to the tension between Mookie (Spike Lee) and his boss, Sal (Danny Aiello). Mookie confronts Sal with his suspicion that Sal is romantically interested in his sister Jaye (Joie Lee). The camera moves so quickly from shots of one character to the other that the intermediate space appears blurred (fig. **5.36**).

A **tilt** refers to the technique of tipping the camera vertically while it remains secured to a tripod. The movement can simulate a character looking up or down, or help to isolate or exaggerate the vertical dimension of an object or setting. In *Citizen Kane*, when Mr. Thatcher (George Coulouris) presents Charles with a sled for Christmas, the young boy unwraps the gift, and then looks up at his guardian. The camera tilts upward, exaggerating the fact that Thatcher towers over the boy. This tilt contributes to a parallel developed over the entire film between Charles and Thatcher. This early tilt shows that Thatcher dominates Charles during his childhood. Later in the film, low angles on Kane suggest that he dominates others in the same way.

5.36 A canted angle precedes a swish pan in *Do the Right Thing.*

5.37 *(left)* A dolly on a track.

5.38 *(right)* Dax ordering his troops into battle in *Paths of Glory*.

Movement in Three Dimensions

Tracking Shots To free the camera further, cinematographers sometimes mount cameras on rolling platforms called **dollies**, which ensure fluid, controlled, motion. A **crab dolly** has wheels that rotate, so the dolly can change direction. Very low-budget filmmakers sometimes use shopping carts as dollies and stand or sit inside holding the camera while being pushed! A **tracking shot** is accomplished by moving the camera, on a dolly, along a specially built track (fig. **5.37**). Tracking shots can trace movement laterally (across the frame) or in and out of the depth of the frame. In Stanley Kubrick's *Paths of Glory* (1957), a tracking shot emphasizes the forward momentum of Colonel Dax (Kirk Douglas) as he strides through the trenches of World War I, ordering his troops into battle (fig. **5.38**). The soldiers stand still as he passes, which further emphasizes Dax's vigorous march.

5.39 A camera mounted on a crane.

Crane Shots Cameras mounted on cranes create sweeping, three-dimensional movements (fig. **5.39**). The long takes that open *A Touch of Evil* and *The Player* are **crane shots**. A crane shot also takes place near the conclusion of Ethan and Joel Coen's

O Brother, Where Art Thou? (2000), when the three bumbling miscreants Everett (George Clooney), Pete (John Turturro), and Delmar (Tim Blake Nelson) are about to be hanged. As Everett drops to his knees to pray, the camera adopts a high-angle position above him and then pulls back and upward, as if his appeal to the almighty has taken flight (figs. **5.40, 5.41**).

Aerial Shots Aerial shots, taken from airplanes and helicopters, allow filmmakers to compose shots from great distances. As Thelma and Louise begin to experience the freedom of leaving their conventional lives behind as they head for Mexico, an aerial shot underscores the sense of openness and contributes to a motif of flight. Aerial shots in *Daughters of the Dust* show vast expanses of beach and ocean, indicating the remote location and unspoiled terrain of the coastal Sea Islands (fig. **5.42**).

Handheld Cameras and the Steadicam In many instances, filmmakers want to capture intimate scenes and subtle camera movements. Conventional motion picture cameras are heavy, however; without a brace, all the motion of the camera operator will be translated into shaky images. By the late 1950s and early 1960s lightweight 35 mm cameras used for recording newsreel footage during the 1940s had found their way into independent filmmaking. The Éclair Cameflex was the favorite of French New Wave filmmakers. In the 1960s, lightweight 16 mm cameras able to record synchronized sound led to a flowering of documentary filmmaking, and, particularly, the non-interventionist **direct cinema** of filmmakers such as Richard Leacock, D.A. Pennebaker, Albert and David Maysles, and Frederick Wiseman in the U.S. and Chris Marker in France. The sense of immediacy produced by **handheld shots** is evident in narrative fiction films as well, including *Medium Cool* (Haskell Wexler 1969), *Reservoir Dogs* (Quentin Tarantino 1991), and *The Blair Witch Project* (Eduardo Sánchez and Daniel Myrick 1999).

5.40 *(top)* Everett drops to his knees in *O Brother, Where Art Thou?*

5.41 *(center)* The camera pulls back and upward, away from Everett in *O Brother, Where Art Thou?*

5.42 *(bottom)* An aerial shot from *Daughters of the Dust.*

Chapter 5: Cinematography

Other innovations in camera technology included the small, lightweight, and quiet Panaflex camera, first used on Spielberg's *Sugarland Express* (1974) to capture handheld shots with dialogue in a moving car. Cinematographer Garrett Brown developed a stabilizing device worn by the camera operator that he patented as the **Steadicam**, first used on *Rocky* (John Avildsen, 1976). The Steadicam permits fluid camera movement, allows greater mobility than tracking shots, and minimizes shakiness (fig. **5.43**). Brown describes the effect of his invention: "the moving camera lets you break into the medium itself—the screen stops being a wall and becomes a space you can play in" (LoBrutto, p. 139). Notable examples of the artful use of a Steadicam include the opening scene of *Bound for Glory* (Hal Ashby 1976), the scene where Danny runs through the hedge maze in *The Shining*, and a number of scenes in *The Fugitive* (Davis 1993). Brown has gone on to develop other devices that allow filmmakers to incorporate fluid movement, such as the underwater moby cam and the SkyCam, a system that involves suspending and moving cameras using cables and pulleys.

5.43 A camera operator wears a Steadicam.

As this discussion suggests, discerning the significance of camera placement and movement requires careful consideration of a shot in context. Broadly speaking, camera movement can function in five ways. It may:

- reveal information in a dramatic fashion, as in *The Life of an American Fireman*.
- establish a character's perspective: the tilt in *Citizen Kane* aligns the viewer with the small boy.
- convey a sense of space: the aerial shot encompasses the Sea Islands in *Daughters of the Dust*.
- suggest mood, as in *The Blair Witch Project*, where a handheld camera translates fear and conflict between characters into a visually upsetting experience.
- emphasize the continuity of time and space (*Gangs of New York*) and expand time and space (the Copacabana scene in *Goodfellas*).

● ●

Techniques in Practice: Patterns of Camera Placement and Movement

In Spike Lee's *Do the Right Thing*, patterns of camera placement and movement establish relationships between the characters. Canted angles, close-ups, and tracking shots communicate the rising tensions among residents of a Brooklyn city block on a summer day.

5.44 A canted angle close-up emphasizes the tension in this scene from *Do the Right Thing*.

Lee and DP Ernest Dickerson use canted angles to emphasize conflict between characters. Canted angles define the confrontation early in the day when Mothersister (Ruby Dee) yells at Da Mayor (Ossie Davis) out her window. The second time these characters interact, Jaye (Joie Lee) is combing Mothersister's hair on the stoop and Da Mayor walks by. Once again, canted angles are used for both Mothersister and Da Mayor, suggesting they are at odds. Their differences are also evident in their contentious dialogue.

A shift in the relationship between these two characters is partially suggested by a shift in camera angle. Late in the day, after Da Mayor has saved a child from being hit by a car, Mothersister praises his heroism. During this conversation, camera angles are level on both characters, hinting that they have called a truce. By the end of the film, they have become friends.

Canted angles and close-ups visually define disputes between other characters. When Radio Raheem (Bill Nunn) buys batteries for his boom box from the Korean grocers, canted angles and close-ups indicate Raheem's impatience at having to repeat himself. Canted angles also show the Korean grocers' anger toward his superior attitude. The first time Raheem enters Sal's pizzeria, canted angles and close-ups emphasize the two men's anger as Sal (Danny Aiello) bellows at Raheem to turn his music down (fig. **5.44**). In the final scene of confrontation, extreme close-ups combine with loud music and raised voices to help viewers recognize that anger is spiraling out of control.

In addition to canted angles and close-ups, Lee uses tracking shots to convey tension among neighborhood residents. In a startling sequence, Lee films Mookie, Pino, a Latino gang leader, a police officer, and the Korean grocer as they face the camera directly and spout racial epithets. As each character expresses these sentiments, the camera tracks in toward the character, ending the shot in a close-up. At the conclusion of this vignette, the camera remains immobile as the love-preaching DJ, Mr. Señor Love Daddy (Samuel Jackson), rolls toward it (figs. **5.45**, **5.46**). He delivers a very different message, asking everyone to "cool out." In this sequence, the shift from the camera tracking in toward

5.45 *(left)* Señor Love Daddy starts to move toward the camera in *Do the Right Thing*.

5.46 *(right)* Señor Love Daddy closes in on the camera in *Do the Right Thing*.

Chapter 5: Cinematography

unmoving characters to Señor Love Daddy moving toward the stationary camera, visually underscores the DJ's attempt to reverse the unrelenting messages of hate.

● ●

● Lenses and Filters: The Frame in Depth

Although the camera may function like an eye as it records images, the camera does not see the world the way that the human eye does. Eyes and cameras both use lenses to focus rays of light. The rays converge, producing an image of the object being observed. The lens of the human eye focuses light rays on the retina. In the camera, the lens focuses the light rays entering the aperture and they converge on the film stock. Camera lenses must be carefully calibrated to produce the desired image. On the set, the **focus puller** carefully measures the distance from the lens to the subject being photographed, then marks the focus ring with tape and moves the camera's focal ring to those marks during filming (focus is precisely determined by measurements, not by looking through the camera lens). Keeping images in focus would seem to be a rather basic element of film-making, but, in fact, DPs use lenses and filters not just to maintain proper focus, but also to shape the environment, create mood, and develop themes.

Cinematographers may use focus to capture the viewer's attention. In *The Graduate*, a motif involving **selective focus** reinforces Benjamin's alienation from the shallow world of upper middle-class Los Angeles. The camera repeatedly singles out Benjamin while others around him are out of focus. During his graduation party, Ben's parents visit his bedroom. Because they are out of focus, they appear to be ill-defined physical obstacles hovering around him. When Benjamin calls Mrs. Robinson from the hotel to arrange a tryst, Ben is in focus but the world outside the phone booth is a blur. After Ben follows Elaine Robinson (Katharine Ross) to Berkeley, he waits for her at an outdoor fountain. The camera captures Ben in focus, but again everything around him is fuzzy (fig. **5.47**). When

5.47 Selective focus on Ben in *The Graduate*.

5.48 *(above)* An illustration of depth of field: the pots are in focus but leaves are not.

5.49 *(below)* A shot taken with a normal lens.

5.50 *(bottom left)* The same shot taken with a wide-angle lens: note the wider angle of vision.

5.51 *(bottom right)* The same shot taken with a telephoto lens: note the blurring of the background.

he spots Elaine leaving a classroom building and turns to look at her, however, the camera zooms in and focuses on Elaine. This effect highlights the way that Ben seems alienated from the world of his peers. He seems to exist in a world of his own. It also hints that his pursuit of Elaine is single-minded and obsessive; the rest of the world doesn't matter to him.

The Visual Characteristics of Lenses: Depth of Field and Focal Length

Lenses allow filmmakers to shape the space of the story (or, in an avant-garde film, the visual field in which images take shape). Different lenses have different visual characteristics. Most important is the **depth of field** (fig. **5.48**), or the "range of acceptable sharpness before and behind the plane of focus" (*American Cinematographer's Manual*, p. 161). Depth of field describes the space in front of and behind the primary subject where objects remain in crisp focus. Understanding the focal properties of lenses helps viewers to assess the frame as a three-dimensional visual field that serves as an environment for the action, that creates the texture of another reality, or externalizes a character's feelings.

Lenses may be **normal**, **wide-angle**, or **telephoto**. Each of these different types of lens produces a distinctive look because the **focal length** of a lens (the measurement, in millimeters, of the distance from the surface of the lens to the surface of the film) in large part determines depth of field (figs. **5.49**, **5.50**, **5.51**). Given the same aperture and focus distance, a lens with a longer focal length will produce a shallower depth of field than a lens with a shorter focal length.

The normal lens (focal length: 27 to 75 mm) approximates the vision and perspective of the human eye. No spatial distortions are apparent. The wide-angle lens, with a focal length of less than 27 mm, produces a wider angle of view than the human eye and exaggerates the frame's depth. Characters (or objects) in the foreground appear larger than they are, and characters (or objects) in the background appear smaller than they are. The viewer reads this discrepancy as enhanced depth: the distance between foreground and background appears greater than it actually is. Also, movement toward the camera appears faster than it is: a character will appear to make more rapid progress through the depth of the frame toward the camera than if a normal lens were used. This lens also accelerates the convergence of parallel lines so they appear to bend more than they do when seen through a normal lens (Zettl, 153).

The opening of Luis Buñuel's *The Diary of a Chambermaid* ("*Le Journal d'une femme de chambre*"; 1964) illustrates all three characteristics of a wide-angle lens: distortion of straight lines, exaggeration of depth, and wide peripheral vision. A shot from a moving train shows a railroad track that appears to bend up at either end (fig. **5.52**). When the train stops and Celestine (Jeanne Moreau) disembarks, the train station in the background can be seen in crisp detail through the windows and door of the train compartment (fig. **5.53**). As Celes-

tine is driven to the estate, the wide-angle of vision depicts the horse and carriage as they speed through the streets of a small village. The wide-angle allows the frame to encompass the buildings on either side of the street (fig. **5.54**).

The optical properties of wide angle lenses can enhance a film's themes. In Peter Weir's *The Truman Show* (1998), wide angle lenses are used to "emulate the style of television commercials and to approximate the superwide look of [. . .] surveillance cameras" (Rudolph, p. 80). This look is appropriate because the film depicts a man, Truman Burbank (Jim Carrey), whose every move is filmed and broadcast to the world, unbeknownst to him.

5.52 *(top)* The railroad track appears to be bent in *The Diary of a Chambermaid* ("*Le Journal d'une femme de chambre*").

5.53 *(center)* The train is stopped in *The Diary of a Chambermaid*: the station is visible in depth.

5.54 *(bottom)* Wide angle of vision captures the space on either side of the carriage in *Diary of a Chambermaid*.

An **extreme wide-angle** or **fish-eye lens** (focal length less than 17.5 mm) dramatically distorts images so that most straight lines appear to be curved. In Darren Aronofsky's *Requiem for a Dream*, a fish-eye lens depicts a scene in which three friends, Harry (Jared Leto), Marion (Jennifer Connelly), and Tyrone (Marlon Wayans), take drugs. The lens distorts the space of their apartment while fast motion distorts the time frame of the conversation; these visual effects mimic the effects of the drugs (fig. **5.55**).

Telephoto lenses, with focal lengths of 75 to 1000 mm, compress the distance between objects at different distances from the lens; that is, the distance between foreground and background appears to be less than it actually is. These lenses slow down the motion of an object or character toward the camera (*American Cinematographer's Manual*, p. 149). The telephoto lens also inhibits the convergence of parallel lines, so they will not appear to curve (Zettl, p. 153).

A telephoto lens is used in *Run Lola Run* just after Lola's father refuses to help her (fig. **5.56**). Lola stands in the street in front of his office building. She is in focus, but people and objects in the foreground and background are not. This shallow depth of field isolates her, separating the in-focus element from background and foreground (as it did in the above example from *The Graduate*). The moment underscores Lola's solitary quest to save her boyfriend; she is on her own. This moment offers a contrast to scenes depicting Lola's frenetic run through the streets of Berlin. There, a wide-angle lens takes in Lola's surroundings and enhances her movement from the background to the foreground, emphasizing her speed (fig. **5.57**).

5.55 *(top)* A fish-eye lens distorts the sense of space in *Requiem for a Dream*.

5.56 *(center)* A telephoto lens used in *Run Lola Run* ("*Lola rennt*").

5.57 *(bottom)* A wide-angle used in *Run Lola Run*.

Chapter 5: Cinematography

The fact that a telephoto lens slows movement toward the camera is used to good effect in *Full Metal Jacket*, when marines in training run through a muddy puddle toward the camera. The additional use of slow motion helps exaggerate the men's physical effort.

Rack focus is a change of focus from one plane of depth to another. In *Blow Out* (Brian De Palma 1981), a scene depicts Jack (John Travolta) as he records sounds outdoors. In the foreground of one shot, an owl appears in focus at screen right (fig. **5.58**). As the owl turns its head, the focus shifts, causing the owl to become blurry and bringing into focus a car in the background before it plunges off a bridge (fig. **5.59**). DP Haskell Wexler used shifting focus artfully in the original version of *The Thomas Crown Affair* (Norman Jewison 1968), when rich businessman Thomas Crown (Steve McQueen) phones five operatives and sends them into action, robbing a bank. A **split screen** combines six separate images (fig. **5.60**). Because several images are out of focus, the screen resembles a collection of abstract paintings. Each man comes into focus only at the moment that Crown gives him the signal to proceed.

The Zoom Lens

Zoom lenses have a variable focal length. Zooming changes the size of the filmed subject without changing the distance between the subject and the camera (*American Cinematographer's Manual*, p. 155). By rotating the barrel of the lens, cinematographers move from wide-angle to telephoto (**zooming in**, which magnifies the subject) or from telephoto to wide-angle (**zooming out**, which makes the subject smaller). When zooming in or out, the subject remains in focus. The opening of Francis Ford Coppola's *The Conversation* makes use of an extended zoom from a position and angle high above the action. In keeping with the film's

5.58 *(top)* An owl in focus in the foreground of *Blow Out*.

5.59 *(center)* Rack focus reveals the car plunging off the bridge in *Blow Out*.

5.60 *(bottom)* A split-screen shot in *The Thomas Crown Affair*: getting the signal to proceed.

5.61 *(above left)* A wide shot at the beginning of a zoom in *The Conversation*.

5.62 *(above right)* A closer shot, later in the zoom in *The Conversation*.

5.63 *(right)* A telephoto shot picks out the couple talking in *The Conversation*. Note the diminished depth and selective focus.

theme of surveillance, the slow zoom in magnifies the people congregating in San Francisco's Union Square. The telephoto lens's shallow depth of field helps to produce selective focus, singling out the couple engaged in the conversation that Harry Caul (Gene Hackman) has been hired to record (figs. **5.61**, **5.62**, **5.63**).

Combining Camera Movement and Lens Movement

Filmmakers sometimes combine camera movement and the zoom lens to create unusual shots. In *Vertigo*, Hitchcock created the **trombone shot**. Initially, the camera was trained on a model of a stairwell, with the zoom fully in so that the stairwell filled the frame. The camera was tracked in toward the model as the lens zoomed out (fig. **5.64**). This combination produces an unsettling physical effect because the stairwell remains the same size (tracking toward it would make it larger, but zooming out counteracts the track), but the apparent depth of the stairs increases (the zoom-out increased the depth of field). Scorsese adapts the same technique in *Goodfellas*, during a scene where Henry meets Jimmy (Robert De Niro) at a diner and learns that Jimmy is actually his enemy. There, the camera zooms in and tracks out, which maintains the size of the characters, but causes the background to lose depth, to flatten, and go out of focus. It appears as if the world is collapsing in on Henry.

Chapter 5: Cinematography

In both cases, the dramatic shot reflects a character's visceral, uncomfortable sensations. In *Vertigo*, the effect simulates panicky feelings of acrophobia (fear of heights) felt by Scottie Ferguson (James Stewart). In *Goodfellas*, Henry realizes that his relationship with Jimmy has irrevocably changed and that his life may be in danger.

Through the Lens: Filters and Diffusers

Filters change the quality of light entering the lens by absorbing certain wavelengths. They affect contrast, sharpness, color, and light intensity. **Neutral-density filters** absorb all wavelengths and permit less light overall to strike the film stock. **Polarizing** filters increase color saturation and contrast in outdoor shots.

Diffusion filters "bend" the light coming into the lens, blurring the image. Mesh, netting, and gauze (silk fabric) placed over the lens also reduce sharpness. They enhance the appearance of the human face (wrinkles and blemishes disappear) and create a filmy, otherworldly look. In Arthur Penn's *Bonnie and Clyde* (1967), they are used to create a distinction between the real world and an ideal world. The bank robbers Clyde Barrow (Warren Beatty) and Bonnie Parker (Faye Dunaway) visit Bonnie's mother after a scene in which Bonnie expresses her fear that she will die an outlaw (fig. **5.65**). Diffusion filters create a soft visual look for the family reunion; the scene represents a nostalgic vision of anonymity and normalcy that Bonnie and Clyde can never regain.

Fog filters have a glass surface with numerous etched spots that refract light, so they create the appearance of water

5.64 *(above)* A trombone shot from *Vertigo*.
5.65 *(below)* A family reunion scene from *Bonnie and Clyde*.

Deep Focus Cinematography

In the late 1930s, "fast" lenses and advances in lighting technology helped cinematographers such as Gregg Toland to perfect **deep-focus cinematography**, in which objects remain in focus from positions very near the camera to points at some distance from it. Working with William Wyler on films such as *Dead End* (1937) and *Wuthering Heights* (1939), Toland experimented with the techniques that later became well known as a result of his collaboration with Orson Welles on *Citizen Kane*. Toland used wide-angle lenses and stopped down the lens, making the aperture smaller to produce greater precision in focus. Wyler, Welles, and John Ford, directors who choreographed actors and arranged sets with several planes of depth, are said to **compose in depth**. These directors rely on deep-focus cinematography—the technique that permits many planes to remain in focus—to accentuate the interplay among several levels of meaning. The frame's three-dimensional space helps to depict Kane's immense power as well as his limited choices.

When Orson Welles composes in depth, he creates spatial motifs. In *Citizen Kane*, Kane is routinely positioned between other people, who make decisions for him, as in the Colorado boarding house scene discussed in Chapter Four. But Kane also frequently occupies the background. In the scene where he signs over the management of his financial interests to Mr. Thatcher, Kane stands between Thatcher and Bernstein (Everett Sloane). But Kane also stands near the back wall of the room (fig. **5.66**). His moving forward to sit at the table with the two men and sign the documents signals that he becomes resigned to his fate (fig. **5.67**). Welles choreographs this scene in three dimensions; at first, Kane is trapped between his financial advisers, yet he also distances himself from their values. He moves forward in this scene, as in several others, to assert himself, although the outcome may be self-defeating. The complexity of the scene—and Welles' ability to develop this spatial motif—depends on Toland's mastery of deep-focus cinematography.

5.66 The paper-signing scene from *Citizen Kane*: Kane in the background.

5.67 The paper-signing scene from *Citizen Kane*: Kane moves into the foreground.

droplets in the air (*American Cinematographer's Manual*, p. 214). An image also can be "fogged" by applying substances such as petroleum jelly to a clear filter in front of the lens. This technique was used in *The Terminator* to create the illusion of motion blur around the robot (Rickitt, p. 161). **Star filters** create points of light that streak outward from a light source (*American Cinematographer's Manual*, p. 215).

Color filters absorb certain wavelengths but leave others unaffected. On black-and-white film, color filters provide contrast control; they can lighten or darken tones. On color film, they can produce a range of effects. Jane Campion's

5.68 Blue and green tones dominate this shot of the woods from *The Piano*.

The Piano makes use of color filters in scenes of the New Zealand forest. The director wanted to achieve the effect of being underwater—which contributes to an ocean motif—by drawing out the blue and green tones of the forest (fig. **5.68**).

Day for night refers to the practice of shooting during the day but using filters and underexposure to create the illusion of nighttime. French cinema theorists call the technique *nuit Américain* (or "American night"). Day-for-night shooting is generally more successful on black-and-white film, using red or yellow filters to darken the blue sky.

● ●

Techniques in Practice: **Lenses and the Creation of Space**

Stanley Kubrick's *Paths of Glory* (1957) and Robert Altman's *M*A*S*H* (1970) chronicle human experiences of war, yet the two filmmakers adopt very different approaches to this subject. One technical feature that offers insight into their differences is the choice of lens. Kubrick uses a wide-angle lens and composes in depth to emphasize the hierarchical structure of the army and its vast reach. In contrast, Altman uses a telephoto lens and frequent zooms to reveal disconnected spaces and to emphasize the chaotic aspects of a military organization.

Paths of Glory concerns three French soldiers during World War I who are charged with cowardice, court-martialed, and executed by a firing squad. Kubrick and cinematographer George Krause frequently employ a wide-angle lens to depict the hypocritical and power-hungry officers as well as the powerless foot soldiers ordered to fight a losing battle. The wide-angle lens and composition in depth not only convey the different experiences of officers and soldiers, but also suggest what binds them together: the highly ordered military system.

The film's opening scene depicts several lines of soldiers marching around the grounds of the stately château that serves as the headquarters of General Mireau (George Macready). The wide-angle lens takes in the vast expanse of open space around the château (fig. **5.69**). Because many planes of depth are in focus, the scene highlights the linear pattern formed by marching soldiers. This scene presents the first instance of a motif: lines of men whose lives are controlled by others. The calm, ordered emptiness of the space suggests the distance of the headquarters from the deadly trenches where the war is being fought.

The wide-angle lens also shapes the viewer's sense of the château's interior. As General Broulard (Adolphe Menjou)

5.69 An exterior shot of the château in *Paths of Glory*.

manipulates the ambitious Mireau into ordering an assault on a well-defended German position, the men occupy a room decorated with exquisite antiques and works of art. The details of the room are clear because the lens allows many planes to remain in focus at the same time. In this scene, Mireau claims that he feels a sense of responsibility for the lives of 8,000 men, but agrees to order the attack after Broulard makes it clear he will earn a promotion if he succeeds. The elegant setting contrasts with the brutal deaths that will result from their plans and establishes the generals' hypocrisy.

The next scene takes place in the trenches, a space that is the polar opposite of the château. The trenches are long, snaking pits cluttered with equipment and lined with soldiers. What little sky is visible above is hazy with the dust and debris from artillery fire. This cramped space is very different from the château, yet the wide-angle lens is equally effective at presenting its characteristics. The motif of powerless men standing in lines reappears as General Mireau marches through the trenches on his way to see Colonel Dax (Kirk Douglas) to order the attack (fig. **5.70**). As the pompous Mireau strides through the trenches (accompanied by a martial drumbeat), the lens enhances the General's vigorous movement forward. This movement contrasts with that of the soldiers he talks to along the way; they are exhausted and stand still. The General repeats the same lines when he greets each soldier, which contributes to the sense that he is unfeeling and mechanical.

When Colonel Dax orders his men into battle, a wide-angle lens and slow tracking shot depict the trenches as an unending series of maze-like passages crowded with men. Once again, the leader moves past men who stand still. However, Colonel Dax and General Mireau are very different military leaders. Dax actually leads his men into "no man's land" between the French and German barbed wire. The futile attack on the well-defended German Ant Hill, however, results in the useless death of many soldiers.

After the failed attack, Colonel Dax valiantly attempts to save the lives of three soldiers in his unit who are accused of deserting because they retreated or were injured. He defends them at their trial, but finally is unable to save them from the firing squad. The trial is held in a room similar to the room where Mireau and Broulard meet: it is enormous, very bright, and full of open space. The trial is arranged in a very orderly way, with the defense and prosecution on either side of the judges. The deep space and symmetrical composition reinforce the hierarchical

5.70 General Mireau in the trenches in *Paths of Glory*.

military power structure and the entrapment of the ordinary man within that system. As each accused man steps forward to be questioned, Kubrick positions him very close to the camera, yet the wide-angle lens maintains in focus the vast space behind him (fig. **5.71**). Each soldier is singled out as an individual, yet each one is also overwhelmed by the space around him. Because they occupy the lowest position in the hierarchy, the ordinary soldiers are doomed to die as pawns in the game played by the generals, the men who plot strategy from the safety of the spacious villa.

5.71 Deep focus in the trial scene in *Paths of Glory*.

Altman and cinematographer Harold Stine adopt a very different approach in their Korean war comedy *M*A*S*H*, using telephoto and zoom lenses to create a sense of decentralization and chaos. The use of the zoom lens suggests that the army hospital unit is composed of numerous eccentric individuals and that no structure or hierarchy exists to control them. The telephoto lens also allows Altman to depict the intimacy among the characters, despite the confusion and clutter of the hospital environment.

During the opening credits, repeated zooms isolate injured soldiers carried to 4077th Mobile Army Surgical Hospital by helicopters. The zooms permit the viewer a brief medium shot or close-up of each wounded man before he is whisked away to the hospital, then the lens zooms out and moves on to another wounded soldier. The zooms establish the disorder of war and the way it threatens to dehumanize soldiers and the doctors. The quick, intrusive zooms act as a metaphor for the way the military doctors are forced to treat the wounded men. The doctors attend to their injuries, usually by cutting into their bodies and then sewing them up. Rarely do doctors and patients interact on a personal level because the soldiers who survive are sent home or back into combat.

The zoom lens frequently singles out the one emblem of a central authority in the film: the camp's public broadcast system. Yet zooms into the loudspeakers turn out to be ironic. The supposedly important messages are retracted, corrected, or make no sense. For example, the loudspeaker announces that all personnel must provide urine samples, then states that no one must do so.

The telephoto lens allows Altman to suggest the distinctive individuality and diversity of the doctors and nurses. In typical Altman style, the cast works as an ensemble. Although Hawkeye Pierce (Donald Sutherland), Duke (Tom Skerritt), and Trapper John (Elliott Gould) occupy center stage, the audience also becomes familiar with a number of minor characters, such as "Painless" (John Shuck), Lieutenant "Dish" (Jo Ann Pflug), and "Radar" (Gary Burghoff). The telephoto lens singles characters out through tight close-ups.

The reliance on close-ups adds to the film's sense of decentralization and lack of hierarchy. Visually the film presents a world without a clear organization. Aside from the early aerial shot of Duke and Hawkeye driving toward the camp, there are no long shots that establish the overall geography of the hospital. Instead, medium shots and close-ups present a cluttered and disorganized shanty town. Visually, space is broken down into small units that don't add up to a coherent whole. Telephoto shots through the screening of the army tents help to create this effect—such as the moment when the chaplain (Rene Auberjonois) speaks to Hawkeye about Painless (fig. **5.72**). This technique places a number of visual impediments between the actors and the viewer to emphasize the divided space. In addition, the telephoto lens compresses the distance between characters and the screens, creating a sense of claustrophobia and entrapment.

These directors and their cinematographers convey ideas and emotions visually through the choice of lenses. The wide-angle lens and compositions in depth in *Paths of Glory* heighten the contrast between generals, who are in control, and soldiers, who are at the mercy of the system. The zooms and telephoto lens in *M*A*S*H* suggest a lack of

5.72 The chaplain talks to Hawkeye in *M*A*S*H*.

Chapter 5: Cinematography

Cinematography on the Set

For most films, the DP collaborates with the director and art director before and during principal photography to think systematically about creating expressive visual images throughout the film. Prior to the production phase, the director and DP confer about camera angles and effects, using the script to map out the specific set-up for each shot. Often, they create storyboards, with drawings, photographs, or computer simulations. During principal photography, the DP is responsible for all aspects of the photographic process, including camera placement, movement, and lighting set-ups. The crew includes: the camera operator, responsible for the operation and maintenance of the camera; the focus puller, who measures, marks, and moves the focus ring on the camera lens; and an assistant camera operator, who records the details of shots; the **gaffer**, the chief electrician, the **best boy**, and assistant electricians are responsible for the

lighting equipment. A **second unit** may be used for filming at a remote location, or for **insert** shots. Directors use a **video-assist**, a video monitor that records the action and allows them to see what the shot looks like on screen (one of film's greatest shortcomings is the length of time it takes to process the photographic images chemically). The film footage exposed in a given day is often printed, and **dailies** are screened to determine whether changes are necessary.

While the DP's job theoretically is complete at the end of shooting, often she will work with the editor during post-production to ensure that the desired look is achieved. Now that visual effects are contracted out to specialized companies, such as Industrial Light and Magic, the visual effects supervisor often acts as a liaison between the director and DP and the company producing visual effects.

order and the difficulty of making connections in a chaotic, decentralized, and claustro-phobic environment.

Film Stock

Another key factor that will influence the final look of the film is the choice of film stock, which will affect, among other things, the color and depth of contrast of the images produced.

Characteristics of Film Stock

Film stock is composed of two parts: the **emulsion**, a light-sensitive chemical layer in which the image is formed, and the **base**, the flexible support material for the emulsion. The base for the earliest films was cellulose nitrate, a highly flammable substance that was replaced in the 1950s by cellulose triacetate.

The attributes of film stock include gauge, speed, and grain. **Gauge** refers to the size of the film, measured horizontally across the film stock (fig. **5.73**). Standard feature films are projected on 35 mm film. This has an image area four times that of 16 mm film, which

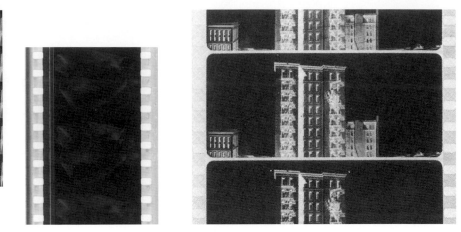

5.73 Different gauges of film: 8 mm, 16 mm, 35 mm, 70 mm (65 mm with soundtrack).

has traditionally been the province of documentary, experimental, and independent film-makers because it offers lighter cameras and less expensive processing. Super 8 and regular 8 film, developed in the 1950s, were used for home movies. Since the advent of inexpensive digital video cameras, Super 8 is now the medium of choice only for experimental filmmakers.

Speed is a measure of a film stock's sensitivity to light and is measured by an index called the ASA or DIN number. The higher the ASA or DIN number, the greater the film's sensitivity to light, and the "faster" the film. **Fast** film stocks, because they are sensitive, require less light to produce an acceptable image. Thus, a fast film stock works well under conditions of low light. A documentary filmmaker who cannot control lighting conditions on the shoot might use fast film to make sure the images will register. Fast stocks, however, are prone to producing grainy images. **Slow** film stocks are relatively insensitive to light but produce high-quality images under optimal lighting conditions. If a filmmaker can exercise a great deal of control over the light, as is the case on a studio set, then slow film renders the sharp, fine-grained images associated with the high **production values** of most commercial Hollywood films.

The **grain** refers to the suspended particles of silver or color-sensitive grains in the emulsion layer. After processing, the grains may become visible as dots. Finer-grained, slow film stock records more detail and renders sharp images with high resolution. Grainy film, with its lower resolution and fuzzier images, is typically associated with fast film stock such as black-and-white **newsreel** and documentary films. But feature filmmakers may deliberately produce grainy images to create a documentary feel, as Welles does in the newsreel that opens *Citizen Kane*, as Woody Allen does in *Zelig* (1983), and as Robert Zemeckis does in *Forrest Gump* (1994).

Light and Exposure

Exposure refers to the amount of light striking the light-sensitive emulsion layer of the film stock. When the **shutter** of the camera opens, light passes through the aperture and strikes the film. The aperture size can be varied to let in a greater or smaller amount of light.

"Appropriate" exposure captures sufficient detail in both bright and dark areas of the frame. **Overexposure** occurs when more light than is required to produce an image strikes the film stock; the resulting image is noticeable for its high contrast, glaring light, and washed-out shadows (fig. **5.74**). Steven Soderbergh often manipulates exposure, as in the overexposed scenes in Miami in *Out of Sight* (1998). One reason Soderbergh overexposes the film is to simulate the harsh sun of south Florida, correcting the look produced by the artificial light of the studio.

Underexposure occurs when too little light strikes the emulsion. Dark areas in an underexposed image will appear very dense and dark (including shadows) and overall contrast will be less than a properly exposed image (fig. **5.75**).

Film Stock and Color

Directors and cinematographers choose their film stock according to the aesthetic effects they are seeking to achieve. For example, occasionally black-and-white and color film stock may be used in the same film, to contrast between past and present, perhaps, or

5.74 *(top)* Overexposure produces glaring light in *Insomnia*.

5.75 *(bottom)* Underexposure produces a dense, dark effect in *Psycho*.

between reality and fantasy. In *The Wizard of Oz*, black-and-white film depicts depression-era Kansas whereas Technicolor film characterizes the fantasy world of Oz. In *A Matter of Life and Death* (*Stairway to Heaven*; Michael Powell and Emeric Pressburger 1946), Heaven appears in black-and-white and Earth in color (figs. **5.76**, **5.77**). Black-and-white sequences indicate past events in *Memento*, and sometimes the distinction between black-and-white and color is arbitrary, as in *If* (Lindsay Anderson 1968).

Filmmaking has always involved color, even before the development of color film stock. The black-and-white one-reelers of French film pioneer Georges Méliès and Pathé Frères were hand-painted (fig. **5.78**), a painstaking and expensive process of painting sections of each frame with one or more colors (Sklar, p. 41). By around 1910, most films used color. The most prevalent technique was **tinting**, which involved bathing lengths of developed film (typically one scene at a time) in dye. Conventions developed so that blue was used for night scenes, amber for candle-lit interiors, and magenta for scenes of romance. By the 1920s, more than 80% of film prints were tinted (Salt, p. 150). Examples include D.W.

Griffith's *The Birth of a Nation* (1915), Wiene's *The Cabinet of Dr. Caligari* (fig. **5.79**), and Murnau's *Nosferatu*. Another practice, called **toning**, replaced silver halide with colored metal salts so that the dark portions of the frame appear in color rather than black. Mordanting involved developing the emulsion with a silver solution able to fix colored dyes (Usai, p. 9).

Even unadulterated black-and-white images vary in their tonal properties. First, black-and-white film stocks possess different properties: the earliest stocks, for example, were sensitive to blue and violet only. **Orthochromatic** film—sensitive to blue, violet, and green—was developed in the 1970s. Because it did not register the red tones of human faces, actors were required to wear heavy theatrical makeup. Black-and-white film stocks that were sensitive to all colors of the spectrum (called **panchromatic**) became the industry standard in the 1930s.

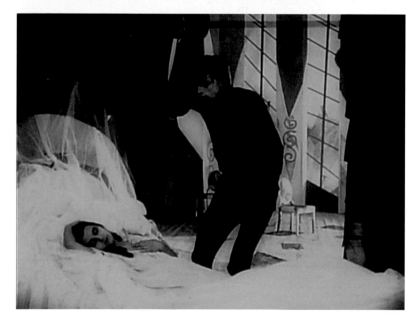

5.76 *(top left)* Earth appears in color in *A Matter of Life and Death* (*Stairway to Heaven*).

5.77 *(top right)* Heaven appears in black-and-white in *A Matter of Life and Death*.

5.78 *(center)* A hand-painted scene from *The Life of Christ*.

5.79 *(bottom)* An example of tinting from *The Cabinet of Dr. Caligari* ("*Das Kabinett des Dr. Caligari*").

Second, filmmakers make different use of the same technologies. When Eastman Kodak and Agfa manufactured faster film stocks in the 1930s, movie studios responded to them differently, which resulted in distinctive visual styles. MGM overexposed the film, and then pulled (underdeveloped) the negative, creating a pearly gray look (fig. **5.80**). But at Twentieth Century Fox, the use of faster film meant DPs could stop down the lens (making the aperture smaller), increasing depth of field and contributing to deep-focus cinematography (Salt, p. 196). Fox thus became known for the clarity of its images (fig. **5.81**).

Although color film processes were developed in the 1930s, it wasn't until after World War II that color film developed into an industry standard. Color cinematography was a commercial and aesthetic enterprise: color was one way U.S. movie studios could compete with television, which was broadcast in black-and-white. In the early 1950s, television viewing cost the film industry 500,000 tickets per week (Seagrave, p. 5). Studios marketed their color spectacles with the phrase "Glorious Technicolor." Between 1947 and 1954, the number of American films made in color rose from one in ten to one in two. By 1979, 96% of American films were made in color (Cook, pp. 462–3).

In 1922 the Technicolor Corporation developed a two-strip additive process. Two strips of negative film were exposed (using a beam splitter in the camera), printed separately on a red and a green layer of film stock, and cemented together for projection. The process was plagued by several problems: during screenings the cement melted under the high-intensity heat generated by projector lamps. Furthermore, over time the colors tended to fade to orange.

In 1928, Technicolor perfected a dye transfer process called imbibition printing, which became the basis for its three-color dye transfer process, the industry standard from 1935

5.80 *(top)* The characteristic pearly appearance of MGM films: *Queen Christina* (1933).

5.81 *(bottom)* Twentieth Century Fox films from the 1930s were known for the clarity of the images: *Slave Ship* (1937).

until the mid-1950s. The process used three strips of negative film from which separate color matrices were made; then the color images were transferred onto a single print. The strengths of Technicolor were vibrant and stable colors that aged well. But Technicolor's *de facto* monopoly and the fact that the process used three times as much film stock as black-and-white cinematography meant that color films were extremely costly to make. Film studios had to rent special equipment, use Technicolor labs to process the film, and pay for expertise directly from the Technicolor Corporation, in the form of **color consultants** to oversee the **color timing** (shot-to-shot color correction).

The development of Eastmancolor also contributed to the widespread adoption of color cinematography. Eastmancolor uses a multilayered film stock. Each of the three layers of emulsion contains **dye couplers** sensitive to a different color: red, blue, and green. When developed, the grains to which the dyes have been coupled release the dye. This method produces sharper prints than the Technicolor process, but its colors are less saturated. The process became popular because film studios could use standard film cameras and process the film in their own labs, saving money. But the widespread use of Eastmancolor produced hidden, long-term costs. Prints made before 1983 are notorious for their unstable color; restoring these faded prints requires resources and technical expertise.

Color—as an element of *mise en scène* and cinematography—allows directors to express ideas, themes, and mood. The lyrical use of color in films from every cinematic tradition—from Coppola's *The Godfather* to Mira Nair's *Salaam Bombay!* (1988), from Jacques Demy's *The Umbrellas of Cherbourg* ("*Les Parapluies de Cherbourg*"; 1964) to Bernardo Bertolucci's *The Conformist* ("*Il conformista*"; 1969), to Kurosawa's *Dreams* ("*Yume*"; 1990)— attests to the fact that color cinematography opened up an entirely new creative aspect of cinema (figs. **5.82**, **5.83**, **5.84**, **5.85**, **5.86**, **5.87**).

When analyzing the use of color in a film, viewers should attend to the specific

5.82 *(top)* Saturated brown colors evoke an era in *The Godfather*.

5.83 *(bottom)* Harsh light and high contrast in *Salaam Bombay!*

5.84 *(top left)* Primary colors create a vivid effect in *Dreams* ("*Yume*").

5.85 *(top right)* An ashen gray is used for the apocalypse sequence in *Dreams*.

5.86 *(center)* Bright, otherworldly colors have a romantic effect in *The Umbrellas of Cherbourg* ("*Les Parapluies de Cherbourg*").

5.87 *(bottom)* Desaturated color gives a sense of alienation in *The Conformist* ("*Il conformista*").

ways color is used in relation to narrative, visual, and sound elements. Some questions to consider include:

- Are there strong areas of color or pronounced contrasts in the frame that demand attention?
- Are tones uniformly saturated or desaturated, producing a vibrant or somber mood? If so, do they act as complement or as counterpoint to the action?
- What are the effects of the *relative* saturation and warmth/coolness of colors in the *mise en scène*?
- Are color motifs developed, perhaps through *mise en scène* and/or cinematography techniques such as pushing, pulling, or flashing (see p. 142)?
- Do colors bear a particular cultural significance? Be sure to test initial associations against the full complement of elements at

work in any film and to conduct research to make sure the cultural context is taken into account. Do not assume, for example, that red equals danger in every aesthetic and cultural situation.

Wide Film and Widescreen Formats

During the 1950s, U.S. movie studios developed **widescreen formats** as part of their campaign to compete with the popular new medium of television by creating larger, more colorful images than TV could. These formats widened the traditional aspect ratio (a measure of the horizontal to the vertical dimension of the image) from the **Academy ratio** of 1.33:1 (also that of traditional television) to 1.85:1 or 2.35:1 (fig. **5.88**). Currently, U.S. movie theaters project films in those two aspect ratios. The aspect ratio for HDTV is 1.78:1 (also referred to as 16:9).

CinemaScope and Panavision use **anamorphic lenses** to create an aspect ratio of 2.35:1 with standard 35 mm film, cameras, and projectors. When used to shoot a film, the anamorphic lens squeezes the image at a ratio of 2:1 horizontally onto a standard film frame. If the film were projected "as is," the image would look stretched from top to bottom and actors would look extremely tall and thin, but using anamorphic lenses on projectors unsqueezes the image (fig. **5.89 B**, **C**, and **D**). The first Cinema-Scope release was Twentieth Century Fox's *The Robe* (Henry Koster 1953).

Other widescreen processes involve changes in cameras and film stock. **Cinerama** uses three cameras, three projectors, and a wide, curved screen. Viewers sitting in the "sweet spot" (in the center of the first ten rows) feel immersed in the image, which reaches past their peripheral vision on either side (fig. **5.90**). The technique was both novel and expensive; only a few films were made in the format, including *This is Cinerama* (Merian Cooper and Gunther von Fritsch 1952) and *How the West Was Won* (Henry Hathaway, John Ford, and George Marshall 1962).

One method for producing a wide screen image without using special lenses or equipment is **masking**. Cinematographers shoot a film using standard film stock at an aspect ratio of 1.33.1, but block out the top and bottom of the frame to achieve an aspect ratio of 1.85:1. However, masking during shooting is rare because it is expensive to modify the camera, and this procedure sacrifices 36% of the image.

Wide film formats use a larger film stock than standard 35 mm stock. IMAX, Omnivax, and Showscan are shot on 70 mm film. The gauge of the film stock (e.g., 35 mm versus 70 mm) is its width, measured across the frame (see fig. 5.73).

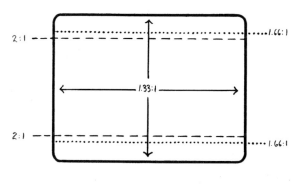

5.88 *(above)* A comparison of four aspect ratios: Academy, 1.85:1, 2.35:1, and 1.78:1.

5.89 *(below)* A squeezed image, created with an anamorphic lens.

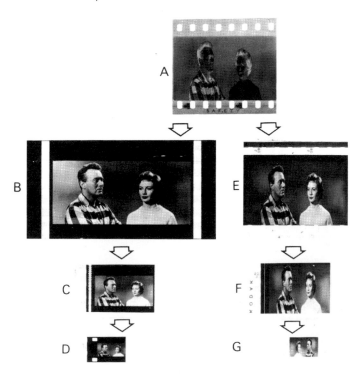

Labels within the illustration (left figure):

FIVE SPEAKERS BEHIND SCREEN

SOUND-CONTROL

ROCKET

SPLASH

PICTURE-CONTROL ENGINEER

AS BOATS LEAVE SCREEN, SOUND FADES AWAY THROUGH THIS SPEAKER

PROJECTOR

EXTRA SPEAKERS FOR OFF-SCREEN NOISES

PROJECTOR

PROJECTOR

MAGNETIC SOUND RECORDER

SOUND FROM SIX MICROPHONES RECORDED ON ONE T...

THREE SEPARATE FILMS

THREE LENSES

THREE MAGAZIN...

146-DEGREE ANGLE OF VIEW

SIX MICROPHONES PICK UP SOUND AS BOATS MOVE

SHUTTER

CAMERA TAKES THREE PICTURES SIMULTANEOUSLY

THREE FILMS

5.90 The Cinerama system.

Vista Vision was an alternative to Cinemascope developed by Alfred Hitchcock that uses standard 35 mm film stock but changes the orientation of the film so that the film moves through the camera horizontally instead of vertically. The larger image is of higher quality than standard processes. Though it was largely abandoned in the 1940s, it was resurrected for special effects work on *Star Wars*.

Processing Film Stock

Once a film stock has been chosen and exposed, cinematographers can achieve unusual visual effects by making choices about processing methods. A number of specific techniques have been developed.

5.91 Bleach bypass printing gives a desaturated, silvery feeling to *Se7en*.

Scratching involves scraping the surface of the film to achieve the look of a home movie. Martin Scorsese's *Mean Streets* (1973) includes one of the characters' home movies, which the director shot and then scratched after processing. Some avant-garde filmmakers scratch films to create patterns or to remind viewers of the material basis of the medium. Stan Brakhage, for example, scratched his name into film stock, signing the film the way painters mark their work. Brakhage also experimented with paint and other substances, using moth wings on the surface of the film and quick cuts to suggest the motion of flight in the three-minute film *Mothlight* (1963).

Pushing a film (also known as overdevelopment) means allowing it a longer time in development, which increases contrast and density. **Pulling** a film negative (underdevelopment) reduces contrast. **Forced development** is a technique used when lighting levels are inadequate for normal exposures. Cinematographers deliberately underexpose the film and then overdevelop, or push, the film. This procedure affects contrast but not colors.

Pre-fogging or **flashing** the negative desaturates color. Before, during, or after shooting, the film stock is exposed to a small amount of light, resulting in an image with reduced contrast. This technique was used for Altman's *McCabe and Mrs. Miller*, a film set at the turn of the twentieth century, to create the visual effect of an old photograph.

Bleach bypass printing means leaving the silver grains in the emulsion rather than bleaching them out. This desaturates the color slightly because it is akin to adding a layer of black-and-white to a color negative. This process was used for David Fincher's *Se7en*, which has an overall dense, silvery cast to it, lending a somber visual feel to a dark storyline (fig. **5.91**).

● Special Visual Effects

Although they are often associated with sci-fi or action films, special **visual effects** have been part of the film experience since the beginning of cinema and are used in all kinds of films. Special visual effects encompass painting, model building, prosthetics, photography, and computer graphics. In industry parlance, special effects are created during production while visual effects are created in **post-production**, but the terms are often used interchangeably.

5.92 Some of the special effects journals and magazines available today.

This section of the chapter presents commonly used visual effects and looks at how they are achieved and why they might be used. Digital visual effects are created with software programs, and practitioners in the field are constantly developing and perfecting new effects with every film project, so any discussion of techniques becomes out of date very quickly. A list of journals (fig. **5.92**) directs readers to publications that explain traditional visual effects and track new developments:

American Cinematographer
Astounding Science Fiction
Cinefantastique
Cinefex
Cinemagic
Cinescape
Photon
SMPTE Journal (Society of Motion Picture and Television Engineers)
SFX

Like any element of film, describing these effects, including the way they support the narrative system or develop a visual motif, contributes greatly to a thorough film analysis.

computer graphics programs to create architectural extensions, adding several stories to existing buildings on location in Seaside, Florida to produce the look of downtown Seahaven. But Chris Evans warns, "software does not replace all the knowledge that has been acquired over the years about light, color, and composition. The computer can take many hours to calculate a realistic lighting effect that a good artist can achieve with a single dab of paint" (Rickitt, p. 209).

5.99 *(above)* A glass shot.

5.100 *(below)* Superimposed images at the conclusion of *Psycho*.

5.101 *(bottom)* Split screen at the opening of *Requiem for a Dream*.

Creating Scene Transitions, Titles, and Credits: The Optical Printer

An optical printer is a device that allows films to be re-photographed and has been used for numerous visual effects, including scene transitions such as fades and dissolves. For a **fade-out**, a scene is copied in the printer, but near the end of the scene, the shutter is closed in increments, reducing the amount of light striking the copy. A **dissolve** results from copying a fade-out at the end of a scene onto the fade-in of the next scene (and is usually accomplished by rewinding the copied film and exposing it twice; see fig. 5.4).

With the optical printer, technicians can create freeze frames such as the famous final shot of *Butch Cassidy and The Sundance Kid* (George Roy Hill 1969) by re-photographing a single frame many times over. Optical printers can also be used to copy a series of frames in reverse order and to produce **superimpositions** such as the one at the conclusion of *Psycho* (fig. **5.100**). (**Double exposures** are achieved in camera by exposing film frames then rewinding the film and exposing them again: see fig. 8.27.)

Another use for the optical printer is to create split-screen effects, by exposing different areas of the frame at different times. Often the same actor is involved, appearing in the image twice. An evocative use of split screen occurs in the opening of *Requiem for a Dream*. Harry steals his mother's television, as he does so, she hides in the closet (fig. **5.101**). The two characters' actions appear on the screen side by side—showing that they inhabit two entirely different worlds, even though they are in the same apartment.

Finally, optical printers can be used to create titles and credits by superimposing black-and-white film with title wording over live-action footage.

Optical and Digital Compositing: Assembling the Elements of the Shot

Compositing refers to the creation of a single image by combining elements filmed separately (also called a process shot). Long the province of the optical printer, compositing is now largely accomplished digitally.

To combine an actor and a background filmed separately, filmmakers mask part of the frame during shooting, creating complementary **mattes** (sometimes called male and female). The matte allows the film to be exposed in one area and prevents exposure in another; the second, or counter, matte then masks the area the first had allowed to be exposed (fig. **5.102**). Mattes can be drawn by hand (and combined with countermatte footage in an optical printer) or created using computer programs.

Blue and **green screen** techniques refer to a compositing method that begins by shooting action against a blue or green background. This background is replaced with an image, called the background plate, through the use of a **traveling matte** (a mask used to cover portions of the image that move from frame to frame). As with most visual effects, compositing is now achieved digitally, by scanning the negative into a digital format, creating the composite on a computer, and scanning the images back out to film. The blue hue is used for optical compositing because there is so little blue in human skin

5.102 A matte shot dramatically alters the landscape.

that achieving the proper color balance for flesh tones in the live action footage is easier. Green screens are used because they provide better resolution on video formats.

A comic scene in *Stuck on You* (Farrelly Brothers, 2003), a film about conjoined twins, shows the blue screen Chroma Key technology used for broadcast television. Bob (Matt Damon) wears a blue suit because he is physically attached to his brother, Walt (Greg Kinnear), an actor in the show. Because he is wearing blue, Bob does not appear in the scene as (depicted on a monitor in the studio), because the television cameras have been adjusted to tune out that hue. As a result, Walt appears to have great powers, since the unseen Bob supports him as he undertakes extreme physical feats.

Digital compositing techniques, on the other hand, use any color background, and are used to blend live action footage with computer-generated images. An example of what can be done with digital compositing is the closing scene of *The Matrix*, where Neo and Morpheus hang from a rope dangling from a helicopter. The actors were shot hanging from a rope in the safety of a studio, and the cityscape of Sydney, Australia, was added later. Ropes and harnesses were digitally "erased" from the final print.

In the opening scene of *The Matrix*, effects artists used a technique that rearranged part of an actor's body. Trinity (Carrie-Anne Moss) flies through space in a corkscrew leap. During production, Moss was twirled around vertically in a rig that bound her feet and hands. In post-production, visual effects technicians "cut and pasted" her legs so they appear to kick. Effects supervisor John Gaeta called it "Frankensteining" her body—a reference to the classic horror story about animating a body composed of dead parts.

Computer-Generated Images

Computer-generated imagery (CGI), made possible by the rapid development of powerful computers during the 1970s, was first used in a feature film in Disney's *Tron* (Steven Lisberger 1982) and first came to attention after it was used by James Cameron to create the watery pseudopod in *The Abyss* (1989). CGI creates background images and objects using a three-part process: developing the spatial characteristics of an object through a 3-D model (also called the **wireframe**), rendering (producing the finished image), and then animating the object and simulating camera movement (frame by frame). Cinematographer Stephen Barclay writes, "the basic terminology may be analogous to the usual photographic and lighting phrases, but what is actually being created exists in an imaginary three-dimensional world, where everything is based on mathematical calculations which attempt to simulate reality" (Barclay, p. 199).

Adding and Subtracting Frames

Morphing is a process that involves the interpolation of frames using a computer program. The process begins with the creation of starting and ending images (say, a face before and after transformation), with specific areas within the images used as anchoring points (eyes, ears, and chin). The program then calculates the way the image must change in order for the first image to become the second over a series of frames (Rickitt, p. 86). The object appears to stretch as it metamorphoses (hence the term) into something else entirely (fig. **5.103**).

The graphic artists working on *The Matrix* pioneered a technique called **recursive action**. John Gaeta calls the effect the "fist bouquet" because Neo's fists seem to multiply in space and time (fig. **5.104**). To achieve this effect, which suggests that Neo is moving faster than his training program can handle, the scenes were shot at 96 frames per second. In post-production, effects editors added and subtracted frames, "laying several images over one another to create a fanning-out effect" (Martin, p. 81).

5.103 *(top)* A morphing pseudopod in *The Abyss*.

5.104 *(bottom)* Recursive action creates a "fist bouquet" in *The Matrix*.

Digital Cinema: Post-Production

The first uses of digital technology were in post-production, where filmmakers replaced chemical processing and optical printing with digital techniques. Portions of a film are scanned into digital file format, so that technicians can correct color, paint out rigs and wires used in action sequences, and restore scratches and imperfections. *O Brother, Where Art Thou?* was among the first major features to use "digital answer printing," where the entire original film print was scanned into digital format, manipulated, and then reprinted on film stock for exhibition. The scanning process took between fifteen seconds and three minutes per frame, with each film frame being exposed three times: once each through red, green, and blue color-separation filters.

For *O Brother*, the digital manipulation mainly influenced the film's color design. The directors and cinematographer Roger Deakins wanted to create a "dustbowl" effect to convey the depression-era 1930s South, with sepia and brown tones dominating. Through digital enhancement, for example, bright green grass became amber. It is actually possible to compare the look of the film before and after digital processing by screening the **trailer** (the short advertising reel for the film) included on the DVD. A difference in the

5.105 *(left)* A still from the trailer of *O Brother, Where Art Thou?*

5.106 *(right)* The same shot from the final cut of *O Brother, Where Art Thou?*

tonal range and saturation of the colors is evident: in the trailer and out-takes, the grass is green and the sky is deep blue, whereas in the final cut of the film, the grass is brown and the sky is a faded gray (figs. **5.105**, **5.106**).

The same idea motivated Vilmos Zsigmond's cinematography for Robert Altman's *McCabe and Mrs. Miller*. Like Deakins, Zsigmond sought to create the look and texture of a particular place and time through visual means. But he created a faded brown and blue palette and a filmy image texture through traditional photographic means, including filters and flashing (fig. **5.107**).

As with all new technologies, some visual effects artists use digital techniques imaginatively, pushing the envelope of film art; others use them to replace standard practices.

5.107 Filmy image textures in the opening of *McCabe and Mrs. Miller.*

Ultimately, digital processes have become integral to commercial filmmaking because they are less expensive than traditional methods and offer a director and art designer greater control. In the 1980s and 1990s, digital visual effects were relatively expensive to create, but improvements in computer graphics capabilities and an increasing number of trained personnel have made digital processes a significant part of commercial film production.

● Digital Cinematography and Film Style

George Lucas, a pioneer in the development of special visual effects, shot *Star Wars Episode II: Attack of the Clones* (2002) digitally, but many theaters screened it through conventional film projection. Lucas plans to release *Episode III* only in digital format. Observers disagree about whether viewers will be able to detect a difference between film and digital projection. But the shift from film to digital images is motivated by a desire not to improve on film images as images, but to take advantage of the convenience and flexibility of digital formats in production and exhibition.

One important question to ask is whether the digital revolution has changed the nature of film as a medium composed of expressive images that are, in narrative fiction films, linked to stories. Has an emphasis on special visual effects in *Twister* (Michael Almereyda 1990), *Independence Day*, *Titanic*, the *Matrix* trilogy, and the *Lord of the Rings* trilogy undercut the importance of character or theme? Is the industry using special effects to compete with sophisticated home viewing technologies (broadband cable, high-speed computer connections, and home theater systems) at the expense of thoughtful narratives? In 1998, film critic Gary Thompson wrote that the latest advances in special effects have left audiences jaded, unable to be amazed by the magic of cinema (quoted in Pierson, p. 1). In 2004, critic David Denby wondered whether three directors whose work focuses on emotional connections (Sofia Coppola, Catherine Hardwicke, and Patty Jenkins) might "pull at least part of our movie culture away from frantic digital spectacle" (Denby, p. 86).

Certain trends in filmmaking—what Denby calls the "digital spectacle"—may emerge because of these technologies. One trend may be the revival of the epic blockbuster, of which *Gladiator* (Ridley Scott 2000) and the *Lord of the Rings* trilogy are examples. Both films were made possible by the fact that CGI allows directors to create huge crowds through duplication. Digital compositing can also change the way landscapes are used—evident in the numerous panoramic shots of the otherworldly Middle Earth landscape in the *Lord of the Rings* trilogy.

But to analyze and interpret individual films, viewers must consider special visual effects as part of the overall system of meaning. Shock, surprise, and delight at optical and digital tricks can make watching films fun. But to unearth a greater underlying significance, those effects must be read in relation to story, character, theme, tone, and style.

Cinematography is a powerful visual tool that has always depended on a mix of old and new technologies. Whether based on photochemical or electronic processes, cinematography works in concert with narrative elements, *mise en scène*, editing, and sound to produce an integrated aesthetic experience.

● Summary

- The camera and time: The long take is a long uninterrupted shot that requires the choreography of actors and camera and produces continuity. By exposing more (or fewer) than 24 frames per second and projecting the exposed and developed footage at 24 fps, directors can create slow- and fast-motion effects, which can extend or shorten the apparent duration of events.
- The camera and space: by selecting camera height, angle, and distance, filmmakers present characters, actions, and locations from a particular visual perspective.

- Camera movement: choreographing camera movements, often with devices built expressly for this purpose, permits the camera to explore the space of the frame in two and three dimensions, detaching the audience from the action or placing them in the midst of it.
- Lenses and filters: lenses affect the perception of the visual field of the frame, particularly in terms of depth. Wide-angle lenses increase the apparent space between objects in the foreground and background. Telephoto lenses do the opposite—they compress that visual distance. Normal lenses approximate human vision. Filters manipulate color and light.
- Film stock: gauge, grain, and speed affect the overall look of a film. Gauge refers to the size of the film, measured horizontally across the strip of film. Grain refers to the grains of silver halide in the film's emulsion. Fast film stocks are very sensitive to light, but may yield images with visible grain. Slow film stocks are relatively insensitive and produce high-quality images when light can be carefully controlled, as on a studio set.
- Special visual effects involve optical illusions and digital techniques used during principal photography and in post-production. This aspect of cinematography includes building models and miniatures, matte paintings or glass shots, or digitally enhancing built sets. It also encompasses optical and digital compositing, where several elements of the frame are produced separately and brought together using an optical printer or computer.

Film Analysis • Cinematography in Documentary Films

This chapter has emphasized the way cinematography creates meaning in narrative fiction films. But cinematography also plays a critical role in documentaries and avant-garde films. The film analysis below discusses the way cinematography conveys meaning in two documentaries.

The author introduces the words and ideas of others in direct quotations and paraphrases. The comments of a film's director, film critics, and film scholars, and lines of dialogue that come directly from the film, all help to clarify descriptive statements about the film, provide historical context, and strengthen an interpretation. It's important to make clear to the reader which ideas are those of the author and which ideas the author is using to strengthen her argument or as a contrast to her own. That way, the reader knows who is responsible for the arguments and ideas.

Study Notes document the sources used, whether they involve direct quotations or paraphrases. Writers using a film as a primary text do not need to cite it in the bibliography, but should make clear in the text the director and year of the film. If the essay draws on audio commentary or extra features on a DVD, the DVD must be cited as a source in the manner detailed below. Always acknowledge sources, including books, journal articles, or websites, and use the proper format. Consult *The Chicago Manual of Style* and the *MLA Handbook* for the correct format for citation.

Cinematography in Two Documentaries

Comparing the visual style of two important documentary films, Leni Riefenstahl's *Triumph of the Will* ("*Triumph des Willens*"; 1934) and Alain Resnais' *Night and Fog* (1955) offers a dramatic contrast in political viewpoint and cinematic vision. Riefenstahl's film, made shortly after Adolf Hitler became Führer of Germany, celebrates the National Socialist Workers' Party Congress in Nuremburg in 1934. Resnais' film, made ten years after World War II, documents the atrocities of the Nazi death camps, where Hitler's regime tortured and killed millions of Jews and "social undesirables," including homosexuals and political dissenters. The two films were made for vastly different reasons and in different historical contexts, but comparing them reveals how cinematography can be used to convey ideas and feelings.

Adolf Hitler commissioned Leni Riefenstahl to direct *Triumph of the Will*. According to her memoir, published 53 years later, Riefenstahl initially refused the project because she was unfamiliar with the subject matter and had never made a documentary film before (p. 158).[1] Hitler insisted, and Riefenstahl, along with eighteen camera operators and a crew of more than 150 people, produced one of the most controversial films ever made.

Employing innovative cinematography and editing techniques, Riefenstahl succeeded in her quest to transcend the ordinary newsreel. Yet did Riefenstahl document reality, or help to fabricate one? Cultural critic Susan Sontag has condemned the film because, she argues, Riefenstahl's images idealize the Nazi Party, rather than documenting it: "Anyone who defends Riefenstahl's films as documentaries, if documentary is to be distinguished from propaganda, is being ingenuous"(p. 83).[2]

In documenting the rally, Riefenstahl's images represent Hitler as an exceptional leader who enjoys great popularity among the German people. They also emphasize the party's military discipline and unity. Riefenstahl's camerawork treats the Führer as an exalted figure, and then brings him down to earth in order to connect Hitler, the Nazi party, and the German people.

Riefenstahl's camerawork contrasts Hitler (an exceptional individual) and his admirers (the common people). She then resolves that tension, showing that Hitler is one with the German people. Riefenstahl's opening sequence—filmed from Hitler's plane—casts the leader as a god-like figure, surveying the city of Nuremburg from above. Overhead shots of the city reveal the precise geometry

1 Paraphrased material from Riefenstahl's memoir provides historical context. Writers need to tell readers where paraphrased material begins and ends. This author signals the paraphrase with the words "According to . . ." and ends the paraphrase with the page number. The source would then be included in a footnote or a works cited list. This source is: Leni Riefenstahl. *Leni Riefenstahl: A Memoir*. New York: St. Martin's Press, 1992.

2 A paraphrase and a direct quotation from Susan Sontag help to present the argument: that the film constructs a reality rather than documenting one. Any quoted material needs to be incorporated into a sentence; it cannot stand on its own. Here the author introduces the Sontag quotation with a paraphrase. Susan Sontag. "Fascinating Fascism." [1974] In *Under the Sign of Saturn*. New York: Vintage, 1981, pp. 73–105.

5.108 *(left)* An overhead cityscape shot from *Triumph of the Will* ("*Triumph des Willens*").

5.109 *(right)* Marching troops in *Triumph of the Will*.

5.110 Hitler seen from behind in *Triumph of the Will*.

of marching legions of SA and SS (figs. **5.108**, **5.109**). These opening shots suggest that Hitler is a divine figure and that the party, trained and disciplined, resembles a military organization.

Riefenstahl composes shots of Hitler so that he appears larger than the people around him. She shoots him from behind as he motors along the streets, greeting the cheering crowds of people (fig. **5.110**); his proximity to the camera exaggerates his physical size. The camera also circles him from a low angle (fig. **5.111**), magnifying his stature and adding a dynamic physicality to his performance.

Although she at first presents Hitler as a heroic, messianic, figure, Riefenstahl then uses camera distance and editing to link him to the common people. Before his arrival in Nuremberg, a tracking shot depicts the crowds that await him, singling out individual faces in close-ups, then fragmenting body parts in a rush as onlookers wave and salute their leader when he arrives (figs. **5.112, 5.113**). The close-ups, extreme close-ups, and rapid editing suggest the fevered pitch of shared anticipation.

But rather than maintain the distinction between Hitler the individual and the masses of the people, Riefenstahl singles out individuals and associates them with Hitler. During his address to the SA, long shots of the rigidly organized troops dominate the scene. But close-ups of one young

Chapter 5: Cinematography

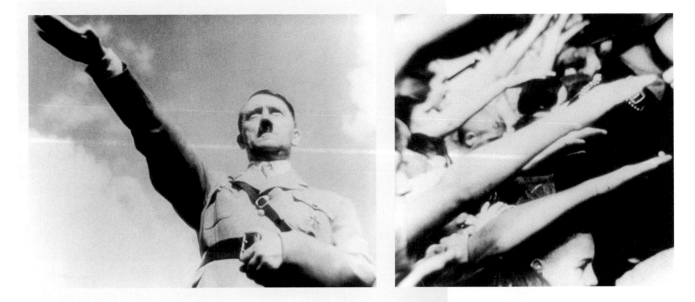

man are juxtaposed with close-ups of Hitler, an editing choice that reveals the emotional impact of his presence on his devoted followers and forges a mystical connection between Hitler, the German people, and Germany's future.

Depicting Hitler as a unifying force makes Riefenstahl vulnerable to the criticism that she has constructed an image rather than documenting a reality. Sontag raises this issue when she labels the film propaganda rather than documentary. The Nazi agenda was not a vision of unity, premised as it was on policies of racial division, including the physical displacement and destruction of Jews and other targeted groups. Many historians, film scholars, and filmmakers have argued that Riefenstahl staged many of the images (thus violating the principle of documentary film) and have challenged her one-sided representation of the Nazi project.

One such filmmaker is Alain Resnais. The opening shot of Resnais' *Night and Fog* rhymes with the opening of Riefenstahl's film. A static shot of a cloudy blue sky moves downward in a slow tilt that brings into the frame the rusted barbed wire of a former concentration camp (figs. **5.114**, **5.115**). Whereas Riefenstahl simulates Hitler's "god's eye" point of view, Resnais recreates the point of view of Hitler's victims.

5.111 *(top left)* A low-angle shot of Hitler in *Triumph of the Will.*

5.112 *(top right)* A fragmented close-up of the crowd in *Triumph of the Will.*

5.113 *(bottom)* A close-up of an individual face from the same scene in *Triumph of the Will.*

5.114 *(left)* A static shot of the sky at the beginning of *Night and Fog* ("*Nuit et Brouillard*").

5.115 *(right)* The barbed wire of a former concentration camp in *Night and Fog*.

3 This paraphrase provides insight into visual oppositions. Reserve direct quotations for those passages where the original wording is important; in all other cases, summarize and paraphrase. Annette Insdorf. *Indelible Shadows: Film and the Holocaust*, 3rd edn. Cambridge University Press, 2003.

This shot makes a pointed reference to Riefenstahl's film to suggest one of the film's central themes: the simultaneous importance and impossibility of representing the point of view of those who experienced the Holocaust. Film scholar Annette Insdorf writes that the film contains a dual perspective, that of a witness to the horrors of the camps (Jean Cayrol, the film's narrator) and that of a visitor (Resnais, who had no direct experience of the camps) (p. 201).[3] With this opening image, Resnais refuses to allow Riefenstahl's film to have the last word.

Resnais uses film stock to create a dialogue of sorts between Riefenstahl's world and that of postwar Europe. He differentiates past and present, juxtaposing black-and-white footage from *Triumph of the Will*, black-and-white stills from the Nazi period, and color scenes filmed ten years after the war.

Resnais also contrasts past with present through composition. In scenes from the war, the frame is filled with images of people being deported (fig. **5.116**), standing behind camp fences, and being liberated by the Allies. In the color footage, Resnais emphasizes the emptiness of the postwar landscape (fig. **5.117**). This contrast signifies an important difference between the Nazi era and its aftermath: the haunting absence of millions of people. All that remain are the historical documents (including photographs and films) and visual reminders, such as the

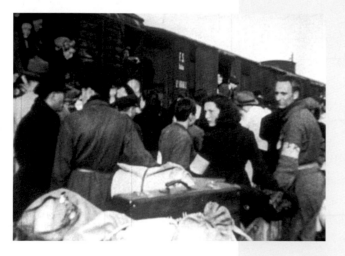

5.116 People being deported in *Night and Fog*: a crowded frame.

5.117 *(top)* A tracking shot captures the emptiness of the postwar landscape in *Night and Fog.*

5.118 *(bottom)* Precise use of a camera angle subtly reveals horror in *Night and Fog.*

indentations left from fingernails scratching at the concrete ceiling of the gas chamber.

Some of Resnais's most powerful images document the mechanisms that enabled the horrifying transition from the densely populated prewar images to the empty postwar landscape. These shots reveal the way the Nazi regime turned people into objects. Resnais presents images of personal items (eyeglasses, shoes) and body parts (hair) that the Nazis collected as they conducted mass exterminations (fig. **5.118**). These images show how living individuals were transformed into and equated with inanimate objects; they present a stark counterpoint to Riefenstahl's images of individuals joyously celebrating Hitler as their leader. The precise camera angle on a roll of carpeting made of human hair allows the viewers to see individual filaments protruding from it—more

evidence of the unspeakable horrors of the era Riefenstahl idealized.

Ultimately, by design, the contrast Resnais establishes between past and present collapses. Past (the memory of the witness) and present (the current reality of the visitor) cannot remain radically distinct in an ethical world. Resnais focuses on the architecture of the camp, which narrator Cayrol refers to as "a semblance of a city," to point out the apparently mundane and functional aspects of running the camp.[4] The image of a so-called hospital still standing in 1955 attests to the continued existence of the architecture of the Nazi era, and,

The author uses a direct quotation from *Night and Fog* because precise wording is important. The narrator compares Nazi death camps to everyday life in a city for specific reasons—to suggest that only a small distance may separate normalcy (a city) from abject horror (the camps) and to hint that the ideologies that created the camps may linger but remain hidden within seemingly ordinary structures of existence.

Direct quotations from a film used as a primary source do not have to be cited and documented in a bibliography. Include information on the director and year of release at the first mention of the film, as follows: (Alain Resnais 1955).

If the writer had cited a director's commentary track from a DVD, he or she would need to include a citation in the text and list the source in the bibliography. For example, the textual citation for the director's commentary for *Out of Time* would read: (Franklin, "Director's Commentary"). The

by implication, the survival of the ideology underlying the Nazi project of extermination.

The cries of the victims, the film implies, must be kept alive by revisiting the past, no matter how painful, and by recognizing that aspects of the past linger in the present. It is not acceptable, the closing narration states, to relegate the Nazis to the past. There may well be seeds of genocide being sown even as the world of the 1950s breathes a sigh of relief.[5] Resnais's cinematography encourages viewers to compare past and present, to experience the perspectives of witness and visitor, and, ultimately, to consider whether the present has truly freed itself from the terror and trauma of the recent past.

bibliography entry would read: Franklin, Carl. "Director's Commentary." *Out of Time*. MGM Home Entertainment DVD, 2004. The commentary of a film critic or historian (or cinematographer, editor, or actor) should be listed under his or her name, for example: Kenny, Glenn. "Commentary." *The 400 Blows*. Dir. Francois Truffaut. Fox Lorber DVD, 1999.

With all issues of documentation, become familiar with the standards expected, whether the writing is produced within an academic context or for a popular publication.

5 The two preceding sentences summarize the narration in the conclusion of the film.

Works Consulted

American Cinematographer's Manual. Hollywood, CA: ASC Press, 1993.

Arden, Darlene. "The Magic of ILM." www.darlenearden.com/articleILM.htm. 6/22/04.

Ascher, Steven, and Edward Pincus. *The Filmmaker's Handbook: A Comprehensive Guide for the Digital Age*. New York: Plume, 1999.

Barclay, Steven. *The Motion Picture Image: From Film to Digital*. Boston: Focal Press, 2000.

Cook, David. *A History of Narrative Film*. New York: Norton, 1996.

Crafton, Donald. "Tricks and Animation," in *The Oxford History of World Cinema*, ed. Geoffrey Nowell-Smith. Oxford and New York: Oxford University Press, 1997, pp. 71–8.

Denby, David. "Killer: Two Views of Aileen Wuornos," *The New Yorker*, January 26, 2004, pp. 84–6.

"Focus on Jim Jarmusch." Interview with Elvis Mitchell. Independent Film Channel, January 18, 2004.

Haines, Richard W. *Technicolor Movies: The History of Dye Transfer Printing*. Jefferson, NC: McFarland, 1993.

Handy, Bruce. "This is Cinerama." *Vanity Fair*, 488 (April 2001), pp. 258–74.

Hiltzik, Michael. "Digital Cinema Take 2." *Technology Review*, September 2002, pp. 36–44.

LoBrutto, Vincent. *Principal Photography; Interviews with Feature Film Cinematographers*. London and Westport, CT: Praeger, 1999.

Magid, Ron. "Vision Crew Unlimited's Artisans Lay Scale-model Keels for *Titanic*," *American Cinematographer*, 78/12 (December 1997), pp. 81–85.

Martin, Kevin H. "Jacking into the Matrix," *Cinefex*, 79 (October 1999), pp. 66–89.

Mast, Gerald, and Bruce Kawin. *A Short History of the Movies*, 6th edn. Boston and London: Allyn and Bacon, 1996.

Modleski, Tania. *The Women Who Knew Too Much: Hitchcock and Feminist Theory*. London and New York: Routledge, 1988.

Monaco, James. *How to Read a Film: Movies, Media, Multimedia*, 3rd edn. Oxford and New York: Oxford University Press, 2000.

Nowell-Smith, Geoffrey. *The Oxford History of World Cinema*. Oxford and New York: Oxford University Press, 1997.

Perisic, Zoran. *Visual Effects Cinematography*. Boston: Focal Press, 2000.

Pierson, Michele. *Special Effects: Still in Search of Wonder*. New York: Columbia University Press, 2002.

Rickitt, Richard. *Special Effects: The History and Technique*. London: Virgin Publishing, 2000.

Rogers, Pauline. *Contemporary Cinematographers on Their Art*. Boston: Focal Press, 1998.

Rudolph, Eric. "This is your Life." *American Cinematographer*, 79/6 (June 1998), pp. 74–85.

Salt, Barry. *Film Style and Technology: History and Analysis*, 2nd edn. London: Starword, 1992.

Schaefer, Dennis, and Larry Salvato. *Masters of Light: Conversations with Contemporary Cinematographers*. Berkeley, CA: University of California Press, 1984.

Sklar, Robert. *Film: An International History of the Medium*, 2nd edn. Upper Saddle River, NJ: Prentice Hall and Harry N. Abrams, 2002.

Spoto, Donald. *The Art of Alfred Hitchcock: Fifty Years of His Motion Pictures*. New York: Doubleday, 1979.

Street, Rita. *Computer Animation: A Whole New World*. Gloucester, MA: Rockport Publishers, 1998.

Usai, Paolo Chechi. "The Early Years," in *The Oxford History of World Cinema*. Oxford and New York: Oxford University Press, 1997, pp. 6–13.

Von Sternberg, Josef. *Fun in a Chinese Laundry*. New York: Macmillan, 1965.

Wheeler, Paul. *High Definition and 24p Cinematography*. Oxford: Focal Press, 2003.

Zettl, Herbert. *Sight, Sound, Motion: Applied Media Aesthetics*, 3rd edn. Belmont, CA: Wadsworth Publishing Co., 1999.

6

Editing

One must learn to understand that editing is in actual fact a compulsory and deliberate guidance of the thoughts and associations of the spectator.

V.I. Pudovkin

Throughout Peter Jackson's *Return of the King* (2003), the crusaders trying to defeat the evil necromancer Sauron find themselves divided into multiple camps, each isolated from the other. While Aragorn (Viggo Mortensen), Legolas (Orlando Bloom), and Gandalf (Ian McKellan) each try to muster up the forces needed to fight Sauron's army, Frodo (Elijah Wood) and Sam (Sean Astin) fend for themselves in their attempt to destroy the magical ring Sauron needs to consolidate his evil powers. When Gandalf fears that Frodo and Sam's attempt has been thwarted, audiences too would be

6.1 The highway patrolman in *Psycho*: a subtle low-angle shot.

left wondering whether or not the brave hobbits were still alive, were it not for Jackson's ability to reveal Frodo and Sam's whereabouts.

Jackson's ability to move the audience back and forth among the various locations—the Path of the Dead in Rohan, the enclave of Minas Tirith, and the hills of Mordor, where Frodo and Sam carry out their arduous task—is evidence of his mastery of editing, the process of joining together two or more shots. Editing has several practical functions: it makes the logistics of crafting feature-length films (involving multiple lines of action) possible; it makes scenes easier to choreograph; and it cuts down on production costs.

Because a traditional motion picture camera magazine holds less than fifteen minutes' worth of film stock at a time, making a conventionally shot feature film would be impossible without editing multiple shots together. Only recently has the development of digital video and computer technology made the concept of a full-length, one-shot film possible, as demonstrated by Aleksandr Sokurov's *Russian Ark* (2002)—a celebration of the history of Russia's Hermitage Museum filmed in a single 96-minute shot.

Furthermore, editing allows filmmakers to simplify the choreography in each shot. Any continuous shot of more than a minute—called a long take—demands perfect choreography; actors and actresses must remember their lines of dialogue and blocking, while the camera operators must move the camera in perfect timing with the cast. If anyone on the set misses a cue, then the entire shot has to be redone, which can be time-consuming and expensive since, unlike videotape, once film is exposed, it cannot be reused.

Tom DiCillo's *Living in Oblivion* (1994) is a comedy about a director trying to film one seemingly simple long take. One disaster leads to another: actors forget lines, lights explode, and a smoke machine is a little too effective. Finally the director decides to settle for a scene composed of two shots instead of the long take he had been committed to. The director's ability to create a scene by using portions of two different takes also illustrates how editing allows filmmakers to choose the best moments from various takes and combine them into one ideal scene—even if the decision is made out of necessity.

Editing also contributes to the aesthetic quality of a film. Music videos typically involve many short takes and thus demonstrate how a film can assemble a variety of images to enhance its visual appeal. The rapidly changing images and the rhythm created in the shift from shot to shot complement the lyrics, tone, and beat of the song they accompany. But, in narrative films, editing also emphasizes character development, establishes motifs and parallels, and develops themes and ideas.

At its core, editing involves the manipulation of three things: the graphic qualities of two or more shots, the tempo at which these shots change, and the timing of each shot in relationship to other elements of the film. After examining each of these three elements of editing, this chapter looks first at how editing can be used in narrative films to construct the meaning of the story that the viewer sees unfolding on screen, and then at how editing can produce meaning at a more abstract level, by defying audience expectations and by creating visual associations.

The Kuleshov Effect

One of the basic theoretical principles of editing is that the meaning produced by joining two shots together transcends the visual information contained in each individual shot. In other words, the meaning of a sequence of shots is more than the sum of its parts. In 1917, Soviet filmmaker Lev Kuleshov, a pioneer in editing techniques, began publishing articles on film as an art form. Eventually he established the "Kuleshov Workshop" to study the effects of editing on audiences. In one experiment, he cut back and forth between the same found footage of a man's (Ivan Mozhukhin) expressionless face and a succession of three other images: a bowl of soup, a woman's corpse in a coffin, and a young girl with a teddy bear. When he screened the sequence of shots for various audiences, they claimed that the man's facial expression registered an emotional response to each of the objects on screen. Kuleshov documented their comments:

> The public raved about the acting of the artist. They pointed out the heavy pensiveness of his mood over the forgotten soup, were touched and moved by the deep sorrow with which he looked on the dead woman, and admired the light, happy smile with which he surveyed the girl at play. But we knew that in all three cases the face was exactly the same. (quoted in Cook, p. 137)

His discovery illustrated that the meaning of a shot was determined not only by the material content of the shot, but also by its association with the preceding and succeeding shots. This general principle of editing is called the **Kuleshov Effect**.

● The Attributes of Editing: Creating Meaning Through Collage, Tempo, and Timing

Joining Images: A Collage of Graphic Qualities

Editing forms a collage, an assortment of images joined together in a sequence. When images are joined, audiences formulate ideas and derive meaning by comparing the visual details of each shot. A comparison of two shots can reveal important changes in *mise en scène*, including setting. In Ernst Lubitsch's *Trouble in Paradise* (1932), for example, two thieves find true love when they meet one another, and skillful editing suggests the sexual tryst that unfolds on the night of their first encounter. In a two-shot, Gordon Monescu (Herbert Marshall) casually seduces Lily (Miriam Hopkins) while she reclines languorously on a couch (fig. **6.2**). In the following shot, the couch is empty (fig. **6.3**). The combination of images is a not so subtle suggestion that, as the evening has worn on, the couple has adjourned to the bedroom. The editing underscores important differences in *mise en scène* to illustrate succinctly how this romantic interlude evolves over the course of a night.

Editing can also encourage audiences to compare and contrast the cinematographic qualities of each shot. Consider the scene in *Psycho* when Mother murders the detective Arbogast (Martin Balsam). As the attack begins, audiences see an overhead shot of the detective reaching the top of the stairs and Mother running out to stab him (fig. **6.4**). Then there is a cut to a close-up of Arbogast's face (fig. **6.5**). According to director Hitchcock,

the main reason for raising the camera [to an overhead shot] was to get the contrast between the long shot and the close-up of the big head as the knife came down on him. It was like music, you see, the high shot with the violins and suddenly the big head with the brass instruments clashing. (Truffaut, p. 276)

Hitchcock's quote suggests how the director was acutely aware of the way abrupt changes in camera positioning can evoke an emotional response.

Of course, two juxtaposed shots do not have to be so dramatically different in order to be evocative. On the surface it may even appear as if a scene involving dialogue between two characters does not exploit changes in visual information from one shot to the next. In fact, such scenes commonly depict participants in a conversation from similar vantage points. If one character speaks in a medium close-up, then a character who responds to the first character is also filmed in a medium close-up or close-up (figs. **6.6**, **6.7**). Because of the lack of graphic distinction between such shots, audiences tend to overlook how such combinations powerfully evoke the continuity of a conversation, even when the completed scene may be composed of many performances filmed over a week.

Analyzing Interactions between Characters

Careful attention to the editing in what appears to be a purely functional scene in *Psycho* will demonstrate how many elements of the visual system a director can bring into play during a scene that revolves around the restrained dialogue between two characters.

6.2 *(above left)* Monescu and Lily on the couch in *Trouble in Paradise*.

6.3 *(above right)* The vacated couch: romance blooms by night's end.

6.4 *(below)* Arbogast and Mother on the stairwell in *Psycho*.

6.5 *(bottom)* A close-up of Arbogast suddenly facing terror.

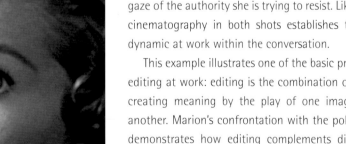

6.6 *(top)* A close-up of Frodo in *Lord of the Rings: Return of the King.*

6.7 *(center)* A close-up of Gollum creates continuity in *Lord of the Rings: Return of the King.*

6.8 *(below)* A reverse shot of Marion in *Psycho*: a high-angle shot.

Marion Crane, on the lam after stealing $40,000 from her boss, is awakened and questioned by a highway patrolman after spending the night in her car. As the officer begins his interrogation, we see him via Marion's point of view. The shot is a slightly low-angle close-up of the officer as he leans toward Marion. He is wearing dark sunglasses, preventing the audience (and Marion) from seeing exactly what he is looking at (fig. **6.1**, p. 160). When the scene cuts to a **reverse shot**—a shot taken from the reverse angle to the preceding shot— audiences see Marion from a slightly high-angle medium close-up, emphasizing her weakness (fig. **6.8**). She is anxious, as becomes evident in her sudden attempt to drive away and her large, frightened eyes.

In alternating between these two shots, Hitchcock encourages his audience to adopt Marion's nervous response to the officer's presence. The *mise en scène* in the shots of the officer emphasizes his power. He is physically imposing, as he leans into Marion's space, and coldly impersonal: his sunglasses, uniform, and stern expression all suggest that he is a tough, "by the book" officer. In contrast, the reverse shot emphasizes Marion's sense of entrapment and helplessness, thanks to the tight framing and her wide-eyed stare. Taken together, these shots suggest that Marion is helpless prey, trapped within the predatory gaze of the authority she is trying to resist. Likewise, the cinematography in both shots establishes the power dynamic at work within the conversation.

This example illustrates one of the basic principles of editing at work: editing is the combination of imagery, creating meaning by the play of one image against another. Marion's confrontation with the police officer demonstrates how editing complements dialogue by shaping visual information to evoke a response from the audience on emotional and intellectual levels.

Graphic Similarities between Shots

Editing can also emphasize similarities between shots, establishing a point of comparison between two people, places, or things. A **graphic match** is when two shots are juxtaposed in a way that emphasizes their visual similarities. At the end of the first segment of *Run Lola Run*, Lola's boyfriend throws a red bag full of money up into the air (fig. **6.9**). This shot is followed by a shot of a red telephone receiver that Lola tosses upward each time she begins her run (fig. **6.10**). The graphic match establishes a visual connection between the two segments of the film.

Stanley Kubrick's *2001* demonstrates how a graphic match can convey an idea. The film begins with a society of apes discovering how to use a discarded bone as a weapon. The bone gets hurled triumphantly into the air when, as the next shot begins, it "turns into" a revolving space station orbiting the Earth. The graphic match emphasizes how aeronautical technology is the logical extension of primitive weaponry, thus introducing the film's theme of humanity's reliance on (and abuse of) technology.

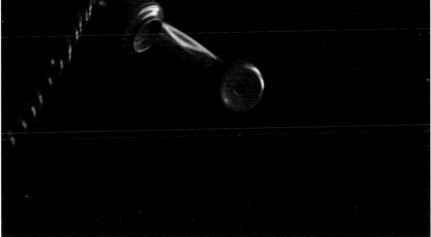

6.9 *(top)* Graphic match: the red bag full of money thrown into the air in *Run Lola Run* ("*Lola rennt*").

6.10 *(bottom)* The telephone receiver thrown in the air, from *Run Lola Run*.

Adjusting the Tempo

Filmmakers also encourage emotional and intellectual responses by adjusting tempo. The tempo in editing can be affected by two factors: the length of each shot and the type of shot transition—the visual effect used to move from one shot to the next.

Shot Length

The most obvious way that editors adjust tempo is by controlling the length of each shot: long takes tend to slow down the pace of a scene, while short takes quicken pace and intensity. Most movies combine long takes and short takes to allow for more variation and sophistication in the narrative pacing. Action scenes tend to rely on very short takes to convey excitement, while romantic scenes in the same movie unfold in longer takes at a more relaxed pace.

Scholars have studied the **average shot length** in films and discovered that the average shot in contemporary films is shorter than the average shot in older films. The difference between the rapid-fire editing of a modern action film such as *The Fast and the*

Furious (Rob Cohen 2001) and classic romance such as Casablanca (Michael Curtiz 1943) may seem obvious. But recent studies have shown that, with the advent of new digital editing devices, shots are increasingly becoming shorter. According to film scholar Michael Brandt, "films cut traditionally [have] an average shot length of 5.15 seconds, compared to 4.75 seconds for the electronically cut films," a difference of almost 10%. Brandt goes on to suggest that editing at this rate allows audiences to respond only to rhythm, since the brevity of each shot does not allow audiences fully to comprehend the visual information before them:

> Other studies have shown that it takes an audience anywhere from 0.5 to 3 seconds to adjust to a new shot. If it takes the audience three seconds just to adjust to a cut to a shot, what happens when the average shot length is so short that the audience is never given a chance to catch up? . . . Certainly, as each viewer picks and chooses the shots he or she pays attention to, there must be shots which audience members never fully absorb. (Brandt)

The tendency to rely on such rapid editing in recent films may explain why younger audiences are not initially receptive to older films: they seem slow-paced.

Shot Transitions

The second way in which filmmakers adjust the rhythm of editing is through **shot transitions**. A shot transition is the method of replacing one shot on screen with a second. The most common shot transition is the cut, when Shot A abruptly ends and Shot B immediately begins. A second common shot transition is the fade-out/fade-in, in which Shot A gradually darkens until the screen is completely black (or white, or red, or some other solid color) and then Shot B gradually appears. A third common shot transition is the **dissolve** (sometimes called overlapping, or lap dissolve), in which Shot A gradually disappears, while, simultaneously, Shot B gradually appears. Unlike fades, with a dissolve, the two shots will temporarily be superimposed. The viewer sees the two images overlapping one another (figs. **6.11**, **6.12**, **6.13**).

Two other shot transitions are less common in contemporary films: the **wipe** and the **iris in/iris out**. A wipe is when Shot B appears to push Shot A off the screen; that is, a portion of Shot B will appear on one side of the screen and will move across the screen until Shot A disappears altogether. Unlike a dissolve, the two images do not overlap; instead they appear divided, as in split-screen cinematography, and the second shot appears to

6.11 (top) Carrie prays to Jesus in Carrie: a fluid dissolve.

6.12 (center) The exterior of the house in Carrie: illuminated windows.

6.13 (bottom) The Jesus statue with illuminated eyes in Carrie: a graphic match.

expand to push the first shot out of the way (fig. **6.14**). An iris in/iris out occurs when a circular mask—a device placed over the lens of the camera that obscures part of the image—appears over Shot A. The circular mask gradually constricts around the image until the entire frame is black, at which point Shot B appears within a small circular mask. The circle, or iris, expands outward until Shot B takes up the entire screen. The iris in/iris out appears throughout *The Cabinet of Dr. Caligari* (fig. **6.15**). This technique functions in a similar way to the wipe and dissolve, in that iris shots are typically used as a transition from one scene to the next.

One function of these transitions is to help convey the passage of time, but they also affect the pacing of a scene. Cuts are almost invariably used within scenes because they connote an instantaneous change. They immediately alter the image, quickening the pace of the action. Even in a scene that relies primarily on long takes (and, hence, slow pacing), a cut often suggests a sudden change in mood or character dynamic. Such is the case in the scene from *Notorious* when Devlin returns to meet Alicia after learning that her assignment is to seduce a Nazi spy. While Alicia tries to make the evening romantic, the editing in the scene emphasizes how Devlin's seething jealousy contaminates the intimate mood. In a medium two-shot, Alicia embraces Devlin as she asks him why he is so distracted (fig. **6.16**). This long take contributes to the scene's relaxed pace and complements Alicia's casual playfulness as she questions him. But after Alicia jokingly suggests that Devlin must want to end their affair because he's secretly married, he replies bitterly, "I'll bet you've heard that line often enough," revealing his jealously over Alicia's sexual past. At this point, the scene cuts to a close-up of Alicia (fig. **6.17**; an example from *Citizen Kane* is in figs. **6.18**, **6.19**). The abrupt change draws attention to the sudden shift in the emotional weight of the scene: Devlin's words have devastated Alicia.

Using shot transitions to join scenes affects the pace of a sequence or an entire movie. Fades can have an especially pronounced effect on the pace of a film because they give audiences a literal visual pause in the action. Jim Jarmusch's *Stranger than Paradise* (1984) is a pronounced example of how fades can slow the pace of a film. In order to evoke the lackadaisical, meandering lifestyle of his main characters, Jarmusch uses only fades to link each scene—to the point of frustration for some viewers. In contrast, George Lucas uses wipes throughout *Star Wars* (1977). Since wipes in the film move quickly across the screen, the editing maintains a visual dynamism that mirrors the film's lively action.

6.14 *(top)* *Star Wars* uses wipes as transitions.

6.15 *(bottom)* An iris out shot from *The Cabinet of Dr. Caligari* ("*Das Kabinett des Dr. Caligari*").

6.16, **6.17** Romantic tension builds during a long take in *Notorious*.

Dissolves, fades, irises, and wipes rarely occur within scenes, since most scenes take place over an uninterrupted period of time. When they do occur within scenes, they usually introduce a memory or a fantasy. On rare occasions, these transitions are used within scenes without signaling a shift to a different time and place. When this occurs, the transitions dramatically slow down the pace of the scene.

A scene from *Fight Club* illustrates how fades suggest a more conspicuous protraction of time. When Tyler Durden (Brad Pitt) leaves the unnamed narrator (Edward Norton) after months of close friendship, his final words are presented in eight shots, the first four of which are connected by fades. Tyler wakes the narrator up in the middle of the night to deliver the news. After Tyler stands up to leave the room, the remaining shot transitions are cuts. The effect is hypnotic, conveying the narrator's dreamlike state of mind. Interestingly, the scene was originally edited using only cuts, but the filmmakers opted for the more narcotic feel of fades. The DVD includes both versions and allows audiences to compare them. The scene illustrates how the atypical use of fades within scenes slows

6.18, **6.19** An abrupt cut to a close-up emphasizes emotional shift in *Citizen Kane*.

the pace to suggest emotional detachment or a dreamy lack of engagement with the world.

Adjusting the Timing of Shot Transitions

The third way filmmakers use editing to produce meaning is by placing shot transitions so that they coincide with other visual and sound elements. The placement of shot transitions in relationship to these elements can punctuate the emotional and intellectual content of a scene. In narrative films, cutting within scenes tends to correspond to lines of dialogue, so that the editing draws attention to how characters are responding to what is being said.

In *The 400 Blows*, juvenile delinquent Antoine Doinel reads a passage from nineteenth-century French novelist Honoré de Balzac. For most of the scene, Truffaut uses a long shot to show Antoine reclining on a couch, smoking. A voice-over reads Balzac's words, suggesting that the boy is so entranced with the book that he can literally hear the author's voice speaking to him. As the story moves to its climax and the tone of the voice-over intensifies, Truffaut cuts to a shot of the book itself from Antoine's point of view. The editing underscores Antoine's passionate involvement with the story. As the narrator repeats the character's dying words (Archimedes' "Eureka! I have found it.") Truffaut cuts to a close-up of Antoine. As he "hears" the words, his eyes lift to the sky in amazement. Cutting on a line of dialogue emphasizes the degree to which Balzac moves Antoine. The timing of the cut also adds a layer of meaning to the story's last line. Not only have Archimedes and the dying character "found it," but so has the boy: he has discovered his love for art, which he mistakenly assumes will help him succeed in school.

Shot transitions may also correspond to visual cues. At the end of *The Graduate*, Benjamin Braddock arrives at the church to prevent Elaine's marriage. From the sanctuary's balcony, where Benjamin stands, a high-angle shot zooms in on the couple as they kiss. The scene then cuts back to Benjamin, showing the audience his distraught response; he has arrived too late to stop the wedding. Editing may be timed to coincide with action, a character's gaze, or lines of dialogue. Filmmakers employ editing to produce meaning through collage (joining images to invite comparison and contrast), creating and adjusting tempo (selecting average shot length and shot transitions), and by using shot transitions as punctuation (coordinating them with other visual and sound elements).

● ●

Techniques in Practice: Using Contrasting Imagery and Timing to Romanticize the Outlaws in *Bonnie and Clyde*

Audiences in 1967 flocked to see Arthur Penn's new gangster film *Bonnie and Clyde*. Although the film was panned by a number of influential film critics, young viewers were drawn to the two characters. In retrospect, the popularity of the film isn't hard to explain, given the fact that in America the 1960s counter-culture youth movement was in full swing. The ad campaign said of Bonnie and Clyde, "They're young! They're in love! And they kill people!"

But the film's depiction of the two outlaws emphasizes their youth and romantic ideals far more than their violent acts. The film makes it clear that the gang of outlaws robs only from the wealthy banks that are foreclosing on poor farmers' properties. In contrast, the film's authority figures—bounty hunter Frank Hamer, Ivan Moss, and the banks—represent a stifling system that encourages ruthless self-interest. An analysis of two crucial scenes from the film illustrates how Penn uses editing to draw a contrast between the honesty, openness, and altruism of the outlaws and the dishonesty and hypocrisy of the establishment.

Late in *Bonnie and Clyde*, three remaining members of the gang of outlaws—Bonnie, Clyde, and C.W.—recuperate at C.W.'s father Ivan's house after being ambushed by the law. Bonnie (Faye Dunaway), Clyde (Warren Beatty), C.W. (Michael J. Pollard), and Ivan Moss sit on the porch discussing the newspaper's coverage of the police assault on the Barrow gang, which left Clyde's brother mortally wounded. As C.W. reads the paper, he asks why he is always listed as an "unidentified suspect." The scene cuts to a medium two-shot of Bonnie and Clyde, so that we see Clyde's response to C.W.'s question. He tells C.W. to be glad "that's all you are." While Clyde is still talking, the scene cuts to a medium close-up of Ivan. At this point the audience can see his devilish grin appear when he hears Clyde tell C.W., "as long as they don't know your last name." The timing of the cut emphasizes Ivan's realization that he can double-cross Bonnie and Clyde without jeopardizing his son. Ivan, at this point, becomes one of the many authority figures that the film condemns for being hypocritical.

A subsequent pairing of images underscores Ivan's duplicity. In one medium long shot, Bonnie and Clyde rest in one

6.20 *(top)* An image of tenderness in *Bonnie and Clyde*, as the two outlaws rest on the front porch.

6.21 *(bottom)* A sharply contrasting image from *Bonnie and Clyde*, as Ivan beats C.W.

another's arms on the front porch, enjoying the peace, tranquility, and sunshine (fig. 6.20). As the shot continues, C.W. and his father, Ivan, go inside to fix lunch; Ivan stops in the doorway and tells the young couple to stay as long as they want. Bonnie and Clyde sit for a few seconds longer in the sun. Then the scene abruptly cuts to a shot of the interior of the house, where Ivan is beating C.W. and berating his son for bringing such "trash" to his home (fig. 6.21). The juxtaposition of the two shots is jolting. Penn uses the contrast between the two images (tranquility vs. violence; hospitality vs. condemnation; sunshine vs. a dingy interior) to emphasize Ivan's hypocrisy, and to distinguish his untrustworthiness from the young couple's loyalty to one another and their friends.

Indeed, the use of editing to compare the youthful honesty and innocence of the two lovers with the self-interested double-dealing of authority figures is a motif running throughout the film. The motif continues when a scene of Bonnie and Clyde making love in an open field is juxtaposed with a shot of Ivan making a deal with law officer Frank Hamer, sealing the couple's tragic fate. The radical shift in *mise en scène* from lovemaking to deal making once again emphasizes Ivan's betrayal. The shift in cinematographic details also illustrates the difference between the couple's zest for freedom and authority's claustrophobic containment. The first shot ends with a wide-angle view of two newspapers blowing across the open field, and the second begins with a disorienting telephoto shot of a city wall—a shot that slowly pans left until it finds the two men hunched over a table in an ice-cream parlor.

The editing throughout *Bonnie and Clyde* underscores the integrity of the Barrow gang in contrast to the deceitfulness of the authority figures who pursue them. In linking the couple's innocence and moral integrity with images of tranquility and openness, the film romanticizes the two outlaws, who are ruthlessly gunned down by a corrupt establishment.

Story-Centered Editing and the Construction of Meaning

All films consisting of multiple shots, even those that do not tell stories, draw on the three attributes of editing discussed above. But almost all popular films revolve around a story, and, as Chapter Three emphasizes, stories usually unfold over a period of time greater than the screen time and take place in a number of different spaces. In narrative films, editing's primary functions are to shape the audience's sense of time and to draw the audience's attention to important details of the story space.

Editing and Time

Narrative films tell stories by splicing (joining together) multiple shots to convey the cause and effect logic of the plot. The order in which an audience sees shots determines how the audience perceives the storyline. At the simplest level, as editors arrange shots within a scene, they have to create the illusion that the succession of shots depicts continuously flowing action. The arrangement of images to depict a unified story time is called **narrative sequencing**.

Out of Sight begins with Jack Foley walking out of a building and furiously throwing his necktie to the curb of a busy street. He then proceeds to cross the street to rob a bank. Despite the apparent simplicity of the sequence, Soderbergh actually used nine different shots (in 26 seconds) to document Jack's actions. Yet, viewers perceive the fragmented movement as one continuous action because the shots are joined.

In addition to creating the illusion of chronological time, narrative sequencing allows filmmakers to shape the audience's perception of time in three ways: to condense or expand time; to suggest the simultaneity of events happening in different settings; and to rearrange the order in which audiences see events.

Condensing and Expanding Time

The most obvious way narrative sequencing shapes how audiences perceive narrative time is by cutting out unnecessary events. The *syuzhet* in most narrative films shows us only those actions and events that directly affect the outcome of the storyline. Billy Wilder's *Some Like it Hot* (1959) illustrates how narrative sequencing can simultaneously eliminate extraneous material, focus the audience's attention on the central conflict motivating the characters, and emphasize character development. Two musicians, Joe (Tony Curtis) and Jerry (Jack Lemmon), witness a mob hit. Fearing for their own lives because they are eyewitnesses, they don women's clothing and join an all-woman musical troupe that is leaving Chicago for Florida. When they call the agent in charge of hiring, we see and hear Joe adopting his best feminine voice as he inquires about the job. The shot dissolves into a close-up of four legs in high heels and stockings, clumsily walking down a train station's loading platform.

This example illustrates how narrative sequencing often achieves a purely functional purpose—it keeps the audience's attention from flagging. In just two shots, Wilder efficiently emphasizes how Joe and Jerry are going to get out of Chicago. He does not show the audience the two men scrambling for an entire wardrobe of women's clothing.

But in the process of manipulating time, narrative sequencing can also help a film develop emotional and/or intellectual intricacy. Changes in time and space invite audiences to make an immediate comparison between two distinct points in time. Changes in time may mark the presence of central conflicts or emphasize important stages in character development. They may even allude to a film's themes. Transitions that signal important shifts in time do more than just cut out unnecessary events; they also help develop motifs, emphasize parallels, or indicate abrupt changes in patterns.

Wilder's use of editing draws attention to an important change in Joe and Jerry. Earlier scenes in the film depict them as conniving womanizers. Ironically, despite their sudden physical proximity to women (especially to Sugar, played by Marilyn Monroe), Joe and Jerry's masquerade makes it difficult for them to get physically intimate with them. From this point on, their characters evolve as they become more emotionally intimate with their fellow musicians.

Eliding time can also emphasize more abstract themes. In Ingmar Bergman's *The Seventh Seal* ("*Det sjunde inseglet*"; 1957), Death (Bengt Ekerot) comes to claim the life of a knight (Max von Sydow) who has just returned from the Crusades. But the knight convinces Death that the two should play a game of chess; the victor wins the knight's life. Early in the film, Bergman films a close-up of the chessboard the knight has set up on a rock near the ocean. A dissolve makes it appear as if the ocean's tide is washing away the chessboard. In narrative terms, the dissolve indicates the passage of time. The sun is setting on the horizon in the second shot, and clearly the knight has spent the entire day on the shoreline.

But the dissolve also carries with it a more profound symbolic meaning. Given the significance of the chessboard in the film, the editing emphasizes the frailty of life. Human life is as tenuous as chess pieces toppled by the sea. The editing's emphasis on the movement of the sun in this context also lends symbolic weight to the imagery; the end of the day clearly connotes the ending of life (fig. **6.22**).

Sometimes filmmakers use a **montage sequence** to indicate the passage of time. Instead of merely excising a period of time altogether via a dissolve or a fade-out, a montage sequence emphasizes the actual process of passing time (albeit in a condensed form). Montage sequences consist of several shots, each one occurring at a different point in time, and each joined together by an appropriate shot transition. A montage sequence can span hours, one day, a few months, or years.

In *Spider-Man*, a montage sequence depicts the hours that Peter Parker spends dreaming up the costume he will wear, which will complement his recently acquired powers. The film exploits the language of the montage sequence for comic effect when, after showing the amount of time Peter spends fantasizing about a sleek, form-fitting body-suit, the film reveals what he actually wears for his first public performance: a baggy red and blue sweatsuit and a ski mask.

In addition to condensing or eliminating time, editing also allows filmmakers to expand time by arranging multiple overlapping shots of a single action, so that portions of the action are repeated as it unfolds. In *Shoot the Piano Player* ("*Tirez sur le pianiste*"; François Truffaut 1960), amateur pianist Edouard Saroyan (Charles Aznavour) is invited to his first professional audition. When he arrives at the studio, he pauses nervously outside the

6.22 Superimposed images add symbolic significance to *The Seventh Seal* ("*Det sjunde inseglet*").

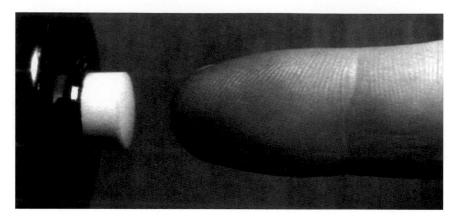

door, and when he finally decides to ring the bell, the film presents his action in three consecutive and overlapping extreme close-up shots of his hand as it reaches for the button (fig. **6.23**). The editing effectively triples the amount of time it takes Saroyan to ring the doorbell and, by exaggerating a gesture that would otherwise be an inconsequential detail, suggests how much emotional investment he stakes in the audition.

6.23 An extreme close-up of Saroyan's finger, from *Shoot the Piano Player* ("*Tirez sur le pianiste*"): editing exaggerates the gesture.

Suggesting the Simultaneity of Events

Narrative sequencing also involves arranging the order in which audiences see events. For example, editing can suggest multiple lines of action unfolding simultaneously. **Parallel editing**, sometimes called cross-cutting, is when a filmmaker cuts back and forth between two or more events occurring in different spaces, usually suggesting that these events are happening at the same time.

Often filmmakers use parallel editing to create suspense. Action films inevitably include parallel editing to suggest multiple lines of action that are converging on the same space, as in a car chase or rescue sequence. Sometimes a filmmaker uses parallel editing to compare two or more lines of action. In addition to suggesting that the depicted events are occurring simultaneously, such sequences also help develop themes. In *Billy Elliot*, Billy (Jamie Bell), the son of an out-of-work miner, develops a love for ballet, much to the dismay of his father, who has hopes that Billy might pursue boxing. At one point, a parallel editing sequence humorously suggests how Billy's entire family, with the notable exception of his father, expresses a love for music through movement. As the soundtrack plays T Rex's "Jitterbug Boogie," the sequence cross-cuts between four separate spaces: Billy practices his ballet routine in the local gym; his brother Tony listens to the same song and plays air-guitar in his bedroom; his grandmother practices long-forgotten ballet movements downstairs; and his father sits on the toilet gargling. The father's lack of engagement with the tune—and the fact that he sits on the commode, of all places, while everyone else dances—points to his preference for unrefined pursuits over the arts and helps explain his refusal to allow Billy to continue practicing ballet.

Arranging the Order of Events

Editing can also allow filmmakers to rearrange the sequence in which events are shown. Editing makes possible the expressive potential of those moments when a film's *syzuhet* reorders chronology to suggest a similarity between two points in time or a cause-and-effect relationship. The most common example of this is the flashback, when events taking place in the present are "interrupted" by images or scenes that have taken place in the past. Typically filmmakers give audiences a visual cue, such as a dissolve or a fade, to clarify that the narrative is making a sudden shift in chronology. Usually a flashback is motivated by the plot, as when a character—any of the narrators in *Citizen Kane*, for example—recalls a memory.

Flashbacks typically emphasize important causal factors in a film's *fabula*. In the exposition of *Mystic River* (Clint Eastwood 2003), two child molesters abduct Dave Boyle. He eventually escapes, but his life is forever tainted by these memories. When the film reveals Boyle as an adult (Tim Robbins), he is a withered, timid shell of a man, and the film repeatedly flashes back to an image of him as a child fleeing from his abductors as if to suggest that he is still trying to evade his own past.

Editing also allows filmmakers to reveal a character's dreams or fantasies. Like a flashback, a dream is usually signaled by a shot transition that indicates the boundary between reality and fantasy. In *Walkabout* (Nicholas Roeg 1971), a teenage girl from the city and her young brother are stranded in the Australian outback. Eventually they are rescued by a young aboriginal male who guides them back to the industrialized world. Despite the mutual sexual attraction between the girl and her guide, they never overcome the cultural barriers that separate them; their desires remain unspoken. The film's resolution reveals that, on returning home, the girl has grown up and married a young professional. As he babbles on about his impending promotion, the camera slowly zooms in to her glazed eyes (fig. **6.24**). Then the scene dissolves into a shot of the aborigine, naked and diving into a lake in the outback. He swims over to a small island where the girl and her brother are sitting and laughing, also naked (fig. **6.25**).

The scene of the three characters frolicking together is clearly not a flashback, because the girl was never comfortable enough around her guide to express her affection for him, much less to take off her clothing in front of him. Instead, the scene is a fantasy, a longing for what could have been. Indeed, the editing in the remainder of the sequence emphasizes the sharp contrast between the happiness that she fantasizes about and the boredom of her daily routine. The jubilant laughter,

6.24 *(top)* The girl's eyes glaze over in *Walkabout*.

6.25 *(bottom)* Reality gives way to fantasy in *Walkabout*.

unselfconscious nudity, and her playful demeanor are the antithesis of the dissatisfied gaze (complete with glassy eyes and blank expression), made-up face, and lack of interest with which she greets her husband. The idyllic landscape in her fantasy also contrasts with the blandness of her apartment in real life. The clash of the *mise en scène* in each shot indicates that she realizes she has sacrificed freedom and affection for sterile predictability.

On rare occasions, filmmakers will insert a flashforward, interrupting the events taking place in the present by images of events that will take place in the future. By their nature, flashforwards can be disorienting since they can only be understood as such after the "future" event occurs. Sometimes a flashforward may be logically explained by the narrative, as when a character has a premonition of upcoming events.

However, flashforwards are seldom logically justified in terms of the narrative; their significance is usually far more ambiguous. At one point in *Easy Rider* (Dennis Hopper 1969), Captain America (Peter Fonda) is interrupted as he talks by an inexplicable and brief shot of burning debris on the side of a road. Only later will viewers recognize that the debris they had seen earlier is the wreckage from Captain America's motorcycle crash, which occurs at the end of the film.

Editing and space

One of the many distinctions between film and theater is film's ability to draw audiences into the story space. When viewers see a play, their perspective is determined and limited by the distance between their seats and the stage. Early filmmakers relied largely on the **tableau shot**, a long shot in which the frame of the image resembles the proscenium arch

6.26 A tableau shot from *The Great Train Robbery*: the audience observes from a distance.

of a stage (fig. **6.26**). The audience's perspective, in other words, is consistently distanced from the action onscreen, as it would be if they were watching a play.

But film has the unique ability to focus the audience's attention on anything from the microscopic—as in *Three Kings* (David O. Russell 1999), when we see how muscle fiber reacts when a bullet enters the body—to the grand—as in *Return of the King*, when editing and camera movement trace the lighting of pyres across a mountain range in a majestic call to arms. Editing allows filmmakers to shift the camera's position and draw the audience's attention to the most crucial information in the story space. For example, because editing can draw attention to a character's facial expression, it plays a significant role in helping audiences understand the emotional content of a scene. In *American Beauty*, Lester Burnham begins his revolt against what he sees as a stifling, middle-class lifestyle when his supervisor calls him into his office to discuss the importance of "cutting corners" to save money. Lester responds to his supervisor's plea for understanding by mentioning that one of the executives has used the company charge account to hire prostitutes. As he begins his tirade, he is filmed with a long shot. But when Lester's supervisor claims that the story is an "unsubstantiated rumor," the scene cuts to a medium shot of Lester as he says, "That's 50,000 dollars. That's somebody's salary. That's somebody who's going to get fired." By adjusting the camera's proximity to Lester, the editing stresses the emotional intensity of his words, and encourages the audience to recognize how furious he is at the hypocrisy of the company's executives.

As filmmakers cut within scenes, they can draw the viewer's attention to four things: how characters respond to lines of dialogue; the elements of the *mise en scène*; the group dynamics of a scene; and important elements of the *mise en scène* that will influence the plot or contribute to themes.

Shot/Reverse Shot

One of the most important editing techniques within a scene is the **shot/reverse shot**, a standard shot pattern that directors use to film conversations between two characters. This method dictates that a shot of a character speaking will be followed by a shot of another character's response, taken by a camera placed at the reverse angle of the first shot (fig. **6.27**). This pattern rarely uses actual point-of-view shots because characters would appear to directly address the camera. In general actors avoid looking at or speaking to the camera, because doing so acknowledges the audience's presence and destroys the illusion of a naturally unfolding story. As the analysis of Marion's encounter with the trooper in *Psycho* demonstrated, this pattern—so common in narrative films that most viewers take its expressive power for granted—can define the emotional dynamics of a scene.

6.27 Diagram of the shot/reverse shot technique. Cameras A and B, on the left, shoot the conversation. Camera C, on the right, does not.

A more detailed analysis of Marion's conversation with Norman in his parlor will reveal two specific ways that the shot/reverse shot accentuates the emotional content of a scene. First, the timing of the cuts corresponds to the pattern of dialogue, shifting the audience's perspective so that it remains focused on how characters respond to the spoken word.

The scene between Norman and Marion lasts for several minutes, and the camera largely volleys back and forth between two shots: an eye-level medium shot of Marion eating her sandwich and an eye-level medium shot of Norman reclining in a chair. The lack of exaggerated camera angles in these shots suggests the conversation has a pleasantly innocuous tenor. The editing emphasizes how each character responds to what the other has said. When Marion asks if Norman goes out with friends, the scene cuts to Norman so the audience can see his body's involuntary

withdrawal as he offers his timid response that "a boy's best friend is his mother." When Marion says that she is looking for her "own private island" to escape to, the camera immediately cuts to Norman as he leans forward and asks, "what are you running away from?" His response marks a sudden shift in the dynamics of the conversation: now Marion is put into a defensive position, and Norman's leaning into the foreground offers a clear indication of his aggression, which is beginning to emerge. In other words, the timing of the cuts to Norman draws attention to elements of the *mise en scène* as they change in relation to the dialogue. The cuts reveal which words affect him most and the specific physical and emotional responses he has to them.

A second way that editing can help visualize the emotional undercurrents of dialogue is by exploiting sudden shifts in a scene's established visual patterns, as this scene demonstrates. Typically, the visual details of the alternating shots in a shot/reverse shot sequence create a somewhat repetitious pattern. That is, when filmmakers return to a reverse angle, they often use a shot that is more or less consistent with the previous reverse-angle shot. However, editing can signal important shifts in the emotional dynamics of a scene by suddenly altering this pattern.

Through much of *Psycho*'s parlor scene, Hitchcock consistently employs the same eye-level medium shots of Marion and Norman (figs. **6.28**, **6.29**). But when the undertone of the conversation becomes more loaded with Marion's and Norman's personal baggage, the editing emphasizes the (suddenly apparent) unspoken seriousness of the interchange. When Marion comments on overhearing Mother's vicious critique of Norman, the reverse shot of Norman marks a radical departure from the pattern that has been established previously. Instead of shooting Norman from an eye-level medium shot, Hitchcock films him from a low-angle profile shot (fig. **6.30**). So, when Norman says he gets the urge to "leave her forever, or at least defy her," the audience sees him from a very disquieting vantage point. The sudden rupture in the shot/reverse shot sequence hints at the dark underside of Norman's submissive relationship with Mother, which Marion's inquisitiveness has just prodded. Moreover, the change in the camera's perspective positions Norman underneath a stuffed owl in the background, as if Norman were the bird's prey. The editing and the *mise en scène* coincide to create a visual metaphor for Norman's entrapment under Mother's watchful gaze.

The shift in the shot/reverse shot pattern allows Hitchcock to reframe the scene's physical space to illustrate disruptions in the scene's emotional space. In a sense, this scene paves the way for the more radical fissures in emotional space that will appear in the film's famous shower sequence.

6.28 *(top)* Norman talks to Marion in the parlor in *Psycho*.

6.29 *(center)* A reverse shot of Marion in the same scene from *Psycho*.

6.30 *(bottom)* The atmosphere changes in the parlor in *Psycho*.

Eyeline Match

A second key technique editors sometimes use to shape the audience's understanding of the geography of a scene is the **eyeline match**. This match cut uses a character's line of sight to motivate the cut. If a filmmaker wants to emphasize that a character is looking at a particular prop or another person, she will include a shot of the character looking offscreen, followed by a shot of the object or person that the character observes. This sequence of shots makes spatial relationships clear to the audience and guides viewers through a character's thought process. Sometimes the filmmaker will begin with the shot of the object or person, and then follow it with a shot of the character who is looking at it. In either case, the editing—via the eyeline match technique—allows audiences to understand what has captured the character's attention.

In *O Brother, Where Art Thou?* escaped convicts Pete and Delmar face Everett as the three men argue about who should be in charge, when the sound of barking dogs begins to intrude upon their conversation. Everett looks offscreen, startled (fig. **6.31**). The scene cuts to a shot of a forest tree line in the distance (fig. **6.32**) and then cuts back to a shot of Pete and Delmar looking offscreen toward the forest (fig. **6.33**). The eyeline match efficiently tells audiences what the barking signifies (that the law is nearby) and where it is coming from (the forest in the distance). As the example illustrates, the eyeline match can convey the geography of a scene. The shots of the woods roughly approximate the convicts' vantage point. However, eyeline matches are not necessarily point-of-view shots. Here, the shots of the forest approximate the perspective of the three characters, but do not depict the subjectivity of any one character.

The eyeline match is a powerful storytelling device because it may provide audiences access to a character's feelings. A scene from *The Pianist* reveals how effective editing can be at drawing audiences into a character's emotional state. The film details the tragic ordeal of Wladyslaw Szpilman (Adrian Brody), a Polish Jew living in Warsaw during Germany's occupation of the city who, after escaping from the Jewish Ghetto, is shuttled from one hideout to another by a well-meaning but powerless resistance movement. Throughout the film, Polanski uses eyeline matches to draw audiences into Szpilman's perspective, emphasizing his emotional and physical vulnerability.

As the tides begin to turn for the Allies in the war, a benefactor (Valentine Pelka) moves Szpilman to a new hideout "right at the heart of the lion's den"—across the street from a German hospital and next door to the police. In a medium close-up, Szpilman looks out the window onto the street below, turning his head to screen left when he hears the

6.31 *(top)* An example of eyeline match from *Oh Brother, Where Art Thou?*: Everett looks offscreen.

6.32 *(center)* The camera cuts to the forest.

6.33 *(bottom)* The camera cuts back to Pete and Delmar, looking offscreen right. Note how editing (separate shots) and *mise en scène* (they look to the right) separate these two from Everett, helping to establish him as the leader.

6.34 *(top left)* Szpilman looks out the window offscreen in *The Pianist.*

6.35 *(top right)* Szpilman's benefactor packs up in *The Pianist.*

6.36 *(bottom left)* Szpilman alone at the window in *The Pianist.*

6.37 *(bottom right)* The benefactor closes the door behind him in *The Pianist.*

jangle of keys offscreen (fig. **6.34**). The scene cuts to the benefactor, who is packing up to leave Szpilman alone (fig. **6.35**). The scene cuts back to a medium long shot of Szpilman standing alone by the window (fig. **6.36**) and then cuts back to the benefactor as he creeps down the room's entrance hall, exits, and closes the door behind him (fig. **6.37**). When the door latches, the scene cuts back to the medium long shot of Szpilman standing alone and dejected by the window. He turns and stares out the window, at which point audiences see another eyeline match of the street below, bustling with the activities of German soldiers. Taken together, this series of eyeline matches powerfully evokes Szpilman's feelings of helplessness after being abandoned in a tiny sphere of complete isolation amid a hostile environment. In this case, eyeline matches guide the audience into a character's physical environment and emotional state.

Cutting to Emphasize Group Dynamics

In scenes involving more than one or two characters, filmmakers sometimes cut to specific areas of the *mise en scène* to help suggest complex group dynamics. This occurs frequently in scenes where the characters have conflicting goals and distinct character traits, where editing can help portray a complex interweaving of different emotions, types of behavior, and physical responses to stimuli.

One example is the scene in *Stagecoach* when the passengers gather around the table to have dinner in Dry Fork. As all the characters approach the table to find a seat, a medium long shot frames the three representatives of the American upper class:

Gatewood, Lucy, and Hatfield (fig. **6.38**). Ringo and Dallas—the outlaw and the prostitute—are noticeably absent. Then the scene cuts to a two-shot of them on the opposite side of the table as Ringo asks Dallas to have a seat facing Lucy (fig. **6.39**). The cut, in this context, isolates the two ostracized members of the group and establishes the class conflict that will govern the rest of the scene. Once Dallas accepts Ringo's offer, the reverse shot shows Gatewood's, Lucy's, Hatfield's, and even Doc Boone's shocked response. The shot/reverse shot, in other words, makes palpable the disdain Gatewood, Lucy, and Hatfield feel for Dallas and Ringo.

Cutaways

Editing may also draw attention to non-human elements of the *mise en scène* that will influence the plot or help develop the theme of a film. Shots that focus the audience's attention on precise details are called **cutaways**. Unlike an eyeline match, a cutaway is not character-centered; the onscreen appearance of an object does not depend on a character having to "see it" in the previous shot.

In Dreyer's *The Passion of Joan of Arc*, an eyeline match reveals that Joan sees a shadow in the shape of a cross on the floor of her prison cell. She interprets the shadow as a sign from God. Later, Dreyer films a close-up shot once again, so that viewers see the feet of a church interrogator as he enters her cell and steps on the shadow. The imagery foreshadows how he

6.38 *(top)* A medium long shot of Gatewood, Lucy, and Hatfield in *Stagecoach*.

6.39 *(bottom)* The cut to a two-shot of Ringo and Dallas in *Stagecoach* establishes them as outsiders.

will betray Joan's trust. For the second shot of the shadow, Dreyer uses a cutaway without an eyeline match, emphasizing that Joan does not see the interrogator tread on the shadow and so does not witness his defilement of her symbol of faith.

In short, editing offers filmmakers a powerful tool for drawing the audience's attention to what is important within the diegetic space. It allows filmmakers to bring the audience's perspective closer to (or further from) the action that unfolds in the story space and tells the audience what it should notice and when.

● Beyond Narrative: Creating Meaning Outside the Story

So far this chapter has focused largely on the ways editing can generate story-centered meaning: how editing helps filmmakers indicate the passage of time and how editing emphasizes important narrative details in a scene. But there are two significant means by which editing can produce abstract ideas: it can defy audience expectations by departing from the "rules" of continuity editing, and it can associate two images with one another to produce meaning on the level of metaphor.

Continuity Editing: Conventional Patterns and "Bending the Rules"

Chapter Two discussed how audiences carry with them certain expectations when they go to see movies: expectations based on the leading actor or actress in a movie, expectations shaped by marketing strategies, and expectations based on their assumptions of how a story should be told. Sometimes a filmmaker will deliberately upset, or at least complicate, these expectations in order to generate a particular emotional or intellectual response—for example by casting an actor against type.

Similarly, audiences have expectations about how editing should function in a narrative film, and sometimes a filmmaker will deliberately upset those expectations. For many audiences, expectations about what editing should do are shaped by the Hollywood standard, which is often called **continuity editing**, or invisible editing: editing which is intended to flow so smoothly from one shot to the next that audiences are not even conscious of the shot transitions.

One major concern of continuity editing is to ensure that audiences have a clear sense of the geography of a scene. Because editing is a collage of collected images, changing shots can cause confusion. Any time a scene cuts to a new shot, the image becomes fragmented and the scene's coherence could potentially rupture. Continuity editing works to hide this fragmentation by employing two strategies: it relies on a systematic order for presenting shots and it maintains the consistency of direction on screen. These standard practices help ensure that audiences perceive the story space as unified and coherent.

The Standard Shot Pattern

To begin, editors usually rely on a **standard shot pattern**, which helps to orient audiences to the setting and spatial characteristics of a scene. Typically a scene begins with an **establishing shot**, which is usually (but not always) a long shot designed to clarify when and where the scene is taking place in relation to the previous scene and to provide an

6.40 *(top)* An establishing shot of the church in *High Noon*.

6.41 *(center top)* A high-angle shot of the congregation inside the church focuses on the location of the action in *High Noon*.

6.42 *(center bottom)* Kane addresses the congregation in *High Noon*: tensions arise.

6.43 *(bottom)* A point-of-view shot from the pulpit in *High Noon*.

overview of the entire setting. Once the audience has a clear sense of where the characters are and how they are positioned in relation to one another, the filmmaker can cut to closer shots to emphasize important details. Continuity editing demands that filmmakers rely on standardized techniques—the shot/reverse shot and the eyeline match—to ensure that audiences understand why they are being shown this information. In other words, when Marilyn Monroe suddenly appears onscreen in *Some Like it Hot*, the use of the eyeline match justifies her presence: she has caught the eye of Joe and Jerry. As a scene ends, there is often a **re-establishing shot**, another long shot that reorients viewers to the environment, that offers closure to the scene, paving the way for the next scene. Longer scenes often include re-establishing shots midway through to reorient audiences when characters move about the setting.

In *High Noon* (Fred Zinnemann 1951), Marshal Will Kane (Gary Cooper) interrupts a church service to solicit the congregation's help in defending the community against Frank Miller (Ian MacDonald), a recently paroled outlaw who will arrive in town at noon. The scene begins with an establishing shot of the exterior of the church (fig. **6.40**). Kane walks into the frame and approaches the building. There is a cut to the interior of the church, a high-angle long shot of the congregation taken from behind the pulpit (fig. **6.41**). Kane enters the background of this shot. After a cut to a medium shot of him addressing the man in the pulpit and an eyeline match that reveals Kane's view of the pulpit, the congregation on either side of the aisle turns to gaze at the camera/Kane. The rest of the scene depicts the escalating tensions within the room when Kane addresses the parishioners via a series of shot/reverse shots and eyeline matches (figs. **6.42**, **6.43**). Eventually one member of the church stands up and demands that the children should leave the room before the discussion continues. At this point, there is a cut to a high-angle long shot of the congregation as the children get up to leave. Finally, there is a re-establishing shot of the exterior of the church, showing the children scampering joyfully out of the building. As is typical in continuity editing, the scene begins with the broadest details before it focuses on the more subtle interactions among the various characters involved.

The 180-degree Rule and Jump Cuts

Another way for filmmakers to ensure that audiences do not lose track of the setting's spatial arrangement as the scene moves from shot to shot, is by following the **180-degree rule**. This rule dictates that, within a scene, once

6.44 *(top)* The TV executive faces screen right in *Bamboozled*.

6.45 *(bottom)* In the next shot from *Bamboozled*, the TV executive faces screen left. Note the different backgrounds.

the camera starts filming on one side of the action, it will continue filming on that same side of the action for the rest of the scene unless there is a clearly articulated justification for crossing "the axis of action." If, in fig. 6.27, the director starts filming the conversation between these two characters with camera A, he can also film the dialogue with camera B. But cutting to camera C would reverse the direction of the action onscreen. Suddenly the characters would be facing in the opposite direction.

Another side effect of crossing the axis of action, or breaking the 180-degree rule, is that the background of the scene is suddenly changed. If, in the diagram, camera A begins filming, audiences will see a white background and the two main characters in the foreground. Camera B would also show the white background behind the characters. If camera C begins filming, audiences will see a gray background. In short, the 180-degree rule helps maintain consistent screen direction and spatial unity. Within a scene, the axis of action may shift. If characters move, or if new characters enter the scene, the line adjusts accordingly, through reframing and, perhaps, a re-establishing shot. Still, most filmmakers conscientiously work to ensure that audiences perceive the direction of movement as consistent across shots. Spike Lee intentionally breaks the rule in *Bamboozled* (2000), during the scene in which a television executive (Michael Rapaport) berates his staff. One shot shows him sitting at the end of a conference table at screen left, facing right (fig. **6.44**), but the next shot is a close-up of him facing screen left (fig. **6.45**). The disorientation suggests confusion, and serves as a distancing device to undercut the authority of his words.

In addition to maintaining a coherent story space, continuity editing also works to maintain the audience's sense of linear time. Because cutting out passages of time is such an integral part of the editing process, editing itself threatens to destroy continuity. With every cut, audiences could potentially lose track of their sense of how the story time is unfolding. One basic rule of continuity editing, as has been suggested earlier, is to use an appropriate shot transition to emphasize when time is being excised as a film moves from scene to scene. An abrupt, inexplicable shift in the time and place of an action which is not signaled by an appropriate shot transition such as a dissolve or a fade-out/fade-in is called a **jump cut**.

Consider, for example, the difference between two scenes in which characters drive a considerable distance in cars. In the classically edited *The Maltese Falcon* (John Huston 1941), Sam Spade (Humphrey Bogart) takes a taxi cab across town to investigate a mysterious address. In the first shot, Spade hires a cab to take him to the address. This shot dissolves to a close-up of a car wheel, which in turn dissolves into a shot of the cab pulling to the side of a curb in a dark San Francisco neighborhood (the address, it turns out, is a hoax). In three quick shots, Huston takes the action across town while maintaining the illusion of linear time. As Robert Ray points out, the dialogue complements the editing to help convey how much storytime is being depicted on screen: "Spade's question to the cabbie, 'You got plenty of gas?' tells the viewer that the forthcoming trip is a relatively long one" (Ray, p. 46).

By comparison, Jean-Luc Godard's *Breathless* ("*A Bout de Souffle*"; 1960) radically disrupts continuity in the scene when the thief Michel (Jean-Paul Belmondo)–who idolizes Humphrey Bogart (see fig. 10.6)–flees Paris in a car he has stolen. As Michel drives down the road, passing cars and talking to himself, several jump cuts disorient the viewer's sense of time and space, since there is no clear indication of how long he has been driving over the course of the sequence or how far he gets from Paris. Michel steals the car on a crowded street in Paris, and as he drives off, a jump cut suddenly places him in the outskirts of the city. Later, surrounding traffic suddenly disappears via jump cuts. The scene's depiction of time and space, in other words, is far more fragmented than Huston's in *The Maltese Falcon*.

Continuity Errors

Even within scenes, filmmakers generally work to create the illusion of time passing in a linear order, even when (as is often the case) shots and scenes are filmed out of order. Most film crews contain at least one **continuity editor** (sometimes called the **script supervisor**) whose job is to maintain consistency of action from shot to shot. If shot A ends with a character standing beside a trash can smoking a pipe, shot B (assuming it is a continuation of the same scene) should begin with that character in the same position, still smoking a pipe. Any unintentional noticeable discrepancy from shot to shot—for example, an inexplicable change in location, in costume, in posture, in hairstyle—is called a **continuity error**. In John Frankenheimer's *Seconds* (1966), "Tony" Wilson (Rock Hudson) receives a pillow from a stewardess. The close-up of Hudson makes it clear that he places the pillow behind his head (fig. **6.46**). There is a cut to the reverse shot of the stewardess, and then a cut back to Hudson—only now the pillow has disappeared (fig. **6.47**). A reverse shot reveals the stewardess, and when the scene cuts back to Hudson, the pillow is once again in place! Some audiences take great pleasure in finding such continuity errors, and some films, such as Ed Wood's *Plan 9 from Outer Space* (1959), develop cult followings because the continuity errors are so numerous and glaring.

6.46 *(top)* A continuity error from *Seconds*: the stewardess has given Hudson a pillow.

6.47 *(bottom)* In this next shot from *Seconds* the pillow has mysteriously disappeared!

Continuity and Chronology

Continuity editing also dictates that events be presented so as to be understood chronologically. Most films are constructed so that

Continuity Editing

During principal photography, the continuity editor (or script supervisor) maintains a record of each shot to guarantee consistency from take to take. Her notes would specify each actor's costume and position, and the arrangement of the *mise en scène* in general at the end of each take. After the principal photography is completed, the **editor** works with the director to combine and cull the footage. To build a scene, directors and editors combine **master shots**—takes that cover the entire scene—with reaction shots, cutaways, and **B-roll** (secondary footage that may depart from the main subject of a scene, such as an exterior shot of the building where a scene takes place). For *Cold Mountain* (Anthony Minghella 2003), editor Walter Murch whittled 113 hours of material down to a two-and-a-half-hour film (Cellini, p. 3).

Because any single take may be filmed from multiple vantage points simultaneously, editors study footage on an editing deck that allows them to watch several takes at once before deciding which is the best one for the scene. Sometimes the editor will only use part of one take, selecting the best moments of an actor's performance from it.

An **assistant editor** catalogs all the takes, inspects the condition of the negative, and supervises the creation of optical effects (often contracted out). A **negative cutter** assembles the entire negative and cuts and splices it together, adhering to the editor's decisions. Positive prints are then made from the negative.

As digital post-production technologies have become the norm, the tools available to the editor have changed. Walter Murch cut *Cold Mountain* on Final Cut Pro, a professional editing software program which has become an industry standard. In an interview, he notes several differences using digital technology: he could show dailies to director Minghella on the set in Romania on a laptop and send a DVD of them to producer Sidney Pollock in Los Angeles. And the affordability of computer workstations relative to flatbed editing machines meant that he had four workstations functioning simultaneously rather than two. But Murch also acknowledges certain advantages of working with film. "When you actually had to make the cut physically on film, you naturally tended to think more about what you were about to do," Murch states, "which—in the right proportion—is a good thing to do." He misses the spontaneity of scanning through footage in search of a specific shot. "Inevitably before you got there, you found something that was better than what you had in mind. With random access, you immediately get what you want. Which may not be what you need." (Cellini)

the appearance of the events onscreen replicates the order in which they occur in the *fabula*. Any exceptions to this precept are almost always motivated by characters or events. For example, the *syuzhet* of *Citizen Kane* makes radical jumps back and forth in time, but this departure from chronological order is explained by the fact that Thompson is gathering this information from the various narrators. So, even though Kane's life is presented "out of order," Thompson's quest is presented in chronological order. Moreover, whenever the film makes a radical leap in time, an appropriate shot transition helps the viewer understand how the chronology is being rearranged.

Finally, in continuity editing, events happen onscreen only once. In *Do the Right Thing*, Spike Lee breaks this rule twice. When Mookie delivers a pizza to his girlfriend Tina, he throws the pizza box down on the table and moves to embrace her—then the same shot is repeated again. Later, when Mookie decides to throw the trashcan through Sal's window, an exterior shot shows the trashcan shattering the glass, and then Lee cuts to an interior shot that also shows the trashcan shattering the glass. The same event appears twice, but from different perspectives. The repetition emphasizes the action, and is in keeping with the film's interest in the opposite forces of love and hate.

By today's standards, Lee's use of repetition is a self-conscious departure from the norm. Generally, if events happen more than once on screen, narrative elements motivate the repetition.

Underscoring Emotional Content

Finally, the Hollywood model of editing assumes that a scene will rely on editing that is carefully calibrated with the action on screen, as opposed to following Bazin's *mise en scène* aesthetic (see pp. 90–93). Bazin advocated the use of long takes so that audiences experience an unfolding of reality through unmediated access to characters in their environment. Jim Jarmusch's *Stranger than Paradise* refuses to use any editing within scenes. Every scene consists of a single long take. One scene depicts a poker game in which two of the main characters are accused of cheating. Instead of relying on eyeline matches and shot/reverse shots to accentuate the tension in the room, Jarmusch films the scene in a single three-minute shot. Most filmmakers adhering to the Hollywood standard would use editing to draw the audience's attention to the shifting emotional dynamics of the scene.

The underlying philosophy in continuity editing is that every shift to a new shot must serve a narrative function. In other words, continuity editing should tell the story with the greatest emotional impact and the most clarity.

Two Case Studies in "Breaking the Rules"

Because continuity editing is the norm, most film scholarship does not concern itself with considering or discussing how a film adheres to the Hollywood standard. But viewers, critics, and scholars do notice when a film departs from these standards. While some films accidentally break the rules, some filmmakers such as Spike Lee intentionally choose to break them. Because audiences are so used to seeing films that conform to the "rules" of continuity editing, films can have a powerful impact when they depart from these rules.

Two scenes demonstrate how filmmakers can intentionally confuse the audience's sense of time and place for dramatic effect. In *Walkabout*, Nicolas Roeg disrupts the continuity of space to suggest the main character's psychological trauma. The scene emphasizes the film's exploration of cultural incompatibility.

Disrupting the Continuity of Space in *Walkabout*

Late in the film, an Australian aborigine finds his life endangered while stalking a water buffalo calf:

1. Long shot: the aborigine approaches the calf with a club in hand and places the club on the calf's head in an offensive maneuver (fig. **6.48**).

2. (cut) Close-up: the calf struggles against the club placed firmly between its horns.

3. (cut) Long shot: two adult buffalo run in the distance (fig. **6.49**).

4. (cut) Long shot: the hunter grabs the horns of the buffalo and tries to wrestle it to the ground.

5. (cut) Medium long shot: the hunter pulls the prey to the ground.

6. (cut) Extreme long shot: two adult buffalo run in the distance.

7. (cut) Long shot: a handheld camera rapidly approaches the hunter, who is still wrestling with his prey. When the camera has moved to a medium close-up of the hunter, he drops his club and rolls backward in a defensive maneuver. The camera rapidly tilts downward to film the soil (fig. **6.50**).

8. (cut) Medium close-up: an out-of-focus shot of a white male behind the wheel of a vehicle. His eyes and his forehead are offscreen as he moves from screen right to screen left (fig. **6.51**).

9. (cut) Medium close-up: the hunter continues to topple backwards.

10. (cut) Medium close-up: a water buffalo runs from screen left to screen right.

11. (cut) Medium shot: two white men pass in a jeep. As they drive away from the camera, it becomes apparent that the jeep is pulling a trailer loaded with a carcass. They too are hunters.

12. (cut) Close up: the aborigine hunter lifts his head in a bewildered reaction shot.

After this sequence of twelve shots, the hunters stop the jeep and use their rifles to kill a water buffalo in the distance. The aborigine witnesses the kill and is clearly disturbed by the mechanical quality of their hunting technique.

6.48 *(top)* The aborigine puts the club on the calf's head in *Walkabout.*

6.49 *(center top)* Two adult buffalo in the distance begin to charge in *Walkabout.*

6.50 *(center bottom)* The camera tilts down as the aborigine wrestles with his prey in *Walkabout.*

6.51 *(bottom)* Men in a jeep appear from nowhere in *Walkabout.*

On seeing this sequence for the first time, audiences are bound to be perplexed by the sudden appearance of the men in the jeep. The scene is disorienting, as it intentionally plays with the audience's understanding of how editing constructs spatial coherence. Roeg uses the logic of continuity editing to suggest that, while the aborigine is wrestling with the buffalo (shots 2, 4, and 5), two more adult buffalo are charging to protect the calf (shots 3 and 6). Following shot 6, shot 7 appears to be a point-of-view from the charging animals' perspective as they approach the aborigine. But then Roeg disrupts the flow of events in shot 8. Instead of cutting to a reverse shot of the charging animals, he introduces a heretofore unseen element into the setting: the white hunter. In disturbing the continuity of space, Roeg conflates the buffalo charge with the white hunters' vehicle, suggesting that the real threat to the aborigine is not the animal but the descendants of the colonizers who are destroying his way of life. Following the image of the aborigine violently toppling backwards, shots 10 and 11 further emphasize Roeg's metaphor: the hunters are assaulting the aborigine's space.

The Discontinuity of Time in *The Limey*

In *The Limey*, the British thug Wilson (Terence Stamp) comes to the United States to find Valentine (Peter Fonda), who Wilson believes is responsible for his daughter's death. After the opening credits, which prominently feature a close-up shot of Wilson on an airplane, Wilson settles into his Los Angeles hotel room and pulls out an envelope with the return address for Ed Roel (Luis Guzmán). Suddenly, in what appears to be a flashforward, Wilson introduces himself to Roel. The scene cuts back to Wilson's approximate point of view looking at the envelope in his hotel room. Shortly afterwards, Wilson takes a cab to Roel's house, and Soderbergh shows Wilson introducing himself once again. In the middle of an extensive discussion about Roel's connection to Wilson's daughter, Soderbergh inserts the close-up shot of Wilson on the plane in what appears to be a flashback.

This opening sequence is indicative of how the first third of *The Limey* freely rearranges the order of events and shows events multiple times. The plot is so convoluted that most audiences cannot determine exactly when these events take place in relationship to one another: is this all a fantasy that Wilson has on his flight to L.A.? When he talks to Roel, is Wilson suddenly remembering his flight? The film's resolution begins with the same close-up shot of Wilson on an airplane, which suggests that the entire film is a flashback. But throughout the film Soderbergh has refused to clarify the relationship between past, present, and future. By the climax, Wilson realizes that he is partially responsible for his daughter's death. The film depicts Wilson's agonizing guilt at having spent much of his daughter's childhood in prison. One of its major themes, then, is that past, present, and future all interact simultaneously. All of the characters in the film are constantly haunted by their pasts, and they allow the past to control their actions in the present. Editing allows Soderbergh to depict the mind's process of interweaving past memories with present-day experiences. Lem Dobbs, the film's screenwriter, says of its unusually fragmented structure, "One of the great clichés of filmmaking [. . .] is that, unlike novels, in films you can't show thinking. [. . .] It's a total lie. I think movies are great at showing someone thinking. [. . .] I think it's very novelistic to do this kind of fragmentation" ("Screenwriter Commentary").

Associational Editing: Editing and Metaphor

One of the great challenges of spoken language is finding a way to articulate abstract feelings or ideas. Writers run up against the limitations of the word when they are faced with having to describe something as basic, yet as abstruse, as romantic longing or fear. Authors use metaphors and similes to help their readers visualize what would otherwise be an indescribable feeling. Poet Robert Burns compares his love to "a red, red rose," and Madonna compares the sensation of physical desire for a new lover to making her "feel like a virgin." Both examples describe the indescribable by associating it with something that is concrete and comprehensible. Editing also has the power to encourage audiences to meditate on equally abstract ideas.

A graphic match in Charlie Chaplin's short film *Sunnyside* (1919) demonstrates how the expressive potential of editing is so powerful that it can evoke the physical sensations of the characters onscreen. In one scene, the Little Tramp has been jilted by his would-be lover, and he decides to kill himself by standing in front of an oncoming car. He puts his fingers in his ears, turns around, and bends over so that the car will hit him solidly in the rear. Just as the car is about to hit, a second shot shows us a drowsy Little Tramp having his rear kicked by his demanding boss. The Tramp had actually just fallen asleep on the job (standing up, conveniently) and had dreamed his melodramatic suicide attempt. The graphic match is what makes the sequence so comic: it transfers the sensation of the Tramp's experiences in his physical world into his dreamworld.

Soviet Montage

Whereas the graphic match exploits the visual similarities between shots to produce meaning, **Soviet montage** is a style of editing built around the theory that editing should exploit the *differences* between shots to produce meaning. It was developed and perfected in Russia during the silent film era of the 1920s, when the Soviet regime had just come to power. Soviet leaders believed that film was an effective political tool, and filmmakers saw editing as the key to involving the audience in political and intellectual revolution. Exploiting the Kuleshov effect became the guiding principle of three of the major Soviet filmmakers in the 1920s: V.I. Pudovkin, Dziga Vertov (born Denis Kaufman), and Sergei Eisenstein. All three directors experimented with the notion that, just as audiences could derive an emotional meaning from the juxtaposition of two completely unrelated shots, so, too, they could understand abstract political ideas.

A careful analysis of four shots from the famous "Odessa Steps sequence" from Eisenstein's *Battleship Potemkin* illustrates how the intentionally jolting collision of images elicits both an emotional and an intellectual response. In this scene, set in Russia in 1905, the peaceful citizens of Odessa have gathered near the harbor to honor the mutinous sailors on board the battleship *Potemkin*. The sailors have revolted against their officers and, by extension, the Tsar. The Tsar sends troops to break up the congregation of citizens at the harbor. The troops fire on the civilians, and the peaceful protest turns into a massacre. Eisenstein based the scene on an actual historic event, which left 70 dead and 200 injured (Figes, p. 185). But rather than filming the sequence as an objective document of the event, Eisenstein's use of editing turns the conflict into a symbol of the oppression that only revolution can overturn. Throughout the sequence, Eisenstein uses editing to expand time, prolonging the impact of the Tsar's brutality by crosscutting among multiple lines of action and by showing pivotal moments of violence several times. When the troops begin to fire their guns, Eisenstein shows one victim's head snapping backward with the force of the bullet. The same shot is repeated three times in rapid succession to underscore the horror of the moment.

Four shots appear midway through the sequence. In the first, a row of faceless soldiers fires down on the civilians, who are offscreen (fig. **6.52**). Next, a high-angle shot depicts throngs of civilians running scattershot down the steps, from screen left to screen right (fig. **6.53**). A third shot shows the soldiers progressing in a line down the steps (fig. **6.54**). The fourth shot is a medium close-up of a woman clutching her son to her chest and walking defiantly towards the soldiers (fig. **6.55**).

A careful analysis reveals that Eisenstein exploits *mise en scène* to suggest opposition, as evident in the character movement in each shot. While the soldiers march in unison, the crowd disperses chaotically. The opposition is equally apparent in shot composition. The soldiers' boots create a rigid, seemingly impenetrable diagonal line, which sweeps across the screen with mechanical precision. The crowd, on the other hand, peppers the stairway at random as it scatters so that, instead of moving in unison, each civilian moves as an individual. This clash of opposing imagery suggests Eisenstein's main point: the troops represent a unified and oppressive force, lashing out against a disorganized array of ordinary citizens.

An abrupt contrast in shot distance also emphasizes opposition. In the third shot, the soldiers are filmed with a long shot. The camera's perspective leaves them faceless, while

6.52 *(left)* Faceless soldiers fire in *Battleship Potemkin* ("*Broneonosets Potyomkin*").

6.53 *(right)* Civilians scatter down the steps in *Battleship Potemkin*.

6.54 *(left)* Soldiers march down the steps in *Battleship Potemkin.*

6.55 *(right)* A mother clutches her son in *Battleship Potemkin.*

the close-up of the woman in the fourth shot emphasizes her defiant facial expression and her son's drooping body (he has been trampled amid the confusion). In splicing this shot with that of the faceless, unidentified soldiers, Eisenstein elicits an intellectual response: the troops represent a brutal, callous, and oppressive Tsarist regime which torments helpless individuals.

At the climax of the sequence, the eponymous battleship rises up in revolt and defends the citizens of Odessa against the oppressive regime. After the battleship fires on the Tsar's troops, Eisenstein adds three consecutive shots of statues of lions, each one in a different pose: one is asleep, the second has its head raised (figs. **6.56**, **6.57**), and the third lion is standing up. The effect is purely symbolic: the three shots create the effect of a sleeping lion (representing the people of Russia) awakening and rising up (against the Tsar).

Eisenstein's 1928 film *October* ("*Oktober*" or *Ten Days That Shook the World*) is even more bold in its use of editing to stimulate intellectual responses detached from any narrative cause-and-effect logic. The film depicts the period during the Russian Revolution between the overthrow of the Tsar and the installation of the Leninist government. During this time, the moderate communist Kerensky established an interim government, which Eisenstein clearly depicts as obstructionist—a threat to the people's revolution. Late in the

6.56 *(left)* The sleeping lion statue in *Battleship Potemkin.*

6.57 *(right)* A statue of a lion with its head raised in *Battleship Potemkin.*

Chapter 6: Editing

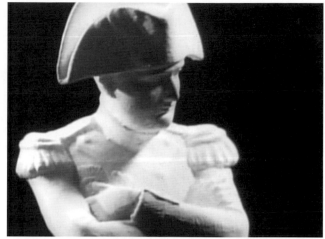

film, Eisenstein depicts Kerensky ordering the arrest of the revolution's leader Lenin and then signing a decree reinstating the death penalty. In a subsequent series of shots, Kerensky climbs the stairs of the Tsar's palace, where he has taken up residence, and pauses to overlook the room below, confidently crossing his arms at his chest (fig. **6.58**). The scene then cuts to a shot of a statue of Napoleon, likewise represented with his arms crossed (fig. **6.59**). The clear implication is that Kerensky, in signing these orders, has become the new emperor; he is not a leader of the people but an egotistical despot. To emphasize the point, Eisenstein cuts to a general who turns to salute, then cuts to a naval officer who turns to salute. Eisenstein isn't depicting the story space following the standards for continuity, since neither officer is actually in the room (nor is the statue of Napoleon). Instead of functioning literally, these officers become symbolic of Kerensky's control over the military elite—and not, significantly, the military's foot soldiers, who, the film makes clear, are suffering in the trenches of World War I (fig. **6.60**).

6.58 *(top left)* Kerensky with arms crossed in *October* ("*Oktober*").

6.59 *(top right)* The camera cuts to the statue of Napoleon in *October*.

6.60 *(bottom)* A saluting officer symbolizes Kerensky's control throughout *October*.

Variation within the Soviet School

Among the chief practitioners of montage editing there was some contentious debate about how editing conveys ideas to the audience. Eisenstein's editing self-consciously created visual collisions. He advocated what he called a "dramatic principle" of editing, by which "montage is an idea that arises from the collision of independent shots—shots even opposite to one another" (Eisenstein, p. 49). Eisenstein described how Pudovkin, on the other hand, believed in an "epic principle," which held that "montage is the means of *unrolling* an idea with the help of single shots" (Eisenstein, p. 49). In other words, Pudovkin maintained that editing had the greatest power as an integral part in a series of narrative events.

Film Style and Culture: The Influence of Marxism on Montage Editing

In keeping with Marxism's belief in communal action, Soviet films during Lenin's time often avoided valorizing characters acting in isolation. In contrast to Hollywood's tendency to focus on the heroics of individual characters, the Soviet directors tend to deflate, or negate altogether, the importance of people acting in isolation.

In the same vein, one school of thought contends that the Soviet approach to editing dismantles the filmmaker's traditional authority to govern the audience's response to the information onscreen. Soviet montage collapses the hierarchical relationship between filmmaker and audience by demanding that the spectator participate in the production of meaning. Eisenstein doesn't guide his audience through a cause-and-effect relationship from shot to shot. As the series of shots from *October* demonstrates, audiences have to be more self-conscious and active in order to grasp the film's metaphorical connections between Kerensky and Napoleon. An opposing view holds that editing overtly manipulates the audience's attention and response. But Eisenstein's film demonstrates how, at its most ambitious, the Soviet theory of dynamic juxtaposition demands the spectator's intellectual involvement, and audiences become critically important to the generation of meaning.

6.61 Pavel on the ice in *Mother* ("*Mat*").

Comparing the climactic sequence of Pudovkin's *Mother* ("*Mat*"; 1926) with the editing in *October* illustrates how his approach to editing differs from Eisenstein's. In *Mother*, Pavel (Nikolai Batalov), a man imprisoned for his revolutionary political beliefs, breaks out of his cell to join a parade of revolutionaries. During Pavel's escape, Pudovkin repeatedly cuts away to show images of ice breaking up on the river outside the prison. Like the juxtaposition of Kerensky with the statue in *October*, the cutting here conveys a metaphorical meaning; when combined with images of Pavel's escape, the break-up of the ice and the flow of the river come to symbolize the growing revolt and the dissolution of the Tsar's oppressive control. But unlike the shots in *October*, the imagery also has a narrative function: Pavel has to leap across the floes to join the protesters on the opposite side of the river (fig. 6.61). The metaphorical power of the editing arises within the cause-and-effect logic of Pavel's story—not from the collision of two images with no narrative context.

Techniques in Practice: Soviet Montage Aesthetic in *The Godfather*

Soviet montage never caught on as a popular approach to filmmaking. It eventually fell out of favor under Stalin's regime, and even at the height of his productivity, Eisenstein's films weren't necessarily popular among audiences in the Soviet Union. Nevertheless, this aesthetic approach has had a lingering impact on other filmmakers. While Hollywood filmmaking is still largely wedded to the priority of telling a good, gripping story, some films do incorporate Soviet montage as a means of offering shorthand commentary on characters, or of adding a layer of complexity to theme.

By and large, Francis Ford Coppola's *The Godfather* adheres to the standards of continuity editing. Nevertheless, the film provocatively combines continuity editing and montage editing to add layers of complexity to the story. In particular, Coppola uses montage editing to show that the Mafia justifies its dishonorable activities (murder) by linking them to honorable values (the importance of family and loyalty).

The film's opening dialogue establishes the film's principal theme: that the Corleone family uses violence to buttress the family. An undertaker explains how two men brought dishonor to his family when they raped and beat his daughter, leaving her permanently scarred. He asks powerful Mafia boss Don Vito Corleone (Marlon Brando) to deliver justice by killing the men. Corleone eventually agrees to help (though he refuses to have the men killed) as long as the undertaker pledges his loyalty to the godfather and promises to return the favor in the future.

The scene emphasizes the contradiction at the heart of Corleone's philosophy. He agrees to act on the undertaker's behalf only after the undertaker is brought into "the family." Only then can committing an act of violence become synonymous with honor and loyalty. Yet Corleone wants to keep his business affairs and family life separate and believes he can do so. But, as this scene makes clear, violence and family honor are inextricably linked.

This contradiction is underlined by the editing. The cut from Don Corleone's office to the next scene draws attention to the connection between violent business and family life. After the undertaker leaves the room, the camera cuts to a medium close-up of Corleone as he says to the others in the dimly lit room, "We're not murderers, despite what this undertaker says." At this point there is a cut to an establishing shot of the next scene—the wedding of Corleone's daughter Connie, which is taking place at the same time the Don was meeting with the undertaker. The change of setting emphasizes con-

6.62 Vito sniffs the rose in his lapel in *The Godfather*.

trast in a dramatic shift from darkened interior and hushed voices to the brightly lit exterior and noisy hubbub of the wedding. The visual contrast between the two images highlights the opposition between the activities taking place inside Corleone's office and those taking place outside. The *mise en scène* of the first shot emphasizes the close confines and soft, low-key lighting of the interior setting, along with the slow, methodical movement of Corleone as he sniffs the rose on his lapel (fig. **6.62**). The medium close-up complements the emphasis that the *mise en scène* places on confinement. In the next shot the bright, natural lighting, exterior setting, festive dancing,

and camera placement (an extreme long shot) stand in stark contrast to the tightly framed shots of Corleone.

The disparities between shots suggest Corleone's attempt to keep family and business separate. But as the movie progresses, the two become increasingly indistinguishable from one another, as the wedding scene foreshadows. A wedding photographer tries to arrange a family portrait. Don Corleone refuses to let the picture be taken until his son Michael (Al Pacino) arrives. Michael is in the army, far removed from the Corleone business dealings. After his return, he is pulled into his father's "business" just as he is pulled into the wedding portrait. In the end the Don's attempt to keep family separate from business fails. Michael enters the picture, so to speak, and he becomes the new godfather.

The film's climax, an extended parallel editing sequence, juxtaposes images of another traditional ritual—a baptism—with images of multiple mob hits to suggest the final collapse of the boundary between the family and its business: violence. Michael has agreed to become the godfather of Connie's son, and simultaneously has ordered a series of murders to avenge those who have betrayed the Corleones. The acts confirm that he has replaced Vito as head of the family and the business. He is a new godfather in both senses of the word, but he is less successful than Vito at separating family and violence. Despite the apparent differences between the act of baptism and the act of murder, the parallel editing suggests an affinity between the honorable act of baptism and the dishonorable act of killing.

As the infant's hood is removed, Coppola cuts to a close-up shot of a gun being taken out of its case. As the priest anoints the infant with oil, Coppola cuts to a barber applying shaving lotion to one of the hit men, grooming himself for his job. The editing continues to cross-cut between the baptism ceremony and the killers' preparation, suggesting the ritualistic qualities of both. Finally, the priest asks Michael, who holds the baby, if he renounces Satan. Coppola immediately cuts to a shot of the first hit being carried out. The

6.63 The murder of the baby's father in *The Godfather*.

scene then cuts back to a close-up of Michael as he responds, "I do." The scene then cuts to the murder of the second victim. Coppola continues to juxtapose Michael's renunciations of Satan with images of the hits that he has ordered, including the killing of Carlo, the baby's father (fig. **6.63**).

Like its opening, the climax of *The Godfather* illustrates how the boundary between family honor and corruption collapses. As the priest pours the holy water over the baby's head, the camera cuts to a series of shots that tallies up all the victims of Michael's orders. Just as Connie's son has been baptized with holy water, Michael has been baptized in blood.

Editing synthesizes the cinematography and *mise en scène* of individual shots into a series of images that, when taken as a whole, transcend the limitations of any one of the images in isolation.

Editing is the last of film's three visual elements described in this book. While this chapter has emphasized how a film creates meaning by combining images, the next chapter will explore how film creates meaning by combining images with sound.

● Summary

- This chapter has emphasized how all editing, even that used in completely abstract films, consists of three attributes: collage, tempo, and timing.
- In narrative films, editing helps shape the way audiences perceive time and space.
- Editing shapes the way time is presented onscreen in four ways: suggesting continuously flowing action; manipulating the length of time; suggesting the simultaneity of events; and arranging the order of events.
- Editing can draw the audience's attention to important details of the narrative space by employing three different devices: the shot/reverse shot; the eyeline match; the cutaway.
- Many films follow the standards of continuity editing, a method for clearly presenting space and time.
- Editing can suggest more abstract ideas that transcend the literal scope of a film's narrative in two ways: by departing from the conventional rules of continuity editing and by employing associational editing.

● ●

Film Analysis ● Editing for Association

The essay below analyzes a short film by one of America's most important avant-garde filmmakers, Maya Deren. In particular, the essay discusses how Deren uses associational editing to transform everyday objects into symbols of marital dissatisfaction. Study Notes accompanying the essay discuss strategies for effective paragraph organization.

When children begin reading and writing, they learn that paragraphs are units of organization that help distinguish the main ideas of a piece of writing and play a pivotal role in helping readers assimilate information. While there is no standard ideal length for a paragraph (indeed, variation is an important writing strategy), longer paragraphs run the risk of incorporating too many ideas, all struggling for attention at the same time. Shorter paragraphs, on the other hand, often introduce important ideas without offering enough developed discussion to support those ideas or explain their importance.

For this reason, good writers take great pains to organize paragraphs to underscore their importance as markers of the essay's major ideas. The sidebars stress how each paragraph is structured in order to foreground the author's most important ideas, helping him emphasize the importance of his interpretive claims over his descriptive ones. This helps the reader follow the argument's main ideas.

Editing in *Meshes of the Afternoon*

Maya Deren's short experimental film *Meshes of the Afternoon* (1943) depicts what would otherwise appear to be the most innocuous sequence of events. A woman returns home on a sunny afternoon, settles down to take a nap, and begins dreaming. But Deren's experimental visual techniques transform this everyday activity into a surreal, horrific event, allowing viewers to interpret the film as a meditation on the disintegration of her relationship with her husband, Alexander Hamid (who also helped shoot the film and who appears in the movie, along with Deren). Throughout the film, Deren's editing techniques transform tranquil images of domesticity into threatening portents of destruction, suggesting how the unnamed main character (Deren) feels trapped in a suffocating relationship.[1]

The plot of the film simply repeats and expands on a woman's routine after returning home: as she walks up the sidewalk toward her house, she sees a man in the distance. She fumbles with her key and enters the house. After surveying the room (noticing several everyday domestic items: a record player, a telephone, a bread knife), she settles down for a nap in an easy chair, which allows her to look out a window and onto the sidewalk below. Once she falls asleep, this same routine is repeated in her dream state three times—with creative variation—suggesting how her subconscious is reflecting on and interpreting the psychological ramifications of this daily activity.

Once the woman enters her dream state, Deren exploits the conventions of continuity editing to undercut the apparent normalcy of the activities.[2] Each new cycle in the film's repetitive progression begins with an eyeline match of the woman looking out of her window to the image of herself below (fig. **6.64**). In other words, she sees herself running up the sidewalk after a mysterious, cloaked figure that resembles the Grim Reaper and which has "replaced" the anonymous male figure she saw at the beginning of the film (fig. **6.65**). At one point,

1 Notice how the last sentence of the introductory paragraph announces the main idea that the rest of the essay will prove. Everything else that follows this clearly demarcated thesis statement is subordinate to this main idea.

2 This sentence expresses the main idea of the paragraph—it functions much like a thesis statement for the rest of the paragraph. Such a sentence is called a "topic sentence." Topic sentences do not always have to be the first sentence of a paragraph; nor do they have to be limited to one sentence. But the strongest paragraphs will begin with a topic sentence or two. The reason why skimming an article or reviewing an assignment by reading the first sentence of each paragraph can be effective is that the most important ideas appear at the beginning.

6.64 The woman looks out of the window in *Meshes of the Afternoon*.

the woman enters the house and, in another eyeline match, sees two other images of herself gathered around a table.[3] The repeated use of eyeline matches to create the illusion that the woman is looking at herself emphasizes how detached and alienated she is from her own identity. In her dreams, she sees herself in the third person repeating her daily activities, as if her domestic identity is disembodied from other aspects of her personality.

More dramatically, Deren's use of collage reveals how the woman's dream reinterprets tokens of domesticity as ominous portents of death and destruction. At one point in the film, three apparitions of the woman gather around a table and take turns picking up the key to the house from the center of the table. When the third figure picks up the key and turns her hand over, the key rests in her outstretched palm (fig. **6.66**).

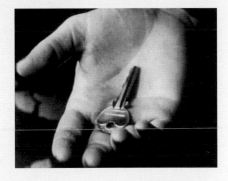

Deren then cuts to the same outstretched hand in the same position, but the palm holds a knife instead of the key (fig. **6.67**). The editing makes it appear as if the key, a quintessential image of domesticity since it connotes a shared personal space, magically transforms into the knife, an image of violence. This graphic match equates marriage with violence or destruction.[4]

This film's intimation of violence becomes much more explicit at this point, as the figure with the knife in her hand stands up from the table with the weapon drawn in attack mode. She approaches the reclining woman, and the film's use of eyeline match and point-of-view shots makes it clear that the standing woman is intent on stabbing her

6.65 The woman sees herself pursuing the shrouded figure in *Meshes of the Afternoon*.

3 Notice the overall structure of the paragraph up to this point. After the topic sentence, the author includes three descriptive sentences. This serves as the evidence for the paragraph's main claim as articulated in the topic sentence. What follows is analysis, which explains the logical link between this evidence and the main claim. This is a standard organizational pattern in academic writing: claim, evidence, analysis. Notice how the author's phrasing ("The repeated use of eyeline matches . . .") helps the reader connect the descriptive detail to the analysis.

6.66 The symbolic key in *Meshes of the Afternoon*.

6.67 A knife replaces the key in *Meshes of the Afternoon*.

4 Once again the paragraph begins with a claim and then offers evidence. Which sentence moves the essay from describing details from the film to offering analysis of those details? How does the author's wording emphasize the shift from description to analysis?

sleeping self-image. At this point, the editing's collage once again encourages viewers to associate domesticity with violence. One shot is a close-up profile of the reclining woman as the shiny knife blade slowly approaches her mouth. Deren then cuts to an extreme close-up of the reclining woman's eyes as they open in shock; the glare of the knife blade is reflected in her face. The editing here makes it clear that the sleeping woman is about to be stabbed by the image of herself. But then Deren cuts to an extreme close-up of a man's face (presumably the husband, played by Hamid) retreating from the camera, suggesting that the shot is the woman's point of view of her husband, who has awakened her with a kiss. More importantly, the sequence of shots draws a parallel between the imagined murder/suicide and the husband's tender kiss, once again associating domesticity with violence and destruction.

Some may be tempted to interpret the film as a depiction of domestic violence, but careful analysis of the imagery reveals that the film is really interested in the psychological trauma of marriage rather than physical abuse. After all, when the husband appears, he seems quite benevolent (carrying a flower, kissing the woman, tucking her into bed). Moreover, the figure that does appear threatening to the woman is herself. But Deren's use of an intentionally jolting collage of images transforms the couple's domesticated relationship and the husband's seemingly tender actions into harbingers of death. The suggestion is not that the woman in the film feels physically threatened by her husband, but that marriage itself has led to something just as terrifying: the loss of her identity.

Works Consulted

Bazin, André. "The Evolution of the Language of Cinema," in *Film Theory and Criticism*, ed. Gerald Mast *et al.*, 4th edn. New York: Oxford University Press, 1992, pp. 155–67.

Brandt, Michael. "Traditional Film Editing vs. Electronic Nonlinear Film Editing: A Comparison of Feature Films." *Nonlinear 4: The Website of Digital Video and Film Editing*. http://www.nonlinear4.com/brandt.htm. May 16, 2002.

Cellini, Joe. "An Interview with Walter Murch." http://www.apple.com/pro/film/murch/index.html. June 16, 2004.

Cook, David. *A History of Narrative Film*. New York: Norton, 1996.

Dobbs, Lem. Commentary track. *The Limey* (DVD), dir. Steven Soderbergh. Artisan, 1999.

Eisenstein, Sergei. "A Dialectic Approach to Film Form." *Film Form*. San Diego, New York, and London: Harcourt Brace Jovanovich, 1949, pp. 45–63.

Ellis, Jack C., and Virginia Wright Wexman. *A History of Film*, 5th edn. Boston: Allyn and Bacon, 2002.

Figes, Orlando. *A People's Tragedy*. New York: Viking, 1997.

Kenez, Peter. *Cinema and Soviet Society: From the Revolution to the Death of Stalin*. New York: I.B. Tauris, 2001.

Leyda, Jay. *Kino: A History of the Russian and Soviet Film*. Princeton: Princeton University Press, 1960.

Pudovkin, V.I. *Film Technique and Film Acting*. New York: Grove Press, 1970.

Ray, Robert. *A Certain Tendency of the Hollywood Cinema, 1930–1980*. Princeton: Princeton University Press, 1985.

Truffaut, François. *Hitchcock*, rev. edn. New York: Touchstone, 1993.

Tsivian, Yuri. "Dziga Vertov," in *The Oxford History of World Cinema*, ed. Geoffrey Nowell-Smith. Oxford and New York: Oxford University Press, 1996, pp. 92–3.

Chapter 7

Sound

Audiovisual analysis must rely on words, and so we must take words seriously . . . Why say "a sound" when we can say "crackling" or "rumbling" or "tremolo." Using more exact words allows us to confront and compare perceptions and to make progress in pinpointing and defining them.

Michael Chion

*I*n Terry Jones's comedic period film *Monty Python's Life of Brian* (1979), Roman soldiers pursue Brian, a woebegone sad sack trying to shrug off claims that he's a messiah. In an instant of poor judgement, Brian flees up a set of stairs, which dead-

7.1 Cody Jarrett in flames in *White Heat*.

ends at the top of a decrepit tower. Terrified, Brian falls from the top of the tower. As he plunges toward his seemingly inevitable death, he falls into the seat of a space ship, which is being pursued . . . by another space ship. The chase advances to outer space, and the squeal of tires on pavement rings out as the two ships round sharp "corners" in the celestial chase scene (fig. **7.2**).

This wildly anachronistic, hilarious episode points to how integral sound is to the construction of cinematic imagery. The scene parodies the way the sounds of grinding gears and tires hitting the blacktop are as important in an action sequence as the image of automobiles careening around corners. In this scene rubber does not literally touch asphalt, but Jones obliges—and ridicules—his audience's expectation that any good chase sequence will include the sound of roaring engines and squealing tires.

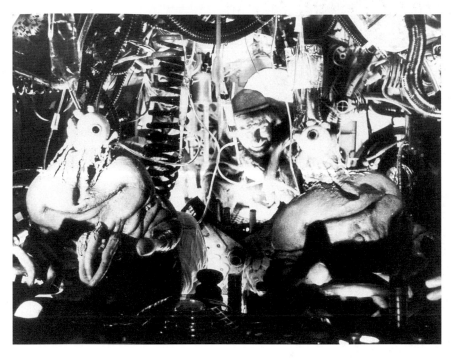

7.2 The comic space chase in *Monty Python's Life of Brian*.

The film also illustrates how sound in a film does not always correspond to what's happening onscreen. It is an expressive element of film capable of operating independently from images. Often filmmakers encourage intellectual and emotional responses by including sounds that do not logically or literally correspond to the image. In this particular scene, Jones encourages laughter by exploiting the discrepancy between what the audience sees and what the audience hears.

But not all sounds differ so dramatically from the image being shown; nor do they all stimulate laughter. What emotional response does George Lucas encourage with the sound associated with the light sabers in *Star Wars*? What sound in this context might have produced laughter?

Though many film critics and scholars focus most of their attention on the narrative and visual elements of films, this chapter emphasizes how sound is an evocative element in its own right. As the above example suggests, sound plays a critical role in determining how audiences react to images, and so this chapter stresses the importance of learning how to think, talk, and write about sound, using concrete, analytical language.

This chapter begins with a brief history of the use of sound in films, followed by a discussion of the technical aspects of the sound track, which is generally created completely independently from the visual image. Then there is an examination of the different relationships that a filmmaker can create between sound and image. The last section looks at the three components of film sound in terms of the way filmmakers manipulate the relationship between sound and image.

A film **soundtrack** is composed of three elements: dialogue, music, and sound effects. These components are recorded separately from the images and from one another. **Mixing** is the process of combining the three elements of film sound into one soundtrack, which is added to the image track in post-production. Although the early years of cinema (1896–1927) are referred to as the silent era, the next section explains that films have always depended upon the relationship between image and sound, which involves aesthetic principles, technological innovations, and commercial considerations.

● Film Sound: A Brief History

Contrary to popular assumption, movies were never "silent." In practice, a variety of sounds accompanied the exhibition of early films. When movie theaters emerged as sites of exhibition after 1908, live narration, organs, and sound effects machines accompanied most films. Eventually some big-budget films, such as *Birth of a Nation*, had their own **scores** (music specifically composed or arranged to accompany a film). More prosperous exhibitors could hire entire orchestras to transform screenings into elaborate gala events. From the earliest days of the cinema, then, movies provided audiences with the three elements of film sound: dialogue, sound effects, and music.

The idea of combining pre-recorded sound that could be synchronized with images motivated many early experiments with sound, but the process of developing a workable system for doing so spanned several decades.

An early system capable of synchronizing sound and image was Vitaphone's sound on disc system, where sound was recorded and played on separate discs. But it wasn't until 1927 that a group of exhibitors (Loew's, Universal, First National, Paramount, and Producers Distributing Corporation) signed the "Big Five Agreement," which stated that the signatories would jointly agree to adopt the single film sound system that they decided was the best one for the industry. Realizing that the introduction of several incompatible film sound systems would limit distribution and, ultimately, studio profits, they wanted to ensure technological standardization (Gomery, p. 13). As a result, by 1929, nearly 75% of Hollywood films included pre-recorded sound (Cook, p. 249).

By 1930 sound-on-film systems replaced sound on disc. Sound-on-film systems were based on the conversion of sound to electronic signals that were recorded as light impulses on film stock. These optical soundtracks appear as wavy lines along the edge of the film print. The sound information is read by a photoelectric cell on the projector as light from an exciter lamp passes through the soundtrack.

Film historians do not necessarily herald the shift from silent to sound filmmaking as an unqualified step forward for the art. The need to record dialogue on the set affected the mobility of the camera, which, in turn, had an impact on film style. Motion picture cameras had to be encased in soundproof booths so that microphones did not record the sound of their motors (fig. **7.3**). But, in the booth, the camera could pan only about 30 degrees to the right or left (Salt, p. 38). Marsha Kinder and Beverle Houston write, "the three elements that had been so crucial to the artistic development of the silent cinema—visual composition, camera movement, and editing—were severely restricted" (Kinder and Houston, p. 52). For these reasons, "talkies seemed bare and clumsy by comparison with the dazzling inventions of the late silent cinema" (Bordwell, p. 37). In the early 1930s, studios devised techniques for "blimping" cameras to allow for more extensive movement.

The high costs of conversion to sound film hit independent producers particularly hard because it became more difficult to compete with better-financed, vertically integrated studios. Whereas African-American producers George and Noble Johnson of the Lincoln Motion Picture Company had lost their struggle to maintain their independence from Hollywood by the mid-1920s, Oscar Micheaux managed to continue making films into the 1930s and 1940s. Due in part to the cost of sound technology, Micheaux declared bankruptcy in 1928 but re-emerged with new investors in 1931 to make his first sound film. Jesse Algernon Rhines describes the sound films of Micheaux as "a miracle of entrepreneurial determination" although "they were not successful competitors with white productions even for an African American audience" (Rhines, p. 31).

In the late 1930s, the practice of re-recording, or post-synchronization, freed sound films from the idea that "everything seen on the screen must be heard on the soundtrack" (Cook, p. 271). The practice of re-recording allowed filmmakers to manipulate sound and to experiment with the relation of sound to image. Now almost all commercial films, even those whose aim is a realistic depiction of conversation, use dialogue recorded in postproduction. The freedom engendered by post-synchronization has allowed filmmakers to transform film sound into a vital component of cinematic expression, completely independent of, and at times more weighty than, a film's visual information.

7.3 A camera in a soundproof booth.

Repeatedly, advances in film sound technology have promised greater fidelity and a heightened sense of audio realism. In the 1950s (with the advent of magnetic tape recording), films began featuring multichannel soundtracks, which allowed filmmakers to add layers of sounds. Dolby and wireless eight-track recording contributed to the complex sound mixes of the Hollywood Renaissance filmmakers of the early 1970s. Multi-track recording and Dolby noise reduction produced sound with better definition and individuation, permitting a greater degree of detail. When *Star Wars*—one of the first major releases in Dolby—was in theaters, Dolby-equipped theaters earned more box office revenue than non-Dolby theaters (Shreger,

Film Sound: A Brief History

p. 353). As a result, the industry responded: at the beginning of 1978 there were 700 Dolby-equipped theaters, but during that year the number grew at a rate of 500 per month (Shreger, p. 354). More recently filmmakers have shifted to digital sound reproduction in the form of THX, Dolby Digital, and DTS systems. This latest sound revolution extended to include products for the home viewing market: the Digital Video Disc (DVD) and the home theater, complete with sophisticated surround sound system.

Audiences' attraction to the recent proliferation of digital sound systems, which promise increased fidelity and more realistic sound, suggests a lingering, common misperception: that film sound should replicate the sounds one would experience in "real life." But film sound is an expressive element, as carefully composed as the image. Film sounds do not reproduce reality—they provide an aesthetic experience, in conjunction with the images onscreen.

● Freeing Sound From Image

Sound effects (any noise that forms part of the film soundtrack, apart from dialogue and music) are seldom recordings of the actual events the audience is being shown. Otherwise Hollywood would leave an awful lot of corpses in its wake, given the popularity of gunfights in films! Instead, **Foley artists** produce many of a film's sound effects by creatively manipulating various materials (fig. **7.4**) (The position was named for Jack Foley, who created the first sound effects studio in the 1950s.) For the nautical thriller *The Hunt for Red October* (John McTiernan 1990), sound designer Frank Serafine recorded himself playing in a friend's pool: "I'd swim around for the torpedo . . . I created propellers by doing a cannonball dive into the water—*scroooom*" (LoBrutto, p. 224). In *Rush* (Lili Fini Zanuck 1991), the sound effect of a striking match was created when Gary Rydstrom unclogged the nozzle of a can of compressed air: "It made this great explosive air release, which to me sounded like a very big match flare up" (LoBrutto, p. 229). Even the sound of footsteps in film isn't "real." In fact, the most common manufactured sound effect in films is walking, which is why Foley artists are often called "Foley walkers" (Cook, p. 966).

Comparing the sound of punches in *Rocky*, *Raging Bull*, and *Fight Club* illustrates how filmmakers conceive of sound differently, even when the effects are linked to the same visual event. These sound effects do not recreate the noise

7.4 Foley artists at work.

Sound Recording and Dubbing in Production and Post-production

The sound designer plans the sound for a film and oversees the entire recording process.

During the production phase of filming, a boom operator extends the microphone at the end of a long pole, or boom, to record dialogue on the set. The cable person manages the equipment. The location sound mixer, or production sound mixer, controls the recording and mixing during the shoot.

During post-production, Foley artists and effects editors experiment with making and recording sound effects. The ADR supervisor re-records flawed or inadequate lines of dialogue. Meanwhile, the film's music supervisor determines how much prerecorded and original music the film will be able to include. The composer or arranger scores the film, often watching dailies for inspiration. When the score is complete, the composer works with the music editor to record the score. Together they determine when the music should enter the soundtrack, and when it should leave. The re-recording mixer combines and mixes all three elements of the film's soundtrack. The supervising sound editor supervises the entire process of editing the soundtrack, making sure that the dialogue, sound effects, and music are synchronized with the images.

of punches that one would actually hear at a boxing match or a street fight. Instead, the filmmakers choose the sound effect for the emotional effect it will have on the audience. Even when sound effects are recorded on location (called **direct sound**), they are remixed and remastered in post-production so that they achieve the desired result.

The human voice is similarly prone to post production manipulation. While a scene containing dialogue is usually recorded by the camera and sound equipment, if a technical glitch or inappropriate inflection mars the delivery of a particular line, that line can be replaced during post-production using a process called **ADR**, or automatic dialogue replacement. During this process, sometimes called **looping**, actors re-read their lines as they watch footage of the scene that needs to be reworked. In fact, the voice that audiences hear is not necessarily that of the actor who appears to be speaking onscreen. While James Prowse plays Darth Vader onscreen in *Star Wars*, audiences hear the voice of James Earl Jones whenever Vader speaks.

Finally, the third component of the soundtrack—music—is often quite obviously freed from the image. In fact, much film music is non-diegetic, or played outside the world the characters inhabit. Even when songs are part of the diegesis, as in musicals where characters break out into song and dance routines, audiences hear separately recorded orchestrations that transcend the limitations imposed by the mechanics of film production. Professional singers often perform the musical numbers instead of the stars onscreen (whose voices may prove inadequate), a fact that Stanley Donen's *Singin' in the Rain* (1952) and Julie Dash's *Illusions* (1982) use as an element of the plot.

In post-production, the sound characteristics of dialogue, music, and sound effects can be altered to achieve specific effects. Because filmmakers have the ability to select and manipulate every sound on the soundtrack, audiences should be as attentive to what they hear as they are to what they see, and consider how it contributes to the overall aesthetic impact of the film.

● The Relationship Between Sound and Image

Filmmakers often take advantage of the fact that sound and image are recorded separately. Whenever filmmakers construct a soundtrack, they must consider what audiences will hear at any given time and whether dialogue, music, or sound effects gets the most emphasis. Because dialogue conveys so much information, speech gets the most emphasis in most mainstream films. Rarely do sound effects or music overwhelm the dialogue. At the end of the gangster film *White Heat* (Raoul Walsh 1949), Cody Jarrett (James Cagney) can clearly be heard saying, "Top of the world, Ma!" even while a chemical plant explodes and burns around him (fig. **7.1**, p. 202). The sound is clearly calibrated to prioritize his dialogue.

Of course, some filmmakers have experimented with intentionally obscuring pivotal lines of dialogue. In Hitchcock's *Rear Window*, L.B. Jeffries (James Stewart) spies on his neighbors while he spends his days stuck in his apartment, recuperating from a broken leg. While his neighbors often appear onscreen talking (or arguing), much of their dialogue is inaudible; audiences can hear their voices, but cannot understand their words. Hitchcock's use of sound demands that the audience share Jeffries's perspective. The audience can only speculate about what the other characters are saying, based on their tone of voice and their body movements.

In Woody Allen's comedy *Bananas* (1971), two thugs assault Fielding Mellish (Allen) in a subway car. In an unusual move, Allen does not include any dialogue or sound effects on the soundtrack, only non-diegetic music. Audiences hear a type of music reminiscent of silent movie era slapstick. The inclusion of such music rather than the thugs' threatening words or the sound of the subway's roar through the tunnel tells the audience to read the scene as comic instead of tragic or exciting.

These two examples illustrate how filmmakers carefully choose which sounds to include on the soundtrack, knowing that emphasizing a particular sound helps to shape the audience's perspective and to determine the emotional dynamics of a scene.

In addition to selecting what sounds an audience will hear, filmmakers also consider how these sounds will correspond to the imagery. Usually the soundtrack will offer an acoustic equivalent to the visual effect on the screen. For example, when the massive ship hits the iceberg in *Titanic*, the soundtrack conveys the sound of ice wrenching and tearing the ship's steel hull.

But there are five ways that sound may differ from the imagery onscreen. Filmmakers can choose to create contrasts between:

- onscreen space and **offscreen space**
- objective images and subjective sound

- diegetic details and non-diegetic sound
- image time and sound time
- image mood and sound mood.

Emphasizing the Contrast between Onscreen and Offscreen Space

Sound is a powerful tool for helping filmmakers create the illusion that the world of the story extends beyond the boundaries of the frame. Sound often points to action that happens offscreen—details that are unseen, but which are important factors shaping the storyline. After Marion Crane checks into her room at the Bates Motel in *Psycho*, she hears Mrs. Bates berating Norman (fig. **7.5**). While the audience never sees their argument, the soundtrack clarifies that mother and son are carrying out their squabble in the dark, gothic mansion on top of the hill. The fact that Mother's voice bleeds into Marion's room also reaffirms what the *mise en scène* has already suggested: that the eerie house and its inhabitant (Mother) pervade the hotel below. Crucially, audiences don't see Mother yelling at Norman; it's not the images that suggest her dominance, but sound emanating from offscreen space.

7.5 Marion hears an argument taking place offscreen at the window in *Psycho*.

Emphasizing the Difference between Objective Images and Subjective Sounds

Sound gives audiences access to what a character is thinking, even while the images continue to show what the character is doing or experiencing at an objective level. Sound can depict a character's subjectivity without the need to dissolve to a fantasy or flashback sequence. In *Psycho*, as Marion flees Phoenix with the $40,000 she has stolen, she imagines what others are saying about her mysterious disappearance. Onscreen, Marion continues to drive her car, nervously but cautiously. But audiences hear, via the use of a voice-over, the voices she imagines, primarily those of her boss and the client from whom she's stolen. These voices do not exist in the external, objective world of the film. This use of sound to indicate character subjectivity is a motif running throughout the film, which suggests an important parallelism between Norman and Marion. Audiences ultimately recognize that both characters act out their guilt in their minds.

Emphasizing the Difference between Diegetic Details and Non-diegetic Sound

Sound and image can differ in terms of their relationship to the story world. Using the terminology set out in Chapter Three, anything that the characters involved in the story can experience can be called diegetic sound, while anything outside the story space can be referred to as non-diegetic sound. By far the most common non-diegetic sound is music, but non-diegetic sound also includes, for example, sound effects that don't actually occur within the diegesis. In *Requiem for a Dream*, for example, a variety of sound effects simulate the experience of using drugs. In one montage sequence, the sound of a plane flying overhead accompanies fragmented images depicting the process of shooting heroin. While voice-overs are usually diegetic—examples include Martin Scorsese's *Goodfellas* and Sam Mendes' *American Beauty*—some films include a voice-over narration that is non-diegetic: that is, someone from outside the world of the story delivers the voice-over, as in *A.I.* (Steven Spielberg 2001) or *The Royal Tenenbaums*.

Non-diegetic sounds generally function as a form of direct address, wherein the filmmaker offers explicit commentary on the image. By noticing whether or not sounds are diegetic or non-diegetic, therefore, audiences can determine the degree to which the filmmaker is directly addressing them. In *Grosse Pointe Blank* (George Armitage 1997), when hired hit man Martin Q. Blank (John Cusack) goes to his high school reunion, he discovers that a cookie-cutter convenience store has been built where his parents' house used to stand. When he first realizes that his house is gone, audiences hear the chorus to the rock song "Live and Let Die" and recognize its dog-eat-dog philosophy. The music is non-diegetic: no visual cues indicate that Blank is listening to the song on a radio. His facial expression upon seeing the store registers his shock, however, and the music's lyrics and chords underscore his feelings of anger, cynicism, and dismay.

Diegetic sounds, on the other hand, help define an environment whose traits the characters must recognize to some degree. In the same film, when Blank enters the store, a silly muzak version of the same song plays over the tinny store speakers. This diegetic music helps to define the character of a store that has replaced a distinctive dwelling (Blank's home) with a bland, commercial setting and an array of cheap junk food.

Often diegetic music reveals character traits. When a character plays a song on a jukebox or listens to music on the radio, that music is an outward symbol of her taste or emotional state at a given point in time. In *Grosse Pointe Blank*, Blank's former girlfriend Debi Newberry (Minnie Driver), whom he jilted in high school, now works as a radio DJ. Throughout the film, she plays pop music from the 1980s in honor of the upcoming high school reunion—and nostalgically reminisces about her high school lover.

Emphasizing the Difference between Image Time and Sound Time

Combining sound and image allows filmmakers to present two different points in time simultaneously, as when a voice-over narration describes past events. In *Double Indemnity* (Billy Wilder 1944), the voice of Walter Neff (Fred MacMurray), speaking from the present, explains the visual images and actions of Neff's past. In *The Princess Bride* (Rob Reiner 1987), a grandfather (Peter Falk) narrates a story to his young grandson (Fred Savage). Falk's voice-over narration reminds viewers that the world onscreen is a fantasy, lovingly concocted by the interaction between the author, the storyteller, and the boy.

Discrepancies in time that are signaled by sound and image also occur during transitions between scenes. On occasion, the dominant sound at the end of one scene will carry over into the next scene, forming the aural equivalent of a dissolve called a **sound bridge**. Alternatively, some scenes end with the gradual emergence of the next scene's dominant sound. Such moments suggest the powerful aura of an event, as the sound acts as a reminder of its lingering presence or anticipates an event's arrival. In *Medium Cool* (Haskell Wexler 1969), TV cameraman John (Robert Forster) takes nurse Ruth (Marianna Hill) to the roller derby on a date. As they watch the competitors skate and beat one another, the crowd chants "kill her," and "hit her in the back." When the scene fades to the next, the crowd continues to chant, even while John and Eileen make love in his apartment. The lingering sounds of the crowd's demand for violence emphasize the cultural turbulence and sexual tension that serve as the backdrop for the couple's romance.

Emphasizing Differences in Image Mood and Sound Mood

Finally, combining sound and image can produce a jolting contrast on an emotional level. While typically the soundtrack corresponds to the action and accentuates the mood evoked by visual details, sometimes filmmakers will pair an image with a sound that seems wildly inappropriate, producing a noticeable tension between aural and visual information. Such disjunctures can occur within the diegesis, as when Alex (Malcolm McDowell) sings "Singing In the Rain" while he rapes Mrs. Alexander in *A Clockwork Orange*, or when Jules (Samuel L. Jackson) talks about fast food before he assassinates a man in *Pulp Fiction* (Quentin Tarantino 1994). In both cases, the conflict between comic or absurd sound and a disturbingly violent image suggests the perpetrator's indifference to his victim's plight.

Filmmakers may also choose non-diegetic sounds to work against the imagery. The result may be irony, as in the conclusion of *Dr. Strangelove*, when the soundtrack plays "We'll Meet Again," to images of nuclear annihilation. Told that a Doomsday device has destroyed the world, audiences must realize there is no possibility of what the song's lyrics promise: that two lovers will be able to meet again. The irony is a fitting conclusion to the film's repeated suggestion that the nuclear arms race is one expression of aggressive masculine sexuality.

Filmmakers can and do exploit all five variants of the relationship between sound and image. Sometimes the most creative use of film sound goes beyond simply trying to mirror the images onscreen or clarifying narrative events; the most profound examples of film sound often exploit the soundtrack's ability to add intellectual or emotional depth to the visual image. To develop valid interpretations of a film, viewers must be able first to define the relationship between sound and image and then describe its effect on the film's meaning.

● Three Components of Film Sound

In narrative films, the words a screenwriter gives to his characters, the music they listen to, and the sounds in their environment all convey a wealth of information.

Dialogue

Dialogue forwards the narrative, giving voice to characters' aspirations, thoughts and emotions, often making conflicts among characters evident in the process.

Text and Subtext

The primary function of spoken dialogue is to externalize a character's thoughts and feelings, bringing motivations, goals, plans, and conflicts to the surface. Screenwriters are careful to avoid dialogue that reiterates information already made clear by the image. Clunky dialogue that states the obvious is called **on-the-nose dialogue**.

The most effective dialogue works on several levels to suggest character motivations, even when characters are not fully aware of those feelings themselves. Dialogue makes meaning through the **text** (the words a characters says), the **line reading** (the way an actor says the line, including pauses, intonation, and emotion), and the **subtext** (the unstated meaning that underlies spoken words).

Dialogue often works in a roundabout fashion and depends upon audiences to discern the subtext (what isn't stated directly) which eloquently reveals a character's complexity. In the character drama *In the Bedroom* (2000), written by Rob Festinger and Todd Field, Ruth Fowler (Sissy Spacek) grieves over the death of her son Frank, who was shot by his girlfriend's estranged husband. In a brief scene where Ruth talks with her priest, the two characters communicate through both text and subtext. At the textual level, Father Oberti (Jonathan Walsh)—renamed Father McCasslin in the film—reminds Ruth that she isn't the only woman to have lost a child and Ruth asks questions about another grieving mother:

> FATHER OBERTI
> Louise McVey lost a child a few years back. Maybe you remember.
>
> RUTH
> *(searching)*
> Mmm she had four—it was the youngest girl, wasn't it?
>
> FATHER OBERTI
> Yes. She told me about a vision she had when she found out her daughter had died . . . she saw herself at a great distance from the earth—and encircling it, an endless line—as she got closer she saw that it was made up of mothers—traveling forward.[. . .] She said she knew—that all the millions of women on her side—were the mothers who had lost children . . . she seemed to find great comfort in that.
>
> *Ruth doesn't react*

RUTH

How did she die?

FATHER OBERTI

A drowning—some kind of swimming accident.

RUTH

Oh.

(Festinger and Field, pp. 61–2)

At the subtextual level, Ruth's questions defy the priest's attempt at consolation. By reminding him that the other mother had four children and asking "How did she die?", Ruth refuses to equate her loss with that of Louise McVey. Frank was an only child, killed in a violent encounter. Ruth believes that his tragic death sets her apart from everyone else, although she never states this belief directly. By refusing to compare Frank's death with that of the McVey girl, Ruth also rejects any association with Louise McVey, a woman who is comforted by the realization that she is not alone. Without using words, Ruth powerfully asserts her commitment to her solitary suffering.

Dialogue plays an important role in establishing character. It can also be used to emphasize setting, or a character's cultural background. It can define a character's relationship to others in terms of age, authority, or class. It can also reveal a character's level of education, or portray the level of a character's emotional and intellectual engagement with the story events. Finally, the voice can define a character's environment, and his relationship to that environment.

Dialogue vs. Voice: The Emotive Power of the Human Voice

Although the dominant sound in most narrative films is that of the human voice, most viewers don't consider in specific terms what it is that allows the voice to convey so much information so quickly. Listening to dialogue involves more than noting what words are spoken. Characters in books "speak" as well—but films allow audiences actually to *hear* qualities of speech, making the experience far more dynamic than that of reading words printed on the page.

The suggestive power of the human voice is so persuasive that often it contradicts and outweighs the literal meaning of words in and of themselves. In *Citizen Kane*, Mary Kane says that she has had her son Charles's "trunk all packed for a week." Read literally, her words might suggest that she's indifferent (or even excited) about his impending departure. But Agnes Moorehead's soft, slightly distracted delivery of the lines and the fact that her voice "breaks" when she calls out her son's name, tell the audience what her words do not: she's heartbroken.

The human voice has four sonic attributes that invest words with emotional and intellectual depth: volume, pitch, vocal characteristics, and acoustic qualities. Each of these is examined below, along with one particular use of the voice that deserves special attention: the voice-over.

Volume

It almost goes without saying that volume reflects the level and the type of a person's engagement with her surroundings. Generally, the louder a person speaks, the greater the emotional intensity of her words. Sigourney Weaver's vocal performance as Ripley in *Alien* is restrained. Through much of the film, she delivers her lines softly, conveying her calm, rational demeanor. After the alien has killed the captain, leaving Ripley in charge, she meets with the remaining crew members to decide what they should do. Tempers flare, and for the first time in the film, Ripley raises her voice to command the others' attention. Once her authority is established and the others calm down, Ripley lowers her voice again, conveying her methodical, carefully considered approach to solving the crew's dilemma. Only after the remainder of her crew is killed and she fails to stop the ship's self-destruct sequence does Ripley scream out in frustration, implying a momentary lapse in confidence and resolve.

Volume suggests the emotional vigor of dialogue. Loudness usually connotes a character experiencing intense emotion, such as anger, fear, or passion. Softness, on the other hand, usually connotes a more timid or carefully considered emotional response: tenderness, diffidence, sophistication, fear, or even guile.

Pitch

A sound's pitch refers to its frequency, or its position on a musical scale. In music, the lowest (or deepest) pitch is bass, and the highest pitch is soprano. While one immediately thinks of pitch as being a musical term, it can also be used to evaluate the quality of the speaking voice.

Typically, audiences associate deep voices (basses or baritones) with power or authority. Inspector Vargas (Charlton Heston) in *Touch of Evil*, Sean Connery's James Bond, and Marsellus Wallace (Ving Rhames) in *Pulp Fiction* are all characters whose deep voices convey dignity, restraint, and authority. However, deep voices can also be associated with evil or duplicity, such as the killer's menacing (and electronically altered) voice in the *Scream* series (Wes Craven 1996, 1997, 2000).

Characters with high-pitched voices, on the other hand, are often associated with weakness or indecisiveness. Consider how the difference between Charles Foster Kane's booming voice and Susan Alexander's piercing voice helps to define the nature of their relationship: Kane treats Susan like a little girl. Furthermore, Emily Kane's lower pitched voice emphasizes the age and class differences between Kane's wives. In *Bonnie and Clyde*, Blanche Barrow (Estelle Parsons) spends much of the film shrieking in an undecipherable, shrill voice, which helps to convey her fear of the outlaw existence and her lack of commitment to the group. Bonnie, meanwhile, speaks in a lower pitch, conveying her self-confidence and honor.

Speech characteristics

The way a character speaks does more to define her individual persona than perhaps any other characteristic of the human voice. Her cultural background, her class, her interests, her aspirations, and even her limitations can all be revealed by subtle qualities of the voice such as accent, diction, and vocal tics.

Accent and Dialect A character's accent is a powerful indicator of background and social status. Through language, audiences readily recognize a character's nationality, for example. Meryl Streep has earned a reputation for her ability to adopt the accent of her characters, and the national identities of her broad array of roles include Italian American (*The Bridges of Madison County* [Clint Eastwood 1995]), Irish (*Dancing at Lughnasa* [Pat O'Connor 1998]), Polish (*Sophie's Choice* [Alan J. Pakula 1982]), and Danish (*Out of Africa* [Sydney Pollack 1985]). Some audiences may not initially recognize that, in *Dr. Strangelove*, Peter Sellers plays three different roles: Mandrake, a British officer; Muffley, the American president; and the German scientist Dr. Strangelove. Sellers's stellar performance in the film relies on his ability to adopt three distinct accents so flawlessly. Actors train with dialect coaches to perfect their pronunciation. For his role as Viktor Navorski in Steven Spielberg's *The Terminal* (2004), Tom Hanks and his coach chose Bulgarian as the root language for the fictional country of Kracozhia. Hanks practiced for several months, perfecting the sounds a speaker of a Slavic language would make when speaking English.

But a character's accent usually contributes more to a film's storyline than just indicating where a person was raised. Often this background information plays a crucial role in helping audiences to understand a character's motivations or in helping a film explore broader themes. In British films, especially those about the effects of class-bound culture, such as *The Loneliness of the Long Distance Runner* (Tony Richardson 1962), *This Sporting Life* (Lindsay Anderson 1963), and *Sleuth* (Joseph L. Mankiewicz 1972), cockney accents are an immediate mark of the urban working class and a symbol of the characters' social and economic entrapment. In Wong Kar-Wai's *Chungking Express* ("*Chongqing Senlin*"; 1994), a lonely, heart-broken Cop 223 in Hong Kong tries desperately to start a conversation with a stranger in a bar. When she doesn't respond to his pick-up line, he repeats the same phrase in several different dialects, drawing attention to Hong Kong's multi-cultural makeup, which Cop 223 must negotiate if he is to establish an emotional connection.

American films frequently use accents to define characters according to regional background. In the fish-out-of-water comedy *My Cousin Vinny* (Jonathan Lynn 1992), a fledgling Brooklyn lawyer (Joe Pesci) comes to Wahzoo City, Alabama, to get his cousin out of jail. The film's humor frequently derives from the southern characters' inability to understand Pesci's thick Brooklyn accent. In *Three Kings*, a rural Southern accent distinguishes Conrad Vigs (Spike Jonz) from the other soldiers in his unit, who are urban Northerners. The film frequently associates Vigs's accent with his lack of intelligence and poor upbringing (thus perpetuating a common Southern stereotype).

Diction A character's diction—his choice of words—can also reveal his economic status or level of education. Consider how the foul language that spills out of the mouths of the thugs in Quentin Tarantino's *Reservoir Dogs* or *Pulp Fiction* distinguishes

7.6 Michael tries to make himself understood through actions, not words, in *The Deer Hunter*.

them from the more elite and sophisticated criminals (who rarely curse), such as Auric Goldfinger in *Goldfinger* (Guy Hamilton 1964) or Thomas Crown in *The Thomas Crown Affair* (Norman Jewison 1968; John McTiernan 1999).

A character's inability to find the right words can also speak volumes. In Michael Cimino's Vietnam War epic *The Deer Hunter* (1978), a group of friends—all of them steelworkers in industrial Pennsylvania—go on one last hunting trip together before going off to war. When the careless Stanley (John Cazale) forgets his boots, the leader of the group, Michael (Robert De Niro), reprimands him for his irresponsibility. But words fail Michael as he tries to explain to Stanley the importance of responsibility (fig. **7.6**). The only way he can impart his knowledge to Stanley is to hold up a bullet and say, "Stanley, see this? This is this. This ain't something else. This is this. From now on, you're on your own." Michael is unable to articulate his code of honor, which dictates that men have to take care of themselves. For him, actions are more important than words.

In *Rushmore* (Wes Anderson 1998), tenth-grader Max Fischer (Jason Schwartzman) tries to rise above his blue-collar background by becoming the renaissance man of his private academy. Max's diction clearly separates him from his peers, as he tends to speak in formal, seemingly erudite phrases, although the occasional misuse of words points to his limitations. Early in the film Max meets with his best friend's mother. When she thanks Max for taking care of her son, Max replies, "Dirk's a great kid, and I'm just trying to impart some of the experiences I've accrued to help him." Max's elaborate language here clearly implies that he sees himself on the same level as his elder. He too is a parental figure, more mature than his peers in school.

Vocal tics Finally, the human voice can be characterized by vocal tics particular to specific individuals. Marilyn Monroe, for example, is famous for her high, breathy voice, which audiences have associated with sensual fragility. In contrast, Katharine Hepburn in films such as *Holiday* (George Cukor 1938), *The African Queen* (John Huston 1951), *Rooster Cogburn* (Stuart Millar 1975), and *On Golden Pond* (Mark Rydell 1981) has a gravelly, quavering voice that helps to connote her characters' independence and strength.

Jimmy Stewart's voice is recognizable for its slow drawl, and its propensity to get higher in pitch as his characters become agitated. Stewart's unique voice complements his tendency to play characters notable for their humility and honor, as in *Mr. Smith Goes to Washington* (Frank Capra 1939), in which Stewart is an idealistic but naïve politician who combats corruption when he arrives in Washington. The contrast between Stewart's "aw-shucks" delivery and Grace Kelly's more crisp and refined voice helps suggest the class differences that divide the couple when they appear together in *Rear Window*.

In contrast, Humphrey Bogart tends to speak through his teeth and pursed lips without much modulation in his voice, contributing to the macho image he projects in films such as *The Maltese Falcon*, *Casablanca* (Michael Curtiz 1942), *Treasure of Sierra Madre* (John Huston 1948), and *The African Queen*.

Some actors' voices are immediately recognizable for their rhythm. Jack Nicholson (*The Shining* [Stanley Kubrick 1980], *Batman* [Tim Burton 1989]) and Owen Wilson (*Meet the Parents* [Jay Roach 2000], *The Royal Tenenbaums*) speak in slow, fluid phrases. The carefully paced rhythm of their delivery often suggests quirkiness or lackadaisical menace. In contrast, Woody Allen (*Manhattan* [Woody Allen 1979]) and Ben Stiller (*Meet the Parents*, *The Royal Tenenbaums*) speak in quick bursts, suggesting their characters' hysterical anxiety. Bette Davis (*Jezebel* [William Wyler 1938], *Whatever Happened to Baby Jane?* [Robert Aldrich 1962]) is noted for the staccato or percussive quality of her voice, which often conveys overwrought emotions or maniacal hostility. Julia Roberts (*Mystic Pizza* [Donald Petrie 1988], *Erin Brockovich* [Steven Soderbergh 2000]) is famous for a boisterous laugh that suggests her characters' self-confident love of life.

Acoustic Qualities

Manipulating the acoustic quality of the human voice can help filmmakers convey perspective and details about the surrounding environment. The way voices sound can suggest the distance between characters, or the mood, aura, or atmosphere of a place—its ambience. The quality of a sound's movement through a particular space—what might be called a sound's acoustic properties can help determine whether that space feels cozy and intimate, or sterile and alienating.

Sound engineers can toy with the acoustic qualities of voices by adjusting microphones (for example, placing microphones away from an actress to suggest distance), and by making adjustments during mixing after the primary shooting is completed. At this point, the sound editor can freely manipulate the volume, balance (the relative volume coming from each speaker), and other acoustic properties of each sound, including the dialogue. When mixing the sound, the sound editor may add reverb (an echo) to the voices in a scene. This effect usually encourages audiences to imagine that the setting is expansive, and that the sounds are reverberating from distant walls.

In *The Conversation*, Harry Caul (Gene Hackman) and Meredith (Elizabeth McRae) retreat from a group of revelers to have a one-on-one conversation. They wander into the middle of Caul's mammoth workshop—a large, vacant warehouse. At first Caul is unable to overcome his reclusive tendencies, and he responds to Meredith's questions perfunctorily. The camera films them in a long shot. Their voices echo, emphasizing the vast emptiness of the setting and the loneliness of Caul's self-imposed isolation. Soon Caul begins to open up to Meredith, and the scene cuts to a series of medium close-up tracking shots. As the scene becomes more intimate, sound engineer Walter Murch reduces the reverberation considerably, using the acoustic qualities of their voices to draw attention to the couple's temporary sense of physical and emotional closeness. When drunken revelers interrupt their conversation by revving a motor scooter, the scene cuts to a rapid reverse

7.7 Inside the coffin in *The Vanishing* ("*Spoorloos*").

tracking shot that ends on an extreme long shot of the couple and the circling scooter, suggesting the sudden loss of intimacy.

Conversely, a sound editor may also dampen (or muffle) vocal reverberation and remove other background, or ambient, noises to imply a tightly enclosed space, to evoke intimacy or create a claustrophobic ambience, as in George Sluizer's *The Vanishing* ("*Spoorloos*"; 1988). At the climax of the film, Raymond Lemorne (Bernard-Pierre Donnadieu) finds himself trapped in an extremely confined space—a coffin (fig. **7.7**). Sound editor Piotr van Dijk completely removes any reverberation and amplifies the character's breathing. Complementing the scene's tight framing, the soundtrack emphasizes Lemorne's entrapment.

Through the mixing process, sound editors are able to conjure a broad array of audio illusions. By manipulating the acoustic characteristics of voices, a sound editor can create the effect of a character speaking from across a great distance, on the telephone, broadcasting via radio, speaking from behind a wall, and so on.

Addressing the Audience: the Voice-Over

Because of its ability to encourage audience identification with characters onscreen, the voice-over deserves special attention. Diegetic voice-overs may function as a character's meditation on past events, as in Billy Wilder's *Sunset Boulevard*. Wilder's film begins with a third-person discussion about a corpse floating in a swimming pool. The film then launches into a flashback, at which point the voice-over switches to Joe Gillis's first-person account of the series of events that led to his own murder. Gillis's voice-over focuses the audience on Gillis as the point of identification during the flashback. Only at the film's conclusion does the audience realize that he is the corpse. The film demonstrates how voice-overs can guide viewers through a series of events they might not otherwise understand. Interestingly, the voice-over contributes to the audience's surprise upon realizing that the main character dies. Because Gillis speaks in third person during the exposition, he directs the audience's attention away from himself as the corpse.

Voice-overs can also allow audiences access to a character's immediate thoughts, as in *Mean Streets*, when audiences hear Charlie (Harvey Keitel) praying in several voice-overs throughout the film. Again, such voice-overs allow audiences to experience a more profound level of engagement with that character. And voice-overs in the present tense grant access to the character's immediate thoughts, feelings, and perspective.

The famous post-production history of *Blade Runner* offers a telling example of how profoundly a voice-over can affect audience identification. The science-fiction film is about a former cop, Deckard (Harrison Ford), living in Los Angeles in 2019, who is hired to find and destroy four androids roaming the streets of the city. When the film was originally screened for test audiences, it contained no voice-over. Audiences were confused, and they found Ford's character inscrutable and unlikeable. The studio added a voice-over narration (and a happy ending) before releasing the film to the general public.

The difference between the two versions of the film is striking. Both versions are now available on VHS and DVD, offering fans the opportunity to compare the two different effects. The director's cut does not have a voice-over. By refusing access to Deckard's thoughts and feelings, this version invites the audience to question whether or not this apparently unfeeling character is actually an android. The inscrutability (to which audiences reacted negatively) is entirely appropriate. The theatrical release, on the other hand, underscores the humanity of the character, tracing his spiritual transformation as he slowly begins to sympathize with the androids he is pursuing. The addition of the voice-over encourages close identification with the character because the audience is privy to his thoughts and emotions.

Some filmmakers upset the audience's expectation that a voice-over will offer a stable point of identification. Terrence Malick's films, for example, tend to emphasize that the voice-over narration may not offer the most accurate or perceptive account of the events onscreen. In *Badlands* (1974), Kit (Martin Sheen) and Holly (Sissy Spacek) go on a killing spree across the American Midwest. The film is narrated by Holly after her arrest, and her delivery of the lines is detached and riddled with romantic clichés. Their killing spree begins when Kit kills Holly's father. Holly expresses no real regret over her father's death. Instead, she tells the audience in a deadpan, affectless voice how she "sensed that her destiny now lay with Kit, for better or worse, and that it was better to spend a week with someone who loved [her] for what [she] was than years of loneliness." Rather than understanding and regretting the violence she has participated in, she sounds numb and ignorant.

Malick's World War II film *The Thin Red Line* (1998) uses multiple voice-overs that prevent the audience's attention from settling on any one character. Whereas war movies generally tend to focus on one or a few individuals, Malick's film jumps back and forth between multiple perspectives, weaving a complex tapestry of accounts of the battle for Guadalcanal. One character's voice-over meditates on the relationship between war and natural events. Another's focuses on memories of his wife. Yet another's contemplates the value of his attempts to please his superiors. The film jumps from one perspective to the next, often without providing an image that clarifies whose voice is speaking. The overall effect is to suggest that battles aren't one soldier's story, but every soldier's story. The story of a battle is not simply a linear one, because battles involve hundreds or thousands of soldiers. Malick's experimentation with sound illustrates the degree to which more conventional uses of voice-over direct the audience's attention to a single character.

Sound Effects

Because dialogue is the element of film sound that usually receives the most emphasis on screen (and in spectators' minds), some viewers may be tempted to think that sound effects are a minor, cosmetic component of a film's soundtrack. However, sound effects play an important role in shaping the audience's understanding of space and in characterizing an environment.

Functions of Sound Effects

Sound effects can contribute to the emotional and intellectual depth of a scene in three ways: they can define a scene's location; they can lend a mood to the scene; and they can suggest the environment's impact on characters.

Define Location Sound effects play an important role in helping audiences understand the nature of the environment that surrounds the characters. From the beeping car horns of an urban thoroughfare in *Manhattan* to the swirling wind of a North African sandstorm in *The English Patient* (Anthony Minghella 1996), sound effects can depict a wide array of environments.

Usually, sound effects define location rather generically. Urban films rely on the constant buzz of traffic in the background to evoke the hustle and bustle of the city, for example, while Westerns rely on the jangle of spurs and the howl of a coyote to connote the lonely, arid plains where the action will unfold.

In some films, however, sound effects define the setting more specifically, alluding to particular places at specific points in time. In *Raging Bull*, the pop of flashbulbs dominates the soundtrack, evoking an era when sports coverage was largely limited to newspapers rather than television. The sound of whirling helicopter rotors plays a crucial role in depicting the American conflict in Vietnam (*The Deer Hunter*, *Apocalypse Now* [Francis Ford Coppola 1979], *Platoon* [Oliver Stone 1986]) because the war marked the first time that helicopters were used extensively in combat.

7.8 A pastoral moment in *The Scent of Green Papaya* ("*Mui du du xanh*").

The Scent of Green Papaya ("*Mui du du xanh*"; Anh Hung Tran 1995), is a film set in Vietnam between 1951 and 1961, just before the entry of American troops into the country. The sound effects at the beginning of the film are limited to rustling leaves and chirping birds (fig. **7.8**). Eventually these natural sounds are disrupted, and careful viewers will hear the sound of airplanes flying overhead, suggesting impending military activities. This subtle use of sound effects adds a layer of complexity to a seemingly naïve romantic story, transforming the film into an ode to a family's tranquility that will soon be ravaged by war.

These examples of sound effects do not have an immediate bearing on the plot. They do, however, give audiences a greater sense of the physical environment and historical circumstances that surround the characters.

Lend Mood to an Environment As Chapter Four explored, the visual attributes of a setting can create the emotional tenor of a scene. Sound effects can likewise contribute to the mood established by the *mise en scène*. Perhaps the most obvious examples of this effect can be found in horror films, where a common device for evoking fear is a pronounced clap of thunder. For example, in the scene in *Frankenstein* where Dr. Frankenstein creates life, his laboratory comes alive with crashes of thunder and the persistent buzz of electric transformers (fig. **7.9**). The justifiably famous sound effects in the scene help create an eerie atmosphere, and the parallel between the lightning and the electrical current in the machinery provides a potent symbol for the doctor's ability to harness nature in the name of science.

In *Saving Private Ryan* (Steven Spielberg 1998), an American soldier moves about on the top floor of an abandoned building as he readies himself for the climactic battle with the Germans. In addition to the subdued rumble of tanks in the distance, audiences can hear the sound of strong wind whistling through the broken window-panes. The sound is ominous, and underscores the soldier's isolation, as he prepares to fulfill his patriotic obligation alone.

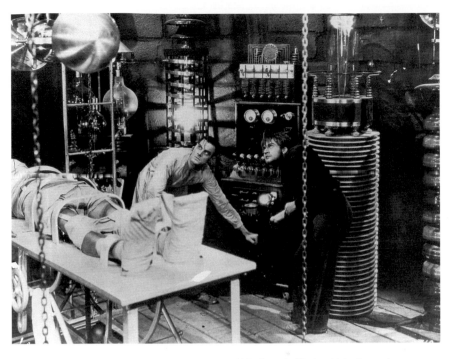

7.9 Sound effects add to the eerie atmosphere in *Frankenstein*.

Of course, sound effects can produce a wide variety of moods. The persistent clinking of dishes and rattle of silverware in the exposition of *Thelma and Louise* evokes the hectic, working-class environment of the diner where Louise works. The sound of the rushing elevated train in *The Godfather* suggests Michael's intensifying nervousness as he prepares to commit his first murder. The sound of lapping water in *Cast Away* (Robert Zemeckis 2000) emphasizes the isolation that Chuck Noland (Tom Hanks) feels. Sound effects can create a romantic environment or a terrifying one, an intimate setting or an alienating one.

Portray the Environment's Impact on Characters Sound effects can help illustrate how the environment has a direct impact on characters. Action/adventure films, which typically feature characters being bombarded by hostile forces around them, provide some fruitful examples. In a famous sequence from Alfred Hitchcock's thriller *North by Northwest* (1959), Roger Thornhill (Cary Grant) finds himself alone near a desolate cornfield, hoping to meet the mysterious George Kaplan. Shortly after he arrives, a crop duster appears in the distance. At first, the small, single-engine plane hums innocently in the background, but soon it approaches Thornhill, its engine growing louder and louder until it begins firing bullets. Then the sound of the engine starts to fade as the plane flies past. But, when the sound begins to grow louder again, audiences know before they see it that the plane has turned around and is once again flying toward Thornhill.

Three Components of Film Sound

But this function of sound effects is certainly not limited to action films. In the drama *Red Desert* ("*Il deserto rosso*"; Michelangelo Antonioni 1964), the sound of approaching boats is an important motif. The characters associate the sound with two potential threats that ocean liners present: disease (which the international ships transport, along with their cargo) and loneliness (the film implies that the male characters are frequently absent because of their business travel). This motif demonstrates the way sound effects are a powerful and sometimes subtle device for establishing how surroundings have a direct impact on people.

To suggest that sound effects have these three functions, however, is, in some cases, to impose an artificial distinction between the roles sound plays in films. Particularly expressive sound effects may serve all three functions simultaneously, defining location, creating mood, and portraying the environment's relation to characters.

Characteristics of Sound Effects

A crucial component of any analysis of a sound effect is a careful description of how that effect is created. To write with precision, film scholars take particular note of four characteristics of sound effects: acoustic qualities, volume, regularity, and verisimilitude.

Acoustic Qualities In order to analyze sound effects it is important to be able to describe exactly what the audience hears, and to write about it with precision. As an example of subtly differing sound effects, consider the noises made by the opening and closing doors in *Alien* and the *Star Wars* series. When Captain Dallas (Tom Skerritt) pursues the alien in the former film, circular hatches close behind him one by one, sounding like sheets of grimy steel grating against one another. The clunky, mechanical sound effect befits the industrial aura of the starship *Nostromo*. In contrast, when doorways open and close on the Death Star in *Star Wars*, the only sound is of decompressing air (fig. **7.10**). The hydraulic sound conveys the space station's efficient and sterile environment. Given the contexts in which these sounds appear, the difference between them is entirely appropriate.

As they do with the human voice, sound editors can also adjust the acoustic qualities of a sound effect to help characterize the surrounding environment. For example, when the soldiers jump into the water as they assault the beach in *Saving Private Ryan*, a series of underwater shots combined with the muffled sound of explosions evokes the experience of being submerged. At one point the camera breaks the surface of the water and then goes under again (repeatedly), and the acoustic properties of the sound effects changes accordingly. When the camera is above the surface, the sound effects are clear and piercing; when it is underwater, the sound effects are dampened. The result is to give the audience a vivid sense of the horror of having to struggle onto the beach at Normandy.

Volume Because dialogue tends to overwhelm sound effects, those rare moments when sound effects do compete with dialogue are particularly important. They suggest an environment that engulfs the characters within it.

Sometimes, however, filmmakers will diminish the volume of sound effects for expressive purposes. When Captain Miller (Tom Hanks) lands on the beach in *Saving Private Ryan*, the cacophony of explosions and shouting nearly disappears. The sonic frenzy is replaced by ominous white noise, which sounds like air blowing through an empty corridor. Because the shift in volume accompanies a medium close-up of Miller, audiences recognize that the soundtrack expresses the soldier's subjectivity. The horror of war has left him dazed. When one of Miller's subordinates asks him, "What do we do now sir?" audiences have to read the soldier's lips, because Miller does not hear the words. A whistle appears on the soundtrack. It grows louder

7.10 A door closes on the Death Star in *Star Wars: Episode IV—A New Hope.*

and higher in pitch until it gives way to the sound effects of explosions and gunfire, and thus functions as an audio symbol of Miller's being "snapped back into reality." The experimentation with volume (which reappears in the climactic battle scene) develops the film's central theme: the importance of duty and self-sacrifice. Miller cannot let himself retreat from the horror he has witnessed; his subordinate's question reminds Miller that he has an obligation to guide the younger, inexperienced soldiers.

The expressive potential of adjusting the volume of sound effects goes well beyond war films, however. Kubrick's sci-fi epic *2001* employs restrained volume to suggest the emptiness of space, as when Dr. Frank Poole (Gary Lockwood) conducts a space walk and all audiences can hear is the sound of his breathing. When the ship's computer cuts Poole's life support, the breathing suddenly gives way to a

7.11 Harry Caul cowers in the corner in *The Conversation.*

disturbing silence. In *The Conversation*, Harry Caul is riding an elevator when he encounters the woman whom he thinks is going to be murdered. Rather than warning her, he cowers in the corner (fig. **7.11**). During the scene, the whoosh of air rushing through the elevator shaft grows louder, signifying Caul's paralyzing fear.

Regularity By and large, sound effects occur sporadically and without regularity, because in real life most sounds do not follow a set, repetitious pattern. Thus, when a sound effect does appear with rhythmic consistency, its persistence draws

attention to a rigid order that runs counter to more sporadic rhythms of daily life. Consider how in films such as *Paths of Glory* (Kubrick 1957), the sound of soldiers' marching feet brings a mechanical precision that stands in contrast to the more irregular noises of warfare later in the film.

Rosemary's Baby uses repetitive sound effects to suggest that the main character is suspended in time, unable to effect change. Indeed, the inexorable unfolding of time itself becomes a theme in the film. Rosemary (Mia Farrow) learns about, and unwillingly becomes involved in, a devious plot to deliver Satan's offspring to the world. Repeatedly, Polanski draws attention to the sound of a clock ticking mindlessly in the background. The sound effect complements other motifs in the film involving the passage of time and natural cycles: Rosemary and others monitor her pregnancy; and the film emphasizes the changing seasons, thus drawing attention to the passage of time.

The film's emphasis on time wryly suggests that the delivery of Satan's child isn't supernatural. On the contrary, it is almost routine, and the ticking of the clock casually counts down the minutes until the end of the world. As with many sound effects that occur with regularity, the clock's preternatural rhythm emphasizes the contrast between the main character's hardship and the indifferent, business-as-usual mentality of her environment. In other contexts, however, repetitive sound effects may offer comfort.

Verisimilitude Typically Foley artists and sound editors try to produce sounds with a high degree of verisimilitude. That is, audiences assume that the sounds that accompany images are true to life—that the creaking timbers in *Master and Commander: The Far Side of the World* (Peter Weir 2003) accurately represent the experience of life in the hull of a British frigate in the Napoleonic era, for example, or that the light sabers in *Star Wars* sound like what a light saber *would* sound like in that faraway world. But on occasion, filmmakers will disregard verisimilitude altogether, and provide instead a sound that strives to be more expressive than representative.

For example, in *After Hours* (Martin Scorsese 1985), staid computer programmer Paul Hackett (Griffin Dunne) goes on a blind date in New York's funky Soho district, but the evening goes dangerously awry. By the end of the night, he is running for his life from a violent mob. When he first arrives at his date's apartment, her roommate tosses Hackett the keys from several flights up, so he can let himself into the building. But rather than hearing the innocent jangle of keys hurtling through the air, audiences instead hear the menacing rumble of thunder. Scorsese abandons verisimilitude, and thus transforms the image into an ominous portent of things to come.

In Andrei Tarkovsky's science fiction epic *Solaris* (1972), a woman is brought back to life after having committed suicide. When she realizes that she is inhuman, she kills herself again, only to be resuscitated once more. As viewers see this process, they hear the sound of breaking glass. The sound effects "suggest that she is constituted of shards of ice; in a troubling, even terrifying way, they render both the creature's fragility and artificiality" (Chion, p. 39).

As these two examples suggest, departures from verisimilitude have the potential to transcend representations of physical reality. They can allude to metaphorical or psychological truth rather than the sounds of everyday experience.

● ●

Techniques in Practice: Sound Effects and the Construction of Class in *Days of Heaven*

American literature and film usually portray the plains of the Southwest as a rugged landscape that offers a liberating alternative to the Midwest's noisy, claustrophobic, and industrialized urban areas. In Terrence Malick's *Days of Heaven* (1978), lovers Bill (Richard Gere) and Abbey (Brooke Adams), along with Bill's younger sister (Linda Manz), flee Chicago. The three abandon the crowded city in favor of the spacious plains of the Texas panhandle, but they soon discover that the lush farmland too is industrialized. As in the city, Bill and Abbey find themselves at the very bottom of the class ladder. Rather than pastoral escape, the working-class lovers find only hard labor in the wheat fields of the Southwest.

The film's portrayal of industrialized spaces as noisome is apparent in the opening scene, in which Bill assaults his foreman at a Chicago foundry. The two men argue, but their dispute remains a mystery because the sound of pounding metal completely overwhelms their speech. The volume, acoustic characteristics, and regularity of the sound effects all work to convey the idea that Bill is consumed by this industrial space. The metal (an industrial material) clangs loudly and monotonously, evoking the maddening repetition associated with factory work. As the argument becomes more heated, the noise becomes louder, linking Bill's anger and frustration with mechanization. The pounding of steel also parallels the pounding of men's bodies in the fight, thus connecting the brutality of the argument with the brutality of the work space and the modern, industrialized world.

Later, when the three characters arrive in Texas, they find the migrant lifestyle anything but tranquil. One sequence depicting a day's work on the farm begins with the faint rustle of a breeze and the soft chirp of crickets. But the sound of a blacksmith banging a horseshoe soon disrupts the serenity. The noise echoes the sound of the foundry and thus establishes a parallel between the two spaces. Eventually the sound of the blacksmith gives way to the louder sound of the thrasher harvesting the wheat. Once again, the rhythmic sound of machinery overwhelms the dialogue, and the characters are swallowed by their work environment (fig. **7.12**). Later, a close-up shot reveals a shovel feeding coal into the engine of the thrasher. This image mirrors an earlier shot in the foundry, confirming the parallel between Chicago and Texas.

By contrast, the unnamed Farmer (Sam Shepard) is associated with tranquility. His prosperity allows him the privilege of avoiding the industrial noise and spaces, thus establishing the class conflict that propels the film's main storyline. In one scene, the Farmer reclines on a divan in the middle of one of his fields while he listens to the foreman

7.12 *(left)* The start of day on the farm in *Days of Heaven.*

7.13 *(right)* The Farmer takes it easy in *Days of Heaven.*

(Robert J. Wilke) tally up his profits (fig. **7.13**). The only sound effects in the scene are the faint rustle of wind through the wheat and the "ka-ching" sound of the adding machine. The sound of the machine situates the Farmer as part of the industrial system that engulfs Bill and Abbey, but the relative quiet clearly suggests his comfortable position in the upper class.

Both sound effects and images in *Days of Heaven* suggest that, by the turn of the century, the American West was already an industrialized region. While the Farmer can enjoy the privilege of a pastoral experience on his farm, Bill, Abbey, and the Girl remain trapped in their industrialized, working-class milieu.

Music

On the set of *Lifeboat* (1944), Alfred Hitchcock questioned the logic of scoring a film set entirely on a lifeboat in World War II. Hitchcock wryly asked, "But where is the music supposed to come from out in the middle of the ocean?" Hearing of the director's reluctance to include a score, composer David Raksin suggested that Hitchcock should be asked "where the cameras come from" (quoted in Prendergast, pp. 222–3).

The exchange between Hitchcock and Raksin points to the central challenge film composers face. Most narrative films rely on music to engage the audience's attention, yet the same music threatens to make the artificiality of any film obvious. The composer's charge is to add soundtrack music that complements the imagery on screen without calling attention to itself. In fact, film scholar Claudia Gorbman calls this music "unheard melodies" because audiences should not be *too* aware of the composer's work for fear of interfering with the story.

Functions of Film Music

In many cases, the only function of a score is to provide background music, which sustains audience attention and lends coherence to a scene as it moves from shot to shot. Composer Aaron Copland said that this music "helps to fill the empty spots between pauses in a conversation. . . . [It] must weave its way underneath dialogue" (quoted in Prendergast, p. 218).

But, like the other elements of a film, music can develop systematically. It can establish motifs and parallels, and it can evolve with narrative context. In *The Lord of the Rings: The Fellowship of the Ring* (Peter Jackson 2001), when audiences first see Frodo Baggins (Elijah Wood), the soundtrack plays a faintly Gaelic tune, which represents the bucolic life in the Shire where Frodo lives. Later, when Frodo and Sam (Sean Astin) leave the Shire, Sam comments on how he will be going farther from home than he has ever gone before. While he talks, a melancholy French horn repeats the musical theme (a melody that becomes a motif), signaling their departure and Sam's impending homesickness. During the film's resolution, when Frodo and Sam agree to travel together on a quest to destroy the ring, a flute plays the theme. The instrumentation, with its Gaelic flair, conveys how the communal spirit of the Shire follows these two friends as they vow to work together to combat evil. Shore chose Celtic music, "one of the oldest [forms of] music in the world" to give the score "a feeling of antiquity" befitting the bygone era of the Shire (Otto and Spence D).

Such systematic use of film music can contribute to the emotional and intellectual complexity of a film in five ways: it can establish the historical context for a scene; it can help depict the a scene's geographical space; it can help define characters; it can help shape the emotional tenor of a scene; and it can provide a distanced or ironic commentary on a scene's visual information.

Establish Historical Context Music offers filmmakers an efficient means of defining a film's setting. Audiences should associate diegetic music with the story's time period, since, in the name of historical accuracy, most filmmakers will try to ensure that the music characters listen to would have been popular during the time when the story takes place. Throughout *The Last Picture Show* (Peter Bogdanovich 1971), the music of Hank Williams seeps out of car radios and jukeboxes, evoking the mood of a dying Texas town in the 1950s. The country music legend's lyrical emphasis on broken relationships and loneliness reflects the character's alienation. In *Saving Private Ryan*, the soldiers enjoy a brief respite from battle listening to the love songs of Edith Piaf. The choice of music is highly evocative of the story's setting in France, since Piaf had been an unofficial symbol of France and its resistance against Germany during World War II. The use of intentional anachronisms in *Moulin Rouge!* (Baz Luhrman 2001), in which characters sing popular rock songs from the late twentieth century even though the story is set in the late nineteenth century, is extremely rare in popular films, in part because music plays such an important role in situating the audience in the narrative's place and time.

Shaping space Diegetic music can be used to help audiences perceive the geography of the setting. Consider how, in *Notorious*, Hitchcock underscores Alicia and Devlin's precarious situation as they investigate the wine cellar, spying on Alicia's suspicious husband. By lowering the volume of the party music on the soundtrack, the film emphasizes the cellar's proximity to the festivities upstairs. By using diegetic music to remind audiences of the geography of Sebastian's manor, Hitchcock invests the scene with a considerable amount of tension.

The loud country/rock music in the Silver Bullet in *Thelma and Louise* emphasizes the crowded confines of the bar. In contrast, the soft music playing in the background through much of *Rear Window* contributes to the audience's understanding that Jeffries's open window looks out onto a busy courtyard. The barely perceptible music points to the fact that, although he is surrounded by neighbors, Jeffries is simultaneously cut off from them.

Music can even suggest the specific cultural makeup of a setting's location. The celebrated opening tracking shot in the re-released version of *Touch of Evil* contains an eclectic assortment of diegetic music, whereas the studio's original release included only a non-diegetic title song by Henry Mancini. An elaborate crane shot begins a tour of the streets of a town on the U.S./Mexican border. As the camera passes various buildings, the soundtrack music changes, establishing that the town is full of bars playing loud music. Moreover, by having each bar play a different style of music, the soundtrack highlights the multi-cultural makeup of this border town.

Defining Character Just as many people express themselves through the music they listen to, so filmmakers use music to define characters. A particular song, artist, or type of music may function as a motif that informs audiences of a character's taste, demeanor, or attitude. In music terminology, the leitmotif (leading motif) was first used to describe the compositional strategies of Karl Maria von Weber and Richard Wagner, who used distinctive musical phrases and themes to define character and present ideas. Fritz Lang's thriller *M* (1931) offers one of the cinema's first (and most disturbing) examples of how music can define a character. The child killer (Peter Lorre) whistles Edvard Grieg's sinister "In the Hall of the Mountain King" from *Peer Gynt*. In *Billy Elliot*, young Billy spends his days listening to the songs of the rock band T Rex while he fantasizes about becoming a ballet dancer. Given Billy's rejection of traditional gender roles and his ambiguous sexuality, T Rex is an appropriate choice, since the band's lead singer, Marc Bolan, was noted for his glam-rock androgyny. Howard Shore integrated more than forty motifs in his score for Peter Jackson's *Lord of the Rings: The Return of the King* (2003). "It's based on Wagner's storytelling," says Shore. "It's okay to feel something when you hear music and to attach motifs to characters" (Otto and Spence D).

Often composers score non-diegetic music so that main characters are associated with a particular musical motif, or theme. For *Once upon a Time in the West*, Ennio Morricone composed a haunting, almost tuneless song built around the lone wail of a harmonica.

Throughout the film, this song is associated with the character called, appropriately enough, Harmonica (Charles Bronson). The theme is intimately connected to the character's personality. He plays the instrument himself, and a flashback eventually reveals that a harmonica played a pivotal role in a traumatic childhood event, which has haunted him ever since (fig. **7.14**).

Harmonica's nemesis, Frank (Henry Fonda), is associated with an electric guitar that suggests the character's methodical menace. But submerged under the main melody of Frank's theme is the wail of the harmonica, suggesting the sadistic past these two men share. When the two characters finally meet for a cli-

7.14 Harmonica in *Once upon a Time in the West*.

mactic shootout, the two musical themes compete for audio space, representing the central conflict between two strong wills. While most scores are composed after shooting is completed, Morricone composed the score before shooting on the film began. Leone then played the score on the set during filming, so that each actor could move to the music. The unusual process Leone and Morricone adopted indicates how closely they tied the characters to the score's musical themes (Frayling, pp. 280–1). Similarly, Coppola uses two distinct themes to identify Vito and Michael Corleone in *The Godfather*.

Shaping Emotional Tenor Music plays an important role in helping audiences know how to interpret the mood of a scene. Consider how the score for the famous opening scene of *The Sound of Music* (Robert Wise 1965) differs from the first chase scene from *Terminator 2* (James Cameron 1991). The comparison of such wildly divergent films may seem ludicrous, but remember that the primary visual image in both scenes is of people running. However, there is a dramatic difference of mood between the two scenes. As Maria (Julie Andrews) begins singing the second chorus of "The Sound of Music," an expansive swell of the orchestra accompanies her movement as she gallops across the Austrian mountain range, establishing the sense of liberation and happiness that music offers her. In contrast, the more sparsely orchestrated, urgent, uptempo, and percussive score for *Terminator 2* appropriately contributes to the scene's emphasis on action and suspense.

John Williams's score for *Jaws* (Steven Spielberg 1975) offers a good example of how music can help a filmmaker emphasize dramatic shifts in emotional tenor from scene to scene within a single film. The famous main theme—a sinister melody played primarily by low strings and based on an eerie, two-note progression—precedes each of the shark's attacks, and thus contributes to its horrific menace. But later, when Sheriff Brody (Roy Scheider) hits the high seas with two compatriots in pursuit of the shark, Williams's score is often more uptempo (fast) and lushly orchestrated to suggest the sheriff's sense of excitement and adventure.

Distancing the Audience Music sometimes exploits a contrast between sound and image. The effect of such a contrast is to distance the audience—to sever the connection between sound and image, so that the audience sees the images from a more critical perspective.

Sometimes, filmmakers use this technique to offer wry, satirical commentary. *Dr. Strangelove* begins with images of bomber planes refueling in mid-flight, a process that requires one plane to release fuel through a long tube into the tank of the bomber. Instead of using military music to accompany the image, Kubrick uses the airy, romantic tune "Try a Little Tenderness." The odd juxtaposition of sound and image transforms the military operation into a mechanical mating ritual, pointing to one of the film's central tenets: that weaponry is an absurd substitute phallus and that the arms race between the Soviet Union and the United States is a dangerous contest to see who has the biggest "equipment."

On other occasions, filmmakers exploit the juxtaposition of music and image to suggest the world's complete indifference to a character's plight. In *Face/Off* (John Woo 1997), a child listens to the song "Somewhere over the Rainbow" on headphones, oblivious to the bloody shootout taking place around him. In *Blue Velvet* (David Lynch 1987), a character is brutalized by a group of thugs to the tune of Roy Orbison's haunting ballad "In Dreams" (fig. **7.15**). And in Sam Fuller's *Naked Kiss* (1964), a woman discovers her fiancé sexually molesting a child while a record of children singing a lullaby plays in the background. According to Claudia Gorbman, such instances "testify to the power of . . . music which blissfully lacks awareness or empathy; its very emotionlessness, juxtaposed with ensuing human catastrophe, is what provokes our emotional response" (Gorbman, p. 24). In other words, such blatant inappropriateness draws attention to the contrast between the music's complete lack of response and the audience's (hopefully) more empathetic response to these characters' predicaments.

Obviously, a piece of film music can carry out more than one of these functions simultaneously. To help recognize how a piece of music functions, audiences should train their ears to recognize five characteristics of film music.

7.15 Thugs attack in *Blue Velvet*, to the accompaniment of a haunting ballad.

Five Characteristics of Film Music

Film music is notoriously difficult to write about. Despite a song's uncanny ability to sweep audiences up into the romantic (or exciting, or tragic) sentiment unfolding onscreen, few people have the ability to describe how the music accomplishes this. Those who have formally studied music are perhaps best equipped to describe and analyze film music. For those who haven't spent years training their ears to dissect a tune into its individual components, the danger in trying to write about music is that the discussion will be too imprecise to inform or convince other readers. Vague adjectives such as "romantic" or "scary" are of little value when describing a melody.

Still, it is possible for non-musicians to talk and write concretely about film music. In order to think and write about film with specificity, begin by concentrating on these five attributes of film music: patterns of development; lyrical content; tempo and volume; instrumentation; and cultural significance.

Patterns of Development Like other elements of film, music develops systematically. Musical themes are often repeated, establishing motifs and parallels. And as musical motifs evolve, they signal important changes in the story. Consequently, perhaps the most important strategy for actively listening to and thinking about film music is to notice when a musical theme appears. Does the theme come to be associated with particular characters or settings? With particular emotions? With particular visual imagery?

In his score for *Star Wars*, John Williams developed two distinct melodies. The film's familiar main theme is associated with the idealism of the Rebel Alliance, whereas a more foreboding and militaristic theme (the tune is in a minor key and its plodding rhythm sounds like bootsteps) signals the presence of the evil Empire. In the James Bond cycle, two distinctive brassy notes of John Barry's famous theme song introduced in *Dr. No* (Terence Young 1962) often punctuate Bond's dramatic triumphs onscreen. The musical motif accentuates the character's cocky bravado. In *He Got Game* (Spike Lee 1998), several montage sequences depicting basketball games are accompanied by Aaron Copland compositions, including "Appalachian Spring," and "Fanfare for the Common Man" from *Symphony no. 3*. The repetition of music and image elevates games of street ball to the status of high art. Copland's music famously refashioned "folk" melodies into high art just as Lee's film presents basketball as a vibrant urban art form. In each case, the musical theme is repeatedly linked to a particular character, environment, or event.

Musical motifs can function in more abstract ways as well, helping viewers to draw connections between characters, settings, or ideas. In *Jules and Jim* ("*Jules et Jim*"; François Truffaut 1962), the two title characters become fixated on a mysterious statue. When they see the statue for the first time, the sound of a melancholy flute accompanies the image. Later, when Jules (Oskar Werner) and Jim (Henri Serre) see Catherine (Jeanne Moreau) for the first time, the same tune plays in the background. The motif thus points to the mysterious opacity that Catherine shares with the statue, and which will fascinate the two men for twenty years.

Lyrics Since the late 1960s, soundtrack music has relied more on self-contained popular songs instead of scored material. Often (but not always) filmmakers choose songs whose lyrics are relevant to the image on screen. Consequently, an analysis of film music should consider the possible significance of any lyrics.

For example, Public Enemy's "Fight the Power" plays over the opening credits of *Do the Right Thing* and occurs throughout the film whenever Radio Raheem emerges with his blaring boom-box. In general, the song's militant sentiment reflects the escalating racial tension among the neighborhood's residents and foreshadows the riot that erupts after the police kill Radio Raheem. Moreover, the lyrics' emphasis on American culture's refusal to commemorate important African-American leaders and artists reflects one of the central conflicts in the film: Buggin' Out's demand that Sal put pictures of African-American heroes on the wall of his pizzeria.

Lyrics can be powerful indicators of mood or turning points in plot. In *Thelma and Louise*, after Thelma finally gathers the courage to ignore Darryl's orders and accompany Louise on a weekend getaway, the soundtrack plays Van Morrison's "Wild Night." The lyrics mirror Thelma and Louise's actions as each packs her bags in a parallel editing sequence:

> As you brush your shoes, you stand before your mirror
> And you comb your hair, grab your coat and hat

More importantly, the lyrics speak to the giddy anticipation both women feel over the prospect of escaping their humdrum daily routines.:

> And every thing looks so complete
> When you're walking down on the streets
> And the wind, it catches your feet
> Sets you flying, crying
> Ooh ooh-ooh wee, wild night, is calling

> ©1971 (Renewed) WB Music Corp. (ASCAP), and Caledonia Soul Music
> (ASCAP). All rights on behalf of Caledonia Soul Music (ASCAP). Administered
> by WB Music Corp. All rights reserved. Used by permission.

Importantly, the soundtrack plays Martha Reeves' version of the song, emphasizing how this moment captures the excitement of women's liberation. Furthermore, the lyrics' emphasis on flying establishes one of the central motifs in the film: flight into open space as a metaphor for empowerment. In short, the use of the song effectively ends the film's exposition, as both women have made the first step away from their gender roles as housewife and waitress.

Tempo and Volume Tempo (speed) and volume are two attributes of music that are readily describable even to the untrained ear. They also play a significant role in determining the emotional intensity of a song (and, by extension, a scene).

Uptempo, or fast, melodies tend to convey frenetic energy and rapid movement. Chase scenes in action films, for example, usually rely on non-diegetic uptempo melodies. Slow melodies, on the other hand, suggest a more relaxed pace, or a lack of energy. Perhaps no scene exemplifies the distinction as effectively as when Benjamin hurries to prevent Elaine's marriage in *The Graduate*. As he drives from Berkeley to Santa Barbara—frantically stopping along the way to ask directions—a quickly strummed acoustic guitar corresponds to Benjamin's speed and anxiety. But soon the tempo of the music slows considerably, telling the audience exactly when Benjamin's car starts to run out of gas. Eventually the music putters out altogether, suggesting that his quest may be futile.

Like tempo, volume can also affect the intensity of a scene. But whereas tempo usually comments on a character's movement, volume usually characterizes the aura of space surrounding characters. Loud music seems to swallow characters, whereas soft music connotes more intimacy.

One scene in *Apocalypse Now* exemplifies how altering volume can radically modulating the dynamics of a scene. A squadron of helicopters on a bombing raid approaches the target village, led by the demented racist Lt. Kilgore (Robert Duvall). The soldiers blast Wagner's "The Ride of the Valkyries" on an elaborate speaker system designed to terrify the enemy. The choice of music is an intertextual reference to *The Birth of a Nation*, whose original score featured Wagner's music accompanying the Ku Klux Klan's triumphant charge. The choice of music emphasizes Kilgore's racism and bigotry. Wagner dominates the mix on the soundtrack and offers audiences a sense of the soldiers' simultaneous fear and excitement. The music transforms what would otherwise be the confined space of a helicopter into a position of authority and dominance; the blaring music is an act of aggression that exceeds the physical space of the helicopter itself.

7.16 Helicopters approach the village in *Apocalypse Now*.

The sequence then cuts to the targeted village, whose silence is disrupted by the comparatively quiet ringing of a bell. Eventually Wagner's music can be heard on the soundtrack accompanying images of the village (fig. **7.16**). It gradually gets louder, culminating in the helicopters' attack. The abrupt movement from loud to soft shifts the audience's identification, so that the excitement audiences might otherwise share with the soldiers onscreen gives way to empathy for the villagers. Sound editor Walter Murch's manipulation of volume in this scene puts audiences in the position of the attacked, as well as the attacker.

Three Components of Film Sound

The tempo and volume of non-diegetic music can also help paint internal space. In *Psycho*, as Marion leaves Phoenix, the score is played quite loud and establishes her nervousness. Moreover, multiple melodic lines unfold in differing rhythms and suggest the dual facets of Marion's personality. At a lower pitch, the strings play a rapid progression of notes characterized by their sharp, distinct (staccato) sound. It is the dominant strain in the melody, which begins immediately after Marion's boss crosses the street in front of her car; his perplexed look makes it clear that he wonders why Marion is not home sick in bed, as she said she would be. As Marion continues her drive the next night, the plucking of the strings corresponds to the blinding rain and slashing windshield wipers, which clearly distract Marion, leading her to the Bates Motel. This line is clearly associated with Marion's fear as she leaves town and evades the law.

The second melodic line is higher pitched. The violins play a *legato* (notes that are smooth and connected) melody at half the speed of the lower notes. Given the narrative context, this upper melodic line seems to correspond with Marion's attempt to remain calm—or rather, to act calm when under the surface she is almost paralyzed with fear. In this regard, the two distinct melodic lines reflect one of the film's most important motifs: personalities torn asunder by conflicting desires. The volume and tempo of Bernard Herrmann's score are, in other words, a musical representation of psychosis.

Instrumentation It is not difficult to make generalizations about what instruments are used to perform a piece of music. Does an orchestra play the music? A brass ensemble? A string quartet? Do the musicians use electric or electronic instruments? Do the musicians sample and manipulate pre-recorded sounds? Bernard Herrmann's score for *Psycho* would have had a very different effect had he included brass instruments to temper the sound of the strings, especially during the piercing notes that accompany Marion's violent death. Different instruments create different moods, so the choice of instrumentation can play a dramatic role in creating an environment for a scene.

Instrumentation can suggest a film's time period and setting. For example, when Bill, Abbey, and the Girl flee Chicago at the beginning of *Days of Heaven*, an acoustic guitar accompanies images of the three riding southwest on a train. The instrument's association with folk music (and rural space) is an efficient way to emphasize the film's early twentieth-century time period and to signal the characters' movement from an urban to a rural locale. In contrast, Howard Shore's score for the opening credits of *Se7en* helps to establish the urban setting and grim tone by utilizing distorted electric and electronic instruments and sampled sound effects.

Some instruments may also portray more subtle emotional states. In Wong Kar-Wai's *In the Mood for Love* (2002), Su Li-zhen (Maggie Cheung) and Chow Mo-wan (Tony Leung) turn to one another for comfort after discovering their respective spouses are having an affair. On the verge of becoming romantically involved themselves, the would-be lovers separate, leaving their tentative love unrequited. Michael Galasso's score suggests the couple's unspoken longing for one another through the use of a cello "because it is such an evocative instrument, able express strong emotions"; a low bass drum accompanies the cello, sounding like a "subliminal heartbeat" (Galasso, quoted in Lee).

Instrumentation can also suggest important character traits. John Carpenter's score for his slasher film *Halloween* (1978) is notable for its spare arrangement, revolving around the rapid repetition of two notes on the piano. The ominous simplicity reflects the terrifying incongruity that opens the film: the stalker/killer in the exposition is a child. The rudimentary piano sounds like a child doodling on the keyboard, but the staccato notes and rapid tempo suggests the character's violent, insistent energy.

Marx Brothers' films offer many comic examples of how instruments can be associated with a character. In these films, Harpo Marx never utters a word. His primary means of communication are his mischievous smile and an oversized bicycle horn, which he frequently honks in exclamation (fig. **7.17**). Yet the chaotic frenzy of a Marx Brothers' film is always tempered by Harpo's romantic side, which appears when he tenderly serenades the audience with a harp. The character's quirky humor arises from the bizarre juxtaposition of low-brow (the honking horn) and high-brow (the harp).

7.17 Harpo Marx (with blonde hair) is always associated with a horn or a harp.

Cultural Significance Finally, filmmakers can add complexity to a film by using music that bears a specific cultural significance. A specific song or type of music may conjure up shared cultural knowledge, as in *Stagecoach* (1939), when John Ford uses a familiar musical theme to tell audiences that Native Americans are near. According to Claudia Gorbman, the film's "Indian music" produces meaning in part because of its "cultural-musical properties—[the] rhythmic repetition in groups of four with accented initial beat . . . [which] *already* signify 'Indian' in the language of the American music industry" (Gorbman, p. 28).

Music that functions in this way often relies on stereotypes to produce meaning. The music in Ford's film is not authentic Apache music; it is a cliché that became a substitute for the authentic artifact because of its repetition in film, radio, and eventually TV.

Mel Brooks's comedy *Blazing Saddles* (1974) parodies Hollywood's tendency to rely on musical stereotypes. Early in the film, the white foreman of a crew of African-American railroad workers asks his workers to sing an authentic folk spiritual: "I don't hear no spirit. When you were slaves you sang like little birds." When the crew sings a carefully

7.18 Music adds layers of meaning in *The Royal Tenenbaums*.

harmonized version of Cole Porter's "I Get a Kick Out of You," the foreman complains that the song is not authentic enough. To illustrate his point, he sings "Swing Low Sweet Chariot," and all the white workers then break into a jolly version of "The Camptown Races." They are so caught up in song that they dance away, leaving the rest of the crew in peace. The episode suggests that the white workers are the only ones who have anything invested in false stereotypes.

Filmmakers may also use songs whose production history holds some cultural significance. In *The Royal Tenenbaums*, after Richie Tenenbaum (Luke Wilson) unsuccessfully attempts to commit suicide, Nick Drake's recording of "Fly" plays softly in the background. The fact that Drake committed suicide adds poignancy to the scene beyond the melancholy of the tune itself. (fig. **7.18**)

In *Chungking Express*, the soundtrack includes a hefty selection of music of various national origins: reggae, Indian raga, and American pop music all become sound motifs. In most cases, these motifs are diegetic music. The music pours out of jukeboxes and portable radios, suggesting the eclectic mix of ethnicities in Hong Kong. At the time of filming, Hong Kong was a bustling hub for multinational trade, destined to become reintegrated with mainland China when Great Britain relinquished control on July 1, 1997. But residents greeted this change with skepticism since Hong Kong had been a British colony for over 150 years. The assortment of diegetic music underscores the territory's fluid cultural makeup and its pronounced diversity.

Even the non-diegetic music evokes Hong Kong's troubled concept of nationhood. Faye Wong's adaptation of the Cranberries' song "Dreams" plays twice on the soundtrack, and the choice of music resonates on a number of levels. The Cranberries are an Irish rock band, so the song alludes to Hong Kong and Ireland's shared history as British colonies. But the concept of national identity is further undercut by the fact that Wong uses an adaptation of the song, rather than the original; is the song British? Irish? Cantonese? The music, in other words, explores the way Hong Kong's identity is no longer defined by place or history.

● ●

Techniques in Practice: Bernard Herrmann's Score and Travis Bickle's Troubled Masculinity in *Taxi Driver*

In Martin Scorsese's *Taxi Driver*, Robert De Niro plays Travis Bickle, a lonely New York cab driver who is simultaneously sickened by the moral decay he sees everyday and obsessed with political campaigner Betsy (Cybill Shepherd). When his romance with Betsy fizzles out, Travis tries unsuccessfully to assassinate the political candidate Betsy works for. After he fails, Travis murders a pimp and several street hustlers in order to rescue the thirteen-year-old prostitute Iris (Jodie Foster) (fig. **7.19**). He becomes a local hero in the process. Travis's obsessions seem paradoxical: on one hand, he's a hopeless romantic, and on the other hand he's an explosive cynic who can only see the city's decay. But Bernard Herrmann's score emphasizes that Travis's romantic and violent sides are interrelated.

Herrmann's score for *Taxi Driver* (his last score in a career that began with *Citizen Kane* in 1941) introduces two dominant themes during the opening credits. The soundtrack alternates between the two, seemingly antithetical, non-diegetic themes. The first theme is spare and militaristic. It is built around two low, descending notes. Often the tonal progression is punctuated by the tapping of a snare drum, whose tempo gradually increases until the high note gives way to the low note. The second theme is a slow, lilting jazz tune played on a tenor saxophone. Onscreen, the image cuts back and forth between extreme close-ups of Travis's eyes and blurry, oversaturated point-of-view shots of New York City. This suggests immediately that the music reflects two halves of his personality, and that Travis's perspective of the city is distorted.

Throughout the film, the militaristic theme is associated with Travis's seething anger. The foreboding theme, largely played on low brass instruments, reflects his military background in Vietnam, and his voice-over emphasizes that Travis will eventually use this background on the domestic front. As he contemplates how sordid the city has become, Travis's voice-over speaks of his hopes for a "real rain [to] come and wash all the scum off the streets." The militaristic theme typically accompanies these thoughts, suggesting that he, the lone stalwart against the "scum and the filth" of the city, might just be the "real rain" to clean up the street.

7.19 Iris—the child prostitute Travis "saves" in *Taxi Driver*.

Yet, from the opening credits, the film clearly emphasizes that his condemnatory view of the city is a distorted and destructive one. Several scenes emphasize that Travis directs most of his hostility toward African-Americans. Also, Travis repeatedly points weapons (or his fingers, as if they were a weapon) at innocent strangers: people walking on the streets, dancers on television, and women onscreen at the local porno theater.

Coming on the heels of Travis's fuming over the moral decay of the city, the romantic theme initially suggests that love could, perhaps, alleviate some of his anger and cynicism. It appears more frequently in the first half of the film, whenever Travis thinks longingly about Betsy. For example, when he sees Betsy for the first time, the music plays and Travis's voice-over explains, "She appeared like an angel out of this filthy mass". In his eyes, she stands apart from the rest of the city. Audiences may assume that her love, then, could save Travis from his anger. Once she rejects him, the theme is associated with Iris, suggesting that she becomes a substitute for Betsy.

But the film makes clear that Travis's psychotic ranting and his romantic longing, far from being opposites, are actually complementary. Travis's tirades against the city's culture, his love for Betsy, and his desire to rescue Iris are nothing more than means for him to prop up a wounded ego. What Travis really desires is to assert his dominance, by acting as the supreme moral force over an entire city and by protecting two women whom he sees as too helpless to defend themselves. His first thoughts of Betsy are notable for their misguided chivalry, and when he asks Betsy out, he promises to protect her. When Betsy rejects Travis, he turns his attention to Iris, someone who, he thinks, is in need of rescue. To underscore that Travis's motivations are selfish, the film depicts how Travis decides to rescue Iris only after he has failed to assassinate the politician Palantine—Travis's rival for Betsy's attention. Travis's attitude toward Betsy and Iris is rooted in insecurity and is thus closely linked to an undercurrent of male retribution and violence.

After the film's bloody shootout, the two musical themes fuse, drawing attention to this connection between romance and violence. As the camera slowly tracks down the hallway of the hotel, tallying up the carnage Travis has left in his wake, the non-diegetic romantic tune once associated with Betsy is played by low brass instruments and accentuated by pounding percussion. The romantic has combined with the militaristic. The film's producer, Michael Phillips, says that Herrmann "explained that the reason he did it was to show that this was where Travis's fantasies about women led him. . . . His illusions, his self-perpetuating way of dealing with women had finally brought him to that bloody, violent outburst" (quoted in S. Smith, p. 15).

The film's score emphasizes that Travis's romantic longing for Betsy, his hatred for the city, and his rescue of Iris are all interrelated. His romantic ideals are essentially violent, since they require the subjugation of everyone's will to Travis's ego. The fact that the public lauds Travis as a hero at the end of the film is a crucial ironic twist. Scorsese suggests that Americans still valorize chivalry—a value system the film shows to be outdated, violent, self-serving, and destructive.

This discussion of sound concludes our book's coverage of the five technical aspects of film art (narrative, *mise en scène*, cinematography, editing, and sound). By and large this chapter (along with chapters Three through Six) has explored how these elements function in narrative films. Because sound lacks shape and form, writing about its use in cinema is in some ways more difficult than writing about narrative and visual content, but it is no less important.

Yet even films that don't tell stories can use sound to complement images onscreen, even when those images are abstract. While sound in such cases won't contribute narrative information such as historical context or a character's upbringing, the characteristics of the human voice, sound effects, and music will still be relevant. The next chapter takes up in more specific detail two such alternatives to narrative filmmaking: documentary and avant-garde cinema.

● Summary

- The history of sound technology has seen several major developments, each one an attempt to provide higher fidelity.
- Because sound is added or altered during post-production, it is freed from the image.
- There are five common image–sound relationships: onscreen vs. offscreen sound; subjective vs. objective sound; diegetic vs. non-diegetic sound; image time vs. sound time; image mood vs. sound mood.
- The three components of film sound are: dialogue, sound effects, and music.
- In addition to the content of an actress's lines of dialogue, the four characteristics of her voice contribute to film's overall impact: volume, pitch, speech characteristics, and acoustic qualities.
- The voice-over is a powerful storytelling technique that can help maintain narrative coherence and provide a point of identification.
- Sound effects have three common functions in narrative films. They can define location, lend mood to an environment, and portray the environment's impact on characters.
- To be precise when describing sound effects, film scholars pay attention to four characteristics of sound effects: acoustic qualities; volume; regularity; verisimilitude.
- Five common functions of film music are: to establish historical context; to shape the audience's perception of space; to define character; to shape the emotional tenor of a scene; to distance the audience.
- It is possible to write concretely about music in film by noting these five characteristics: patterns of development; lyrics; tempo and volume; instrumentation; cultural significance.

Film Analysis • Sound and Language

The essay below examines the way sound emphasizes a common humanity among the prisoners and guards occupying a P.O.W. camp in Jean Renoir's *The Grand Illusion* ("*La Grande Illusion*"; 1937).

The Study Notes that accompany this film analysis focus on strategies for writing introductions and conclusions. These paragraphs are notoriously difficult to write, largely because writers fear they may be redundant. However, introductions are important since they establish what the rest of the paper will cover, and conclusions often summarize the main argument. From the reader's perspective, these paragraphs aren't repetitive—they clarify. Introductions guide the reader into the argument, letting her know what main point(s) will be addressed in the body of the paper. Conclusions reiterate this main point in light of the ideas that have been developed throughout the paper.

Instructors look to introductions and conclusions to gauge how well students have synthesized their ideas. Researchers look to introductions and conclusions to help weed through piles of material quickly, since they offer a good indication of the scope of the essay. If a scholar doing research stumbles across a poorly written introduction or conclusion—one that fails clearly to delineate the specific issues covered in the article—there's a good chance he could ignore the whole piece, assuming that it doesn't address relevant topics.

How does the introduction in this essay prepare the reader for the main argument that follows? How does the conclusion reiterate the logic that connects the essay's major claims?

Language, Nationality, and Class in *The Grand Illusion*

Jean Renoir's drama *The Grand Illusion* depicts the hardships and occasional pleasures in the lives of French soldiers in two German prisoner of war camps during World War I.[1] The French prisoners include an aristocratic officer, Captain de Boïeldieu (Pierre Fresnay); a mechanic turned pilot, Lieutenant Maréchal (Jean Gabin); and a Jewish schoolteacher, Rosenthal (Marcel Dalio).[2] Thrown together by the war, the three men learn to respect and cooperate with one another while trying to escape from the camps. Renoir uses sound—especially dialogue—to depict prison camps riven by national, ethnic, class, and religious partitions. His use of language repeatedly emphasizes how the camp allows such superficial barriers to overwhelm the common bond of humanity that should unite the men.[3]

The opening sequences use sound to establish parallels between the French and German officers. The opening shot begins with a close-up of a gramophone and tilts upward to introduce Maréchal, who is standing in a French officers'

---

1 Even though introductory paragraphs begin an essay, many authors actually write them after the body of the argument has been completed. This is because, during the writing process, a writer's argument usually evolves, or changes altogether, and it's difficult to introduce an argument that hasn't been completely formulated yet. Consequently, many students find that, when they have difficulty getting started on a paper, the best strategy is to skip writing the introduction until a rough draft is finished.

2 The general purpose of an introduction is to establish a general foundation on which to build the rest of the argument. Save the specific details and claims (except for your thesis statement, of course) for the body of the paper. This author adopts a fairly common strategy: he offers a brief plot summary, which leads to the thesis statement. But notice how this plot summary emphasizes each character's background. The reader's awareness of these cultural differences plays an important role in shaping the rest of the paper. The plot summary isn't just "filler" or empty information for readers who haven't seen the film; rather, it is preparing the reader for the thesis, which follows.

3 Thesis statements almost always conclude introductory paragraphs in academic writing. Readers, at least in Western cultures, are trained to look at the end of introductions for these all-important sentences. This is why it is crucial for writers to spend so much time crafting precise thesis statements and to place these sentences at the end of the introduction (not in the beginning, and not in the middle). Be aware that an introduction does not have to be limited to one paragraph. In longer papers, an introduction might be several paragraphs—or even several pages—long. But in general, short papers (fifteen pages or less) require short introductions.

7.20 *(left)* French officers and a gramophone in *The Grand Illusion* ("*La Grande Illusion*").

7.21 *(right)* The German officers' mess in *The Grand Illusion*: parallel spaces.

mess enjoying the music (fig. **7.20**). Minutes later, after a brief sequence explaining that Maréchal will fly his superior officer Captain de Boïeldieu on a reconnaissance mission, the setting changes to a German officers' club. Here the audience is introduced to Commandant von Rauffenstein (Erich von Stroheim), who has just shot down the two French pilots (fig. **7.21**). The *mise en scène* and sound in the German officers' mess are remarkably similar to their French counterparts: a gramophone plays diegetic music in the background, the officers enjoy drinks, and the camera surveys a collection of posters on the wall. The parallel underscores a central irony running throughout the film: French and German soldiers share similar tastes and appetites, but arbitrary national differences divide them.

This point is emphasized in the dialogue moments later, after Maréchal and de Boïeldieu's captors invite the French prisoners to dine with them. One of the German officers tells Maréchal that he used to work in France as a mechanic. Just as Maréchal is about to say that he shares the same professional background, he is interrupted in mid-sentence by the arrival of a wreath commemorating a fallen French pilot. As both men are discovering their shared humanity, the war intrudes; the moment of intimacy is lost.

Throughout the film, language defines and divides characters according to nationality. Many of the French prisoners cannot communicate with their German guards. In one poignant scene, Maréchal has been in solitary confinement for several days when a guard enters the cell to try and comfort the French prisoner. When the guard speaks German, Maréchal explodes in anger, frustrated that he hasn't been able to hear anyone speak French in so long. Despite the guard's attempt to forge a bond, Maréchal feels alone. Eventually the guard exits, but he leaves a harmonica with Maréchal, who begins to play when the guard is out of the room. The following shot reveals that on the other side of the door, unbeknownst to Maréchal, the German guard listens to the offscreen sound and begins humming along. The two men are drawn to the same tune, which becomes a non-verbal form of communication not bound by national identity. The thick cell door that divides the two men qualifies this connection, however. Once again, the symbols of warfare interrupt camaraderie.

Linguistic differences even isolate allies from one another. On the eve of having successfully completed a tunnel out of the prison camp, one group of French prisoners is informed that they are immediately being transferred to another camp. Not wanting their efforts to go to waste, Maréchal attempts to tell an incoming prisoner about the nearly completed tunnel. But the prisoner is English and fails to understand his comrade's French. The tunnel will be forgotten. This moment points to how arbitrary boundaries such as nationality divide men who otherwise share a common humanity.

But national boundaries aren't the only impediments to fraternity. Renoir's film emphasizes that Europe is rife with other social systems that produce conflict. In *The Grand Illusion*, class has the most profound impact on how the men relate to one another. Two officers in the camp, Boïeldieu and von Rauffenstein, are aristocrats. They are fighting on opposing sides in the war, yet they respect one another because they are of the same class. Language is an important symbol of their upper-class background, as both men are multilingual. The fact that they both speak French, German, and English implies their camaraderie and further underscores the absurdity of warfare, since these two men are able to overlook cultural differences.

Ironically, however, their multilingualism and the aristocratic status that it represents separate them from the other soldiers in the camp. Early in the film, the other French prisoners doubt whether they can trust Boïeldieu because of his position in the upper class. They are surprised that he willingly participates in their efforts to tunnel out of the camp. Dialogue underscores these tensions between Boïeldieu and the other men. Film scholar Jeffery Alan Triggs points out, for example, that Boïeldieu is separated from the other officers by the particular highly formal French dialect he employs. His strict adherence to formality is particularly evident when Maréchal asks why, after eighteen months in prison together, Boïeldieu still addresses Maréchal with the formal "*vous*." Boïeldieu replies, "I say *vous* to my mother and my wife." He cannot get beyond the courtliness of his upper-class dialect to verbalize his emotional connection to Maréchal. Such tension is evident throughout the film, alluding to the way that class, like nationality, is another barrier that isolates people from one another.

The last third of the film emphasizes how people can transcend the pain and horror of war if they learn to overlook nationality and class. In a profound act of charity, Boïeldieu sacrifices his own life so that Maréchal and Rosenthal can escape. The pair's escape is further facilitated by a widowed German, Elsa (Dita Parlo), who lies to a patrol of German soldiers to protect them. Elsa also offers the men shelter and food and is obviously pleased to have their companionship (she and Maréchal share a romantic relationship). In other words, only the spirit of cooperation across class and national barriers helps the two men escape the war.

But this camaraderie is short-lived, and the film ends on a profoundly bittersweet note. Their sense of national obligation lures Maréchal and Rosenthal away from Elsa's secluded farm—back to the war from which they had managed to escape. As the men flee across the snow-covered mountains, a German patrol spots them and one soldier aims his gun at the escapees. But another soldier stops him and says, "Forget it. They're in Switzerland." On the one hand, the ending is happy, since the two men have escaped with their lives. On the other hand, the dialogue emphasizes how the soldier's decision not to fire is predicated on his honoring arbitrarily defined national borders. Ironically, the very system that saves their lives also serves as the philosophical underpinning of war.

Renoir's film suggests that the forces dividing humans are nothing but "grand illusions."[4] The film's use of diegetic music and dialogue illustrates how class and national differences are at best superficial. But Renoir does not casually propose that people are able to overlook these differences. Maréchal and Rosenthal's escape points to the possibilities of benign human interaction, but the film's resolution implies, as if with a sigh of resignation, that the hope of a permanent *esprit de corps* is also little more than a "grand illusion."[5]

4 Many writers find conclusions the most difficult part of the paper to write because the purpose of the conclusion is to summarize the paper's main argument *without* sounding repetitious, being long-winded, or introducing a new idea altogether. Notice how this author discusses an element of the film heretofore ignored (its title) as a way of reiterating the main point. The author avoids using a self-announcing phrase, such as "In conclusion," to begin the paragraph. Such phrases are clunky and distracting.

5 Again the author refers to the title of the film, but with a twist: the title takes on two different meanings. In effect, the author has introduced a new idea in the concluding paragraph. In general, writers try to avoid introducing new ideas in the conclusion. But here the new idea encapsulates the rest of the paper. Other writers might provide a more straightforward summary. Some conclusions point to the need for further research on the topic at hand, or ask readers a provocative question designed to make them contemplate the main argument further.

Works Consulted

Bordwell, David. *On the History of Film Style*. Cambridge, MA: Harvard University Press, 1997.

Chion, Michel. *Audio-Vision: Sound on Screen*. New York: Columbia University Press, 1994.

Cook, David. *A History of Narrative Film*. New York: Norton, 1996.

Festinger, Rob, and Todd Field. *In the Bedroom*. New York: Hyperion, 2002.

Frayling, Christopher. *Sergio Leone: Something to Do with Death*. London: Faber, 2000.

Gomery, Douglas. "The Coming of Sound; Technological Change in the American Film Industry," in *Film Sound*, ed. Elizabeth Weis and John Belton. New York: Columbia University Press, 1985, pp. 5–24.

Gorbman, Claudia. *Unheard Melodies: Narrative Film Music*. Bloomington: Indiana University Press, 1987.

Kinder, Marsha, and Beverle Houston. *Close-Up: A Critical Perspective on Film*. New York: Harcourt, Brace, Jovanovich, 1972.

Lee, Joanna. "The Music of *In the Mood for Love*." *In the Mood for Love*. Dir. Wong Kar-Wai. DVD. USA/Criterion, 2002.

Leeper, Jill. "Crossing Borders: The Soundtrack for *Touch of Evil*," in *Soundtrack Available: Essays on Film and Popular Music*, ed. Pamela Robertson Wojcik and Arthur Knight. Durham, NC: Duke University Press, 2001, pp. 226–43.

LoBrutto, Vincent. *Sound on Film: Interviews with Creators of Film Sound*. Westport, CT: Praeger, 1994.

Otto, Jeff, and Spence D. "Howard Shore Interview." *ign.com*. (http://music.ign.com/articles/446/446567pl.html).

Prendergast, Roy M. *Film Music: A Neglected Art*, 2nd edn. New York: Norton, 1992.

Rhines, Jesse Algeron. *Black Films/White Money*. New Brunswick, NJ: Rutgers University Press, 1996.

Salt, Barry, "Film Style and Technology in the Thirties: Sound," in *Film Sound*, ed. Elizabeth Weis and John Belton. New York: Columbia University Press, 1985, pp. 37–43.

Shreger, Charles. "Altman, Dolby, and the Second Sound Revolution," in *Film Sound*, ed. Elizabeth Weis and John Belton. New York: Columbia University Press, 1985, pp. 348–55.

Smith, Jeff. *The Sound of Commerce*. New York: Columbia University Press, 1998.

Smith, Steven. "A Chorus of Isolation." *Taxi Driver*. Dir. Martin Scorsese. Laser Disc. Criterion/Voyager Co. 1990.

Triggs, Jeffery Alan. "The Legacy of Babel: Language in Jean Renoir's *Grand Illusion*." *The New Orleans Review*, 15/2 (1988), pp. 70–74.

Alternatives to Narrative Fiction Film: Documentary and Avant-garde Films

The logic of a work of art is the result of re-relating elements selected from reality into a new relationship so that a new reality is created which, in turn, endows the selected elements with a new value.

Maya Deren

Many moviegoers regard "the fiction feature film *à la* Hollywood [...] as the 'real' cinema, much in the same way as an American tourist abroad might ask: 'How much is this in *real* money?'" (Stam, p. 5). But alternative filmmaking practices such as documentary and avant-garde cinemas are very real, and a sound grasp of their history and formal organization is crucial to understanding film art and culture. This chapter explores the formal characteristics of documentary and avant-garde films and emphasizes the way they differ from narrative, feature-length commercial fiction films.

8.1 Errol Morris's *The Fog of War*, an extended interview with former US Defense Secretary Robert McNamara.

Three Modes of Filmmaking: A Comparison

Documentary and avant-garde film depart from commercial fiction films in several ways, including their purpose, mode of production, exhibition venues, and their formal organization and visual style. Commercial films (whether screened in theaters, on video or DVDs, or purchased on cable or satellite) are designed to appeal to a mass audience in order to make profits for the companies that produce, distribute, and exhibit them. The parties involved—including writers, directors, actors, producers, studio executives, distributors, and exhibitors—treat films as products that entice the viewing public to spend money on films, concessions, and related toys and games. Not all commercial films turn out to be financially successful, of course, but profitability is the primary goal of the large corporations that produce, distribute, and exhibit them.

By contrast, documentary films present contemporary or historical events, not fictional stories. Documentary filmmakers may be motivated by many reasons unrelated to profitability: they may be interested in educating viewers about a pressing social issue, in introducing viewers to extraordinary people and their achievements, in capturing the humor and pathos of everyday life, or in using the tools of their craft to create a profound experience. Most documentary filmmakers do not treat profits as a primary objective; usually they are pleased if they can just make a living as filmmakers!

The goals of avant-garde filmmakers, like those of documentary filmmakers, vary widely, but two principal concerns dominate the cinemas gathered under this heading. The first is the desire to explore the artistic and technological capabilities of the medium, usually by rejecting the conventional use to which film has been put: telling stories. Like many modern artists, avant-garde films highlight the medium's "materials" (film, light, sound) and technology; these films often draw on connections to painting, sculpture, dance, music, and photography. The second major concern of many avant-garde, experimental, and underground filmmakers is to question orthodoxies beyond the realm of aesthetics. Avant-garde films often challenge conventional thinking about politics, culture, gender, race, and sexuality. These filmmakers are not focused on profits. Instead, they use film as a means of personal expression to address important social issues and to expand the aesthetic vocabulary of film art.

Another way to differentiate commercial film from documentary and avant-garde film is to consider their methods of production and exhibition. Documentaries are not produced in the industrial context of Hollywood, where corporate executives, stars (and their management companies), guilds, and unions interact as part of a complex, profit-oriented system. Instead, individuals or small groups of people work together, raising funds, renting equipment and space, and managing restrictive budgets. Documentary filmmakers spend weeks, months, or even years conducting research, doing interviews, and recording sound and images. Documentary films often have lower production values than commercial fiction films, owing in part to their having smaller budgets. Also, unless a documentary filmmaker works exclusively with archival materials, the spontaneity of real world events often prevents him from taking a "perfect" shot or recording flawless sound.

Screening options for documentaries are limited, and, with a few exceptions, most distributors of documentaries spend only a small amount on advertising. Documentaries are most likely to be seen on public television or on subscription cable or satellite networks (such as The History Channel and A&E). A select few earn theatrical release in art house cinemas or even multiplexes. Recent examples of these exceptions include *The Fog of War* (Errol Morris 2003; fig. **8.1**), *Capturing the Friedmans* (Andrew Jarecki 2003), *Spellbound* (Jeffrey Blitz 2003), and *Bowling for Columbine* (Michael Moore 2002). Several international film festivals are dedicated to screening documentary films, including the Full Frame Documentary Festival in Durham, North Carolina, and the IDFA in Amsterdam, the Netherlands. The peripheral status of documentary film relative to the Hollywood industry is reflected by the fact that there are just two Academy Awards for documentaries: one for short and one for full-length documentary.

Avant-garde films are made in an artisanal mode, often by just one person. Although many avant-garde filmmakers use technology in unconventional ways to produce new visual and sound experiences, the goal is not necessarily to make conventionally beautiful images, but, rather, to create thought-provoking sensual and aesthetic experiences. Experimental filmmakers may eschew synchronized soundtracks, sets, and even actors. The prospects for screening avant-garde films are very limited: their unusual subject matter, short length, and limited distribution channels mean they are only rarely screened in commercial movie theaters. Most experimental films are screened in art galleries, on university campuses, at cinemathèques, film clubs, and theaters devoted to art and avant-garde cinema (such as the now-defunct Cinema 16 in New York) and at film festivals such as Madcat in San Francisco and Flicker (an organization with chapters around the U.S. devoted to Super-8 filmmaking). Two important institutions devoted to preserving and distributing experimental films are the Filmmakers' Cooperative in New York and Canyon Cinema in San Francisco. Because high-speed internet connections make it possible to view trailers and short personal films with ease on the iFilm Network or through the microcinema.com website, access to experimental and avant-garde films may improve.

Avant-garde films should not be confused with independent film, although filmmakers working in both of these modes may self-consciously reject the commercial film production process. Independent feature filmmaking is not always synonymous with an anti-industry perspective, however, as avant-garde filmmaking almost always is. During the Hollywood studio era, independent producers such as Samuel Goldwyn and David O. Selznick circumvented the studio system and worked with directors such as Hitchcock, William Wyler, and William Wellman to make popular films. American directors Stanley Kubrick, Robert Altman, Alan Rudolph, John Sayles, Charles Burnett, Julie Dash, and Steven Soderbergh have made feature films without studio involvement, often by forming their own production or distribution companies. But these directors are not experimental filmmakers. Although they sometimes challenge Hollywood conventions, they produce feature-length narrative fiction films for wide distribution. Although some documentaries depict characters and stories, and some avant-garde films are interested in the way narratives work, neither type of film is *primarily* concerned with telling stories. Thus, they do not obey the rules of narrative form discussed in Chapter Three.

After looking at the history and motivation behind the rise of the documentary as a genre, the remainder of this chapter focuses on documentary form and conventions. It then discusses one particular type of documentary, the ethnographic. This is followed by a discussion of issues relating to avant-garde cinema. Because documentary and avant-garde films have a lower commercial profile than mainstream narrative films, they can prove difficult to track down. The last section of this chapter therefore gives some tips on research in this area.

● Documentary Film: "The Creative Treatment of Actuality"

Most films made before 1907 were not narrative fiction films but short documentaries. These *actualités*, as they were known, were "shot around the world, nominally 'unstaged', although many were documents of performances, dances, processions, and parades" (Russell, p. 52). Moments from daily life, as well as trips to foreign locales, were the frequent subject of the earliest films, including the works of Auguste and Louis Lumière from the 1890s. The novelty of moving images meant that simple vignettes of everyday activities such as a train leaving a station fascinated audiences.

8.2 Workers leaving a factory, an early Lumière brothers *actualité*.

As non-fiction films based on real world events, these *actualités* were precursors to the documentary film. Yet these films vary in the way they present their images: some early Lumière films record everyday acts, such as workers leaving a factory at the end of the day (fig. **8.2**). In others, subjects self-consciously acknowledge the camera, and the filmmakers develop rudimentary narratives. *The Waterer Gets Watered* ("*L'Arroseur arrosé*"; 1895), for example, depicts the travails of a gardener attempting to do his job, while a young boy plays tricks on him (fig. **8.3**). The film has a beginning, middle, and end, and a comic twist. The legitimate question arises: at what point does a documentary film cease to be a document of reality and become instead a fictional creation?

The term "documentary" was coined by John Grierson, founder of the British documentary movement in the 1920s, who famously described documentary film as "the creative treatment of actuality." In his work for government agencies in Britain, Grierson argued that documentary film was superior to fiction film because it presented the real world, not a fantasy, but should do so with greater imagination than a standard newsreel. His deceptively simple phrase suggests the double-edged nature of documentary form. Filmmakers inventively shape the material of "real life" by selecting the subject matter, choosing angles and shots, making editing decisions, creating re-enactments, and adding music or voice-over narration. The outright scripting or staging of events during shooting is precluded. But a tension remains between an ideal—that documentaries capture unmediated reality—and the practical fact that making a film about a topic may well affect the behavior of subjects and the outcome of events.

The purpose of documentary film is to engage viewers by showing them some aspect or aspects of the real world. A documentary filmmaker captures and organizes visual images and sound to convey some truth of that real world situation. Barbara Kopple's *Harlan County USA* (1977), for example, depicts a struggle by coal miners who want to unionize and mine owners who oppose the union (fig. **8.4**). In one dramatic scene, Kopple captures the mine owner's agent driving through the picket line at night shooting at picketers. Without any commentary, the scene effectively makes the argument that the mine owners disregard the lives of the miners and explains why the miners need the union to

8.3 *(top)* A gardener is distracted by a young boy in *The Waterer Gets Watered* ("*L'Arroseur arrosé*").

8.4 *(bottom)* A mine owner's agent shoots at picketers in *Harlan County USA*.

protect themselves. Kopple captures and presents this moment of heightened reality in a way that encourages viewers to draw certain conclusions about the mine owners' unfair and dangerous labor practices, and to take sides. Kopple, whose many non-fiction films cover subjects from the U.S. labor movement to rock music to celebrities such as Woody Allen and Mike Tyson, received the American Film Institute's Lifetime Achievement Award in 2004.

A documentary film director's choices regarding organization and editing influence the conclusions viewers may draw. Unlike Kopple, the director of *Capturing the Friedmans* (2003), Andrew Jarecki, edits interviews in a way that makes it difficult for viewers to form conclusive judgments. The film concerns a family whose lives are irrevocably changed when two family members are accused of sexually abusing neighborhood children. Jarecki repeatedly interrupts the flow of individual testimonies and juxtaposes conflicting statements made by other interviewees. Because of the editing, viewers constantly question the truthfulness of statements that family members, victims, police officers, and experts make (see fig. 5.29).

Some documentaries trace the lives of individuals, such as the Friedmans or the coal miners, and as a result they resemble stories with characters, goals, and obstacles. But even such narrative documentaries do more than simply present a good story. They also say something about the real world.

Narrative Documentaries

Narrative documentaries rely on cause–effect logic and present subjects who seem like characters. But story elements are based on real world events, and any powerful narrative documentary ultimately refers the viewer not just to a satisfying story but also to a complex reality. *Lost in La Mancha* (Keith Fulton and Louis Pepe 2002) tells the story of a grandiose but failed film production: Terry Gilliam's *Don Quixote*. The documentary treats Gilliam as a character with a primary conflict: he faces an uphill struggle to realize his dream of making the film (fig. **8.5**).

8.5 Terry Gilliam's frustrated attempts to make a film become the subject of *Lost in La Mancha*.

The filmmakers shaped this narrative of heroic failure after the fact; this was not the story they had intended to tell. When they began production, they had every intention of completing a "making-of" documentary about Gilliam's successful production. The finished documentary draws parallels between Gilliam and the fictional Quixote (both are men who try to do the impossible) as well as between Gilliam and Orson Welles (famous for his strong directorial vision and his own failed Quixote project). These parallels add to the building sense of doom as the production gradually falls apart.

In this narrative documentary, Gilliam's story serves the filmmakers' argument that visionary artists such as Gilliam and Welles—idealistic, quixotic figures—face insurmountable obstacles in realizing their visions because the industry is driven by finance and insurance interests. This is the complex reality behind the story the directors present.

● Documentary Form

Film scholar Bill Nichols has developed a useful framework for evaluating the documentary's formal mode of organization. Nichols writes, "the logic organizing a documentary film supports an underlying argument, assertion, or claim about the historical world"

(Nichols 2001, p. 27). The simplest argument a documentary film can make is that the images depicted in the film are real: that the film has captured some aspect of existence that is worthy of contemplation. Documentaries may also make other arguments: they may assert that the subject matter of the documentary is worthy of greater scrutiny (the issue has more sides than have been represented); that a social or economic practice has caused, or is causing, problems that need to be addressed; that a subculture is of interest because it resonates with culture at large (or, conversely, because it represents the profound diversity of humanity); that a forgotten but important cultural or historical figure needs to be given her or his due; that previous explanations of a historical event have not fully captured its complexity, or have deliberately ignored certain facts and viewpoints.

Documentaries present this wide variety of arguments through rhetorical devices that appeal to logic, ethics, and emotions. Some documentaries use obvious strategies for argumentation, such as charts, facts, and expert witnesses. Others address viewers on an emotional level, encouraging them to see aspects of the world differently because they identify with a subject of the documentary. Some documentaries do both.

Viewers may be surprised that arguments often are presented through images, not words. For example, *Winged Migration* makes the case that birds are fascinating creatures with remarkable physical strength and distinctive personalities. The film does so entirely through images. The film follows migrating birds as they make their annual trek north and then return home. By focusing exclusively on the birds' behavior—accompanying them in flight, observing them interact with one another—the film suggests that birds are a great source of wonder, and their beauty and complexity are easily overlooked. The inclusion of a jarring scene where hunters shoot several birds out of the sky casts a pall over that sport, since numerous close-ups have enabled the audience to develop an intimacy with the birds.

Documentary filmmakers employ a number of rhetorical strategies to support their assertions about the world. The rest of this section examines four of those strategies—the voice of authority, talking heads, direct cinema (also known as *cinéma vérité*), and self-reflexivity—and the way they are mocked in the popular style of pseudo-documentary called the mockumentary.

Voice of Authority

One of the most basic strategies employed by documentary filmmakers is to combine voice-over narration with images (which function as evidence) in order to convince the audience of a particular claim about the world. Well-known political figures, respected celebrities, and actors with commanding vocal qualities may be employed to narrate these films in an authoritative style. Examples include Ken Burns's televised documentaries on baseball, jazz, and the U.S. Civil War. Burns gathers still photographs, archival footage, and other visual evidence, sewing these images and sounds together with voice-over narration.

8.6 The *Why We Fight* series was highly influential during World War II.

Films that rely exclusively on this strategy include nature documentaries such as the IMAX film *Africa: The Serengeti* (George Casey 1994) and combat films in the *Why We Fight* series. Directed by Hollywood director Frank Capra during the 1940s, these newsreels offered American audiences images of World War II battles combined with scripted narration that persuaded Americans of the appropriateness of the military campaign (fig. **8.6**).

Documentaries made with the sole intent to persuade of the rightness of a single view are referred to as **propaganda films** because they advertise a single position without any allowance for competing perspectives. Some documentary filmmakers attempt to offer a balanced perspective by including competing views, while others feel that their own deeply held beliefs justify them in making the strongest argument possible for one point of view. In any event, it is always useful for viewers to consider the precise claim to authority represented by the narration. Is the author of the textual information an expert on the subject, or does the narrator's commanding voice alone convey authoritative knowledge?

Talking Heads and Director–Participant

8.7 The radical Bernardine Dohrn from *The Weather Underground*.

A second rhetorical strategy combines images with verbal testimony from individuals affected by or interested in the subject matter of the documentary. This strategy allows real people, not a designated off-screen authority, to make assertions about the subject. Documentaries that rely exclusively on interviews are often called "talking heads" documentaries.

Interviews allow for a range of ideas to be presented and may convince the viewers that the reality the filmmaker has presented is as complex as the real world. It also captures the personal feelings of interview subjects, which may invite viewer identification. *Store Wars* (Micha Peled 2001) uses interviews with engaging subjects who discuss the disruptive impact of the attempt by the large discount chain Wal-Mart to build a store in their community. *The Weather Underground* (Sam Green and Bill Siegel 2003) combines archival footage from the 1960s and 1970s with contemporary interviews of Weather Underground radicals, along with activists who disagreed with their tactics, providing a vantage point from thirty years after the events (fig. **8.7**).

A documentary film director may edit images and sound to corroborate *or* to call into question the statements made by subjects. *Fast, Cheap,*

and Out of Control (Errol Morris 1998) looks at four individuals and their work. Each of the four subjects works with animals or animal facsimiles: one is an animal trainer with the circus, another is a mole-rat expert, one is a topiary gardener who fashions enormous animals from shrubbery, and another is a scientist who creates robotic machines.

Morris adopts a bemused perspective on his subjects: his ironic distance is made evident through editing. He juxtaposes images of one subject with sound from interviews with another, so it seems as if the people he interviews are making comments about the lives and work of others. For example, in one scene, circus music plays over images of robots. Later, Morris cuts to images of circus performers, but the sound that accompanies the images comes from statements made by the mole-rat expert and robot scientist (figs. **8.8**, **8.9**). By pairing a subject's statements with seemingly unrelated images, Morris adds depth and dimension to the interviews, introducing ideas that none of his subjects has voiced. Morris gets at one truth by allowing the interviewees to tell their own stories, yet his editing encourages the audience to make unusual connections. For example, are human and mole-rat societies similar, because they both have sharply delineated roles such as king, queen, soldier, worker? Are circus performances akin to robotic movements? Are the robot scientist's concerns that he is too controlling relevant to other social contexts?

Unlike Morris, who presents complex ideas subtly, Michael Moore includes his own pointed commentary as well as interviews with others. Moore's controversial *Fahrenheit 911* (2004), which won the *Palme d'Or* at the 2004 Cannes Film Festival (a prize rarely bestowed on documentary films), is an unapologetic critique of American foreign policy since the terrorist attacks of September 11, 2001. In the film, Moore makes clear his feelings toward government leaders through antagonistic encounters with politicians. In one scene, he accosts members of Congress, asking them to volunteer their children for active duty in the ongoing military operation in Iraq. His actions imply that politicians may find it easy to pursue military options because they don't make the personal sacrifices that ordinary citizens make. Moore acts as narrator and participant, making his point of view clear to the audience (fig. **8.10**).

8.8 *(left)* Robot scientist voice-over in *Fast, Cheap, and Out of Control*: "Sometimes I feel like Yoda—I have to say 'I feel the force, don't try to control the robot.'"

8.9 *(right)* Mole-rat expert voice-over in *Fast, Cheap, and Out of Control*: "To me, it's this incredible mammal that breaks all the rules. A mammal with a queen, king, soldiers, workers, all playing roles."

8.10 Michael Moore.

8.11 Spurlock weighs in in *Super Size Me.*

8.12 The district manager gives a pep talk in *Salesman.*

Super Size Me (2004) follows a similar strategy of directorial participation combined with interviews. Interested in dramatizing the health effects of fast food, director Morgan Spurlock meets with his doctors before embarking on a month of an all-McDonald's diet. Spurlock humorously narrates the changes in his body, interviews people ranging from Big Mac addicts to his own girlfriend, and returns to his doctors for periodic check-ups (fig. **8.11**). A little more than halfway through the month, all have grave concerns about the diet's health effects, which include weight gain, high cholesterol, elevated blood sugar, and liver distress. In this film, the director, his friends, and his doctors testify to the fact that fast food is unhealthy. The argument literally is presented through the director's body as well as in interviews and images.

Direct Cinema

A third rhetorical strategy represents a radical shift from talking heads documentaries, especially those that feature the personal involvement of the director. Observational documentaries (also called direct cinema and *cinéma vérité*, which means "cinema of truth") present events without any evidence of the director's perspective or judgments. In short, filmmakers attempt to make themselves invisible. They shoot events with minimal intrusion (lighting, cameras, microphones) and do not supply voice-over commentary that might influence the viewer's interpretation. The development of this intentionally unobtrusive style of documentary during the 1960s owed a great deal to the introduction of lightweight 16 mm cameras and the portable Nagra tape recorder, which helped directors capture unfolding events with as little intervention as possible. A number of important observational films emerged from that decade, including David and Albert Maysles's *Salesman* (1966), D.A. Pennebaker's *Don't Look Back* (1967), and Frederick Wiseman's *High School* (1968).

Two of direct cinema's visual techniques—the static camera and the long take—strongly connote the idea that viewers are invisible observers watching events unfold. The Maysles brothers' classic *cinéma vérité* documentary *Salesman* uses long takes and a static camera to depict Bible salesmen in the Northeastern U.S. The camera captures the boredom of some salesmen at district meetings as well as the anxiety of those whose sales figures have not been adequate (fig. **8.12**). A scene immediately after the district manager's "pep talk" shows the manager storming out of the room, repeating some of the phrases from his talk. The camera becomes mobile as the filmmakers follow the subject down the hallway, eavesdropping on his conversation, which involves a somewhat misappropriated quotation of civil rights activist Fannie Lou Hamer's famous line about fighting for social justice: "I'm sick and tired of being sick and tired."

Despite the desire of some *vérité* directors to make themselves invisible during production, they do make choices and employ

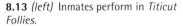

8.13 *(left)* Inmates perform in *Titicut Follies.*

8.14 *(right)* Staff members perform in *Titicut Follies.*

techniques in production and post-production that convey implicit ideas. Directors choose the subject matter, select the framing of shots, and juxtapose scenes through editing. In many regards, editing is the cinematic technique that offers the documentary filmmaker the greatest influence over the material. In Wiseman's controversial *Titicut Follies* (1967), for example, the editing and framing make it difficult to distinguish between the staff and inmates at a mental institution (figs. **8.13**, **8.14**). Wiseman's camerawork and editing thus present a subtle argument that those deemed mentally unstable may not be so different from the rest of society, or that such institutions force the sane and insane to behave the same way.

Self-reflexive Documentary

A fourth rhetorical strategy departs dramatically from direct cinema by including the process of filmmaking as part of the subject matter of the film. Bill Nichols calls this "self-reflexive documentary" because, like formalist narrative films, these films refer to the process of filming and expose the way the medium constructs reality. They challenge audiences to reconsider the relationship between documentary images and reality. Shirley Clarke's *Portrait of Jason* (1967), for example, questions the nature of cinematic truth by taking as its subject a young hustler who tells stories about his life, but then contradicts them, undermining the viewer's ability to take his statements at face value. For example, he introduces himself as Jason, and then confesses to the camera that his real name is not Jason, but Aaron Payne. From the outset, the film calls into question the process of uncovering identity by interviewing someone on film. Self-reflexive visual techniques (such as bringing Jason in and out of focus between scenes) also undercut the veracity of the process (fig. **8.15**).

8.15 A close-up emphasizes issues of identity in *A Portrait of Jason.*

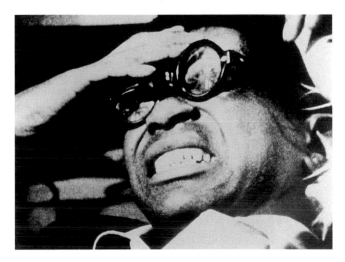

As these examples suggest, documentary filmmakers can and do make creative use of reality for a number of purposes: to inform viewers about extraordinary or mundane aspects of reality, to encourage viewers to draw conclusions about world events, to change the audience's understanding of social issues, and to question the way the film medium constructs reality.

● Avant-garde Film

Like documentary film, avant-garde film—called experimental film in the 1940s and '50s and underground cinema during the 1960s and '70s—represents an extraordinarily diverse array of filmmaking practices. Some avant-garde films tell bizarre stories, others focus on the abstract qualities of the film images, while still others may choose to explore one particular technical aspect of film, such as slow motion, and to exploit its effects to the full. Many avant-garde filmmakers have been associated with art and social change movements, including Surrealism, Minimalism, feminism, and gay and lesbian liberation.

If viewers think of cinema solely in terms of narrative film, then avant-garde films may put them off. These films ask viewers to interpret images and sounds that are not organized according to narrative form and thus require a different set of skills for interpretation. Scott MacDonald argues that avant-garde films may evoke frustration because "these films confront us with the necessity of redefining an experience we were sure we understood" (MacDonald, p. 2).

What kind of redefined film-going experience does MacDonald refer to? Avant-garde films rarely present straightforward stories or characters. Instead, they approach the film medium as an aesthetic, philosophical, and/or political means of expression. They often isolate elements of film art—including cinematography, sound, and editing—and subject them to intense scrutiny. Avant-garde films often reject traditional methods for combining images and sound, startling the viewer with new possibilities. They may explore such things as: the way light achieves certain photographic effects; the influence of abstract shapes and color on emotions; how superimposition connects two images; how repetition inspires certain thoughts; how rapid editing overwhelms perceptual capacities; and whether an image means the same thing to viewers when is it paired with an unlikely soundtrack.

Avant-garde filmmakers self-consciously break new ground in film aesthetics and cultural politics. The techniques experimental filmmakers use to challenge convention include time-lapse photography, fast, slow, and reverse motion, negative images, scratching and painting on the emulsion, superimposition, electronic soundtracks, and non-synchronized sound. Film scholar William Wees considers these devices "gestures of rebellion against the conventions of popular cinema [. . .] They confront the viewer with a more complex and dynamic experience of visual perception than is normally the case in film viewing" (Wees, p. 4). In other words, they ask viewers to pay close attention to images and sounds as sensual, emotional, and aesthetic experiences, meaningful on their own terms, not because they obey the logic of character development and cause and effect.

The sections below examine several important styles and traditions in avant-garde filmmaking, including Surrealism, abstract film, the city symphony, structuralist film, and the compilation film. This examination is suggestive rather than comprehensive; an annotated list of resources for further research directs readers to sources for exploring the gamut of avant-garde filmmaking practices.

Surrealist Cinema

One film convention that early European avant-garde filmmakers rebelled against was narrative form. Surrealist film culture, centered in Paris, grew out of Dada and Surrealist currents in performance (Hugo Ball and Tristan Tzara), photography (Man Ray), and literature (André Breton). Surrealist filmmakers explored the irrational, unconscious mind "beneath" the surface of reality.

Surrealist films are rife with humor, sexuality, and scandalous images. They reject conventional morality and poke fun at bourgeois values through form and content. *Un Chien andalou* ("*An Andalusian Dog*"; Luis Buñuel and Salvador Dalí 1929), *Entr'acte* (René Clair 1924) and *Ballet Mécanique* (Fernand Léger, Man Ray, and Dudley Murphy 1924) are Surrealist films that subvert chronological time and narrative causality. In *Entr'acte* a series of loosely connected scenes includes a dancing ballerina who becomes a man (fig. **8.19**) and a runaway hearse that incites an absurd chase scene (fig. **8.20**), commenting on World War I as an out-of-control race toward death.

Un Chien andalou vigorously mocks narrative form. The sequence of events is not organized in a coherent fashion; viewers cannot make sense of the events through cause-and-effect logic. While intertitles offer clichéd phrases apparently designed to orient

8.19 *(left)* A ballerina becomes a man in *Entr'acte*.

8.20 *(right)* The fragmented perspective of a runaway hearse in *Entr'acte*.

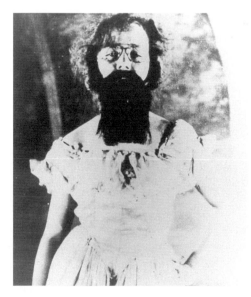

8.21 *(left)* A woman's lover waits on the beach in *Un Chien andalou* ("*An Andalusian Dog*")

8.22 *(right)* The lovers "in the Spring" in *Un Chien andalou.*

viewers to a timeline, the film renders the information useless. Although several intertitles announce that the action is moving backward or forward by years or hours, the events seem continuous. Unnamed characters have few clear goals or conflicts (although motifs include gender fluidity and sexual aggression). The soundtrack parodies the way non-diegetic music is used in commercial narrative cinema to invoke emotions, pairing Wagner's *Tristan and Isolde* with bizarre vignettes that have little to do with romance. Slow motion is used merely for its own sake. One character shoots his double from across the room, and an inexplicable happy ending is tacked on at the conclusion, when a single cut permits a woman to move from an urban apartment location to join her lover on the beach (figs. **8.21**, **8.22**).

During World War II, a number of European artists and filmmakers left occupied Europe and came to the U.S., where an American avant-garde developed, in New York and San Francisco. Within the American avant-garde, some filmmakers expanded on the Surrealist tradition, dismantling narrative by working in a poetic form. Maya Deren's poetic 16-minute film *Meshes of the Afternoon* (1943) explores the dream state, suspending the notion of chronological time while relying on characters, settings, and the semblance of a narrative. Deren and her husband use domestic interiors as the dreamlike and nightmarish location for the dreamer's vivid and self-destructive imagination. (See Film Analysis, pp. 197–200.)

While contemporary filmmaker Sadie Benning does not focus on the dream state *per se*, her intensely autobiographical films depict every day life as surreal. The meditative tone of many of her films reflects her isolation: one response to a world that is hostile to women and lesbians. In her earliest films, made at age fifteen, "her main subject was herself, coming to terms with a pervasive 1980s cultural of junk TV and mindless consumerism" (Morris). In *Flat is Beautiful* (1998), the actors all wear masks. The characters' "authentic feelings and desires continuously strain to break through these rigid, unforgiving, literally constructed identities" (Morris). Benning's work is notable because of her facility with the low-resolution Fisher Price Pixelvision camera (originally marketed as a toy for children), her complex examination of gender and sexuality, and her ability to integrate drawings, masks, video, and film in menacing and poetic ways.

Abstract Film

At the same time as the Surrealists were exploring irrationality, filmmakers such as Man Ray, Walter Ruttmann, and Hans Richter established a very different tradition, one of abstract filmmaking. Their films abandoned human figures altogether. *Opus I–IV* (Walter

Ruttman 1921–5) and *Rhythmus 21* (Hans Richter 1921–4) pay attention to graphic form and rhythmic editing. Their animated, geometrical forms reflect their creators' idea that filmmaking was painting with motion. Man Ray's *Return to Reason* ("*Le Retour à la raison*"; 1923) made use of his signature technique, called rayography, which involved laying objects on unexposed film and exposing them to light briefly, creating contact images without the use of a camera.

San Francisco-trained filmmaker Stan Brakhage made a number of abstract films that reflected his interest in the philosophy and physiology of vision. Brakhage sought to liberate human perception from a "'practical' view of experience in which the goal of amassing material wealth requires conformity in how we see and how we act" (MacDonald, p. 6). Abandoning goal-oriented perception in favor of "open, 'receptive' seeing," Brakhage painted on, bleached, and scraped the film surface to produce "closed-eye" vision; that is, the things people are capable of seeing when their eyes are closed (Wees, p. 126). Brakhage believed that the untutored eye absorbs and creates its own visual field before it learns to recognize familiar objects. Brakhage thought he was, "the most thorough documentary filmmaker in the world because I document the act of seeing as well as everything the light brings me" (quoted in Wees, p. 78).

Viewers may take issue with Brakhage's claim that he makes documentaries because many of his films are abstract. His *Film No. 6* (1975) exemplifies this dual commitment to engaging with the real world and eliciting "untutored vision" from spectators. In that film, time-lapse photography is used to transform close-ups of plants from yellow to green as the sun sweeps across them. "The camera eye has caught what the human eye might miss—or misperceive as ordinary green grass" (Wees, p. 66). Film scholar David Curtis wrote about Brakhage that his films defy all conventional notions of filmmaking. They have "no story, no symbolism, no acting, no posed photographic beauty; the drama is [. . .] the drama of vision, a vision that implies a belief that the first priority is to see and record, the second to structure and interpret" (Curtis, p. 86).

Although described within the abstract tradition here, Brakhage has been called a personal and visionary filmmaker because his work is both poetic and self-referential: for example, a number of his films revolve around his life with his wife, Jane, and their children. His commitment to exploring the possibilities of vision led him to produce more than 300 films, and his *oeuvre* is extraordinarily diverse: *The Act of Seeing with One Own's Eyes* (1971) documents autopsies, whereas *Dog Star Man* (1964) is a multi-part romantic tale of mythic male struggle. The two films discussed in the film analysis at the end of this chapter are pure abstractions, which the filmmaker called "bits of paint painted on film" ("Remarks").

The City Symphony

Beginning in the 1920s, a number of filmmakers celebrated the vibrancy of the modern city with the **city symphony** film, a genre that combines documentary and experimental film. Walter Ruttmann's *Berlin, Symphony of a Great City* ("*Berlin: Die Sinfonie der*

Großstadt"; 1927) and Dziga Vertov and Boris Kaufman's *Man with a Movie Camera* ("*Chelovek s kinoapparatom*"; 1929) are organized by the chronological timeline of a single day. They open with images depicting early morning, and then proceed to document people as they work and carry out leisure activities before concluding in the darkness of the evening.

Ruttmann and Vertov's films present ideas through visual association: images are combined and produce meaning based on their visual attributes, not through the logic of cause and effect. Both filmmakers are fascinated by the movements of modern urban life and edit their films to establish visual comparisons. Ruttmann films a sequence of blinds and store windows opening, marking the synchronicity of actions taken early in the day. At midday, he shows the way lunch interrupts the workday for both wealthy businessmen and factory workers.

Vertov's film reflects his utopian ideas about the machine age. His excitement about the modern industrial world can be inferred from his own assumed name, which means

8.23 *(top left)* An image of rotation from *Man with a Movie Camera* ("*Chelovek s kinoapparatom*"): a sewing machine.

8.24 *(top right)* Another image of rotation from *Man with a Movie Camera*: a turbine engine.

8.25 *(bottom left)* Fluttering images of eyes in *Man with a Movie Camera.*

8.26 *(bottom right)* Blinds in *Man with a Movie Camera.*

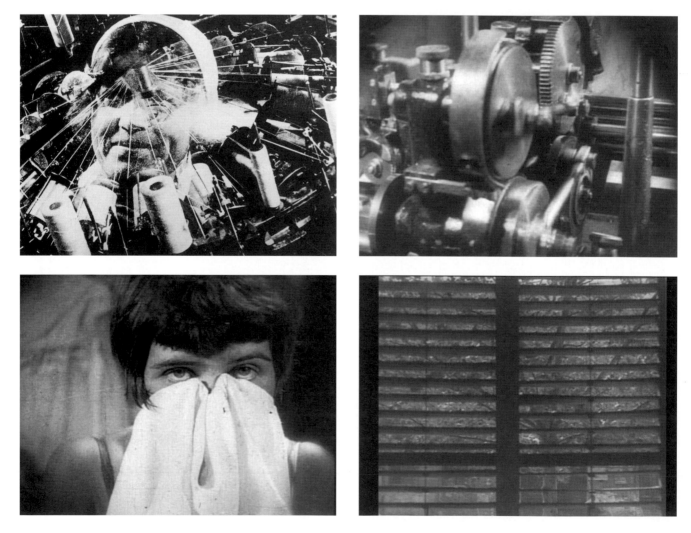

Chapter 8: Alternatives to Narrative Fiction Film

"spinning top." Sequences in *Man with a Movie Camera* transmit the aesthetic intoxication of machines in motion. One series of shots visually compares machines that rotate and spin, from the simple sewing machine to huge turbine engines (figs. **8.23**, **8.24**). The connection between the images lies in the similar circular motion.

Vertov also uses self-reflexive techniques to call attention to the process of making the film. At one point a woman gets out of bed and washes her face at a basin. She looks directly at the camera and blinks her eyes (fig. **8.25**). Vertov cuts to a shot of Venetian blinds opening and closing (fig. **8.26**). After cutting back and forth between the two images, he introduces a third: a close-up of a camera lens as its aperture opens and closes (fig. **8.27**). The editing requires that the viewer take an active part in interpretation: it invites spectators to contemplate the work of the film-maker as an observer of daily life and to note the parallels between the fluttering motion of the eyes, blinds, and the lens as they all let light in and out.

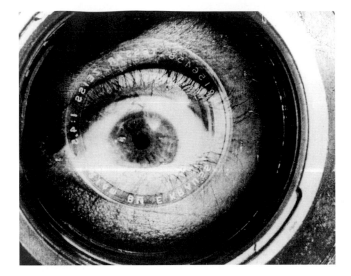

8.27 A camera-eye double exposure, from *Man with a Movie Camera*.

Vertov also includes images of a man with a movie camera traveling around the city and shows the editor (Kaufman's wife) selecting strips of film to splice together. The images she handles appear later in the film. Vertov believed that filmmaking should be a collaborative enterprise made by and for the mass public. For him, the ideal film would consist of many amateur artists shooting footage that would be assembled without regard to realism or continuity. Editors would create visual associations and metaphors that captured the underlying reality of the exciting modern world.

Two short experimental films of the 1950s that grow out of the city symphony tradition are Shirley Clarke's *Bridges Go Round* (1958) and Marie Mencken's *Go Go Go* (1963). Clarke's film offers an interesting lesson in the relationship between image and sound. In this non-narrative 3½-minute film, Clarke plays with images of bridges in New York City. She records the city skyline while driving across bridges, and then repeatedly superimposes the structural steel bridges against the sky. Clarke made two versions of the film; the images are identical, but the musical scores differ. In one, a jazzy score by saxophone player and jazz producer Teo Macero accompanies the images; in the second, Bebe Barron's electronic score plays (Barron scored *Forbidden Planet* [Fred Wilcox 1956] with her husband, Louis). Watching the two versions of Clarke's film can create vastly different impressions because each score emphasizes different elements of the images: the jazz score underlines the pace of editing and the camera movement, whereas the electronic score highlights the abstract patterns created by the images of bridges.

New York filmmaker, painter, and poet Marie Mencken made films that were an extension of her many talents. In them, surface, texture, and rhythm (including camera movement, editing, or fast motion) became central elements. *Go Go Go* uses a handheld camera and stop-motion photography to record the daily activities of New Yorkers.

Structuralist Film

In the 1960s, filmmakers, like painters and Conceptual artists, developed an interest in "a 'metaphysics' of the cinematic apparatus" (MacDonald, p. 37). Structuralist filmmakers explored the material properties of the medium: strips of film, sound waves, cameras, and lenses. Ernie Gehr's *Serene Velocity* (1970) is a 23-minute film of a classroom hallway at the university where Gehr taught. By filming the hallway four frames at a time and then readjusting the zoom lens (working from the midpoint to either end of the lens's focal range), he makes the image appear to pulsate rhythmically. Scott MacDonald describes the film as both violent and contemplative (MacDonald, p. 41).

In *Wavelength* (1967), Michael Snow also manipulates a zoom lens in an attempt to examine film space and time. For Snow, as for Gehr, "the camera is fixed in a mystical con-

8.28 A close-up of a photograph on the wall in *Wavelength*.

templation of a portion of space" (Sitney, p. 350). Throughout the film's 45-minute zoom, the shifting focal length reconfigures the space of a New York loft, from three-dimensional deep space to a two-dimensional flat surface. The shot slowly closes in on a photograph on the wall (fig. **8.28**). The soundtrack is a sine wave that rises in pitch, its own wavelengths shortening over the duration of the film.

Wavelength is a reflection on cinematic form, not an exploration of character or action. Initially, the film appears to offer a narrative: women move a bookcase into an apartment; a man enters the room and falls down; a woman makes a telephone call to report the dead body to someone. But, finally, no story coalesces around these events. Instead, the film invites viewers to focus on the way their perception of time and space shifts as a result of cinematic acts of observation. Scott MacDonald calls the final irony the fact that the long, slow zoom ultimately delivers the viewer to "the absolute nemesis of the conventional cinema: to a still photograph viewed in silence for several minutes" (MacDonald, p. 36).

The Compilation Film

The compilation film reuses pre-existing film footage in an entirely new context to generate innovative ideas. Bruce Conner's *A Movie* (1958) is a classic example of compilation filmmaking. Conner worked as a collage sculptor before turning to film. The use of found footage to stimulate new ideas recalls Marcel Duchamp's subversive aesthetic of ready-mades and *objets trouvés* ("found objects"). The compilation film offers many opportunities for irony: since the images all originate in another context, a distance exists between the images and the viewer's experiences of them (Sitney, p. 298).

In compilation films, themes and ideas emerge from the careful sequencing and juxtaposition of vastly different images. Conner's film exploits irony by juxtaposing shots of a

8.29 *(left)* A submariner and periscope in *A Movie.*

8.30 *(right)* An image of Marilyn Monroe, from *A Movie.*

submariner looking through a periscope (fig. **8.29**) with images of a Marilyn Monroe film (fig. **8.30**). The editing suggests the seaman sees the sexy images. When the submarine fires a torpedo, the explosion yields a mushroom cloud. The sequence turns on the humorous connection between war and sexual aggression but also offers some sobering implications. In Chick Strand's *Cartoon La Mousse* (1979), footage from classic cartoons forms the centerpiece for an eerie meditation on romance and solitude.

A more recent film, *Decasia* (Bill Morrison 2002), hypnotically juxtaposes archival footage from *The Last Egyptian* (L. Frank Baum 1914) with an original symphonic score. The film evokes the cultural importance and neglect of the film medium as well as the ghostly beauty of the degraded images.

● Conducting Research on Documentary and Avant-garde Films: Locating Sources

Locating avant-garde and documentary films may pose a challenge. Documentary and avant-garde films can be difficult to obtain; generally, most DVD and video rental outlets will offer a small selection at best. Some films are available only on film, not in electronic formats. Thus, the research process for scholars pursuing an interest in these films often begins with a detective story: finding film prints or locating an outlet to rent or purchase a video copy or DVD.

Conducting an on-line search for a director or film is one place to begin; but a great deal of information about alternative filmmaking, including articles and reviews, does not appear in on-line indexes. A university library may offer access to print sources that may not be available on-line. And a university reference librarian may be able to locate film, video, and digital materials through interlibrary loan.

The list below is another resource. Many of these sites and organizations make documentary or avant-garde films available through rental and purchase; in some cases, materials do not circulate but may be viewed on the premises.

tones of the paint from one frame to the next. The subtle variations and carefully modulated editing simulate a shimmer of movement.

Brakhage uses two devices to create the illusion of depth. First, he divides the frame into two areas: the color daubs at the outer portions of the frame and black in the center. The composition emphasizes depth: it creates a foreground of color and a background of color-swallowing black in what appears to be the deep center of the frame.[2] Second, the painted splashes that appear to move forward do so at a slower pace than the colors rotating around the periphery. This discrepancy creates an additional layer of depth and also produces a visual tension, a sense of unease that simulates falling. The combination of the moving paint splotches and the two speeds of movement suggests the idea of black ice—something that is unseen but dangerous and that might cause a person to misjudge depth and fall down (see fig. 2.3).

In *Dark Tower*, Brakhage once again relies on the most basic elements of film: dabs of colored paint, a black background, and editing. But the composition and editing produce distinctly different effects. In the first section of the film, a tapered dark shape occupies the center of the frame, with bright paint arranged on either side.[3] Those splashes of color become gashes of light and color, creating a stained-glass effect in the second section (fig. **8.31**).

In the third segment, those thin slices of light and color clash horizontally across the frame, simulating turbulent sword fights. In the fourth section, the composition changes radically: a vertical strip of black appears in the center of the frame, dividing the two sides of the image. This repeats the opening section with the subtle tapered shape, but here the shape is bold. In the film's final section, the clashing splashes of color and light become larger and bolder, and give off white haloes.

8.31 *(left)* Refracted light and color produce a stained-glass effect in *Dark Tower*.

8.32 *(right)* A black line divides the frame in the fourth section of *Dark Tower*.

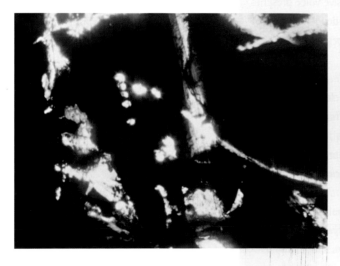

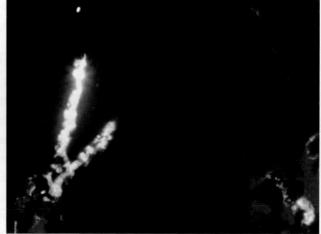

In contrast to *Black Ice*, editing and composition in *Dark Tower* emphasize the division of the frame into right and left, not foreground and background (fig. **8.32**). On the DVD, Brakhage describes this film as "an *homage* to all the dark towers in literary history" (*By Brakhage*). Brakhage sees these divided compositions as abstract versions of the classical image of the medieval tower, an image that may be familiar from the *Lord of the Rings* trilogy. Pursuing this interpretation, one could argue that the editing emphasizes the brutal, physical clash of abstract entities, possibly connoting a mythic struggle between good and evil, light and darkness.

●●●

Works Consulted

Brakhage, Stan. "Remarks." *By Brakhage: An Anthology*. Criterion Collection DVD, 2003.

Brakhage, Stan. *Film at Wit's End: Eight Avant-garde Filmmakers*. New York: McPherson, 1989.

Clark, VeVe, Millicent Hodson, and Catrina Neiman (ed.) *The Legend of Maya Deren*, vol. 1, part 2. New York: Anthology Film Archives/Film Culture, 1984.

Corner, John. *The Art of Record: A Critical Introduction to Documentary*. Manchester and NY: Manchester University Press, 1996.

Curtis, David. *Experimental Cinema: A Fifty Year Evolution*. New York: Dell, 1971.

Gidal, Peter. *Materialist Film*. London: Routledge, 1989.

Horak, Jan Christopher. "The First American Avant-Garde, 1919–1945," in *Lovers of Cinema. The First American Film Avant-Garde 1919–45*, ed. Jan-Christopher Horak. Madison: University of Wisconsin Press, 1995, pp. 14–66.

James, David. *Allegories of Cinema: American Film in the 1960s*. Princeton: Princeton University Press, 1989.

MacDonald, Scott. *Avant-Garde Film: Motion Studies*. Cambridge: Cambridge University Press, 1993.

Moritz, William. "Americans in Paris" in *Lovers of Cinema: The First American Film Avant-Garde 1919–45*, ed. Jan-Christopher Horak. Madison: University of Wisconsin Press, 1995, pp. 118–36.

Morris, Gary. "Behind the Mask: Sadie Benning's Pixel Pleasures." *Bright Lights Film Journal*, issue 24: April 1999. http://www.brightlightsfilm.com/24/benning.html. 2/17/04.

Nichols, Bill. *Introduction to Documentary*. Bloomington and Indianapolis: Indiana University Press, 2001.

Nichols, Bill. *Representing Reality*. Bloomington and Indianapolis: Indiana University Press, 1991.

Peterson, James. *Dreams of Chaos, Visions of Order: Understanding the American Avant-Garde Cinema*. Detroit: Wayne State University Press, 1994.

Rees, A.L. *A History of Experimental Film and Video*. London: British Film Institute, 1999.

Rigney, Melissa. "Sadie Benning." *Senses of Cinema. Great Directors: A Critical Database*. www.sensesofcinema.com/contents/directors/03/benning.html. 2/17/04.

Russell, Catherine. *Experimental Ethnography*. Durham, NC, and London: Duke University Press, 1999.

Sitney, P. Adams. *Visionary Film: The American Avant-Garde, 1943–1978*, 3rd edn. Oxford and New York: Oxford University Press, 2002.

Stam, Robert. *Film Theory: An Introduction*. Malden, MA, and Oxford: Blackwell, 2000.

Sussex, Elizabeth. *The Rise and Fall of British Documentary*. Berkeley and Los Angeles: University of California Press, 1975.

Swann, Paul. *The British Documentary Film Movement, 1926–46*. Cambridge: Cambridge University Press, 1989.

9

Writing About Film

9.1 Appearances are deceiving: the photographer examines his work in *Blow-Up.*

The best critic is one who illuminates whole provinces of an art that you could not see before.

Stanley Kauffman

*T*he proliferation of independent zines and the varied assortment of film-related sites on the internet, not to mention the continued prevalence of newspaper and magazine reviews, mean that casual and avid film buffs alike now have access to a wide array of film writing on a daily basis. Reviews, biographies, box office statistics, behind-the-scenes gossip, and production information are all readily available in print and on-line. Even the descriptive blurbs on the back of video sleeves and DVD jewelboxes are examples of film writing.

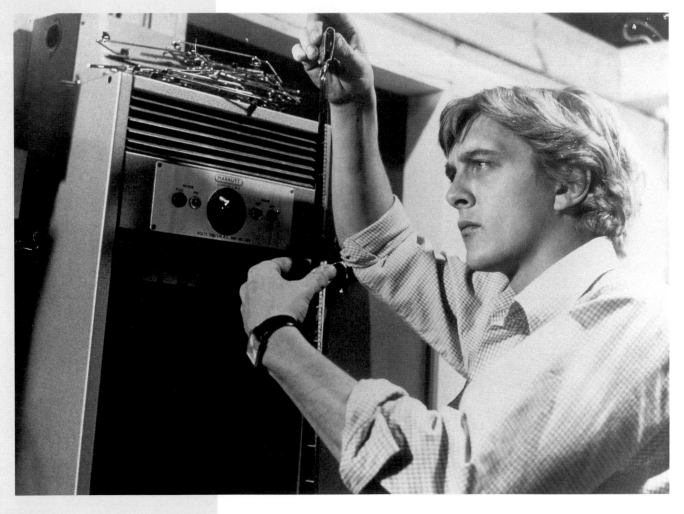

Writing about film in an academic setting, however, differs from the writing that appears in such popular contexts. When a professor asks students to write about film, she requires students to go beyond describing a movie's plot, asserting its entertainment value, or detailing its profitability. While an academic discussion of a film might include this information, most academic assignments ask students to consider how a film (or a group of films) functions as a complex artistic and cultural document. Instructors hope that writing assignments will help students fully appreciate the medium's complexity, artistic potential, and diversity.

This chapter discusses strategies for preparing to write about films, including generating ideas and gathering evidence. Then it explores the four most common genres of writing about film: the scene analysis, the film analysis, the research paper, and the popular review.

● Getting Started

Keeping a Film Journal

The Study Notes accompanying Chapter Two's reading of *Devil in a Blue Dress* discuss the importance of taking notes during screenings. This is the first step in any type of writing about a film, be it a popular review or critical analysis. Some film enthusiasts and scholars also find it helpful to keep a screening journal—a cinephile's version of a diary. In a journal or notebook specifically dedicated to keeping track of viewing experiences, viewers log entries for each film screened.

A typical journal entry should include the film's title and important production information: its release date and studio, its director, its cast, and a brief plot summary. Because journals explore an individual's response to films, entries tend to vary significantly from one film to the next. Some entries might make an evaluative claim ("this film is great") and explain the reasons for it. Others could include interpretive observations, noting among other things a film's motifs and parallels, references to other films, or significant scenes. Some entries might document details of the filmgoing experience: did the spectator see the film in a new venue or while traveling? How did the audience respond to the film? Was going to the movie part of a memorable date?

Because they document a person's most (and least) enjoyable experiences at the movies, film journals provide opportunities for personal exploration and creative thinking and writing. Furthermore, keeping a journal helps film students study for exams (journals can provide detailed information that prods the memory) and generate ideas for papers.

Formulating a Thesis

Because it encapsulates the entire argument of an essay in a sentence or two, the thesis statement is the most crucial element in any written analysis of a film. Consequently, most writers try to develop a working thesis *before* they start to write. Writing a formal analysis of a film (as opposed to an informal, personal journal entry) requires multiple viewings of the film(s) under consideration. Defining the main idea of a paper before undertaking these repeated screenings imposes order on the process by helping clarify what to look for. Obviously the thesis can and will evolve over the course of several viewings of a film. Nevertheless, crafting a provisional thesis statement is a crucial first step in writing a strong essay.

Many writers assume that drafting a thesis is a daunting task. Often students do not know what constitutes a strong thesis, or what a particular instructor looks for in a thesis. While a plot summary is appropriate in newspaper blurbs announcing the movies playing at the local theater, thesis statements go beyond superficial descriptive claims. A strong thesis for an academic paper does more than simply stating what would be obvious to anyone who watched the film; it organizes and interprets the information gleaned from analysis. A strong thesis proposes a debatable argument about a film and reveals the writer's understanding of themes and appreciation of the way cinematic techniques coalesce into a coherent artistic expression.

Below are four common types of thesis statements: each makes an interpretive claim about a single film (fig. **9.2**). The left-hand column briefly summarizes each rhetorical

9.2 Common rhetorical approaches for writing on a single film.

Rhetorical approach	Sample thesis statement
Illustrate how a character (or group of characters) undergoes physical and/or emotional changes to attain a goal. Include visual and/or sound elements as contributing to the film's emphasis on character change.	In *About a Boy* (Chris Weitz and Paul Weitz 2002), Will Lightman comes to realize that life without companionship is empty. The film's narrative, *mise en scène*, and cinematography all emphasize how Lightman gradually changes from a materialistic, self-centered hermit to a benevolent father figure willing to humiliate himself to help a lonely young boy.
Explore how a character's psychological or emotional makeup defines the film's primary conflict. Include visual and sound elements as factors that enhance the film's presentation of psychology and emotions.	Catherine Hardwick's sobering film *Thirteen* (2003) explores how Tracy pursues a friendship with the school's most popular (and most trouble-prone) girl in order to find the emotional security she can't find at home. The girls' experimentation with drugs and crime is a destructive ritual of emotional bonding, a substitute for the parental guidance they lack.
Discuss how a film consistently employs a particular stylistic device to develop its story and themes.	*Dancer in the Dark* (Lars von Trier 2000) employs two distinct styles to differentiate the dismal routine of Selma's real life with the colorful glamor of her musical fantasies. The jolting collision of styles emphasizes how Selma's fantasies, based on the Hollywood musicals she adores, are hopelessly naïve, even while they are her only means of coping with the hostile environment around her.
Argue that a film explores a cultural phenomenon; consider whether or not the film adopts a position on this phenomenon.	The most horrifying thing about *28 Days Later* (Danny Boyle 2003) is its implication that innate human survival instincts are indistinguishable from the anti-social effects of a rage-inducing bacterium that decimates England's population by transforming humans into bloodthirsty zombies.

approach, while the right-hand column offers sample thesis statements. This list is far from exhaustive; in fact, sophisticated claims commonly fuse elements from two or more of these rhetorical approaches.

● Four Types of Writing About Film

The Scene Analysis Paper

The scene analysis is designed to help students identify narrative, visual, and sound elements and to establish the link between minute details and broader patterns of development in a film. With this assignment, the film instructor asks students to analyze one scene from a film carefully, discussing the specific qualities of each individual shot.

This assignment has an essentially academic purpose, since it requires students to demonstrate that they can read significant details and describe them using the language of film studies. In most cases, evaluative claims are irrelevant in this assignment. Rather, the scene analysis relies heavily on descriptive statements. In fact, some instructors require students only to describe the details of each shot's *mise en scène*, cinematography, editing, and sound. Others ask students to develop interpretive claims, by analyzing how the scene contributes to motifs and themes developed over the course of the entire film.

The essay below analyzes a scene from *The Big Heat*, Fritz Lang's brutal *film noir* from 1953. Notice that this essay forwards an interpretive claim. The introduction establishes a theme running throughout the film and ends with a thesis statement linking this particular scene to that theme.

"The Divided Human Spirit in Fritz Lang's *The Big Heat*"

Like many examples of *film noir*, Fritz Lang's *The Big Heat* (1953) focuses on an urban criminal underworld in order to explore the darker side of human existence. In the film, Detective Bannion (Glenn Ford) is an honest, hard-working cop investigating the mysterious suicide of one of his colleagues. As he delves into the case, he begins to suspect that a connection exists between the local crime syndicate and high-ranking members of his own police force. When a bomb meant for Bannion kills his wife instead, Bannion quits the force in a fit of anger. He investigates the case himself, becoming a brooding, increasingly violent vigilante.

During the course of his investigation, Bannion finds an unlikely compatriot in Debbie Marsh (Gloria Grahame), a gangster's moll brutalized and betrayed by her lover, the gangster Vince Stone (Lee Marvin). In one critical scene, Debbie commits murder to help Bannion. But in this *noir* world without moral logic, Debbie's act redeems her at the same time that it points to Bannion's complicity in the killing.

Understanding the scene's positioning within the film's overall narrative structure is critical. Before this scene, the film has emphasized Bannion's willingness to rely on violence in his quest for revenge. He is investigating Bertha Duncan (Jeanette Nolan), the widow of Bannion's dead colleague, and discovers that Bertha's husband had written a confessional letter prior to his suicide, detailing the connection between the police force and the crime syndicate. Bertha, who is using the letter to extort money from the syndicate, refuses to give the information to Bannion. In his frustration, Bannion begins to strangle Bertha and nearly kills her, but he is stopped by two police officers. Bannion has grown bitter over the course of his investigation and there is very little that distinguishes him from the gangsters he is investigating.

In a subsequent scene, Bannion tells Debbie about his investigation, complaining that Bertha's stubbornness has effectively put a halt to his pursuit of justice. At one point he confesses, "I almost killed her an hour ago. I should've." To this Debbie replies, "If you had, there wouldn't be much difference between you and Vince Stone." Herein lies the motivation for the scene at hand: Debbie kills Bertha to prevent Bannion from becoming like Vince Stone. In doing so, she redeems herself.

The scene begins with an establishing shot of Bertha walking down the stairs as the doorbell rings. The long shot captures Bertha's flowing mink coat as well as the spaciousness of the house in general. Together these two elements establish that Bertha Duncan is wealthy; her ill-gotten wealth provides her a lavish lifestyle that the honest Bannion has never been able to afford. The camera pans right as Bertha answers the door, further underscoring the size of her house.

Lang cuts to a medium close-up of Debbie's profile. This shot simulates Bertha's point of view as she looks through the window in the door to see half of Debbie's face. Debbie's face is the most important element of the *mise en scène*, as half of it appears normal, but the other half is covered with gauze. Earlier in the film, Vince Stone had thrown a pot of boiling coffee at Debbie in a fit of rage, scalding the left side of her face. Debbie's face is literally two-sided, becoming a visual representation of duality. Half of Debbie's personality has enjoyed the wealth and glamour afforded by her participation in the gangster lifestyle, but the other half—the pure, untainted half—befriends Bannion and acknowledges the immorality of Vince Stone's world. In this shot, Debbie's "good half" shows. Her scars are turned away from the camera, suggesting her desire to renounce her scarred past.[1]

Lang cuts to a medium long shot as Bertha opens the door and invites Debbie inside. Hard lighting emanating from the streetlights outside casts shadows on the wall, contributing to the film's dreadful *noir* atmosphere. Debbie enters the house, and, as the two walk side by side in a medium long shot, with the camera tracking their movement, an obvious parallel develops: both Debbie and Bertha wear long mink coats (fig. **9.3**). Debbie's dialogue confirms the similarities apparent in the *mise en scène*: "I've been thinking about you and me . . . how much alike we are. The mink-coated girls." Her words reveal Debbie's regret that she, like Bertha, has led an immoral life, pursuing material wealth via corrupt means. Bertha is clearly frustrated by Debbie's opaque pronouncements, and she demands that Debbie explain herself more clearly. She takes an aggressive step toward her visitor. Lang cuts to a medium close-up of Debbie to emphasize the importance of her words: "We should use first names. We're sisters under the mink." Again, Debbie's words reveal her own recognition that she has led a corrupt life just like Bertha's.[2]

1 This essay combines descriptive claims with interpretive claims. Where in this paragraph does the author link description to an interpretive idea? Which phrases make the connection between description and analysis clear?

2 Notice that the final sentence links the ideas in this paragraph to the essay's main argument, established in the thesis statement.

A reverse shot reveals Bertha's increasing ire in a medium close-up, as she accuses Debbie of not making any sense. The camera pans to the right to follow Bertha as she moves to the desk on the other side of the room. Ironically, it was at this desk that Bertha's husband shot himself, plagued by guilt and shame. Now Bertha, perturbed and perhaps frightened by Debbie's presence, uses the phone on the desk to call Vince Stone. Her use of the desk expresses her complete indifference to her husband's death and her calculated refusal to sever the mob ties that killed him. Bertha stands behind the desk in a medium long shot and, as she picks up the phone, she tells Debbie, "You're not well."

The cut to a close-up of Debbie emphasizes the power of her reply: "I've never felt better in my life." Her hands fumble for something in her coat. She draws a gun and fires at Bertha. Crucially, this medium close-up includes Debbie, but the gun remains off-screen. Had the image been a medium or long shot, some attention would have been drawn to it. Instead, Lang keeps the camera's attention on Debbie's face so that the audience focuses on Debbie's self-proclaimed moral redemption rather than on the act of violence she is committing in Bannion's name.[3]

9.3 "Sisters under the mink" in *The Big Heat.*

3 Here, an analysis of dialogue supports the main idea in this analysis. To extend the analysis of film sound, compare the voices of Gloria Grahame (Debbie) and Jeanette Nolan (Bertha) in this exchange. Do vocal differences suggest differences in character?

The final shot of the scene is a medium long shot of Bertha, wincing as the still unseen gun fires. She starts to slump, and the camera tilts down, following her collapse to the floor. Debbie has done Bannion's dirty work for him. She preserves what is left of his moral rectitude by killing Bertha. She also helps him with his investigation: now Bertha's husband's letter will be made public and the thugs responsible for Bannion's wife's death will be arrested. In performing such a selfless act, Debbie—who earlier had no moral qualms about using mob money to supply herself with fancy clothes and a penthouse lifestyle—redeems herself. When she kills Bertha, her sister under the mink, Debbie destroys the vanity and selfishness in herself that Bertha represents.

At the end of the shot, the gun falls into the frame. Again the framing distances Debbie from the violence she has just committed. However, Debbie makes no attempt to hide the gun or her fingerprints; she accepts her guilt and, consequently, confirms her redemption.

Because of her actions, Bannion rids himself of the anger and resentment festering inside him. In the film's resolution, he rejoins the police force, no longer needing to stand apart from society's rules and obligations. Still, the resolution's optimism is qualified by Debbie's death during a climactic shootout and complicated by Bannion's use of violence to seek vengeance. Yes, Debbie and Bannion redeem themselves. But Lang's film suggests that redemption may be a temporary state of being, because even the most honorable men and women are capable of committing horrific acts when they are pushed far enough.

The Film Analysis

Like the scene analysis, the film analysis is a form of academic writing. This assignment demands that students trace an idea as it develops over the course of an entire film. Unlike the scene analysis, the film analysis doesn't require students to analyze every single shot—otherwise, the paper might be hundreds of pages long. Instead, this assignment requires students to develop a thesis about a film and then isolate passages from the film that illustrate that thesis.

In most cases, evaluative claims are irrelevant or inappropriate for this assignment. Usually instructors want students to focus on an interpretive claim. As with the scene analysis, the film analysis should utilize the vocabulary of film studies.

Chapter Two explained how the barbershop scene from Buster Keaton's *Steamboat Bill Jr.* emphasized a parallel between Bill and a female friend. The sample essay below illustrates how one can expand ideas about a single detail into the analysis of an entire film. Taking the ideas in Chapter Two as a starting point, this essay explores how *Steamboat Bill Jr.* links questions about Bill's masculinity to two important themes: the conflict between father and son and Bill Sr.'s unwillingness to accept change.

The only plot summary occurs in the introduction. The summary consists of only a few sentences and functions solely to prod the memory of the reader who has not seen the film recently.

The author develops his ideas not through the detailed analysis of any one scene, but by revealing the patterns evident in four scenes from the film: the opening shot, Bill Jr.'s arrival, the barbershop scene, and the climax. These discussions function as the structural foundation of the essay—they illustrate the most crucial ideas the author wants to convey.

The Anxieties of Modernity in *Steamboat Bill Jr.*

Buster Keaton's last great comedy, *Steamboat Bill Jr.* (1928), might at first glance appear to be a variation on Shakespeare's *Romeo and Juliet.* But in fact, the film is more interested in the troubled relationship between father and son. Bill Jr. (Keaton) visits his estranged father (Ernest Torrence) in a small Southern town. Coincidentally, Bill Jr. bumps into a college sweetheart, Marion (Marion Byron). Unfortunately their romance is temporarily put on hold when they discover that their fathers are business rivals and mortal enemies. The film's primary conflict—the source of tension between Bill Jr. and his father that keeps the lovers apart—is Bill Sr.'s fear of modernity. For Bill Sr., his son's longing for the daughter of the local business magnate represents the boy's abandonment of traditional values and his failure to be a real man. However, by the end of the film, Bill Sr. learns to accept that his son lives in the modern world and to recognize that it has some advantages.[1]

The first image in the film establishes the film's concern with the inevitable passage of time. A high-angle long shot of two fishermen in a canoe on the Mississippi River opens

1 In the introduction, the author moves from a general plot description of the film to the main point.

the film. The pastoral image at first appears to be a romantic depiction of the pre-industrial South. But the camera pans left, past a stand of trees, and finds the dogleg of the river. Here a modern riverboat, not a canoe, belches smoke as it moves upstream. The *mise en scène* and the camera movement in this establishing shot suggest the film's dominant theme: the conflict between past (the canoe) and present (the mechanized boat).

As the scene cuts to closer shots of individual characters, it becomes apparent that past and present are embodied by Bill Canfield and his rival J.J. King (Tom McGuire). Bill is stuck in the past. He wears a ratty sailor's uniform, smokes a corncob pipe, and his ship is called the *Stonewall Jackson*, all signifying his connection to the nineteenth century and the heyday of riverboat navigation. Furthermore, he suffers from an inability to adapt. His boat, as the rest of the film will make clear, is a decrepit relic that is slowly falling apart. Bill has not amassed the wealth he needs to compete with his rival in the steamboat business.

King, on the other hand, has his eyes set on the future. In contrast to Bill, whose attire links him to a rustic past, he wears a shiny top hat and black tuxedo. His fashionable clothing indicates that he is a modern man of wealth—wealth earned not in the field or on the river, like Bill's, but in the city. The film makes this point clear several times, as it emphasizes that King has his hand in many of the town's business operations. He is a modern entrepreneur who doesn't specialize in any one field. Instead, he has invested in everything. At one point in the film, King is seen operating a newspaper stand selling "out of town papers." This detail emphasizes how he is not established in town. He is more cosmopolitan, and represents a world where people, goods, and capital can move across an entire nation quickly and efficiently.

9.4 Bill Jr. displays his carnation to the wrong men in *Steamboat Bill Jr.*

Despite Bill's stubborn adherence to the past, the rest of his family subscribes to King's modern approach. When Bill receives a telegram from his son, who is coming to visit during his vacation from college, the audience realizes that Bill Sr. is estranged from his family. Not a traditional tightly knit family, the Canfields haven't lived together since Bill Jr. was a boy. When the family does communicate, the interaction is made possible by the very technology that Bill seems to fear: the telegram and the railroad, symbols of America's movement into the modern era.

When Bill Jr. arrives, his father doesn't even recognize him. In one of the film's comic set pieces, Bill Sr. tries to identify Bill Jr. by looking for a young man with a white carnation on his lapel (fig. **9.4**). But it's Mother's Day, so *every* male getting off the train is wearing a carnation. The incident speaks volumes about the modern family. Family members are so detached from one another that intimacy is lost, replaced by a mass-produced sentiment propagated by the greeting card and flower industry.

Once father and son meet, the two begin to act out the conflict between past and present, usurping the Canfield–King conflict. Bill Sr. is quite displeased with his son's all-too-cozy connection to the modern world. Bill Jr. is the antithesis of his father. His attending college in Boston clearly goes against his father's stubborn idealization of the rural southern lifestyle. As the two interact, it's evident that Bill Sr. thinks all of his son's so-called "book smarts" have prevented him from learning any real skills, such as running a steam engine or punching a man out. Much of the film's humor derives from Bill Jr.'s awkwardness on board his father's ship. He wears a formal sailor's uniform, much to his father's displeasure; he repeatedly runs into the ship's guidelines; he knocks the life-preserver into the water below (where it promptly sinks); and he accidentally hits a lever that engages the paddle and drives the boat into King's. Bill Jr. is clearly out of his element.

The film repeatedly draws attention to Keaton's small stature to emphasize Bill Jr.'s sense of displacement. He is dwarfed by the engine and by the numerous coils of wires and ropes. And, in one telling shot, Bill Jr. stands between his father and an engineer. He is dwarfed by the two hulking men, illustrating how, from his father's perspective, the boy is hopelessly ineffectual (fig. **9.5**).

In fact, many of the film's gags center around the father's fear that his son is too effeminate. At the train station, when Bill Sr. finally spots his son, the boy is prancing about, trying to appease a crying baby. The father turns to his chuckling first mate and says, "If you say what you're thinking, I'll strangle you." Bill Sr. fears that his effeminate son is gay. To make the boy more masculine, the father tries desperately to change his look: he makes Bill Jr. trade in his striped jacket, baggy pants, and polka-dotted bowtie for working clothes; he demands that Bill Jr. trade in his beret for a new hat; and he makes Bill Jr. shave his pencil-thin mustache.

The scene in the barbershop emphasizes Bill Jr.'s supposed lack of masculinity. Instead of lathering Bill Jr.'s entire face, the barber disdainfully dabs just a little bit of shaving cream onto the minuscule display of facial hair. He removes the mustache with two quick swipes of the razor blade, and then yanks out one remaining hair with a pair of tweezers, as if plucking a

9.5 Bill Jr. dwarfed by his father in *Steamboat Bill Jr.*

woman's eyebrows. The scene then cuts to a long shot of the establishment's two chairs. Bill Jr. is in one, and a woman (who will later turn out to be Marion) is in the other (see fig. 2.8). The *mise en scène* establishes a parallel between the two, clearly suggesting that Bill Jr. is effeminate: both face screen right; both have their head bowed at the same angle; and both wear similar styles of black hair. The parallel is underscored when the two look up and recognize one another from Boston. The fact that Bill Jr.'s sweetheart is J.J. King's daughter infuriates Bill Sr., confirming his assumption that his long-lost son has been corrupted by his urban education.

But Bill Sr. comes to realize that his son's embrace of the modern does not necessarily mean a rejection of the father and his old-fashioned values; nor does it mean that his son lacks bravery and mechanical know-how.[2] After catching his son trying to arrange a midnight rendezvous with Marion, Bill Sr. gives up trying to rehabilitate his son and abruptly sends the boy back to Boston. Immediately afterwards, Bill Sr. is arrested when he gets into a fight with King. Bill Jr. hears that his father is in jail and vows to help him escape; rather than bearing a grudge against the man who disowned him, Bill Jr. remains committed to the family.

Despite his mousy demeanor and small stature, Bill Jr. proves to his father that being an intellectual doesn't mean he can't throw a wallop of a punch. After his initial escape plans fail (he bakes a file into a loaf of bread), Bill Jr. surprises his father and himself when he punches the prison guard and knocks him unconscious. The father's pride in his son is evident later when, after having escaped from prison, he returns to defend his son's honor. He winds up back in jail, thus sacrificing himself for the boy he had previously rejected.

During the climactic moments of the film, Bill Jr. also shows his father that his education (and the modern world that it represents) doesn't mean he is incapable of operating machinery. In fact, Bill Jr. proves to have an even greater capacity with machinery than his father. When a giant cyclone levels the town (and King's boat), Bill Jr. is the only man able to rescue his father, who is stuck inside his prison cell as the entire jail floats down the gushing Mississippi. Bill Jr. takes charge of the *Stonewall Jackson*, stepping into his father's shoes. Because there are no engineers around, he concocts a comically elaborate device for operating the boat. Using a convoluted web of ropes and levers, Bill Jr. is able to control the boat's speed and steer simultaneously. Through his ingenuity, Bill is able to rescue both his father and King.

To his father, Bill Jr. represents the threat of modernity. But his clever use of ropes seems to define modernity as a more sophisticated and refined use of machinery, not the useless or abstract knowledge that Bill fears. Bill Jr. embodies the idea that the conflict between past and present is predicated on a false dichotomy. Even King's entrepreneurial gumption doesn't negate Bill Sr.'s unrefined machinery—it depends on it. The film ends on a suitably romantic note, as the two fathers share a laugh on the deck of the *Stonewall Jackson* while Bill Jr. rescues a preacher, who will, of course, perform an *ad hoc* wedding ceremony. In establishing a union between Bill Jr. and Marion, the film's romantic conclusion also unites symbols of the past and present.

> **2** Here the essay shifts from emphasizing Bill Sr.'s adherence to the past to his acceptance of modernity. What strategies does the author use to emphasize this important transition in the argument?

Taking Notes

After establishing a working thesis, writers should gather details and examples to support the main point. For film scholars, this means watching a movie several times, taking note of how narrative, *mise en scène*, cinematography, editing, and sound contribute to, complicate, or contradict the ideas associated with the working thesis.

Most film scholars rely on a shorthand system as they take notes during screenings. Developing a series of abbreviations helps viewers quickly note the basics of a shot's visual details without taking their eyes off the screen. Consider using the list of common abbreviations below:

Camera placement:
  ls = long shot
  ms = medium shot
  cu = close-up
  xcu = extreme close-up
  ha = high-angle
  la = low-angle

Camera movement:
  ts = tracking shot
  t = tilt
  ps = pan shot
  cr = crane
  hh = handheld
  z = zoom
  sl = screen left
  sr = screen right
  hkl and lkl = high-key lighting and low-key lighting

Editing:
  diss. = dissolve
  s/rs = shot/reverse shot
  ct. = cut
  fi/fo = fade-in/fade-out
  w = wipe

The Research Paper

Unlike the scene analysis or the film analysis, whose primary function is to show that the author has mastered the materials in a professor's course, the research paper is designed to teach students important academic skills. The assignment asks students to read beyond assigned materials to broaden intellectual horizons and generate new ideas; to summarize and synthesize others' ideas to support their own; to acknowledge perspectives that contradict their own; and to argue against these perspectives with intellectual integrity and respect.

When a professor asks students to write a research paper, she wants them to participate in an ongoing scholarly conversation about the subject matter. The research paper requires the writer to draw ideas from a broad array of materials, including original documents, scholarly books and articles, newspapers, magazines, and websites.

A good research paper does not merely collect and repeat the information contained in these sources. Serious research involves a process whereby the writer gathers information and ideas that may support and contest the working thesis; the writer then reassesses the persuasive power of his working thesis in light of the evidence gathered.

Topics for research papers vary widely. A research paper might make an argument about the importance of an individual film's production history or remarkable style. It might analyze one film in relation to other films of the same genre. Some research papers might connect films to other cultural phenomena, or discuss a film in relation to the director's *oeuvre*. Scholars can easily incorporate research to help support an argument that uses any of these approaches and those outlined in fig. 9.2. Figure **9.6** is a table outlining several approaches writers use when they pursue research and synthesize ideas taken from multiple texts (including more than one film, book, article, etc.).

The sample research paper below compares Francis Ford Coppola's *The Conversation* and Tony Scott's *Enemy of the State*, two films made in different historical and industrial contexts. It argues that each film represents a specific era in film history. The author assumes that by comparing and contrasting these films, readers will gain a better understanding of how the eras differed from one another.

Notice the sources this essay relies on. The author cites academic journals or books published by university presses, not popular magazines or books published at popular presses. An academic journal decides to accept (or reject) articles on the basis of the peer review, a professional selection process. One or two scholars in the field read and evaluate the integrity and sophistication of any essays submitted for publication. University presses use the same process, approving manuscripts for publication only after several readers have considered its intellectual merit. Manuscripts are generally chosen for publication based on their originality and intellectual rigor. While popular criticism has its

9.6 Common rhetorical approaches for papers involving research.

Rhetorical Approach	Sample Thesis Statement
Compare and contrast two films that explore a similar subject matter. What factors might account for their similarities or differences? The historical and cultural circumstances of production? The artists responsible for their production? Different source materials?	Both *Mean Streets* and *The Godfather* explore life in the mob, but where the former focuses on the daily routines of small-time hoods passing time, the latter focuses on the grandeur of mafia bosses and their attempts to sustain power. The rough-hewn, independent approach of *Mean Streets* is the result of director Martin Scorsese's quest to make a personal film about a lifestyle he witnessed growing up in the streets of New York City, whereas *The Godfather*'s more classic narrative results from a major studio's quest to produce a popular epic film by adapting an already popular novel.
Situate a film within a larger group of films, such as a genre (horror), historical movement (the French New Wave) or a director's *oeuvre*. How does the film compare to the other films in this grouping in terms of its themes and style?	Many scholars have argued that Stanley Kubrick's last film, *Eyes Wide Shut* (1999), with its focus on contemporary urban married life, represents a departure from his previous work. But analysis of the film in relation to the director's *oeuvre* reveals that his satirical view of human beings and the systems they design is in full evidence in this film.
Research the production history of a film. What obstacles did the filmmakers have to overcome to produce their movie? How did these obstacles influence the final film?	Francis Ford Coppola encountered so many difficulties when making *Apocalypse Now* that the production nearly collapsed upon itself. Nevertheless, the director trudged onward, risking financial and mental ruin in an obsessive quest that closely resembled the war story he was filming.

Resources for Film Scholarship

Libraries and the internet now contain a wealth of resources for film scholars. Here is a selective bibliography that includes some of the materials that may prove helpful to begin a research project.

Bibliographical resources:

Academic fullText Elite: An electronic database that indexes articles from over 3,100 scholarly journals.

The Film Literature Index. Indexes academic and popular articles written on film since 1973.

MLA Bibliography. Indexes academic articles written on literature and film since 1964. Available in an electronic version.

New York Times Film Reviews. Collection of the newspaper's popular reviews from 1913–1968.

Project Muse. Electronic index of scholarly journals in the humanities since 1993.

Scholarly journals:

Cahiers du Cinéma (in French)
Camera Obscura
Cineaste
Cinefex
Cinema Journal
Film Comment
Film Quarterly
Journal of Film and Video
Literature/Film Quarterly
Screen
Sight and Sound
Velvet Light Trap
Wide Angle

Popular and industry magazines:

American Cinematographer
Entertainment Weekly
Photoplay (a Hollywood fan magazine, no longer published)
Variety

place in film scholarship, rarely do successful research papers rely solely on popular materials such as popular books, newspapers, magazines, and websites.

The essay begins by referring to published commentary on *Enemy of the State*. The rest of the essay, in effect, expands and comments on this initial idea. This is a common and effective rhetorical strategy in research papers because it "guides" the reader into the topic. Put another way, it mirrors the way one might be inspired to reflect further on a film after reading someone else's perspective. Research often begins with casual reading; in this case, the review has sent the author to another film (which, in turn, will send the author to a third film). Furthermore it demonstrates that the author is participating in an ongoing public dialogue about the film. The essay doesn't just rehash ideas appearing in the quoted article; instead, it develops and adds to them.

The Evolution of an Idea: The Changing Hollywood Aesthetic in *The Conversation*, and *Enemy of the State*

1 In the introduction, the author uses a popular source, rather than an academic one. Is there a reason why he might have chosen to use popular sources here? Is his decision appropriate? Why or why not?

In her review of Tony Scott's paranoid thriller *Enemy of the State* (1998), about an innocent lawyer running for his life because he has inadvertently received a surveillance tape that documents a Senator's murder, Kim Newman notes the film's connection to Francis Ford Coppola's *The Conversation* (1974):[1]

> Gene Hackman's appearance as [. . .] Brill/Lyle makes it a continuation of *The Conversation* (it even uses a still from *The Conversation* for Lyle's NSA file photo). [. . .] He provides a welcome physical link to what went before but is also shuttled off to one side so Smith can carry the whole thing in an uncomplex '90s way. (Newman)

Indeed, *Enemy of the State* is chock full of references to Coppola's film: one scene mirrors *The Conversation*'s opening moments in San Francisco's Union Square. In another, actor Gene Hackman (as Brill) dons the same translucent raincoat worn by the character he played in *The Conversation*, Harry Caul. Finally, Brill's cage-like workshop looks identical to the one in *The Conversation*.

The Conversation, directly inspired by European art cinema and, more specifically, by Michelangelo Antonioni's *Blow-Up* (1967), is a prime example of Hollywood filmmaking in the late 1960s and early '70s. In that period, the industry rejuvenated itself by funding small, independent projects. They cut production costs and offered more challenging films that appealed to an increasingly sophisticated younger audience. According to film historian David Cook, "Hollywood was strapped for cash and relied on low-budget, independently produced films. Because these films cost less to make, they could take more risks in terms of content and style that borrowed from European art cinema's emphasis on character psychology and complex themes" (Cook, pp. 919–20).[2]

By contrast, *Enemy of the State* exemplifies Hollywood's emphasis on big-budget blockbusters during the 1980s and '90s. After the massive success of *Jaws* and *Star Wars*, studios began to "bank on high-budget pictures crammed with stars and special effects. The big money was to be found in 'home runs'" (Thompson and Bordwell, p. 683). Because such big-budget films have to draw huge crowds to guarantee profitability, they must appeal to a large, general audience. This, in turn, inhibits complexity and innovation. Ironically, *Enemy of the State*'s many references to Coppola's film only emphasize how intellectually neutered the 1990s blockbuster is, compared to the stimulating films of Hollywood's renaissance.

Before examining *The Conversation* and *Enemy of the State*, it's important to understand the way European art films challenged Hollywood filmmaking and how those challenges inspired Coppola. The theme of Antonioni's *Blow-Up* is, by conventional Hollywood standards, remarkably abstract: the film explores the possibilities and limitations of art and perception. *Blow-Up* depicts a self-absorbed fashion photographer who, after enlarging a series of photographs he has taken in a park, discovers he has unknowingly photographed a murder (fig. **9.1**, p. 270). The more the photographer investigates his pictures as a way to solve the murder, the more inexplicable the mystery becomes. The film is a meditation on the limitations of perception, whether associated with the human eye or its mechanical equivalent in photography. "In [*Blow-Up*] I said that I do not know what reality is," stated the director. "Reality escapes us, changes constantly; when we believe we have grasped it, the situation is already otherwise" (quoted in Chatman, p. 14).

Blow-Up develops the theme of the limitations of photography (and by extension, cinematography) through an unconventional narrative structure. Antonioni departs from

2 How does the author organize these paragraphs so that the historical information supports his main ideas?

9.7 More than meets the eye: models in a row in *Blow-Up*.

3 How does the author use other scholars' interpretations?

cause-and-effect logic. A good deal of the film—approximately half, in fact—follows the photographer as he wanders about London, casually taking pictures and avoiding would-be fashion models who want his attention. He has no clearly defined goals or objectives. In fact, he doesn't discover the murder until nearly two-thirds of the way into the film, and even then he flits about London with no clear objective. By the time he gets back to the park to take a picture of the body, it has disappeared. The film's narrative design confounds the logic of cause and effect because several events in the plot (such as the initial trip to the park, or the photographer's pictures taken there) gain significance only in retrospect.

The film's visual style contributes to the idea that no camera can capture reality or show what is truly important. Antonioni's framing frequently obscures important visual information. At one point, the photographer is taking photographs of a lone model standing behind a pane of plexiglass. Then the camera slowly tracks to the right and reveals *several* models standing behind the first one (fig. **9.7**). The layering of the *mise en scène* and the deliberate camera placement and movement point to Antonioni's idea that no single image can ever capture all the information of a given space. As film scholar John Orr observes, when the corpse is visible onscreen, "the spectator is never cued in by either [the photographer] or the director to what is clearly visible" (Orr, p. 62). Only when audiences revisit the film will they notice the body. Antonioni's cinematography actually draws attention to its own limitations.[3]

Blow-Up ends with the photographer's failure and a profound lack of closure. Neither the main character nor the audience has a clear understanding of what transpired in the park. Ultimately the photographer literally disappears from the screen (via a dissolve) like the corpse in the park. Neither the photographer nor Antonioni the filmmaker solves any of life's real mysteries.

Like *Blow-Up*, *The Conversation* is a self-consciously "arty" film, which offers audiences an opaque main character, an open ending, and an intentionally obfuscating style, all in the service of an abstract theme. In Coppola's film a professional surveillance expert, Harry Caul, records a conversation between a woman and her lover. Caul fears that the tapes he has made will lead to her murder, since the woman's husband hired him. In an ironic twist of fate, the two lovers use Caul's tape to murder the husband. Caul actually becomes an unwilling accessory to a different crime from the one he imagined. Rather than providing audiences with an emotionally satisfying happy ending, in which the hero saves the day, Coppola challenges his audience with a protagonist who is somewhat unlikeable and a downbeat ending that reiterates the moral accountability of the "hero" in the murder.

Like *Blow-Up*, *The Conversation* revolves around a character's spying on others and his fundamental misinterpretation of the details of their lives. Whereas the photographer in Antonioni's film misinterprets his pictures, Caul misreads a key line of dialogue; he hears the lovers say, "He'd *kill* us if he had the chance," but the climax's revelation is that the proper intonation was actually "He'd kill *us* if he had the chance." His misinterpretation of the line underscores a solipsistic worldview that allows him to spy on others without feeling any moral qualms: "The error committed by Harry Caul was to fail to understand the position of the speaker [. . .] Locked into his own subjectivity [. . .] he read things as if they had been articulated as pure denunciation, devoid of shading and nuance of discourse" (Turner, p. 12). Finally, like *Blow-Up*, Coppola's film explores an abstract theme: a character's moral responsibility for someone else's murder.

As with many European art films, *The Conversation* abandons standard narrative strategies. For one thing, Caul is far from being a proactive protagonist. Although Caul is aware of the ethical problems inherent in his profession, he fails to alter his behavior. The knowledge that his recordings have contributed to a brutal slaying in the past plagues him, and he is aware that his surreptitious involvement in a love triangle will probably result in yet another murder, yet he refuses to erase the tapes he has made or to alert the police.

Although Caul senses immediately that his recording will cause someone harm, he obsessively continues to remix the layers of tape to achieve the optimum fidelity (fig. **9.8**). When his tapes are stolen, he goes to the hotel where he thinks the murder will take place. But when the violence erupts, Caul turns up the television set and covers his ears so he won't have to hear the noise. His inability to erase the tapes and his subsequent passivity point to his own moral culpability in the murder, and his anguish in the hotel room "springs from a deep well of shame; such violence could and should have been prevented

9.8 Harry listens to tapes in *The Conversation*.

by him, Harry Caul. The woman is *his* victim" (Cowie, p. 91). Harry Caul's guilt derives from his inaction.

The film's visual style also resembles the tendency in *Blow-Up* to obscure visual information to develop a theme. In this case, the theme is surveillance and control. When Caul returns home and calls his landlord to complain about her breaking into his apartment to leave a birthday gift, the camera is placed at a long shot to watch him as he walks across the room. But Caul walks offscreen: the camera doesn't follow the primary action. There is no narrative justification for the static camera—no character remains in the room he has left. The camerawork seems to ask, *what if* there was a spy camera looking at Caul? Are viewers spying on Caul? The technique appears at the end of the film as well, when a high-angled pan "sweeps past [Caul] in his living room like a surveillance camera at work in some supermarket" (Turner, p. 6). The cinematography contributes to the film's theme of surveillance and also aligns the audience with Caul. Like him, viewers spy on an individual's private life—his moral downfall could be ours as well. Like Antonioni, Coppola raises questions about the cinematic medium itself.

The Conversation offers some sense of closure: the audience knows who killed whom and how. Yet the closure is qualified and indefinite, again reflecting European art cinema's influence. The movie shows us the murder scene, but it is played out in Caul's mind, so "it could be argued that what we are seeing is only what he imagines—in his guilty paranoia—to be taking place" (Turner, p. 8). More noticeably, the movie concludes with Caul himself under surveillance. He receives a mysterious phone call, warning him that he is being listened to. He responds by tearing up his apartment, looking in vain for a bug. The movie ends with Caul alone in his ransacked room. The dismal ending, quite unlike a Hollywood happy ending, addresses a psychological and social issue—the invasion of privacy—with intellectual and aesthetic complexity.

The period of the Hollywood renaissance quickly came to an end, and Hollywood began to attract larger audiences by selling a more homogenized, less challenging style of "blockbuster" filmmaking. When compared with its American predecessor, *Enemy of the State*'s conventional narrative and its kinetic but vacuous visual style reflect Hollywood's shift toward the entertainment-oriented action/adventure genre and away from intellectual films.

While Tony Scott's *Enemy of the State* makes gestures towards carrying *The Conversation*'s questions about surveillance into the age of the microchip, it ultimately lacks the complexity of Coppola's film. *Enemy* abandons art film ambiguity in favor of Hollywood-style closure and a plot-centered style. On the most obvious level, Scott's film replaces the slow pace and ominous foreboding of *Blow-Up* and *The Conversation* with non-stop action scenes, revealing itself as the antithesis of the Hollywood renaissance. It is the embodiment of what film scholar Michael Allen calls, a "blockbuster without personal vision"—a large-budget film "lacking any intention of examining serious issues or subjects" (Allen, p. 95).

More specifically, *Enemy of the State* offers a tightly constructed narrative, complete with goal-oriented characters, clearly defined antagonists, and a reassuring closure that circumvents most of the ethical questions the film raises. In the beginning of the film, a friend slips an incriminating computer disk into the bag Robert Dean (Will Smith) is carrying. Soon afterward, Dean finds himself hounded by a government agency that wants to cover up the murder captured on the disk. The agency uses its ubiquitous surveillance equipment (including security cameras, computers, satellites, and bugs) to terrorize Dean and his family to get it back. Dean can shake the agency only after he enlists the help of Brill (Hackman), a former agent and surveillance expert who has gone underground.

Enemy's narrative structure follows the classical Hollywood model, as opposed to the experimentation with narrative organization that characterizes *Blow-Up* and *The Conversation*. The exposition establishes a main character (Dean) and the central conflict he will have to overcome: how will Dean escape the clutches of the men who want the disk he now possesses? The film's resolution also offers closure. The group of operatives that antagonized Dean are caught and punished. Dean and his wife are nuzzling on the sofa and send their precocious son up to play in his room so they can be alone. Brill, a wanted man, has escaped to the tropics and taps into Dean's cable signal just to say hello.

Thus, while the film raises questions about the possible systematic misuse of surveillance technology and stresses how pervasive this technology is—a theme that could be every bit as complex as that of *The Conversation*—the film's tidy resolution naïvely suggests that one heroic person can orchestrate an operation to eradicate any corruption. The film loosens some of the tight closure when a senator appears on TV and promises that he is going to fight for a "security bill" that will allow government agencies more legal access to wire tapping and other forms of covert surveillance. But the film also emphasizes that the operatives pursuing Dean were a rogue group, now being thoroughly interrogated by honest government agents.

Even the film's characterizations reduce questions of surveillance to a simple question of good and evil. Whereas *Blow-Up*'s photographer and *The Conversation*'s Harry Caul are complex characters whose flaws contribute to their failures, Dean is above reproach. Though he is implicated for having spied on others (he is a lawyer and has access to a tape that will help him get leverage in a labor dispute), the film makes it clear that his use of surveillance tapes is morally justified. In other words, whereas *Blow-Up* and *The Conversation* explore the moral and psychological complexities of each of their main characters, *Enemy* presents a simply drawn character with little emotional or psychological depth. He commands the audience's uncomplicated admiration. Whereas Coppola took pains to distance viewers from Harry Caul, Scott encourages the audience to identify with Dean by casting Will Smith, the strikingly handsome and immensely popular star of *Independence Day* (1996) and *Men in Black* (Barry Sonnerfeld 1997). In short, the film's narrative doesn't offer philosophical musings along the lines of *Blow-Up*, nor does it delve into the psychological richness of its main character as *The Conversation* does.

The film's cinematography also lacks the visual poetics of *Blow-Up* and *The Conversation*. Cinematographer Dan Mindel employs a wide range of flamboyant techniques, shifting from color to black-and-white film stock, using disorienting canted angles and swish pans, and employing long, overhead shots. But these techniques are directly linked to the plot: they do not contribute to self-reflexive questions about the film medium or philosophical concerns with human perception, surveillance, and visual representation, as similar techniques had done in *Blow-Up* and *The Conversation*.

When an array of satellites and cameras document Dean's movements, camera angles suggest their point of view. Whereas *The Conversation* mysteriously suggests that there might be someone watching Caul, *Enemy of the State* takes pains to make it clear who is

understand why a reviewer liked a film, so they can determine whether or not to trust the reviewer's judgement. In turn, a reviewer must carefully consider whom she is addressing, and evaluate a film using criteria her audience will recognize and might accept. Reviews in *Rolling Stone* magazine, for example, target the magazine's primary readership: males in their late teens and early twenties. In contrast, readers of *The New Yorker* tend to be older, middle-class intellectuals, and the magazine's film reviews generally address the values of that specific audience. Reviews in political magazines such as *The Weekly Standard* or *The American Prospect* evaluate films in large part based on their political values.

The reasons for liking or disliking a film have to be considered carefully. Anyone who has had the experience of liking a film only after a second viewing understands that one can not always trust an initial response. Any number of factors may limit a viewer's ability to appreciate a movie after just one viewing. Perhaps the theater's environment or other patrons inhibited enjoyment; perhaps the film was simply too complex to comprehend fully after just one screening. When writing a review, try to avoid knee-jerk reactions. Instead, begin by considering what a film is trying to accomplish and how it tries to accomplish these things. The most convincing *evaluative* claims follow careful *interpretive* analysis.

While most popular reviews are easier to read than academic arguments about film, they are not necessarily easier to write. In fact, since effective popular reviews usually take into account a film's thematic concerns and its aesthetic techniques without assuming that the reader has any formal training in film aesthetics, the popular review is, theoretically, more difficult to write than an academic argument.

Consider the following review of Mary Harron's controversial horror film *American Psycho* (2000). Notice how it begins by describing the controversy surrounding the film's release. This rhetorical strategy brings audiences into an ongoing conversation that started a long time ago about the film and, before that, about the novel it was based on. Of course, not all films are controversial, and so not all reviews can situate themselves with or against the tide of public furor. But popular reviews often begin by establishing a film's cultural context, and then proceed to evaluate the film within this context: its production history; historical events coinciding with the release of the film; the level of public anticipation regarding the film's release; or biographical notes of interest regarding key personnel in the film.

American Psycho
Philadelphia City Paper
April 13–20, 2000
by Cindy Fuchs

Cut. This is the first word that comes to mind when seeing Patrick Bateman's incredible physique. Doing stomach crunches while a violent porn film plays on his television monitor, jumping rope in the white-on-white sterility of his starkly furnished living room, stepping out of his perfectly appointed shower (stocked with premium body scrubs and facial masks), into one of his impeccably matched white towels, Patrick (Christian Bale) reveals an upper body to die for (fig. **9.9**). Watching him admire his supercut biceps in the mirror while [. . .] being serviced by . . .] two prostitutes he's procured for the evening, you might think—for a second—that the MPAA had it right, that this is the most unnerving and revolting scene in Mary Harron's film of *American Psycho.*[1]

9.9 Christian Bale as Yuppie slasher Patrick Bateman in *American Psycho.*

The ratings controversy was, of course, only one of many associated with the project. Before Harron cut some 20 seconds from the above sex scene—mostly having to do with Patrick's scary self-admiring—the MPAA judged the film an NC-17. (Now it's an R, with essentially the same murder and mayhem scenes as when it started.) A general anxiety over the movie's violence, sex, and treatment of humans as meat might have been anticipated, given the hate and apprehension inspired by its source, Bret Easton Ellis's well-timed and only half-smart 1991 novel; Simon & Schuster dropped it, NOW condemned it, other feminist groups protested it, and predictably, the book made for its author much money and notoriety.

The long-in-the-making movie version, written by Harron and Guinevere Turner (*Go Fish*), sharpens that insight, so it becomes a kind of baleful glare. The movie refashions by necessity the book's meticulous listings of designer labels and restaurants (most of whom didn't want their names associated with the project), and reduces the details of bloody body parts. [. . .] What's left is a taut, grim and sometimes quite funny (in a sick way, of course) indictment of soul-killing consumer culture, presented here—quite convincingly—as the ongoing legacy of the 1980s.[2]

American Psycho takes aim at most all the terrible trends and traumas of the '80s: whooshy men's haircuts, AIDS, Ronald Reagan, greed, Phil Collins, slasher flicks, women's shoulder pads. Patrick is the consummate conformist, so selfish and self-sculpted that even his own co-workers and acquaintances can't tell him apart from other members of his pack. Consider the breathtaking scene (shot with brutal elegance by Andrzej Sekula [. . .]) in which Patrick and his associates (the similarly clean-cut Bill Sage, Justin Theroux, and Josh Lucas), all do-nothing VPs at an absurdly swank New York brokerage house, compare their outrageously expensive new business cards. The surreally crisp office lighting softens momentarily as each card gets its

1 How does the author use informal language and humor to make her writing enjoyable and accessible?

2 According to Fuchs, what does the movie have that redeems its potentially excessive use of violence?

almost frightening close-up: bone or off-white, raised lettering, platinum carrying case. Startled that one of his rival/friends has outdone him in this competition, Patrick ponders his position (in deadpan voice-over), and comes to the realization, almost as an afterthought, that indeed, he must murder this Paul Allen (Jared Leto) [. . .].

The movie conducts its analysis of status-mongering delicately and provocatively, that is, through Patrick's serial killing. Patrick is such a product of his moment that he literally consumes his friends and associates, and seduces the smarmy detective (Willem Dafoe), who never comes near the truth. When he's bored enough with his glossy socialite fiancée Evelyn (Reese Witherspoon, so glossy she's painful) and junkie socialite mistress Courtney (Samantha Mathis), he turns elsewhere for sensual, even vital, pleasures. He finds control and solace in his detailed enumerations of the virtues of '80s pop (Whitney Houston, Huey Lewis and the News) or more emphatically, in the savage arts he applies, to a homeless black man, his dog, and to his own visitors, those he pays and those he merely invites [. . .].

When, at last, one victim tries to escape, she runs through the outwardly immaculate apartment, discovering body parts hanging in the closet and heads cooling in the fridge. She screams, of course, and Patrick follows her in full-on bloodlust mode, chainsaw roaring and wearing only his red-spattered white cotton briefs. The camera tracks them through the many-roomed apartment and alarmingly austere hallway, as their actions mimic Tobe Hooper's *Texas Chainsaw Massacre* (which Patrick has recently been watching during his morning calisthenics). The scene is delirious, hilarious, and repugnant, and it speaks to Patrick's lunacy, which is at once absolutely strange and absolutely representative.[3]

"Did you know," he demands at one point, "I'm utterly insane?" But in seeking recognition, Patrick—and everyone like him—can only remain utterly unseen. In Ellis's novel, Patrick finds some rudimentary emotional relationship with his excruciatingly loyal secretary; in the movie, Jean (Chloë Sevigny) is only another missed connection, eventually made aware of his monstrosity, but only able to succumb to tears, alone in Patrick's office. This is the severe beauty of *American Psycho*, its relentlessness, its refusal to give you a way to identify with Patrick or any one of his victims. In this way, the film draws comparisons between Patrick and two key figures of his era: Leatherface and Ronald Reagan (who also appears on a background TV, denying Iran–Contra culpability). There is no responsibility and no identification, no self and no way out or in. For all its excesses, the film suggests, consumer culture is really about emptiness. (*Reprinted courtesy of the author.*)[4]

This chapter concludes Part Two of this book by examining four common types of film writing. Despite the obvious differences among them, they all require an appreciation of

3 Does this review recommend the movie or not? What does the author provide the reader to help her decide whether or not to go?

4 Who would disagree with Fuchs's rationale? Would a reader have to share any values with Fuchs to accept her recommendation?

how films systematically use narrative, visual, and sound details to evoke characters, themes, and abstract ideas. Even though popular movie reviews emphasize evaluative claims, they often make interpretive statements about a film's themes and its means of developing them.

Part Three of this book introduces several complex interpretive frameworks that scholars and critics adopt when they move beyond the level of the individual film text. Each of these frameworks takes into consideration the way cinema functions not only as an art form but also as a cultural, economic, and aesthetic institution.

Cinema and Culture

Part III moves readers beyond a focus on textual analysis to consider the relationship between film and culture. These chapters present conceptual frameworks that approach cinema as a cultural, economic, and social institution. The topics of Chapters Ten through Fifteen do not exhaust potential areas of inquiry, but instead introduce several important fields within film studies. These chapters examine the relation between social context and film style, ideology, stardom, genre, auteur theory, and film as an industry. Each one explores ideas and questions that filmmakers, film enthusiasts, critics, and scholars contemplate when they investigate cinema's role in culture. Each chapter also includes examples of writing about cinema as a cultural institution.

By the time readers have completed Part III, they will be prepared to formulate original questions related to cinema as a cultural institution and to conduct independent research on film studies topics.

Together, Parts II and III help readers develop the critical reading, analytical, and rhetorical skills to describe, interpret, and evaluate a film at the textual level and to engage current issues in film and media studies by moving beyond the individual text to consider the broader cultural significance of film.

Alfred Hitchcock in a publicity still for *Psycho.*

Social Context and Film Style

10.1 Marlene Dietrich on set with Josef von Sternberg.

Hollywood was the place where the United States perpetuated itself as a universal dream and put the dream into mass production

Angela Carter

At the turn of the twentieth century, New York City was the center of commercial filmmaking. But by 1910, filmmakers began to move west from New York to Hollywood, drawn to the area's climate, cheap real estate, and the opportunity to avoid paying equipment licensing fees to Thomas Edison's Motion Picture Patents Company. By the end of the decade, film production was a lucrative industry and Wall Street investors helped Hollywood dominate the international film market. Ever since the 1920s, many people have equated Hollywood with moviemaking.

But Hollywood is not the world's only major film industry, and its preference for larger-than-life, escapist fantasies represents only one approach to filmmaking. This chapter discusses several cultural contexts for filmmaking: the Hollywood studio system, international art cinema, Italian Neorealism, and Third Cinema. Each context is associated with an economic, political, and cultural approach to film, and the types of films that have emerged from each of these contexts reflect these differences.

Hollywood's Industrial Context: The Studio System as Dream Factory

American film production and reception were at their height during what has become known as the Hollywood studio era. Though film historians debate the exact dates, many pinpoint 1915 as its beginning. This was the year that D.W. Griffith released *The Birth of a Nation*, one of the first feature-length narrative films to demonstrate the medium's artistic and commercial potential. The end of the Hollywood studio era, though hard to define precisely, was signaled by a 1948 Supreme Court decision. That decision, called the Paramount Consent Decree, ordered the major Hollywood studios to cease their monopolistic business practices.

Between 1915 and 1948, five **major studios** (Metro-Goldwyn-Mayer [MGM], Paramount, Warner Brothers, Twentieth Century Fox, and RKO) and several **minor studios** (Universal, Columbia, and United Artists) perfected a mode of filmmaking that, in turn, generated a standardized film style. Hollywood's efficient mode of production, distribution, and exhibition, known as the **studio system**, gave rise to an instantly recognizable type of film. The next section briefly describes the classical Hollywood style before examining the economic and social practices that gave rise to it.

Classical Style

Classical Hollywood narratives exhibit four important traits, as discussed in Chapter Three. Those traits include clarity (viewers should not be confused about space, time, or events), unity (cause and effect connections are direct and complete), goal-oriented characters (they are active and invite identification), and closure (loose ends are tied up, often through romantic union). All other components of a classical Hollywood film are subservient to narrative. In fact, the classical Hollywood style is often called "the invisible style," because narrative considerations dictate choices involving *mise en scène*, cinematography, editing, and sound. This style relies on "unobtrusive craftsmanship" (Thompson, p. 9), ensuring that viewers will become absorbed in the narrative.

More specifically, in this style of filmmaking, the *mise en scène* depicts an external world that adheres to the norms of "realism" determined by the conditions of the story. The *mise en scène* offers spectators a seemingly objective presentation of the story space, as opposed to the subjectivity of Expressionism. Similarly, the cinematography is

10.2 Sam Spade before he is drugged in *The Maltese Falcon*.

unobtrusive; the style eschews exaggerated angles or flamboyant movement.

On those occasions when a film does employ obvious visual distortions, there is almost always a narrative justification. In *The Maltese Falcon*, when Sam Spade meets his nemesis, Gutman, the image becomes blurry. Cinematography threatens to remind viewers they are looking through a lens. However, the distortion is motivated by the narrative. Spade has been drugged; this is his point-of-view shot (fig. **10.2**).

Classical editing follows the rules of continuity editing, as outlined in Chapter Six. It functions primarily to excise events that aren't immediately relevant to the plot, to create a unified sense of space and time, and to punctuate the emotional content of a scene by drawing attention to characters and their actions.

Finally, a classical Hollywood film privileges dialogue over other sounds because dialogue carries the narrative forward. Dialogue expresses character traits and motivations, helps to explain cause-and-effect logic, and emphasizes the emotional content of a scene. Because narrative information is the most important element in these films, and because dialogue is the sound most directly responsible for moving the plot forward, dialogue tends to be audible above all other sounds. When directors such as Robert Altman began to experiment with **overlapping dialogue** in *M*A*S*H* and *Nashville* (1975), viewers accustomed to the classical style may have been frustrated by their inability to discern everything the characters say.

In short, the classical Hollywood style attempts to guarantee that "at any moment in a movie, the audience [is] to be given the optimum vantage point on what [is] occurring on screen" (Ray, p. 33). The perspective it creates is so ideal that audiences forget they are watching a carefully orchestrated fictional representation. Indeed, some critics call the classical style escapist because it creates the illusion of stories unfolding in real space and time and takes audiences away from their own lives.

It might appear that the classical Hollywood style is the only logical way to approach narrative filmmaking. But as the following sections illustrate, the invisible style was as much a product of economic and political circumstances as it was a set of conscious aesthetic choices.

Economic Practice and Hollywood Convention

The profit-driven studio system was designed to deliver products to consumers as quickly as possible. Its mode of production was, to a large degree, the assembly line of the modern factory system. Studios relied on a division of labor to generate products rapidly and cheaply. At the beginning of the process, producers conferred with studio heads to generate ideas and to determine which projects to pursue. Once they had decided on a project, a team of writers would draft and revise the screenplay while the art director designed the sets, the costume designer fashioned the wardrobe for the cast, and the casting office selected actors.

The project's producer and assistant director oversaw much of this pre-production process, and when it was completed, the director took over, handling most of the decisions during shooting. After shooting was complete, the editor assembled the shots, working to ensure continuity. Sometimes the director was involved in this process, but often he was not. After the final cut was assembled, the score was composed. This is a simplified description of the process, which evolved and became more complex as the industry grew, but it offers some indication of how rationalized and compartmentalized film production was.

This compartmentalization contributed to the standardization of Hollywood's style in several ways. When audiences flocked to see a film, producers tried to rework the same formulas. Eventually, producers discovered that they could reuse production units. At Paramount, for example, Marlene Dietrich, director Joseph von Sternberg (fig. **10.1**, p. 296), screenwriter Jules Furthman, and cinematographer Lee Garmes collaborated on a series of four successful romantic melodramas in the early 1930s: *Morocco* (1930), *Dishonored* (1931), *Blonde Venus* (1932), and *Shanghai Express* (1932). Costumes and sets could be reused as well, saving the studios both money and time. Relying on stories and production practices that had succeeded before facilitated rapid output and relatively consistent quality.

The classical Hollywood conventions for continuity and camera placement do not constitute an inherently superior method of conveying narrative information, but they became Hollywood's standard partly because they contributed to production efficiency. The "rules" provided directors with a predetermined shot set-up for each scene. In other words, Hollywood's visual style was largely shaped by a powerful determinant: the logic of industrial capitalism.

The studios' reliance on stars also reflected the market logic of capitalism on several levels. Stars served as a marketing device, helping the studios to pre-sell a picture to fans. But the star system also facilitated the production and distribution of films. Once a star became associated with a particular type of character, that star could serve as an economical means of shorthand character development. Screenwriters wouldn't have to worry about how to establish important character traits since, theoretically, audiences would already have those traits in mind as soon as the actor walked on screen. Star personas also helped the studios distribute their products to the theaters, since theater owners would have a clear idea of what they were getting with a "Marlene Dietrich picture" or a "Lon Chaney movie." Put simply, in the name of efficiency, character development became typed, or standardized.

Finally, the hierarchical structure of the industry itself and its profit-driven *modus operandi* played a key role in determining a film's narrative structure. Some producers and studio heads would test screen movies and then re-edit, or sometimes reshoot, the films, according to audience response. The practice helped guarantee a crowd-pleasing product—but it also led to the desecration of some profound works of art. Thomas Schatz describes how, on seeing a test screening of *Tess of the D'Urbervilles* (1924), MGM studio head Louis B. Mayer was disappointed because the film concluded with the heroine being hanged for killing the man who had raped her. He demanded a new, happy ending. Director Marshall Neilan protested and sought out the novel's author Thomas Hardy for support, but MGM owned the rights to the novel and Mayer prevailed (Schatz, p. 32).

In short, the filmmaking process affects what audiences see on screen. In a profit-driven industry, financial considerations play a significant role in determining both what audiences see and how they see it.

Censorship and Hollywood Convention

Hollywood's practice of self-censorship illustrates how the profit motive, social mores, and political pressure combine to shape what audiences see. In the early 1920s, Hollywood found itself increasingly under attack from church groups and conservative publications, which denounced the industry because of scandals relating to sexual deviance, avarice, drugs, and alcohol. In 1915, the Supreme Court had ruled that motion pictures were not part of the press and therefore not constitutionally protected from censorship. As a result, the 1920s protests sparked industry-wide anxieties that movies would soon be subject to government censorship.

In response, Hollywood established the Motion Picture Producers and Distributors of America (MPPDA), an organization designed to help the industry regulate its own content. Former Postmaster General Will Hays—a conservative who, in his own words, put his "faith in God, in folks, in the nation, and in the Republican party"—headed the organization (quoted in Maltby, p. 238). While not the equivalent of a state censor, the MPPDA did ensure that the American film industry kept subversive content in check.

Initially the MPPDA offered little in the way of rules regarding appropriate and inappropriate content. Hays drafted a list of "Don'ts and Be Carefuls," which he expected filmmakers to consult as they determined the content of their pictures. The "Don'ts"—subjects that Hays deemed unacceptable "irrespective of the manner in which they are treated"—included profanity, suggestive nudity, miscegenation, scenes of childbirth, and ridicule of the clergy (quoted in Maltby, p. 239). Filmmakers were encouraged to "be careful" when depicting religious ceremonies, criminal behavior, the institution of marriage, and law enforcement.

The end of the 1920s saw another public backlash against Hollywood, in part because of celebrity scandals and the growing popularity of the gangster film. The MPPDA responded by turning its list of "Don'ts and Be Carefuls" into the Production Code, a list of rules prohibiting certain images and scenarios. (The entire text of the code can be found on-line at www.historymatters.gmu.edu/d/5099/.) The most prominent addition to the original list was a preamble that read:

1. No picture shall be produced which will lower the moral standards of those who see it. Hence the sympathy of the audience shall never be thrown to the side of crime, wrongdoing, evil or sin.

2. Correct standards of life, subject only to the requirements of drama and entertainment, shall be presented.
3. Law, natural or human, shall not be ridiculed, nor shall sympathy be created for its violation (quoted in Maltby, p. 242).

Implicit in the preamble is the assumption that any images outside of the dominant value system could have a negative impact on audiences. Crucially, the moral standards that films were supposed to uphold were defined by conservative groups, including members of the Catholic Church.

The preamble dictates that the MPPDA could evaluate and determine not only the content, but also the style of a film. That is, a film's *approach* to its subject matter helped determine whether or not the film was "appropriate." Films could depict criminal activity, as long as the audience is "never thrown to the side of crime, wrongdoing, evil or sin." As such, the gangster films of the 1930s inevitably end with the gangster suffering his (often brutal) punishment for the crimes he committed. Sexuality could be suggested, as long as there was enough ambiguity built into the screenplay for only adult viewers to recognize the implications.

10.3 *The Moon Is Blue* (1953)—one of Otto Preminger's assaults on the Production Code.

Increasingly challenged by directors such as Otto Preminger, who defied the code and released three films in the 1950s without certificates of approval (fig. **10.3**), the Production Code ceased being enforced by the mid-1960s. In 1967, Jack Valenti, President of the Motion Picture Association of America, MPAA (as the MPPDA had been renamed), instituted the ratings system, which remains in effect today. This system solved some problems, but raises other issues, most notably controversies over what deserves an R or an NC17 rating. Originally meant to distinguish adult films from pornographic films, NC17 is effectively an economic kiss of death for any title bearing the rating, since many theaters refuse to show films with this rating.

American Ideology and Entertainment

As the discussion of the studio system and the Production Code suggests, the social context in which a film is produced has a profound effect on its content and style. Critics of Hollywood film contend that its seamless mode of storytelling masks its ideological content. They would claim that even apparently apolitical films made purely to entertain are not free from ideology. An ideology is a worldview: a set of political, moral, and cultural assumptions. An individual or cultural ideology includes, among other things, beliefs about social and economic systems, race, gender, sexuality, identity, community structure, and the function of government.

Much of a culture's ideology remains unspoken, or implicit. The United States, for example, officially defines its ideology in the Declaration of Independence, the Constitution, and other legal documents. But many of America's dominant ideologies—its privileging of competitive individualism, its belief in capitalism as the ideal economic system, and its celebration of progress over stasis—don't appear in these documents, and these are widely held beliefs that influence American culture.

The Production Code provides an example of how an industry can self-consciously control its output with rules and regulations that uphold a dominant belief system. But not all ideological content is dictated by a licensing authority: most ideologies are maintained subtly through everyday practices and conveyed through a variety of media, including film. A film presents an attitude toward its subject matter, and always reflects a particular perspective. As these components become conventionalized over a broad array of films—repeated unselfconsciously—the ideology too becomes conventionalized, taken for granted rather than questioned. Film scholars, then, sometimes read films as barometers of a culture, or as a "symptoms" of the culture that produced them.

Popular films usually reflect dominant social perspectives in unremarkable ways. For example, watching Harold Lloyd's *The Freshman* (Fred C. Newmeyer and Sam Taylor 1925), audiences may unquestioningly accept its celebration of heroic individualism because it tells a heartwarming tale of an underdog outsider earning social acceptance. But the film uses sports to reinforce dominant ideas about masculinity and individualism.

Bumbling Harold Diddlebock (Lloyd) struggles to fit in with his new college compatriots. He fails miserably until he manages to score the winning touchdown in the season's most important football game (fig. **10.4**). The film's climax revolves around football instead of, say, cricket because American audiences readily accept that the physical challenge of scoring a touchdown defines a masculine rite of passage. "Scoring a boundary" in a cricket match might be a cause for ridicule, since many Americans would assume the level of athleticism required to achieve that goal is limited. By presenting football as a means to male adulthood, *The Freshman* reinforces a dominant cultural assumption that football is the pre-eminent masculine sport.

Furthermore, the tendency for Hollywood films to focus on one or two characters (a stylistic trait enhanced by the star system) is symptomatic of the way American culture privileges the individual over the community. By presenting the victory in terms of Diddlebock's triumph, despite the fact that football is a team sport, *The*

10.4 Harold Diddlebock scores the winning touchdown in *The Freshman*.

Freshman reinforces the importance of competitive individualism. In focusing primarily on individuals, classical Hollywood narratives exemplify American culture's tendency to dismiss community concerns as irrelevant compared to the rights of the individual.

Finally, the climax of *The Freshman*, in which Diddlebock "gets the girl," is also indicative of how American films revolve around heterosexual romance. This was the case throughout the twentieth century. Using a survey of 100 randomly selected studio films, David Bordwell found that "ninety-five involved romance in at least one line of action, while eighty-five made that the principal line of action" (Bordwell, p. 16). The conspicuous absence of explicitly homosexual characters in classical Hollywood films points to the fact that the system's definition of love was markedly rooted in the dominant Judeo-Christian ethic. In short, *The Freshman*, a seemingly simple tale of an individual overcoming social ostracism to become a hero, reflects and contributes to cultural ideologies.

Reaffirming or Resisting Dominant Ideology

The discussion thus far seems to suggest that the Hollywood studio system was a monolithic institution, so powerful that it could stifle any dissent. But the studios recognized that maintaining the popularity of its products required more than just repeating what had worked before. According to Janet Staiger, the industry strove to balance standardization (relying on tried and true devices) with differentiation (experimenting with new plot twists and stylistic maneuvers). They were aware that audiences would be bored by movies that had become too formulaic, and shocked or confused by movies that were radically experimental (Staiger, p. 112).

Contemporary film scholars argue that, consequently, some films from this era actually go "against the grain." That is, some films subtly question American ideology. In his analysis of Billy Wilder's *Double Indemnity* (1944), James Naremore argues that this *film noir* presents a pessimistic view of American culture rather than reinforcing its dominant ideologies. The film concerns an insurance salesman, Walter Neff (Fred MacMurray), who participates in an ill-fated plot to help Phyllis Dietrichson (Barbara Stanwyck) murder her husband. Naremore discusses how Wilder's background as a German *émigré* influenced by Expressionism shaped the film's visual style and its critical perspective on the supposed advantages of modern American life, including the availability of manufactured consumer products. Wilder's take on America transforms the landscape of modern life into an alienating terrain:

> The theme of industrialized dehumanization is echoed in the relatively
> private offices on the second floor of the insurance company, which are
> almost interchangeable, decorated with nothing more than statistical charts
> and graphs. [. . .] The public world is equally massified: when Walter realizes
> that Phyllis wants to murder her husband, he drinks a beer in his car at the
> drive-in restaurant; then he goes to a bowling alley at Third and Weston,
> where he bowls alone in an enormous room lined with identical lanes.
> (Naremore, p. 89)

Wilder's depiction of a supermarket—the epitome of a place where American goods are on display, readily available for mass consumption—shows it to be a space where products and people become anonymous.

> The most surreal instance of mechanical reproduction, however, is Jerry's, "that big market up at Los Feliz," where Walter and Phyllis plan their crime. Walter and Phyllis hold *sotto voce* conversations across aisles filled with baby food, beans, macaroni, tomatoes, and seemingly anything else that can be packaged and arranged in neat rows; they talk about murder in public, but the big store makes them anonymous, virtually invisible shoppers. (Naremore, p. 89)

Finally, Naremore points to the way Wilder's *mise en scène* likens the *femme fatale* to a manufactured product (fig. **10.5**).

> [Phyllis] is blatantly provocative and visibly artificial; her ankle bracelet, her lacquered lipstick, her sunglasses, and above all her chromium hair give her a cheaply manufactured, metallic look. In keeping with this synthetic quality, her sex scenes are almost robotic, and she reacts to murder with an icy calm. (Naremore, p. 89)

10.5 The *femme fatale* (Barbara Stanwyck) as a manufactured product in *Double Indemnity*.

In his detailed analysis, Naremore carefully considers the film itself, but also moves his discussion beyond the text to consider its relationship to culture. When he identifies the theme of industrialized dehumanization, he is positing that Wilder's film is a critique of American culture in the mid-1940s.

Naremore's analysis assumes a certain degree of intentionality on the director's part. A different approach to ideology acknowledges that audiences may be able to read films against the grain, rejecting the dominant messages they contain. The notion of reading against the grain postulates that some films contain inadvertent contradictions that undermine their apparent endorsement of dominant cultural beliefs.

Robin Wood performs this kind of analysis on Frank Capra's *It's a Wonderful Life* (1946), a film that, on the surface, reaffirms small-town American values. In the film, George Bailey (Jimmy Stewart) spends his whole life sacrificing his dreams to help others. Despite his urge to travel the world, George marries, spends his life in his small home town of Bedford Falls, and runs his father's building and loan business. When he loses $8,000 because of an employee's forgetfulness and a rival banker's duplicity, he becomes despondent, resentful, and suicidal. A guardian angel intervenes and shows George what life in Bedford Falls would have been like without him. Run by the corrupt banker Potter, the town is full of vice, bars, and unhappy people. The angel inspires George to return to his family. Upon his return, he finds that the entire community has pooled its resources to help replace the lost money.

On one level, the film emphasizes George's re-commitment to family and middle-class values. But, Wood points out, by depicting an alternative, equally viable *film noir*-style Bedford Falls, the film exposes the unpleasant realities underneath the idealized small town world that George embraces in the conclusion.

> *It's a Wonderful Life* manages a convincing and moving affirmation of the values (and value) of bourgeois family life. Yet what is revealed, when disaster releases George's suppressed tensions, is the intensity of his resentment of the family and desire to destroy it—and with it, in significant relationship, his work (his culminating action is furiously to overthrow the drawing board with his plans for more small-town houses). [. . .] What is finally striking about the film's affirmation is the extreme precariousness of its basis [. . .] [The film] may well be Capra's masterpiece, but it is more than that. Like all the greatest American films—fed by a complex generic tradition and, *beyond that, by the fears and aspirations of a whole culture—it at once transcends its director and would be inconceivable without him.* (Wood, pp. 295–6, emphasis added)

Wood ascribes a latent pessimism to the film's surface optimism. In other words, he reads the film as a critique of the American middle class because it draws attention to suppressed feelings of dread that accompany the American Dream. This critique, he emphasizes, is the product of cultural forces beyond Capra's control. The film embodies the anxieties of a culture over its dominant ideology—ironically, an ideology the film intends to reinforce.

● International Art Cinema

Not all cinema traditions value Hollywood's industrial efficiency and emphasis on narrative. During the 1950s and 1960s, a wave of European and Asian films garnered international reputations because they departed from Hollywood's commercialism, uncomplicated characters, and invisible style. At the height of this era, filmgoers around the world were drawn to films from Sweden, Japan, India, Italy, and France. Many cinephiles referred to these films collectively as the art cinema movement.

The moniker assumes a marked distinction between Hollywood film and art film. Whereas the former is assumed to be escapist entertainment, the latter is seen to have a more serious intellectual purpose and a more sophisticated approach. Indeed, the films produced in this era addressed a number of weighty issues, including the discrepancy between memory and lived experience (*Hiroshima, mon amour* [Alain Resnais 1959]), the plight of the financially, but not spiritually, impoverished (*Pather Panchali* [Satyajit Ray

1955]), the relationship between art and life (*Breathless*), and spiritual doubt in the face of death (*The Seventh Seal*).

These films abandon goal-oriented characters, preferring instead to explore the psychology of complex characters who often have no sense of what they want out of life, much less how to achieve it. Rather than dedicating screen time to action, these films often dwell on capturing time in which little or nothing (physical) happens. Stylistically, they flout Hollywood conventions in bold attempts to depict subjectivity or to draw the audience's attention to film's status as art. By no means is there a consistent narrative or stylistic model to which international art films adhere. The single trait they have in common is their contrast from the Hollywood studio model.

Jean-Luc Godard's *Breathless* ("*A Bout du Souffle*") exemplifies the way art cinema differs from classical Hollywood films. At first glance, the film promises to be a gangster film about Michel Poiccard (Jean-Paul Belmondo), a car thief who somewhat impulsively shoots a policeman (fig. **10.6**). But Michel is far from the conventional outlaw on the lam. Rather than setting to work on a plan to evade the police, he fritters his time away in Paris, alternately trying to seduce his American girlfriend Patricia (Jean Seberg) and take her to the movies. In one extended scene, Michel and Patricia playfully romp half-clothed in bed together, and their dialogue is full of sexual innuendo (fig. **10.7**). This frank depiction of sexuality was in sharp contrast to Hollywood's sanitized bedrooms of the same era, where even married couples slept in separate beds. In fact, one reason for the popularity of art films in the U.S. is that audiences, used to the rigid moral standards imposed by the Production Code, were intrigued and titillated by art cinema's open display of sexuality, occasional nudity, and its characters' youthful insouciance.

By conventional standards, Michel and Patricia's actions are indecipherable and often self-contradictory. At one point Michel inexplicably follows a stranger into a building and up several flights on an elevator. He gets off the elevator and proceeds to steal the man's car, but the film makes no attempt to explain why he follows the man in the first place.

10.6 *(left)* Michel gazes at a poster of Humphrey Bogart in *Breathless* ("*A Bout du Souffle*").

10.7 *(right)* Michel and Patricia romp under the bedcovers in *Breathless*.

Patricia is a college student, but, despite her intellectual bent, she is drawn to the pointedly vulgar Michel. She confesses that she loves him only after discovering that he's a wanted man—and then proceeds to alert the police as to his whereabouts.

In keeping with the disjointed narrative and quirky characters, the film's style is playfully fragmented. Most noticeable is its use of jump cuts throughout, which excise lengthy chunks of time, as when Michel shoots the officer and then abruptly reappears in Paris. Frequently the editing and the soundtrack conceptualize time differently. For example, as Michel drives toward Paris, jump cuts visually interrupt time and condense the amount of time spent on the road, even while Michel's singing runs fluidly. In other words, chronological time is removed from the image, but not from the soundtrack.

10.8 Surreal poetry marks the final circus scene from *8½*.

The film's cinematography resembles that of a documentary, complementing the film's spontaneous feel. Cinematographer Raoul Coutard relied extensively on handheld cameras (then a relatively unheard of approach in fiction films), natural lighting, and an unusual film stock: rolls of fast film made exclusively for still photography spliced together for the 35 mm camera. According to Coutard, Godard's goal was to "escape from convention and even run counter to the rules of 'cinematographic grammar'" (quoted in Neupert, p. 210).

In short, rather than making style subservient to a tightly structured narrative, *Breathless* draws attention to the expressive and aesthetic vitality of cinema: the director "wanted to give the feeling that the techniques of filmmaking had just been discovered or experienced for the first time" (Godard, quoted in Marie, p. 162). Again, by no means does *Breathless* define a common sensibility among all art films. Whereas it revels in playful spontaneity, other films, such as Alain Resnais's *Last Year at Marienbad* or Federico Fellini's *8½*, adopt a highly stylized, formalist approach (fig. **10.8**). Still others, such as *Pather Panchali*, strive for a heightened and poetic sense of realism.

The Ideology of "Art"

To refer to these films as "art cinema" may imply that there were no commercial concerns associated with their production and distribution, which is not the case. Historians attribute the expansion of art cinema in part to the public financing of national cinemas after

World War II, as government policy in many countries financed productions that would stand as visible and marketable documents of national culture (Nowell-Smith, p. 567). While these filmmakers did not work in a highly regimented industrial structure, funding still depended on a project's potential marketability. Art films were produced in the hopes of generating a profit (and indeed they did, often both domestically and abroad), and they successfully competed against the Hollywood juggernaut because their self-conscious artistry helped to distinguish them from Hollywood's more immediate accessibility.

Thus, while many cinephiles appreciate these films as examples of high culture—sophisticated and highly intellectual art—and Hollywood films as mass culture—commercial art appealing to unrefined tastes—the distinction between the two is an oversimplification. In fact, such rote categorization reveals a class-based ideological precept implicit in the art cinema movement: the assumption that popular film is too plebian, crude, and unsophisticated to be considered worthy of serious consideration.

The case of India's film industry illustrates how privileging high art dictates that most international audiences overlook indigenous popular cinemas. India's film industry is the largest film industry in the world in terms of the number of films produced. Dubbed "Bollywood" because of its Bombay location and prodigious size, rivaling Hollywood, the industry produces a remarkable 900 films annually. Many in the West were introduced to Indian cinema in 1956, when the jury at the Cannes Film Festival voted *Pather Panchali*, "Best Human Document." Director Satyajit Ray achieved international fame for his work, and for many Western enthusiasts, Ray's films represent Indian cinema. However, his films represent a departure from the norm in that country.

> Popular Indian films are typically an eclectic hodgepodge of styles: comic interludes, musical sequences, religion, adventure, fights, socio-political considerations—all get mixed up together in commercial (pan-Indian mainstream) cinema, often characterized by the epithet *masala* (spicy). (Thoraval, p. 118)

One of the most popular Indian films ever made, the "curry" Western *Embers* ("*Sholay*"; Ramesh Sippy 1975), exemplifies how Hindi films distinguish themselves by fusing competing narrative strategies and visual styles. The film includes episodes of extreme brutality: one man throws glowing coals on a thief covered in fuel; a gang of outlaws cuts the arms off the policeman. But it also contains absurdly comic sequences: when two men can't decide who should get to ask a woman out, they flip a coin—which stands on its side instead of falling on heads or tails. Bollywood films also rely on elaborate sets and ornate costuming to create a kaleidoscopic visual appeal, which complements the films' elaborate narratives and captivating musical numbers.

In contrast, the highly poetic *Pather Panchali* follows the hardships of a poor Bengali family, focusing on the young children, Apu (Subir Bannerjee) and his older sister, Durga (Uma Das Gupta). Ray's film consists of loosely linked episodes that portray the daily routines of an impoverished family: Apu and Durga see a train for the first time; Apu asks his father for money to buy candy; Apu watches his sister dance in the first rains of the monsoon. When the father leaves home for an extended period of time to find work, a series of tragic events besets the family, culminating in Durga's death from pneumonia. While popular Indian films don't shy away from depicting social problems, their aesthetic approach favors escapist fantasy over the melancholic and provocative realism of Ray's work.

The visual style of *Pather Panchali* also stands in sharp contrast to India's popular cinema. It abandons studio shooting in favor of locations. Ray uses the Indian landscape to capture the family's fleeting pleasures and mounting hardships. Animals and insects wander in and out of the frame to suggest how precariously situated is the family's crumbling homestead (fig. **10.9**). When Apu and Durga experience the excitement of watching a passing train, they must leave the confines of the forest surrounding their home and wander into an open field, enhancing the emotional expansiveness of the incident.

10.9 Apu's family stand amidst nature and disarray in the yard in *Pather Panchali*.

Following the international success of *Pather Panchali*, the Indian government founded the Indian Film Finance Corporation to improve the quality and heighten the international reputation of the country's films. The Indian government hoped to capitalize on Ray's critical success by subsidizing films that might bring more international prestige to the country's film industry.

In effect, Ray's international popularity and the government's subsequent decision to fund "serious" movies established a two-tier system in which international acclaim is lavished on directors whose films meet certain criteria associated with high art. Those criteria may include a bias toward Western art: Ray's most obvious influences were not other Indian film directors, but Americans and Europeans, including David Lean, Frank Capra, John Ford, Sergei Eisenstein, Jean Renoir, and Vittorio De Sica. In fact, Ray secured government financing only after John Huston and representatives from the Museum of Modern Art in New York expressed an interest in *Pather Panchali* (Thoraval, p. 243). Perhaps a film that was less Western might not have received such lavish praise from American critics. Finally, the world premiere of *Pather Panchali* was not in India, but in New York.

While a remarkable cinematic achievement, Ray's film does not reflect the everyday Indian movie-going experience. But the international preference for his work demonstrates how art films often are marketed as more legitimate cultural expressions than mainstream films.

International Art Cinema

In short, the art cinema movement of the 1950s and '60s provided audiences with a wide range of cinematic experiences that differed dramatically from classical Hollywood's standard fare. Still, the production and reception of these films were profoundly shaped by cultural, historical, and economic circumstances. Fig. 10.14 at the end of this chapter offers a brief schematic of these two filmmaking contexts, as well as two others that are discussed below: Italian Neorealism and Third Cinema.

● Italian Neorealism

Italian Neorealism was an influential postwar cinema whose social and economic context defined its style in crucial ways. In Italy after World War II, Roberto Rossellini, Vittorio De Sica, and Luchino Visconti, actors and directors who had trained and worked in the commercial Italian film industry before the war, produced startling and distinctive films that seemed to capture the reality of the physical devastation, the moral degradation, and the human suffering of the war years. In the words of De Sica, "the experience of the war was decisive for us all. Each felt the mad desire to throw away the old stories of the Italian cinema, to plant the camera in the midst of real life" (quoted in Marcus, pp. xiii–xiv).

Neorealism predated (and in many ways influenced) the international art cinema discussed above. Its principles and visual style were even further removed from Hollywood than those of art cinema.

Neorealist filmmaking grew from real-life events—yet the films were fictionalized accounts of experiences during the war and of the hardships of postwar Italy. Although Rossellini's *Rome, Open City* ("*Roma, città aperta*"; 1945) and De Sica's *Bicycle Thieves* were scripted, they convincingly relayed the harsh realities of wartime and its aftermath with a directness and immediacy that seemed to be missing from the escapist Italian and Hollywood films of the 1930s (fig. **10.10**).

According to the theorist and screenwriter Cesare Zavattini, Neorealism presented everyday life through stories involving working-class or poor protagonists, the use of location shooting, long takes, natural lighting, non-professional actors, vernacular dialogue, grainy black-and-white film stock, and unobtrusive editing (Marcus, p. 22). These distinctive characteristics derived partly from the economic circumstances of postwar

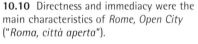
10.10 Directness and immediacy were the main characteristics of *Rome, Open City* ("*Roma, città aperta*").

filmmaking—a lack of equipment, film stock, and studio soundstages—and partly from the directors' commitment to filmmaking with a social purpose.

Neorealist cinema was concerned with telling the stories of ordinary Italian people struggling to survive. Films such as *Bicycle Thieves*—the story of a poor man and his son who attempt to recover their stolen bicycle because it represents the family's economic future—convey the breakdown of traditional social institutions. In terms of narrative form, Neorealist films depict people going about their daily lives. They devote screen time to the depiction of mundane details and favor an elliptical or digressive storytelling style. Peter Lehman and William Luhr describe the difference between De Sica's *Umberto D* (1952; fig. **10.11**) and a Hollywood film in terms of the organization of the action:

10.11 The depiction of minute detail is a stylistic feature of *Umberto D*, a film about an impoverished pensioner.

> De Sica seeks to give a wholeness to the reality he represents. He does not
> break it down into parts, decide what is important and unimportant and
> then only show us the important part. He shows us everything in the belief
> that we can decide what is important [. . .] The [Classical Hollywood] style
> [. . .] uses a continuity system based on eliding unimportant parts of an
> action. (Lehman and Luhr, p. 215)

Italian Neorealist films appealed to audiences and filmmakers around the world. Committed to telling stories about the recent past, often of spirited survival under grim circumstances, Neorealist filmmakers rejected the artificiality of films made on sets, starring matinee idols and revolving around contrived romantic storylines. Yet despite its success with audiences, the period of Italian Neorealism was short-lived. In 1949, the Italian government passed the Andreotti Law, which allowed censors to excise portions of films or to prohibit the export of Neorealist films on the grounds that they did not convey Italy in a good light. The government labeled certain Neorealist films "antagonistic to the national interest" (Marcus, p. 26).

Nevertheless, Italian Neorealism had a significant influence on many postwar cinemas, including Hollywood's *film noir* and social problem films of the 1940s and 1950s, the British New Wave of the 1960s, and Third Cinema movements such as Cinema Novo in Brazil and post-revolutionary Cuban cinema. Its social vision and conventions were taken up by politically committed filmmakers in Africa, Latin America, and Asia during the revolutionary fervor of the 1960s.

10.14 Classical Hollywood, art cinema, Neorealism, and Third Cinema.

	Classical Hollywood	Art Cinema	Neorealism	Third Cinema
Characters	one or two active, goal-oriented characters	one or two psychologically complex characters with unclear goals	everyday individuals who struggle to survive and become heroic in the process	focus is on collective experience, whether represented through an individual or group
Narrative	cause-and-effect logic; three-act or four-part structure; closure	loose cause–effect relations; episodic structure; open-ended	tales of average people struggling in postwar Italy; open-ended	revolutionary stories that resonate at personal and social levels
Visual Style and Sound	studio and location shooting; continuity editing; visual and sound techniques enhance storytelling	studio and location shooting; emphasis on expression and artistry rather than storytelling; self-reflexivity	location shooting, non-professional actors, and direct sound contribute to documentary immediacy	location shooting; non-professional actors; many adopt documentary techniques, others use indigenous art traditions
Mode of Production	industrial studio system	*auteur*-driven studio and government-supported filmmaking	studio-trained directors worked outside industrial system	government-supported, independent, and artisanal productions; many varied national contexts

Works Consulted

Betz, Mark. "The Name above the (Sub)Title: Internationalism, Coproduction, and Polyglot European Art Cinema." *Camera Obscura*, 16/1 (2001). March 8, 2002. http//muse.jhu.edu/journals/camera_obscura/v016/16.1betz.htm.

Bignardi, Irene. "The Making of *The Battle of Algiers*." *Cineaste*, spring 2000, pp. 14–22.

Bordwell, David. "Story Causality and Motivation," in *The Classical Hollywood Cinema: Film Style and Mode of Production to 1960*, ed. David Bordwell *et al.* New York: Columbia University Press, 1985, pp. 12–23.

Carter, Angela. *Expletives Deleted*. London: Chatto and Windus, 1992.

Chanan, Michael. "Tomás Gutiérrez Alea," in *The Oxford History of World Cinema*, ed. Geoffrey Nowell-Smith. Oxford: Oxford University Press, 1996, p. 744.

Cook, David. *A History of Narrative Film*, 3rd edn. New York: Norton, 1996.

Guerrero, Ed. *Framing Blackness: The African American Image in Film*. Philadelphia: Temple University Press, 1993.

Hay, James. *Popular Film Culture in Fascist Italy*. Bloomington: Indiana University Press, 1987.

Heines, Marjorie. *Sex, Sin, and Blasphemy. A Guide to American's Censorship Wars*. New York: The New York Press, 1998.

"John Ford's *Young Mr. Lincoln*." Collective text by the editors of *Cahiers du Cinéma*. *Film Theory and Criticism: Introductory Readings*, 3rd edn., ed. Gerald Mast and Marshall Cohen. New York: Oxford University Press, 1985, pp. 695–740.

Kruidenier, David. "Postcolonialism and Feminism in *The Battle of Algiers*." Unpublished paper. February 2004.

Lehman, Peter, and William Luhr. *Thinking about Movies: Watching, Questioning, Enjoying*. Fort Worth: Harcourt, 1999.

Lewis, Jon. *Hollywood versus Hardcore: How the Struggle over Censorship Saved the Modern Film Industry*. New York: New York University Press, 2000.

Maltby, Richard. "Censorship and Self-Regulation," in *The Oxford History of World Cinema*, ed. Geoffrey Nowell-Smith. New York: Oxford University Press, 1996, pp. 235–48.

Marcus, Millicent. *Italian Film in the Light of Neorealism*. Princeton: Princeton University Press, 1986.

Marie, Michel. "It Really Makes You Sick," in *French Film: Texts and Contexts*, 2nd edn., ed. Susan Hayward and Ginette Vincendeau. London: Routledge, 2000, pp. 158–73.

Naremore, James. *More than Night: Film Noir in its Contexts*. Berkeley: University of California Press, 1998.

Neupert, Richard. *A History of the French New Wave*. Madison: University of Wisconsin Press, 2002.

Nowell-Smith, Geoffrey. "Art Cinema," in *The Oxford History of World Cinema*, ed. Geoffrey Nowell-Smith. New York: Oxford University Press, 1996, pp. 567–75.

Rajadhyaksha, Ashish. "Realism, Modernism, and Post-colonial Theory," in *The Oxford Guide to Film Studies*, ed. John Hill and Pamela Church Gibson. Oxford: Oxford University Press, 1998, pp. 413–25.

Ray, Robert. *A Certain Tendency of the Hollywood Cinema, 1930–1980*. Princeton: Princeton University Press, 1985.

Schatz, Thomas. *The Genius of the System: Hollywood Filmmaking in the Studio Era*. New York: Pantheon, 1988.

Schroeder, Paul A. *Tomás Gutiérrez Alea: The Dialectics of a Filmmaker*. New York and London: Routledge, 2002.

Shohat, Ella, and Robert Stam. *Unthinking Eurocentrism: Multiculturalism and the Media*. London and New York: Routledge, 1994.

Sklar, Robert. *Film: An International History of the Medium*, 2nd edn. Saddle River, NJ: Prentice Hall and Harry N. Abrams, 2002.

Staiger, Janet. "Standardization and Differentiation: The Reinforcement and Dispersion of Hollywood's Practices," in *The Classical Hollywood Cinema: Film Style and Mode of Production to 1960*, ed. David Bordwell *et al*. New York: Columbia University Press, 1985, pp. 96–112.

Sontag, Susan. "The Imagination of Disaster," in *Movies*, ed. Gilbert Adair. London: Penguin, 1999, pp. 170–85.

Thoraval, Yves. *The Cinemas of India*. New Delhi: Macmillan India, 2000.

Vir, Parminder. "The Mother of All Battles." *The New Statesman*. July 8, 2002, pp. 40–2.

Wood, Robin. "Ideology, Genre, Auteur: *Shadow of a Doubt*," in *Hitchcock's Films Revisited*. New York: Columbia University Press, 1989, pp. 288–303.

Film and Ideology

11.1 As Mammy, Hattie McDaniel reluctantly does Scarlett's bidding in *Gone with the Wind*.

Film drama is the opium of the people.

Dziga Vertov

*L*ike Chapter Ten, this chapter broadens the scope of film analysis by considering the relationship between film and cultural context. More specifically, it introduces several topics within ideological criticism and offers examples of the way film critics and scholars write about the ideologies that pervade popular films.

Ideological criticism posits that films are structured and patterned according to ideologies or worldviews: systems of belief that purport to describe the world but, in fact, also shape the world. Ideologies are beliefs, and they are not always amenable to rules of

logic or evidence. They are formed and influenced by family, cultural background and experiences, education, and popular culture (music, films, television, and the internet). Usually, they seem so "commonsensical" as to appear obvious and natural. But they form an unquestioned basis for individual and group decisions about the proper organization of society, from the economic system to social roles for men and women to the significance of perceived sexual and racial differences.

Ideological critics assume that films influence what filmgoers think and how they act when they aren't watching movies. Jonathan Rosenbaum, an exemplary critic using the ideological approach, presents the reason why some critics are committed to using this method. "What is designed to make people feel good at the movies has a profound relation to how and what they think and feel about the world around them" (Rosenbaum, p. 3).

Ideological critics consider the potential impact of ideologies on audiences. Their work overlaps that of reception studies. Reception studies scholars survey audience members about their actual responses to films. Together, ideological criticism and reception studies consider the way popular films celebrate and/or challenge the dominant ideologies of the culture that produced them and assess the way viewers accept, resist, or reinterpret those ideologies.

Disagreement exists about the precise way ideologies in films affect viewers. Inspired by Theodor Adorno and the Frankfurt School of critical theory, active in the mid-twentieth century, some ideological critics view popular films as a "culture industry," or as entertainment contaminated with repressive ideologies. In this view, films purvey the conservative values of the powerful interests that control the film corporations. Critics associated with the British film journal *Screen* during the 1970s argued that commercial cinema seduces naïve audiences into compliance because films perpetuate oppressive class divisions, making the status quo appear to be the only state of affairs possible.

In the last two decades, film scholars and critics have begun to argue that popular films carry contradictory messages about class, capitalism, technology, gender, and race. Cultural studies, a field pioneered by Stuart Hall and Angela McRobbie, suggests that viewers are not passive receptacles of a film's ideology. Instead, they sometimes join in a dominant reading—one aligned with dominant values—but also may recognize, question, and resist dominant ideologies. Scholars of reception also consider what accounts for different interpretations, asking what elements within the films (say, open endings rather than closure) or the viewer's profile (education, training, cultural experiences) contribute to resistant readings.

One reason critics consider ideology in Hollywood films to be important is the enormous cultural impact those films have had in the U.S. and around the world. From the 1920s through the 1950s, movies were a major socializing force in American culture, influencing the way people looked, talked, and acted (Kellner, p. 128). Hollywood's social influence persists, now on a global scale.

Like all film critics, ideological critics evaluate films according to certain criteria. These criteria, however, emphasize political and cultural issues along with aesthetic merit. For example, one critic might argue that technically sophisticated Hollywood action films

11.2 A twist? Femininity as physical dominance in *Terminator 3*.

promote an image of the U.S. as a military power-house that resorts to violence only when necessary. The critic may commend these films for promulgating an ideology of justified violence. Another critic might agree with the first critic's description but disagree with the evaluation. The second might condemn the films for presenting masculinity as synonymous with physical dominance, arguing that this ideology is potentially damaging to both men and women viewers. A third critic might consider the implications of the way male and female characters use violence to dominate others (fig. **11.2**).

The readings and analyses below illustrate ideological criticism at work. They all address popular U.S. films, partly because ideologies are culturally specific, and it is inappropriate to generalize across cultural and national contexts. Also, U.S. films dominate the global market, so the ideological thrust of American films carries a particular force. Of course, the range of subjects examined here—race, gender, sexuality, class, and national identity—does not exhaust the topics for which the ideological criticism is relevant.

● Ideologies of Racial Difference

Historically, in the U.S. and Europe, there was a dominant, mistaken belief that there were several biologically distinct races, and that the white race was superior to all others. In the U.S. and elsewhere, this white supremacist ideology accompanied and supported practices such as slavery, segregation, and discrimination: the legally sanctioned exploitation and disenfranchisement of African people. The ideology of white supremacy is apparent in films such as D.W. Griffith's *The Birth of the Nation*, which depicts African-Americans as foolish, servile, or menacing; the white characters meanwhile are, with one exception, noble and courageous. (The one ignoble white character is a politician who advocates freeing the slaves and the "mixing" of the races.)

The film's scandalous treatment of black people and its validation of Ku Klux Klan violence made it controversial in its day. The NAACP (National Association for the Advancement of Colored People) organized protests. Griffith sought to address the criticism in his next film, *Intolerance* (1916), an epic that casts oppression and inhumanity among four ancient cultures in a negative light but made no reference to contemporary America.

Films such as *The Birth of the Nation*, *The Little Colonel* (David Butler 1935), and *Gone with the Wind* (Victor Fleming 1939) reinforce the idea of racial hierarchy. First, the plot-lines revolve around white characters because their lives and concerns are presumed to be appealing and universal. Most Hollywood films before the 1970s ignore the fact that African-American characters have lives independent from their white employers. *Émigré* director Douglas Sirk treated this convention of American films with irony in *Imitation of Life* (1959), where he populated the funeral of the black maid Annie (Juanita Moore) with hundreds of mourning friends whom her white employer never knew about during Annie's life.

Second, in most Hollywood films before the 1970s African-American people appear as types rather than as individuals. Donald Bogle identifies the vicious stereotypes most often used to represent black people in commercial U.S. cinema: Toms, Coons, Mammies, Mulattos, and Bucks. Hattie McDaniel's Mammy characters in *The Little Colonel* and *Gone with the Wind* represent the nurturing but feisty black female caretaker, who unselfishly (but not uncomplainingly) ministers to the needs of white folks (fig. **11.1**, p. 316). Film scholar Ed Guerrero points to child star Shirley Temple's dance routines with Bill "Bojangles" Robinson in *The Little Colonel* and *The Littlest Rebel* (David Butler 1935) as products of a white perspective. They were "resented by black spectators and critics as demeaning renditions of the myths and stereotypes inflicted on blacks by an indelible culture of racism" (Guerrero, p. 19).

One counterargument about stereotypes asserts that they are impossible to avoid: all films condense action and characterizations, sometimes resorting to shorthand. But stories that depend heavily on stereotypes—whether negative or positive—should be questioned on both ideological and aesthetic grounds.

Fortunately, white supremacist ideology is not the only set of beliefs about racial difference. Many people believe that perceived cultural differences between black and white people—and other historical minorities such as Latinos, Asian Americans, and Native Americans—must be carefully considered in terms of the history of racial oppression, in particular, the centuries-long dominance of white Europeans. One implication is that different stories and styles of storytelling may be needed to express the experiences of different cultural groups. Whereas a black male coming-of-age story might look like *Boyz N the Hood* (John Singleton 1991), a white male coming-of-age story might look like *A Bronx Tale* (Robert De Niro 1993), and a Native American coming-of-age film looks like *Smoke Signals* (Chris Eyre 1998).

A third ideology of racial difference rejects distinctions altogether. A belief that all people are fundamentally the same and that superficial differences should play no role in social practices underpins films that show white and black people with common hopes, fears, and aspirations: for example, *Grand Canyon* (Lawrence Kasdan 1991) or the *Lethal Weapon* series (Richard Donner 1987–98).

An ideological critic interested in the way historical circumstances contribute to film aesthetics might examine the history of African-Americans in film. While black performers were never excluded from the industry *per se*, the number and quality of roles were limited. Out of 1364 Oscar nominations between 1927 and 2002, only 35 went to African-Americans. Of those, seven African-American actors have won eight awards: Hattie McDaniel, Sidney Poitier, Lou Gossett, Jr., Denzel Washington (who won Best Supporting Actor for *Glory* [Edward Zwick 1989] and Best Actor for *Training Day* [Antoine Fuqua 2001]), Cuba Gooding, Jr, Whoopi Goldberg, and Halle Berry.

Until the 1970s, industry practices of discrimination prevented black filmmakers from directing and producing films and denied them membership in technical guilds. Film scholar Melvin Donalson argues that the history of stereotyped images and a lack of an economic base in the industry prevented African-Americans from directing Hollywood films until the late 1960s (Donalson, p.5). Yet filmmakers such as Oscar Micheaux, Spencer Williams, Ivan Dixon, Ossie Davis, Melvin Van Peebles, Charles Burnett, and Julie Dash have made, and continue to make, films outside Hollywood. An ideological critic might ask whether films made by independent African-American filmmakers differ from films made by white independent filmmakers in content or style and consider the reasons for those differences.

The reading below concerns the racial politics and aesthetics of *Mississippi Burning* (Alan Parker 1988), a film based on an actual incident involving the killing of three civil rights workers in Mississippi in 1964. The film deviated from the actual events by creating two fictional characters, white FBI agents, who become the focal points of the action.

Misplaced Heroism in *Mississippi Burning*

Jonathan Rosenbaum's review of *Mississippi Burning* focuses on the film's celebration of the two fictional FBI agents, Anderson (Gene Hackman) and Ward (Willem Dafoe; fig. **11.3**).

> It's emblematic of the entire approach of Parker and screenwriter Chris Gerolmo that the movie focuses almost exclusively on the investigation of the murders by two FBI agents, . . . and that they're the only good guys in sight. (Rosenbaum, p. 119)

Black characters are marginalized, treated as children rather than agents of social change.

> Needless to say the blacks are given no voice at all in the debate; they're essentially treated like children, and emotionally speaking Ward and Anderson are the parents who have to decide what's best for them. (Rosenbaum, p. 120)

11.3 Gene Hackman and Willem Dafoe as Anderson and Ward in *Mississippi Burning*.

Although no overtly negative stereotypes are used, black characters are treated as a group, not as individuals.

> Ward, Anderson, and the deputy's wife are the only figures with any density in the plot. The nameless murder victims, seen only in the opening sequence, are never allowed to exist as characters, and the local blacks—noble, suffering icons without any depth or personality—hardly fare better. (Rosenbaum, p. 121)

Rosenbaum deflects the argument that Hollywood films never reproduce reality by saying he can accept some creative license. But he finds that the director's focus on white heroes makes the film unnecessarily simple.

> It's not enough to counter that any Hollywood movie entails a certain amount of distortion [. . .] I wouldn't expect a docudrama of this sort to deal with the literal truth [. . .] But Parker has stuck so exclusively to his white heroes that he has drained all complexity out of everyone else, blacks and racists alike. (Rosenbaum, pp. 120–22)

Rosenbaum addresses the film's aesthetics through its politics. He argues that the drama lacks complexity because the filmmakers have chosen to foreground two white characters and their struggles while painting all others as victims or evildoers.

Ideologies of Gender

Many cultures treat the gender difference between men and women as a fundamental organizing principle. Evolutionary biologists claim that biological differences define male and female: men are competitive and violent, seeking to dominate other men in order to acquire the largest number of mates possible, whereas women are nurturing and loyal, preferring the stability of a relationship with one opposite sex partner with whom to raise children. The presumption, akin to the pop catch phrase that "men are from Mars, women are from Venus," is sometimes accompanied by the belief that one sex (in most cases, the male) is superior. Although these views are contradicted by the fact that in biological terms men and women are more alike than they are different (they share 99% of the same DNA), they influence ideas about sex differences and the means for dealing with them.

A society structured by ideologies of male supremacy is sometimes described as "patriarchal." In patriarchies, men exercise power and authority over women, who are excluded from full participation on the grounds that it would be unnatural for women to perform certain tasks. Patriarchal social practices range from women's exclusion from political life (women were not permitted to vote in the U.S. until 1918) to economic inequities (women currently earn 70% of what their male counterparts earn) to exclusion from certain civic activities (women were excluded from combat service until 1991) to the circulation of stereotypes about women (the common claim that they are bad drivers). Gender stereotyping affects both men and women by assigning a limited number of expected or acceptable traits to each gender: men must appear strong, for example, and women nurturing.

Many social scientists contend that socialization processes impose meaning on anatomical sex differences. In other words, they argue, masculinity and femininity are learned behaviors called gender roles. In this view, male and female children must be taught gendered behaviors. This belief suggests that not all men do (or should) act out the stereotype of masculinity (strong, aggressive, breadwinner figures) and that not all women do (or should) exhibit traditional notions of femininity (emotional innocents, seductive sirens, or nurturing mothers). The belief that genders are learned questions the idea that men and women are ordained by nature to be "opposite" and complementary sexes. Thus, it allows for the possibility that both men and women might learn and enact a range of behaviors that once were thought of as belonging to two categories, masculine and feminine.

Yet another view of sex differences is that they are (or should be considered) irrelevant—that the humanity men and women share outweighs (or ought to outweigh) superficial differences.

What are the implications of these ideologies of sexual difference for film criticism? Just as practices of racial exclusion limited African-American participation, practices of gender exclusion have affected would-be women filmmakers. Over 100 women directed silent films during the 1910s and 20s, but during the Hollywood studio era, only two remained: Dorothy Arzner and Ida Lupino. As of 2004, only three women directors (Lina Wertmuller, Jane Campion, and Sofia Coppola) had been nominated for Best Director Academy Award, and none has won the Oscar for directing.

One of the most influential strains in ideological criticism is feminist criticism, an approach that examines the way films differentially represent women and men. In the 1960s and 1970s, feminist film theorists such as Molly Haskell and Laura Mulvey leveled a powerful critique at Hollywood films, arguing that they present an active male hero, with whom audiences are encouraged to identify, and cast women as objects, passive spectacles on display for male characters and audience members. Women's sexuality threatens men, Mulvey conjectured, and as a consequence, men take action to eliminate that threat. Male characters on screen, and men in the audience, exercise the power of "the male gaze" to control women, turning them into objects. Mulvey's arguments stimulated a great deal of discussion and debate. Although many of her ideas have been questioned, qualified, and in some cases rejected, her work continues to inform feminist criticism.

Feminist Criticism and Alien Mothering

The following passages are excerpted from Barbara Creed's book on representations of motherhood as monstrous. In her chapter on *Alien*, Creed argues that this science fiction film expresses male anxieties about women's power over reproduction. In *Alien*, the powerful, archaic mother—generator of life and wielder of death—threatens male power, so she must be eliminated. Creed asserts that the archaic mother first becomes evident within the film's *misc cn scène*. Creed analyzes the *mise en scène* closely, arguing that it represents a fantasy of childbirth that excludes the mother.

The first birth scene occurs at the beginning of the film, where the camera/spectator explores:

> the inner space of the mother-ship whose life support system is a computer
> aptly named—"Mother." This exploratory sequence of the inner body of the
> "Mother" culminates with a long tracking shot down one of the corridors
> which leads to a womb-like chamber where the crew of seven are woken up
> from their protracted sleep by Mother's voice monitoring a call for help
> from a nearby planet. The seven astronauts emerge slowly from their sleep

pods in what amounts to a re-birthing scene which is marked by a fresh, antiseptic atmosphere. In outer space, birth is a well-controlled, clean, painless affair. There is no blood, trauma or terror. This scene could be interpreted as a primal fantasy in which the human subject is born fully developed—even copulation is redundant. (Creed p. 259)

11.4 A shot from *Company of Wolves*. Birth scenes—common in horror films—refer to monstrous maternity.

Creed describes in detail the way the *mise en scène* suggests a sanitized, technological birth. She identifies an instance where an act of birth eliminates the human mother: when the alien creature bursts out of one character's stomach. The mother has been replaced, yet her image haunts the setting.

> Although the "mother" as a figure does not appear in these sequences—nor indeed in the entire film—her presence forms a vast backdrop for the enactment of all the events. She is there in the images of birth, the representations of the primal scene, the womb-like imagery, the long winding tunnels leading to inner chambers, the rows of hatching eggs, the body of the mother-ship, the voice of the life-support system and the birth of the alien. (Creed, p. 260)

Creed argues that the film represents "an attempt to appropriate the procreative function of the mother, to represent a man giving birth" (Creed, p. 261). Many horror films recast the act of birth as a frightening scene (fig. **11.4**).

Some viewers may contend that the hero of the film—and of the entire series—is a woman (Lt. Ellen Ripley, played by Sigourney Weaver), and that therefore *Alien* presents a progressive vision of gender roles. Yet Creed questions the film's vision because it revels in the violent appropriation of the mother's power while it eliminates her as a human presence. The maternal imagery in *Alien* returns in *Aliens* (James Cameron, 1986), the second film of the series. In that film, unscrupulous male characters motivated by their allegiance to the company use female characters as incubators for aliens. In *Aliens*, the company plans to appropriate the power of the mother to propagate alien creatures that might be useful as weapons. Creed's reading of the first film thus unearths themes that the second film presents overtly.

Feminist film criticism has broadened to include ideologies associated with masculinity and film representations of men. Furthermore, the field of feminist criticism, along with gay and lesbian studies, has contributed to Queer Theory; a body of thought and writing that examines sex and gender differences within a comprehensive analysis of sexuality.

● Ideologies of Sexuality

Just as certain ideologies purport to explain the difference between men and women, so some related ideologies explain differences among people in terms of sexual orientation. For much of the twentieth century, only two categories of sexuality were recognized: homosexual (gay and lesbian) versus heterosexual (straight). Moreover, homosexuality was considered deviant, "the love that dare not speak its name." As with race and sex differences, beliefs and theories accounting for perceived differences range from the biological to the bizarre (and sometimes both).

In terms of film representation, the belief that heterosexuality is the natural state of being produces films that unquestioningly celebrate heterosexual romance as a worthy goal for all people. As Chapter Ten points out, a familiar convention of Hollywood films is the heterosexual coupling at the conclusion. Most popular films ignore homosexuality completely or, if they do include gay or lesbian characters, relegate them to the background, implicitly discounting their emotional lives and sexual bonds.

Ideologies of sexuality underlie all kinds of films, not just films about gay and lesbian characters. Beliefs about proper sexual conduct inform even films that seem to be exclusively about heterosexuality. Thus, criticism that examines ideologies of sexuality may consider films that are primarily concerned with homosexual characters and story lines such as *Go Fish* (Rose Troche and Guinevere Turner 1994), *Bound* (Andy Wachowski and Larry Wachowski 1996), or *Mulholland Drive*; films that acknowledge only heterosexuality (*Gladiator* or *The Lord of the Rings*); and films that seem to avoid issues of sexuality altogether (*The Wizard of Oz*).

Gay Male Sexuality and Mr. Ripley's Talent

The Talented Mr. Ripley (Anthony Minghella 1999) concerns Tom Ripley (Matt Damon; fig. **11.5**), a young middle-class man who vacations with, becomes emotionally attached to, and then kills his wealthy friend Dickie Greenleaf (Jude Law). Ripley assumes Dickie's identity and travels through Europe, killing two more people in order to keep his secret. The conclusion implies that he must remain isolated to sustain his charade, and that he may find it necessary to kill again.

James Keller writes that casting choices offer one way to discern a shift away from traditional ideologies of sexuality and gender: "the casting of Matt Damon as a character with homosexual longings [Ripley] virtually guaranteed the film's success, a fact that exposes a change in Hollywood's construction of masculinity" (Keller, p. 77).

He also argues that the film develops sexuality itself as a complex theme by establishing a parallel between Ripley's crimes and his sexuality.

> The "talent" referred to in the title is Ripley's ability to remain unseen in plain sight. The film draws a parallel between the notorious ability of serial killers to walk among us undetected and the similar ability of gay men to blend into mainstream society, a quality that accounts for Mr. Ripley's talent. (Keller, p. 69)

Keller spends some time examining the way Ripley departs from a familiar stereotype of the gay killer, prominent in films such as *Strangers on a Train* (Alfred Hitchcock 1951), *Rope* (Alfred Hitchcock 1948), *Looking for Mr. Goodbar* (Richard Brooks 1977), *Cruising* (William Friedkin 1980), *Dressed to Kill* (Brian De Palma 1980), and *Silence of the Lambs* (Jonathan Demme 1990). In contrast to the psychotics in these films, Ripley is "motivated not by a secret gratuitous obsession for blood, but by a desire to improve his station in life" (Keller, p. 69). But Keller ultimately finds that the film does reiterate certain clichés about gay men:

> When viewed as a portrait of a gay man's struggle for inclusion, the film is somewhat troublesome. Tom is, after all, a sociopath and a serial killer, driven to desperate measures by Dickie's rejection. This pattern is a cliché within the traditions of homophobic rhetoric. The homosexual is so desperate for an unavailable heterosexual man that he resorts to violence and subterfuge. (Keller, p. 79)

Yet, Keller argues, the film allows Ripley to gain some sympathy, which makes its sexual politics somewhat less offensive:

> The portrait would be offensive were it not for the screenwriter/director's ability to direct the sentiments and support of the audience toward Tom Ripley, who—although he goes too far—is more likeable than most of the people he kills. (Keller, p. 69)

Keller uses his interpretive skills to show that, despite the film's troubling reiteration of some stereotypes, the complex and sympathetic treatment of Ripley's character (including the casting of Damon) tempers some of the clichés.

11.5 Matt Damon challenges Hollywood masculinity as Ripley in *The Talented Mr. Ripley*.

● Ideologies of Class

Class-based approaches to film criticism derive from Marxist theory. In the mid-nineteenth century, Karl Marx posited that the economic organization of a society formed the framework for its social relationships. Marx rejected the dominant ideology that market capitalism was the best possible economic system. He believed industrial capitalism created two unequal social classes: workers, who sell their labor, and owners of capital, who profit from exploiting workers.

Rather than see the poor and the working classes as inherently inferior (a view held by many thinkers of his day), Marx criticized the terrible living conditions they had to endure and their lack of access to education, which he saw as consequences of capitalism. Marx asserted that the political situation was unstable and that the system would eventually defeat itself. He posited a future of socialism (state ownership of property) and, eventually, communism (property owned in common by all).

Marx's ideas have influenced art, literary, and film criticism. They continue to serve as a foundation for critics who examine representations of social class in films. They also influence film critics who make direct connections between industry structure and film content and argue that economic relations are the key to all aspects of social life.

The American ideology of class mobility suggests that, with hard work, anyone can succeed. Thus it stands in direct opposition to Marx's idea that, within capitalism, power derives from inherited capital and connections. Conservative films support the capitalist status quo by suggesting that individuals can escape from the working class and ascend to the middle class. Liberal films often challenge that notion, suggesting that groups of people can and should work together to effect meaningful change. Both conservative and liberal films may imply that upward mobility isn't all it's cracked up to be, drawing on stereotypes of the unhappy rich or romantic visions of working-class family values. In many Hollywood films, from *Stella Dallas* (King Vidor 1937) to *Wall Street* (Oliver Stone 1987), characters pay a price if they rise too far above their humble origins.

Class Mobility and Racial Conflict in *Rocky*

Sylvester Stallone's *Rocky* series began with the exploits of washed-up street fighter Rocky Balboa (Sylvester Stallone) and his bid for success and love through a courageous comeback. In the first film, he challenges and nearly beats the world heavyweight champion, African-American boxer Apollo Creed (Carl Weathers). In the second (Sylvester Stallone 1979), Rocky defeats him (fig. **11.6**).

Michael Ryan and Douglas Kellner see the film as a fantasy of class transcendence, one that conforms to the conservative model where the individual succeeds through hard work. These critics establish that the first two *Rocky* films were successful at the box office and attribute that success to their hopeful message of class mobility:

> The popularity of the *Rocky* movies (number 2 in box office gross in 1977, number 3 in 1979, and all among the top fifty money-makers of all time) suggests that they appeal to widespread desires for class transcendence. Yet the films also indicate that such desires tend to get channeled toward the ideal of the accumulation of wealth, which merely reinforces the system of class oppression. (Ryan and Kellner, p. 112)

Although Rocky stages a comeback and accumulates wealth, his individual actions do nothing to address the system that produced the conditions in which he formerly lived. He has merely moved up the ladder.

> The Rocky series offers a fantasy of transcending working-class life through individual initiative. *Rocky* (1976) depicts Rocky Balboa (Sylvester Stallone) as a palooka, a bum boxer, who gets a lucky shot at a title match against the black champion. Through faith, effort, and love from his girlfriend, he

gets in shape and succeeds against tremendous odds. But the film is something more than a gratifying success story. (Ryan and Kellner, p. 111)

Ryan and Kellner argue that the film addresses very specific historical concerns: Rocky's plight spoke to white viewers who saw black workers as a threat to their jobs. Rocky's transcendence is predicated on his triumph over a black boxer, with whom he manages to go the distance, fighting the full fifteen rounds.

Made during the second major recession of the decade, [Rocky] transcodes white male working-class fears and desires, offering a vision of hope at a distressing time. Yet the edifying story of accomplishment just barely hides the spirit of resentful white working-class racism that motivates it. Rocky's attack against black power in the ring metaphorically mobilizes white working-class resentment of the sort that was prevalent throughout the seventies. One scene in which Rocky is obliged to give up his locker to a black contender suggests the literal, metonymic origin of that racism, at least as it appeared in the seventies, in fears of losing scarce jobs to blacks. (Ryan and Kellner, p. 111)

11.6 A boxing match from *Rocky*.

In arguing that the tale of class mobility rests on a fundamentally racist vision of hope, the critics refer to specific scenes and also provide a context for those scenes by relating them to contemporary events (economic recession) and social anxieties (white working-class concern over jobs).

● Ideologies of National Identity

Just as Hollywood films encode ideologies of race, gender, sexuality, and class, so they also purvey ideas about national identity. They may support the idea that essential differences exist between people of different nationalities, suggesting that citizens of a nation possess a distinctive national character based on biology and/or history.

A different view of national identity grows out of the belief that national boundaries are little more than fictions—a view suggested by the conclusion of *Casablanca*, when Rick (Humphrey Bogart) and Captain Renault (Claude Rains) leave Morocco together to join the fight against Hitler's Germany. *Three Kings* (David O. Russell 1999) depicts American soldiers in the Gulf War (1991) who learn how much they have in common with the Iraqi people they were supposed to be fighting.

In the reading below, film critic Andre O'Hehir argues that *Black Hawk Down* (Ridley Scott 2001) oversimplifies historical events and uses stereotypes of national identity to support its portrayal of American soldiers as heroes.

National Identity: *Black Hawk Down*

Andrew O'Hehir uses concepts of national identity to discuss *Black Hawk Down*. The film depicts actual events that occurred during a 1993 military operation in Mogadishu, Somalia. When two Black Hawk helicopters were shot down, U.S. troops came under attack from heavily armed Somalis. Even the troops sent to rescue the downed soldiers were trapped in the city for fifteen hours. The battle resulted in the deaths of almost one thousand Somalis.

O'Hehir begins by questioning the director's goals: does he want to celebrate the U.S. military in unabashed fashion or to offer insight into the morality of warfare?

> While the episode seems ripe with both dramatic potential and
> contemporary relevance, Scott can't decide whether to make the film a
> propaganda shoot-'em-up or a moral docudrama, and it ends up as a half-
> assed neither-nor. (O'Hehir)

He finds that Americans and Somali characters alike are drawn with such broad brush-strokes that they become caricatures. Americans are wisecracking civilizers; Somalis are violent primitives.

> On one hand, the film version of *Black Hawk Down*, unlike the book,
> provides virtually no context for the famine and civil war in Somalia, and
> presents the citizens of Mogadishu as a teeming, vicious horde, an angry
> black tide that engulfs the lonely emissaries of civilization. On the other
> hand, none of the movie's American characters (some of whom are
> composites, while others bear the name of real soldiers) amounts to much
> more than a wisecrack, a typical gesture or an attitude. (O'Hehir)

In their focus on American heroism, according to O'Hehir, the filmmakers avoid painful questions:

> Inevitably, Scott and the producers have attempted to recast *Black Hawk
> Down* as a story of American military heroism, rather than a grim fable of a
> Murphy's-law mission doomed by arrogance, incompetence and sheer bad
> luck. (I don't know whether the film was recut after Sept. 11, but I wouldn't
> be surprised.) (O'Hehir)

O'Hehir faults British-born director Scott who, by virtue of his nationality, might be expected to offer a more critical appraisal of U.S. policy, for choosing not to depict tragic events that would shed light on the larger significance of the situation:

> I can understand why Scott avoided the most mythic and primal image from
> the Mogadishu battle: the half-naked corpse of Master Sgt. Gary Gordon

being dragged through the streets to be kicked and spat on by the very people he was theoretically there to help. All the same, there's something dishonest about leaving it out. As unpleasant as it might be for Americans to see that image again, it contains a kind of truth that is both literal and symbolic. Like pictures of Ground Zero in New York, it reminds us of things we'd rather not be reminded of, but that we can't always avoid. It's not clear—at least, not to me—that we are honoring the memories of Gordon and his comrades, or of the thousands in the World Trade Center, by sanitizing our memories and sugaring our emotions, by thinking only the thoughts about our country that we wish were true. (*Reprinted courtesy of Salon.com*)

He proposes that films about military operations and terrorist attacks have an obligation to do more than honor the memory of those who have been killed. Difficult as it may be, they must address the complex causes and effects of warfare and terrorism, rather than presenting only those thoughts that people wish were true.

O'Hehir speculates that the film may have been re-edited to reflect a change in the mood of the U.S. public after the terrorist attacks of September 11, 2001. He suggests that filmmakers may have anticipated that the public would reject the film if it did not perpetuate the ideology of the U.S. as a beloved nation of heroic individuals that is a civilizing force internationally.

As these examples of ideological criticism reveal, moving beyond textual analysis to ask whether a film challenges received wisdom about politics, economics, and social identities offers many rewards. Well-crafted ideological criticism integrates research and interpretation. It combines careful textual analysis, historical research, and theoretical concepts drawn from film, humanities, and social science fields to examine the critical role ideologies play in culture.

Works Consulted

Creed, Barbara. "Horror and the Monstrous Feminine: An Imaginary Abjection," in *Feminist Film Theory*, ed. Sue Thornham. New York: New York University Press, 1999, pp. 251–66.

Donalson, Melvin. *Black Directors in Hollywood*. Austin, TX: University of Texas Press, 2003.

Guerrero, Ed. *Framing Blackness: The African American Image in Film*. Philadelphia: Temple University Press, 1993.

Keller, James R. *Queer (Un)friendly Film and Television*. London and Jefferson, NC: McFarland, 2002.

Kellner, Douglas. "Hollywood Film and Society," in *American Cinema and Hollywood*, ed. John Hill and Pamela Church Gibson. Oxford and New York: Oxford University Press, 2000, pp. 128–38.

O'Hehir, Andrew. "Fog of War," Salon.com
dir.salon.com/ent/movies/review/2001/12/28/black_hawk_down/index.html

Rosenbaum, Jonathan. "A Perversion of the Past," in *Movies as Politics*. Berkeley: University of California Press, 1997, pp. 118–24. Originally published in *Chicago Reader*, December 16, 1988.

Ryan, Michael, and Douglas Kellner. *Camera Politica: The Politics and Ideology of Contemporary Hollywood Film*. Bloomington: Indiana University Press: 1988.

Stam, Robert. *Film Theory: An Introduction*. Malden, MA, and Oxford: Blackwell, 2000.

Vertov, Dziga. "Provisional Instructions to Kino-Eye Groups," in *The European Cinema Reader*, ed. Catherine Fowler. London and New York: Routledge, 2002.

Chapter *12*

Film Stardom as a Cultural Phenomenon

12.1 Gwyneth Paltrow looks glamorous in *Shakespeare in Love.*

Among the strange characteristics of the tribes who populate this continent, North America, is the one by which its inhabitants choose specific stars for themselves and live their lives in worship of them.

Sergei Eisenstein

Throughout the United States, images of James Dean are still ubiquitous half a century after his tragic death in an automobile accident. For audiences of all ages, Dean's name is synonymous with modern angst and youthful rebellion. Although he starred in only three feature films, Dean is such a pervasive component of American popular culture that, without a doubt, many who have not seen one of his movies have some sense of Dean's magnetic persona (see fig. 4.17).

America's lingering obsession with Dean is, in many ways, the embodiment of the star culture central to the economic success of Hollywood and other major film industries. As anyone who owns the poster for Dean's *Rebel without a Cause* can attest, audiences do not just appreciate a star's performance onscreen, they also consume the offscreen image that a star gradually acquires over the course of a career. Fans are so drawn to these larger-than-life figures that they will imitate the attire and mannerisms of their favorite stars, scour gossip magazines looking for them, and even vote them into political office (as evidenced by Ronald Reagan's political career and Arnold Schwarzenegger's successful gubernatorial campaign in California). For many fans, stars embody desires about everything from beauty and wealth to masculinity and femininity.

To state the obvious, "actor" is not synonymous with "star." In film, actors play characters onscreen, and good actors can create complex characters. But a star's presence transcends the performance; a star doesn't just make her character believable—a star also possesses a publicly acknowledged magnetism that lures audiences to the film and lingers in viewers' memories after they leave the theater. While stars may come by this magnetism naturally, in most cases studio heads, talent agencies, publicity outlets, and the stars themselves carefully cultivate the public's admiration.

Stars are an integral part of every major film industry and play a pivotal role in production and marketing. For producers, a star is raw material—talent capable of producing consistent and worthy performances. Occasionally writers, directors, and producers design a project specifically with a particular star in mind, hoping to capitalize on audience expectations and further develop the star's growing reputation. Such projects are called "star vehicles," because they showcase that star's persona—a vehicle to be driven by the star, so to speak. Some consider *Master and Commander* a star vehicle for Russell Crowe, or *Erin Brockovich* a vehicle for Julia Roberts.

Industry insiders evaluate a star's appeal by measuring his box office draw, and today fan magazines such as *Entertainment Weekly* regularly feature analysis of star track records. Of course, Hollywood isn't the only film industry to rely on stars. Hong Kong's film industry, for example, has had a number of internationally recognized stars, including Bruce Lee, Jackie Chan, Chow Yun-Fat, and Maggie Cheung. Britain has made stars out of Sean Connery, Hugh Grant, and Julie Christie, among others. France's art cinema turned Brigitte Bardot, Jeanne Moreau, and Jean-Paul Belmondo into world-renowned stars.

Stars also represent a significant portion of a film's overhead, and often their status as paid labor is governed by complex contracts in which pay comes in the form of up-front fees, percentages of grosses, and/or percentages of profits. In short, a star can play a significant role in determining the profitability and the profit margin of a film.

From its early days the film industry has recognized the importance of the star. A bizarre promotional campaign for silent movie "starlet" Florence Lawrence served as an early attempt to draw audiences to a film by marketing the biographical details of its key player. According to film historian Richard DeCordova, in 1910 the *St. Louis Post-Dispatch* supposedly reported that Lawrence had been killed by a New York streetcar (although no one has ever produced a copy of this original article). On March 5,

Lawrence's studio, Independent Motion Picture Company (IMP), purchased an ad in *Moving Picture World*, decrying that "the blackest and at the same time the silliest lie yet circulated by enemies of 'Imp' was the story foisted on the public of St. Louis last week to the effect that Miss Lawrence . . . had been killed by a street car" (quoted in DeCordova, p. 58). DeCordova hypothesizes that IMP itself intentionally began circulating the story of Lawrence's death. More importantly, IMP's subsequent denial of the rumor demonstrates a two-tiered strategy to generate public interest in Lawrence's films. By dispelling the rumor, IMP drew public attention to the star. And, by painting its competitors as mendacious perpetrators of an outrageous lie, IMP sought to generate public sympathy for the primary victims of the deception: IMP Studios and, of course, Florence Lawrence.

This often cited episode in the rise of Hollywood's star culture underscores how the film industry relies on stardom to lure audiences into the theater by marketing an actor's biography (fictionalized or not).

Star studies explores how stardom attracts audiences and affects what audiences respond to onscreen. The appeal of celebrity is an integral part of music, sports, television, and politics in many cultures. Some of the earliest, best, and most systematic analyses of celebrity come out of film studies approaches. This chapter will introduce five basic approaches scholars use to analyze the star system: stars and the movie industry; performance; the star persona; stardom and ideology; and stars and subcultures.

● Stars and the Movie Industry

Stars are so instrumental that they influence the economic viability of not just individual films but entire film industries. Some film scholars explore topics such as the economic impact of studio contracts versus the "free agency" stars now enjoy, and how these trends affect overall industry output and profitability.

For example, the abolition of lengthy studio contracts following the disintegration of the Hollywood studio system in the 1950s helped facilitate a growth in independent productions. Producers were now able to arrange star contracts for a single film or for a small cluster of films (as opposed to the old system, where stars were bound to a particular studio for years). This arrangement—called the package-unit approach to production, since stars were "packaged" with individual projects—led to the subsequent proliferation of talent agents responsible for managing star careers (Thompson and Bordwell, p. 336).

When a studio invests heavily in a star package, one single performance's relative success or failure can guarantee or shatter the economic stability of the studio. The following excerpt of Paul McDonald's analysis of Arnold Schwarzenegger's work in *Last Action Hero* (John McTiernan 1993) demonstrates how a star persona can play a pivotal role in determining the content and marketing of, and the public response to, a film. McDonald argues that, through the 1980s, Schwarzenegger's career was defined by two different roles: action heroes (*Conan the Destroyer*, *Predator*, *Total Recall*) and comic characters (*Twins*, *Kindergarten Cop*).

Columbia developed *Last Action Hero* in an attempt to fuse these two roles, hoping to attract fans of Schwarzenegger's violent shoot-'em-ups and audiences drawn to his comedies (fig. **12.2**). The studio spent $87 million producing the film and another $30 million on advertising and distribution. When the film opened, it took in only $15.3 million at the box office, jolting Columbia pictures and its parent company Sony:

> Reviewing the film, Vincent Canby remarked in *The New York Times* that the film "tries to be too many things to too many different kinds of audiences, the result being that it will probably confuse and perhaps even alienate the hard-core action fans" while "more sophisticated audiences are likely to never see the film's occasionally funny gags at the expense of movies the action fans have never heard of" (1993:96). At the centre of the project's failure were the impossible demands made to stretch the appeal of the Schwarzenegger image. In attempting to entertain all audiences, the film and its star arguably satisfied none [. . .] Rather than the valuable franchise Sony hoped would make the company a profitable front-runner in the film market, the Schwarzenegger image became an unmarketable concept that nearly drove Sony to make an early exit from the film business. (McDonald 2000, pp. 91–3)

12.2 Arnold Schwarzenegger in *Last Action Hero.*

McDonald shows that *Last Action Hero* can be analyzed not only at the textual level but also as a combination of Schwarzenegger's star persona, marketing strategy, and capital investment. He implies that Sony/Columbia banked much of its economic stability on a single star performance. The failure of that performance to attract an audience demonstrates what a powerful economic force stardom is within the industry. Schwarzenegger's career recovered with James Cameron's *True Lies* (1994), but his return to the cyborg character that made him famous (in *Terminator 3: Rise of the Machines* [Jonathan Mostow 2003]) underscores a star's best strategy for recuperating a flagging career: go back to what's tried and true.

● The Dynamics of Performance

One aspect of a star's appeal is, quite obviously, her performance onscreen. Why are audiences still mesmerized by Audrey Hepburn (and not, one might add, George Peppard) in *Breakfast at Tiffany's* (Blake Edwards 1961)? Why did fans suddenly scour the internet for

12.3 *FoxTrot* pokes fun at the star system. FoxTrot © Bill Amend. Reprinted with permission of Universal Press Syndicate. All rights reserved.

pictures of Orlando Bloom after seeing his performance in *The Return of the King* (Peter Jackson 2003)? Rather than attributing a star's appeal to an enigmatic, indefinable talent, film scholars are interested in trying to explain what makes a particular performance memorable.

Stars create a following by developing a memorable and recognizable persona (fig. **12.3**). Two elements of that persona are the roles a star plays and the techniques he uses to create these roles. While character actors play a variety of different roles and experiment with various acting techniques depending on the type of characters they play, many stars often play one type of character and perfect one style of performance. Audiences automatically associate Keanu Reeves (*The Devil's Advocate*, *The Matrix*) with his unique, wooden vocal delivery, and Tom Cruise (*Minority Report*, *The Last Samurai*) with his wildly gesticulating hands and his tendency to snap his head back and smile to suggest frustration and surprise. In other words, stars often formulate onscreen techniques which they then repeat.

Charlie Chaplin is one of the few silent film stars still recognized by mainstream audiences today, because his signature character, the Little Tramp, still appeals to viewers. One of Chaplin's best-loved scenes comes in *The Gold Rush* (Charles Chaplin 1925), when, stuck in the dead of winter in the middle of the Yukon with nothing to eat, the Little Tramp dresses a boot to eat. James Naremore considers this scene indicative of Chaplin's work, and, in this excerpt from his analysis of Chaplin's acting, he argues that Chaplin's performance not only evokes both laughter and sympathy from the audience, but also resonated for audiences who recognized the down-and-out Tramp as a victim of capitalism. Naremore argues that the humor in the scene arises from the Tramp's meticulous attention to formality; even though he is serving a boot for dinner, he maintains "extravagant table manners."

> And yet even though this famous scene can be used as a definition of comedy, it has another quality as well. The situation is pitched near to real horror, and the camera watches Chaplin from a relatively close vantage, framing his spot at the table and bringing us near to the character's

Chapter 12: Film Stardom as a Cultural Phenomenon

suffering. His makeup is a visible, chalky pancake with heavy black circles beneath the eyes, but there is an authentically glassy, hallucinated look on his face. [. . .]

The mixed effect is basic to Chaplin's work. Although he seldom invites the audience to identify with his character in the same way they would with the protagonists of realistic drama, he involves them in a more complex way than the other silent comics. *The Gold Rush* can be read not only as a slapstick comedy but also as an allegory of Capital, full of symbolic implications about Greed, Fate, and the *condition humaine*; hence, the Tramp is designed to elicit the audience's sympathy more directly than the typical clown. (Naremore, pp. 124–6)

12.4 Charlie Chaplin's performance in *The Gold Rush* earned plaudits.

Naremore's analysis draws attention to particular aspects of the performance—his exaggerated mimicry, his facial expression—to explain why this is such a powerful performance (fig. **12.4**). When Naremore argues that the mixture of comedy and horror "is basic to Chaplin's work," he suggests that this approach is an integral part of Chaplin's persona. It is a recognizable characteristic of Chaplin's career onscreen. Naremore's discussion does not just consider Chaplin's performance; it also pays careful attention to other elements of *mise en scène* (the boot, Chaplin's makeup) and cinematography (the close-up) that complement the actor's physical presence.

This approach to star studies synthesizes much of the material covered in Part II of this book. But rather than analyzing how a film's narrative, visual, and sound systems develop themes, this approach emphasizes how these cinematic elements help create the screen persona that audiences come to recognize as the star's signature.

● The Star Persona

Richard Dyer argues, "the star phenomenon depends upon collapsing the distinction between the star-as-person and the star-as-performer" ("Four," p. 216). The performances by Nicole Kidman and Tom Cruise in *Eyes Wide Shut* (Stanley Kubrick 1999) are obvious examples. The film explores the sexual dynamics of a young married couple, played by Cruise and Kidman (who were married when the film was released). When it opened, audiences flocked to theaters expecting to see the couple's real-life sparks on screen. The original television ad campaign exploited these expectations to attract audiences. It began with "Cruise" written in bold red letters against a black background, then cut to a shot of

12.6 A shot of Bette Davis from *Little Foxes*.

shift away from stardom, he argues, allows audiences, critics, and actors to pay more attention to the specific qualities of performances. The validity of Scott's argument remains to be seen; however, his position does emphasize how stardom transcends the parameters of any single performance and speaks to larger cultural concerns.

Academic scholarship in this area typically defines the specific dimensions of a star's image and explores how her films, promotional materials, publicity, and criticism all converge to create this persona. Film scholar Maria LaPlace's analysis of Bette Davis's star persona as a strong, assertive woman (fig. **12.6**) serves as an effective example of how film criticism can study the way a star's persona is constructed via multiple intersecting sources of public information:

> In cinema the Independent Woman falls into two categories: one is the "good" strong woman, noble, generous, sympathetic; the other is "evil," aggressive, domineering, sexual, "neurotic." Both convey strength and take action.
>
> Davis's film roles are almost all one or the other Independent Woman. Some of her famous early roles are the latter type—"bitches" Dyer calls them: *Of Human Bondage* (1934), *Dangerous* (1935, Oscar for Davis), *Jezebel* (1938, Oscar for Davis) and *Little Foxes* (1941). In the years just preceding *Now, Voyager*, there were a growing number of "good" women [. . .]: *Marked Woman* (1937, which actually combined both roles), *The Sisters* (1939), *Dark Victory* (1939), and *All This and Heaven, Too* (1941).
>
> What links these roles is Davis's performance style. Characterized by a high level of intensity, energy, and charged emotionality, it conveys a specific "personality" that interacts with each film role. The Davis style consists in a deliberate, clipped vocal inflection; darting eye movements and penetrating stares; a swinging, striding walk; gestures such as clenching fists and sudden, intense drags on cigarettes; and quick shifts in mood and register. These connote assertiveness, intelligence, internal emotional conflict and strength. (LaPlace, pp. 135–6)

LaPlace also illustrates how Davis's promotional materials and publicity emphasize these same qualities in her private life. Notice how LaPlace cites original publicity materials (specifically, biographical information) to show how Bette Davis was presented to the general public:

[T]he Davis "story" is of a plucky, resourceful, "self-made" woman whose success is due not to beauty, but to personal qualities of talent, determination, and down-to-earth self-awareness. The product of a fatherless, mother-supported, lower-middle-class family, Davis [. . .] meets and surmounts adversity because she knows who she is and what she wants [. . .]. Thus, [her] image is strongly marked by attributes of strength and independence, constructed in another way through the depiction of Davis as anti-glamour and anti-consumerism, eschewing all the trappings of stardom:

> Davis dislikes equally the stuffed shirts and glamour girls of Hollywood and makes no effort to please them . . . Her social circle is made up of non-professionals, including her sister; her closest approach to a hobby is her interest in dogs. Informality is her keynote . . . she no longer dyes her hair and she never diets. ("Bette Davis," *Life*, January 8, 1939)

Work is the privileged aspect of the Davis image; she is portrayed as completely dedicated to her career. (LaPlace, p. 136; *excerpts reprinted courtesy of BFI*)

LaPlace begins by describing the common characteristics of Davis's characters and identifying the acting techniques that help Davis portray each of these similar characters (her stride and clipped voice). She then shows how contemporary publicity painted a picture of Davis's personality that is remarkably similar to that of her typical character.

This approach to star studies does not assume that actors play themselves onscreen; nor does it posit the idea that a star's persona is defined solely by the roles she plays. Rather, a star's persona the image that lures audiences to theaters, that attracts their attention in fan magazines, that sells products in endorsement campaigns—is created by the interplay between the screen, media coverage, and the (selective) biographical details to which audiences gain access. In effect, the real Bette Davis is supplanted by a public image.

● Stardom and Ideology

Chapter Eleven argues that films inevitably bear some relationship to the political and social values of the culture that produces and consumes them. Mainstream narrative films tend to express popular sentiment and often reflect the dominant ideological assumptions of their culture. Scholars in star studies frequently explore how stars function as cultural barometers, embodying the political, moral, and cultural assumptions of those fans who consume their images.

At the most obvious level, the idealized star's body—the visible image that fixates and arouses spectators—may reinforce dominant ideas about sex and gender. Film scholar Heather Addison argues that film culture in the 1920s helped to transform national ideals

fantasy of feminine sexuality. Clint Eastwood, Brad Pitt, Russell Crowe, and Will Smith have all laid claim to representing a masculine ideal.

On occasion, however, a star can appeal to a discrete subculture, a group of fans that defines itself through its position outside of mainstream society. Al Pacino's performance as Tony Montana in *Scarface* (Brian De Palma 1983) is still heralded as iconic in gangster rap circles more than twenty years after its release (fig. **12.8**). While Pacino is certainly a mainstream star, rappers latch onto his performance in *Scarface* (and not, say, his role as a television news producer in Michael Mann's *The Insider* [1999]), reading his character as a forerunner of the gangster rapper. Rather than adopting the mainstream interpretation of the film as a cautionary tale about organized crime, rappers identify with Tony Montana's status as an outsider who accumulates a considerable amount of wealth and prestige despite the odds stacked against him. In fact, the 2004 DVD release of the film includes a documentary in which Sean "Puffy" Combs, Andre 3000, Big Boi, Snoop Dogg, and Method Man, among others, discuss the influence the film has had on their own stage personas. At one point in the documentary, Kevin Liles, president of Def Jam Music Group, explains, "I look at Scarface . . . as a ghetto tale. I don't look at *Scarface* as a drug movie" (*Origins*).

As Liles's quote illustrates, when a subculture appropriates a star's image, it often reads "against the grain," drawing a significance from that image that may be overlooked by mainstream audiences. As Paul McDonald points out, subcultures define themselves through a common value system that sets them apart from the mainstream, and some star images come to embody this value system. To mainstream audiences, singer/actress Judy Garland—star of *Meet Me in St. Louis* (Vincent Minnelli 1944), *Broadway Melody of 1938* (Roy Del Ruth 1937), and *The Wizard of Oz*—represents virtue and innocence. But gay audiences, aware of the discrepancy between Garland's innocent onscreen image and her personal battles with drug and alcohol addiction, consider her an icon because she represents the artificiality of "all-American wholesomeness" (McDonald 1998, p. 192).

Scholars explore why a subculture reveres a star's image in ways that defy mainstream expectations by evaluating the sometimes contradictory details that make up a star's persona, examining historical context (of both the period of image production and the period of public consumption of that image), and cataloging viewer responses to a star's persona. In this excerpt from her analysis of country music legend, actress, and theme park owner Dolly Parton, Chris Holmlund explains how Parton, through adroit professional choices, has positioned herself to be revered by both fundamentalist Christians and lesbian fans.

12.8 Al Pacino as Tony Montana in *Scarface*, a gangster-rap prototype.

Chapter 12: Film Stardom as a Cultural Phenomenon

Holmlund argues that most of Parton's films reflect traditional attitudes about the importance of heterosexual romance and family (fig. **12.9**). *Best Little Whorehouse in Texas* (Colin Higgins 1982), *Rhinestone* (Bob Clark 1984), *Steel Magnolias* (Herbert Ross 1989), and *Straight Talk* (Barnet Kellman 1992) all culminate in the formation or reunification of nuclear families.

But at the same time, most of the films are overtly feminist and covertly queer. The most successful—*Nine to Five* and *Steel Magnolias*—demonstrate how much fun Dolly's uppity, independent characters have with other women [. . .] The ability to engage audiences interested in "divine guidance" *and* audiences attuned to "queer speak" via "straight talk" entails a balancing act that Dolly manages better than most: few other media personalities can please both right-wing fundamentalists and drag queens. Trust is key, and [. . .] films and interviews alike foreground her candor. Yet *what* Dolly says in interviews necessarily depends on what she is asked. In a recent *Knoxville News Sentinel* article entitled "The Gospel Side of Dolly," for example, East Tennesseeans [Tennessee is Parton's home state] are assured that she repeats the Lord's Prayer and reads Scripture daily. [. . .]

12.9 Dolly Parton appeals to different fans through careful image management.

[Yet] Her manager, Sandy Gallin, is gay. Rumors have it her constant companion and best and oldest friend, Judy Ogle, is lesbian. Judy says nothing; Dolly volunteers merely that she and Judy "always sleep in one double bed," and that "I am closer to Judy than I am to Carl [her husband]." Periodically she refutes charges that she herself is gay, but she vehemently opposes conservative religious edicts which hold that homosexuality is a sinful activity: "I believe in . . . the Scripture, 'judge not, lest ye be judged.' I have many gay friends who I love dearly. I have also lost some very special friends to AIDS." (Holmlund, pp. 163–5)

Holmlund's discussion makes it clear that Parton's "straight" fans see a different image from her "queer" fans. She suggests that this is in part explained by the fact that Parton, perhaps self-consciously, addresses one audience differently than the other. Her image-making acumen has ensured that "Dolly emerges as the ultimate media model and pomo-retro mix, a down-home sophisticate who is equally comfortable in a shack as in a mansion" (Holmlund, p. 170). She is the perfect example of how stars can mean different things to different people.

Fan Culture

One important element of star system economics is fan culture. In order for stars to function as commercial products, a loyal fan base must be cultivated that will consume the films, products, and magazines that relay information about their favorite stars. Film scholars have studied the behavior of fans and theorized about the emotional investment of fans in film stars and other celebrities.

Fan cultures create communities; they also create further opportunities for profit-making, as is the case with a community of fans devoted to the *Lord of the Rings* trilogy organized through TheOneRing.net (TORn). The site, owned by four fans, sponsored parties for the Academy Awards in 2002, 2003, and 2004, inviting fans and stars to attend and using proceeds to maintain the website. In 2004, a competing party was held by the official *Lord of the Rings* fan club, which was licensed by New Line Cinema (the distributor of the films) and run by a private corporation.

Such fan communities underscore how stars help advertise films and may make it easier for studios to do so. Marketing campaigns rely on star images to differentiate one film from the next. Audiences, for example, expect a Tom Cruise vehicle to differ from a Ben Stiller vehicle. A film's star helps determine how a film is marketed, and to whom a marketing campaign is addressed. Marketing campaigns for movies featuring older stars, such as *Calendar Girls* (Nigel Cole 2003), starring Helen Mirren, will target a more mature audience, whereas campaigns for youth movies such as *American Pie* (Paul Weitz and Chris Weitz 1999), starring Jason Biggs, will address teenagers and young adults.

In addition, given the prevalence of product tie-ins in many Hollywood films, stars often help market products. When *Lara Croft Tomb Raider: The Cradle of Life* (Jan de Bout 2003) was released, star Angelina Jolie appeared on television commercials and in magazine ads for Jeep motor vehicles and Panasonic digital video cameras—both of which also received highly visible product placement throughout the film and in ads for the film. Indeed, ads for the movie were virtually indistinguishable from those for the products.

This chapter has focused on what is, to many viewers, the most immediately visible and emotionally compelling element of a film: its stars. It has emphasized that when audiences pay attention to a star, they watch more than a performance—they see acting technique, an accumulation of onscreen and offscreen roles that the actor has played, and the market force of that star's persona. Stars' ability to hold audiences in their sway underscores the power of celebrity as a cultural and economic institution.

Works Consulted

Adair, Gilbert. "Eistenstein on Disney," in *Movies*. London: Penguin, 1999.

Addison, Heather. "Capitalizing their Charms: Cinema Stars and Physical Culture in the 1920s." *The Velvet Light Trap*, 50 (fall 2002), pp. 15–34.

Collins, Nancy. "Lust and Trust." *Rolling Stone*, July 8, 1999. *Academic Search Elite*. Online. Ebsco. January 9, 2004.

DeCordova, Richard. *Picture Personalities: The Emergence of the Star System in America*. Urbana: University of Illinois Press, 1990.

Dyer, Richard. "Four Films of Lana Turner," in *Star Texts: Image and Performance in Film and Television*, ed. Jeremy G. Butler. Detroit: Wayne State University Press, 1991, pp. 214–39.

Dyer, Richard. *Heavenly Bodies: Film Stars and Society*. New York: St. Martins, 1986.

Dyer, Richard. *Stars*. 2nd edn, London: BFI, 1998.

Holmlund, Chris. *Impossible Bodies: Femininity and Masculinity at the Movies*. London: Routledge, 2002.

LaPlace, Maria. "Stars and the Star System: The Case of Bette Davis," in *The Film Studies Reader*, ed. Joanne Hollows *et al*. New York: Oxford University Press, 2000, pp. 134–39. Originally published in Christine Gledhill (ed.), *Home is Where the Heart Is*. London: BFI, 1987.

Majumdar, Neepa. "The Embodied Voice," in *Soundtrack Available: Essays on Film and Popular Music*, ed. Pamela Robertson Wojcik and Arthur Knight. Durham, NC: Duke University Press, 2001, pp. 161–81.

McDonald, Paul. Afterword ("Reconceptualising Stardom"), in *Stars*, 2nd edn. London: BFI, 1998, pp. 177–211.

McDonald, Paul. *The Star System: Hollywood's Production of Popular Identities*. London: Wallflower, 2000.

Naremore, James. *Acting in the Cinema*. Berkley: University of California Press, 1988.

Origins of a Hip Hop Classic. Dir. Benny Boom. *Scarface*. DVD Supplementary Material. Universal. 2003.

Scott, A.O. "The New Golden Age of Acting," *The New York Times*, February 15, 2004, 2Λ: pp. 1, 25.

Thompson, Kristin and David Bordwell. *Film History: An Introduction*, 2nd edn. Boston: McGraw-Hill, 2003.

13

Genre

> *Critics have ignored genre films because of their prejudice for the unique.*
>
> Leo Braudy

13.1 Will Kane in *High Noon*—a typical Western hero.

Most filmgoers choose movies they would prefer to see (and others they would like to avoid) without reading any reviews. They do so because films can be categorized according to genre, and audiences have grown so accustomed to what these categories represent that genres play a significant role in shaping audience expectations. A musical will feature romance and songs; a Western will involve horses and shootouts; a thriller will contain fast-paced action set in big cities; a screwball comedy

will depict characters who get into a tight situation because of a misunderstanding. Each of these can be seen as a distinct genre.

The origin of the word can be traced back to the Greek philosopher Aristotle, who in the fourth century BC defined drama according to three types: epic poetry, tragedy, and comedy. Subsequently, genre has become a familiar tool for classifying works of art. In film culture, audiences draw on these categories to help make informed choices. Distributors and marketers employ genre designations to target specific demographics. Filmmakers rely on audience assumptions about genres to impart critical character traits and other narrative information efficiently.

This chapter explores, first, what makes a genre—what aspects of a movie audiences, critics, and filmmakers are looking at when they categorize it as belonging to a specific genre. The chapter then examines some of the major American movie genres. It ends with a discussion of the relation between genre, film production, and audiences.

● What Makes a Genre?

In film studies, a genre refers to a group of films that share a set of narrative, stylistic, and thematic characteristics or conventions. While not every film in a given genre will exhibit all of the genre's conventions, every film in a given genre will exhibit at least some of them. This allows for a certain amount of ambivalence when critics try to define whether or not a particular film is part of a genre, and such ambivalence often leads to spirited debates. Despite the slipperiness of genre categories, film industry personnel, scholars, critics, and audiences inevitably begin any discussion of genre by considering conventions.

For many, the Western is the quintessential Hollywood genre. Even while younger audiences today see few Westerns at the theater, most are familiar with the genre's stories and visual style. Being one of the most important and recognizable genres in American cinema, the Western exemplifies how a set of conventions can link a group of films.

Influential film scholar Thomas Schatz postulates that narrative conventions are among the most important criteria for defining a genre. Films that belong to the same genre will often share plot events and character types. Thus plotlines in Westerns, for example, often build toward a climactic shootout between a protagonist and villainous antagonists. This is often preceded by some combination of events along these lines: villains terrorize a group of innocent victims; the hero arrives in a new town and reluctantly involves himself in the conflict between the townspeople and the villain, coming to the rescue of the helpless; the hero tentatively confronts the villains, often in a crowded bar room; and the hero retreats to gather his wits and/or to recuperate before launching his final assault on the villains. The resolution often depicts the hero, who never seems able to settle down, wandering off into the distance alone.

Similarly, Westerns frequently include the following character types: a male hero, often an outsider who is reluctant to get too entangled in a community's problems; a brutal male villain who gleefully uses violence to amass wealth and/or power; a band of vicious, blood-thirsty Native Americans, bent on destroying white settlements; a band of benevolent Native Americans who willingly cooperate and assist white settlers; and a good-hearted woman, often a prostitute, who empathizes with the hero's inability to fit into "normal society." Not all Westerns have all of these character types, but most have several of them.

In addition to sharing similar narrative characteristics, films from the same genre often exhibit the same stylistic traits, for example using *mise en scène* as a shorthand means of expression. The Western relies on the visual traits of the spacious, post-Civil War, American frontier setting to emphasize the individual and the community's struggles to survive in an inhospitable environment. To this end, props (six-shooters, horses, whiskey glasses), costumes (cowboy hats, spurs, dirty work-wear), and location (the arid plains of the American Southwest) play an integral role in defining the characters' rugged independence. Film scholar Lawrence Alloway argues that the repetition of such images makes them iconographic—readily identifiable to the audience. In turn, audience familiarity with these images invests them with unspoken cultural value. Visual conventions, in other words, function as cultural symbols (Hutchings, p. 62).

Films from a certain genre will often share other visual and sound characteristics as well. For instance, the Western makes extensive use of extreme long shots and casually paced pans to emphasize the vast emptiness of the setting. Some genres even have recognizable soundscapes: audiences are likely to associate a howling windstorm, a coyote's call, or the hum of a harmonica with the Western.

The conventions of the Western identified above do not circumscribe every single film within the genre. In fact, critics point to smaller clusters of films, or **subgenres**. For example, one Western subgenre focuses solely on the hero facing a gang of outlaws, as in *High Noon* (Fred Zinnemann 1953; fig. **13.1**) and *A Fistful of Dollars* (Sergio Leone 1964). Another, which includes *The Searchers* and *Little Big Man* (Arthur Penn 1970), portrays the bloody struggle between Native Americans and settlers for control of the land.

The fact that such disparate subgenres can both be considered Westerns illustrates why some critics and audiences rely on more than visual and narrative characteristics to categorize films. In some cases, critics might focus more attention on central themes common among a group of films. Consider the case of Charlie Chaplin's comedy *The Gold Rush*, which has many of the trappings of the Western described above. The film is set in California in the mid-1800s, at the height of the gold rush. A loner (Chaplin) wanders through the Klondike Mountains, struggling for survival against the harsh elements, when he stumbles across "Black Larson" (Tom Murray), California's most notorious brute. On the surface, the film resembles a Western, especially in its use of setting and character types. But in the film's second half, the loner discovers gold, becomes independently wealthy, and wins the heart of the dancer he has admired. The film is a rags to riches saga.

Genre films are linked by common themes as well as by stylistic and narrative conventions. Fans of the Western recognize that not every movie is a Western just because it features horses. Films in the genre typically explore the tension between the contradictory impulses of individual liberty and communal responsibility. Whether the Western hero wards off a gang of violent criminals or a tribe of hostile Native Americans, he does so by getting involved and tempering his desire to remain free from entanglements. As most critics have noted, the Western hero acts out of a *reluctant* sense of obligation. This tension between the longing for the unencumbered freedom of the wilderness and the physical security promised by civilization forms the thematic core of the genre.

The Gold Rush is thus not a Western, because the loner never experiences the conflicting desires for individualism and attachment. More than gold, he seeks love

13.2 *Drums along the Mohawk*—a Western even though it's set in New York state.

and companionship, and the film concludes with his success: he appears in formal attire, surrounded by the press and his lover. On the other hand, John Ford's *Drums along the Mohawk* (1935), set in Revolutionary War-era New York state, is a Western precisely because the family's battle with the Indians acts out this central thematic conflict between attachment and individualism (fig. **13.2**). The family's insistence on establishing their homestead beyond the boundary of white civilization points to an unspoken desire to confront the "wilderness" rather than remain safe within the limits of established society (Altman, p. 31).

As a point of comparison, consider one of the Japanese film industry's important genres. *Jidai-geki* (jee-dye gecky), "stories of the old times," are historical costume dramas, usually set just before or during the collapse of the Japanese feudal system during the late 1800s. (By contrast, *gendai-geki* (gen-dye gecky) feature contemporary stories, from comedies to *yakuza* gangster films.) *Jidai-geki* depict stories of feudal warlords and wandering swordsmen, or *ronin*. One might assume that the slashing samurai is the equivalent of the gunslinger of American Westerns, but an examination of the two character types highlights the differences between American and Japanese film cultures. The *jidai-geki* focuses on the warrior's struggle to live up to his code, or *Bushido*—which demands honor, loyalty, and self-sacrifice—even when this loyalty conflicts with other obligations or desires. For example, in *The Hidden Fortress* (Akira Kurosawa 1958), General Rokurota (Toshiro Mifune) sacrifices his sister and risks his own life to guarantee his princess's survival. The samurai's commitment to familial and community obligation contrasts sharply with the cowboy's spontaneity and individuality. While the cowboy ultimately is swayed by a sense of communal obligation, he accepts this commitment begrudgingly, and with the tacit agreement that the commitment is temporary. The cowboy hero rides off into the sunset alone; Rokurota stays with the princess, a loyal servant for the rest of his life.

The Difficulty of Defining Genre

The discussion above suggests the difficulty of conclusively defining any genre. Films that get lumped together don't always have consistent character types or visual characteristics. Furthermore, even when the conventions of a genre appear absolute, a single film can undermine their legitimacy. For many, *Star Wars* epitomizes the science fiction film, but for others it is a variation on the Western.

Further compounding the problem is the fact that, as genres evolve, some films fuse two or more genres into one **hybrid.** *Blade Runner*, for example, fuses the hard-boiled detective film with science fiction.

In the 1970s, a wave of films featuring Black casts and often (but not always) Black production crews were immensely popular among African-American audiences clamoring for films about powerful African-American characters who reject white domination. Critics and scholars commonly refer to this group of films as a genre called **blaxploitation** (short for "black exploitation"). Film scholar Ed Guerrero defines the blaxploitation formula as a film that features a rebellious Black man who challenges white oppression and wins (Guerrero, p. 86). While blaxploitation is closely associated with action films such as *Sweet Sweetback's Baadasssss Song* (Melvin Van Peebles 1971), *Shaft* (Gordon Parks 1971), and *Superfly*, it also expanded to include horror films such as *Blacula* (William Crain 1972) and gangster films such as *Black Caesar* (Larry Cohen 1973).

The blaxploitation phenomenon suggests how fluid the concept of genre is. On the one hand, these films are commonly referred to as comprising a genre, yet the sheer diversity of filmmaking styles associated with the movement confounds attempts to isolate a single consistent set of conventions running through them. Moreover, blaxploitation pictures influenced the conventions of the genres from which they drew inspiration. The popularity of *Black Caesar*, for example, paved the way for a new kind of gangster film in the 1980s and 1990s, including *Scarface* (Brian De Palma 1983), *Menace to Society* (Allen and Albert Hughes 1993), and *Belly* (Hype Williams 1998).

The definition of any genre is always in flux. Nevertheless, audiences develop notions about genre from their movie-going experiences, from marketing, and from media coverage. Consequently, a viewer has expectations about genre and interprets films according to these expectations, even though these expectations may change over time (Ryall, p. 336). When a viewer considers a film in terms of genre, she is (consciously or not) exploring how it creates meaning via its relationship to other films and other forms of cultural expression.

The next section of this chapter explores five major American film genres: the hard-boiled detective movie, the paranoid conspiracy film, the science fiction film, the horror film, and the screwball comedy. As a survey of American film genres, this list is far from exhaustive. Several of Hollywood's most noteworthy genres (including the musical, the family melodrama, the gangster film, and the action/adventure film) do not appear. But the list below suggests how critics can categorize films by studying the conventions they share, even when these conventions evolve over time.

Major American Genres

The Hard-boiled Detective Movie

Like the cowboy in the Western, the hard-boiled detective is a loner. He is an investigator who stands just outside the law, yet remains the moral center of the film. But the hard-boiled detective doesn't traverse the open plains like the cowboy or venture down lonely roads like the wanderer—his domain is the crowded city street.

The hard-boiled detective film is a genre unlike its more genteel precursors, mysteries featuring investigators such as Sherlock Holmes and Charlie Chan. Whereas Holmes and Chan project an aura of rigorous, intellectual sophistication, hard-boiled detectives such as Philip Marlowe and Sam Spade are streetwise and brash. Holmes and Chan work through mysteries as if they were games of cat and mouse between two foes trying to outwit one another, while Marlowe and Spade solve mysteries by relying on physical stamina. Their investigative prowess relies as much on legwork and street smarts as it does on cognitive skills (Cawelti, p. 185).

In contrast to the rational optimism of Chan and Holmes, the hard-boiled detective embodies the loneliness and alienation of the modern human condition. He has few friends, and he works alone. In John Huston's prototypical film *The Maltese Falcon* (1941), Sam Spade's partner is murdered just after the film's exposition. On hearing the news, Spade buries any emotional response, rationalizing that death is part of the business. Later, viewers learn that Spade had been having an affair with his partner's wife, reflecting how the hard-boiled detective tends to have only tenuous and tortured relationships.

Above all, the hard-boiled detective works apart from the law. In some cases he has worked as a police officer in the past, but inevitably he has quit the force, either out of self-interest or disgust. In short, the hard-boiled detective is a figure of isolation who can trust no one. Given his asocial lifestyle and business practices, very little distinguishes the detective from the outlaws he pursues, save for an abstract (and at times, questionable) moral code.

The criminals he encounters exacerbate the detective's feelings of distrust. These characters tend to be the powerful elite rather than mere criminal thugs; often they carry clout in the political or legal system. The conflict between detective and criminal reflects an unspoken class dichotomy between the honorable (though imperfect) working class and the maliciously deceitful upper class. In *The Maltese Falcon*, for example, Spade's nemesis Kasper Gutman is wealthy enough to squander his time and money looking for the eponymous artifact.

In many ways, the most treacherous character type in the genre is the *femme fatale*, the detective's romantic interest. Quite frequently, she is a liar trying to exploit the hero's sympathy and sexual desires for her gain.

Hard-boiled detective narratives are notoriously convoluted. Just as the detective is confused by a web of deceit, so is the audience. Often the film begins with the detective accepting a simple case, following a series of false leads, then realizing that the crime is far more complex than he suspected. The plot of Howard Hawks's *The Big Sleep* (1946) is so convoluted that, when asked whether or not one of the corpses was murdered or committed suicide, the director reportedly confessed that he didn't know! (Mellen, p. 139).

While recent films such as *Devil in a Blue Dress* and *L.A. Confidential* (Curtis Hanson 1997) set their stories in the 1940s and '50s, others adapt the genre to contemporary settings (*Klute* [Alan J. Pakula 1971], *Who Framed Roger Rabbit* [Robert Zemeckis 1988], *Shaft* [Gordon Parks 1971] or even futuristic ones (*Alphaville* [Jean-Luc Godard 1965], and *Blade Runner*).

The Paranoid Conspiracy Film

In Alfred Hitchcock's *North by Northwest*, ad exec Roger Thornhill (Cary Grant) raises his hand to call for a waiter in a crowded bar in the middle of the afternoon. His request for a phone is ill-timed, as two goons consequently mistake him for an American Secret Service agent they are supposed to eradicate. The turn of events leads Thornhill into an existential nightmare in which he loses his identity (fig. **13.3**), is framed for murdering

13.3 Roger Thornhill causes a commotion in *North by Northwest*.

a U.N. ambassador, and ends up dangling off the face of Mt. Rushmore. Such is the logic of the paranoid conspiracy film: in this world of Cold War espionage and urban anonymity, subtle nuances of everyday behavior may unleash a wave of chaotic and life-threatening repercussions.

The paranoid conspiracy film focuses exclusively on innocent individuals who stumble on a devious plot. These films typically begin by depicting the daily routine of a blissfully ignorant citizen. Through an arbitrary act, he stumbles upon the conspiracy. Those acts include: befriending a kindly old lady in *The Lady Vanishes* (Alfred Hitchcock 1938); a sound engineer recording a car accident in *Blow Out* (Brian De Palma 1981); or a teenager parking his scooter in the wrong place in *Diva* (Jean-Jacques Beineix 1982). The hero of the paranoid thriller differs dramatically from professional spies in other categories of the thriller. Unlike James Bond or Jack Ryan, he is an unwilling participant in violent spy games. He is motivated as much by self-preservation as by any sense of obligation toward his country. The fact that the hero's suspicions are almost always justifiable underscores a central assumption of the genre: the most corrupt members of society are those with power. Ordinary citizens have (or develop) more integrity.

The genre's narrative then unfolds, following a fairly regular pattern. Although the protagonist is initially ignorant of what he has witnessed, he finds himself pursued by the conspirators. He runs for his life in a state of befuddlement, failing to comprehend why others are trying to kill him (fig. **13.4**). When he finally does ascertain the truth, he cannot convince the authorities to help him. The police either refuse to believe the elaborate conspiracy theory, or are actually involved in the plan.

The film builds to its climax when the hero stops passively fleeing danger and begins proactively dismantling the conspiracy, utilizing his unique skills or behavioral idiosyncrasy. Just as Thornhill employs his ad man's adeptness at lying to help him manipulate scenarios to his advantage, singer Jo MacKenna (Doris Day) uses her voice to prevent a political assassination and to locate her kidnapped son in *The Man Who Knew Too Much* (Alfred Hitchcock 1956).

The genre's primary visual characteristic is an urban setting, which is crucial for underscoring the protagonist's justified paranoia: she is surrounded by people, any of whom might be trying to murder her. Complementing the urban setting is the genre's reliance on rapid transportation systems: cars, trains, subways, even scooters. The fact that characters move from place to place so rapidly underscores the all-encompassing nature of the scheme. The further and faster the protagonist runs, the more it becomes apparent that options for escape are nil.

13.4 Jules rides for his life in *Diva*, though he doesn't know why he's being pursued.

13.5 An assassination in broad daylight in *The Parallax View*.

From the 1930s to the early 1960s, paranoid thrillers reflected a preoccupation with the threat to established order posed by external forces, such as the Nazis in *The 39 Steps* (Hitchcock 1935) and *Ministry of Fear* (Fritz Lang 1944), or communists in *North by Northwest* and *Man Hunt* (Fritz Lang 1941). During the politically turbulent 1960s, the genre began to depict evil emanating from within the U.S. government or the corporate world. Paranoid conspiracy films have implicated big business in *The Conversation* and *The Parallax View* (Alan J. Pakula 1974; fig. **13.5**); the medical industry in *Coma* (Michael Crichton 1978), the political process in *Blow Out* and *Bullworth* (Warren Beatty 1994); the secret service in *Enemy of the State* and *The Bourne Identity* (Doug Liman 2002); and the international recording industry in *Diva*.

The Science Fiction Film

Of the many popular film genres, science fiction is perhaps the most difficult to define through a set of conventions. It's possible to associate science fiction with stories about space travel or futuristic societies—stories that take place in settings where technology plays a dominant role in the characters' lives. Yet, such a definition excludes films such as *Back to the Future* (Robert Zemeckis 1985), a comedy in which Marty McFly (Michael J. Fox) travels back in time to 1955 in a mad scientist's sports car.

How can a single genre accommodate *Frankenstein* (James Whale 1931), *The Fly* (Kurt Neumann 1958), *The Thing from Another World* (Christian Nyby and Howard Hawks 1951), and *Star Wars*? The genre does not have the visual and narrative conventions so readily locatable in the Western. Instead, what links the wide array of science fiction films is a thematic interest in the relationship between technology and humanity (fig. **13.6**). Science fiction films explore the potential of human ingenuity and ponder the spiritual, intellectual, and/or physical costs of technological development. They suggest that technology alone is impotent, or worse, destructive, unless its development coincides with an expansion in the human capacity for creativity, empathy, and/or humility.

In the most general terms, science fiction films begin with protagonists confronting a problem associated with their over-reliance on rational thought. In some cases the conflict is literally the product of scientific inquiry, such as Frankenstein's monster or Dr.

Jekyll's alter ego Mr. Hyde in *Dr. Jekyll and Mr. Hyde* (Rouben Mamoulian 1932). Sometimes the protagonists are less directly responsible for the source of conflict, as in alien invasion films such as *Invasion of the Body Snatchers* (Don Siegel 1956) and *The Thing from Another World*. Nevertheless, the arrival of these alien creatures is often associated with society's increasing preference for the rational (and often secular) over an instinctive, ruminative, and spiritual imagination.

The conflict is resolved only when protagonists learn to balance the scientific approach with a more humanistic one. Dr. Frankenstein (Colin Clive) defeats the monster (and his will to power) by joining a community mob and confronting his creation face to face. In *Star Wars*, Luke Skywalker (Mark Hamill) blows up the evil Empire's "Death Star" only after he ignores his computer monitor and follows his own inner "force." Often the solution doesn't necessitate completely abandoning scientific thought. Rather, the protagonist must adopt a balanced approach that utilizes rationality alongside spontaneity, emotions, spirituality, and creativity.

13.6 The horror of scientific exploration in *The Thing from Another World*.

Science fiction can be subdivided into four subgenres, each of which is distinguishable by narrative and visual conventions. Perhaps the most familiar subgenre is the exploration film, which involves a group of travelers exploring different worlds. These travelers are driven by their thirst for knowledge.

The paradigmatic film in this category is Georges Méliès's *A Trip to the Moon* ("*Le Voyage dans la lune*"; 1902), about a group of astronauts that departs for the moon. Others include *Forbidden Planet* (Fred M. Wilcox 1956; fig. **13.7**), *2001: A Space Odyssey*, the *Star Trek* series, and *Pitch Black* (David Twohy 2000). By no means is the subgenre limited to films about travel in outer space. The travelers might find themselves hurtling through time—as in *The Time Machine* (George Pal 1960) and *La Jetée* (Chris Marker 1962)—or venturing into other earthly environments in the present. In *The Fantastic Voyage* (Richard Fleischer 1966), scientists shrink themselves and explore the inside of a human body, and in *Tron* (Steven Lisberger 1982), a computer programmer is sucked into a video game, literally becoming one of the digital combatants. In most cases, these adventurers discover more about themselves than they learn about the world they visit.

13.7 A supernatural monster attacks in *Forbidden Planet*.

Another strain of science fiction is more concerned with invaders encroaching on supposedly safe territory. On occasion the invaders turn out to be benevolent, as in *The Day the Earth Stood Still* (Robert Wise 1951), *E.T.*, and *Brother from Another Planet* (John Sayles 1984). But more often the invaders pose a threat to humanity.

Alien invaders do not necessarily have to be extraterrestrial. Following the distant lead of *King Kong* (Ernest B. Schoedsack and Merion C. Cooper 1933; fig. **13.8**), a wave of monster movies appeared in the 1950s, including *Them!* (Gordon Douglas 1954) and *Tarantula* (Jack Arnold 1955). These films depict humanity threatened by earthly creatures. Typically the monsters demonstrate the destructive folly of human ambition. They are the by-products of scientific inquisitiveness and/or technological development, as in the *Godzilla* series, in which the monster's destructive rampage is linked to radioactivity lingering from the atomic bombs the U.S. dropped on Hiroshima and Nagasaki.

Since invaders, whether alien or not, are physically superior, they can only be conquered by luck or ingenuity. In *The War of the Worlds* (Byron Haskin 1953), bacteria ultimately undo the Martian attack. In many cases it is the everyday citizen (or people banding together), not the brilliant scientist, who succeeds in driving off the foes. In *The Terminator*, a working-class woman defeats a destructive robot from the future, and in *Independence Day*, a hodgepodge assortment of outcasts launches a counter-offensive on attacking aliens. Invasion films value cooperation, ingenuity, and sheer tenacity over advanced technology and firepower.

The third subgenre explicitly criticizes unbridled scientific inquiry. This subgenre grows out of the legendary Faust myth, in which an alchemist trades his soul to Mephistopheles for knowledge. After he sacrifices his eternal soul for fleeting, earthly knowledge, Faust learns that knowledge divorced from wisdom is destructive. In science fiction, this premise is reformulated in stories of reclusive, often mad, scientists who are so fixated on their quests for scientific discovery that they fail to recognize the self-destructive ramifications of their behavior. Notable examples include *The Invisible Man* (James Whale 1933) and both versions

13.8 *(top)* An earthly monster in *King Kong*.

13.9 *(bottom)* Books are ceremonially burned in *Fahrenheit 451*.

of *The Fly* (Kurt Neumann 1958; David Cronenberg 1986). In these films, brilliant scientists are threatened or destroyed by their audacious experiments.

The fourth subgenre, films about dystopias, suggests how an entire society can be corrupted if "progress" goes unchecked. In Fritz Lang's seminal film *Metropolis* (1926), industrial technology has run amok and workers are reduced to mere drones, ceaselessly providing for the towering factory machinery. In *Fahrenheit 451* (François Truffaut 1966), books are outlawed (fig. **13.9**). The logical extreme of science fiction dystopias is George Lucas's *THX 1138* (1971), which depicts a world in which emotions are outlawed and citizens are given drugs to make them passive, content to live in a colorless, underground world. In these films, societies devoid of emotions are devoid of humanity. *The Matrix* is a popular update of this formula.

In short, science fiction is a diverse genre unified by a central conceit—to explore the possibilities and potential dangers of technological advancement.

The Horror Film

The distinction between science fiction and horror is often difficult to discern. Where, for example, does one categorize a film like *Alien*, in which a small cluster of astronauts is terrorized by a murderous stowaway alien? Are the zombies in *Night of the Living Dead* (George A. Romero 1968), associated with toxic waste and radioactivity, the stuff of science fiction or of modern horror? Indeed, many critics would argue that some of the films discussed above—*Frankenstein*, *The Thing*, the *Godzilla* films—belong in the genre of horror rather than science fiction.

13.10 A human monster in *Peeping Tom*.

One key difference between the two genres is articulated by the name of the latter: horror. The primary function of the genre is to elicit a particular emotional response from its audience: disgust, revulsion, fear . . . horror. Yet even this distinction remains nebulous, as audiences' propensity for shock evolves. Whereas audiences in 1931 may have found Boris Karloff's portrayal of Frankenstein's monster frightening, contemporary audiences probably see the character as pathetic, not terrifying. As *Frankenstein* suggests, horror and science fiction occasionally overlap, and in some cases the distinction between the two is impossibly blurred.

The monster—the most crucial character type in a horror film—embodies the revulsion and fear so important to the genre. A survey of horror films reveals a wide assortment of monsters. In some films, the source of terror is supernatural. Protagonists find themselves haunted by ghosts from beyond the grave or by demon spirits. Some monsters are ghouls, beings painfully suspended between two different biological states: human and animal, living and dead. Werewolves, zombies, vampires, and mummies are all banished from society for their inhuman bloodlust, even though they may have good intentions. Michael Powell's *Peeping Tom* (1960) and *Psycho* introduced the human monster in the form of the psycho killer (fig. **13.10**). These characters are purely human (although some, such as the Michael Myers character in *Halloween*, possess supernatural strength), yet they are driven to murderous rampage by inexplicable emotions.

A standard narrative convention of horror films is that the exposition portrays a character or small group of characters venturing into a strange and ultimately threatening setting. Jonathan Harker (Alexander Granach) goes into the Carpathian Mountains to make a business deal with the mysterious Count Orlock in *Nosferatu*, and a group of teenagers investigates an abandoned family farmhouse in *The Texas Chainsaw Massacre* (Tobe Hooper 1974). Stumbling into this setting unleashes the monster's energies, threatening the lives of the protagonist and those closest to her.

13.11 A hostile environment inside the castle in *Frankenstein*.

The genre's visual style emphasizes the ominous quality of the setting. As potential victims abandon the safety of familiar territory, *mise en scène* and cinematography emphasize that the characters have entered a dark, dangerous, and abnormal world. The setting's barren and labyrinthine qualities underscore the unknowability and hostility of the environment (fig. **13.11**). The cinematography, in turn, makes use of hard, low-key lighting and exaggerated camera angles to make the space

13.12 The suburban setting of *Halloween*.

appear even more threatening—sometimes because audiences cannot see what's there. Moreover, sound often draws attention to what audiences can't see, evoking the audience's fear by suggesting that danger lurks nearby while withholding its specific location.

More and more frequently, horror films do not distinguish so-called "normal" space from horrific space. Some films instead locate horror in the most innocuous of places. In *Rosemary's Baby* and *The Exorcist* (William Friedkin 1972), the devil pesters (to say the least) his victims in the privacy of their urban dwellings. In *It's Alive* (Larry Cohen 1974), a woman gives birth to a cannibalistic mutant in a Los Angeles hospital. In *Halloween* and *Scream* (Wes Craven 1998), knife-wielding slashers terrorize bland suburban households (fig. **13.12**).

The horror film's shift in location from the gothic and overtly grotesque to the normal and everyday coincided with a shift in what it defined as horrific. Many critics argue that the monster has always represented the repressed desires of its potential victims. Vampire films, for example, often equate monstrosity with unbridled sexual desire. Nevertheless, in the gothic horror films, the monster is visibly different from humans and is readily identifiable as evil. Film scholar Robin Wood has argued that the more recent trend in urban and suburban horror suggests that evil can erupt anywhere, or, more horrifyingly, that evil is indistinguishable from everyday behavior. Indeed, in some cases horror is an integral part of the American family.

The Screwball Comedy

In Howard Hawks's *Bringing Up Baby*, stodgy paleontologist David Huxley (Cary Grant) is focused on two things: the intercostal clavicle bone he needs to complete his reconstruction of a brontosaurus skeleton and his imminent marriage to the rigid Alice Swallow (Virginia Walker). While playing a round of golf with a museum donor, David stumbles upon an absent-minded socialite, Susan Vance (Katharine Hepburn), who is immediately entranced by the soon-to-be-married scientist. The rest of the film follows Susan's zany exploits as she simultaneously tries to prevent David's marriage and to win his heart. She tries to take his golf ball, makes him slip on an olive she has accidentally dropped on the floor of a crowded restaurant; and convinces him to escort her and "Baby"—a tame leopard—from New York to Connecticut, where, after an entire night of pratfalls, they are both arrested. After being bailed out, David returns to his brontosaurus in New York, his engagement called off. Susan comes to visit him one last time. When they finally both profess their love for one another, Susan's clumsiness sends the massive dinosaur skeleton tumbling to the ground. Of course, the brief plot summary of the film does absolutely no justice to its comic content or to the subtle intricacies of the story. Yet the difficulty of briefly summarizing *Bringing Up Baby*, a screwball comedy, points to two distinctive characteristics of the genre.

First, the genre features wildly chaotic plotlines, wherein characters find themselves in one untenable situation after another as they stumble their way toward marriage. One film scholar asserts that the genre combines the rapid-fire dialogue of the romantic comedy with the frenzy of slapstick comedy (Lent, p. 327). Hence, the genre's name, suggesting a wild, out-of-control baseball pitch.

Second, the screwball comedy's humor relies on fast-paced, overlapping dialogue, full of puns, word play, and *double entendres*. A brief summary cannot possibly capture the comic appeal of the sexual innuendo of David's desperate search for his intercostal clavicle on the eve of his ill-fated marriage ("My bone! It's rare . . . it's precious!").

Most historians divide screwball comedies into two distinct subgenres based on the work of Stanley Cavell: the marriage, or commitment comedy and the remarriage, or reaffirmation comedy. Marriage comedies (*It Happened One Night* [Frank Capra 1934], *Holiday* [George Cukor 1938], *Bringing Up Baby*) generate romantic tension by focusing on a

13.13 *(top)* Walter (Cary Grant) discovers bizarre complications in *His Girl Friday*, a remarriage comedy.

13.14 *(bottom)* Antagonism turns to love in *It Happened One Night*, a marriage comedy that crosses class boundaries.

couple who at the start of the film do not realize they are in love with one another. These films inevitably conclude with their impending marriage.

Marriage comedies such as these follow a remarkably consistent pattern. The films begin with a flawed couple, such as David and Alice in *Bringing Up Baby*. The film introduces the ideal partner (Susan) who vows to pursue the object of her affection. Eventually the two are trapped in a situation beyond their control. Because they are stuck together and must cooperate to extricate themselves from the sticky situation, they realize their love for one another (Karnick, pp. 134–6).

The less common remarriage comedy (*The Philadelphia Story* [George Cukor 1940], *His Girl Friday* [Howard Hawks 1940]) begins with a couple separated, or on the verge of separation (fig. **13.13**). After a series of romantic trials and errors with other partners, they discover that they want to remain together.

Perhaps the most crucial element of the screwball comedy is the characterization of the main characters as opposites. Their initial antagonism gradually turns into romantic love. Some film critics argue that the genre's emphasis on romance triumphing over difference offered Depression-era audiences a utopian resolution of class conflict (fig. **13.14**). Even when not dealing explicitly with socioeconomic tension, the genre translates all kinds of differences into the zany idiosyncrasies of character, which initially put the would-be lovers at odds with one another (Schatz, pp. 139–42).

Indeed, the genre thrived during the Great Depression and ground to a halt after World War II. While there are a few notable post-war screwball comedies, most critics agree that the genre gave way to other comedic formulas by the 1950s. Recent attempts to revitalize the genre include *What's Up, Doc?* (Peter Bogdanovich 1972), *Meet the Parents* (Jay Roach 2000), and *Punch-Drunk Love* (Paul Thomas Anderson 2002).

● Genre, Film Production, and Audiences

The proliferation of genres in Hollywood's studio era can be explained, at least in part, by the major studios' industrial filmmaking strategies, described in Chapter Ten. Genre films allowed the studios to conceptualize, produce, market, and distribute their products efficiently and rapidly. For any given genre film, a studio might be able to reformulate popular storylines and reuse sets, costumes, and even production units. In turn, genre films lured audiences into theaters by offering them familiar pleasures. Thus, repetition was, and still is, a crucial component of any genre, from both the industry's and the audience's perspectives.

Because genre films depend on repetition and are so closely linked to Hollywood's industrial practices, critics overlooked their aesthetic and intellectual potential until the 1960s. Until then, genre automatically connoted mindless, homogeneous entertainment. Now genre films inspire a wide array of provocative academic analysis and popular criticism. The remainder of the chapter will explore four approaches that critics employ when they contemplate genre films: the use of repeated formulae; the social implications of adhering to convention; the way genres themselves are prone to change; and the relation of the individual filmmaker to the established conventions of the genre.

Genre Film and Aesthetic Appeal: Cliché or Strategic Repetition?

Popular film critics regularly measure the degree to which a given film relies on conventional plot devices and visual details. While following convention is an integral part of any genre film, good genre films rely on more than sheer repetition. Any film that merely rehashes tried and true strategies quickly lapses into cliché. Genres thrive when filmmakers find ways to modify the conventions. So, while audiences carry a set of expectations with them whenever they attend a genre film, for most audiences, one of these expectations is that the film will surprise them by *upsetting* some of their expectations.

For most critics, the most pronounced criterion for evaluating a film is how much originality it injects into the formula without totally abandoning the conventions of the genre. Genre films shouldn't sacrifice the pleasures of familiarity for obtuseness; nor should they mindlessly repeat every property of films past.

Peter Stack argues that horror fans will love *Scream* because of its original approach to generic conventions.

> [*Scream*] plays lively games with the macabre. It's the sort of creepy hemoglobin shocker that peaked in the 1980s when horror movies were all the rage, before they turned into endless series of laborious, half-baked sequels.
>
> *Scream* derives much of its freshness from satirizing the *Friday the 13th*s and *Halloween*s and dopey sequels of yesteryear. Craven, formerly a college professor, obviously relishes poking fun at his own contributions (*Last House on the Left, The Hills Have Eyes*). (*Republished with permission of the* San Francisco Chronicle, *from "Satirical* Scream *is Out for Blood," Peter Stack. Dec. 26, 1996. Permission conveyed through Copyright Clearance Center, Inc.*)

Stack begins his review by suggesting that, by the end of the 1980s, horror movies had lost their aesthetic edge by becoming too repetitive. Much of *Scream*'s appeal, he implies, comes from its ability to repeat the formula while providing new twists. His review illustrates how fans and critics alike measure the success of a genre film by evaluating how well it balances the old with the new.

Genre and the Status Quo

Another approach to genre criticism considers the social implications of a reliance on repetition. This perspective assumes that, because genre films are a popular, mass-produced form of entertainment, they are a modern version of cultural mythology.

Robert Warshow, for example, argues that the characteristics of the Western hero—his solitude, his commitment to unfettered movement across the plains, his reluctant but morally clarified use of violence—make him "the last gentleman." Inevitably, the cowboy is presented as brave, independent, and considerate, and the reappearance of these qualities in film after film suggests how the cowboy functions as a symbol of a national heritage (real or imagined). Warshow argues that repetition in genre films is imperative to their success (Warshow, p. 457).

Often a more ideological perspective informs this approach. Marxist film scholar Judith Hess Wright, for example, argues that genre films lull audiences into complacency by their promise to be nothing more than mere entertainment. As a result, viewers are little more than passive receptacles, mindlessly absorbing a reassuring cultural mythology that celebrates the status quo: "Genre films produce satisfaction rather than action, pity, and fear rather than revolt. [. . .T]hey throw a sop to oppressed groups who [. . .] eagerly accept the genre film's absurd solutions to economic and social conflicts" (Wright, p. 41).

In the Western, she argues, such a conflict arises over the issue of whether violence is justifiable. The genre naïvely solves this conflict by boiling its characters down into two simplistic types: guilty and innocent. Violence is always justified when it is inflicted on the guilty in the name of justice. The result is a genre that justifies vigilantism, ignoring questions regarding the environmental causes of antisocial behavior (Wright, pp. 42–3).

These perspectives share the assumption that, at their core, genre films contain certain unchanging elements. What makes a genre potent, in other words, is its consistency. By analyzing this consistency one can measure its aesthetic and social impact. Both approaches also assume that viewers' responses are standardized—that audiences are only capable of reading a film according to dominant cultural values.

Genres as Culturally Responsive Artifacts

Another mode of criticism measures how genres gradually change, or evolve. While on one level genres retain their basic conventions, over time certain conventions will give way to others. An obvious example is the horror film's depiction of monsters. The more obviously grotesque products of nature or science have been replaced by serial killers who appear perfectly normal.

Some critics try to account for and evaluate such shifts in convention by exploring how a popular genre at a given point in time reflects the *immediate*, albeit unacknowledged, concerns of its audience. This approach is predicated on the assumption that genre films attract audiences because they appeal to popular sentiment, whether or not viewers are aware of their concerns and anxieties. Consequently, the subtext of a genre at any point in time may grant critics and filmgoers alike access to a culture's approach to complex social issues. Genre films are akin to a mass-produced ritual, wherein cultures see their fantasies acted out onscreen. When the culture's fantasies evolve, so do generic conventions.

For example, the hard-boiled detective film came of age during and just after World War II, and some film critics link the genre to the unspoken cynicism of a culture that had come face to face with the horrors of industrialized genocide. The 1970s saw a new wave of detective films reinvigorate the formula: *The Long Goodbye* (Robert Altman 1973), *Night Moves* (Arthur Penn 1975), and *Farewell, My Lovely* (Dick Richards 1975). Thomas Schatz links the nostalgic flair apparent in this revitalization to America's longing for the bygone days of the 1940s and '50s. But the nostalgia of these films was accompanied by an unremitting pessimism even more pronounced than that of their predecessors. This pessimism has been cited as evidence of the emotional and psychological by-products of the Vietnam War, urban blight, political corruption, and racial strife:

> [T]he detective-hero necessarily reflected the change in values. As did his '40s prototype, the screen detective of the 1970s accepted social corruption as a given and tried to remain isolated from it, still the naïve idealist beneath the cynical surface. *But the new* detective of the '70s inhabited a milieu he was unable to understand or to control [. . .]. (Schatz, p. 149, emphasis added)

When a film such as *Chinatown* radically modifies a genre's conventions, critics refer to it as **revisionist**. *Devil in a Blue Dress*, with its depiction of postwar Los Angeles from an African-American perspective, is a revisionist detective film. Rather than living as an outsider by choice, as the more conventional detectives do, Easy Rawling struggles to maintain his position in the middle class. He begins to work as a private eye only after he is laid off from his defense industry job, and his primary motivation is to earn enough money to make house payments.

Instead of assuming that genres remain static, this approach focuses on the way the flexibility of a genre's conventions ensures its adaptability for popular culture's shifting interests.

Genre and Film Authorship

In his interviews with François Truffaut, Alfred Hitchcock explains how he developed the idea for the famous crop-dusting sequence in *North by Northwest*, where Roger Thornhill finds himself nearly gunned down in a cornfield by a crop-dusting plane:

I found I was faced with the old cliché situation: the man who is put on the spot, probably to be shot. Now, how is this usually done? A dark night at a narrow intersection. The waiting victim standing in a pool of light under the street lamp. . . . The slow approach of a black limousine, et cetera, et cetera. Now, what was the antithesis of a scene like this? No darkness, no pool of light, no mysterious figures in windows. Just nothing. Just bright sunshine and a blank, open countryside with barely a house or tree in which lurking menaces could hide. (quoted in Truffaut, p. 256)

Hitchcock's quote suggests how a filmmaker can work within a genre while at the same time self-consciously working against its conventions, upsetting audience expectations and providing a richer cinematic experience in the process.

A fourth approach to genre criticism looks at how notable directors or *auteurs* work with genre conventions to assert a personal vision. This approach assumes that good genre films distinguish themselves from the rest, and that a director may be responsible for a genre film's originality.

In his review of Martin Scorsese's musical *New York, New York* (1977), the critic Richard Combs argues that the director brings a particular set of ideas to the musical genre. At first glance, Scorsese's decision to film a musical seems like a radical departure from his usual interest in gangster films and male violence. But, as Combs points out, *New York, New York* is informed by the director's interest in the self-destructive male psychology.

Situated in fantasy, Jimmy Doyle (Robert De Niro) . . . becomes uniquely blessed among Scorsese heroes—he is allowed to achieve his ambition, the fulfillment of what he calls the "major chord," when you have everything in life that you want. But Scorsese plays the figure not as fantasy but as a character streaked by the same self-destructive fanaticism, unwavering drive and crippling ambivalence as any of his street punks on the make—and compresses the psychology of the character not into the predictable narrative of breakdown and break-up, but most tightly into the scenes where one most expects relaxation, i.e., the musical numbers. (Combs, p. 252)

13.15 *New York, New York* matches Scorsese's other films for psychological intensity.

Combs finds consistency in the way Scorsese's films evoke masculine emotional and psychological intensity, and this intensity is evident even in a musical (fig. **13.15**). His analysis demonstrates how some critics value some genre films over others because a director created a unique vision while working with a genre's conventions.

The work of the *auteur* underscores the complexities of genre criticism. On the one hand, definitions of genres require stasis and consistency. On the other hand, economic, cultural, and artistic forces inevitably undermine such assumptions. The next chapter explores in more detail the theoretical underpinnings (and the fallacies) of the *auteur* theory—the argument that some directors have the ability to inscribe their own personal signature on the films they direct.

Works Consulted

Altman, Rick. "A Semantic/Syntactic Approach to Film Genre," in *Film Genre Reader*, ed. Barry Keith Grant. Austin: University of Texas Press, 1986, pp. 26–40.

Brandy, Leo. "Genre: The Conventions of Connection," in *Film Theory and Criticism*, 4th edn. New York: Oxford University Press, 1992.

Cavell, Stanley. *Pursuits of Happiness: The Hollywood Comedy of Remarriage*. Cambridge, MA: Harvard University Press, 1981.

Cawelti, John G. "*Chinatown* and Generic Transformation in Recent American Films," in *Film Genre Reader*, ed. Barry Keith Grant. Austin: University of Texas Press, 1986, pp. 183–201.

Combs, Richard. "New York, New York." *Sight and Sound*, fall, 1977, pp. 252–3.

Cook, David. *A History of Narrative Film*, 3rd edn. New York: Norton, 1996.

Corrigan, Timothy. *A Cinema without Walls: Movies and Culture After Vietnam*. New Brunswick: Rutgers University Press, 1991.

Guerrero, Ed. *Framing Blackness*. Philadelphia, PA: Temple University Press, 1993.

Hutchings, Peter. "Genre Theory and Criticism." *Approaches to Popular Film*, ed. Joanne Hollows and Mark Jancovich. Manchester and New York: Manchester University Press, 1995, pp. 59 77.

Kawin, Bruce. "Children of the Light," in *Film Genre Reader*, ed. Barry Keith Grant. Austin: University of Texas Press, 1986, pp. 236–57.

Lent, Tina Olsin. "Romantic Love and Friendship: The Redefinition of Gender Relations in Screwball Comedy," in *Classical Hollywood Comedy*, ed. Krisine Brunovska Karnick and Henry Jenkins. London: Routledge, 1995, pp. 314–31.

Mellen, Joan. "Film Noir," in *The Political Companion to American Film*, ed. Gary Crowdus. Chicago: Lakeview Press, 1994, pp. 137–44.

Neale, Steve. *Genre and Hollywood*. London: Routledge, 2000.

Richie, Donald. *Japanese Cinema: An Introduction*. New York: Oxford University Press, 1990.

Ryall, Tom. "Genre and Hollywood," in *The Oxford Guide to Film Studies*, ed. John Hill and Pamela Church Gibson. London: Oxford University Press, 1998, pp. 327–37.

Schatz, Thomas. *Hollywood Genres: Formulas, Filmmaking, and the Studio System*. Philadelphia: Temple University Press, 1981.

Solomon, Stanley J. *Beyond Formula: American Film Genres*. San Diego: Harcourt Brace, 1976.

Sontag, Susan. "The Imagination of Disaster," in *Film Theory and Criticism*. 3rd edn., ed. Gerald Mast and Marshall Cohen. New York: Oxford University Press, 1985, pp. 451–65.

Stack, Peter. "Satirical *Scream* is Out for Blood—And Lots of It." *San Francisco Chronicle*. December 26, 1996. *SFGate.com*. February 13, 2003.

Truffaut, François. *Hitchcock*, rev. edn. New York: Touchstone, 1984.

Warshow, Robert. "Movie Chronicle: The Westerner," in *Film Theory and Criticism*. 4th edn., ed. Gerald Mast, Marshall Cohen, and Leo Braudy. New York: Oxford University Press, 1992, pp. 453–66.

Wood, Robin. *Hollywood from Vietnam to Reagan*. New York: Columbia University Press, 1986.

Wood, Robin. "Introduction," in *The American Nightmare: Essays on the Horror Film*, ed. Andrew Britton, Richard Lippe, Tony Williams, and Robin Wood. Toronto, Canada: Festival of Festivals, 1979, pp. 7–28.

Wright, Judith Hess. "Genre Films and the Status Quo," in *Film Genre Reader*, ed. Barry Keith Grant. Austin: University of Texas Press, 1986, pp. 236–57.

Chapter

14

Film Authorship

14.1 Charlie Chaplin on the outside looking in, from *The Gold Rush*.

The studio had expected this to be a nice little murder mystery, an ordinary kind of picture. Well you don't have Orson Welles and have an ordinary anything. He could only make it extraordinary.

Janet Leigh on Touch of Evil

How do people decide which films to see? They read film reviews in newspapers, magazines, and journals, and on websites. They listen to their friends. Or they may see a film, no matter what friends and critics say, because certain individuals are associated with it. Many fans flock to see movies featuring their favorite star; others line up for a film by a director whose work they enjoy. These viewers use their knowledge of the director's *oeuvre* as well as historical and biographical information to analyze, interpret, and evaluate her latest film.

The common practice of using a film's director as an organizing principle is based upon the *auteur* theory, developed by French cinephiles in the 1940s and 1950s. At its most basic, the theory proposes that a director is the author of the film: *auteur* translates as "author." The term implies that the director is the primary creative source and, therefore, his films express his distinctive vision of the world. Just as "Dickensian" describes Charles Dickens' literary style, so "Wellesian" might be used to describe a film exhibiting certain traits of Orson Welles's style, such as deep-focus cinematography and fluid camerawork.

The connection between the film director and literary author derives from the fact that, historically, French film directors wrote or co-wrote the films they made. But the French critics who argued on behalf of the *auteur* did not just extol the work of recognized French writer–directors. Instead, they argued for the artistry of Hollywood directors. Their theory claimed that even commercial Hollywood directors (whose films others disparaged as mass entertainment, made in an assembly-line fashion) should be viewed as artists.

More than fifty years after the *auteur* theory emerged, it seems unremarkable to assume that the director is the primary creative force behind a film. Directors, studios, and film critics all encourage this notion. But the customary use of the *auteur* approach to film should be tempered by an understanding of its full implications. This chapter examines the idea of film authorship as it developed in France and, later, in the U.S., and at the way the idea of the *auteur* can be used as a marketing tool. Then it looks at the practical application of this approach when writing about film and gives examples of the use of the *auteur* theory in film criticism. This discussion reveals both the value and limitations of the *auteur* approach.

● The Idea of the *Auteur*: From *Cahiers du Cinéma* to the Sarris–Kael Debate

The *auteur* theory emerged from a specific cultural milieu: postwar France. During the 1940s and '50s in Paris, intellectuals who loved cinema used it to explored aesthetic and philosophical questions. Many of these cinephiles—including François Truffaut, Eric Rohmer, Jean-Luc Godard, and Claude Chabrol—also made important films. Others, including André Bazin and Alexandre Astruc, contributed to film theory. Their early arguments in favor of the *auteur* approach to film criticism were published in the influential film journal *Cahiers du Cinéma*.

Alexandre Astruc looked at film as a medium of personal expression, like literature, elaborating this idea in a 1948 essay, where he used the phrase "*caméra-stylo*," which literally means "camera pen." In 1954 Truffaut published "A Certain Tendency of French Cinema," a *Cahiers* essay that endorsed Astruc's ideas by advocating the *auteur* approach. In the essay, Truffaut argued that the average, unremarkable film director merely translates a pre-existing work (a novel or screenplay) onto film, but an *auteur* transforms the material. In the process, he makes it his own (an especially remarkable feat when accomplished by directors working within the commercial Hollywood studio system). Writer–directors *and* directors who shape pre-existing material according to a distinctive, creative sensibility are *auteurs*.

Truffaut favorably compared Hollywood films with the French cinema's "tradition of quality." To him, Hollywood provided models for daring cinematic creativity whereas the latter produced dull translations of literary works. Truffaut and Bazin elevated filmmakers within the Hollywood studio system who they thought had been neglected, though Bazin warned against making the director a cult hero.

The *auteur* theory challenged the prevailing view of the aesthetic superiority of European cinema over American. As Robert Stam notes:

> Filmmakers like Eisenstein, Renoir and Welles had always been regarded as *auteurs* [. . .] The novelty of *auteur* theory was to suggest that studio directors like Hawks and Minnelli were also *auteurs* (Stam, p. 87).

The *auteur* approach focused attention on the artistry of Hollywood, not on what many saw as its crass commercialism.

The theory not only reconsidered popular films as potential works of art; it also spurred debates about which directors deserved to be called *auteurs*. In the United States the discussion of authorship appeared in the journal *Film Culture* and *The New Yorker* magazine, in a well-known debate between film critics Andrew Sarris and Pauline Kael.

In "Notes on the Auteur Theory in 1962," Andrew Sarris created a version of the *auteur* approach primarily designed to evaluate directors. Sarris's criteria are meant to determine: (1) whether or not an individual director is an *auteur*; and (2) where a director ranks among all *auteurs*. A necessary (but not sufficient) criterion for an *auteur* is technical competence; a director must be capable of creating a well-made film. Second, the director must demonstrate a distinguishable personality. Finally, Sarris argued that the films in an *auteur*'s body of work share an interior meaning, defined as an underlying tension between the director's vision and the subject matter.

Sarris did not define this last criterion to the satisfaction of many critics, but it can be thought of as the continuing elaboration of a director's perspective on the world through the treatment of themes. An example of interior meaning would be Stanley Kubrick's ironic view of imperfect human beings and the flawed technologies they create in their own image. Many of his films satirize the desire for control and transcendence through technology, but they also reveal a grudging respect for the creative potential of human beings.

New Yorker critic Pauline Kael challenged Sarris. She argued that technical competence was a weak criterion: it failed to acknowledge the true masters of technique, such as Antonioni. She also pointed out that the distinguishable personality criterion favored repetition, penalizing directors who risked venturing beyond a familiar genre or style, and she found the "interior meaning" criterion impossibly vague. She pointed out that the *auteur* approach might lead critics to overvalue trivial films, elevating them simply because they had been made by a recognized *auteur*.

Kael also criticized the *auteur* approach for refusing to take into account the collaborative nature of filmmaking. The theory ignores the fact that many people's creative decisions are part of the process of making films. Kael claimed that in many cases the director was not the driving creative force. Although she argued incorrectly that screenwriter Herman Mankiewicz, not Orson Welles, was responsible for the final version of the *Citizen Kane* script (and therefore should be considered its *auteur*), most film historians agree with her point that, like most films, that project was a collaboration. The innovative visual elements of *Citizen Kane* resulted from Welles's collaboration with cinematographer Gregg Toland. A number of film scholars have argued that it is appropriate in certain cases to label producers (Val Lewton, Christine Vachon), actors (Clint Eastwood), and screenwriters (Dudley Nichols) as *auteurs*.

One additional limitation of the approach should be considered. *Auteur* criticism implies that the director possesses conscious intentions and, perhaps, unacknowledged ideas, all of which combine to produce a film, and, eventually, a body of work. The approach views the director as the primary source of meaning.

But film theorists such as Peter Wollen argue that the meaning of any text, whether it is a film, novel, television show, or a billboard, may exceed the intentions of the person or people who created it. Wollen questions whether anyone—even the author—can fix any film's meaning definitively for all time. To him, a strict *auteurist* approach may ignore the complexity inherent in any text by insisting that the only authorized readings be linked to some notion of what a director meant to convey. Wollen cautions against limiting interpretation "since there is no true, essential meaning there can therefore be no exhaustive criticism, which settles the interpretation of a film once and for all" (Wollen, p. 533).

A simple example illuminates Wollen's concerns. It is well known that Orson Welles was intrigued by the idea of making a film based on the life of newspaper magnate William Randolph Hearst. Although pursuing this avenue of research may prove fruitful for analyzing *Citizen Kane*, to constrain an interpretation to this single aspect would exclude the many ideas the film generates about American culture, aging, and the nature of human relationships, as well as other meanings that Welles may or may not have intended.

Despite many shortcomings, the *auteur* approach remains central to film scholarship and criticism. Moreover, the powerful notion of film authorship exerts an influence on filmmaking as a cultural practice, as the next section shows.

● *Auteur* as Marketing Strategy: Old and New Hollywood

The commercial exploitation of the *auteur* is evident in many marketing campaigns. In 2003, the publicity surrounding *Alex and Emma* touted its director, Rob Reiner, as "the director of *When Harry Met Sally*," forging links with his earlier, successful romantic comedy. Film critic Rex Reed plugged *When Peggy Sue Got Married* as Francis Ford Coppola's best film since *The Godfather*. DVD box sets are packaged by director: Hitchcock, Kubrick, and Truffaut. As André Bazin feared, the film director has become a cult celebrity.

Q & A with Independent Filmmaker Kevin Cournoyer

Pramaggiore/Wallis: Why do you reject the idea of the film director as an *auteur*?

Kevin Cournoyer: When you see credits like "a so and so film" or "a film by so and so," you're seeing an ego on parade. Nothing more. To belabor the obvious, filmmaking is a collaborative enterprise. There's absolutely no rational basis for the possessory credit on any film in the history of cinema.

It's amusing that this illusory precept—director as *auteur*—is derived, in large part, from a group of film critics at *Cahiers du Cinéma* who aspired to be directors. Here were film lovers who dreamed of being filmmakers. You could view *la politique des auteurs* as a form of wish fulfillment. An American critic, Andrew Sarris, simply reified this grand delusion by affixing the word "theory" after it.

No one filmmaker solely "authors" a film like a writer "authors" a novel. Filmmaking is not the pure, organic process of fiction writing. Film enthusiasts often make references like "a Hitchcock film" or an "Altman film." Such references suggest either an historically expedient convenience or a profound misunderstanding of filmmaking—or both. To point out just one demonstrable flaw with such a reference: Hitchcock stopped writing after 1946. To call a film directed by Hitchcock a "Hitchcock film" is a deplorable insult to everyone else who helped create it,

from the writer to the cinematographer to the production designer to the actors.

A filmmaker who writes, pre-visualizes, directs, and edits her or his own film comes as close as is possible to the notion of authorial identity. Some have called such a person a "holistic" filmmaker.

P/W: Why has the idea of the *auteur* had such lasting appeal?

KC: One reason why the *auteur* is so difficult to relinquish is that it's easy to say Altman's *Nashville* (and consequently consign the writer, Joan Tewkesbury, to the cutting room floor of cinema history). Also, cinema studies is an offshoot of literary studies—born in the bowels of English departments. Literary and film studies' approaches to textual analysis and authorial identity are identical and ironclad. That's a shame: there's a great need for more accurate evaluative criteria with regard to the study of films and filmmakers.

As for filmmakers—or, more to the point, directors—I think they persist in this delusion because it's good for their egos and it's good for their careers. And for moviegoers, the *auteur* theory has become a way to legitimate hero worship.

Kevin Cournoyer is a filmmaker and teacher.
He directed *Olanda's Wish*.

But in fact, commerce has always informed the idea of film authorship. The next section looks at the careers of Orson Welles and Alfred Hitchcock to examine the way the *auteur* has been used by the commercial industry during the studio era and in post-studio Hollywood.

Studio-era *auteurs*: Welles and Hitchcock

Orson Welles personified the creativity and fierce independence of the *auteur*. When he began making films in the 1940s, the U.S. film industry was in its heyday. Although the hierarchical organization of the major studios positioned directors as mere studio employees, a unit production system that had emerged in the 1930s offered some latitude to certain directors and producers. The demand for features was so great that studios also hired independent producers and directors, as RKO did when they hired Welles in 1939.

Welles was well known because of his successful Mercury Theater productions (including the legendary radio broadcast of H.G. Wells's *The War of the Worlds*). Because of Welles's reputation, RKO studios granted him unprecedented creative control to make three films. His first, *Citizen Kane*, was well received critically, but did not achieve box office success. During the editing of his second film, *The Magnificent Ambersons* (1942), Welles was filming a documentary in Brazil. In his absence, studio executives excised 40 minutes of footage and appended a happy ending. The film was not commercially successful; nor was Welles' third film, *Journey into Fear* (1943), and the director was

●●●

Creating an Author-Driven Cinema: Young German Cinema

In postwar West Germany, the concept of the *auteur*, or *Autor*, had a specific meaning that reflected that country's historical circumstances. The concept gave rise to the Young German Cinema of the 1960s and the New German Cinema (*das neue Kino*) of the 1970s. In 1962, hostility toward the highly conventional German film industry of the 1950s, a rejection of Hollywood (arising in part from the U.S. occupation), and a desire to break completely with the troubled German past led a group of 26 critics and filmmakers to sign the Oberhausen Manifesto, a document that set out an agenda for a new German film practice. The manifesto rejected "papa's cinema" and called for an anti-industrial cinema where the director would work entirely free of commercial influence. Film historian Anton Kaes states that the manifesto "points to a Romantic notion of authorship not bound by economics or the expectations of an audience" (Kaes, p. 614).

One tangible result of the Oberhausen manifesto was the establishment of a government funding agency, the *Kuratorium Junger Deutscher Film*. Thus, "the conditions for an *auteur* cinema were deliberately cultivated (in conjunction with certain industrial, political, and cultural developments)" (Johnston, p. 122). Between 1965 and 1967, the *Kuratorium* supported twenty productions and used as an explicit criterion the independence of the director. During the 1960s, Alexander Kluge, Volker Schlöndorff, and Jean-Marie Straub and Daniele Huillet produced "a cinema of resistance—against the mass-produced entertainment industry of the Nazi period and the 1950s, against the visual pleasure of lavish productions, and against the ideology of conformism that flourished in the decade of the economic miracle" (Kaes, p. 617). A number of remarkably innovative films (the government financed about twenty-four in all) dealt with the politics and aesthetics of German history, including Kluge's *Yesterday's Girl* ("*Abschied von Gestern*"; 1966), and *Artist under the Circus Dome: Clueless* ("*Die Artisten in der Zirkuspel: Ratlos*"; 1968), both of which blended documentary and fiction elements, and Schlöndorff's *Young Törless* ("*Der junge Törless*"; 1966). But by 1968, new laws tied government subsidies to a director's commercial success and a film's potential to bring in 500,000 Deutschmarks at the box office.

Despite its early demise, the Young German Cinema laid the groundwork for the New German Cinema of the 1970s, associated with directors Wim Wenders, Werner Herzog, and Rainer Werner Fassbinder. By 1982, with Fassbinder's death and a new government minister who refused to subsidize "elitist" films, came the end of New German Cinema. In what may be an inevitable cycle, German directors of the 1980s came to see the radical pioneers of the 1960s and 1970s as an older generation against whom they defined their own "new" vision.

unceremoniously fired by RKO. Over the course of the next three decades, Welles rejected the notion that studio executives knew how to make films, but periodically he submitted to studio discipline (as an actor and director) in order to make his own films.

Because his films were formally audacious and challenging, and because he clashed with executives who sought to exert their creative control, Welles became notorious as an outsider reviled by the Hollywood power structure. No other American director before or since has so epitomized the genius who flouted the profit-oriented commercial system. He directed films at B studios and in Europe, before returning to Hollywood to make *Touch of Evil* for Universal in 1958, yet another production that generated conflict between Welles and studio executives.

One example of Welles's importance as a marketing tool is the 1998 re-release of *Touch of Evil*. As was the case with most of his studio films, Welles clashed with Universal over its decisions regarding editing and sound. He wrote a detailed memo urging the studio to make a number of changes before releasing the film. Welles's 58-page memo to Universal studio head Edward Muhl formed the basis for the film's restoration in 1998. Film critic Jonathan Rosenbaum (who participated in the restoration) explained the process:

> Rick Schmidlin concocted a wild scheme: to follow all of the memo's instructions for the first time and put together the *Touch of Evil* Welles had had in mind. After Schmidlin showed Universal an edited sample of one of Welles's suggestions, the studio saw a way to get more value out of an old chestnut. (Rosenbaum, pp. 134–5)

The impetus for the project was financial gain: Universal would "get more value out of an old chestnut." Thus, Universal used Welles's reputation as a fiercely independent creative artist to entice viewers to see the restored film, one that promised to be superior to the original because it hewed more closely to the *auteur*'s intentions. The "revamping" project would be a worthwhile endeavor in any case, but the Welles name made it feasible to a profit-driven corporation. A lesser director's work might not receive the same commitment.

Like Orson Welles, Alfred Hitchcock is a celebrated *auteur*. Edward R. O'Neill notes that Hitchcock's very image is famous and that his name "has passed into the vernacular in the word 'Hitchcockian'" (O'Neill, p. 310). Like Welles, Hitchcock clashed with producers and corporate executives in Hollywood, and particularly the independent producer David O. Selznick.

Unlike Welles, however, Hitchcock earned a reputation as a popular and prolific director. His steady output—53 features between 1925 and 1976—seemed to confirm his persona as a craftsman rather than a tortured genius. This reputation was so entrenched that influential critics such as Claude Chabrol, Eric Rohmer, François Truffaut, and Robin Wood had to argue forcefully in order for Hitchcock's work to be taken seriously.

Hitchcock's authorial persona was used to market his films at the time they were released. A lengthy trailer advertising his 1960 film *Psycho* follows the director around the set, mugging for the camera and exaggerating his dour personality as he hints at the shocking events that take place in the hotel, in the shower, and in the gothic mansion where Norman Bates lives (fig. **14.2**). In this trailer, Hitchcock performs his "Master of Suspense" persona to entice viewers to see the film. In the trailer, Universal used the audience's idea of Hitchcock—and not the stars, genre, or plot line—as the hook. In other words, even during the studio era, some directors were celebrities used as fodder for the studio marketing machine.

Blockbuster *Auteurs*: Spielberg and Lucas

The shift to a corporate entertainment environment in the 1980s and '90s did not eradicate the idea of the *auteur*, but modified its profile. Jon Lewis cites Steven Spielberg (fig. **14.3**) and George Lucas (fig. **14.4**) as examples of the successful blockbuster *auteur*. This is the director who is just as savvy about the financing of a film as he is about translating a creative vision to the screen. Film scholar Jon Lewis writes:

> corporations began to insist that films be efficiently distributed in a variety of forms and format to better exploit the vertically and horizontally integrated marketplace. Lucas and Spielberg were the first and best at the very sort of filmmaking designed to succeed under such an economic policy. (Lewis, p. 25)

The *auteur* is alive and well and "bound up with the celebrity industry of Hollywood" according to Tim Corrigan (Corrigan, p. 39). The director functions as a brand name to market films, to signify a consistent product. Corrigan claims that the *auteur* is needed to assure blockbuster profits by doing interviews and television appearances.

Another economic and technological development that exploits the *auteur* as brand name is the marketing of DVDs. The director's cut solidifies the director as *auteur*, particularly on commentary tracks where the director describes the film in detail. Without disputing the value of a director's insight, this practice speaks to entertainment conglomerates' ability continually to reap the financial benefits of the *auteur* as celebrity and brand name.

Thus far, this chapter has concentrated on the origins and implications of film authorship. The remainder of the chapter examines methods of incorporating the approach into film analysis and presents examples of the auteur approach in film criticism on established and up-and-coming *auteurs*.

14.2 Alfred Hitchcock in a publicity still for *Psycho*.

14.3 *(left)* Steven Spielberg.
14.4 *(right)* George Lucas.

Using the *Auteur* Approach to Interpret and Evaluate Films

When a film critic adopts the *auteur* approach, the director's life and career become the frame of reference for describing, interpreting, and evaluating individual films or groups of films. One could look for patterns that recur in Hitchcock's silent and sound films, assuming there will be similarities because they were made by the same director, despite the differences of historical era, location (Britain versus Hollywood), and technology. Scholarly books may examine all the films of an individual director, whereas a popular review would compare one or two films in order to give readers a point of comparison.

A common claim writers make when they adopt the *auteur* approach is that an individual film is typical of (or an aberration in) the director's *oeuvre*. This process requires that a profile of the director be compiled from a wide sample of her other films. Often, critics treat a director's career as an evolution, with the implicit expectation that early work is potentially immature but inspired and that a mid-career period of consistency guarantees the director's place in posterity. Of course, the real world exigencies of filmmaking do not always conform to this abstract model of maturing artistry.

Another goal of *auteur* analysis might be to compare the work of two directors, to note similarities and differences, or to rank them. In addition to comparing directors, critics trace the influence of one director on another. One of the most famous lines in film history is Orson Welles's statement that his only preparation for a filmmaking career was watching John Ford's *Stagecoach*. An earnest critic might attempt to explain what Welles meant through an analysis of Ford's and Welles's films.

A director's work might be reconsidered through examinations of influence. Todd Haynes's *Far From Heaven* (2002), a film set in the 1950s that deals with the breakdown of a comfortable suburban couple's marriage owing to taboo sexual desires (fig. **14.5**), made conscious references to Douglas Sirk's 1950s melodramas, including *All That Heaven Allows* (1955) and *Written on the Wind* (1956). Criticism calling attention to Sirk's influence on Haynes may have educated filmgoers about Sirk's films (fig. **14.6**).

14.5 Saturated color in *Far from Heaven* represents a homage to Douglas Sirk.

Finally, the *auteur* approach can be used to strengthen the interpretation of a film. The approach provides a framework for locating consistent narrative patterns and determining their relationship to visual techniques—for example, comparing several Welles films allows a critic to recognize that his fascination with individuals corrupted by great power informs *Citizen Kane* as well as *Lady from Shanghai* (1947) and *Touch of Evil*. Welles's interest in the inner struggle of powerful but flawed figures is revealed through composition in depth and a mobile camera.

In contrast to the wealthy and powerful men that Welles's films examine, Charlie Chaplin's films focus again and again on outsiders, misfits, and the mistreated. They reveal with great admiration the pluck and gumption of downtrodden individuals, using humor to emphasize the resources that allow them to resist dehumanizing situations. His camerawork relies on the static tableau, not on the sweeping crane shots that characterize Welles's style. These tableaux accentuate the fact that Chaplin's characters occupy marginal positions, on the fringes or at the bottom of the hierarchy (fig. **14.1**, p. 366).

Although considering a film as part of a director's *oeuvre* may be useful to interpretation, it is important to remember that no one interpretation—even one based on the director—is definitive. Interpretation always engages both textual evidence and persua-

14.6 Sirk's characteristic rust colors in *All That Heaven Allows*.

sion. Why else would film scholars still be discussing films such as Welles's *Citizen Kane*, Ford's *The Searchers*, or Hitchcock's *Psycho*? While a director remains an important source for building interpretations, the *auteur* approach is just one of many frameworks that help writers to move their analysis beyond textual interpretation, including genre, historical period, star studies, and national cinema approaches. Combining research on a film's director with one of these methods is likely to enrich any film analysis.

● Readings in *Auteur* Criticism

The readings below show how film critics use the *auteur* approach to describe, compare, evaluate, and interpret works by important directors. Five *auteurs* are examined: two well-established directors (Akira Kurosawa and Ousmane Sembene) and three emerging directors (Jafar Panahi, Sofia Coppola, and Wong Kar-Wai).

Akira Kurosawa (1910–1998)

Despite the existence of a thriving Japanese film industry for more than forty years, it was not until 1950 that Japanese cinema achieved international recognition. Kurosawa's *Rashomon*, a tale of irreconcilable realities, earned the Golden Lion at the 1951 Venice Film Festival and the Academy Award for best foreign film in 1952 (fig. **14.7**). Trained as a painter, Kurosawa's films are remarkable for their visual texture, partly the result of his mastery of composing for the wide screen, use of a telephoto lens, and expressionist treatment of color. He is best known for his samurai films (*jidai geki*, or "stories of the old times") and for his adaptation of Western literature to historical and contemporary Japanese contexts, including *High and Low* ("*Tengoku to jigoku*" or "King's Ransom"; 1963), *Throne of Blood* ("*Kumonosujo*" or "Macbeth"; 1957), and *Ran* ("King Lear"; 1985).

In an essay in *Film International*, Tadao Sato combines the *auteur* approach with a national cinema perspective, suggesting that Kurosawa's films—along with those of his contemporaries—drew on Japanese and Western aesthetics. Sato compares several Japanese directors in terms of the genres in which they worked:

14.7 Akira Kurosawa.

Interestingly enough, neither Akira Kurosawa nor Kenji Mizoguchi, or Masaki Kobayashi, came from those [studios that] specialized in *jidai geki* movies. Rather they started their career by making contemporary dramas and then moved on to make some *jidai geki* masterpieces. (Sato, p. 62)

According to Sato, these directors generated a "new" style by combining the realism of the contemporary dramas they made with the rigidly conventional *jidai geki*. Sato singles out Kurosawa, however, explaining what it was about his *jidai geki* films that was new:

> The *jidai geki* films have stylized all the minute expressions of the manners and customs between the master and the followers [. . .] and these stylized forms have become a tradition themselves. The *jidai geki* films of Kurosawa are, on the other hand, characterized by the fact that they have broken all these stylized patterns. (Sato, p. 62)

Sato places Kurosawa the *auteur* within traditions of Japanese aesthetics, but also describes the way his work, and *Rashomon* in particular, combines Japanese and Western elements:

> [In Kurosawa's films] a traditional Japanese sense of beauty is merged with a most progressive Western sense of beauty, making his pictures neither Japanese nor Western, but rather uniquely original [. . .] while containing the elements inherited from the traditional [. . .] Kabuki play (the part related to the behaviors of proud men), *Rashomon* analyzes them in light of modern individualism. (Sato, p. 63)

Sato combines an *auteurist* approach with specific cultural knowledge to enrich the analysis of Kurosawa's films.

Select Filmography: *Sugata Sanshiro* (1943), *Rashomon* (1950), *Ikuru* (1952), *Seven Samurai* ("*Shichinin no samurai*"; 1954), *Throne of Blood* (1957), *Hidden Fortress* ("*Kakushitoride no sanajunin*"; 1958), *Yojimbo* (1961), *Red Beard* ("*Akahige*"; 1965), *Derzu Usala* (1975), *Kagemusha* (1980), *Ran* (1985), *Dreams* ("*Yume*"; 1990).

Further Reading: David Desser, *The Samurai Films of Akira Kurosawa*; Donald Richie, *The Films of Akira Kurosawa*.

14.8 Ousmane Sembene.

Ousmane Sembene (b. 1923)

In 1963, novelist and essayist Ousmane Sembene (fig. **14.8**) turned to filmmaking, partly because he realized that most of his fellow Senegalese were illiterate. He trained at Moscow's Gorky film school. Sembene made the first African feature, *Black Girl* ("*La Noire de . . .*") in 1966. His style has been influenced by Italian Neorealism and indigenous Senegalese traditions; his films often critically examine French colonialism as well as life in post-independence Senegal. Still making films at the age of 81, Sembene took home the *Prix un Certain Regard* at the 2004 Cannes film festival for *Moolaade*, a film about female genital excision.

Sembene's *Camp Thiaroye* ("*Camp de Thiaroye*"; 1988) concerns the experiences of African troops who fought for France in World War II but are detained at a transit camp on their return home to Dakar, Senegal. Caryn James refers to a common theme in the director's *oeuvre*; the depiction of Senegalese and African histories:

> This film continues Mr. Sembene's complex career long treatment of African identity [. . .] its believable central character [Diatta] comes to embody all the dilemmas of African nations in the decades just before and after the collapse of colonial rule [. . .] "The Camp at Thiaroye" is not simply a revision of the historical past. The figure of Diatta looks forward, suggesting that though globalism may have replaced colonial rule, African identity is no simpler an issue than ever. (*James, p. C16; reprinted courtesy of* The New York Times)

Like James, John Pym combines historical context with the *auteur* approach. He uses biographical details to connect the film's protagonist and director:

> It is not reading too much into this character [Diatta] to see in him [. . .] a portrait of the principled young Sembene, the one-time union organizer of the Marseille waterfront who went on to write, among other books in French, *Les bouts de bois de Dieu*, a novel set against the 1947–48 French railway strike. (Pym, p. 280)

Pym educates the audience about Sembene's career as a novelist and political activist, arguing for the relevance of those biographical details for this film.

Georgia Brown uses the *auteur* approach to consider Sembene's influence on other directors:

> Thriving on debate, putting the emphasis on community and identity, Spike Lee seems to be following in the giant footsteps of the Senegalese master Ousmane Sembene. As polemicist and provocateur, Sembene has a running start on him, even though he didn't begin making films until almost 40. (Brown, p. 64)

Here the reviewer provides the reader with a new context for thinking about the films of another important director, Spike Lee. Generally discussed in the context of contemporary U.S. film, Lee's work can be productively examined in relation to African films.

Select Filmography: *Black Girl* ("*La Noire de . . .*"; 1966), The *Money Order* ("*Mandabi*"; 1968), *God of Thunder, Lord of the Sky* ("*Emitaï*"; 1971), *Xala* (1974), *The People* ("*Ceddo*"; 1977)

Further reading: Sheila Petty (ed.), *A Call to Action: The Films of Ousmane Sembene* (1996); David Murphy, *Sembene* (2001)

The three directors examined below began producing their films in the late 1980s and 1990s. They have fewer works, yet critics have hailed them for presenting astonishing new visions.

Jafar Panahi (b. 1958)

Although his first film, *The White Balloon* ("*Badkonak-e Sefid*"; 1995), won a Golden Camera award at the Cannes Film Festival, Jafar Panahi lacks the reputation of Abbas Kiarostami, perhaps the best-known contemporary Iranian filmmaker and Panahi's some-time collaborator. Reviewers typically locate Panahi's work as part of a recent wave of Iranian cinema and use Kiarostami as a point of reference when discussing Panahi's films.

One reviewer mentions the work of several contemporary Iranian directors when reviewing Panahi's third film, *The Circle* ("*Dayereh*"; 2000), which was financed by Italian sources and banned in Iran: "Certainly there are earlier Iranian films that have dealt with the plight of women, but none that I know of approaches the uncompromising bluntness of *The Circle*" (Johnson). The reviewer goes on to mention films by Dariush Mehrjui (*Leila*; 1997), Ebrahim Mokhtari (*Zinat*; 1994), Mehdi Fakhimzadeh (*The Spouse*; 1994), Mohsen Makhmalbaf (*The Day I Became a Woman*; 2000), and Samira Makhmalbaf (*The Apple*; 1999), emphasizing the varied approaches to similar subject matter.

The same reviewer suggests the work of international directors as points of comparison. He describes one scene in *The Circle* as being "as tense as any in a Hitchcock film:"

> The comparison with Hitchcock is not arbitrary. When Panahi was a student
> at Tehran's College of Cinema and Television, he says, "I liked studying
> Hitchcock to see if he made any mistakes." (Johnson)

Johnson uses one recognized *auteur*—Hitchcock—to posit Panahi's status as another. The review illustrates that, for critics who subscribe to this approach, an *auteur*'s vision can transcend national boundaries.

Filmography: *The White Balloon* ("*Badkonak-e Sefid*"; 1995), *The Mirror* ("*A'ineh*"; 1997), *The Circle* (2000), *Crimson Gold* ("*Talaye sorkh*"; 2003)

Further Reading: Richard Tapper (ed.), *The New Iranian Cinema*; Hamid Dabashi, *Close Up: Iranian Cinema Past Present and Future*

14.9 Sofia Coppola.

Sofia Coppola (b. 1971)

Sofia Coppola (fig. **14.9**) began her career helping her father, Francis Ford Coppola, write and direct one segment of *New York Stories* (1989). After a critically reviled performance as Michael Corleone's daughter in *Godfather III*, she turned to visual art and eventually, film directing. About her 1999 debut film, *The Virgin Suicides*, Graham Fuller wrote:

> Her meticulously faithful transposition of Jeffrey Eumenides' incantatory
> prose to the screen has resulted in nothing less than a timelessly romantic
> suburban myth that could become a cult classic. (Fuller)

In 2004, David Ansen of *Newsweek* called Coppola a "new visionary." Her second film, *Lost in Translation*, earned Oscar nominations for Best Actor (Bill Murray—for whom she wrote the part), Best Screenplay, and Best Film. She won a Golden Globe and an Academy Award for her original screenplay and was named Best Director by the Boston Society of Film Critics and the Independent Spirit Awards. Coppola told Ansen that she intentionally avoided working through a major studio in order to maintain control:

> I wrote the script and I wanted to keep the budget really low so I didn't have a boss—and I wouldn't have gotten final cut if I brought it to a studio [. . .] So we did foreign sales and raised the money. (Ansen)

Her comments suggest that even film directors who do not wish to become blockbuster *auteurs* must be well versed in the business side of filmmaking. Although they depend on the financial input of others, would-be *auteurs* such as Coppola try to limit their creative input.

Filmography: *The Virgin Suicides* (1999), *Lost in Translation* (2003)

Further Reading: Graham Fuller, "Death and the Maidens,"; David Ansen, "The New Visionaries."

Wong Kar Wai (b. 1958)

Whereas Coppola's *Lost in Translation* focuses on the cultural dislocation of foreigners in Japan, Hong Kong director Wong Kar Wai's films depict a multicultural world where everyone experiences dislocation. Many films of Wong Kar Wai address cultural anxieties surrounding the transfer of Hong Kong from British colonial rule to China in 1997. Wong is celebrated for the way he integrates popular culture, music, and images into stories about cultural displacement. He also is known for radical camerawork that involves experiments with color and fast and slow motion. Wong won Best Director at Cannes for *Happy Together* ("*Cheun gwong tsa sit*"; 1997), the story of two gay men from Hong Kong who try to rejuvenate their relationship by traveling to Argentina. His science fiction film about Hong Kong fifty years after the transition, entitled *2046*, premiered at Cannes in 2004.

Charles Taylor, writing about the film for Salon.com, sees Wong's repeated use of pop culture as a joke about cultural homogenization:

> It's one of the recurring jokes in Wong's movies that no matter where the characters travel, they end up in the same crummy bars and apartments and fast-food joints. That every place looks like every place else is both Wong's comment on the way pop culture has remade the world and a comic rejoinder to "one world, one people" platitudes. (Taylor)

He also credits the cinematographer's contribution, noting a consistency with an earlier Wong film:

> As he did in *Chungking Express*, cinematographer Christopher Doyle uses slow-motion bursts of pixilated movement. (Taylor)

Jonathan Rosenbaum also refers to this collaboration, but also argues that the art director contributes to Wong's consistency:

> But [Wong's] films, like [Woody] Allen's, have a particular "look" that derives from his using the same collaborators again and again—Doyle and art director William Chang. (Rosenbaum 1998/2004)

Ironically, while Wong has earned an international reputation as an *auteur*, these critics reveal the fact that the distinctive visual style for which he is known results from collaboration between director and cinematographer.

Select Filmography: *Ashes of Time* ("*Dong Xie Xi Du*"; 1994), *Days of Being Wild* ("*A-Fei Zhengchuan*"; 1990), *Chungking Express* (1994), *Fallen Angels* ("*Duoluo Tianshi*"; 1995), *Happy Together* (1997), *In the Mood For Love* ("*Fa yeung nin wa*"; 2000).

Further Reading: Poshek Fu and David Desser (ed.), *The Cinema of Hong Kong: History, Arts, Identity*

Works Consulted

Ansen, David, and Jeff Giles. "The New Visionaries," *Newsweek*, 143/6 (September 2, 2004). Online. Academic Search Elite. February 26, 2004.

Appelo, Tim. "Chasing the Chador," *The Nation*, 272/17 (April 30, 2001). Online. Academic Search Elite. February 25, 2004.

Brown, Georgia. "Heart of Darkness," *Village Voice*, 35 (September 11, 1990), p. 64.

Cineaste. Editorial, 28/1 (winter 2002). Online. Academic Search Elite. February 25, 2004.

Cook, David. *A History of Narrative Film*, 3rd edn. New York and London: W.W. Norton, 1996.

Corliss, Richard. "Gay and Gaudy," *Time*, 150/17 (October 27, 1997), p. 111.

Corrigan, Timothy. "*Auteurs* and the New Hollywood," in *The New American Cinema*, ed. Jon Lewis. Durham, NC: Duke University Press, 1998, pp. 38–63.

Cousins, Mark. *Scene by Scene*. London: Laurence King, 2002.

Economist, The. "On screen it's Iran's Shout," 336/7921 (January 7, 1995). Online. Academic Search Elite. February 25, 2004.

Fuller, Graham. "Death and the Maidens," *Sight and Sound*, new series, 10/4 (April 2000). Online. Humanities Art Database. February 26, 2004.

Gargan, Edward. "Hong Kong's Master of Internal Pyrotechnics," *New York Times*, Sunday October 12, 1997, Section 2, pp. 13, 29.

Iwasaki, Akira. "Kurosawa and his Work," in *Focus on Rashomon*, ed. Donald Richie. Englewood Cliffs: Prentice Hall, 1972, pp. 21–31.

James, Caryn. "Loyalties Scalded by Humiliation," *The New York Times*, September 5, 1990, p. C16.

Johnson, William. "The Circle," *Film Quarterly*, 54/3 (spring 2001). Online. Communication and Mass Media Complete. February 25, 2004.

Johnston, Sheila. "The Author as Public Institution," in *The European Cinema Reader*, ed. Catherine Fowler. London and New York: Routledge, 2002, pp. 121–31.

Kaes, Anton. "The New German Cinema," in *Oxford History of World Cinema*, ed. Geoffrey Nowell-Smith. Oxford and New York: Oxford University Press, 1996, pp. 614–27.

Magombe, P. Vincent. "Ousmane Sembene," in *Oxford History of World Cinema*, ed. Geoffrey Nowell-Smith. Oxford and New York: Oxford University Press, 1996, pp. 668–9.

Murphy, David. *Sembene*. Oxford and Trenton, NJ: Africa World Press, 2001.

"The Oberhausen Manifesto," in *The European Cinema Reader*, ed. Catherine Fowler. London and New York: Routledge, 2002, p. 73.

O'Neill, Edward R. "Alfred Hitchcock," in *Oxford History of World Cinema*, ed Geoffrey Nowell-Smith. Oxford and New York: Oxford University Press, 1996, pp. 310–11.

Pym, John. "Soldier's Pay," *Sight and Sound*, 58/4 (autumn 1989), p. 280.

Rosenbaum, Jonathan. "*Touch of Evil* Retouched," in *The Best American Movie Writing 1999*, ed. Peter Bogdanovich. New York: St Martin's Griffin, 1999, pp. 133–6.

Rosenbaum, Jonathan. "The Problem with Poetry," in *Movies as Politics*. Berkeley: University of California Press, 1997, pp. 183–94.

Rosenbaum, Jonathan. "Cult Confusion," *The Chicago Reader*, January 9, 1998. February 25, 2004. http://www.chireader.com/movies/archives/1998/0198/01238.html

San Filippo, Maria. "Lost in Translation," *Cineaste*, 29/1 (winter 2003). Online. Academic Search Elite. February 25, 2004.

Sato, Tadao. "The Films of Akira Kurosawa and the Japanese People," *Film International*, 6/2 (1998), pp. 61–4.

Stam, Robert. *Film Theory: An Introduction*. Malden, MA, and Oxford: Blackwell Publishers, 2000.

Taylor, Charles. "Hong Kong Tango," Salon.com. October 31, 1997. September 10, 2002. http://www.salon.com/ent/movies/1997/10/31happy.html?CP=SAL&DN=110.

Wollen, Peter. "From *Signs and Meaning in Cinema*: The Auteur Theory," in *Film Theory and Criticism,* 5th edn, ed. Leo Braudy and Marshall Cohen. Oxford: Oxford University Press, 1999, pp. 519–35.

Cinema as Industry: Economics and Technology

The movie business is macabre. Grotesque. It is a combination of a football game and a brothel.

Federico Fellini

Well before *Titanic* hit screens in 1997, headlines trumpeted the film's costly special effects and its bloated budget. The publicity helped lure spectators to theaters, and the film became the highest-grossing film of all time. By contrast, when Richard Rodriguez released his first movie, *El Mariachi* (1992), publicists emphasized how the project was a triumph of low-budget filmmaking (fig. **15.2**, p. 384). Initial production costs were reportedly less than $10,000. The film received an expensive overhaul in post-production, funded by the studio that picked up and distributed it. The news created a buzz in independent film circles, and the movie became a cult hit. For

15.1 *Easy Rider* engaged a new generation of filmgoers.

many budding *cinéastes* (filmmakers), it was a potent symbol of how quirky, personal film-making was still possible in an age of special effects extravaganzas.

Though *Titanic* and *El Mariachi* seem to be polar opposites, the media coverage surrounding each film's release was remarkably consistent. Stories focused on production costs and box office receipts, on the struggle of one director (Cameron) to justify his extravagance and of the other (Rodriguez) to transcend the limitations of "guerrilla" film-making. In other words, the discourse about the two films emphasized the fact that cinema is an industry.

Although economic practices have always shaped the film industry, increasingly, the business side of filmmaking determines the way film lovers and casual fans think and talk about movies. Magazines such as *Vanity Fair* and *Entertainment Weekly* routinely publish articles on the powerful players in Hollywood, many of whom are not movie stars, but financially successful producers and executives. Newspapers, television news, and entertainment magazines all publicize statistics on opening box office receipts, promising that a film's financial success or failure gets more public scrutiny than aesthetic considerations.

Whereas Part II of this book focused on films as texts to be watched, studied, and thoughtfully interpreted and Part III has looked at film and culture, this final chapter considers films from a strictly economic perspective, as products to be consumed. It looks at films as commodities whose quality, appeal, and profitability are shaped by the structure of the industry, by methods of production, distribution, and marketing, and by technological developments. More specifically, the discussion focuses on important changes in the structure of the film industry and in business practices—notably industry consolidation—that have shaped film and culture in the post-studio era. It concludes by examining a major technological development that has complemented industry consolidation—digital technology—and considers its impact on the way viewers experience films.

● The Changing Structure of the Film Industry

From Oligopolies to Conglomerates

During Hollywood's golden age, from the 1920s through the 1940s, five major studios dominated the industry. **Vertical integration**—where a few powerful companies controlled the industry from the top down by making, distributing, and exhibiting films in their own theaters—helped the studios guarantee stable box office receipts through practices such as **block booking** (forcing exhibitors to rent a studio's less lucrative films along with the sure box office successes). But the Supreme Court's 1948 Paramount Decree declared that the five majors and three minors had been engaged in monopolistic practices, colluding to keep independent producers out of their theaters. This decision forced Paramount, Warner Bros., Loew's/MGM, Twentieth Century Fox, and RKO to divest themselves of their theater holdings. But although the majors relinquished their theater chains,

15.2 Low-budget action from *El Mariachi*.

they maintained their hold over distribution and began to seek methods for increasing profits through distribution.

The majors began investing in and distributing smaller, independent films rather than producing their own. This defensive economic practice had implications for film style and culture more generally. Studios used this strategy because it reduced risk; independent productions with small budgets didn't have to rely on huge audiences to turn a profit. At the same time, independent directors were emboldened to explore challenging subject matter and to experiment with style. During the late 1960s and 1970s, American films became more adventurous. Films such as *Easy Rider*, *The Wild Bunch* (Sam Peckinpah 1969), *Medium Cool*, and *Woodstock* (Michael Wadleigh 1970) shook up the industry and engaged younger audiences (figs. **15.1**, p. 382, **15.3**). "Hollywood Renaissance" filmmakers addressed social and political issues head-on and rejected the classical style in favor of more daring approaches borrowed from international art cinema directors.

By the early 1970s, Hollywood studios had made significant headway in reviving themselves commercially through the work of independent directors. This revival was solidified in 1972, when audiences swarmed to Paramount's *The Godfather*. Director Francis Ford Coppola was, like many of his peers, an independent committed to making personal films. Coppola accepted Paramount Studio's offer to direct a screen adaptation of Mario Puzo's novel *The Godfather* in order to finance his production studio, Zoetrope, and his next personal project, *The Conversation*. Paramount's gamble paid off, and the film surpassed *Gone with the Wind* as the top box office grossing film of all time, taking in $86.2 million (Biskind, p. 163).

The film marked the studios' re-emergence and renewed an emphasis on production. That interest was facilitated by conglomeration, which began in 1966, when Gulf and Western bought Paramount. Since then, all of the major studios

15.3 *Woodstock*—another film that attracted young audiences.

Chapter 15: Cinema as Industry

and several minors—including Paramount, Warner Bros., MGM/UA, Twentieth Century Fox, Universal, and Columbia—have been absorbed into larger media corporations as part of a wide array of holdings. Under the *laissez-faire* economic policies of the Reagan administration in the 1980s, studios were allowed to merge with conglomerates that also owned theater chains.

Media conglomeration effectively re-established vertical integration because mergers provided studios with distribution and exhibition outlets, including cable and satellite television, video and DVD rental chains, and internet service providers. Rupert Murdoch, who owns the Fox television network, CBS/Fox video distribution, and Deluxe film labs, purchased Twentieth Century Fox. In 1993, Viacom added Paramount to its list of holdings, which included MTV, Nickelodeon, Showtime, and various television stations. Viacom went on to buy Blockbuster, "creating for itself an automatic distribution outlet for its product" (Allen, p. 37). Pro-business government policies effectively rendered the Paramount Decree irrelevant and encouraged virtual monopolies on production and distribution, only now on a global scale.

Horizontal Integration and Synergy

The corporate mergers that began in 1966 and continued unabated through the 1980s and 1990s not only revived vertical integration; they also produced **horizontal integration**, aligning complementary businesses and allowing companies to expand "across" the entertainment industry. This industrial shift has influenced the way films function as cultural experiences: for one thing, movies rarely are seen as discrete aesthetic experiences but, rather, are part and parcel of large-scale acts of consumption.

The reason for this is that studios take advantage of market synergy: they use movie releases to make money in many venues simultaneously. Film scholar Jon Lewis describes how Time-Warner earned massive profits from *Batman* (Tim Burton 1989) by licensing the DC comic character; taking a share of profits from shirts, toys, and other merchandise sold at Warner Bros. outlet stores and elsewhere; showing the film on Time-Warner's cable companies throughout the country; selling the soundtrack album through Time-Warner record labels; and selling videos, DVDs, and laser discs through a Time-Warner label. All of these profits were over and above the film's $250 million gross from theatrical exhibition. Not only did this merchandising add to profits—it also marketed the film. Of course, the film also received free promotional coverage via Time-Warner's news magazines: *Time*, *Life*, and *Entertainment Weekly* (Lewis, p. 103).

Globalization

Another effect of the wave of mergers has been the globalization of the Hollywood film industry. As of 2004, Universal Studios and its subsidiaries are part of France's conglomerate Vivendi; Columbia Pictures and its subsidiaries are owned by Japan's Sony Corporation; and Twentieth Century Fox is part of Australian Rupert Murdoch's ever-burgeoning

15.4 Audiences line up to see a Hollywood blockbuster.

empire. Though still based within the United States, the other three major studios—Warner Bros., Disney, and Paramount—are part of international conglomerates. Of course, the nature of corporate structure is transitory. In 2003, the cable company Comcast made an unsuccessful bid to become the world's largest media corporation by acquiring Disney through a hostile takeover, suggesting the ongoing nature of media conglomerization.

Corporate conglomeration has bolstered Hollywood's ability to compete in the domestic and foreign markets; its position of dominance is unrivaled (fig. **15.4**). Currently, American films capture between 80% and 90% of Continental Europe's box office returns (Cohen). American films took in 90% of Britain's box office receipts in 1990 (Hill, p. 101). In Spain, one of Europe's largest film markets, American films took 78.9% of the box office receipts in 2002 (Riambau, p. 56).

In country after country, Hollywood gained a foothold thanks to three business practices. First, the studios built multiplex theaters in foreign markets to guarantee an adequate number of screens for Hollywood's products. These attracted new patrons by promising them a luxurious setting, allowing the studios to raise ticket prices (Thompson and Bordwell, p. 709). Second, the industry's horizontal and vertical integration gave the major studios economic advantages over smaller, local companies who couldn't afford to invest in saturation marketing campaigns. Finally, the industry hired lobbyists to negotiate for more lenient trade agreements that favored American exports.

Some nations took steps to check the American juggernaut. France, traditionally regarded as the purveyor of one of the most intellectually stimulating film cultures, has repeatedly led Europe's charge to limit Hollywood's influence. The European Union succeeded in keeping film out of the General Agreement on Tariffs and Trade when it was finalized in December 1993, yet Hollywood's power grew unabated. In 1994, the major Hollywood studios earned more money abroad than domestically (Thompson and Bordwell, p. 709).

Industry Labor Practices

As in any industry, the film industry's labor force, its location, and its wages all play critical roles in determining the quality and profitability of the product. In the contemporary Hollywood industry, three trends have emerged as a result of the global marketplace for labor and ideas: the **outsourcing** of labor, **runaway productions**, and the concentration of creative and intellectual control.

Outsourcing

In the studio era, major studios kept production within the confines of studio back lots, which contained the sets, equipment, costumes, and personnel needed to complete a project. If a scene required location shooting, cohesive units traveled together to complete the work. Under the unit production system, an effective team of technicians would work together on project after project. Today, studios outsource much of the labor involved in shooting a picture. On a given production, one independent firm might handle lighting, while another might construct the required sets. The motivation for sub-contracting the work is financial. For example, Asian inkers and colorists do much of Disney's animation work at a fraction of the wages American workers would demand (Thompson and Bordwell, p. 707).

The highest proportion of labor costs is paid to movie stars in the form of exorbitant fees and percentages of the profits. Popular stars cannot be replaced or outsourced, and their involvement can make or break a movie at the box office. However, some industry insiders and film scholars have begun to examine the economic, social, and psychological implications of digitally rendered performers and stars, called **synthespians**. Will audiences respond to computer-generated characters the same way they respond to human stars? While the much reviled Jar Jar Binks of *Phantom Menace* (George Lucas 1999) offers one answer (no!), the enthusiasm with which fans received Gollum in the *Lord of the Rings* trilogy suggests audiences can respond to computer-generated figures.

Furthermore, the popularity of reality television programming—where ordinary people perform rather than movie stars—is another trend that threatens to undermine the traditional star system. Reality TV made its way onto the big screen with films such as *The Real Cancun* (Rick de Oliveira 2003), the tagline for which reads, "No script, no actors, and no rules."

Runaway Productions

For studio executives, runaway productions (films shot outside the U.S.) make economic sense, because it is often cheaper to fly an entire crew overseas to shoot in a one-off set (or on location) using local technicians, than it is to pay the requisite union wages in the United States. In 2002, Canada earned more money through foreign-financed productions than any other country—a total of $1.7 billion (Seguin). Rather than shooting the Civil War epic *Cold Mountain* (Anthony Minghella 2003) in the hills of North Carolina, where the novel is set, Miramax opted to film in the Carpathian Mountains in Romania (fig. **15.5**).

15.5 The Carpathian Mountains of Romania were the location used for *Cold Mountain*, a story set in North Carolina.

But these decisions put studio executives at odds with domestic industries, because the money local economies would have taken in during a shoot is instead spent outside the U.S. If it had been made during the 1990s, *Cold Mountain* might have been shot in North Carolina, which had been recognized as a hospitable climate for filmmaking through tax incentives designed to lure production teams into the state.

Creative Centralization

Although the film industry's labor force is now decentralized via the practice of outsourcing, the production of ideas has become more centralized, owing to the horizontal organization of the industry. Unless screenwriters work for one of the massive media conglomerates, there are fewer and fewer markets for their ideas. The expenditures of six media companies account for three-quarters of the total spending on screenwriting in the U.S. ("Tangled Webs"). Fearing the intellectual consequences of the conglomerates' increasing control of content production, The Writers Guild of America recently argued that the current market place stifles creativity, either by absorbing new, creative talent into impersonal conglomerates that churn out standardized product or by ignoring this talent altogether.

As outsourcing, runaway productions, and creative consolidation illustrate, film industry practices that may at first glance seem to have little to do with social or aesthetic issues do in fact have a significant impact on film and culture.

● Films as Products

To illustrate the way industrial practices shape viewers' experiences of film, this section discusses how film industry practices of the 1970s and '80s created the **blockbuster** and the **high concept film**. Those industrial products, and the saturation marketing used to promote them, in turn prompted a backlash: the independent film culture of the late 1980s.

The Blockbuster

The Godfather taught the studios the importance of the blockbuster: a film that swamps all competition, in part based on the sheer number of prints in circulation at once.

The Godfather, *Jaws*, and *Star Wars* transformed the way Hollywood distributed and marketed its product to the public. During the 1950s and '60s, studios commonly used a tactic called **roadshowing**. The film would have a lengthy run in a few premier theaters to generate word-of-mouth publicity before being distributed more broadly. With *The Godfather*, studios began booking prints in as many theaters as possible, saturating the market with a single film to make a film's opening weekend an event. Studios realized that they could count on the press to cover its opening weekend, luring audiences into the theater with peer pressure: "Everyone else is seeing the film, so I guess I should too."

In fact, one of the economic justifications for the multiplex was not to offer patrons more diversity or convenience but, rather, to guarantee that major releases could open on more screens simultaneously. Universal opened *Jaws* in 495 theaters nationwide. By the year 2000, major releases typically opened on two to three thousand screens.

The goal of guaranteeing a blockbuster has had a tremendous impact on film style. Hollywood catered to general audiences by producing less risky material, often based on novels or television series that have a built in or "pre-sold" audience. *The Godfather* was based on Mario Puzo's already popular novel. *Jaws*, also a popular novel, appealed to an even broader audience, becoming a family event. In fact, a survey of several influential blockbusters of the 1970s reveals a steady trend away from intellectual and moral complexity and toward fantasy: *The Godfather* (1972; fig. **15.6**), *Jaws* (1975), *Star Wars* (1977), *Raiders of the Lost Ark* (1981), and *E.T.* (1982; fig. **15.7**). That trend has continued in the late 1990s, with *Titanic*, and in 2001–3 with the *Lord of the Rings* trilogy.

15.6 *The Godfather* was one of many films from the 1970s based on a successful novel.

15.7 *E.T.* was part of a trend toward fantasy in the 1980s.

The High Concept Film

Hollywood's movement away from complexity and ambiguity and toward simple entertainment coalesced in the high concept film, which fuses star power, genre appeal, and a basic scenario into a bankable package. *Titanic*, for example, could be, "Romeo and Juliet meet on the ill-fated luxury liner." High concept appropriates and combines the most identifiable

traits from other films, stars, and popular trends into a 25-word marketable pitch that appeals to financially minded studio executives. According to screenwriter Howard Rodman, pitching a screenplay has become tantamount to "writing a prospectus for a stock offering" (quoted in Maltby, p. 38).

The practice allows studios to combine already established and successful ingredients into one enticing morsel that the domestic and international markets will find easy to digest. The appeal of the high concept film is that audiences, both domestic and foreign, can readily understand its basic premise and admire its stars, improving its chances of profitability.

Saturation Marketing

The rise of the blockbuster film coincided with the rise of national marketing campaigns. Studios launched nationwide marketing blitzes, which bombarded the public with ads in newspapers, magazines, television, and radio.

The winning synergetic strategy for marketing a blockbuster, according to MCA/Universal marketing executive Elizabeth Gelfand, is to make merchandising deals in three venues: toys, fast food, and video games (quoted in Seagrave, p. 242). Steven Spielberg's *Jurassic Park* still stands tall as one of the monsters of market synergy (fig. **15.8**). By the time MCA/Universal released the film in 1993, the studio had made licensing deals with toy company Kenner Products, McDonald's, Sega games, Nintendo games, K-Mart, Weetabix, Pepsi, Coca-Cola, and Nisson foods; "sales of licensed merchandising passing $1 billion nine months after the film's release" (Seagrave, p. 242). As film historian Peter Bart puts it, movie releases are highly orchestrated events: "Today a movie is unveiled, not with a quietly orchestrated build, but with a cosmic paroxysm, a global spasm of hype involving giant marketing partners like McDonald's and a profligate network on the Super Bowl or the Olympics" (quoted in Allen, p. 55).

Saturation marketing has led to the expansion of advertising budgets for most Hollywood productions: the advertising budget for *Austin Powers: The Spy Who Shagged Me* (Jay Roach 1999), for example, outweighed its production budget (Thompson and Bordwell, p. 684).

15.8 *Jurassic Park* took market synergy to new levels.

Independent Film Culture

Independent filmmaking has always been a part of American film culture, but in the 1980s, audiences and filmmakers alike began to identify a movement opposed to corporate filmmaking. A number of independent filmmakers who debuted low-budget,

idiosyncratic films in the 1980s have garnered larger audiences and international reputations for their work, including Charles Burnett (fig. **15.9**), Joel and Ethan Coen, Todd Haynes, Jim Jarmusch, David Lynch, John Sayles, and Steven Soderbergh, whose *Sex, Lies, and Videotape* (1989) was a breakthrough film for contemporary independent production.

In the most literal sense, an independent film is not financed by a major Hollywood studio. Independent filmmakers secure funds by seeking out sponsors, drumming up investors, or borrowing money from friends and relatives. They often present an alternative sensibility, in terms of both their low production values and their autonomy from large-scale corporate interests.

Independent filmmakers are freer to explore complex topics and social issues that may be off-limits to major studios afraid of offending their general audience. The New Queer Cinema of the early 1990s offered complex representations of gay and lesbian culture in Haynes's *Poison* (1990), *Paris Is Burning* (Jennie Livingston 1990; fig. **15.10**), and *My Own Private Idaho* (Gus Van Sant 1991). Jim Jarmusch's portrayals of foreigners adrift in American culture (*Down by Law* [1986], *Mystery Train* [1989]), John Sayles's exploration of race relations and labor politics (*Matewan* [1987]), and Mary Harron's feminist re-evaluation of the cult of Andy Warhol (*I Shot Andy Warhol* [1996]) are far more critical of American culture than mainstream films. Smaller independent films can earn less gross but still make a profit. For example, Darren Aronofsky's downbeat thriller π (1998) made a 4 million dollar return on a 300,000 dollar investment (Thompson and Bordwell, p. 696).

Two Independent Institutions: Sundance and Miramax

In 1981 actor and director Robert Redford founded the Sundance Institute, a non-profit organization providing training and financial support for emerging screenwriters and directors. The institute was long associated with the Sundance Film Festival in Park City, Utah, a showcase for independent filmmaking. The independent movement gained momentum in the early 1990s, when a string of small films became box office hits—most notably *The Crying Game* (Neil Jordan 1992), *Pulp Fiction, Clerks* (Kevin Smith 1994), and *Sling Blade* (Billy Bob Thornton 1996).

Audiences in the 1990s gained greater access to independent films, thanks to an increasing number of film festivals as well as more opportunities to see independent films on cable and satellite TV. By the end of the decade, independent film was a household phrase, familiar even to those with the most conventional tastes.

Some critics argue that the popularity of the movement has made independent cinema just another part of the mainstream, threatening the idiosyncratic approach to filmmaking that attracted audiences in the first place. Large conglomerates now seek to maximize profits by distributing lower-budget independent films. This phenomenon played itself out in the case of *The Blair Witch Project* (Daniel Myrick and Eduardo Sánchez 1999). Made for $20,000, the film was picked up by Artisan entertainment for $1 million at the 1999 Sundance Film Festival and became one of the most successful independent films ever, grossing more than $200 million.

Connections between Sundance and studio conglomerates have created a perception (accurate or not) that the festival showcases only directors with potentially profitable films or who are interested in making conventional industry films. The philosophy that such corporate connections compromise creativity inspired the Slamdance Festival, an alternative to the alternative, whose name suggests its derisive attitude toward Sundance.

The history of Miramax pictures contributes to the perception that truly independent cinema is a thing of the past. Disney acquired Miramax, a pioneer in independent film, in the mid-1990s, and many critics allege that the parent company's need to promote "family values" has overshadowed any alternative perspectives. Miramax became infamous for mounting lavish campaigns designed to promote its Academy Award-nominated films. As of 2004, the relationship between parent company (Disney) and subsidiary (Miramax) had frayed to the point of unraveling. At issue was the decision by Disney head Michael Eisner not to release Michael Moore's controversial documentary *Fahrenheit 911* and Harvey and Bob Weinstein's desire to distribute the film, which they finally did through another company.

In short, the industry's horizontal and vertical integration has filmmakers, film lovers, and film scholars alike wondering whether alternative forms of filmmaking will continue to challenge Hollywood hegemony in any meaningful way.

● Film and the New Technology

As with any industry, the film industry relies on technological advances to facilitate production and distribution of the product. While the impact of newer digital technology on filmmaking has been discussed in Chapter Five, it's also the case that digital technologies and the convergence of communication and information technologies promise to play an important role in marketing and exhibition. Digital technology is literally changing films themselves, as well as the circumstances of their consumption.

From an economic perspective, films are just one among many entertainment commodities in the market place. Whereas early film exhibitors created beautiful movie palaces, contemporary studios, eager to sell movies as both experiences and products, have embraced new exhibition technologies such as cable, broadband, and DVD. They maximize profits by selling a film many times over. However, in the process, they are changing the way the medium is perceived as an aesthetic and cultural institution.

Until the advent of television in the 1950s and the VHS tape in the 1970s, movie theaters were the primary venues for seeing Hollywood films. In 1946, the average American filmgoer saw twenty-nine films in the theater every year; in 1984, that number had dropped to five. Although the industry has initially feared that every new development in viewing technology will undermine profitability, these fears repeatedly prove to be unfounded. Audiences haven't stopped going to the movies. More importantly, the studios have learned how to diversify and capitalize on each new development, for example by selling network broadcast rights to their films and repackaging different versions of the same film on DVDs. In 1995, the home video market accounted for more than half of the major film corporations' revenues worldwide, whereas theatrical releases accounted for one fourth and television for around one fifth of revenues (Seagrave, p. 192).

The Rise of the DVD

Home-viewing technology entered the digital age in the 1990s. DVDs allow studios to sell films multiple times: at the theater, with the initial DVD release, and with any subsequent releases of "Collector's Editions" that include new bonus features.

For the industry, one significant advantage of the technology is its ability to augment synergetic market forces. DVDs allow studios to advertise other products better than videotapes. Videotape technology had limited the film industry's ability to sell space. The Frito-Lay corporation complained to MPAA President Jack Valenti that the company would not pay top-tier advertising rates for ads placed on videotapes because the fast forward button allowed viewers to skip commercials! Ever able to use technology in the service of profits, the industry learned from this experience. DVD technology has "solved" that problem from the film industry's standpoint. Digital encoding can actually prevent viewers from forwarding through the advertising section of a DVD.

For the viewer, DVD technology represents a significant shift from the videotape. Unlike the videotape, where moving among scenes requires rewinding and fast forwarding, DVDs permit viewers to jump from scene to scene instantaneously. Furthermore, the immense capacity of disks to store digitized information means that bonus materials and commentary tracks by directors and cinematographers are made available to viewers. These features have now become part and parcel of the marketing of DVDs.

DVD technology has provoked a number of debates. Film scholar Thomas Doherty explores the DVD's apparent advantages over videotape as a consumer product and argues that, whether or not the advantages are exaggerated is, in fact, irrelevant. As consumers must do when any industry engages in technological innovation, they are in the midst of

The Dream Palaces

The earliest venues for watching a program of short one-reelers were vaudeville theaters, lecture halls, and churches. Around 1905, permanent storefront theaters called nickelodeons emerged. Then, after the popular success of Italian spectacles such as *Quo Vadis?* (Enrico Guazzoni 1913) and *Cabiria* (Giovanni Pastrone 1914), the industry turned to feature-length films.

As comic shorts gave way to these dramatic feature-length epics, exhibitors built monumental movie theaters to attract and accommodate middle-class audiences (fig. **15.11**). The Regent and Strand theaters in New York City, which opened in the 1910s, were the first such "dream palaces." With more than 3,000 seats and a thirty-piece orchestra, the Strand's lavish interior was appointed with a marble foyer and crystal chandelier (Cook, p. 39). By the late 1920s, most movie theaters were air-conditioned and summertime became the peak season for film going (Gomery, p. 51).

15.11 A publicity still of a typical early movie palace.

a conversion cycle and must accept the inevitable shift to the new technology. Doherty admits:

> Of course, not everyone welcomes the tyranny of DVD technology. To many educated consumers, and consumer educators, compulsory conversion seems but another sinister media-conglomerate racket. Still, whether welcomed with open arms or eyed with Luddite suspicion, resistance is as futile as the cycle is predictable. Buy the new hardware, purchase shelves of new DVDs [. . .] and then repeat the process upon the arrival of a brand-new format. (Doherty)

Not everyone considers technological change neutral in its impact on the film medium. Rather than focusing on the DVD as part of a consumer cycle, James Morrison suggests that the DVD has adversely affected film culture. The DVD's ability to store vast amounts of information, including a "director's cut," may ultimately compromise a director's vision. Directors must sign contracts that restrict the content of their films when they are screened in theaters, because studios expect to "put back in the DVD what was banned in the theatrical release, and use it as a selling point" (Morrison, p. 52). Morrison also questions the value of the supplementary material on DVDs because it emphasizes the commercial rather than the aesthetic possibilities of the medium:

> If the advent of DVD has contributed a greater awareness to many filmgoers' experience of movies, it's of a very specific kind, a cultish type of knowledge, in which localized background detail used to sell the disc, or production tidbits commemorated in the filmmakers' commentaries on DVDs, turn into a new form of mythology. (Morrison, p. 52)

In his view, the DVD encourages commodity fetishism (endowing consumer goods with mystical qualities), enabling viewers to think of films as collectible items prized only for their connection to celebrated personalities.

A case in point might be Fox Studios' 2003 release of *The Alien Quadrilogy*, a collector's set of nine discs containing 58 hours of *Alien*. Such an overwhelming amount of deleted scenes and "making of" documentaries doesn't attract casual fans as much as *Alien* "completists," bent on owning the latest—and longest—version of the films and fixated by the directors' personal accounts of production history. Much like an "all you can eat buffet," such DVDs attract consumers by selling quantity of material, not necessarily quality.

Film and the Internet: Blurring Boundaries

DVD players and televisions are no longer the only hardware appropriate for home viewing. Personal computers provide an array of viewing experiences. Beyond playing DVDs, computers grant access to trailers and full-length films on the internet. Cinephiles and critics widely tout the internet's ability to democratize film culture by providing a means to distribute movies that by-pass commercial theaters.

The internet does offer a host of new possibilities, but it has primarily been used as a marketing device. The following excerpt from J.P. Telotte's analysis of the marketing campaign for *The Blair Witch Project* demonstrates the way films have been absorbed by new entertainment and communication technologies. Telotte argues that the marketing campaign blurred the distinction between watching films and surfing the internet. If seeing a film is indistinguishable from absorbing information from a computer monitor, what are the implications for film as an aesthetic form and social institution?

Telotte describes the film's website, which had links to a number of other sites that purveyed the fiction that three documentary filmmakers had disappeared while in search of the Blair Witch:

> All of these elements, the film's backstory, if you will, elaborately propagate the notion of authenticity, attesting to the film as, quite literally, a "found footage" type of documentary rather than a fictional work, and more particularly, as a different sort of attraction than the movies usually offer

15.12 *The Blair Witch Project*—a film for the internet age.

[. . .] [T]hey suggest we see the film not as film, but as one more artifact, along with the materials gathered together at the website, which we might view in order to better understand a kind of repressed or hidden reality.

Thus, the Blair Witch site [. . .] points in various ways away from the film's privileged status as a product of the entertainment industry. Or, more precisely, its "project" is [. . .] to suggest, in effect, that this particular film is as much a part of everyday life as the Internet, that it extends the sort of unfettered knowledge and access that the Internet seems to offer, and that its pleasures, in fact, closely resemble those of the electronic medium with which its core audience is so familiar. (Telotte)

Telotte argues that, through the website, the film presented itself not as a film but as something more akin to a story being circulated on the internet—the electronic medium so familiar to its core audience (fig. **15.12**). This blurring, Telotte argues, is a portent of cinema's future in the digital age. The internet "threatens, much as television did, to supplant the film industry, in part by offering its own pleasures to a young audience that has grown up with electronic narratives" (Telotte). In other words, digital technology isn't merely changing the special effects in movies; nor is it simply shifting the viewing practices of audiences. It's also changing a culture's ideas about movies and stories and their place in everyday life.

Digital Projection

Digital technology isn't just altering the dynamics of home viewing. The movie theater is also gradually treading on digital terrain or **digital cinema**. During the 1990s, American movie theaters made large-scale conversions to digital sound systems with relative ease, appealing to an audience that favored action films dominated by sound and visual effects. On June 18, 1999, during the premieres of *Star Wars, Episode 1: The Phantom Menace* and *An Ideal Husband* (Oliver Parker 1999), audiences were treated to the first public screenings using digital projection.

Since its debut, there has been much debate regarding the feasibility of digital projection and its merits. Above all, its advocates promise viewers sharp, unblemished images that cannot be damaged or destroyed by the dirt, scratches, and deterioration that plague celluloid film prints. In late 2003, film scholars Nigel Culkin and Keith Randle predicted that "d-cinema will overtake the quality of conventional cinema within the next two years" (Culkin and Randle, p. 79). But there are financial advantages of digital projection as well. Currently, studios spend in the neighborhood of $2,000 per celluloid print, so the distribution costs for wide releases of a film can exceed $5 million (Carvell). Digital systems will allow for immediate, inexpensive electronic distribution of films. Furthermore, the system would provide theater owners with more flexibility. If, for example, a title becomes a sudden sleeper hit, multiplex owners could re-route its screenings to a bigger theater with a simple keystroke instead of having to dismantle cumbersome reels of celluloid.

Some industry insiders, however, are wary about the costs of conversion to digital projection. If the price of digital projectors dropped to $50,000 per machine, converting the estimated 33,000 screens in the U.S. would cost $1.6 billion (Carvell). As of 2002, cost estimates for new projectors were still between $150,000 and $180,000 apiece (Belton). These estimates say nothing about converting cinemas in foreign markets. Needless to say, there is much debate over who should pay for this conversion, and how.

Some scholars and critics also raise aesthetic arguments against digital projection. One of the advantages of digital projection systems is that they will allow theaters to broadcast sporting events or televised concerts. While such dramatic changes in programming would surely attract more diverse audiences, they would also fundamentally alter the social function of the movie theater, transforming screens into glorified television sets. Furthermore, cinema purists such as Roger Ebert proclaim that seeing a digital film simply does not measure up to the experience of seeing a 35 mm print. In fact, Ebert has championed a new film format, MaxiVision 48, which "produces a picture so breathtakingly clear it is like 3-D in reverse" and would "handle any existing 35 mm film format—unlike digital projection, which would make obsolete a century of old prints" (Ebert). Finally, film preservationists are concerned that film culture will be lost if it is stored as digital data. Whereas polyester safety film has a shelf life of approximately a hundred years, current methods for storing digital information have an effective shelf life of five to ten years (Belton).

These debates regarding the merits of digital projection underline the key tenets of this chapter: that aesthetic and cultural concerns in film studies are inextricably tied to the industry's structure and technology. Analysis of film as an art form should not discount its status as an industrial product. Given mainstream films' entertaining narratives, dynamic images, and lush soundtracks, audiences often forget that any movie is a complexly layered work: an aesthetic experience, a form of cultural expression, and an industrial product. Because it influences the way people experience and consume them, the film industry plays a major role in determining the cultural meaning of films.

Works Consulted

Allen, Michael. *Contemporary US Cinema*. Edinburgh Gate: Longman/Pearson, 2003.

Belton, John. "Digital Cinema: A False Revolution," *October*, 100 (2002). Academic Search Elite. Online. Ebscohost. January 21, 2004.

Biskind, Peter. *Easy Riders, Raging Bulls: How the Sex-Drugs-and Rock 'n' Roll Generation Saved Hollywood*. New York: Simon and Schuster, 1998.

Carvell, Tim. "Hello, Mr. Chips (Goodbye, Mr. Film)," *Fortune*, 140 (1999). Academic Search Elite. Online. Ebscohost. January 21, 2004.

Cohen, Tyler. "Cinema: Ticket for One?" *Forbes*, April 28, 2003: n. page. Online. Safari. February 6, 2004.

Cook, David. "Auteur Cinema and the 'Film Generation' in 1970s Hollywood," in *The New American Cinema*, ed. Jon Lewis. Durham, NC: Duke University Press, 1998, pp. 11–37.

Cook, David. *A History of Narrative Film*. New York: Norton, 1996.

Cowie, Peter. *Coppola: A Biography*. New York: Da Capo, 1994.

Culkin, Nigel, and Keith Randle. "Digital Cinema: Opportunities and Challenges." *Convergence*, 9/4 (2003), pp. 79–98.

Denby, David. "The Moviegoers: Why Don't People Love the Right Movies Anymore?" in *The Best American Movie Writing 1999*, ed. Peter Bogdanovich. New York: St. Martin's, 1999, pp. 6–19.

Doherty, Thomas. "DVD, PDQ," *The Chronicle of Higher Education*, April 26, 2002: n. page. Online. Safari. May 1, 2002.

Ebert, Roger. "Start the Revolution Without Digital," *volksmovie.com*. http://www.volksmovie.com/rants/archive/rogerebert.html

Ellis, Jack, and Virginia Wright Wexman. *A History of Film*, 5th edn. Boston: Allyn and Bacon, 2002.

Fellini, Federico. *Fellini on Fellini*. Trans. Isabel Quigley. Cambridge and New York: Da Capo Press, 1996.

Gomery, Douglas. "The Hollywood Studio System," in *The Oxford History of World Cinema*, ed. Geoffrey Nowell-Smith. Oxford and New York: Oxford University Press, 1996, pp. 43–53.

Hill, John. "British Film Policy," in *Film Policy: International, National, and Regional Perspectives*, ed. Albert Moran. London: Routledge, 1996, pp. 101–13.

Kramer, Peter. "Post-Classical Hollywood," in *American Cinema and Hollywood*, ed. John Hill and Pamela Church Gibson. New York: Oxford University Press, 2000, pp. 63–83.

Lewis, Jon. "Money Matters: Hollywood in the Corporate Era," in *New American Cinema*, ed. Jon Lewis. Durham, NC: Duke University Press, 1998, pp. 87–121.

Maltby, Richard. "'Nobody Knows Everything': Post-Classical Historiographies and Consolidated Entertainment," in *Contemporary Hollywood Cinema*, ed. Steve Neale and Murray Smith. London: Routledge, 1998, pp. 21–57.

Morrison, James. "Buzz Factor: The DVD Release of Todd Solondz's *Storytelling* itself Tells a Story about Contemporary Film Culture," *The Independent Weekly*, 19/30 (July 17–23, 2002), p. 52.

Riambau, Esteve. "Public Money and Private Business (Or, How to Survive Hollywood's Imperialism): Film Production in Spain (1984–2002)," *Cineaste*, 29/1 (2004), pp. 56–61.

Riding, Alan. "Filmmakers Seek Protection from U.S. Dominance," *New York Times*, February 5, 2003, p. B3.

Rosenbaum, Jonathan. *Movies as Politics*. Berkeley: University of California Press, 1997.

Schamus, James. "A Rant," *The End of Cinema As We Know It: American Film in the Nineties*, ed. Jon Lewis. New York: New York University Press, 2001.

Schatz, Thomas. *The Genius of the System: Hollywood Filmmaking in the Studio Era*. New York: Pantheon, 1988.

Seagrave, Kerry. *American Films Abroad: Hollywood's Domination of the World's Movie Screens from the 1890s to the Present*. Jefferson: McFarland, 1997.

Seguin, Denis. "The Battle for Hollywood North." *Canadian Business*, 76 (2003). Academic Search Elite. Online. Ebscohost. January 21, 2004.

Sklar, Robert. *Film: An International History of the Medium*, 2nd edn. Upper Saddle River, NJ: Prentice-Hall, 2002.

"Tangled Webs." *The Economist*, 363 (2002). Academic Search Elite. Online. Ebscohost. January 21, 2004.

Telotte, J.P. "*The Blair Witch Project* Project," *Film Quarterly*. 54 (2001). Academic Search Elite. Online. Ebscohost. January 21, 2004.

Thompson, Kristin, and David Bordwell. *Film History: An Introduction*, 2nd edn. Boston: McGraw-Hill, 2003.

Vasey, Ruth. "The Worldwide Spread of Cinema," *The Oxford History of World Cinema*, ed. Geoffrey Nowell-Smith. Oxford: Oxford University Press, 1996, pp. 53–62.

Wyatt, Justin. "From Roadshow to Saturation Release: Majors, Independents, and Marketing/Distribution Innovations," in *New American Cinema*, ed. Jon Lewis. Durham, NC: Duke University Press, 1998, pp. 64–86.

Glossary

180-degree rule A continuity editing rule for positioning the camera in order to maintain consistent screen direction. The camera does not move across an imagined line drawn between two characters, for example, because to do so would reverse their positions in the frame.

Academy ratio The aspect ratio of 1.33:1, standardized by the Academy of Motion Picture Art and Sciences until the development of widescreen formats in the 1950s. See also **Aspect ratio**.

ADR (Automatic dialogue replacement) A technique for recording synchronized dialogue in post-production, using a machine that runs forward and backward. Also called "looping," because it is achieved by cutting several identical lengths of developed film and having actors record the dialogue repeatedly.

Aerial shot A shot filmed from an airplane or helicopter.

Analog video A videotape system that records images onto magnetic tape, using electronic signals.

Anamorphic lens A technique for creating a widescreen aspect ratio using regular 35mm cameras and film. During shooting, an anamorphic lens squeezes the image at a ratio of 2:1 horizontally onto a standard film frame. During projection, an anamorphic lens on the projector unsqueezes the image, creating a widescreen aspect ratio during presentation. See also **Aspect ratio**.

Animation Creating the appearance of movement by drawing a series of frames that are projected sequentially, rather than photographing a series of still images.

Anime A style of Japanese animation, distinguished primarily by the fact that it is not all geared for young audiences.

Antagonist A character who in some way opposes the protagonist, leading to protracted conflict.

Aperture A small, variable opening on a camera lens that regulates the amount of light entering the camera and striking the surface of the film.

Aspect ratio The shape of the image onscreen as determined by the width (horizontal dimension) of the frame relative to its height (vertical dimension). An image with an aspect ratio of 1.33:1 (Academy ratio) will be thirty-three percent wider than it is high. See also **Academy ratio**.

Assistant editor A member of a film crew who assists the editor with various tasks, including taking footage to the lab, checking the condition of the negative, cataloguing footage, and supervising optical effects, often produced by an outside company.

Auteur Translates as "author." A term for film directors that was popularized by French film critics and refers to film directors with their own distinctive style.

Available light Also called "natural light," the process of using sunlight rather than artificial studio lights when filming.

Avant-garde film Also called "experimental film" or "underground cinema." The goal of avant-garde filmmakers is not commercial success, but artistic invention. Avant-garde films are generally made by one person or a small group, distributed in very limited ways, and exhibited at specialized venues such as universities, museums, and cinema clubs.

Average shot length The average length in seconds of a series of shots, covering a portion of a film or an entire film. A measure of pace within a scene or in the film as a whole.

Backstory The details of a character's past that emerge as the film unfolds, and which often play a role in character motivation.

Base A flexible celluloid strip that, along with the emulsion layer, comprises 35mm film stock.

Best boy A crew member who assists the gaffer in managing lighting and electrical crews.

Blaxploitation An action film cycle of the late 1960s and early 1970s that featured bold, rebellious African American characters.

Bleach bypass A process of film development that involves leaving the silver grains in the emulsion rather than bleaching them out. This produces desaturated color.

Block booking An outlawed studio era practice, where studios forced exhibitors to book groups of films at once, thus ensuring a market for their failures along with their successes.

Blockbuster A large-budget film whose strategy is to swamp the competition through market saturation.

Blocking A production term referring to coordinating actors' movements with lines of dialogue.

Blue screen A technique used during production to create traveling mattes for special visual effects. Live action is filmed in front of a blue screen and a matte (black mask) created for use when filming a separate background. The live-action footage is joined with the background footage (which essentially has a black hole that the live action fills). See also **Green screen**.

Brechtian distanciation Drawing attention to the process of representation (including narrative and characterization) to break the theatrical illusion and elicit a distanced, intellectual response in the audience.

B-roll Secondary footage that is interspersed with master shots, sometimes in the form of footage shot for another production or archival footage.

Cameo A short screen appearance by a celebrity, playing himself or herself.

Camera distance The space between the camera and the subject it is filming. The effect of camera distance depends on other visual, narrative, and sound details and patterns. While, for example, long shots (with a large distance between camera and subject) may evoke a sense of a character's powerlessness, the specific effect must be considered in relation to a film's overall ideas and themes.

Canted angle Also called a "Dutch angle," a shot resulting from a static camera that is tilted to the right or left, so that the subject in the frame appears at a diagonal.

Cel A transparent sheet on which animation artists draw images. The sheet is laid over an unchanging background, allowing animation artists to draw only the elements that change from frame to frame.

Character actor An actor whose career rests on playing minor or secondary quirky characters rather than leading roles.

Charge coupler device The chip in a video camera that converts the incoming light to an electronic signal.

Chiaroscuro The artful use of light and dark areas in the composition in black and white filmmaking.

Cinerama A widescreen process that uses three cameras, three projectors, and a wide, curved screen.

City symphony A type of short film that blends elements of documentary and avant-garde film to document and often to celebrate the wonder of the modern city.

Classical style A style associated with Hollywood filmmaking of the studio and post-studio eras, in which efficient storytelling, rather than gritty realism or aesthetic innovation, is of paramount importance.

Close-up A shot taken when the camera is so close to a subject that it fills the frame. It is most commonly used for a shot that isolates and encompasses a single actor's face, to emphasize the expression of emotion.

Closure A characteristic of conventional narrative form, where the conclusion of the film wraps up all loose ends in a form of resolution, though not necessarily with a happy ending.

Color consultant A specialist who monitors the processing of color on the set and in the film lab.

Color filter A type of filter that absorbs certain wavelengths but leave others unaffected. On black and white film, color filters lighten or darken tones. On color film, they can produce a range of effects.

Color timing Because film stock is sensitive to the color of light, directors work with film labs in post-production to monitor the color scheme of each scene in a film, making adjustments for consistency and aesthetic effect.

Compilation film A film composed entirely of footage from other films.

Compositing Creating images during post-production by joining together photographic or CGI material shot or created at different times and places.

Composition in depth A technique of arranging the actors on the set to take advantage of deep-focus cinematography, which allows for many planes of depth in the film frame to remain in focus.

Composition The visual arrangement of objects, actors, and space within the frame.

Computer-generated imagery (CGI) Images that originate from computer graphics technology, rather than photography.

Continuity editing Also called "invisible editing," a system devised to minimize the audience's awareness of shot transitions, especially cuts, in order to improve the flow of the story and avoid interrupting the viewer's immersion in it.

Continuity editor A crew member whose job is to maintain consistency in visual details from one shot to the next.

Continuity error Any noticeable but unintended discrepancy from one shot to the next in costume, props, hairstyle, posture, etc.

Crab dolly A wheeled platform with wheels that rotate, so the dolly can change direction.

Crane shot A shot taken from a camera mounted on a crane that moves three-dimensionally in space.

Cut An abrupt shot transition that occurs when Shot A is instantaneously replaced by Shot B. A cut joins two non-consecutive frames of film.

Cutaway A shot that focuses audience attention on precise details that may or may not be the focus of characters.

Dailies Also called "rushes," footage exposed and developed quickly so that the director can assess the day's work.

Day for night The practice of shooting during the day but using filters and underexposure to create the illusion of nighttime.

Deep-focus cinematography A cinematography technique that produces an image with many planes of depth in focus. It can be accomplished by using a small aperture ("stopping down the lens"), a large distance between camera and subject, and/or a lens of short focal length (wide-angle lens).

Dénouement The falling or unraveling action after the climax of a narrative that leads to resolution.

Depth of field The distance that appears in focus in front of and behind the subject. It is determined by the aperture, distance and focal length of lens.

Desaturated Muted, washed out color that contains more white than a saturated color.

Descriptive claim A neutral account of the basic plot and style of a film, a part of a film, or a group of films.

Diegesis The imagined world of the story.

Diffusion filters These filters bend the light coming into the lens, softening and blurring the image.

Digital cinema Also called "d-cinema." Not to be confused with digital cinematography (shooting movies on digital video), this term refers to using digital technologies for exhibition.

Digital compositing Creating an image by combining several elements created separately using computer graphics rather than photographic means.

Digital set extension Using computer graphics to "build" structures connected to the actual architecture on set or location.

Digital video A system for recording images on magnetic tape using a digital signal, that is, an electronic signal comprised of 0s and 1s.

Direct cinema Also called *cinéma vérité*, a documentary style in which the filmmaker attempts to remain as unobtrusive as possible, recording without obvious editorial comment.

Direct sound Sound recorded on a set, on location or, for documentary film, at an actual real-world event, as opposed to dubbed in post-production through ADR or looping.

Director The person in charge of planning the style and look of the film with the production designer and director of photography, working with actors during principal photography, and collaborating with the editor on the final version.

Dissolve A shot transition that involves the gradual disappearance of the image at the same time that a new image gradually comes into view.

Dolly A platform on wheels, used for mobile camera shots.

Double exposure A technique of exposing film frames, then rewinding the film and exposing it again, which results in an image that combines two shots in a single frame.

Dutch angle See Canted angle.

Dye coupler A chemical embedded in the emulsion layer of film stock that, when developed after exposure, releases a particular color dye (red, green, or blue).

Editor A person responsible for putting a film together from a mass of developed footage, making decisions regarding pace, shot transitions, and which scenes and shots will be used.

Emulsion A chemical coating on film stock containing light-sensitive grains.

Episodic A non-standard narrative organization that assumes a "day in the life" quality rather than the highly structured three-act or four part narrative, and that features loose or indirect cause–effect relationships.

Establishing shot In a standard shot sequence, the establishing shot is the first shot. Its purpose is to provide a clear representation of the location of the action.

Ethnographic film A type of documentary film whose purpose is to present the way of life of a culture or subculture.

Evaluative claim A statement that asserts a judgment that a given film or group of films is good or bad, based on specific criteria, which may or may not be stated.

Exposition Dense accumulation of detail conveyed in the opening moments of a film.

Exposure Light striking the emulsion layer of the film, activating light-sensitive grains.

Exposure latitude The measurement of how "forgiving" a film stock is. It determines whether an acceptable image will be produced when the film stock is exposed to too little or too much light.

Extra An uncredited actor, usually hired for crowd scenes.

Extradiegetic Also called "non-diegetic," any element in the film that is not a part of the imagined story world.

Extreme close-up A shot taken from a vantage point so close that only a part of the subject is visible. An extreme close-up of an actor might show only an eye or a portion of the face.

Extreme long shot A shot that makes the human subject very small in relation to his or her environment. The entire figure from head to toe is onscreen and dwarfed by the surroundings.

Extreme wide-angle lens Also called a "fish-eye lens." With a focal length of 15mm or less, this lens presents an extremely distorted image, where objects in the center of the frame appear to bulge toward the camera.

Eye-level shot A shot taken from a level camera located approximately 5' to 6' from the ground, simulating the perspective of a person standing before the action presented.

Eyeline match A continuity editing technique that preserves spatial continuity by using a character's line of vision as motivation for a cut.

Fabula A chronological and complete account of all the events in a narrative. Also referred to as the "story." See *Syuzhet*.

Fade-out A shot transition where shot A slowly disappears as the screen becomes black before shot B appears. A fade-in is the reverse of this process.

Fast A description of film stock that is highly sensitive to light.

Fast motion Recording images at a slower speed than the speed of projection (24 frames per second). Before cameras were motorized, this was called undercranking. Fewer frames are exposed in one minute, so, when projected at 24 f.p.s., that action takes less than a minute on screen and appears unnaturally rapid.

Figure placement and movement The arrangement of actors on screen as a compositional element that suggests themes, character development, emotional content, and visual motifs.

Film stock Thin, flexible material comprised of base and emulsion layers, onto which light rays are focused and which is processed in chemicals to produce film images.

Filter A device used to manipulate the amount and/or color of light entering the lens.

First-person narration A story narrated by one of the characters within the story, using the "I" voice.

Fish-eye lens See Extreme wide-angle lens.

Flashback The non-chronological insertion of events from the past into the present day of the story world.

Flashing Also called "prefogging," a cinematographic technique that exposes raw film stock to light before, during, or after shooting, resulting in an image with reduced contrast. This effect can also be created using digital post-production techniques.

Flashforward The non-chronological insertion of scenes of events yet to happen into the present day of the story world.

Focal length The distance in millimeters from the optical center of a lens to the plane where the sharpest image is formed while focusing on a distant object.

Focus puller A crew member whose job is to measure the distance between the subject and the camera lens, marking the ring on the camera lens, and ensuring that the ring is turned precisely so that the image is in focus.

Fog filter Glass filters whose surface is etched with spots that refract light, so they create the appearance of water droplets in the air.

Foley artist A crew member who works in post-production in a specially equipped studio to create the sounds of the story world, such as the shuffling of shoes on various surfaces for footsteps.

Forced development A technique of "pushing" the film (overdeveloping it) to correct problems of underexposure (resulting from insufficient light during shooting) by increasing image contrast.

Forced perspective A system of constructing and arranging buildings and objects on the set so that they diminish in size dramatically from foreground to background, which creates the illusion of depth.

Formalist style An alternative to classical and realist styles, formalism is a self-consciously interventionist approach that explores ideas, abstraction, and aesthetics rather than focusing on storytelling (as in classical films) or everyday life (as in realist films).

Four-part structure A contemporary modification of the standard three-act structure that identifies a critical turning point at the halfway mark of most narrative films.

Frame narration The plotline that surrounds an embedded tale. The frame narration may or may not be as fully developed as the embedded tale.

Freeze frame Projecting a series of frames of film with the same image, which appears to stop the action.

Front projection A technique to join live action with pre-recorded background images. A projector is aimed at a half-silvered mirror that reflects the background, which the camera records as being located behind the actors.

Frozen time moment A visual effect achieved through the use of photography and digital techniques that appears to stop time and allow the viewer to travel around the subject and view it from a multitude of vantage points.

Gaffer A crew member who reports to the Director of Photography (DP) and is in charge of tasks involving lighting and electrical needs.

Gauge The gauge of the film stock is its width, measured across the frame. Typical sizes are 8mm, 16mm, 35mm and 70mm.

Genre A class or type of film, such as the Western or the horror movie. Films belonging to a particular genre share narrative, visual, and/or sound conventions.

Genre conventions The rules of character, setting, and narrative that films belonging to a genre—such as Westerns, horror films, and screwball comedies—generally obey.

German Expressionism A film style that emerged in the 1910s in Germany. It was heavily indebted to the Expressionist art movement of the time and influenced subsequent horror films and *film noir*.

Glass shot A type of matte shot, created by positioning a pane of optically flawless glass with a painting on it between the camera and scene to be photographed. This combines the painting on the glass with the set or location—seen through the glass—behind it.

Go-motion A digital technique developed by Industrial Light and Magic, which builds movement sequences from single frames of film.

Grain Suspended particles of silver in the film's emulsion, which may become visible in the final image as dots.

Graphic match A shot transition that emphasizes the visual similarities between two consecutive shots.

Green screen A compositing method that allows cinematographers to combine live action and settings that are filmed or created separately. Actors are filmed against a green or blue background. During post-production, this background is filled in with an image through the use of a travelling matte. See also **Blue screen**.

Handheld shot A shot taken by a camera that is held manually rather than supported by a tripod, crane, or Steadicam. Generally, such shots are shaky, owing to the motion of the camera operator.

Hard light Light emitted from a relatively small source positioned close to the subject. It tends to be unflattering because it creates deep shadows and emphasizes surface imperfections.

High–angle shot A shot taken from a camera positioned above the subject, looking down at it.

High concept film A post-studio era Hollywood film designed to appeal to the broadest possible audience by fusing a simple story line with major movie stars and mounting a lavish marketing campaign.

High-key lighting Lighting design that provides an even illumination of the subject, with many facial details washed out. High-key lighting tends to create a hopeful mood, in contrast to low-key lighting.

Horizontal integration A term that refers to the organization of an industry wherein one type of corporation also owns corporations in allied industries, for example, film production and video games.

Hue Color. The strength of a hue is measured by its saturation or desaturation.

Hybrid A film that fuses the conventions of two or more genres.

Insert A shot that interrupts a scene's master shot and may include character reactions or cutaways.

Interlaced scanning A property of older television monitors, where each frame was scanned as two fields: one consisting of all the odd numbered lines, the other all the even lines. If slowed down, the television image would appear to sweep down the screen one line at a time.

Interpretive claim A statement that presents an argument about a film's meaning and significance.

Intertextual reference A narrative, visual, or sound element that refers viewers to other films or works of art.

Iris in A form of shot transition, generally concluding a scene, where a circular mask constricts around the image until the entire frame is black.

Iris out The reverse of Iris in: an iris expands outward until the next shot takes up the entire screen.

Jump cut An abrupt, inexplicable shift in time and place of an action not signaled by an appropriate shot transition.

Kuleshov effect A mental phenomenon by which viewers derive more meaning from the interaction of two sequential shots than from a single shot in isolation.

Lens A glass element on a camera that focuses light rays so that the image of the object appears on the surface of the film.

Letterboxing A process of transferring film to video tapes or DVDs so that the original aspect ratio of the film is preserved.

Line of action The narrative path of the main or supporting characters, also called a plotline. Complex films may have several lines of action.

Line reading The way an actor delivers a line of dialogue, including pauses, inflection, and emotion.

Long shot A camera shot taken at a large distance from the subject. Using the human body as the subject, a long shot captures the entire human form.

Long take A relatively long, uninterrupted shot, generally of a minute or more.

Looping See ADR.

Loose framing A technique of leaving empty space around the subject in the frame, in order to convey openness and continuity of visible space and to imply off-screen space.

Low-angle shot A shot taken from a camera positioned below the subject.

Low-key lighting Lighting design in which the greater intensity of the key light makes it impossible for the fill to eliminate shadows, producing a high-contrast image (with many grades of light and dark), a number of shadows, and a somber mood.

Major studios The five vertically integrated corporations that exerted the greatest control over film production, distribution, and exhibition in the studio era: MGM, Warner Brothers, RKO, Twentieth Century Fox, and Paramount.

Masking A method for producing a wide screen image without special lenses or equipment, using standard film stock and blocking out the top and bottom of the frame to achieve an aspect ratio of 1.85:1.

Master positive The first print made from a film negative.

Master shot A single take that contains an entire scene.

Matte A black masking device used to block out a portion of the frame, usually for the insertion of other images. See also **Blue screen** and **Traveling matte**.

Matte painting A painting used on the set as a portion of the background.

Medium close-up A shot that includes a human figure from the shoulders up.

Medium long shot A shot that depicts a human body from the feet up.

Medium shot A shot depicting the human body from the waist up.

Method acting A style of stage acting developed from the teachings of Constantin Stanislavsky, which trains actors to get into character through the use of emotional memory.

Minor studios Smaller corporations that did not own distribution and/or exhibition companies in the studio era, including Universal, Columbia, and United Artists.

Mixing A process of blending the three elements of the sound track (dialogue, music, and effects) in post-production.

Mockumentary A fiction film (often a comedy) that uses documentary conventions on fictional rather than real-world subject matter.

Montage sequence A series of related scenes joined through elliptical editing that indicates the passage of time.

Morphing An animation technique that uses a computer program to interpolate frames to produce the effect of an object or creature changing gradually into something different. The program calculates the way the image must change in order for the first image to become the second over a series of frames.

Motif Any narrative, visual, or sound element that is repeated and thereby acquires and reflects its significance to the story, characters, or themes of the film.

Narrative A story; a chain of events linked by cause-and-effect logic.

Narrative sequencing The arrangement of images to depict a unified story time.

Natural-key lighting Lighting design where the key light is somewhat more intense than the fill light, so the fill does not eliminate every shadow. The effect is generally less cheerful than high-key lighting, but not as gloomy as low-key lighting.

Natural light See Available light.

Negative Exposed and developed film stock from which the master positive is struck. If projected, the negative would produce a reverse of the image, with dark areas appearing white and vice versa or, if color film, areas of color appearing as their complementary hue.

Negative cutter A technician responsible for splicing and assembling the film negative to the editor's specifications.

Neutral-density filter A filter that simply reduces the amount of light entering the lens, without affecting the color characteristics.

Newsreel A short documentary on current events, shown in movie theaters along with cartoons and feature films beginning in the 1930s.

Non-diegetic A term used for any narrative, sound, or visual element not contained in the story world. Also called "extradiegetic."

Normal lens Any lens with a focal length approximately equal to the diagonal of the frame. For 35mm filmmaking, a 35–50mm lens does not distort the angle of vision or depth. See also **Wide-angle lens** and **Telephoto lens**.

Offscreen space A part of the story world implied by visual or sound techniques rather than being revealed by the camera.

Omniscient narration The technique of telling the story from an all-knowing viewpoint rather than that of one individual character. Films that use restricted narration limit the audience's perception to what one particular character knows, but may insert moments of omniscience.

On-the-nose dialogue Dialogue that re-states what is already obvious from images or action.

Open-ended A term describing a conclusion that does not answer all the questions raised regarding characters or storylines, nor tie up all loose ends.

Optical printer A machine used to create optical effects such as fades, dissolves, and superimpositions. Most are now created digitally.

Orthochromatic A term for film stock used in early cinema that was insensitive to red hues.

Outsourcing The practice of Hollywood studios contracting out post-production work to individuals or firms outside the U.S.

Out-take A scene filmed and processed but not selected to appear in the final version of the film.

Overexposure An effect created when more light than is required to produce an image strikes the film stock, so that the resulting image exhibits high contrast, glaring light, and washed out shadows. This effect may or may not be intentional on the filmmaker's part.

Overhead shot A shot taken from a position directly above the action, also called a "bird's eye shot."

Overlapping dialogue Sound design that blends the speech of several characters talking simultaneously, used to create spontaneity, although it may also confuse the audience.

Pan The horizontal turning movement of an otherwise immobile camera across a scene from left to right or vice versa.

Panchromatic A type of film stock that is sensitive to (in other words, registers) all tones in the color spectrum.

Panning and scanning Also called "full screen," the technique of re-shooting a widescreen film in order to convert it to the original television aspect ratio of 1.33 to 1. Rather than reproduce the original aspect ratio, as a letterboxed version does, a panned and scanned copy eliminates some of the visual information and introduces camera movement and editing that are not in the original.

Parallel A similarity established between two characters or situations that invites the audience to compare the two. It may involve visual, narrative, and/or sound elements.

Parallel editing A technique of cutting back and forth between action occurring in two different locations, which often creates the illusion that they are happening simultaneously. Also called "cross cutting."

Persistence of vision An optical effect whereby the eye continues to register a visual stimulus in the brain for a brief period after that stimulus has been removed.

Phi phenomenon An optical effect whereby the human eye fills in gaps between closely spaced objects, so that two light bulbs flashing on and off are understood as one light moving back and forth.

Pixel A picture element, a measure of image density. There are approximately 18 million pixels in a frame of 35mm film and 300,000–400,000 in a video image.

Pixilation Also called "stop motion photography." A technique of photographing a scene one frame at a time and moving the model between each shot.

Plot summary A brief chronological description of the basic events and characters in a film. It does not include interpretive or evaluative claims.

Plotline See Line of action.

Point-of-view shot A technique in which the audience temporarily shares the visual perspective of a character or a group of characters. The camera points in the direction that the character looks, simulating the character's field of vision.

Polarizing filters Filters that increase color saturation and contrast in outdoor shots.

Post-production The period after principal photography during which editing and looping take place, and special visual effects are added to the film.

Pre-fogging See Flashing.

Pre-production The period of time before principal photography during which actors are signed, sets and costumes designed, and locations scouted.

Product placement An agreement made between filmmakers and those who license the use of commercial products to feature those products in films, generally as props used by characters.

Production values A measure of the visual and sound quality of a film. Low-budget films tend to have lower production values because they lack the resources to devote to expensive pre- and post-production activities.

Progressive scanning An attribute of newer television monitors, where each frame is scanned by the electron beam as a single field. If slowed down, each frame would appear on the monitor in its entirety on the screen, rather than line by line, as is the case with interlaced scanning.

Promotion Materials intentionally released by studios to attract public attention to films and their stars. Promotion differs from publicity, which is information that is not (or does not appear to be) intentionally disseminated by studios.

Propaganda film A documentary or occasionally a narrative film that presents only one side of an argument or one approach to a subject.

Prostheses Devices that attach to actors' faces and/or bodies to change their appearance.

Protagonist A film's main character, one whose conflicts and motives drive the story forward.

Pulling A technique of underdeveloping exposed film stock (leaving it in a chemical bath a shorter amount of time than usual) in order to achieve the visual effect of reducing contrast.

Pushing A technique of overdeveloping exposed film stock (leaving it in the chemical bath longer than indicated) in order to increase density and contrast in the image.

Rack focus A change of focus from one plane of depth to another. As the in-focus subject goes out of focus, another object, which has been blurry, comes into focus in either the background or the foreground.

Realist style A film style that, in contrast to the classical and formalist styles, focuses on characters, place, and the spontaneity and digressiveness of life, rather than on highly structured stories or aesthetic abstraction.

Rear projection A technique used to join live action with a pre-recorded background image. A projector is placed behind a screen and projects an image onto it. Actors stand in front of the screen and the camera records them in front of the projected background.

Recursive action A technique of shooting a scene at a very high speed (96 frames per second), then adding and subtracting frames in post-production, "fanning out" the action through the overlapping images.

Re-establishing shot A shot that appears during or near the end of a scene and re-orients viewers to the setting.

Reframing A technique of shifting the camera angle, height or distance to take into account the motion of actors or objects within the frame.

Release prints Reels of film that are shipped to movie theaters for exhibition. Digital cinema, which can be distributed via satellite, broadband, or on media such as DVDs, may soon replace film prints because the latter are expensive to create, copy, and distribute.

Restricted narration A narrative approach that limits the audience's view of events to that of the main character(s) in the film. Occasional moments of omniscient narration may give viewers more information than the characters have at specific points in the narrative.

Reverse shot A shot in a sequence that is taken from the reverse angle of the shot previous to it.

Revisionist A genre film that radically modifies accepted genre conventions for dramatic effect.

Roadshowing A marketing strategy of screening a blockbuster prior to general release only in premier theaters.

Rotoscope A device that projects photographs or footage onto glass so that images can be traced by hand to create animated images.

Runaway production Film productions shot outside the U.S. for economic reasons.

Running time The length in minutes for a film to play in its entirety (for example, 120 minutes). Also referred to as "screen time."

Saturation The measure of intensity or purity of a color. Saturated color is purer than desaturated color, which has more white in it and thus offers a washed-out, less intense version of a color.

Scanning See Panning.

Scene A complete narrative unit within a film, with its own beginning, middle and end. Often scenes are unified, and distinguished from one another, by time and setting.

Score A musical accompaniment written specifically for a film.

Scratching A technique of intentionally adding scratches in a film's emulsion layer for aesthetic purposes, such as to simulate home movie footage.

Screen time See Running time.

Screenplay The written blueprint for a film, composed of three elements: dialogue, sluglines (setting the place and time of each scene), and description. Feature-length screenplays typically run 90–130 pages.

Script supervisor A crew member responsible for logging the details of each take on the set so as to ensure continuity.

Second unit A production crew responsible not for shooting the primary footage but, instead, for remote location shooting and B-roll. See also **B-roll**.

Selective focus A technique of manipulating focus to direct the viewer's attention.

Set-up The individual arrangement of lighting and camera placement used for each shot.

Shooting script The annotated script, containing information about set-ups used during shooting.

Shot The building block of a scene; an uninterrupted sequence of frames that viewers experience as they watch a film, ending with a cut, fade, dissolve, etc. See also **Take**.

Shot/reverse shot A standard shot pattern that dictates that a shot of one character will be followed by a shot of another character, taken from the reverse angle of the first shot.

Shot transition The use of editing techniques, such as a fade or dissolve, to indicate the end of one scene and the beginning of another.

Shutter A camera device that opens and closes to regulate the length of time the film is exposed to light.

Slow A term applied to film stock that is relatively insensitive to light. This stock will not yield acceptable images unless the amount of light can be carefully controlled.

Slow motion A technique of filming at a speed faster than projection, then projecting the footage at normal speed of 24 frames per second. Because fewer frames were recorded per second, the action appears to be speeded up.

Soft light Light emitted from a larger source that is scattered over a bigger area or reflected off a surface before it strikes the subject. Soft light minimizes facial details, including wrinkles.

Sound bridge A scene transition wherein sound from one scene bleeds over into the next scene, often resulting in a contrast between sound and image.

Soundtrack Everything audiences hear when they watch a sound film. The soundtrack is the composite of all three elements of film sound: dialogue, music, and sound effects.

Soviet montage An alternative to continuity editing, this style of editing was developed in silent Soviet cinema, based on the theory that editing should exploit the difference between shots to generate intellectual and emotional responses in the audience.

Spec script A screenplay written and submitted to a studio or production company without a prior contract or agreement.

Special visual effects Optical illusions created during production, including the use of matte paintings, glass shots, models and prosthesis.

Speed A measure of a film stock's sensitivity to light. "Fast" refers to sensitive film stock, while "slow" film is relatively insensitive.

Split screen An optical technique that divides the screen into two or more frames.

Standard shot pattern A sequence of shots designed to maintain spatial continuity. Scenes begin with an establishing shot, then move to a series of individual shots depicting characters and action, before re-establishing shots re-orient viewers to the setting.

Star filter A filter that creates points of light that streak outward from a light source.

Star persona Public identity created by marketing a film actor's performances, press coverage, and "personal" information to fans as the star's personality.

Star system A system initially developed for marketing films by creating and promoting stars as objects of admiration. The promotion of stars has now become an end in itself.

Steadicam A device worn by a camera operator that holds the motion picture camera, allowing it to glide smoothly through spaces unreachable by cameras mounted on a crane or other apparatus.

Stop motion photography See Pixilation.

Storyboard A series of individual drawings that provides a blueprint for the shooting of a scene.

Studio system A model of industrial organization in the film industry from about 1915 to 1946, characterized by the development of major and minor studios that produced, distributed and exhibited films, and held film actors, directors, art directors, and other technical crew under contract.

Subgenre A group of films within a given genre that share their own specific set of conventions that differentiate them from other films in the genre. For example, the slasher film is a subgenre of the horror genre.

Subtext An unstated meaning that underlies and is implied by spoken dialogue.

Superimposition A technique of depicting two layered images simultaneously. Images from one frame or several frames of film are added to pre-existing images, using an optical printer, to produce the same effect as a **Double exposure**.

Swish pan A pan executed so quickly that it produces a blurred image, indicating rapid activity or, sometimes, the passage of time.

Synthespian A computer-generated actor that some speculate will replace flesh and blood actors in the not so distant future.

Syuzhet The selection and ordering of narrative events presented in a film, as distinct from the *fabula*, which is the chronological accounting of all events presented and suggested.

Tableau shot A long shot in which the film frame resembles the proscenium arch of the stage, distancing the audience.

Take A production term denoting a single uninterrupted series of frames exposed by a motion picture or video camera between the time it is turned on and the time it is turned off. Filmmakers shoot several takes of any scene and the film editor selects the most appropriate one to use. See also **Shot**.

Telecine A machine that converts film prints to videotape format.

Telephoto lens A lens with a focal length greater than 50 mm (usually between 80mm and 200mm), which provides a larger image of the subject than a normal or wide-angle lens but which narrows the angle of vision and flattens the depth of the image relative to normal and wide-angle lenses.

Text The term for a film's spoken dialogue, as opposed to the underlying meaning contained in the subtext.

Third-person narration Literary narration from a viewpoint beyond that of any one individual character.

Three-act structure The classical model of narrative form. The first act introduces characters and conflicts; the second act offers complication leading to a climax; the third act contains the *dénouement* and resolution.

Three-point lighting An efficient system developed for film lighting. In a standard lighting set-up, the key light illuminates the subject, the fill light eliminates shadows cast by the key light, and the back light separates the subject from the background.

Tight framing A visual effect created when the subject in the frame is restricted by the objects or the physical properties of the set.

Tilt A vertical, up-and-down, motion of an otherwise stationary camera.

Time-lapse photography A technique of recording very few images over a long period of time—say, one frame per minute or per day.

Tinting An early color process, involving bathing lengths of processed film in dye one scene at a time.

Toning An early color process that replaced silver halide grains with colored salts.

Tracking shot A technique of moving the camera, on a dolly, along a specially built track. Such shots often trace character movement laterally across the frame or in and out of the depth of the frame.

Trailer A short segment of film used to promote an upcoming release.

Traveling matte A system for combining two separately filmed images in the same frame that involves creating a matte (a black mask that covers portion of the image) for a live action sequence and using it to block out a portion of the frame when filming the background images. See also **Blue screen**.

Trombone shot A shot combining two kinds of movement: the camera tracks in toward the subject while the lens zooms out.

Turning point A narrative moment that signals an important shift of some kind in character or situation.

Two-shot A shot that contains two characters within the frame.

Typecasting The practice of repeatedly casting actors in similar roles across different films.

Undercranking A technique of running the motion picture camera at a speed slower than projection speed (24 frames per second), in order to produce a **Fast motion** sequence when projected at normal speed. The term derives from early film cameras, which were cranked by hand.

Underexposure An effect created when too little light strikes the film during shooting. As a result the image will contain dark areas that appear very dense and dark (including shadows) and the overall contrast will be less than with a properly exposed image.

Vertical integration A business model adopted by the major studios during the Hollywood studio era, in which studios controlled all aspects of the film business, from production to distribution to exhibition.

Video assist A device attached to the film camera that records videotape of what has been filmed, allowing the director immediate access to video footage.

Vista Vision A film process that uses 35mm film stock but changes the orientation of the film so that the film moves through the camera horizontally instead of vertically. The larger image is of higher quality than standard 35mm processes.

Visual effects Optical illusions created during post-production.

Voice-over A direct vocal address to the audience, which may emanate from a character or from a narrating voice apparently unrelated to the diegesis.

Wide-angle lens A lens with a shorter focal length than a normal or telephoto lens (usually between 15mm and 35 mm). The subject appears smaller as a result, but the angle of vision is wider and an illusion is created of greater depth in the frame.

Wide film A format that uses a larger film stock than standard 35mm. IMAX, Omnimax, and Showscan are shot on 70mm film. See also **Gauge**.

Widescreen Processes such as Cinemascope and Cinerama, developed during the 1950s to enhance film's size advantage over the smaller television image.

Wipe A scene transition in which the first frame of the incoming scene appears to push the last frame of the previous scene off the screen horizontally.

Wireframe The first step in the process of creating CGI. The wireframe is a three-dimensional computer model of an object, which is then rendered (producing the finished image) and animated (using simulated camera movement frame by frame).

Zoom in A technique of moving a zoom lens from a wide-angle position to a telephoto position, which results in a magnification of the subject within the frame, and keeps the subject in focus.

Zoom lens A lens with a variable focal length that allows changes of focal length while keeping the subject in focus.

Zoom out A technique of moving from the telephoto position to the wide-angle position of a zoom lens, which results in the subject appearing to become smaller within the frame, while remaining in focus.

Bibliography

Adair, Gilbert. "Eistenstein on Disney," in *Movies*. London: Penguin, 1999.

Addison, Heather. "Capitalizing their Charms: Cinema Stars and Physical Culture in the 1920s," *The Velvet Light Trap*, 50 (fall 2002), pp. 15–34.

Allen, Michael. *Contemporary US Cinema*. Harlow, UK, and NY: Longman/Pearson, 2003.

Altman, Rick. "A Semantic/Syntactic Approach to Film Genre," in *Film Genre Reader*, ed. Barry Keith Grant. Austin: University of Texas Press, 1986, pp. 26–40.

American Cinematographer's Manual. Hollywood, CA: ASC Press, 1993.

Ansen, David, and Jeff Giles. "The New Visionaries," *Newsweek*, 143/6 (September 2, 2004). Online. Academic Search Elite. February 26, 2004.

Appelo, Tim. "Chasing the Chador," *The Nation*, 272/17 (April 30, 2001). Online. Academic Search Elite. February 25, 2004.

Arden, Darlene. "The Magic of ILM." www.darlenearden.com/articleILM.htm. 6/22/04.

Ascher, Steven, and Edward Pincus. *The Filmmaker's Handbook: A Comprehensive Guide for the Digital Age*. New York: Plume, 1999.

Barbarow, George. "*Rashomon* and the Fifth Witness," in *"Rashomon": Akira Kurosawa, Director*. New Brunswick and London: Rutgers University Press, 1987, pp. 145–8.

Barclay, Steven. *The Motion Picture Image: From Film to Digital*. Boston: Focal Press, 2000.

Bazin, André. *Jean Renoir*. New York: Simon and Schuster, 1971. Trans. 1973.

Bazin, André. "The Evolution of the Language of Cinema," in *Film Theory and Criticism*, ed. Gerald Mast *et al.*, 4th edn. New York: Oxford University Press, 1992, pp. 155–67.

Belton, John. "Digital Cinema: A False Revolution," *October*, 100 (2002). Academic Search Elite. Online. Ebscohost. January 21, 2004.

Berrettini, Mark. "Private Knowledge, Public Space: Investigation and Navigation in *Devil in a Blue Dress*," *Cinema Journal*, 39/1 (fall 1999), pp. 74–89.

Betz, Mark. "The Name above the (Sub)Title: Internationalism, Coproduction, and Polyglot European Art Cinema," *Camera Obscura*, 16/1 (2001). March 8, 2002. http//muse.jhu.edu/journals/camera_obscura/v016/16.1betz.htm.

Bignardi, Irene. "The Making of *The Battle of Algiers*," *Cineaste* (spring 2000), pp. 14–22.

Biskind, Peter. *Easy Riders, Raging Bulls: How the Sex-Drugs-and Rock 'n' Roll Generation Saved Hollywood*. New York: Simon and Schuster, 1998.

Bizony, Piers. "Shipbuilding," in *The Making of "2001: A Space Odyssey."* New York: Random House, 2000, pp. 43–54.

Bordwell, David. *On the History of Film Style*. Cambridge, MA: Harvard University Press, 1997.

Bordwell, David. "Story Causality and Motivation," in *The Classical Hollywood Cinema: Film Style and Mode of Production to 1960*, ed. David Bordwell *et al*. New York: Columbia University Press, 1985, pp. 12–23.

"Brad Pitt goes to extremes in *Troy*." Reuters. May 13, 2004. http:msnbc.msn.com/id/4953083. 6/20/2004.

Brakhage, Stan. "Remarks." *By Brakhage: An Anthology*. Criterion Collection DVD, 2003.

Brakhage, Stan. *Film at Wit's End: Eight Avant-garde Filmmakers*. New York: McPherson, 1989.

Brandt, Michael. "Traditional Film Editing vs. Electronic Nonlinear Film Editing: A Comparison of Feature Films," *Nonlinear 4: The Website of Digital Video and Film Editing*. http://www.nonlinear4.com/brandt.htm. May 16, 2002.

Brandy, Leo. "Genre: The Conventions of Connection," in *Film Theory and Criticism*, 4th cdn. New York: Oxford University Press, 1992.

Brown, Georgia. "Heart of Darkness," *Village Voice*, 35 (September 11, 1990), p. 64.

Buscombe, Edward. *Stagecoach*. London: British Film Institute, 1992.

Carter, Angela. *Expletives Deleted*. London: Chatto and Windus, 1992.

Carvell, Tim. "Hello, Mr. Chips (Goodbye, Mr. Film)," *Fortune*, 140 (1999). Academic Search Elite. Online. Ebscohost. January 21, 2004.

Cavell, Stanley. *Pursuits of Happiness: The Hollywood Comedy of Remarriage*. Cambridge, MA: Harvard University Press, 1981.

Cawelti, John G. "*Chinatown* and Generic Transformation in Recent American Films," in *Film Genre Reader*, ed. Barry Keith Grant. Austin: University of Texas Press, 1986, pp. 183–201.

Cellini, Joe. "An Interview with Walter Murch." http://www.apple.com/pro/film/murch/index.html. June 16, 2004.

Chanan, Michael. "Tomás Gutiérrez Alea," in *The Oxford History of World Cinema*, ed. Geoffrey Nowell-Smith. Oxford: Oxford University Press, 1996, p. 744.

Chatman, Seymour. *Antonioni: or, The Surface of the World*. Berkeley, CA: University of California Press, 1985.

Chion, Michel. *Audio-Vision: Sound on Screen*. New York: Columbia University Press, 1994.

Cineaste. Editorial, 28/1 (winter 2002). Online. Academic Search Elite. February 25, 2004.

Clark, VeVe, Millicent Hodson, and Catrina Neiman (ed.) *The Legend of Maya Deren*, vol. 1, part 2. New York: Anthology Film Archives/Film Culture, 1984.

Cocks, Jay, and Martin Scorsese. *"The Age of Innocence": The Shooting Script*. New York: Newmarket Press, 1995.

Cohen, Tyler. "Cinema: Ticket for One?" *Forbes* (April 28, 2003): n. page. Online. Safari. February 6, 2004.

Collins, Nancy. "Lust and Trust," *Rolling Stone*, (July 8, 1999). *Academic Search Elite*. Online. Ebsco. January 9, 2004.

Combs, Richard. "New York, New York," *Sight and Sound*, (fall 1977), pp. 252–3.

Cook, David. "Auteur Cinema and the 'Film Generation' in 1970s Hollywood," in *The New American Cinema*, ed. Jon Lewis. Durham, NC: Duke University Press, 1998, pp. 11–37.

Cook, David. *A History of Narrative Film*, 3rd edn. New York: Norton, 1996.

Corliss, Richard. "Gay and Gaudy," *Time*, 150/17 (October 27, 1997), p. 111.

Corner, John. *The Art of Record: A Critical Introduction to Documentary*. Manchester and NY: Manchester University Press, 1996.

Corrigan, Timothy. *A Cinema without Walls: Movies and Culture After Vietnam*. New Brunswick: Rutgers University Press, 1991.

Corrigan, Timothy. "*Auteurs* and the New Hollywood," in *The New American Cinema*, ed. Jon Lewis. Durham, NC: Duke University Press, 1998, pp. 38–63.

Cousins, Mark. *Scene by Scene*. London: Laurence King, 2002.

Cowie, Peter. *Coppola: A Biography*. New York: De Capo Press. 1994.

Crafton, Donald. "Tricks and Animation," in *The Oxford History of World Cinema*, ed. Geoffrey Nowell-Smith. Oxford and New York: Oxford University Press, 1997, pp. 71–8.

Creed, Barbara. "Horror and the Monstrous Feminine: An Imaginary Abjection," in *Feminist Film Theory*, ed. Sue Thornham. New York: New York University Press, 1999, pp. 251–66.

Culkin, Nigel, and Keith Randle. "Digital Cinema: Opportunities and Challenges," *Convergence*, 9/4 (2003), pp. 79–98.

Curtis, David. *Experimental Cinema: A Fifty Year Evolution*. New York: Dell, 1971.

DeCordova, Richard. *Picture Personalities: The Emergence of the Star System in America*. Urbana: University of Illinois Press, 1990.

Denby, David. "Killer: Two Views of Aileen Wuornos," *The New Yorker* (January 26, 2004), pp. 84–6.

Denby, David. "The Moviegoers: Why Don't People Love the Right Movies Anymore?" in *The Best American Movie Writing 1999*, ed. Peter Bogdanovich. New York: St. Martin's, 1999, pp. 6–19.

Denby, David. Review of *Ali*. *The New Yorker* (January 28, 2002), p. 27.

Dobbs, Lem. Commentary track. *The Limey* (DVD), dir. Steven Soderbergh. Artisan, 1999.

Doherty, Thomas. "DVD, PDQ," *The Chronicle of Higher Education* (April 26, 2002): n. page. Online. Safari. May 1, 2002.

Donalson, Melvin. *Black Directors in Hollywood*. Austin, TX: University of Texas Press, 2003.

Dyer, Richard. "Four Films of Lana Turner," in *Star Texts: Image and Performance in Film and Television*, ed. Jeremy G. Butler. Detroit: Wayne State University Press, 1991, pp. 214–39.

Dyer, Richard. *Heavenly Bodies: Film Stars and Society*. New York: St. Martins, 1986.

Dyer, Richard. *Stars*, 2nd edn. London: BFI, 1998.

Ebert, Roger. "Start the Revolution Without Digital," volksmovie.com. http://www.volksmovie.com/rants/archive/rogerebert.html

Economist, The. "On screen it's Iran's Shout," 336/7921 (January 7, 1995). Online. Academic Search Elite. February 25, 2004.

Eisenstein, Sergei. "A Dialectic Approach to Film Form." *Film Form*. San Diego, New York, and London: Harcourt Brace Jovanovich, 1949, pp. 45–63.

Eisner, Lotte. *The Haunted Screen*. Berkeley, CA: University of California Press, 1952. Trans. 1969.

Ellis, Jack C., and Virginia Wright Wexman. *A History of Film*, 5th edn. Boston: Allyn and Bacon, 2002.

Elsaesser, Thomas. *Weimar Cinema and After: Germany's Historical Imaginary*. New York: Routledge, 2000.

Fellini, Federico. *Fellini on Fellini*, trans. Isabel Quigley. Cambridge and New York: Da Capo Press, 1996.

Festinger, Rob, and Todd Field. *In the Bedroom*. New York: Hyperion, 2002.

Figes, Orlando. *A People's Tragedy*. New York: Viking, 1997.

"Focus on Jim Jarmusch" interview with Elvis Mitchell. Independent Film Channel, January 18, 2004.

Frayling, Christopher. *Sergio Leone: Something to Do with Death*. London: Faber, 2000.

Fuller, Graham. "Death and the Maidens," *Sight and Sound*, new series, 10/4 (April 2000). Online. Humanities Art Database. February 26, 2004.

Gargan, Edward. "Hong Kong's Master of Internal Pyrotechnics," *New York Times*, Sunday October 12, 1997, Section 2, pp. 13, 29.

Gibson, Pamela Church. "Film Costume," in *The Oxford Guide to Film Studies*, ed. John Hill and Pamela Church Gibson. Oxford and New York: Oxford University Press, 1998, pp. 36–42.

Gidal, Peter. *Materialist Film*. London: Routledge, 1989.

Gomery, Douglas. "The Coming of Sound; Technological Change in the American Film Industry," in *Film Sound*, ed. Elizabeth Weis and John Belton. New York: Columbia University Press, 1985, pp. 5–24.

Gomery, Douglas. "The Hollywood Studio System," in *The Oxford History of World Cinema*, ed. Geoffrey Nowell-Smith. Oxford and New York: Oxford University Press, 1996, pp. 43–53.

Gorbman, Claudia. *Unheard Melodies: Narrative Film Music*. Bloomington: Indiana University Press, 1987.

Gorky, Maxim. "The Kingdom of Shadows," in Gilbert Adair, *Movies*, pp. 10–13. London and New York: Penguin, 1999.

Gras, Vernon and Marguerite (ed.). *Interviews: Peter Greenaway*. Jackson, MI: University of Mississippi Press, 2000.

Guerrero, Ed. *Framing Blackness: The African American Image in Film*. Philadelphia: Temple University Press, 1993.

Haines, Richard W. *Technicolor Movies: The History of Dye Transfer Printing*. Jefferson, NC: McFarland, 1993.

Handy, Bruce. "This is Cinerama." *Vanity Fair*, 488 (April 2001), pp. 258–74.

Hay, James. *Popular Film Culture in Fascist Italy*. Bloomington: Indiana University Press, 1987.

Heines, Marjorie. *Sex, Sin, and Blasphemy. A Guide to America's Censorship Wars*. New York: The New York Press, 1998.

Hill, John. "British Film Policy," in *Film Policy: International, National, and Regional Perspectives*, ed. Albert Moran. London: Routledge, 1996, pp. 101–13.

Hiltzik, Michael. "Digital Cinema Take 2." *Technology Review*, September 2002, pp. 36–44.

Holmlund, Chris. *Impossible Bodies: Femininity and Masculinity at the Movies*. London: Routledge, 2002.

Horak, Jan-Christopher. "The First American Avant-Garde, 1919–1945," in *Lovers of Cinema: The First American Film Avant-Garde 1919–45*, ed. Jan-Christopher Horak. Madison: University of Wisconsin Press, 1995, pp. 14–66.

Horn, John. "Producers Pursue a *Potter* with Pizzazz." *Raleigh News and Observer* (January 25, 2004), p. 3G.

Hutchings, Peter. "Genre Theory and Criticism." *Approaches to Popular Film*, ed. Joanne Hollows and Mark Jancovich. Manchester and New York: Manchester University Press, 1995, pp. 59–77.

Iwasaki, Akira. "Kurosawa and his Work," in *Focus on Rashomon*, ed. Donald Richie. Englewood Cliffs: Prentice Hall, 1972, pp. 21–31.

James, Caryn. "Loyalties Scalded by Humiliation," *The New York Times* (September 5, 1990), p. C16.

James, David. *Allegories of Cinema: American Film in the 1960s*. Princeton: Princeton University Press, 1989.

"John Ford's *Young Mr. Lincoln*." Collective text by the editors of *Cahiers du Cinéma. Film Theory and Criticism: Introductory Readings*, 3rd edn., ed. Gerald Mast and Marshall Cohen. New York: Oxford University Press, 1985, pp. 695–740.

Johnson, William. "The Circle," *Film Quarterly*, 54/3 (spring 2001). Online. Communication and Mass Media Complete. February 25, 2004.

Johnston, Sheila. "The Author as Public Institution," in *The European Cinema Reader*, ed. Catherine Fowler. London and New York: Routledge, 2002, pp. 121–31.

Kaes, Anton. "The New German Cinema," in *Oxford History of World Cinema*, ed. Geoffrey Nowell-Smith. Oxford and New York: Oxford University Press, 1996, pp. 614–27.

Karnick, Kirstine Brunovska. "Commitment and Reaffirmation in Hollywood Romantic Comedy," in *Classical Hollywood Comedy*, ed. Kristine Brunovska Karnick and Henry Jenkins. London: Routledge, 1995, pp. 123–146.

Kawin, Bruce. "Children of the Light," in *Film Genre Reader*, ed. Barry Keith Grant. Austin: University of Texas Press, 1986, pp. 236–57.

Keller, James R. *Queer (Un)friendly Film and Television*. London and Jefferson, NC: McFarland, 2002.

Kellner, Douglas. "Hollywood Film and Society," in *American Cinema and Hollywood*, ed. John Hill and Pamela Church Gibson. Oxford and New York: Oxford University Press, 2000, pp. 128–38.

Kelly, Mary Pat. *Martin Scorsese: A Journey*. New York: Thunder's Mouth Press, 1991.

Kenez, Peter. *Cinema and Soviet Society: From the Revolution to the Death of Stalin*. New York: I.B. Tauris, 2001.

Kinder, Marsha. "Antonioni in Transit." *Sight and Sound*, 36 (summer 1967), pp. 132–7.

Kinder, Marsha, and Beverle Houston. *Close-Up: A Critical Perspective on Film*. New York: Harcourt, Brace, Jovanovich, 1972.

King, Barry. "Articulating Stardom," *Screen*, 26/5 (1985), pp. 27–50.

Kracauer, Siegfried. *From "Caligari" to Hitler: A Psychological History of the German Film*. Princeton, NJ: Princeton University Press, 1971.

Kramer, Peter. "Post-Classical Hollywood," in *American Cinema and Hollywood*, ed. John Hill and Pamela Church Gibson. New York: Oxford University Press, 2000, pp. 63–83.

Kruidenier, David. "Postcolonialism and Feminism in *The Battle of Algiers*." Unpublished paper. February 2004.

LaPlace, Maria. "Stars and the Star System: The Case of Bette Davis," in *The Film Studies Reader*, ed. Joanne Hollows *et al*. New York: Oxford University Press, 2000, pp. 134–39. Originally published in Christine Gledhill (ed.), *Home is Where the Heart Is*. London: BFI, 1987.

Lee, Joanna. "The Music of *In the Mood for Love*." *In the Mood for Love*. Dir. Wong Kar-Wai. DVD. USA/Criterion, 2002.

Leeper, Jill. "Crossing Borders: The Soundtrack for *Touch of Evil*," in *Soundtrack Available: Essays on Film and Popular Music*, ed. Pamela Robertson Wojcik and Arthur Knight. Durham, NC: Duke University Press, 2001, pp. 226–43.

Lehman, Peter, and William Luhr. *Thinking about Movies: Watching, Questioning, Enjoying*. Fort Worth: Harcourt, 1999.

Lent, Tina Olsin. "Romantic Love and Friendship: The Redefinition of Gender Relations in Screwball Comedy," in *Classical Hollywood Comedy*, ed. Krisine Brunovska Karnick and Henry Jenkins. London: Routledge, 1995, pp. 314–31.

Lewis, Jon. *Hollywood versus Hardcore: How the Struggle over Censorship Saved the Modern Film Industry*. New York: New York University Press, 2000.

Lewis, Jon. "Money Matters: Hollywood in the Corporate Era," in *New American Cinema*, ed. Jon Lewis. Durham, NC: Duke University Press, 1998, pp. 87–121.

Leyda, Jay. *Kino: A History of the Russian and Soviet Film*. Princeton: Princeton University Press, 1960.

Lipton, Lenny. *Independent Filmmaking*. New York: Simon and Schuster, 1983.

LoBrutto, Vincent. *Principal Photography: Interviews with Feature Film Cinematographers*. London and Westport, CT: Praeger, 1999.

LoBrutto, Vincent. *Sound on Film: Interviews with Creators of Film Sound*. Westport, CT: Praeger, 1994.

McDonald, Paul. Afterword ("Reconceptualising Stardom"), in *Stars*, 2nd edn. London: BFI, 1998, pp. 177–211.

McDonald, Paul. "Film Acting," in *The Oxford Guide to Film Studies*, ed. John Hill and Pamela Church Gibson. Oxford and New York: Oxford University Press, 1998, pp. 30–36.

McDonald, Paul. *The Star System: Hollywood's Production of Popular Identities*. London: Wallflower, 2000.

MacDonald, Scott. *Avant Garde Film: Motion Studies*. Cambridge: Cambridge University Press, 1993.

Magid, Ron. "Vision Crew Unlimited's Artisans Lay Scale-model Keels for *Titanic*," *American Cinematographer*, 78/12 (December 1997), pp. 81–5.

Magombe, P. Vincent. "Ousmane Sembene," in *Oxford History of World Cinema*, ed. Geoffrey Nowell-Smith. Oxford and New York: Oxford University Press, 1996, pp. 668–9.

Majumdar, Neepa. "The Embodied Voice," in *Soundtrack Available: Essays on Film and Popular Music*, ed. Pamela Robertson Wojcik and Arthur Knight. Durham, NC: Duke University Press, 2001, pp. 161–81.

Maltby, Richard. "Censorship and Self-Regulation," in *The Oxford History of World Cinema*, ed. Geoffrey Nowell-Smith. New York: Oxford University Press, 1996, pp. 235–48.

Maltby, Richard. "'Nobody Knows Everything': Post-Classical Historiographies and Consolidated Entertainment," in *Contemporary Hollywood Cinema*, ed. Steve Neale and Murray Smith. London: Routledge, 1998, pp. 21–57.

Marcus, Millicent. *Italian Film in the Light of Neorealism*. Princeton: Princeton University Press, 1986.

Marie, Michel. "It Really Makes You Sick," in *French Film: Texts and Contexts*, 2nd edn., ed. Susan Hayward and Ginette Vincendeau. London: Routledge, 2000, pp. 158–73.

Martin, Kevin H. "Jacking into the Matrix," *Cinefex*, 79 (October 1999), pp. 66–89.

Mast, Gerald, and Bruce Kawin. *A Short History of the Movies*, 6th edn. Boston and London: Allyn and Bacon, 1996.

Mellen, Joan. "Film Noir," in *The Political Companion to American Film*, ed. Gary Crowdus. Chicago: Lakeview Press, 1994, pp. 137–44.

Modleski, Tania. *The Women Who Knew Too Much: Hitchcock and Feminist Theory*. London and New York: Routledge, 1988.

Monaco, James. *How to Read a Film: Movies, Media, Multimedia*, 3rd edn. Oxford and New York: Oxford University Press, 2000.

Moritz, William. "Americans in Paris," in *Lovers of Cinema: The First American Film Avant-Garde 1919–45*, ed. Jan-Christopher Horak. Madison: University of Wisconsin Press, 1995, pp. 118–36.

Morris, Gary. "Behind the Mask: Sadie Benning's Pixel Pleasures." *Bright Lights Film Journal*, 24 (April 1999). http://www.brightlightsfilm.com/24/benning.html. 2/17/04.

Morrison, James. "Buzz Factor: The DVD Release of Todd Solondz's *Storytelling* itself Tells a Story about Contemporary Film Culture," *The Independent Weekly*, 19/30 (July 17–23, 2002), p. 52.

Mottram, James. *The Making of "Memento."* London: Faber and Faber, 2002.

Murphy, David. *Sembene*. Oxford and Trenton, NJ: Africa World Press, 2001.

Murray, Edward. *Nine American Critics*. New York: Frederick Unger, 1975.

Naremore, James. *Acting in the Cinema*. Berkeley, CA: University of California Press, 1990.

Naremore, James. *More than Night: Film Noir in its Contexts*. Berkeley: University of California Press, 1998.

Neale, Steve. *Genre and Hollywood*. London: Routledge, 2000.

Neupert, Richard. *A History of the French New Wave*. Madison: University of Wisconsin Press, 2002.

Newman, Kim. "Enemy of the State," *Sight and Sound* (January 1999): n. pag. Online. Netscape. June 28, 2003.

Nichols, Bill. *Introduction to Documentary*. Bloomington and Indianapolis: Indiana University Press, 2001.

Nichols, Bill. *Representing Reality*. Bloomington and Indianapolis: Indiana University Press, 1991.

Nowell-Smith, Geoffrey. "Art Cinema," in *The Oxford History of World Cinema*, ed. Geoffrey Nowell-Smith. New York: Oxford University Press, 1996, pp. 567–75.

Nowell-Smith, Geoffrey. *The Oxford History of World Cinema*. Oxford and New York: Oxford University Press, 1997.

"The Oberhausen Manifesto," in *The European Cinema Reader*, ed. Catherine Fowler. London and New York: Routledge, 2002, p. 73.

O'Hehir, Andrew. "Fog of War," Salon.com dir.salon.com/ent/movies/review/2001/12/28/black_hawk_down/index.html

O'Neill, Edward R. "Alfred Hitchcock," in *Oxford History of World Cinema*, ed Geoffrey Nowell-Smith. Oxford and New York: Oxford University Press, 1996, pp. 310–11.

Origins of a Hip Hop Classic. Dir. Benny Boom. *Scarface*. DVD Supplementary Material. Universal. 2003.

Orr, John. *Cinema and Modernity*. Cambridge: Polity Press, 1993.

Otto, Jeff, and Spence D. "Howard Shore Interview." ign.com. http://music.ign.com/articles/446/446567pl.html

Perisic, Zoran. *Visual Effects Cinematography*. Boston: Focal Press, 2000.

Peterson, James. *Dreams of Chaos, Visions of Order: Understanding the American Avant-Garde Cinema*. Detroit: Wayne State University Press, 1994.

Pierson, Michele. *Special Effects: Still in Search of Wonder*. New York: Columbia University Press, 2002.

Prendergast, Roy M. *Film Music: A Neglected Art*, 2nd edn. New York: Norton, 1992.

Pudovkin, V.I. *Film Technique and Film Acting*. New York: Grove Press, 1970.

Pym, John. "Soldier's Pay," *Sight and Sound*, 58/4 (autumn 1989), p. 280.

Rajadhyaksha, Ashish. "Realism, Modernism, and Post-colonial Theory," in *The Oxford Guide to Film Studies*, ed. John Hill and Pamela Church Gibson. Oxford: Oxford University Press, 1998, pp. 413–25.

Ray, Robert. *A Certain Tendency of the Hollywood Cinema, 1930–1980*. Princeton: Princeton University Press, 1985.

Rees, A.L. *A History of Experimental Film and Video*. London: British Film Institute, 1999.

Rhines, Jesse Algernon. *Black Films/White Money*. New Brunswick, NJ: Rutgers University Press, 1996.

Riambau, Esteve. "Public Money and Private Business (Or, How to Survive Hollywood's Imperialism): Film Production in Spain (1984–2002)," *Cineaste*, 29/1 (2004), pp. 56–61.

Richie, Donald. *Japanese Cinema: An Introduction*. New York: Oxford University Press, 1990.

Richie, Donald, ed. *"Rashomon": Akira Kurosawa, Director*. New Brunswick and London: Rutgers University Press, 1987.

Richie, Donald, ed. *Focus on "Rashomon"*. Englewood Cliffs, NJ: Prentice-Hall, 1972.

Rickitt, Richard. *Special Effects: The History and Technique*. London: Virgin Publishing, 2000.

Riding, Alan. "Filmmakers Seek Protection from U.S. Dominance," *New York Times* (February 5, 2003), p. B3.

Rigney, Melissa. "Sadie Benning," *Senses of Cinema. Great Directors: A Critical Database*. www.sensesofcinema.com/contents/directors/03/benning.html. 2/17/04.

Rogers, Pauline. *Contemporary Cinematographers on Their Art*. Boston: Focal Press, 1998.

Rosenbaum, Jonathan. "Cult Confusion," *The Chicago Reader* (January 9, 1998). February 25, 2004. http://www.chireader.com/movies/archives/ 1998/0198/01238.html

Rosenbaum, Jonathan. *Movies as Politics*. Berkeley, CA: University of California Press, 1997.

Rosenbaum, Jonathan. "A Perversion of the Past," in *Movies as Politics*. Berkeley, CA: University of California Press, 1997, pp. 118–24. Originally published in *Chicago Reader*, December 16, 1988.

Rosenbaum, Jonathan. "The Problem with Poetry," in *Movies as Politics*. Berkeley CA: University of California Press, 1997, pp. 183–94.

Rosenbaum, Jonathan. "*Touch of Evil* Retouched," in *The Best American Movie Writing 1999*, ed. Peter Bogdanovich. New York: St Martin's Griffin, 1999, pp. 133–6.

Rosenbaum, Jonathan. "The World According to Harvey and Bob," in *Movies as Politics*, pp. 159–65. Berkeley and Los Angeles, CA: University of California Press, 1997.

Rudolph, Eric. "This is your Life," *American Cinematographer*, 79/6 (June 1998), pp. 74–85.

Russell, Catherine. *Experimental Ethnography*. Durham, NC, and London: Duke University Press, 1999.

Ryall, Tom. "Genre and Hollywood," in *The Oxford Guide to Film Studies*, ed. John Hill and Pamela Church Gibson. London: Oxford University Press, 1998, pp. 327–37.

Ryan, Michael, and Douglas Kellner. *Camera Politica: The Politics and Ideology of Contemporary Hollywood Film*. Bloomington: Indiana University Press: 1988.

Salt, Barry. *Film Style and Technology: History and Analysis*, 2nd edn. London: Starword, 1992.

Salt, Barry, "Film Style and Technology in the Thirties: Sound," in *Film Sound*, ed. Elizabeth Weis and John Belton. New York: Columbia University Press, 1985, pp. 37–43.

San Filippo, Maria. "Lost in Translation," *Cineaste*, 29/1 (winter 2003). Online. Academic Search Elite. February 25, 2004.

Sarris, Andrew. *The Primal Screen*. New York: Simon and Schuster, 1973.

Sato, Tadao. "The Films of Akira Kurosawa and the Japanese People," *Film International*, 6/2 (1998), pp. 61–4.

Schaefer, Dennis, and Larry Salvato. *Masters of Light: Conversations with Contemporary Cinematographers*. Berkeley, CA: University of California Press, 1984.

Schamus, James. "A Rant," in *The End of Cinema As We Know It: American Film in the Nineties*, ed. Jon Lewis. New York: New York University Press, 2001.

Schatz, Thomas. *Hollywood Genres: Formulas, Filmmaking, and the Studio System*. Philadelphia: Temple University Press, 1981.

Schatz, Thomas. *The Genius of the System: Hollywood Filmmaking in the Studio Era*. New York: Pantheon, 1988.

Schroeder, Paul A. *Tomás Gutiérrez Alea: The Dialectics of a Filmmaker*. New York and London: Routledge, 2002.

Scott, A.O. "The New Golden Age of Acting," *The New York Times* (February 15, 2004), 2A: pp. 1, 25.

Scott, Walter. "Personality Parade," *Parade Magazine* (June 13, 2004), p. 1.

Seagrave, Kerry. *American Films Abroad: Hollywood's Domination of the World's Movie Screens from the 1890s to the Present*. Jefferson: McFarland, 1997.

Seguin, Denis. "The Battle for Hollywood North," *Canadian Business*, 76 (2003). Academic Search Elite. Online. Ebscohost. January 21, 2004.

Shohat, Ella, and Robert Stam. *Unthinking Eurocentrism: Multiculturalism and the Media*. London and New York: Routledge, 1994.

Shreger, Charles. "Altman, Dolby, and the Second Sound Revolution," in *Film Sound*, ed. Elizabeth Weis and John Belton. New York: Columbia University Press, 1985, pp. 348–55.

Sitney, P. Adams. *Visionary Film: The American Avant-Garde, 1943–1978*, 3rd edn. Oxford and New York: Oxford University Press, 2002.

Sklar, Robert. *Film: An International History of the Medium*, 2nd edn. Upper Saddle River, NJ: Prentice Hall and Harry N. Abrams, 2002.

Smith, Jeff. *The Sound of Commerce*. New York: Columbia University Press, 1998.

Smith, Steven. "A Chorus of Isolation," *Taxi Driver*. Dir. Martin Scorsese. Laser Disc. Criterion/Voyager Co. 1990.

Solomon, Stanley J. *Beyond Formula: American Film Genres*. San Diego: Harcourt Brace, 1976.

Sontag, Susan. "The Imagination of Disaster," in *Film Theory and Criticism*, 3rd edn., ed. Gerald Mast and Marshall Cohen. New York: Oxford University Press, 1985, pp. 451–65.

Sontag, Susan. "The Imagination of Disaster," in *Movies*, ed. Gilbert Adair. London: Penguin, 1999, pp. 170–85.

Spoto, Donald. *The Art of Alfred Hitchcock: Fifty Years of His Motion Pictures*. New York: Doubleday, 1979.

Stack, Peter. "Satirical *Scream* is Out for Blood—And Lots of It," *San Francisco Chronicle* (December 26, 1996). SFGate.com. February 13, 2003.

Staiger, Janet. "Standardization and Differentiation: The Reinforcement and Dispersion of Hollywood's Practices," in *The Classical Hollywood Cinema: Film Style and Mode of Production to 1960*, ed. David Bordwell *et al.* New York: Columbia University Press, 1985, pp. 96–112.

Stam, Robert. *Film Theory: An Introduction*. Malden, MA, and Oxford: Blackwell, 2000.

Street, Rita. *Computer Animation: A Whole New World*. Gloucester, MA: Rockport Publishers, 1998.

Sussex, Elizabeth. *The Rise and Fall of British Documentary*. Berkeley and Los Angeles, CA: University of California Press, 1975.

Swann, Paul. *The British Documentary Film Movement, 1926–46*. Cambridge: Cambridge University Press, 1989.

"Tangled Webs," *The Economist*, 363 (2002). Academic Search Elite. Online. Ebscohost. January 21, 2004.

Taylor, Charles. "Hong Kong Tango," Salon.com. October 31, 1997. September 10, 2002. http://www.salon.com/ent/movies/1997/10/31happy.html?CP=SAL&DN=110

Telotte, J.P. "*The Blair Witch Project* Project," *Film Quarterly*, 54 (2001). Academic Search Elite. Online. Ebscohost. January 21, 2004.

Thompson, Kristin. *Storytelling in Film and Television*. Cambridge: Harvard University Press, 2003.

Thompson, Kristin. *Storytelling in the New Hollywood*. Cambridge: Harvard University Press, 1999.

Thompson, Kristin, and David Bordwell. *Film History: An Introduction*, 2nd edn. Boston: McGraw-Hill, 2003.

Thoraval, Yves. *The Cinemas of India*. New Delhi: Macmillan India, 2000.

Triggs, Jeffery Alan. "The Legacy of Babel: Language in Jean Renoir's *Grand Illusion*," *The New Orleans Review*, 15/2 (1988), pp. 70–74.

Truffaut, François. *Hitchcock*, rev. edn. New York: Touchstone, 1993.

Tsivian, Yuri. "Dziga Vertov," in *The Oxford History of World Cinema*, ed. Geoffrey Nowell-Smith. Oxford and New York: Oxford University Press, 1996, pp. 92–3.

Turner, Dennis. "The Subject of *The Conversation*." *Cinema Journal*, 24/4 (1985), pp. 4–22.

Usai, Paolo Chechi. "The Early Years," in *The Oxford History of World Cinema*. Oxford and New York: Oxford University Press, 1997, pp. 6–13.

Vasey, Ruth. "The Worldwide Spread of Cinema," *The Oxford History of World Cinema*, ed. Geoffrey Nowell-Smith. Oxford: Oxford University Press, 1996, pp. 53–62.

Vertov, Dziga. "Provisional Instructions to Kino-Eye Groups," in *The European Cinema Reader*, ed. Catherine Fowler. London and New York: Routledge, 2002.

Vir, Parminder. "The Mother of All Battles," *The New Statesman* (July 8, 2002), pp. 40–2.

Von Sternberg, Josef. *Fun in a Chinese Laundry*. New York: Macmillan, 1965.

Warshow, Robert. "Movie Chronicle: The Westerner," in *Film Theory and Criticism*, 4th edn., ed. Gerald Mast, Marshall Cohen, and Leo Braudy. New York: Oxford University Press, 1992, pp. 453–66.

Wheeler, Paul. *High Definition and 24p Cinematography*. Oxford: Focal Press, 2003.

Wollen, Peter. "From *Signs and Meaning in Cinema*: The Auteur Theory," in *Film Theory and Criticism*, 5th edn, ed. Leo Braudy and Marshall Cohen. Oxford: Oxford University Press, 1999, pp. 519–35.

Wood, Robin. *Hollywood from Vietnam to Reagan*. New York: Columbia University Press, 1986.

Wood, Robin. "Ideology, Genre, Auteur: *Shadow of a Doubt*," in *Hitchcock's Films Revisited*. New York: Columbia University Press, 1989, pp. 288–303.

Wood, Robin. "Introduction," in *The American Nightmare: Essays on the Horror Film*, ed. Andrew Britton, Richard Lippe, Tony Williams, and Robin Wood. Toronto, Canada: Festival of Festivals, 1979, pp. 7–28.

Wright, Judith Hess. "Genre Films and the Status Quo," in *Film Genre Reader*, ed. Barry Keith Grant. Austin: University of Texas Press, 1986, pp. 236–57.

Wyatt, Justin. "From Roadshow to Saturation Release: Majors, Independents, and Marketing/Distribution Innovations," in *New American Cinema*, ed. Jon Lewis. Durham, NC: Duke University Press, 1998, pp. 64–86.

Zettl, Herbert. *Sight, Sound, Motion: Applied Media Aesthetics*, 3rd edn. Belmont, CA: Wadsworth Publishing Co., 1999.

Zunser, Jesse. Review of *Rashomon*, in *Focus on "Rashomon."* Englewood Cliffs: Prentice-Hall, 1972, pp. 37–8.

Picture Credits

Every effort has been made to trace and contact all copyright holders. Any images not listed below were deemed to be in the public domain. The publishers apologize for any unintentional omissions or errors and will be pleased to insert the appropriate acknowledgement to any companies or individuals in any subsequent edition of this book.

p. xvi © 2001 Twentieth Century Fox.
1.2 © MMIII New Line Productions. All Rights Reserved.
2.1 © 1968 Turner Entertainment Co. A Warner Bros. Entertainment Inc. Company. All Rights Reserved.
2.2 © 1963 Columbia Pictures Industries, Inc. All Rights Reserved.
2.4 © 2001 Twentieth Century Fox.
2.6 Courtesy of Castle Hill Productions, Inc.
2.7 © 1941 RKO Pictures Inc. All Rights Reserved.
2.13 © Paramount Pictures Corporation. All Rights Reserved.
2.14 © Paramount Pictures Corporation. All Rights Reserved.
2.15 © 2000 Gramercy Films LLC, Universal Studio Licensing LLLP & Initial Entertainment Group, Inc.
2.16 © 1958 Universal City Studios, Inc., & Hitchcock Estate.
2.17 © 1958 Universal City Studios, Inc., & Hitchcock Estate.
2.18 Courtesy of Perdido, Inc.
2.19 © 1963 Columbia Pictures Industries, Inc. All Rights Reserved.
2.20 © 1963 Columbia Pictures Industries, Inc. All Rights Reserved.
2.21 © 1963 Columbia Pictures Industries, Inc. All Rights Reserved.
2.22 © 1998 Courtesy Miramax Films.
2.23 © 1998 Courtesy Miramax Films.
2.25 © 2004 Entertainment Weekly, Inc. Used by permission.
2.26 © 1995 Columbia Pictures Industries, Inc. All Rights Reserved.

p. 30 © 1971 Warner Bros. Inc. All Rights Reserved.

3.1 © 2000 Warner Bros. A division of Time Warner Entertainment Company. All Rights Reserved.
3.2 © 2001 Touchstone Pictures. All Rights Reserved.
3.3 © 1988 Metro-Goldwyn-Mayer Studios, Inc. All Rights Reserved. Courtesy of MGM Clip+Still.
3.5 Courtesy of Newmarket Capital Group & Summit Entertainment.
3.6 © 1986 Twentieth Century Fox.
3.7 Courtesy of Castle Hill Productions Inc.
3.8 Courtesy of Castle Hill Productions Inc.
3.9 Courtesy of Castle Hill Productions Inc.
3.10 Courtesy of MK2 S.A.
3.11 © 1946 Turner Entertainment Co. A Warner Bros. Entertainment Inc. Company. All Rights Reserved.
3.12 © ABC, Inc. All Rights Reserved.
3.13 © ABC, Inc. All Rights Reserved.
3.16 © 1992 Courtesy of Miramax Films.
3.17 © 1960 Shamley Productions, Inc., & Universal Studios LLLP.
3.18 © 1960 Shamley Productions, Inc., & Universal Studios LLLP.
3.19 © 1960 Shamley Productions, Inc., & Universal Studios LLLP.
3.20 © 1960 Shamley Productions, Inc., & Universal Studios LLLP.
4.1 © Paramount Pictures Corporation. All Rights Reserved.
4.2 © Paramount Pictures Corporation. All Rights Reserved.
4.3 Courtesy of Pathé International. All Rights Reserved.
4.4 © Paramount Pictures Corporation. All Rights Reserved.
4.5 Courtesy of Corinth Films. Inc.
4.6 © 2000 Tiger Aspect Pictures (Billy Boy) Limited & Universal Studios LLLP.
4.7 Courtesy of Newmarket Capital Group & Summit Entertainment.
4.8 © 1987 Warner Bros. Inc. All Rights Reserved.
4.9 © 1987 Warner Bros. Inc. All Rights Reserved.

5.70 © 1957 Harris Kubrick Pictures, Corp. All Rights Reserved. Courtesy of MGM Clip+Still.

5.71 © 1957 Harris Kubrick Pictures, Corp. All Rights Reserved. Courtesy of MGM Clip+Still.

5.72 © 1970 Twentieth Century Fox.

5.74 Courtesy of Norsk Filmstudio AS.

5.75 © 1960 Shamley Productions, Inc., & Universal Studios Licensing LLLP.

5.76 © Carlton International Media Ltd & London Features International Ltd.

5.77 © Carlton International Media Ltd & London Features International Ltd

5.79 Bundesarchiv. Filmarchiv / Transit Film GmbH.

5.80 © 1934 Turner Entertainment Co. A Warner Bros. Entertainment Inc. Company. All Rights Reserved.

5.81 © 1937 Twentieth Century Fox.

5.82 © Paramount Pictures Corporation. All Rights Reserved.

5.83 Courtesy of Channel 4 Films, Cadrage S.A., National Film Development Corp, & Mirabel Films Ltd. Courtesy of MGM Clip+Still.

5.84 © Warner Bros. Inc. All Rights Reserved.

5.85 © Warner Bros. Inc. All Rights Reserved.

5.86 Courtesy of Cine-Tamaris.

5.87 © Paramount Pictures Corporation. All Rights Reserved.

5.91 © MCMXCV New line Productions, Inc. All Rights Reserved.

5.92 Courtesy of ADC Holdings Corp. "Cinescape" and "Cinefex" covers courtesy of the publishers.

5.93 © 1956 Columbia Pictures Industries, Inc. All Rights Reserved.

5.94 © 1997 Twentieth Century Fox & Paramount Pictures Corporation.

5.96 © 1964 Geoffrey Stanley, Inc., & Universal Studio Licensing LLLP.

5.97 © 1968 Turner Entertainment Co. A Warner Bros. Entertainment Inc. Company. All Rights Reserved.

5.100 © 1960 Shamley Productions, Inc. & Universal Studios Licensing LLLP.

5.101 Courtesy of Lions Gate Entertainment.

5.103 © 1989 Twentieth Century Fox.

5.104 © 1999 WV Films LLC. All Rights Reserved.

5.105 © 2000 Touchstone Pictures & Universal Pictures. All Rights Reserved.

5.106 © 2000 Touchstone Pictures & Universal Pictures. All Rights Reserved.

5.107 © 1971 Warner Bros. Inc. All Rights Reserved.

5.108 Bundesarchiv, Filmarchiv / Transit Film GmbH.

5.109 Bundesarchiv, Filmarchiv / Transit Film GmbH.

5.110 Bundesarchiv, Filmarchiv / Transit Film GmbH.

5.111 Bundesarchiv,.Filmarchiv / Transit Film GmbH.

5.112 Bundesarchiv, Filmarchiv / Transit Film GmbH.

5.113 Bundesarchiv, Filmarchiv / Transit Film GmbH.

5.114 © 1956 Argos Films.

5.115 © 1956 Argos Films.

5.117 © 1956 Argos Films.

6.1 © 1960 Shamley Productions, Inc., & Universal Studios Licensing LLLP.

6.2 © 1932 Paramount Publix Corporation & Universal Studios Licensing LLLP.

6.3 © 1932 Paramount Publix Corporation & Universal Studios Licensing LLLP.

6.4 © 1960 Shamley Productions, Inc., & Universal Studios Licensing LLLP.

6.5 © 1960 Shamley Productions, Inc. & Universal Studios Licensing LLLP.

6.6 © MMIII New Line Productions, Inc. All Rights Reserved.

6.7 © MMIII New Line Productions, Inc. All Rights Reserved.

6.8 © 1960 Shamley Productions, Inc., & Universal Studios Licensing LLLP.

6.9 © Bavaria Media GmbH.

6.10 © Bavaria Media GmbH.

6.11 © 1976 Metro-Goldwyn-Mayer Studios, Inc. All Rights Reserved. Courtesy of MGM Clip+Still.

6.12 © 1976 Metro-Goldwyn-Mayer Studios, Inc. All Rights Reserved. Courtesy of MGM Clip+Still.

6.13 © 1976 Metro-Goldwyn-Mayer Studios, Inc. All Rights Reserved. Courtesy of MGM Clip+Still.

6.14 Courtesy of Lucasfilm Ltd. © "Star Wars: Episode IV—A New Hope" 1997. All Rights Reserved. Used under authorization.

6.15 Bundesarchiv, Filmarchiv / Transit Film GmbH.

6.16 © ABC, Inc. All Rights Reserved.

6.17 © ABC, Inc. All Rights Reserved.

6.18 © 1941 RKO Pictures, Inc. All Rights Reserved.

6.19 © 1941 RKO Pictures, Inc. All Rights Reserved.

6.20 © 1967 Warner Bros., Seven Arts & Tatira-Hiller Productions. All Rights Reserved.

6.21 © 1967 Warner Bros., Seven Arts & Tatira-Hiller Productions. All Rights Reserved.

6.22 Courtesy of Svensk Filminstittut.

6.23 Courtesy of MK2 SA.

6.24 Courtesy of Euro London Films Ltd.

6.25 Courtesy of Euro London Films Ltd.

6.28 © 1960 Shamley Productions, Inc., & Universal Studios Licensing LLLP.

6.29 © 1960 Shamley Productions, Inc., & Universal Studios Licensing LLLP.

6.30 © 1960 Shamley Productions, Inc., & Universal Studios Licensing LLLP.

6.31 © 2000 Touchstone Pictures & Universal Pictures. All Rights Reserved.

6.32 © 2000 Touchstone Pictures & Universal Pictures. All Rights Reserved.

6.33 © 2000 Touchstone Pictures & Universal Pictures. All Rights Reserved.

6.34 Courtesy of Roman Polanski.

6.35 Courtesy of Roman Polanski.

6.36 Courtesy of Roman Polanski.

6.37 Courtesy of Roman Polanski.

6.38 Courtesy of Castle Hill Productions, Inc.

6.39 Courtesy of Castle Hill Productions, Inc.

6.40 © Paramount Pictures Corporation. All Rights Reserved.

6.41 © Paramount Pictures Corporation. All Rights Reserved.

6.42 © Paramount Pictures Corporation. All Rights Reserved.

6.43 © Paramount Pictures Corporation. All Rights Reserved.

6.44 © MMII New Line Productions, Inc. All Rights Reserved.

6.45 © MMII New Line Productions, Inc. All Rights Reserved.

6.46 © Paramount Pictures Corporation. All Rights Reserved.

6.47 © Paramount Pictures Corporation. All Rights Reserved.

6.48 Courtesy of Euro London Films Ltd.

6.49 Courtesy of Euro London Films Ltd.

6.50 Courtesy of Euro London Films Ltd.

6.51 Courtesy of Euro London Films Ltd.

6.52 Courtesy of Contemporary Films Limited.

6.53 Courtesy of Contemporary Films Limited.

6.54 Courtesy of Contemporary Films Limited.

6.55 Courtesy of Contemporary Films Limited.

6.56 Courtesy of Contemporary Films Limited.

6.57 Courtesy of Contemporary Films Limited.

6.58 Courtesy of Contemporary Films Limited.

6.59 Courtesy of Contemporary Films Limited.

6.60 Courtesy of Contemporary Films Limited.

6.62 © Paramount Pictures Corporation. All Rights Reserved.

6.63 © Paramount Pictures Corporation. All Rights Reserved.

6.64 Courtesy of Mystic Fire Video.

6.65 Courtesy of Mystic Fire Video.

6.66 Courtesy of Mystic Fire Video.

6.67 Courtesy of Mystic Fire Video.

7.1 © 1949 Turner Entertainment Co. A Warner Bros. Entertainment Inc. Company. All Rights Reserved.

7.2 Courtesy of Python Monty Pictures Ltd.

Index